THE QUALITY OF FREEDOM

THE QUALITY OF FREEDOM

MATTHEW H. KRAMER

OXFORD

UNIVERSITY PRESS

OXFORD
UNIVERSITY PRESS

Great Clarendon Street, Oxford OX2 6DP

Oxford University Press is a department of the University of Oxford.
It furthers the University's objective of excellence in research, scholarship,
and education by publishing worldwide in

Oxford New York

Auckland Cape Town Dar es Salaam Hong Kong Karachi
Kuala Lumpur Madrid Melbourne Mexico City Nairobi
New Delhi Shanghai Taipei Toronto

With offices in

Argentina Austria Brazil Chile Czech Republic France Greece
Guatemala Hungary Italy Japan Poland Portugal Singapore
South Korea Switzerland Thailand Turkey Ukraine Vietnam

Oxford is a registered trade mark of Oxford University Press
in the UK and in certain other countries

Published in the United States
by Oxford University Press Inc., New York

British Library Cataloguing in Publication Data

Data available

Library of Congress Cataloging in Publication Data
Kramer, Matthew H., 1959-
The quality of freedom / Matthew H. Kramer.
p. cm.
Includes bibliographical references and index.
1. Liberty. I. Title.
JC585 .K74 2003   320′.01′1—dc21   2002192566

Typeset by SPI Publisher Services, Pondicherry, India
Printed in Great Britain
on acid-free paper by
CPI Antony Rowe, Chippenham, Wiltshire

ISBN 978–0–19–924756–1 (Hbk.)
978–0–19–954573–5 (Pbk.)

3 5 7 9 10 8 6 4 2 1

To
Hillel Steiner and Ian Carter

Preface

Only one terminological caveat is necessary here. Throughout this book, I use the terms 'liberty' and 'freedom' (and 'liberties' and 'freedoms') interchangeably. In construing those terms as synonyms, I am in accordance with much of everyday parlance and with most philosophical writings on social and political freedom. To be sure, theorists have sometimes distinguished between 'liberty' and 'freedom', and the resultant analyses have occasionally been illuminating. (For a perceptive example, see Jonathan Wolff, 'Freedom, Liberty, and Property', 11 *Critical Review* 345 (1997).) Nonetheless, for two main reasons, my treatment of those terms as synonyms is advisable within this book. First, it averts the stylistic rigidity and monotony that would ensue if 'freedom' and 'liberty' were not employed interchangeably. Second, if I were to differentiate between those familiar terms in order to mark conceptual distinctions, I would perhaps seem to be implying that those distinctions—and the patterns of usage that signal them—are consistently upheld in ordinary discourse. Any such appearance would be unfortunate. For one thing, as has already been noted, 'freedom' and 'liberty' are often used interchangeably in everyday pronouncements. Moreover, although ordinary usage is a starting point that certainly cannot be ignored, it is a decidedly imperfect guide for philosophical analysis. It is neither exact nor univocal. For the highlighting of conceptual distinctions, then, my reliance on terms and phrases less familiar than the unadorned 'freedom' and 'liberty' is warranted on more than stylistic grounds.

Several excerpts from Chapters 2 and 3, with many modifications, have been published in the following journals: *Journal of Political Philosophy* ('Freedom, Unfreedom, and Skinner's Hobbes'), published by Blackwell Publishing; *Inquiry* ('On the Unavoidability of Actions'), published by Routledge; *Political Studies* ('Why Freedoms Do Not Exist by Degrees'), published by Blackwell Publishing; *Current Legal Problems* ('Freedom as Normative Condition, Freedom as Physical Fact'), published by Oxford University Press; and *Politics, Philosophy, and Economics* ('On the Counterfactual Dimension of Negative Liberty'), published by Sage Publications. I am very grateful to these journals for permitting me to republish the aforementioned excerpts, with numerous alterations. I am likewise indebted to these journals' anonymous readers for their salutary comments.

I have presented some short portions of Chapters 2, 3, and 5 as talks in the following locations: the University of Glasgow Philosophy Department; the University of Edinburgh Philosophy Department; the Political Studies Association Conference at the University of Manchester; the University College London Faculty of Laws; and the University of Pavia Political and Social Studies Department. I am grateful to the people who attended each of these talks, and especially to the organizers: Jimmy Lenman, Gonzalo Rodriguez-Pereyra, Michael Menlowe, Hillel Steiner, Michael Freeman, and Ian Carter. Many people have offered helpful advice or have posed insightful questions during my writing of this book. I wish to extend warm thanks to Alex Bird, Brian Bix, Jerry Cohen, Julie Dickson, Keith Dowding, Neil Duxbury, Ronald Dworkin, Cécile Fabre, Michael Freeman, Jerry Gaus, Robert Goodin, Alastair Hannay, Martin van Hees, Richard Holton, Paul Kelly, Raf Kinston, Kristján Kristjánsson, Rae Langton, Brian Leiter, Jimmy Lenman, Roni Mann, Matt Matravers, Michael Menlowe, Emran Mian, Chris Mothersole, Serena Olsaretti, Eric Olson, Mike Otsuka, Richard Parker, Amanda Perreau-Saussine, Joseph Raz, Mark Reiff, Gonzalo Rodriguez-Pereyra, Nigel Simmonds, Quentin Skinner, Rob Weekes, Wil Waluchow, Jo Wolff, and Richard Wright. I am very grateful as well to Dominic Byatt, Gwen Booth, and Michael James for their excellent handling of editorial matters, and I am especially indebted to my father Alton Kramer for his unremitting encouragement. My work on this book has been facilitated immeasurably by a generous Fellowship from the John Simon Guggenheim Memorial Foundation for the 2001–2 academic year. I am extremely grateful to the Guggenheim Foundation for its support.

My heartiest thanks, however, must go to the two people to whom this volume is dedicated. Each of them has commented extensively and invaluably on this book as its chapters have materialized, but I am even more obliged to them for the inspiration supplied by their own work. For three decades, Hillel Steiner's pioneering reflections on freedom have stood out both because of their rigour and because of their imaginativeness. Several of his writings on the topic are classic essays that have significantly contributed to his stature as one of the world's foremost political philosophers. Those essays are what sparked my interest in producing a book on freedom. Ian Carter's writings have emerged more recently, during the past decade. However, as will be apparent to any reader of the present book, the importance of his work for my own thinking about many issues is immense. His theorizing is a model of philosophical acuity and profundity.

In the absence of Ian's work as a stimulus, my book on freedom would have been very different from what it is—and it would have been markedly inferior. In the absence of Hillel's work, I very likely would not have written a book on freedom at all.

Matthew H. Kramer
Cambridge, England
July 2002

Contents

1

Introduction

1. Some General Remarks

Like any of the other fundamental concepts of political thought, the concept of freedom is both familiar and obscure; and its obscurity derives not least from its familiarity.[1] It figures prominently in countless discussions of the social and political arrangements within which people live and interact. Whether or not the participants in such discussions attach much value to liberty, they can hardly omit altogether to advert to it as one of the reference points for their judgements. Issues relating to freedom are indeed among the abiding preoccupations of modern Western political disputation, with abundant references to such issues in virtually every context where people reflect on their sundry relations with one another. Yet, precisely because the concept of liberty is so much a part of everyday thinking and debating, its contours and implications are quite murky on many of the occasions when it is invoked. Notwithstanding that the give-and-take of ordinary discourse yields some fine distinctions along the way, it is generally not very conducive to precision and consistency. Our ready acquaintance with the concept of freedom can therefore lead us astray as much as it can assist us. We have all become accustomed to numerous conflicting applications of that concept, of which some are helpfully illuminating whereas others are confusing and undiscriminating. Though we acquire a lot of sound intuitions about freedom through those day-to-day applications of the concept, we also acquire a number of misconceptions that cannot withstand philosophical

[1] As I have stated in the Preface, I use the terms 'freedom' and 'liberty' (and 'freedoms' and 'liberties') interchangeably throughout this book.

scrutiny. Not infrequently, even the sound intuitions are rough and in need of elucidation. Hence, this book's presentation of a systematic theory of socio-political liberty is an endeavour to expose and dispel some widespread misunderstandings as much as an endeavour to reinforce and refine some widespread insights. While the elaboration of any such theory must trade on the fact that readers are already familiar with the concept of freedom in many respects, it must also to some degree unfold as a process of de-familiarization: a process of revealing the untenability of some commonplace ideas about freedom.

Moreover, the difficulties confronting a theory of socio-political liberty go beyond the need to disentangle the subtler and coarser threads of everyday thought. Within the general concept of freedom there are markedly different varieties and conceptions that cannot all be subsumed under a single coherent theory; any comprehensive treatment of those varieties and conceptions must involve an acknowledgment of their irreducible divergences. Most famous among those divergences, of course, is the distinction between negative liberty and positive liberty. That distinction will be examined at length in my second chapter. Suffice it for now to say that this book expounds a theory of negative liberty, a theory that construes liberty as a state of unpreventedness rather than as the exercise of certain faculties or the reaching of certain decisions or the attainment of certain objectives or the following of certain procedures. Whereas positive liberty is a matter of accomplishments, negative liberty is a matter of opportunities. Yet, although my next chapter will argue that the ideal of positive liberty should be redesignated with tags that more informatively convey its nature, the characterization of it as a type of liberty is not preposterous. Someone who achieves positive liberty can credibly claim to have been unconstrained by any factors—such as base desires—that might have blocked such an achievement. It is scarcely an abuse of language to say that an autonomous person has become free in the sense of not having allowed himself to be swayed by the diverse influences that could have rendered him heteronomous. Such a description is not optimal, but it is far from unintelligible or ridiculous. Precisely because the classification of positive liberty as a kind of liberty is not ridiculous or unintelligible, the theses of its exponents must be addressed seriously within a theory of negative liberty. By contrast, if those theses could not plausibly be presented as a conception of freedom at all, they could safely be ignored in this book. However, given that the doctrine of positive liberty and the doctrine of negative liberty are genuinely in competition as ways of fleshing out the general concept of freedom, the differences between them must indeed be investigated herein.

Other divergences within that very broad concept will likewise receive considerable attention in this volume. For example, Chapter 2 will explore the distinction between freedom as the normative state of unforbiddenness and freedom as the physical state of unpreventedness. Although some of my analyses throughout this book will apply to normative liberty as well as to non-normative (physical) liberty, my focus lies chiefly on the latter. Indeed, that focus is apparent in each of the two basic postulates that structure my enquiries, for in each of them we find modal categories rather than deontic categories.

Let us consider first the F Postulate, which declares what is necessary and sufficient for the existence of any particular freedom:

F Postulate: A person is free to φ if and only if he is able to φ.

In this formulation, the Greek letter 'φ' (which stands for any germane verb or set of verbs plus any accompanying words) can denote one's performance of some action or one's existence in some condition or one's undergoing of some process. Any ability of a person, to which the F Postulate refers, will consist not only in his power to φ—that is, his power to φ if left unimpeded—but also in the very condition of unforeclosedness that leaves open at least one opportunity for the exercise of his power to φ. To be free to φ is both to be capable of φ-ing and to be unprecluded from exerting that capability, whether one actually exerts it or not. Alternative formulations of the F Postulate are 'A person is free to φ if and only if it is possible for him to φ' and 'A person is free to φ if and only if he is unprevented from φ-ing'.

Just as important as the necessary and sufficient conditions for the existence of particular freedoms are the necessary and sufficient conditions for the existence of particular unfreedoms. Let us consequently ponder an additional postulate:

U Postulate: A person is unfree to φ if and only if both of the following conditions obtain: (1) he would be able to φ in the absence of the second of these conditions; and (2) irrespective of whether he actually endeavours to φ, he is directly or indirectly prevented from φ-ing by some action(s) or some disposition(s)-to-perform-some-action(s) on the part of some other person(s).

A person *P* who is unfree to φ would be able to φ if left unconstrained by everyone else, but is prevented from φ-ing by some action(s) which at least one other person performs or which at least one other person is disposed to perform in the event of *P*'s attempting to φ.

The F Postulate and the U Postulate are fundamental tenets of my theory of freedom, but they are not dogmas propounded without substantiation or explanation. My subsequent chapters will seek to justify the content of each of those postulates, by indicating why alternative specifications of the conditions necessary and sufficient for the existence of particular freedoms or unfreedoms would be unacceptable. Those chapters will likewise plumb some of the implications of the F Postulate and the U Postulate that are far from evident at first glance, and will develop aspects of those postulates that are not inferable from their abstract formulations alone. What we should notice here is that each postulate is modal rather than deontic in its tenor. That is, each postulate concentrates on the possibility or impossibility of some occurrence(s) rather than on the permissibility or impermissibility thereof. Thus, although the focus throughout this book is on socio-political freedom, the freedom usually under investigation is physical unforeclosedness rather than normative unforeclosedness.[2] To ascertain whether some person P is free to φ—in the sense relevant to the paramount concerns of this book—we have to ask not whether he is unprohibited from φ-ing by authoritative norms, but instead whether he is unprevented from φ-ing by physical incapacities or restrictions.

Given that this book trains its scrutiny not principally on freedom as a normative condition but mainly on freedom as a physical fact, it is perhaps departing slightly from what might be expected of a treatise on socio-political liberty. It departs therefrom in some other respects as well, which should be noted before we consider the respects in which this volume is nonetheless indeed a work of political philosophy. In the first place, as will be discussed more extensively at the outset of Chapter 3, the methodology that informs my discussions is austere. Under the terms of the F Postulate and the U Postulate, the existence of any particular freedom or unfreedom is a matter of fact that can be verified or disconfirmed without any recourse to moral-political considerations. Moreover, the conception of particular freedoms and unfreedoms encapsulated in those two postulates does not itself derive from moral-political considerations, save at a highly abstract level that will be expounded shortly. Thus, no political vision with more than the barest concreteness is driving the analyses that are undertaken here. My aims are to vindicate the coherence of an array of political debates and to clarify some of the issues that are mooted therein, without taking substantive stands on those issues. In accordance with a distinction well known to political philosophers, this book's theorizing is conceptual rather than normative. It does not venture to prescribe

---

[2] As will become evident in each of my next two chapters, 'physical' is used here (and elsewhere) solely in contrast with 'normative' rather than in contrast with 'mental'.

which freedoms should be secured, nor how various freedoms should be apportioned. *A fortiori*, consequently, it does not venture to recommend institutional arrangements that could optimally give effect to such prescriptions.

Furthermore, in keeping with each of the last two paragraphs, the words 'liberty' and 'freedom' are not used here in some of the morally tendentious ways in which those words have occasionally been used by other theorists. Sometimes people use the term 'liberty' (or 'freedom') to refer to principles for distributing liberty, and therefore their complaints about violations of liberty are in fact complaints about violations of those principles. When the concept of liberty is invoked in this fashion, its referent is not the condition of liberty itself but instead a situation of justice pertaining to that condition. No such conflation will occur here. My references to freedom are always references to opportunities or to combinations of opportunities—that is, to states of unpreventedness or to combinations of such states—rather than to criteria for distributing opportunities. Likewise rejected here is the morally fraught use of 'freedom' or 'liberty' to designate only certain types of freedom. Sometimes theorists maintain that the referential scope of each of those terms does not encompass the unpreventedness of illegitimate activities such as theft. According to those theorists, then, the preclusion of illegitimate activities does not involve the elimination of any liberties. According to them, licence rather than liberty has been abridged by any such preclusion.[3] Alternatively or additionally, some theorists maintain that legitimate obstacles which prevent some activities do not thereby remove any liberties, even if the thwarted activities would themselves have been legitimate. In the eyes of these theorists, a permissible curtailment of somebody's freedom is not a curtailment of her freedom at all. For such theorists, that is, a person's freedom-to-φ consists in her not being prevented from φ-ing by impermissible constraints rather than in her not being prevented from φ-ing *tout court*. Still other analysts use the term 'liberty' or 'freedom' to refer only to the sorts of liberties that are typically covered by bills of rights. Like the other morally skewed patterns of usage just recounted, this confinement of the concept of freedom to certain favoured freedoms is discountenanced in this book. As has been remarked in my brief explication of the F Postulate, the 'φ' variable in that postulate and the U Postulate can designate the performance of

[3] For some criticism of this manoeuvre, see Bernard Williams, 'From Freedom to Liberty: The Construction of a Political Value', 30 *Philosophy and Public Affairs* 3, 13–14 (2001).

any action or the undergoing of *any* process or the sustainment of *any* condition that might be performed, undergone, or sustained by some person. Questions of legitimacy and illegitimacy do not arise when we are attempting to determine whether somebody is free to φ. Similarly, when engaging in any such determination, we do not have to ask whether φ-ing is classifiable as the exercise of a precious civil liberty or not.

In all of the foregoing respects, each of which will be emphasized in one or more of my subsequent chapters, this book can appositely be described as apolitical. For the sake of analytical clarity and exactitude and comprehensiveness, my theory of freedom eschews many of the conceptual/terminological manoeuvres to which quite a few other theories of socio-political liberty have resorted. Why, then, should this book be regarded as a work of political philosophy at all, given that it strives for political inscrutability? The answers to this question will emerge at several later junctures, but a few key points should be briefly underscored at this stage.

Among the reasons for holding that this book's account of freedom concentrates on the domain of social and political philosophy—a domain comprising human interrelationships in all their multifarious-ness—is that some major features of the account have been devised by reference to the boundaries of that very domain. One of those features has already surfaced in the shape of the U Postulate. As is straightaway evident, that postulate singles out human actions as distinctively im-portant sources of restrictions on anyone's freedom. Only restrictions directly or indirectly caused by such actions are unfreedoms. Other restrictions eliminate various liberties, or various combinations of conjunctively exercisable liberties, without giving rise to unfreedoms. Hence, although natural limits on anyone's freedom are by no means ignored or discounted in my analyses, and although they certainly play a huge role in determining the level of anyone's overall liberty, their role is here staked off from that of humanly imposed constraints. Of course, any social or political philosopher must take account of rela-tions between human beings and their natural environments; but, as a social or political philosopher, he will focus primarily on relations among human beings themselves as a distinctive object of investigation and concern. That primary focus is exactly what the U Postulate exemplifies, as it distinguishes between the inabilities of any person that are due partly to other people's actions and the inabilities of any person that are due solely to natural forces and to her own conduct.

What also exhibits that focus is my general approach to the meas-urement of each person's overall liberty, which will be adumbrated in

Chapter 2 and developed fully in Chapter 5. In the calculations required under that approach, unfreedoms occupy a special place. Unlike other limits on what a person can do or be or undergo, unfreedoms do not merely form the perimeter of a person's latitude in application to which the relevant calculations proceed; in addition, the numerical expressions of the unfreedoms enter into those calculations directly. As will be seen, they have a distinctively diminutional bearing on the quantification of anybody's overall liberty. Because unfreedoms have such a bearing, and because they are themselves defined by reference to the domain of social and political philosophy, the freedom-measuring enterprise envisaged in this book is centred firmly on that domain.

Yet another aspect of my theory of freedom that derives from its preoccupation with the aforementioned domain is the theory's detachment from debates over the existence of free will. Again we encounter a far-reaching divide within the general concept of freedom. Here the pertinent distinction lies between socio-political liberty and metaphysical liberty. As will become clear in Chapter 3, this book's whole account of freedom prescinds from the disputes between the champions and the opponents of the doctrine of strict determinism. That is, it sedulously avoids taking any stand on the question whether each person's choices and decisions are thoroughly determined by all the events and states of affairs that have anteceded those choices and decisions. Such a question can and should be left in abeyance, in a manner which my third chapter explains. Precisely because that question is left in abeyance, there is room for a theory of socio-political freedom that goes beyond recounting merely what has happened and what will happen; such a theory indispensably recounts what could have happened and what could happen.

Perhaps even more important than any of the preceding factors that earmark this volume as a work of political philosophy is the volume's fundamental purpose or impetus. Its central aim is to uphold the view that the overall liberty of each person is rigorously measurable in principle. Indeed, virtually every element of my theory has been shaped in one way or another by that overriding objective. That objective in turn is prompted by the need for its fulfilment if we are to make sense of most credible theories of justice. Whatever else might be apportioned by virtually any reasonable set of principles of justice, one of the distribuenda should be the property of overall liberty. To be sure, liberties of certain specific types will also be among the distribuenda; but, because of the content-independent valuableness of freedom (which will be highlighted in Chapter 5), those particular liberties will never entirely crowd out the property of overall freedom as something to which virtually any plausible principles of justice should directly pertain. This point about overall liberty can be glimpsed in the following comment by G. A. Cohen, who was a Marxist at the time when he published it: 'There is freedom under capitalism, in a plain, good sense, and if socialism will not give us more of it, we shall rightly be disappointed.'[4] Yet, given that virtually any worthy precepts of justice should provide for the distribution of the desideratum of overall freedom, the coherence of those precepts will hinge *pro tanto* on the coherent measurability of that desideratum. After all, whatever might be this or that specific prescription for the distribution of freedom, it will require measurements for its implementation. Whether the proposal is to maximize each person's level of overall liberty, or to maximize the aggregate level of overall liberty in a society, or to maximize the average level of overall liberty, or to equalize people's levels of overall liberty, or to equalize and maximize those levels of liberty, or to maximize the lowest levels of liberty among the people in a society—or to satisfy some other criterion— the very realizability of any such prescription will depend on the measurability of overall freedom. If freedom is not measurable even in principle, then none of the prescriptions just broached is intelligible.

Of course, some of the prescriptions are more demanding than others in what they require of a freedom-measuring enterprise. Some might be susceptible to implementation in principle even without fine-grained precision in the requisite measurements, and some would depend only on ordinal comparisons rather than on cardinal calibrations. Nevertheless, none of the prescriptions can make sense unless the idea of the measurability of freedom itself makes sense. Accordingly, vindicating the intelligibility of that idea is essential for vindicating the meaningfulness of a key strand in contemporary debates about justice. In so far as most of the prominent positions within those debates apply to the desideratum of overall freedom, they

[4] G. A. Cohen, 'Illusions about Private Property and Freedom', in John Mepham and David-Hillel Ruben (eds), *Issues in Marxist Philosophy*, iv (Hassocks: Harvester Press, 1981), 223, 235. For a much longer treatment of the matters touched upon fleetingly in this portion of my Introduction, see Ian Carter, *A Measure of Freedom* (Oxford: Oxford University Press, 1999), Ch. 3. My justification of my conceptual analyses can be understood in part as a riposte to the wary view of conceptual analysis expressed in W. J. Norman, 'Taking "Free Action" Too Seriously', 101 *Ethics* 505 (1991); Wayne Norman, 'Comment on Kristjánsson: Can You Teach the Old Dog New Tricks?', 10 *Journal of Theoretical Politics* 285 (1998).

presuppose the possibility in principle of ascertaining the extent to which each person is endowed with that desideratum. Underlying my book is the aspiration to uphold the soundness of such a presupposition and thus to uphold the solidity of the aforementioned debates. Although this book does not enter into those debates at all and does not espouse any positions within them, it does indeed contribute importantly to them. It thereby contributes to political philosophy notwithstanding its aloofness from the jousting among substantive moral-political positions.

Moreover, this book's endeavour to affirm the in-principle measurability of people's levels of overall liberty is a project oriented towards the domain of political and social philosophy in another significant respect. Although my discussions will not squarely tackle the normative issues addressed by proponents of theories of justice, my conception of the freedom-measuring enterprise is partly evaluative. That is, as will be argued at length in Chapter 5, the level of each person's overall freedom cannot be ascertained without any reliance on evaluative assumptions—specifically, assumptions concerning the content-dependent valuableness of each person's particular freedoms in connection with the fostering of certain ideals such as individual autonomy and development and well-being. Whereas the existence of any particular freedom or unfreedom is strictly a matter of fact, the extent of anyone's overall liberty is a partly evaluative phenomenon. It is determined principally by the sheer physical proportions of the latitude residing in the combinations of options that are available to a person, but it is also determined by the qualitative importance of those combinations in tending to further the ideals just mentioned. So my fifth chapter will contend; and it will do so on the ground that a starkly non-evaluative approach to the measurement of freedom cannot suitably capture the distinctiveness of freedom as a socio-political desideratum.[5] A strictly non-evaluative approach, in other words, cannot come up with appropriate answers to the 'how free' questions asked about anybody by social and political philosophers. By insisting on this point, in opposition to some of the most powerful recent writings on the concept of freedom, this book does more than vindicate the coherence of the substantive moral disputation in which social and political philosophers engage. In addition, albeit indirectly and on a high plane of abstraction, it joins that disputation.

[5] For some broadly similar doubts about strictly non-evaluative approaches to the measurement of freedom, see Philippe van Parijs, *Real Freedom for All* (Oxford: Clarendon Press, 1995), 50.

2. *A Succinct Conspectus*

The next three of this book's four remaining chapters deal chiefly with matters relating to the existence of particular freedoms and unfreedoms, before the final chapter devotes sustained attention to the matter of gauging the extent of each person's overall liberty. This sequence is amply predictable, since our ability to ascertain the level of anyone's overall freedom depends on our ability to ascertain the existence of his or her particular freedoms and unfreedoms, but not vice versa. Grappling with the complexities that surround the existence of particular freedoms and unfreedoms is thus not only a worthwhile undertaking in itself. It is also crucial for the accomplishment of this book's prime ambition, to establish the measurability of freedom. Furthermore, the division between those two tiers of my theory is by no means entirely hermetic or rigid. As will be evident in each of my next few chapters, a number of the potential snags that complicate enquiries into the existence of particular freedoms or unfreedoms must be resolved by reflection on what is indispensable for the measurability of anybody's overall liberty. When one is zeroing in on the necessary and sufficient conditions for the existence of particular freedoms or unfreedoms, one must be guided to some degree by the implications of one's determinations for the tenability of one's freedom-measuring project.

Chapter 2 introduces a lot of the major lines of thought that compose my theory of freedom, though it touches on some of them only fleetingly. It differs from the later chapters in its continual engagement with the work of Quentin Skinner and (to a lesser extent) Philip Pettit. Although each of the subsequent chapters takes exception to the work of various other theorists from time to time, my criticisms in those subsequent chapters are usually brief and are always secondary to the elaboration of my own theory. In Chapter 2, by contrast, my challenges to Skinner's analytical and exegetic claims are nearly on a par with the development of my own theory. The reason for the inclusion of several lengthy confrontations with the writings of Skinner and Pettit is quite straightforward. In recent years they have expounded a civic-republican conception of freedom and have lauded its merits in comparison with those of the negative conception (that is, the conception of freedom as unpreventedness). Their championing of the civic-republican position has somewhat overshadowed the positive-liberty theories that have traditionally been the most conspicuous rivals of the negative conception. Hence, although my second chapter does assail the positive conception of liberty, it trains its critical scrutiny mainly on the civic-republican approach. By arguing that the insights of that approach can all be perfectly well accommodated within the negative conception of freedom, and by therefore maintaining that the civic-republican position does not stand as a genuine alternative to the negative conception, Chapter 2 clears the ground for the full unfolding of my theory of negative liberty in the subsequent chapters.

Chapter 2 is more than a ground-clearing exercise, however. As has been suggested, it delineates many of the basic ideas that form my conception of liberty. Though it broaches some of those ideas only glancingly, it explores a number of them in depth. Apart from marking the differences between the negative conception and the positive conception of freedom, and apart from highlighting the weaknesses in the latter conception, the chapter commends the F Postulate and the U Postulate in preference to some alternative versions of negative-liberty doctrines—versions which equate 'unfree' with 'not free,' and 'free' with 'not unfree'. Likewise, it investigates the distinction between non-normative freedom and normative freedom; it ponders the bearing of time on the existence and contents of particular freedoms; it underscores the importance of the divide between each person's particular freedoms/unfreedoms and each person's overall freedom; it emphasizes the desire-independence of the existence of particular liberties and unfreedoms; and it considers the role of probabilities in one's ascriptions of freedoms or unfreedoms to any person. Each of these themes is probed at some length in Chapter 2 and is then amplified in the later parts of the book. Sundry other topics receive attention more briefly, including some points that foreshadow my final chapter's approach to the measurement of freedom.

The third chapter begins with a few methodological reflections that expand on some of the observations in this opening chapter. It then tackles a host of difficulties relating to the existence of particular freedoms and unfreedoms. Among the topics addressed are the range of the contents of particular freedoms and unfreedoms (that is, the range of the occurrences and states to which freedoms and unfreedoms can pertain), the counterfactual dimension of liberty (that is, the ways in which each person's freedoms and unfreedoms are determined partly by potential events which could have occurred but which do not actually materialize), the existence of freedoms that pertain to the undergoing of irresistible processes or states, the distinction between the value of doing X and the value of being free to do X, the degree to which doctrines of metaphysical or natural determinism can be reconciled with socio-political liberty, and the freedom-curtailing effects of certain psychological incapacities. As has been noted, several of these issues concerning the existence of particular freedoms or unfreedoms are mulled over by reference to their implications for the measurability of each person's overall liberty.

Chapter 4 addresses a set of problems that are raised by my U Postulate. As is manifest from even a cursory inspection of that postulate, any effort to apply its two prongs will have given rise to a number of causal questions. We need to distinguish between the constraints on the freedom of any person P that are due partly to other people's actions and the constraints on the freedom of P that are due solely to natural forces and to P's own conduct. One's fleshing out of that basic distinction must consist in the elaboration of criteria that will enable us to attribute causal responsibility for freedom-impairing states of affairs. Those criteria separate unfreedoms from mere inabilities, and thereby significantly influence one's calculations of people's levels of overall liberty. As will become apparent, the task of formulating such criteria is much more knotty than it might at first seem. Nonetheless, the various cruxes that must be overcome are far from insurmountable; the chapter comes up with a comprehensively applicable test for the ascription of causal responsibility. Among the conclusions reached in the chapter is that inabilities caused only by other people's omissions and not by their actions are mere inabilities rather than unfreedoms. Only other people's actions are sources of unfreedom.

Chapter 4's elaboration of causal criteria brings to a close my focus on particular freedoms and unfreedoms. While this book's final chapter of course presupposes the conclusions at which the other chapters have arrived, it shifts the focus to the enterprise of gauging people's levels of overall liberty. In order to ascertain such a level for each person P, we have to ascertain every combination of conjunctively exercisable freedoms that is available to P (in other words, every combination made up of freedoms that can be exercised together by P either simultaneously or sequentially). We likewise have to ascertain every combination of opportunities which are not conjunctively exercisable by P and which lack conjunctive exercisability because of some action(s) by some other person(s). A key portion of the chapter explains how the elements in each combination are to be individuated, so that every combination can be expressed numerically. Moreover, as has already been remarked, the second half of the chapter argues that the level of anyone's overall liberty is determined in part by qualitative considerations, which can themselves be expressed numerically. Those considerations concern the extent to which certain types of freedoms tend to promote the realization of some specified ideals and the extent to which certain types of unfreedoms tend to retard the realization of those ideals. My conceptual analysis is not prescriptive but is partly evaluative, as it singles out the quality of freedom as a political desideratum.

In sum, although this book is long, it follows a pretty smooth trajectory. Its discussions in Chapter 2 introduce a lot of my central ideas, and pave the way for the more detailed articulation of those ideas in subsequent chapters. On both analytical and exegetical grounds, the chapter impugns the theory that has emerged as the foremost alternative (or ostensible alternative) to theories of negative liberty. My more detailed exposition of the properties of negative liberty then proceeds apace in Chapters 3 and 4 with a focus on particular freedoms and unfreedoms, and in Chapter 5 with a focus on the measurability of overall freedom. The middle three chapters look ahead frequently to the final chapter, which in turn draws quite heavily on them. Hence, while the involutions of my theory are many, its basic course is largely straightforward. The numerous distinctions drawn throughout this book are all ultimately oriented toward the upshot of the fifth chapter, with its endeavour to establish that each person's overall freedom is both rigorously measurable and evaluation-sensitive. That upshot, which serves to vindicate the coherence of contemporary controversies about the just distribution of freedom, is the book's *fil conducteur*.

2

Fine Distinctions: Some Rejoinders to Quentin Skinner's Attacks on the Modern Doctrine of Negative Liberty

In an array of writings stretching over the past two decades, Quentin Skinner has repeatedly challenged the modern conception of negative liberty developed by Isaiah Berlin and many other theorists.[1] He has sought to draw attention to some once vibrant but now largely peripheral traditions of thought—especially the civic-republican or neo-Roman tradition—in order to highlight what he sees as the limitedness and inadequacies of the currently dominant ways of thinking about freedom. Most of his publications on this topic overlap quite

---

[1] The principal writings by Skinner that will be explored herein are 'Machiavelli on the Maintenance of Liberty', 18/2 *Politics: Journal of the Australasian Political Studies Association* 3 (1983) [hereinafter cited as Skinner, 'Maintenance']; 'The Idea of Negative Liberty: Philosophical and Historical Perspectives', in Richard Rorty, J. B. Schneewind, and Quentin Skinner (eds), *Philosophy in History* (Cambridge: Cambridge University Press, 1984) [Skinner, 'Idea'], 193; 'The Paradoxes of Political Liberty', in Sterling McMurrin (ed.), *The Tanner Lectures on Human Values*, vii (Cambridge: Cambridge University Press, 1986) [Skinner, 'Paradoxes'], 225; 'Thomas Hobbes on the Proper Signification of Liberty', 40 *Transactions of the Royal Historical Society* 121 (1990) [Skinner, 'Signification']; 'The Republican Ideal of Political Liberty', in Gisela Bock, Quentin Skinner, and Maurizio Viroli (eds), *Machiavelli and Republicanism* (Cambridge: Cambridge University Press, 1990) [Skinner, 'Republican'], 293; 'On Justice, the Common Good and the Priority of Liberty', in Chantal Mouffe (ed.), *Dimensions of Radical Democracy* (London: Verso, 1992) [Skinner, 'Justice'], 211; *Liberty Before Liberalism* (Cambridge: Cambridge University Press, 1998) [Skinner, *Liberty*]. For the most powerful riposte to Skinner heretofore, see Alan Patten, 'The Republican Critique of Liberalism', 26 *British Journal of Political Science* 25, 28–36 (1996) [Patten, 'Critique'].

extensively, but his views have undergone some notable modifications that will be duly taken into account herein.

The present chapter will endeavour to defend the modern understanding of negative liberty against Skinner's strictures. My approach to the matter is predominantly philosophical, and I only intermittently joust with Skinner in his status as an eminent intellectual historian. Not under scrutiny at all here is the accuracy of his synopses of the ideas propounded by civic-republican thinkers (especially Machiavelli); similarly, at only three or four junctures is there any doubt cast upon the correctness of his summaries of the ideas advanced by the early liberal opponents of civic republicanism (especially Hobbes).[2] Indeed, this chapter will occasionally even acquiesce in Skinner's brief recapitulations of the views expressed by twentieth-century theorists who have championed the doctrine of negative liberty. Quite apart from the fact that any challenges to the accuracy of those recapitulations must be primarily exegetical rather than philosophical, such challenges are sometimes problematic because of the striking diversity of the positions adopted by negative-liberty theorists. A few of Skinner's criticisms undoubtedly have some force when levelled against certain of those theorists. Not every proponent of the idea of negative liberty has put forward a tenable set of theses. Nonetheless, what will be maintained here is that a suitable exposition of negative liberty along modern lines can withstand all of Skinner's objections, either by rebutting them or by defusing and accommodating them.

As has been indicated in Chapter 1, the following two postulates form the core of my account of negative liberty, at the level of particular freedoms and unfreedoms:

F Postulate: A person is free to φ if and only if he is able to φ.
U Postulate: A person is unfree to φ if and only if both of the following conditions obtain: (1) he would be able to φ in the absence of the second of these conditions; and (2) irrespective of whether he actually endeavours to φ, he is directly or indirectly prevented from φ-ing by some action(s) or some disposition(s)-to-perform-some-action(s) on the part of some other person(s).

As should be clear from what has been said in the preceding paragraph, my conception of particular freedoms and unfreedoms does not purport to be a distillation of tenets that have been accepted by all or most negative-liberty exponents. Among those heterogeneous exponents, a number of the theses that figure in my analysis of liberty have quite

---

[2] I should note, however, that a number of other remarks by Skinner strike me as exegetically dubious. See for example Skinner, 'Maintenance', 5, where he implies that David Hume equated 'passions' with 'present desires'.

often been neglected or even rejected. Hence, although my position is broadly in accordance with the multitudinous doctrines that would normally be classified as theories of negative liberty, it differs from quite a few of them in myriad respects and from nearly all of them in some respects (varying respects). Its claims on one's attention derive not from its somehow encapsulating all the stances favoured by other theorists, but from its serviceability as an account that can overcome or circumvent the difficulties which have frequently been thought to afflict doctrines of negative freedom.

One significant difference between certain other negative-liberty theories and this book's exposition of freedom should be flagged straightaway, in accordance with some remarks made in my opening chapter. What follows is indeed an investigation into the nature of freedom, rather than a set of prescriptions concerning (say) how freedom ought to be distributed or how far any particular freedoms ought to be protected through the conferral of legal rights. None of my contentions about the essential features of liberty will rest on moral-political considerations of the sort just mentioned. By contrast, some negative-liberty theorists such as J. P. Day have endeavoured to incorporate such considerations into their analyses of the nature of freedom. Day, for example, based some of his analytical conclusions on the premise that each person has a moral right to the enjoyment of liberty.[3] Confronting Day's assertions on this point, Skinner can quite aptly declare that—in the absence of any substantiating arguments from Day—those assertions 'are mere dogmas'.[4] By disentangling matters of conceptual explication from matters of moral-political prescription, my discussions avoid both Day's dogmatism and the need for any straightforwardly moral-political reasoning that might vindicate his position in a suitably non-dogmatic manner.

After the first main section of this chapter has elaborated and clarified several of the complex strands in my conception of freedom—in the course of responding to some of Skinner's observations and arguments—the next main section turns to the principal objections which Skinner has raised against modern understandings of negative liberty. We shall first quite briefly examine his arm's-length defence of theories of positive liberty. Some aspects of my ruminations on that defence will re-emerge in my longer rejoinders to his two chief criticisms of present-day thinking about freedom. Throughout his work on this topic,

---

[3] J. P. Day, 'Individual Liberty', in A. Phillips Griffiths (ed.), *Of Liberty* (Cambridge: Cambridge University Press, 1983), 17, 18.
[4] Skinner, 'Idea', 18.

Skinner has submitted that contemporary theorists fail to grasp the instrumental connection between civic virtue and the preservation of liberty; as a consequence of that failure, he contends, those theorists are unattuned to the possibility that people will sometimes (indeed, often) have to be forced to retain their freedoms. Much more recently, while continuing to complain that modern liberals are blind to the instrumental freedom-preserving role of civic virtue, Skinner has additionally maintained that the modern conception of freedom is itself inadequate. Whereas previously he had presumed that civic republicans were at one with present-day liberals in taking freedom to be a negative condition of unconstraint, he now differentiates between them with reference to the breadth of the category of 'constraint'. According to him, the civic republicans were more perspicacious than the twentieth-century thinkers in recognizing the freedom-impairing effects produced by conditions of domination and dependence. This new claim by Skinner about domination, as well as his long-standing claim about the connection between popular political participation and the sustainment of liberty, will occupy our attention in the second half of this chapter. As will be seen, the same basic misstep underlies the accusations that stem from each of those claims.

1. Some of the Essentials of Negative Liberty

1.1. The Avoidability of Actions

Some readers, who might wonder whether the 'φ' variable in the U Postulate is supposed to cover instances of forgone action as well as instances of action, would press for an affirmative answer to this question. They would declare that, when someone is irresistibly obliged to carry out an action *A* by the conduct of somebody else, he is *ipso facto* prevented from eschewing *A*. He is therefore unfree to eschew *A*. His unfreedom in that respect is just as plain as his unfreedom-to-do-*A* when he is prevented from undertaking *A* rather than from forgoing it. So runs a line of reasoning which I shall have to rebut.

This facet of my conception of unfreedom is in need of emphasis because Skinner has upbraided some contemporary theories of negative liberty for overlooking the putative fact that a person can be made unfree to refrain from undertaking some particular action(s). Contrasting those theories with the prototypical liberal account of negative freedom propounded by Hobbes, Skinner writes: 'Although Hobbes agrees that an agent may be said to lack freedom if an action within his powers has been rendered impossible, he does not think that this is the only way in which unfreedom can be produced. The agent will also lack freedom if he is tied or bound to act in such a way that he cannot forbear from acting.'[5] Although Skinner is correct in thinking that some or all negative-liberty theorists have distanced themselves from the position which he ascribes to Hobbes, few if any of those theorists have sought squarely to gainsay that position.[6] Such an endeavour of contestation is requisite here. (As will become evident toward the end of this subsection, my critique of Skinner on this point will submit that his reading of Hobbes is far from unassailable.)

In respect of unfreedom, actions and abstentions are not on a par; there is an asymmetry between them. Because an agent can always elect to cease his activity as an agent, the ostensible inescapability of certain actions is not the same as the outright inescapability of certain instances of *in*action. To see this point, we should look at an example that may initially seem to cut in the other direction—that is, an example that may initially seem to lend support quite plainly to Skinner's position. Let us explore a situation broadly similar to that described near the end of Edgar Allan Poe's short story *The Pit and the Pendulum*.

Suppose that a man possessed of no special handicaps or strengths has been locked in a room with formidably unyielding walls and with neither windows nor unsealed doors. Given the constraints of the situation, his departure from the room is physically impossible for him. Throughout the period during which he is unable and thus unfree to leave the room, the inability/unfreedom is a matter of physical impossibility. His unavoidable abstention from walking beyond the

---

[5] Skinner, 'Signification', 127, footnote omitted.

[6] Indeed, one of the three philosophers whom Skinner chides for neglecting the ostensibly Hobbesian point about unavoidable actions has himself seemingly endorsed that point in a subsequent work. See Hillel Steiner, *An Essay on Rights* (Oxford: Blackwell, 1994) [Steiner, *Essay*], 8 n. 2. For one of the few forthright denials of the claim that actions can be unavoidable, see G. A. Cohen, *History, Labour, and Freedom* (Oxford: Clarendon Press, 1988) [Cohen, *History*], 244–6. As will become evident in the final main section of Chapter 3, my present discussion does not relate at all to the subtle issues raised by Harry Frankfurt, 'Alternate Possibilities and Moral Responsibility', 66 *Journal of Philosophy* 828 (1969). Frankfurt's ingenious article, which has given rise to a large body of responses, is concerned with debates over determinism and the metaphysical/natural freedom of the will. By contrast, my focus throughout this book is on social and political freedom.

confines of the room is unavoidable in precisely that sense. Let us now suppose that, as a result of the fiendish designs of the immured man's captors, the northern and southern walls of the large room begin to move slowly inward. The unfreedom of the man is clearly increasing, and his freedom is decreasing commensurately; he remains unable to go beyond the walls, and the area within which he can still walk is contracting. What we must consider is the following crux. As the northern or southern wall reaches the place where the man is standing, is he forced to move himself away from it? He is unable and thus unfree to continue standing there, because the wall's inward progress is inexorable. Is he therefore obliged to retreat? *Pace* Skinner, the answer is 'no'. The man could opt to let himself be pushed along by the wall as if he were a lifeless physical object. In such an event, he would not be engaging in any active movement but would instead be passively driven back by the impetus of the wall. Since this alternative to the act of moving himself away is available, the man is not irresistibly forced to undertake that act. If he does choose to walk/crawl/run away in lieu of allowing himself to be shoved along like an insensate object, that bit of his conduct is not a matter of physical necessity. Because he has the option of declining to perform such an act, his self-powered withdrawal is not unavoidable. In that respect, it differs from his staying within the confines—the ever diminishing confines!—of the locked room.

A variation on this example will illuminate this point further. Suppose that a man in a locked room is under constant surveillance. He is told that, if he desists from walking around the room and stands still at any point during the next two hours, he will be shot to death immediately. Suppose, moreover, that the threat is fully genuine; were the man even briefly to stop moving, he would be shot to death instantly. (Powerful rifles are trained on him through openings near the high ceiling.) Is he therefore irresistibly obliged to continue walking around? Is the walking a matter of physical necessity? Once again the answer is 'no'. If the man persists in his perambulations, he does so not because of an utter lack of alternatives but because of his desire to shield himself from the sole ghastly alternative that is open to him. Should he become inclined to taste death at any juncture during the two hours, he can cease his pacing and be killed forthwith. His continuation of the pacing is thus not unavoidable for him, in the way that his remaining within the room is unavoidable. Just as the man in the earlier situation could elect to relinquish his active agency in preference to moving away (of his own volition) from the menacing wall, so

too the man in this new situation can relinquish his very life in preference to continuing his trudging around the room.

Other predicaments might combine the chief elements of the two
situations sketched in the foregoing scenarios. What is particularly
important about those scenarios is that the circumstances depicted in
them are maximally favourable to Skinner's claim that people can be
irresistibly compelled to undertake actions. In each scenario, after all,
someone is able to forgo a certain action only by straightaway surrendering his self-determination or life—that is, only by straightaway
becoming a passive object or a corpse. Even in such a plight, however,
the forgoing of the action in question is not physically impossible; in
other words, the performance of the action is not physically inevitable.
Even when the lone alternative to the doing of A by some person is an
immediate loss of his active agency or his life, we should not conclude
that he is unfree to abstain from doing A. The extreme unpleasantness
of an alternative does not strip it of its status as an alternative. So long as
an option other than A is available, the performance of A is not
unavoidable. All the more manifest is the avoidability of A when the
circumstances under consideration are less dire than those portrayed
above (that is, when the harmful consequences of abstaining from A are
less grave or less imminent).

In connection with the argument of this subsection, three caveats or
qualifications are important:

1.   First, the argument has relied on a distinction that will be
sustainedly highlighted in the second half of this chapter—the distinction between particular freedoms or unfreedoms and overall freedom
or unfreedom. This discussion has concerned particular unfreedoms
relating to particular omissions, each of which we can designate as the
unfreedom to refrain from doing A. My concern has been to show that
there are no such unfreedoms. Because anyone can always elect to
remain passive (even if remaining passive involves the immediate surrender of his self-determination or life), there is always an alternative
to doing A; and hence, given that everyone is able to forgo A, no one is
ever strictly unfree to forgo it. To say as much, however, is certainly not
to say that the overall freedom of the man in each scenario above is
unimpaired by the moving walls or the trained rifles. Patently, his
overall liberty is severely restricted. Still, that impact on his overall
liberty is perfectly consistent with the continued existence of his
freedom- to-abstain-from-walking, not least because he can exercise
that particular freedom only at the cost of sharply reducing his subsequent overall freedom (especially in the second scenario). When seek-

ing solely to ascertain whether a person is endowed with some particular liberty, we should not allow ourselves to be distracted by the nature of the context within which that liberty is held—a context that may involve the choking off of virtually all of the person's other liberties. Conversely, of course, when our concern is solely to ascertain whether a person's overall freedom is harshly cabined, we should not allow ourselves to be distracted by the fact that he is free in some particular respect.

2. A second caveat pertains to the occurrence of non-volitional movements of people's bodies. If we are to take cognizance of such movements, must we carve out exceptions to the thesis for which this subsection has argued? In addressing this question, let us first consider the situations in which people's non-volitional movements are due to the wielding of their bodies as instruments or objects or playthings by other people. Suppose that John grabs Herbert's arm and slaps Ronald's face with it. Suppose further that, because of Herbert's bewilderment or John's superior strength—or both factors—Herbert could not have released his arm from John's grip. In these circumstances, he was clearly unfree to withhold his arm from smiting Ronald's face. He was unable to withhold the arm, and his inability was causally attributable to the conduct of someone else. Does his unfreedom along those lines constitute a counter-example to the conclusions of this subsection? Plainly, the answer is 'no'. What this subsection has argued is that nobody is ever unfree to refrain from performing this or that action A. In advancing such a thesis, my discussion has issued a riposte to the claim by Skinner that a person can be made unfree to forbear from engaging in certain actions; Skinner's claim is about actions rather than about bodily movements that are wholly non-volitional and therefore unclassifiable as actions. Yet the motion of Herbert's arm against Ronald's face is indeed entirely non-volitional. It is attributable to John as part of *his* conduct rather than to Herbert as part of his. Herbert is not performing an act when his hand hits Ronald. Instead, he is being acted upon by John. In this respect, he is in basically the same position—the position of a passive object—as the man who is propelled toward the centre of a room by the moving wall in my earlier scenario. (In fact, the passivity of Herbert is more pronounced, since he does not even elect to assume the status of an object.) Thus, the fact of Herbert's unfreedom-to-withhold-his-hand-from-Ronald's-face is unproblematically compatible with my insistence that nobody can ever be made unfree to abstain from acting in a particular way.

Herbert is not acting, and thus his situation does not run athwart my thesis.

Complications could be introduced into the example of John and Herbert and Ronald, without altering its upshot. Suppose that Herbert initially feels startled when his arm is grabbed by John and is tugged toward Ronald's face, but that Herbert willingly cooperates in the assault by the time that his hand actually makes contact with Ronald. Let us presume that the example remains otherwise unchanged. Specifically, let us presume that Herbert could not have released his arm from John's grip if he had tried, and that he was therefore unfree to keep his hand away from Ronald's face. In this modified scenario, then, the following two facts obtain: (1) Herbert is engaging in an act by the time of the occurrence of the slap; and (2) Herbert was unfree to hold his arm back from slapping Ronald. Should we infer that the modified scenario recounts an instance of a compelled action, an action that could not have been eschewed by the person who has performed it? A negative answer is warranted here, for the action of slapping could certainly have been eschewed by Herbert even though the slap itself could not have been. Herbert is able to abstain from the act of slapping by simply not cooperating at all in what is being done with his arm by John. The assault will still occur, but it will not be caused by any aspect of Herbert's conduct (as opposed to John's conduct). Hence, if Herbert does willingly thrust his hand against Ronald's face, the volitionality of the blow—and thus the very status of the blow as an action taken by Herbert—will not have been due to an absence of alternatives.

We should next turn our attention to non-volitional movements of people's bodies that are traceable to diseases or other medical conditions. Such movements do not pose any difficulties for my thesis that no one can ever be made unfree to forbear from undertaking some particular act. In the first place, those movements—which are strictly non-volitional—do not qualify as actions in distinction from mere motions. A spasmodic fit, for example, is not a piece of conduct but is instead something that happens to the person who suffers from it. Hence, the claims by Skinner about irresistible actions do not gain any support from the existence of medical problems of this sort. Moreover, many such problems are not causally attributable to anything done by other people; many of them derive solely from natural causes. Accordingly, even if we were to put aside the fact that any uncontrollable movements arising from illnesses are not actions, we often could not maintain correctly that people are unfree to abstain from those movements. They are not free to abstain therefrom, but, in many cases, they are not *un*free to abstain. People afflicted with such maladies are neither free nor unfree to forgo the twitchings to which they are subject. (The divide between 'not free' and 'unfree' will be highlighted in a later subsection.)

Having made no concessions so far, this discussion should now broach a few limited exceptions to my general position on the unavoidability of actions. Suppose first that a man's mind has been completely taken over by some other people, through sophisticated electronic or chemical or surgical means. Not only the man's volitional movements, but also the very volitions that lead to those movements, now lie within the control of other human beings. Suppose that these captors of his mind have caused the man to form an intention to undertake some action *A*—such as the scratching of his nose—which he does indeed perform. Should we accept that he was unfree to abstain from that action (at least in the absence of external obstacles that would have precluded his carrying out of *A*)?

Chapter 3 will explore at greater length the complexities raised by the possibility of the wholesale appropriation of a person's mind. My present discussion will offer no more than a few terse observations. Let us consider two main potential ways of coming to grips with the prospect of the out-and-out control of a person's mind by somebody else. On the one hand, we might maintain that the person whose mind has been taken over is no longer acting at all. According to such a line of analysis, a human being whose volitions are generated and manipulated by other people is no more a veritable agent than is a robot or any other machine. Yet, when a person is merely an ersatz agent and the plaything of others, he does not perform any real actions. Movements of his body that might appear to be voluntary exertions are in fact attributable to the conduct of other people rather than to any authentic conduct of his own. Hence, given that he is not carrying out any actions—given that his bodily movements are events brought about by other people through the use of him as a vehicle—his inability to keep himself from pursuing the designs of his masters does not mean that he is unfree to abstain from undertaking certain actions. So would run one potential line of thought on this matter.

Another route for dealing with the possibility of mind-control is to allow that instances of such control do indeed constitute exceptions to the general thesis that no one can ever be made unfree to forbear from an action. (In my next chapter's more detailed treatment of this issue, I shall argue for the superiority of the current line of thought vis-à-vis that recounted in the preceding paragraph.) Because the person whose mind has been seized away will nonetheless thereafter be forming intentions and seeking to give effect to those intentions, his posture is that of someone who acts—even though he is free to engage only in certain courses of conduct and is unfree to refrain from engaging therein. To be sure, the intentions of the person in question are chosen for him by the people whose marionette he is; but his interaction with the world does proceed largely through beliefs and intentions rather than solely through the stark electrical impulses that impel the workings of a robot. We should consequently accept that many of his bodily movements are actions, and that they are actions which he is unfree to forgo. An acknowledgment of this point will not require the slightest modification in either the F Postulate or the U Postulate. Under the F Postulate we should contend that the manipulated person is free to adopt only those modes of conduct which he actually adopts. And, likewise, under the U Postulate we should contend that that person is unfree to adopt any modes of conduct which would have been feasible for him in the absence of the mind-control and which differ from those that he actually adopts. (In connection with each of the two postulates, we should further note that the manipulated person is free—and is therefore not unfree—to be moved around unwittingly by external forces in countless ways that do not amount to any actions of his.)

Let us now glance at two other categories of marginal exceptions to this subsection's fundamental thesis, in addition to the category of actions performed by people whose minds have been thoroughly overmastered. One such further type of exception resides in modes of behaviour that are on the borderline between actions and non-volitional reflexes. When a bodily movement is in large part a function of an instinctive reflex but is also partly volitional, it is arguably classifiable as an action. If it is indeed properly so classifiable, then it amounts to an action that cannot really be forgone by the person who performs it. For example, at one juncture in the movie *Schindler's List*, a German soldier bellows at his terrified victims in order to induce them to walk faster. He screams with such ferocity that their obedience to his orders—by stepping more quickly—is at least as much an instinctive reflex as a volitional choice. If we nonetheless maintain that the walking at an accelerated pace is arguably an action which each of them undertakes, we should avouch that the first several steps of that accelerated walking arguably constitute an action which the victims are not free to eschew.

One other special exception to my insistence on the avoidability of actions is some of the behaviour impelled by certain mental illnesses.

(We shall look at this matter in greater depth in Chapter 3.) Although many of the bodily movements induced by severe psychological ill-nesses consist in non-volitional twitchings and jerkings, some of the behaviour induced by an illness such as schizophrenia is volitional conduct that cannot really be forgone. Notwithstanding that that conduct is volitional, the volitions which animate it are resistlessly driven by powerful delusions that hold firm sway over the mind of the person who suffers from the illness. Now, although a theory of socio-political freedom cannot take account of *all* constraints on the formation of a person's beliefs and intentions, we can recognize the freedom-curtailing effects of certain profoundly disruptive mental diseases. Among those possible effects is the inability of a victim of one of those diseases to forbear from engaging in some woefully deluded actions.

3. Finally, some defenders of Skinner may feel that he has antici-pated and parried the objections raised in this subsection. A riposte of that sort would draw attention to a footnote in which Skinner avouches that 'Hobbes sometimes speaks as though an action we cannot forbear from performing cannot be treated as an action: it is a case in which we are acted upon, not a case in which we act'. Having made an apparent concession, Skinner then asserts: 'But the implica-tion—that all actions are free by definition—is one that Hobbes else-where rejects.'[7] In support of this assertion, Skinner cites the passage from *Leviathan* where Hobbes suggested that only actions which 'proceed from [a person's] will, proceed from *liberty*'.[8] Hence, Skinner may appear to have adumbrated and deflected the arguments which I have marshalled here. We must consider whether his remarks truly succeed in impugning any of those arguments.

Two rejoinders to the posited defence of Skinner are appropriate. First, even if his account of Hobbes's view on this matter were unim-peachable, we could rightly question why he does not indicate in any way that the attributed view is untenable. Since he invokes that view partly in order to discredit the modern negative-liberty theorists' understanding of Hobbes, he might have been expected to acknow-ledge the unsustainability of what he perceives as Hobbes's genuine stance. After all, the modern theorists could be pardoned for having overlooked an ostensible aspect of Hobbes's work that does not with-stand close analysis. Even if Skinner's exposition were exegetically

---

[7] Skinner, 'Signification', 125 n. 30.
[8] Thomas Hobbes, *Leviathan*, ed. John Gaskin (Oxford: Oxford University Press, 1996) [Hobbes, *Leviathan*], 140 (Ch. 21, para. 4). Skinner's quotation from this passage is—harmlessly—inaccurate.

impeccable, then, it could be faulted for exhibiting insufficient philosophical tenacity. A philosophically probing explication would disclose the unsoundness of any general insistence by Hobbes on the possibility of unavoidable actions.

Second, at any rate, Skinner's reading of Hobbes is dubious or at best misleading. Hobbes did indeed divide actions into the 'voluntary' and the 'involuntary', but his distinction was really between volitional bodily movements—actions properly so called—and non-volitional bodily movements. In his most direct statement of his distinction, within *The Elements of Law*, he expressed his position forcefully: 'VOLUNTARY actions and omissions are such as have beginning in the will; all other are INVOLUNTARY or MIXED. Voluntary such as a man doth upon appetite or fear; involuntary such as he doth by necessity of nature, as when he is pushed, or falleth, and thereby doth good or hurt to another.'[9] If a tornado sweeps Dorothy up and carries her away for several hundred yards, then she is free—in the presence of the tornado—to soar along the trajectory of her flight. Furthermore, she is not free to abstain from so soaring. However, the ideal of analytical clarity will hardly be advanced if we deem the non-volitional airborne journey of Dorothy to be an action on her part. Her ride through the skies is not something which she undertakes, but is instead something which she haplessly undergoes. Far from performing an action, she is wholly overpowered by the tornado and is thereby precluded from acting as an agent at all. We are best advised, then, to eschew Hobbes's terminology while endorsing his analysis. Instead of distinguishing between voluntary and involuntary actions, we should distinguish between volitional and non-volitional movements of the body, and we should classify only the former set of movements as actions. (Of course, like any diremption, a division between volitional and non-volitional movements of the body will leave a grey area of borderline cases. For example, if someone deliberately seeks out an irresistible force by which he wishes to be overpowered, then the bodily movements occasioned by the overpowering of him might well count as elements of an extended action which he himself has undertaken. Although those bodily movements are the consequences of his being carried or pulled or driven along ineluctably, he has willingly placed himself within the sway of the ineluctable impetus.

[9] Thomas Hobbes, *The Elements of Law*, ed. John Gaskin (Oxford: Oxford University Press, 1994) [Hobbes, *Elements*], 71 (Part I, Ch. 12, para. 3). For an apt rehearsal of Hobbes's position on this matter, see A. G. Wernham, 'Liberty and Obligation in Hobbes', in K. C. Brown (ed.), *Hobbes Studies* (Oxford: Blackwell, 1965) [Wernham, 'Liberty'], 117, 122, 123.

At least in some circumstances, then, we shall be warranted in attributing those resistless movements to him as components of an overarching action which he as an agent has chosen.)

This second retort to the defence of Skinner might seem to be little more than a terminological quibble. Given that Hobbes laid stress on essentially the same distinctions as those that have been highlighted in this chapter, and given that he chose to frame his chief distinction as 'voluntary actions' versus 'involuntary actions' rather than as 'actions' versus 'non-volitional movements', why should anyone dissent when Skinner observes that Hobbes perceived certain actions as irresistible? In so asserting, Skinner appears simply to be following Hobbes's own pattern of usage. Why should anyone object, and, in particular, why should anyone maintain that Hobbes has been misrepresented?

To discern the answer to these questions, we need to look at what Skinner does with his synopsis of the Hobbesian conception of freedom and unfreedom (a synopsis that in itself is largely unexceptionable). We have already noted one thing that he does; in a passage partially quoted earlier, he disparages contemporary negative-liberty writers for misconstruing Hobbes's position.

Hobbes's theory of human freedom seems to have been rather widely misunderstood. Hobbes is often singled out as the classic exponent of what is sometimes called the pure negative theory of liberty. He is claimed, that is, to hold the view that an individual is unfree if and only if his doing of some particular action has been rendered impossible. But this appears to be untrue to Hobbes's analysis. . . . Although Hobbes agrees that an agent may be said to lack freedom if an action within his powers has been rendered impossible, he does not think that this is the only way in which unfreedom can be produced. The agent will also lack freedom if he is tied or bound to act in such a way that he cannot forbear from acting.[10]

As has been stated, Hobbes's distinction between voluntary and involuntary actions is essentially the same as my distinction between actions and non-volitional bodily movements. Hence, when the modern negative-liberty theorists cite Hobbes in connection with the latter distinction, they are entirely justified in doing so. To be sure, all or most of them join me in seeing volitionality as an indispensable element of any action, and thus they opt for my parlance—or something closely akin to it—in preference to Hobbes's pattern of usage. That is, they subscribe to the view that the bodily movements designated by Hobbes as 'involuntary actions' should not be characterized as 'actions' at all. Accordingly, those theorists do not accept that there ever arises a

[10] Skinner, 'Signification', 127, footnotes omitted.

situation in which somebody 'is tied or bound to act in such a way that he cannot forbear from acting'. Nevertheless, the disaccord between their position and that of Hobbes on this point is only at a superficial level of terminology. There is no non-trivial substantive divergence between them. By failing to take full account of changes in philosophical discourse over the past few centuries, Skinner has presumed to detect a substantive disagreement where none in fact exists.

Equally inapposite are some of the other remarks by Skinner when he expounds Hobbes's notion of involuntary actions. For example, he submits that Hobbes sought to flesh out that notion 'with such simple instances as that of the man who is "led to prison by force"'.[11] In fact, Hobbes contended that the forcible journey of a man to prison is a mixed action that combines elements of voluntariness and involuntariness (that is, volitionality and non-volitionality). His description of the matter is highly illuminating: '[W]hen a man is carried to prison he is pulled on against his will, and yet goeth upright voluntary, for fear of being trailed along the ground: insomuch that in going to prison, going is voluntary; to the prison, involuntary'.[12] Hobbes's analysis corresponds precisely to my own, though admittedly his vocabulary is different. Just as the man in my scenario of the moving walls is unfree to remain stationary, so too the prisoner in Hobbes's scenario is unfree to stay away from the prison. And just as the man in my scenario is free to decline to move himself away from the wall when it reaches him, so too the prisoner in Hobbes's scenario is free to decline to walk to the jail. The man in the room could choose to be shoved along by the wall, and the prisoner could choose to be 'trailed along the ground'. In each case, the unpalatableness of the eschewed alternative does not render it unavailable as a physically possible alternative. Hobbes aptly recognized as much when he gave due prominence to the volitional aspect of the prisoner's trek to the jail. His attentiveness to that aspect of the situation becomes obscured when Skinner suggests that Hobbes classified the prisoner's journey as straightforwardly non-volitional. Such a suggestion creates the false impression that the Hobbesian view concerning unavoidable actions is substantively at odds with the view espoused by present-day theorists of negative liberty.

More important still is Skinner's contention that 'the category of actions we cannot forbear from performing is of considerable theoretical importance for Hobbes, since he takes it to be the means of

[11]   Skinner, 'Signification', 125.
[12]   Hobbes, *Elements*, 71 (Ch. 12, para. 3).

defining... human bondage'.[13] Skinner recounts Hobbes's analysis of slavery as follows:

According to Hobbes's analysis, both in *De Cive* and [in] *Leviathan*, the lack of liberty suffered by slaves is not simply due to the fact that they are 'kept in prison or bonds'. It is also due to the fact that 'their labour is appointed to them by another' in such a way that their bodies 'are not in their own power'. A slave is thus defined as someone whose lack of freedom is due in part to the fact that he is, literally, a bondsman: someone who is bound or forced to act, and is not at liberty to forbear from acting.[14]

Skinner's interpretation of the relevant passage from *Leviathan* is not tenable. In that passage,[15] Hobbes distinguished between slaves and voluntary servants. We should straightaway notice that he applied the words 'their labour is appointed to them by another'—words quoted by Skinner—to slaves and voluntary servants alike. Indeed, he affirmed that the condition denoted by those words is precisely what slaves and voluntary servants have in common: 'These two kinds of servants [slaves and voluntary servants] have thus much common to them both, that their labour is appointed them by another.' Hence, the fact that a man's labour has been appointed by somebody else plainly does not mean that the labourer is unable to refrain from engaging in his assigned tasks.

More generally, we shall go astray in understanding the relevant passage from *Leviathan* if we assume that the term 'voluntary' therein carries the same meaning as in the much earlier portion of the text where Hobbes differentiated between voluntary and involuntary actions. In the passage on slaves and servants from which Skinner quotes here, Hobbes differentiated between slaves (whose status derives ultimately from their having been captured in war) and voluntary servants (whose status derives solely from their having agreed to work for remuneration or other benefits). He attached the term 'voluntary' to 'servants' presumably because he wished to distinguish these servants from those whom he had discussed at yet another juncture in *Leviathan*.[16] In that earlier discussion of servants and slaves, he had distinguished between two types of people who are captured in combat: those who have agreed to serve their captors in return for their lives and a modicum of liberty, and those who have not agreed to anything. Hobbes labelled the former set of people as 'servants' and the

---

[13] Skinner, 'Signification', 125.
[14] Ibid., footnotes omitted.
[15] Hobbes, *Leviathan*, 431 (Ch. 45, para. 13).
[16] Hobbes, *Leviathan*, 134–5 (Ch. 20, paras 10–13).

latter as 'slaves'. Slaves are of course wholly at the mercy of their conquerors with no obligations owed on either side, but even servants—that is, servants whose status originates in consent after defeat in combat—are almost entirely within the sway (both normative and physical) of their masters. 'The master of the servant, is master also of all he hath; and may exact the use thereof; that is to say, of his goods, of his labour, of his servants, and of his children, as often as he shall think fit. For he [the servant] holdeth his life of his master, by the covenant of obedience'.[17] Hobbes explained that, in the event of any disobedience by a servant, his or her master can justifiably inflict the most severe punishments. Thus, when Hobbes later distinguished between slaves and voluntary servants, and when he remarked that slaves' 'bodies are not in their own power, (their lives depending on the will of their masters, in such manner as to forfeit them on the least disobedience,)',[18] he was apparently using the term 'slaves' to encompass the servants as well as the slaves whom he had mentioned in his earlier discussion. Hence, probably in order to make clear that the servants singled out by the later discussion are not to be equated with the servants/slaves of the earlier analysis, Hobbes attached the adjective 'voluntary' to 'servants' in that later passage.

At any rate, what is apparent is that Hobbes did not present his distinction between slaves and voluntary servants as a distinction between people who are incapable of abstaining from their assigned tasks and people who are not so incapable. Though voluntary servants are indeed free to decline to act in accordance with their employers' instructions, slaves are likewise free to decline to act in accordance with their masters' behests. Hobbes pertinently recognized this point even in *Leviathan*'s earlier analysis of slavery, where he used the term 'slaves' narrowly to encompass only those captives who are owed no obligations at all by the people who have defeated them in combat: '[S]laves that work in prisons; or fetters, do it . . . to avoid the cruelty of their taskmasters.'[19] It should go without saying that the alternatives open to slaves who refuse to work—alternatives such as being killed or undergoing ferocious beatings—are rebarbative. Nonetheless, once again, the repugnant character of those options does not rule them out as physically impossible. They abide as possibilities, however unappealing they may be. If slaves do comply with their masters' dictates, they do so because they want to forestall the consequences of non-compliance

---

[17] Hobbes, *Leviathan*, 135 (Ch. 20, para. 13).
[18] Hobbes, *Leviathan*, 431 (Ch. 45, para. 13).
[19] Hobbes, *Leviathan*, 135 (Ch. 20, para.12).

rather than because they are incapable of acting otherwise. When they engage in the toil which they have been commanded to perform, their work is something which they choose to do in light of the alternatives. It is not something that happens to them willy-nilly.

In short, as Hobbes was well aware, slaves are free to refrain from following the orders of their masters. Their obedience to those orders cannot correctly be placed on the involuntary side of Hobbes's distinction between voluntary and involuntary actions; that is, in modern terms, their obedience is volitional and eschewable rather than non-volitional and unforgoable. When Hobbes contrasted slaves with voluntary servants, he was not thereby suggesting that the labour of slaves is something which they are incapable of declining to undertake. He used the term 'voluntary' at that juncture in his text to indicate the origin of the servants' status rather than the nature of their exertions. (Moreover, he there invested that term with a meaning quite different from its meaning in his discussion of actions. The difference lies in the divergence between a focus on acting uncoercedly and a focus on being free to act—a divergence to which we shall devote further attention later.)

Why has Skinner gone down a false trail on this topic? Perhaps his misstep resides in a conflation of normative freedom and non-normative freedom. In other words, he may have run together the following two conditions or properties: (1) liberty qua permittedness under authoritative norms such as laws and moral precepts, and (2) liberty qua physical unpreventedness. He should be concentrating on the latter kind of liberty, since his remarks on Hobbes's category of unavoidable actions are concerned with physical possibility and impossibility. However, in the passage from Skinner most recently quoted above, there appears to be some slippage from the non-normative to the normative. For instance, the closing words of that passage—'not at liberty to forbear from acting'—form a predicate that is unproblematically applicable to slaves, if the liberty in question is the latitude allowed to the slaves under the legal norms of the society in which they are subjugated. By contrast, the predicate is wholly inapposite if the term 'liberty' instead denotes the non-normative condition of unpreventedness. We here seem to have come upon a swerve by Skinner from a focus on unfreedom-as-a-physical-fact to a focus on unfreedom-as-a-legal-status. We may suspect all the more strongly that something of this sort has happened when we look at some sentences that are located only slightly earlier in his exposition:

The other way in which a man can be hindered from using his powers at will is . . . when he is physically bound or obliged to act in a particular way by the operation of an irresistible external force…If…he cannot forbear from acting, then his action will not be that of 'one that was free.' As Hobbes had already noted in his preliminary discussion in Chapter XIV, 'obligation and liberty are in one and the same matter inconsistent.'[20]

Although Skinner at the outset of these statements is clearly discussing non-normative unfreedom, he is equally clearly oriented toward normative unfreedom—and freedom—at the close of the extract. We may well presume, then, that a similar elision of the normative/non-normative divide has tarnished some other parts of his analysis of Hobbes's views on liberty and constraint.

As this subsection draws to a finish, however, two observations in partial defence of Skinner are in order. First, the person primarily responsible for the aforementioned elision is Hobbes rather than Skinner. Whereas the second paragraph in the 14th chapter of *Leviathan* concentrates on the non-normative dimension by defining 'liberty' as 'the absence of external impediments', the immediately subsequent paragraph in that chapter concentrates on the normative dimension by proclaiming that 'obligation, and liberty…in one and the same matter are inconsistent'.[21] Since Hobbes took so little trouble to guard against the running together of the factual species and the normative species of freedom, it is hardly surprising that his exegetes sometimes succumb to the temptation to effect an easy transition—an unduly easy transition—between an analysis of one of those two types of freedom and an analysis of the other.

Second, although this chapter will later criticize Skinner further for blurring the distinction between normative liberty and non-normative liberty, we should note forthwith that he sometimes evinces a solid grasp of that very distinction. For instance, he aptly takes exception to the terminological sloppiness of a pronouncement in which Hobbes used interchangeably the phrases 'right of nature' and 'natural liberty'.[22] As Skinner observes, Hobbes had earlier made quite clear that the so-called right of nature is in fact the wide-ranging normative liberty of each person in the State of Nature to take all steps which he or she believes to be necessary for his or her own survival.[23] By contrast, Hobbes had most prominently wielded the phrase 'natural liberty' in the same text to designate the non-normative condition of unpreventedness.[24] Hence, a passage that employs 'right of nature' and

[20] Skinner, 'Signification', 124–5, footnotes deleted.
[21] Hobbes, *Leviathan*, 86 (Ch. 14, paras 2, 3).
[22] Hobbes, *Leviathan*, 177 (Ch. 26, para. 8).
[23] Hobbes, *Leviathan*, 86–7 (Ch. 14, paras 1, 4).
[24] Hobbes, *Leviathan*, 140 (Ch. 21, para. 4).

'natural liberty' as synonymous expressions is at best lax and misleading. Skinner is correct to raise a query about it[25]—even though some broadly similar queries can be raised about certain arguments in his own work.

1.2. The Irrelevance of Desire

Even a perfunctory inspection of my F Postulate and U Postulate will reveal that they make no reference to the desires of any person of whom freedom or unfreedom is predicated. When we are inquiring whether some person P is free to φ, P's attitude towards φ-ing (or towards the freedom to φ) is not a relevant consideration; the existence of any particular freedom or unfreedom is desire-independent, in that the favourableness or unfavourableness of P's feelings about φ-ing (or about the freedom to φ) will neither reduce nor increase the likelihood that P is in fact free to φ. If a person is capable of φ-ing and is not prevented from exercising that capability, then she is free to φ even if she has not the slightest inclination to avail herself of that freedom. People's abilities, as opposed to their wishes or values, are the crucial factors that shape their freedom.

Very few negative-liberty theorists would disagree with the claims advanced in the preceding paragraph. Not least among the reasons for the near-consensus on this point is that Isaiah Berlin famously neglected the desire-independence of the existence of freedoms and unfreedoms, near the beginning of the original version of his essay 'Two Concepts of Liberty'. Though he went on to highlight that desire-independence at a number of junctures in the essay, he stated near the outset that 'liberty... is simply the area within which a man can do *what he wants*. If I am prevented by others from doing *what I want* I am to that degree unfree'.[26] As he emphatically maintained in

---

[25] Skinner, 'Signification', 133 n. 84.

[26] Isaiah Berlin, *Two Concepts of Liberty* (Oxford: Clarendon Press, 1958), 7, emphasis added. For some similarly regrettable formulations, see Keith Dixon, *Freedom and Equality* (London: Routledge & Kegan Paul, 1986), 10; Will Kymlicka, *Contemporary Political Philosophy* (Oxford: Clarendon Press, 1990) [Kymlicka, *Contemporary*], 139; D. D. Raphael, *Problems of Political Philosophy*, 2nd edn (Basingstoke: Macmillan, 1990), 56–60. For a partial retraction, though only a partial retraction, see Raphael, *Problems of Political Philosophy*, 61–3. Some early critics of Berlin failed to recognize his misstep as such, and they therefore based a number of misguided rebukes on the premise that particular freedoms are desire-dependent. See for example Marshall Cohen, 'Berlin and the Liberal Tradition', 10 *Philosophical Quarterly* 216 (1960).

the long introduction to the volume in which he published the revised version of his essay,[27] his original specification of the extent of each person's freedom and unfreedom cannot withstand scrutiny. That original specification is not strictly wrong, but it is lamentably misleading and sloppy. Wholly unacceptable is its suggestion—not a logical entailment, to be sure, but a strong suggestion—that unfreedom exists exactly in so far as somebody is prevented by one or more other people from doing what he or she pleases. Any such intimated message, as Berlin forcefully observed in retrospect, is too restrictive. His original formulation correctly submits that a person suffers unfreedom when she is blocked by other people from doing what she pleases, but the formulation fails to indicate that she likewise suffers unfreedom when she is blocked by other people from doing anything within her capabilities irrespective of whether she cares to do it or not. A person's abilities and inabilities, rather than her preferences, form the boundaries of her freedom and unfreedom.

Were we to take a contrary view and contend instead that the existence of any freedom or unfreedom is desire-dependent, we would be committing ourselves to some outlandish conclusions. If freedom consists precisely in being unprevented by other people from doing what one wishes to do, then the freedom of a person does not increase at all when she acquires countless new options of which she does not wish to avail herself. Likewise, if unfreedom consists in being prevented by other people from doing what one wishes to do, then a singularly effective way of reducing one's unfreedom is to eliminate one's desires and hopes as far as is necessary to match the objective constraints of one's situation. Under such a conception of unfreedom, a prisoner who has narrowed his aspirations to the point of being thoroughly contented with his shackled confinement in a small cell is not unfree in any particular. Similarly, a despotic government can avoid the imposition of any unfreedom on the hapless people who are subject to its ruthless sway, if it manipulates their psyches to effect a full reconciliation between their desires and their lot. Should the manipulation succeed, and should the citizens not wish to exercise any of the opportunities that become newly available to them when

---

[27] Isaiah Berlin, *Four Essays on Liberty* (Oxford: Oxford University Press, 1969) [Berlin, *Four Essays*], xxxviii–xl. Very strangely indeed, one commentator has suggested that Berlin in the Introduction to the revised version of his essay conceded that freedom is desire-dependent. See John Christman, 'Liberalism and Individual Positive Freedom', 101 *Ethics* 343, 352–3 (1991) [Christman, 'Liberalism'].

their government subsequently relaxes its repressive grip on power, the relaxation will not have increased the citizens' freedom—that is, their unpreventedness from acting in accordance with their desires—at all. Many equally preposterous conclusions would follow from a doctrine that characterizes the existence of freedoms or unfreedoms as desire-dependent. (Suppose, for example, that some large barricades have rendered a man unable and thus unfree to drive his car down Maple Street. If he divests himself of his desire to journey along that street with his car, he shall cease to be unfree to do so.)

As has been remarked, a large majority of negative-liberty theorists recognize the desire-independence of the existence of any unfreedom.[28] That is, they recognize that a state of unfreedom obtains in so far as one is prevented by others from doing or being or becoming

---

[28] See for example Ian Carter, *A Measure of Freedom* (Oxford: Oxford University Press, 1999) [Carter, *Measure*], 96–7, 133–4; G. A. Cohen, 'Illusions about Private Property and Freedom', in John Mepham and David Hillel-Ruben (eds), *Issues in Marxist Philosophy*, iv (Brighton: Harvester Press, 1981) [Cohen, 'Illusions'], 223, 231; J. P. Day, 'On Liberty and the Real Will', 45 *Philosophy* 177 (1970) [Day, 'On Liberty']; Joel Feinberg, *Social Philosophy* (Englewood Cliffs, NJ: Prentice-Hall, 1973), 5–7; Kristján Kristjánsson, *Social Freedom* (Cambridge: Cambridge University Press, 1996) [Kristjánsson, *Social Freedom*], 36–7; Philippe van Parijs, *Real Freedom for All* (Oxford: Clarendon Press, 1995) [van Parijs, *Real Freedom*], 18–20; Steiner, *Essay*, 10–11; Hillel Steiner, 'Individual Liberty', in David Miller (ed.), *Liberty* (Oxford: Oxford University Press, 1991) [Steiner, 'Individual Liberty'], 123, 124–6; W. L. Weinstein, 'The Concept of Liberty in Nineteenth Century English Political Thought', 13 *Political Studies* 145, 156–7 (1965) [Weinstein, 'Concept']. See also Brian Barry, *Culture and Equality* (Cambridge: Polity Press, 2001), 36–8; Stanley Benn, *A Theory of Freedom* (Cambridge: Cambridge University Press, 1988) [Benn, *Theory*], 131–2, 144–5; Lawrence Crocker, *Positive Liberty* (The Hague: Martinus Nijhoff, 1980) [Crocker, *Positive Liberty*], 43–7; M. M. Goldsmith, 'Hobbes on Liberty', 2 *Hobbes Studies* 23, 29 (1989) [Goldsmith, 'Hobbes']. For a general discussion— not all of which I endorse—see Tim Gray, *Freedom* (London: Macmillan, 1991), 62–73. For a striking assertion of the position which these theorists are rightly attacking, see Richard Norman, 'Liberty, Equality, Property: II', 55 (supp.) *Proceedings of the Aristotelian Society* 193, 199–200 (1981). See also J. Roland Pennock, *Democratic Political Theory* (Princeton: Princeton University Press, 1979) [Pennock, *Democratic*], 18–19; Amartya Sen, 'Well-Being, Agency, and Freedom', 82 *Journal of Philosophy* 169, 203–4, 207 (1985); Amartya Sen, 'Markets and Freedoms: Achievements and Limitations of the Market Mechanism in Promoting Individual Freedoms', 45 *Oxford Economic Papers* 519, 522, 527–32 (1993); G. W. Smith, 'Slavery, Contentment, and Social Freedom', 27 *Philosophical Quarterly* 236 (1977); Bernard Williams, 'From Freedom to Liberty: The Construction of a Political Value', 30 *Philosophy and Public Affairs* 3, 23 (2001). Cf. Richard Flathman, *The Philosophy and Politics of Freedom* (Chicago: University of Chicago Press, 1987) [Flathman, *Freedom*], Ch. 2.

anything within one's capabilities, and not merely in so far as one is prevented by others from doing or being or becoming anything within one's capabilities which one wishes to do or be or become. For most negative-liberty theorists, the distinction between 'not feeling unfree' and 'not being unfree' is axiomatic. What is surprising, then, about the numerous references by Skinner to the position of the negative-liberty theorists is that he repeatedly attributes to them a doctrine which effaces the distinction just mentioned. He seems to believe that they look upon freedoms and unfreedoms as desire-dependent. Only a few instances of this utterly unwarranted suggestion on his part can be adduced here.[29]

In one of his early treatments of the matter, Skinner asserts that negative-liberty theorists regard the condition of liberty as 'the absence of some element of constraint that inhibits the agent concerned from being able to act independently *in pursuit of his chosen ends*'.[30] His wording is virtually identical in a slightly later essay, where he maintains that the proponents of the theory of negative liberty deem freedom to be 'the absence of impediments *to the pursuit of one's chosen ends*' and 'the mere absence of impediments *to the realisation of one's chosen ends*'.[31] In a more recent piece of writing on this topic, he ascribes to Berlin and like-minded theorists the view that 'freedom is enjoyed so long as I am not "prevented by other persons *from doing what I want*"'.[32] In each of these passages and in the many other passages where Skinner uses closely similar language to characterize the stance of negative-liberty theorists, he erroneously conveys the impression that those theorists perceive the existence of freedoms and unfreedoms as desire-dependent. Each of the formulations just quoted will lead to the conclusion that a person who gains a host of new options has not thereby acquired any new freedoms, if he does not wish to take advantage of any of those options. Likewise, if a person's chosen ends are extremely modest—perhaps extending to no more than the latitude to wriggle his toes, for example—then any number of restrictions on his ability-to-act will not count (under the formulations above) as curtailments of his freedom. Now, exactly because these sorts of conclusions are extravagant and unacceptable, the

---

[29] For some of the many other examples, see Skinner, 'Idea', 206, 213; Skinner, 'Signification', 123, 124, 135; Skinner, 'Republican', 293, 294, 299, 301, 302, 307; Skinner, 'Justice', 217; Skinner, *Liberty*, 5, 25–6.

[30] Skinner, 'Idea', 194, emphasis added.

[31] Skinner, 'Paradoxes', 228, 236, emphases added.

[32] Skinner, *Liberty*, 113–14, emphasis added.

negative-liberty philosophers eschew the conception of freedom that generates them. Though in everyday discourse we often say that a person is free inasmuch as he can do what he pleases, a philosophical analysis of the concept of liberty has to be more rigorous and precise. Such an analysis cannot afford to intimate that the bounds of a person's potential freedom and unfreedom are set by his or her desires. Consequently, the crudities of everyday discourse have to be left behind. Negative-liberty theorists are perfectly well aware of this point, despite the obscuring of it in the doctrine which Skinner persistently attributes to them.

Furthermore, in addition to misrepresenting the views held by present-day exponents of the doctrine of negative liberty, Skinner has been far too accommodating in his treatment of Hobbes's quite different view. Hobbes, as is well known, did frequently portray the existence of any freedom as a desire-delimited condition. He maintained, for example, that the liberty of a man 'consisteth in this, that he finds no stop, in doing what he has the will, desire, or inclination to do'.[33] Skinner correctly ascribes this conception of freedom to Hobbes, and he also correctly contends that that conception is not strictly incoherent. However, he goes beyond a minimal defence of the bare coherence of Hobbes's position, for he raises no objections at all to the oddity and confusion of that position. His excessively generous approach to Hobbes on this matter is especially striking when he defends the Hobbesian thesis that well-enforced laws do not constrict people's liberty at all.[34]

Hobbes of course had grasped and indeed had emphasized that well-enforced legal mandates strongly discourage people from acting in ways that are contrary to the mandates' terms. Nonetheless, he appeared to think that such mandates do not curb the liberty of anyone who is subject to their requirements. He based his stance at least partly on the fact that legal directives do not typically render disobedience impossible.[35] In most circumstances, the enforcement of legal norms consists in punishments *ex post* rather than in preventive actions *ex ante*. Accordingly, the people to whom the norms apply are usually free to violate them.

More generally, Hobbes's denial of any freedom-abridging effects of laws can be seen as bound up with his belief in the desire-dependent nature of any liberty. It is this consideration on which Skinner focuses

---

[33] Hobbes, *Leviathan*, 140 (Ch. 21, para. 2).
[34] Skinner, 'Signification', 134–7.
[35] Hobbes, *Leviathan*, 140 (Ch. 21, para. 3).

when defending Hobbes. Skinner seeks to explain why the daunting-ness of the sanctions that back up legal dictates is consistent with people's enjoyment of uncurtailed liberty:

[W]e need only recall [Hobbes's] account of the means by which we are alone capable of forfeiting our liberty in the proper signification of the word. An external impediment must intervene in such a way that we are either stopped from acting or forced to act *contrary to our will and desires*. But neither fear nor any other passion of the soul can possibly count as such an impediment. Rather, a man who acts out of fear performs his action because he wills or desires to avoid various consequences which, he fears, will otherwise befall him.[36]

We should here put aside the regrettableness of the phrase 'forced to act'—a phrase which Skinner is using in this passage as in other passages to indicate that the eschewal of certain actions would be impossible.[37] My previous subsection has sought to expose the serious difficulties in his notion of unavoidable actions. Let us here instead consider two other shortcomings in the Hobbesian claim that well-enforced legal norms do not curtail people's liberty in any way.

First is a conflation that will be deplored sustainedly in the latter half of this chapter: the conflation of questions about each person's par-ticular freedoms and questions about each person's overall freedom. By glancing first at this misstep, however fleetingly, we can then go on to fathom more clearly the extent to which the Hobbesian denial of any freedom-restricting impact of legal directives is premised on a view of the existence of freedoms as desire-dependent. We should distinguish, then, between the following sorts of questions that might be asked about the impingement of legal mandates on people's liberty. On the one hand, we can ask whether a well-enforced legal prohibition on some activity has rendered each person unfree to engage in that activity (if he or she is not currently being detained for having violated the prohibition). As has been noted, the answer to that question is typic-ally negative; punishment or compensation *ex post* is a much more common mode of enforcement than prevention *ex ante*. Hence, each person's particular freedom-to-do-*A* is usually not eliminated by the steady implementation of a legal norm that proscribes the doing of *A*. On the other hand, our concern might be not with each person's particular freedom-to-do-*A*, but with his overall freedom. If we are indeed asking about overall liberty, then the answer to our question is

---

[36] Skinner, 'Signification', 136, emphasis added.
[37] Skinner, 'Signification', 125 n. 26.

that a well-enforced legal prohibition on A does constrain each person's freedom in important respects. As applied to each person, a diligently monitored legal mandate will block him from exercising various combinations of particular liberties, and will *pro tanto* have curtailed his overall freedom.[38] Though each liberty will very likely continue to be exercisable by him separately, the liberties in any one of the aforesaid combinations will not be exercisable by him conjunctively. Thus, for example, although each person can still exercise the freedom to do A, he cannot any longer exercise both (1) the freedom to do A and (2) the freedom to adopt any mode of conduct that would be precluded by the punishment or the seizure-of-assets that will be imposed on him for having done A. If the former liberty is exercised, the latter liberty disappears. In other words, the legal mandate that forbids A has thereby made each person unfree to carry out any combination of actions of the kind just mentioned (as well as any larger array of actions which includes such a combination and which would otherwise be conjunctively exercisable). If the punishment for doing A is severe, and if refraining from A is itself burdensome, then the *pro-tanto* constriction of each person's overall freedom and the *pro-tanto* expansion of each person's overall unfreedom will be substantial. Such a state of affairs is straightforwardly consistent with the fact that everybody remains free to do A.

The second principal shortcoming in the Skinnerian/Hobbesian view of law and freedom is closely connected to the first. What Skinner maintains is that, because the outlawing of A does not prevent people from acting in accordance with their desires, it does not make people unfree in any respect. Plainly, such a contention relies through and through on the notion that the existence of any unfreedom is desire-dependent. Indeed, it relies on a peculiarly narrow variant of that notion, since it presumes that no person can ever become unfree except in connection with an action which he prefers to all alternative actions. The idea is that, if a legal ban on A has altered the preferences of a person P such that he will now choose to abstain from A in order to avoid the penalties for defying the ban thereon, he is acting on the basis of his all-things-considered inclinations and is therefore not unfree at all. 'When such a person acts, it will still be because he possesses the will or desire to act in precisely the way in which he acts. It follows

---

[38] For a highly sophisticated and illuminating treatment of this point, see the eighth chapter of Carter, *Measure*. I should note here that my use of the phrase '*pro tanto*' will be fully elucidated later, when I am discussing Skinner's elision of the distinction between normative freedom and non-normative freedom.

that, even if the cause of his will is fear, the actions he performs out of fear will still be free actions.'[39] To be sure, the statements just quoted can be read in ways that cast them as unobjectionable. If Skinner is simply submitting that P's compliance with the ban on A is volitional, then he is saying nothing to which anyone could reasonably take exception. Likewise, if he is simply contending that the legal prohibition on A leaves P free to do A, then of course he is correct. However, neither of those perfectly acceptable claims would go any distance toward supporting the thesis for which Skinner is arguing at this juncture in his analysis: the thesis that a well-enforced legal mandate such as the ban on A does not impair P's liberty at all. Although P remains free to do A, he is not free to do both A and anything that would be precluded by the punishment that will ensue from his doing of A. Consequently, his overall freedom—his ability to undertake sundry modes of conduct in any number of combinations—is indeed reduced *pro tanto* by a well-enforced legal directive that proscribes the doing of A. Thus, the only way of reaching Skinner's intended conclusion is to embrace the Hobbesian premise that the existence of any liberty or unfreedom is desire-dependent. For reasons that have already been adduced, however, such a premise should be rejected (not because it is starkly incoherent, but because it yields preposterous corollaries).

Moreover, as has been remarked, Skinner's Hobbesian premise is strikingly narrow. Instead of connecting the existence of freedoms and unfreedoms to all the desires harboured by each person, it draws the connection to the desire that is most intense in any particular context. To apprehend how oddly confining that conception of freedom and unfreedom is, we should ponder the following example. Suppose that Jane is walking toward three doors, which lead respectively to an art exhibition, a clothing shop, and a library. Each door is the lone available entrance for the place to which it provides access. Though the art exhibition and the library are attractive to Jane, she currently wants to go to the clothing shop for a few hours in order to admire the garments on display. Now, suppose that somebody comes along and locks the door to the library and also the door to the exhibition. Under the typical version of the thesis that the existence of any freedom or unfreedom is desire-dependent, we would conclude that Jane has been made unfree to enter the library or the exhibition at present. After all, each of those places is desirable to her—though not currently as desirable as the clothing shop—and each of them is now closed off to her, at least temporarily. Under the Skinnerian/Hobbesian version of the thesis about desire-dependence, by contrast, we must conclude that Jane has not been made unfree at all. Notwithstanding that the library and the art exhibition are attractive to her as options, they are not as appealing as the clothing shop. Hence, according to the Skinnerian/ Hobbesian approach, the sealing off of her access to the less favoured places does not engender any unfreedom for her.

Of course, the usual version and the Skinnerian/Hobbesian version of the thesis about desire-dependence can tally as well as diverge. For instance, let us suppose that Jane comes upon four doors—rather than three—and that the fourth door leads to a storage area for malodorous garbage. Jane has no desire whatsoever to enter that storage area, and indeed she strongly desires to stay away from it and its stench. Hence, if somebody comes along and locks the fourth door, both versions of the thesis about desire-dependence will generate the conclusion that Jane has not been rendered unfree to go into the garbage-storage area. Nonetheless, although the two positions converge in their handling of this new aspect of the scenario, they can lead to contrary verdicts in regard to numerous other matters—as my last paragraph has made clear. In so far as the two positions do diverge, the Skinnerian/Hobbesian stance is especially prone to the formidable difficulties which Berlin and others have highlighted in the notion that the existence of any freedom or unfreedom is desire-dependent. If the typical conception along those lines is profoundly problematic, the Skinnerian/Hobbesian conception is even more markedly so.

1.3. The Unexcluded Middle

As should be evident from some of the earlier discussions in this chapter, the predicates 'free' and 'unfree' are contraries rather than contradictories. They are not bivalent or jointly exhaustive. In other words, 'not free' is not invariably equivalent to 'unfree', and 'not unfree' is not invariably equivalent to 'free'. Frequently we cannot correctly ascribe either freedom or unfreedom to some particular person(s) concerning some particular action(s) or state(s). In such circumstances, both the proposition 'P is free to φ' and the proposition 'P is unfree to φ' are incorrect. Accordingly, both the proposition 'P is not free to φ' and the proposition 'P is not unfree to φ' are true. The inappositeness of any attribution of freedom or unfreedom to the particular person concerning the particular action(s) or state(s) is not due—or is not perforce due—to some ambiguity in his situation. Instead, it is due to the unambiguous inapplicability of the predicates 'free' and 'unfree' to the particular aspect(s) of his condition. Myriad facts occupy a middle ground between the extensions of those predicates.

The key to that middle ground lies in the distinction between unfreedoms and mere inabilities. When a person P is unable to do or be or become something, and when the inability is caused by P himself or by natural phenomena rather than by some other person(s), the inability is not an instance of unfreedom. It is a mere inability, in connection with which the predicates 'free' and 'unfree' do not apply. Thus, for example, if we inquire whether an ordinary human being is free to fly from England to the South Pole without the aid of any apparatus or devices other than his own limbs, the correct response is that he is neither free nor unfree to undertake the flight. It is not the case that he is free to fly, and it is not the case that he is unfree to fly. Instead, he is merely unable to do so. His inability has not been caused by anyone else; it is a natural limitation. Consequently, 'unable' in this context is not equivalent to 'unfree'. The relevant predicates, rather, are 'not free' and 'not unfree'.

As has been observed in Chapter 1, a full explication of this distinction between unfreedoms and mere inabilities would require the formulation of appropriate tests or criteria for the allocation of causal responsibility. That explication will materialize in Chapter 4. For present purposes, however, no precise causal tests or criteria are needed. We shall here be probing the distinction between unfreedoms and mere inabilities at an abstract level, without having to explore how it ought to be operationalized. At that abstract level, Skinner's work can be found wanting in certain respects. Let us begin with a point that relates to the assignment of causal responsibility.

1.3.1. Causation as Opposed to Location   Skinner occasionally implies that some contemporary negative-liberty theorists have emphasized an internal/external dichotomy when analysing the conditions for the existence of freedoms and unfreedoms. That dichotomy, with regard to any human agent of whom freedom or unfreedom is to be predicated, consists in a separation between incapacities internal to the agent and impediments or restraints outside him. For theorists who draw upon such a distinction when seeking to ascertain the applicability of the predicates 'free' and 'unfree,' one's inabilities arising from internal incapacities are not instances of unfreedom. At least twice,[40] Skinner attributes a position of exactly this sort to

---

[40]   Skinner, 'Paradoxes', 228 n. 3; Skinner, 'Republican', 293 n. 4.

Hillel Steiner. In fact, however, Steiner nowhere propounds such a view. Rather, in the essay of his which Skinner cites, he declares simply that an inability is an instance of unfreedom if and only if it has been caused by somebody other than the person who partakes of the inability.[41]

Steiner is wise to shy away from the thesis (a Hobbesian thesis) which Skinner ascribes to him, for the internal/external dichotomy is largely a red herring. Skinner's misattribution runs together the matter of an inability's location or character and the matter of an inability's causal origin. If a person P is unable to φ, and if the causes of his inability do not lie at all in the actions of any other person(s), then the inability is not an instance of unfreedom—regardless of whether the key preventive factor is an internal incapacity or an external obstacle. Even more important in the present context is the converse situation: if at least one action by at least one other person is a sine qua non of P's inability, then P is indeed unfree to φ. The status of his inability as an instance of unfreedom is not affected at all by the character or location of the key factor that precludes his φ-ing.

Suppose, for example, that Tony breaks Jack's leg so badly that Jack is unable to walk at all for eight weeks. During the period of incapacitation, Jack is unfree to walk and not merely unable to do so. Likewise, if Tony's conduct inflicts damage on Jack's brain of such severity that Jack is unable to learn how to read, then the incapacity is an instance of unfreedom. Conversely, if Jack's inability to walk very far is due to the fact that a natural landslide has trapped him in a small cave, the external obstacle to his perambulations has not given rise to any unfreedom on his part. His inability is a mere inability. Similarly, if Jack lives in a rural area, and if he is effectively trapped in his house by a ferocious bear which has wandered in from some nearby hills and which will kill him post-haste if he ventures outside, the external obstacle in the form of the bear has deprived him of many freedoms without making him unfree. He is not free to walk more than a short distance outside his door, but he is not unfree, either; he is merely unable to do so. In respect of each of these situations, then, the classification or non-classification of a state of preventedness as a state of unfreedom does not hinge at all on the internal/external dichotomy. Causal questions, rather than locational questions, are the key to determining the presence or absence of unfreedom. (Perhaps the internal/external distinction is of some evidentiary significance, albeit slight. That is, perhaps when some person P is prevented from φ-ing by an internal incapacity, the character of the inability generates a rebuttable presumption—a

---

[41] Steiner, 'Individual Liberty', 123.

readily rebuttable presumption—to the effect that nobody else's doings have been causally responsible for *P*'s debilitated condition. Still, even this minimal role for the internal/external divide may be inordinate.)

But, a reader might reply, why should one accept the classificatory delimitations that have been recommended here? Why are they preferable to the internal/external demarcation? We can best understand these questions as asking firstly why any classificatory delimitations at all are requisite, and secondly why the specific distinctions presented here are to be endorsed. On the first point, the answer is quite straightforward: we need to distinguish between unfreedoms and mere inabilities in some way if we are to avoid the conclusion that everyone's overall unfreedom is infinitely extensive. After all, if an ordinary human agent (or even an extraordinary human agent!) is unable to fly from England to the South Pole without the assistance of any apparatus or devices other than his own limbs, then *a fortiori* he is unable to soar to distant galaxies—with or without the aid of mechanical devices. There is no limit whatsoever to the sweep and number of the things which each person is unable to do. Ergo, if there is no distinction between unfreedoms and mere inabilities, then the particular unfreedoms and the total unfreedom of each person will be infinitely expansive.

Hence, should we fail to separate unfreedoms from mere inabilities, we would be committing ourselves to a thesis (a wildly implausible thesis) that would undermine any project of measuring freedom and comparing overall levels of freedom. Even the roughest and simplest comparisons—among individuals or among societies—would be wholly untenable. After all, as will be argued in Chapter 5, any satisfactory measurement of each person's overall liberty will involve a ratio expressible as a fraction in which the following two sets of parameters are respectively the core of the numerator and the core of the denominator: (1) the range of each person's combinations of conjunctively exercisable freedoms, and (2) the range of each person's combinations of conjunctively exercisable freedoms plus the range of each person's combinations of consistent unfreedoms.[42] Any apt measurement or comparison of levels of overall liberty, however rough, must implicitly or explicitly draw upon some ratio(s) of the sort just described. Yet this whole enterprise of measurement will be rendered futile for anyone who accepts the thesis that the particular unfreedoms

---

[42] In Chapter 5, I shall elucidate fully my approach to measurement. For the moment, I shall simply mention *en passant* that the figure in the numerator of the specified fraction must be squared.

and overall unfreedom of each person are limitless in extent. Given that thesis, the overall liberty of every person would be exactly the same as everyone else's—a ratio expressible as an infinitesimally small fraction. Additions or subtractions of various freedoms and unfreedoms would make no difference to anyone's overall standing. If we are to reject these highly unpalatable implications of the thesis concerning limitless unfreedom, and if we are thereby to salvage any prospects for meaningful measurements and comparisons of levels of overall liberty, we shall have to stake off unfreedoms from mere inabilities. A distinction along those lines is indispensable for any adequate theory of freedom.

Nothing said so far, however, is directly supportive of the claim that the appropriate basis for the aforementioned distinction is causal responsibility—as opposed to some alternative basis such as the internal/external dichotomy. To grasp why causal tests are indeed the apposite vehicles for demarcating unfreedoms from mere inabilities, we have to understand which kind of unfreedom is the object of my attention throughout this book. Here we come to a topic that will be investigated in greater depth at the outset of Chapter 5. My focus throughout this volume lies on the property of social and political unfreedom in its non-normative manifestation, which consists in relationships of preventedness among human beings. That species of unfreedom arises when at least one action by some human being(s) has ruled out some option(s) that would otherwise have been available to some other human being(s). Such unfreedom, in its interpersonal dimension, is to be distinguished from any strictly intrapersonal inhibitions or incapacities. The relationships of preventedness obtain between human agents rather than solely between different facets of a single human agent. Likewise, the interpersonal character of social and political unfreedom is what differentiates that unfreedom from any state of preventedness that has been brought about by natural forces. Although somebody who is prevented from φ-ing by the workings of nature is thereby not free to φ, he is not thereby unfree to φ. Were we to infer that he has been made unfree to φ, we would be failing to recognize that the category of 'unfreedom' explored in this book—a straightforwardly socio-political category—is applicable to human beings vis-à-vis one another and not to human beings vis-à-vis the natural world.

An inability's causal provenance, rather than its location, is the pertinent touchstone for determining whether or not the inability is an instance of unfreedom. After all, as has just been maintained, social and political unfreedom consists in relationships of preventedness between human beings. Now, when we endeavour to ascertain whether some person *P* has been prevented from φ-ing by somebody else's actions, we are engaged in a causal enquiry. We are asking whether some other person's actions have contributed to bringing about a state of affairs that precludes *P* from φ-ing. To judge whether *P*'s inability-to-φ is an instance of socio-political unfreedom, we have to answer precisely that causal question. By contrast, an inquiry about the location of *P*'s inability—an inquiry asking whether the key preventive factor is a feature of *P*'s environment or is instead a feature of *P*'s body or psyche—is of no relevance. That is, the internal/external dichotomy is of no relevance.

Let us think back to the scenario in which Tony's action has caused damage of such severity to Jack's brain that Jack is unable to learn how to read. As has been observed, Jack's inability in these circumstances is an instance of unfreedom; his learning how to read has been prevented by Tony's action. (I am of course assuming that Jack would have been able to learn how to read had the infliction of damage by Tony not occurred.) For the task of determining whether the inability is correctly classifiable as an unfreedom, the location of the inability in Jack's brain and mind is utterly inconsequential. The lone decisive point is that at least one action by another human being—Tony—was causally responsible for the incapacitation of Jack. An ascription of unfreedom to Jack (the unfreedom-to-learn-how-to-read) rests on an ascription of causal responsibility to Tony. Basically comparable causal attributions underlie all sound attributions of socio-political unfreedom.

1.3.2. Losing Freedom without Becoming Unfree   The foregoing discussion of the non-equivalence of 'not free' and 'unfree' enables us to detect certain weaknesses in some of Skinner's remarks about Hobbes's conception of liberty. (As will be seen, however, Skinner goes on to evince a largely accurate understanding of the matter—albeit in a fashion that is exegetically doubtful.) Skinner more than once leaves himself vulnerable to ripostes when he expounds Hobbes's distinction between liberty and power. Let us begin with that distinction as Hobbes himself developed it. Having defined 'liberty' as 'the absence of opposition; (by opposition, I mean external impediments of motion;)', Hobbes proceeded to explicate the liberty/power distinction as follows:

For whatsoever is so tied, or environed, as it cannot move, but within a certain space, which space is determined by the opposition of some external body, we say it hath not liberty to go further. And so of all living creatures, whilst they are imprisoned, or restrained, with walls, or chains; . . . we use to say, they are not at liberty, to move in such manner, as without those external impediments they would. But when the impediment of motion, is in the constitution of the thing itself, we use not to say, it wants the liberty; but the power to move; as when a stone lieth still, or a man is fastened to his bed by sickness.[43]

Let us note straightaway that Hobbes obviously relied on the internal/external dichotomy in order to distinguish between an absence of liberty and an absence of power. He said nothing about any causal enquiries. We shall presently reflect further on that shortcoming in his account. For the moment, however, we should simply seek to apprehend clearly his analysis of power and liberty.

On the basis of the foregoing passage alone, we cannot tell whether Hobbes used 'power' to denote only an internal capacity or whether he instead wielded that term to denote an ability comprising both an internal capacity and an absence of external impediments. We can settle this matter in favour of the latter alternative, however, if we have recourse to a passage earlier in *Leviathan*. Hobbes there proclaimed that external impediments 'may oft take away part of a man's power to do what he would; but cannot hinder him from using the power left him'.[44] On the one hand, to be sure, it is not entirely inconceivable that Hobbes in this comment was suggesting that an absence of liberty could destroy or diminish a capacity; he might have had in mind, for example, the atrophying of limbs that are held in shackles. On the other hand, it is much more likely that he was using the term 'power' to denote an ability that consists of both an internal capacity and an external liberty (that is, an external state of unobstructedness). Given such a pattern of usage, the ascription of a power-to-do-A to a man entails the ascription to him of a liberty-to-do-A, but the latter ascription does not entail the former. If a man is bereft of the capacity-to-do-A yet is unimpeded from exercising that capacity, then he enjoys the liberty but lacks the power to do A. (Near the end of this subsection I shall examine a pronouncement by Hobbes that may appear to conflict with the interpretation offered here.)

In the course of probing Hobbes's account of liberty and power, Skinner submits that 'if we follow a Hobbesian analysis, we are bound to say of a man who is capable of exercising the power to act in some particular way that he is also at liberty to act in that way. In this case, the man's power and liberty amount to the same thing'.[45] Although my main concern at present is with a warning by Skinner that immediately

---

[43] Hobbes, *Leviathan*, 139 (Ch. 21, para. 1).
[44] Hobbes, *Leviathan*, 86 (Ch. 14, para. 2).
[45] Skinner, 'Signification', 126.

follows the statements in this extract, a one-paragraph digression on these statements themselves is worth our while. The first of the quoted statements if correct is oddly pleonastic, whereas the second is plainly incorrect. In the first statement, the phrase 'capable of exercising the power to act' is probably equivalent to 'having a capacity-to-act which one is not prevented from exercising by any external restraint or obstacle'. If so, then the statement is sustainable. However, it is likewise exceedingly odd—since its predicate 'capable of exercising the power to act' fully comprehends the predicate 'at liberty to act', even though the word 'also' in the statement implies that the latter predicate is not completely encompassed by the former. By contrast, if 'capable of exercising the power to act' means 'having the capacity to act if left unimpeded', then the statement is unsound. Within Hobbes's schema, an internal capacity is not necessarily accompanied by an external liberty. Still more clearly incorrect is the second of the quoted statements by Skinner. Even when a person has a power and thus a liberty to act, the power and the liberty do not 'amount to the same thing'; within the Hobbesian schema, a power is the combination of an internal capacity and an absence of prevention by external restraints or obstacles, while a liberty consists only in the absence of external prevention.

Let us turn to the warning that follows the passage on which we have just been concentrating. Skinner cautions against 'a temptation to add...that if a man...lacks the power to act, he must also lack the liberty'. Contending that '[t]his is certainly a temptation to which "negative" theories of liberty have regularly fallen prey in the twentieth no less than in the seventeenth century',[46] he delivers a rejoinder that must be quoted at some length:

[A]s Hobbes rightly observes, it may or may not make sense to claim that an agent who lacks power also lacks liberty. It will not make sense where the impediment to motion lies 'in the constitution of the thing itself.' To take Hobbes's own example, a man 'fastened to his bed by sickness' lacks the power to move, but it makes no sense to say that he also lacks the liberty. The reason he cannot be said to be unfree is that nothing is impeding him from moving; he is simply incapable of movement. This contrasts with the predicament of someone 'imprisoned or restrained with walls.' His plight is similar to that of the sick man in that he is unable to leave. But the sick man would still be unable even if the prison doors were to be opened, whereas the prisoner is only unable because the doors remain locked. He possesses an underlying power or ability to leave which has been 'taken away' from him. So while the sick man merely lacks ability, the prisoner lacks freedom.[47]

[46] Skinner, 'Signification', 126–7.
[47] Skinner, 'Signification', 127, footnotes deleted.

Now, although this passage is wholly unexceptionable as a recountal of Hobbes's views and terminology, its scrupulousness in that respect is not sufficient to shield it from criticism. After all, Skinner prefaces the passage with his rebuke to contemporary exponents of negative-liberty doctrines. Hence, his remarks should be judged not only by reference to his faithfulness as an exegete of Hobbes (a state of faithfulness that is here unimpeachable), but also by reference to his effectiveness in advancing a critique of modern theories of negative liberty. When assessed on the basis of the latter standard, his remarks will be found wanting—partly because they miss their target, and partly because the present-day account of negative liberty is demonstrably superior to the Hobbesian account.

Of course, as was stated near the beginning of this chapter, contemporary debates in political philosophy have witnessed the emergence of many competing conceptions (albeit overlapping conceptions) of negative liberty. We shall examine Skinner's comments against a background of only one such conception, the one that has been advocated herein. Under my F Postulate, a person is free to φ if and only if he is able to φ. Hence, some person P who lacks the power-to-act must *ipso facto* lack the liberty-to-act. To say that P lacks the power-to-act is to say that he is unable to act, which in turn is to say that he is not free to act. To determine whether he is unfree to act, we need to ascertain what has led to his lack of power. Such an enquiry hinges not on the location of the key preventive factor—its presence inside or outside P—but on the causal provenance of that factor.

According to my theory of negative liberty, then, it is necessarily the case that somebody devoid of the power to do A is devoid of the liberty to do A. Skinner errs if he thinks that such a thesis 'makes no sense'. Obviously, that thesis is false if the terms 'power' and 'liberty' are defined as Hobbes defined them; but his definition of 'liberty' is precisely what my theory rejects. An acceptance of the Hobbesian definition is hardly a talismanic precondition for making sense or for stating truths.

Judged by the lights of my non-Hobbesian theory, Skinner's analysis of the respective situations of the sick man and the prisoner is infelicitous. Given that both the sick man and the prisoner are unable to leave, neither of them is free to leave. Each of them lacks the liberty to do so. The lack of freedom on the part of the sick man is perfectly consistent with the fact that he is not impeded at all by any external obstacles such as the bars and locked doors that immure the prisoner. He is thwarted by his own illness from leaving, and that very state of preventedness in itself amounts to the deprivation of his freedom to leave. Hence, if there is any difference between the sick man and the prisoner, it does not reside in the putative fact that only the latter has been deprived of freedom. Instead, what might differentiate them is that only the latter has been made unfree. Clearly the prisoner is unfree to walk away, since his confinement has been brought about partly by the actions of other people. By contrast, the sick man might not be unfree to walk away, since the causal responsibility for his ailment might be attributable solely to the workings of nature rather than to the actions of anybody else. If so, then he is not free to leave but is not unfree to leave, either. As applied to him, the predicate 'not free' is unequatable with 'unfree'; he has suffered a loss of freedom but has not thereby incurred any additional unfreedom.

To some readers, the last few paragraphs may initially seem to be little or nothing more than the substitution of one set of stipulative definitions for another. As has been readily acknowledged, the most recently quoted passage from Skinner is irreproachable when taken as an explication of Hobbes's conceptual/terminological framework. Only when Skinner's remarks are handled as if they were an attempted explication of my own conceptual/terminological framework, do they become problematic. What is the point of gauging the soundness of his analysis in this manner? As has already been intimated, there are two main replies to this question. First, and less important, Skinner presents his analysis as a rectification of errors committed by contemporary negative-liberty theorists. He maintains that the people who commit those ostensible errors are taking a position that 'makes no sense'. Thus, someone defending the modern doctrine of negative liberty is wholly warranted in endeavouring to show that the non-Hobbesian position derided by Skinner is fully coherent and unconfused. The claims denounced by Skinner as mistakes have turned out not to be mistakes at all when they are investigated within a pertinent analytical framework—the analytical framework in which they have been articulated. Consequently, even if there were no grounds for believing that my own conception of liberty is superior to Hobbes's, there would likewise be no grounds for believing that Skinner has revealed any respect in which the latter conception is superior to the former.

In fact, however, there are ample grounds for favouring my non-Hobbesian analysis of the concept of freedom. My riposte to Skinner is by no means an arid exercise in upholding one set of stipulative definitions in lieu of another. Even if we put aside the numerous instances of confusion and equivocation that detract from Hobbes's accounts of liberty in *Leviathan* and other works,[48] we should reject his equation of 'free to do *A*' with 'not prevented from doing *A* by any external obstacles or restraints'. That is, we should not join Hobbes in thinking that a person such as an invalid is free-to-do-*A* merely because he or she has not been obstructed from doing *A* by any external impediments. We should instead take the view that, if doing *A* lies beyond the capacities of a person, then *ipso facto* he or she is not free to do it. Why is such a position preferable to that of Hobbes? The answer to this question ought to be apparent from my earlier argument concerning the inadvisableness of classifying mere inabilities as unfreedoms. As was contended in that discussion, a classification along those lines would undercut any satisfactory project of measuring (and comparing) people's levels of overall freedom. Much the same is true of Hobbes's conception of liberty—a conception that classifies mere inabilities as freedoms—though the specific difficulties posed are slightly different.

Recall that the task of measuring and comparing levels of overall freedom (of individuals or of societies) involves the specification of some ratios. Roughly stated, each such ratio obtains between (1) the square of the range of a person's combinations of conjunctively exercisable freedoms and (2) the aforementioned range plus the range of the person's combinations of consistent unfreedoms. Now, if we subscribe to Hobbes's analysis of liberty, we shall once again find that the ratio just delineated is useless for the measurement of anyone's overall socio-political freedom. My earlier discussion has pointed out that the range of each person's combinations of consistent unfreedoms will become limitlessly expansive when mere inabilities are classified as unfreedoms. In my present discussion, not surprisingly, a parallel problem arises in connection with the range of each person's combinations of conjunctively exercisable freedoms.

Nobody is holding Mary back from flying around and around all the galaxies in the universe. She of course is unable to engage in such an escapade, but her inability is not due to anyone else's actions. It is instead a mere inability, an inability rooted in her natural finitude as a human being. If we are to follow Hobbes in classifying every such inability as an instance of freedom, then we shall have to conclude that the range of the combinations of conjunctively exercisable freedoms for Mary is infinitely extensive; completely unlimited, after all, is the scope of the activity which she is utterly unable to undertake but which

---

[48] A number of these instances are deftly exposed in Wernham, 'Liberty'—though I disagree with a few of Wernham's analyses.

she is also unobstructed from undertaking. The same will be true of every other person.

Indeed, somebody adhering to the Hobbesian position will not be able to preserve more than a hollow role for the category of 'unfreedoms'. Let us briefly consider a paradigmatic instance of unfreedom, the situation of a man who is shackled in a jail cell. Given the man's current capacities, his escape has been prevented by the actions of other people. However, the Hobbesian theorist cannot take as given the continuation of the prisoner's current capacities. If the prisoner could straightaway grow strong enough to burst free from his chains and the confines of his cell, he would not be prevented from leaving and would thus not be unfree to leave. Obviously, he is not in fact able to acquire Herculean strength in that manner. He lacks the capacity to do so. Yet that incapacity—as opposed to his inability to depart from his cell through the use of his current capacities—is not due to anyone else's actions. It is a mere inability, one of his natural limitations as a human being. Hence, the Hobbesian theorist will have to classify the prisoner's inability-to-gain-immense-strength-without-delay as an instance of freedom. And therefore such a theorist will have to classify the prisoner's inability-to-leave-the-jail-cell as an instance of freedom. Because the latter inability would not obtain if the former did not obtain, and because the former inability is a natural incapacity rather than something attributable to the actions of others, the prisoner's immurement must be classified by Hobbesians as a situation of liberty. Within the Hobbesian analysis, indeed, it would appear that the lone residual role for the category of 'unfreedoms' is to enable highly qualified descriptions of certain circumstances. With regard to the prisoner, for example, the Hobbesians can maintain that he is unfree to leave his cell *through the use of his present capacities or any relevantly similar capacities*. Such a contention seems curiously feeble as a way of characterizing the imprisoned man's plight, not least because that contention is fully consistent with the claim that the man is free to walk out of his cell at any time.

Now, if the range of each person's combinations of conjunctively exercisable freedoms is unlimited—as the Hobbesians must deem it to be—then the ratio by which we gauge the overall liberty of each person will always be precisely the same for everyone. In the fraction which expresses that ratio, both the numerator and the denominator will be infinitely large. Hence, the addition or subtraction of any particular freedoms or unfreedoms will make no difference whatsoever to the level of anyone's overall liberty. That level for everyone will stand as infinity divided by infinity, and will be wholly unaffected by the elimination of restraints or obstacles in the actual world. Such is the conclusion to which the Hobbesian account of freedom logically commits its proponents. If we embrace that account, then, we shall be endorsing a line of analysis that rules out any satisfactory measurements and comparisons of overall liberty. No illuminating measurements and comparisons are possible if it is fully settled beforehand that everybody's quantum of overall liberty is exactly the same as everybody else's, and if it is likewise settled that that uniform quantum is not modifiable by any developments in the world of human interrelationships. Ergo, we have strong reasons for favouring my explication of the concept of liberty over Hobbes's explication.

1.3.3. Reflections Philosophical and Exegetical Like the first principal subsection of this chapter, the current discussion should conclude by giving Skinner due credit—albeit credit that will prove to be tinged with censure. On the one hand, Skinner in the long passage quoted most recently above has gone astray by taking for granted the equivalence of 'lack[ing] liberty' and 'be[ing] unfree'. On the other hand, he proceeds almost immediately thereafter to ascribe to Hobbes a view that is unmarred by any such error: '[E]ven if no one is rendering it impossible for an agent to act in a given way, it still does not necessarily follow for Hobbes that the agent is free to perform the action concerned. This is because, as we have seen, the action in question may still be beyond the agent's powers... [F]or Hobbes, the question of whether the action is one that the agent is or is not free to perform simply does not arise.'[49] Skinner elaborates on these statements in a footnote where he quotes M. M. Goldsmith's claim that, for Hobbes, 'to be unfree is to be restrained from acting as one wishes to act'.[50] Skinner admonishes: 'This implies that we remain free so long as no one restrains us from performing an action we may wish to perform. As we have seen, however, Hobbes's view is that, if the action in question is beyond our powers, the question of freedom does not arise.'[51] Let us assume that Skinner is using the term 'implies' in his footnote to mean 'suggests' rather than 'entails'. That is, he believes that Goldsmith sees the states of freedom and unfreedom as contradictory rather than as simply contrary, and he accordingly

---

[49] Skinner, 'Signification', 127–8, footnote omitted.
[50] Goldsmith, 'Hobbes', 24.
[51] Skinner, 'Signification', 128 n. 48.

takes Goldsmith to be supposing that 'free' is tantamount to 'not constrained by other people' just as 'unfree' is tantamount to 'constrained by other people'. So construed, the footnote matches the passage from the text, in which Skinner warns against the equation of 'not constrained by other people' and 'free'. Understood in this manner, his comments serve to acknowledge that people are sometimes neither free nor unfree to φ. Sometimes they are merely unable to φ. In such circumstances they are not free to φ but are not unfree, either.

In so far as Skinner is adhering to the conception of freedom that has just been outlined, his stance—along with Hobbes's stance—is markedly closer to my own than has been indicated heretofore. Nevertheless, these latest extracts throw up some further problems, two of which are philosophical and one of which is exegetical. In the first place, even if all other difficulties are ignored, the fact remains that Hobbes relied on an internal/external dichotomy rather than on causal enquiries for his distinction between an absence of liberty and an absence of power. His focus in that respect was misguided, even if he recognized that 'free' and 'unfree' are not bivalent.

Second, it is not clear what is meant by Skinner's assertion that 'the question of freedom does not arise' for Hobbes in connection with actions that lie beyond an agent's capacities.[52] A question concerning an agent's freedom to perform some particular action is certainly meaningful and pertinent, unlike (say) an inquiry whether the number seven has a good sense of humour. Unlike an inquiry whether the colour yellow is prone to fits of anger, a question about an agent's freedom does not commit any category mistakes. Moreover, there is always a determinate answer to such a question, at least in the circumstances envisaged by Skinner. Within my own analytical framework, the question of an agent's freedom to perform an act beyond his or her capacities should always be answered in the negative. If an agent lacks the capacity to do *A*, then he *ipso facto* lacks the freedom to do *A*. (Whether he is unfree or merely not free to do *A* will depend, of course, on what has caused his incapacity.) Within Hobbes's analytical framework—that is, within his framework as I have interpreted it—the answer to any query about the freedom of an agent in connection with an act *A* beyond her capacities will depend on the existence or inexistence of external obstacles that would thwart the agent from doing *A*. Unless such obstacles exist, the agent is free to perform *A*

---

[52] Skinner's assertion is probably based on a similar claim in Day, 'On Liberty', at 180.

notwithstanding her inability to do so.[53] In short, both within my theory of liberty and within Hobbes's theory, we are referred to clear-cut factors on the basis of which we can determinately answer any questions about the freedom of agents to perform acts that exceed their capabilities. Such questions do arise, and they pose no intractable difficulties. (As will be argued shortly, such questions arise even within Hobbes's analysis as understood by Skinner.)

Third, as should be evident, the comments by Skinner most recently quoted above are rooted in an interpretation of Hobbes quite different from my own. Skinner seizes on a pronouncement in *Leviathan* that appears to be at odds with my exegesis: '[A] FREEMAN, is he, that in those things, which by his strength and wit he is able to do, is not hindered to do what he has a will to'.[54] From this pronouncement Skinner derives the following interpretation of Hobbes's conception of liberty:

As this makes clear, Hobbes sees two essential elements in the concept of human freedom. One is the idea of possessing an underlying power or ability to act. As Hobbes had already observed in Chapter XIV, it is in relation to 'a man's power to do what hee would' that we speak of his being or not being at liberty. The other is the idea of being unimpeded in the exercise of such powers. As Hobbes explains later in Chapter XXI, the freedom of a man 'consisteth in this, that he finds no stop in doing what he has the will, desire or inclination to do.'[55]

Skinner's understanding of the Hobbesian power/liberty distinction is essentially the inverse of my interpretation. I have argued that Hobbes used 'power' as a more inclusive term than 'liberty' when drawing a contrast between them. With the former term Hobbes adverted not only to each person's capacities but also to the state of external unpreventedness—liberty—that enables the person to exert those capacities. So my discussion has maintained. Skinner adopts an opposite perspective and contends in effect that 'liberty' is the more inclusive term. According to him, Hobbes used that term to denote not only the state of external unpreventedness that allows the exercise of a person's capacities, but also the capacities themselves (powers).

---

[53] Skinner appears to endorse this interpretation in some recent reflections on Hobbes, to whom he imputes the view that '[i]f [an] action is not within [someone's] powers, what they lack is not the freedom but the ability to act' (*Liberty*, 7 n. 20).

[54] Hobbes, *Leviathan*, 139 (Ch. 21, para. 2), italics deleted.

[55] Skinner, 'Signification', 123, footnotes deleted.

The rest of this subsection will seek to impugn Skinner's interpretation, and will then maintain that even the correctness of his interpretation would not necessitate any modification of the analytical points advanced herein. What, then, are the grounds for harbouring doubts about the accuracy of his construal of Hobbes's position? Let us begin by observing that the only passage that can plausibly be cited in support of Skinner's reading is the 'FREEMAN' pronouncement. Each of the other statements which Skinner quotes to buttress his interpretation is instead an expression of the Hobbesian view that the existence of any liberty is desire-dependent. (That view has been sustainedly criticized in this chapter, but is not currently under scrutiny.) Only the 'FREEMAN' pronouncement suggests that the existence of any liberty is capacity-dependent. Hence, we have to determine whether that pronouncement is sufficient to resolve the present clash of interpretations in Skinner's favour.

One manifest but easily overlooked feature of the relevant portion of Hobbes's text is that it defines not 'free' or 'freedom' or 'liberty', but 'freeman'. When defining 'liberty' or 'freedom', Hobbes referred strictly to the absence of external impediments and did not include any intimation of capacity-dependence.[56] Only when he sought to explicate the term 'freeman' did he give the slightest indication that individuals' capacities are an essential component of the phenomenon under investigation. Now, among political philosophers, the distinction between being free-to-φ and being a free man is well known. Although the notion of a free man is far too complicated and controversial to be explored fully here, we should note that one trait typically attributed to the free man is that of self-sufficiency. Joel Feinberg, among others, has pointed to many 'traditional conceptions of the free man as...self-reliant, self-sufficient, and self-confident'.[57] If Hobbes had in mind some of those traditional conceptions when explicating the term 'freeman', he would understandably have been led to highlight the free man's capacities as well as the unrestrictedness that enables the exercise of those capacities. Thus, the prominent reference to such capacities in Hobbes's definition of 'freeman'—a reference which clearly tends to convey the message that one's existence as a free man is capacity-dependent—cannot in itself warrant our inferring that Hobbes perceived the existence of freedoms as

---

[56]   Hobbes, *Leviathan*, 86, 139 (Ch. 14, para. 2; Ch. 21, para. 1).
[57]   Joel Feinberg, 'The Idea of a Free Man', in *Rights, Justice, and the Bounds of Liberty* (Princeton: Princeton University Press, 1980), 3, 15.

capacity-dependent. Because of the non-equivalence of 'being free to φ' and 'being a free man', such an inference is far from entirely safe.

Moreover, even if we pretermit the point that has just been made, the Hobbesian definition of 'freeman' does not per se establish that one's capacity-to-φ is a necessary condition for one's freedom-to-φ. It specifies what must be true if a man with the capacity to φ is also free to φ, but it does not directly address at all the situation of somebody who lacks that capacity. To be sure, the definition plainly leaves room for us to infer that the predicate 'free to φ' is not applicable to someone who lacks the capacity to φ. Such an inference is indeed quite plausible (if the observations in my last paragraph are left aside). Nonetheless, also possible is a contrary inference—an inference that would have been closed off if Hobbes in his definition of 'freeman' had written 'in those things *and only those things*, which by his strength and wit he is able to do'. In other words, that definition as it stands does not state conclusively that a free man must have the capacity to do those things which he is free to do. Nowhere did Hobbes unequivocally submit that the existence of any freedom is capacity-dependent.

Furthermore, if we join Skinner in taking the 'FREEMAN' pronouncement as a sufficient basis for his interpretation of Hobbes's conception of liberty, we shall run afoul of some other passages in *Leviathan*. As a prelude to those passages, we should ponder the following definition of 'liberty' in Hobbes's essay 'Of Liberty and Necessity':

> I conceive *liberty* to be rightly defined in this manner: *Liberty is the absence of all the impediments to action that are not contained in the nature and intrinsical quality of the agent.* As for example, the water is said to descend *freely*, or to have *liberty* to descend by the channel of the river, because there is no impediment that way, but not across, because the banks are impediments. And though the water cannot ascend, yet men never say it wants the *liberty* to ascend, but the *faculty* or *power*, because the impediment is in the nature of the water, and intrinsical.[58]

---

[58] Thomas Hobbes, 'Of Liberty and Necessity', in *The Collected Works of Thomas Hobbes*, iv, ed. William Molesworth (London: Routledge/Thoemmes Press, 1992), 229, 273, emphases in original. For an interpretation of this passage from a viewpoint closer to Skinner's, see Ronald Polansky and Kurt Torell, 'Power, Liberty, and Counterfactual Conditionals in Hobbes's Thought', 3 *Hobbes Studies* 3, 12 (1990): '[S]ince there is no possibility that the water will ascend, we do not properly say that the body of water is "not at liberty". That is, because there is no ascending motion in the water at all (no endeavor upwards at all), we cannot affirm that the water would ascend were things different, i.e., were there no external impediment. We therefore cannot say that the water could be "at

One of the pregnant passages from *Leviathan* is the claim (quoted earlier) that external impediments, which negate liberty when present, 'may oft take away part of a man's power to do what he would; but cannot hinder him from using the power left him'.[59] Under my reading of Hobbes, which maintains that he used 'power' to denote both internal capacities and external unimpededness, the claim just quoted is perfectly straightforward. When external impediments reduce a person's liberty, they *ipso facto* reduce the person's power. By contrast, under Skinner's inverse reading—where we are told in effect that Hobbes used 'power' to denote only internal capacities and that he used 'liberty' to denote both internal powers and external unimpededness—the claim just quoted is curious and far-fetched. As was remarked earlier, a narrow construction of the term 'power' leads to the conclusion that Hobbes in this passage was contemplating occurrences such as the atrophying of muscles in limbs that are fettered. To be sure, as was likewise remarked earlier, it is not completely inconceivable that Hobbes had in mind occurrences of that sort when he wrote about the taking away of power by external impediments. All the same, an interpretation along these lines is hardly cogent.

Even more problematic for Skinner is the passage that immediately precedes the 'FREEMAN' pronouncement. In that passage, which we have already plumbed in some depth, Hobbes declared that 'when the impediment of motion, is in the constitution of the thing itself, we use not to say, it wants the liberty; but the power to move; as when a stone lieth still, or a man is fastened to his bed by sickness'.[60] Under my reading of Hobbes, this passage is wholly straightforward. Given the Hobbesian definitions of 'power' and 'liberty,' a person can lack the

---

liberty". Talk of liberty depends somehow on possibilities and counterfactuals.' Though such an interpretation cannot be absolutely ruled out, it is decidedly unpersuasive. Hobbes was clearly depicting a situation where no external impediments prevent the upward movement of the water in a river. Hence, Polanksy's and Torell's equation of 'were things different' and 'were there no external impediment' is wholly inapt. Precisely because of the absence of external impediments to the river's ascendance, Hobbes counselled against our ascribing to the river a lack of the liberty-to-ascend. He would hardly have been inclined to adopt any other position, given that he had just defined 'liberty' as 'the absence of [external] impediments'. (I should note, incidentally, that Polansky and Torell later characterize the power/liberty distinction—at least on a macroscopic level—in terms virtually the same as my own. See Polansky and Torell, 'Power, Liberty, and Counterfactual Conditionals in Hobbes's Thought', 16.)

[59]   Hobbes, *Leviathan*, 86 (Ch. 14, para. 2).
[60]   Hobbes, *Leviathan*, 139 (Ch. 21, para. 1).

power to do *A* without lacking the liberty to do *A*; the sick man described by Hobbes is in exactly such a condition. Skinner, however, cannot construe the passage along these lines at all. According to his interpretation of Hobbes, a person can lack the liberty-to-do-*A* without lacking the power-to-do-*A*, but not vice versa. According to his interpretation, that is, anyone devoid of the power-to-do-*A* is devoid of the liberty-to-do-*A*. Such an approach cannot explain why Hobbes would decline to affirm that the man fastened to his bed by sickness is bereft of the liberty to walk around.

Contrary to what Skinner maintains, the question of a person's freedom to perform actions beyond her capabilities does arise within the Hobbesian analysis even when that analysis is understood in the way that Skinner recommends. Such a question about a person's freedom is fully intelligible and germane, and it will always be determinately answerable. We are told by Skinner that, for Hobbes, any ascription to someone of the liberty-to-do-*A* must presuppose an ascription to her of the power-to-do-*A*. Consequently, the question of a person's liberty to do things beyond her powers will always be straightforwardly answerable in the negative—which means that the person will always lack the liberty to do any of those things. Quite mysterious, then, is Hobbes's counselling against our saying that the bedridden man lacks the liberty to walk away. In short, if we accept Skinner's account of the Hobbesian power/liberty distinction, we shall find that the passage on the sick man has been rendered inexplicable. The question of the sick man's liberty is as pertinent within Skinner's account as within my own, but Skinner's account obliges us to conclude that Hobbes handled the question wrongly.

At any rate, even if Skinner's exposition of the power/liberty distinction were inexpugnable as an interpretation of Hobbes's work, it would leave intact all the analytical points that have been advanced herein. My primary concern in this subsection and throughout this book is to clarify the concept of social and political liberty. Any such task of conceptual refinement involves the drawing of quite a few subtle distinctions. Those distinctions, such as that between 'unfree' and 'not free', are entirely unaffected by any exegetical jousting over the meanings of various passages in Hobbes's texts. Although his texts can undoubtedly serve to illuminate sundry aspects of the concept of freedom—through his arguments that are sound and perceptive, and also through his arguments that are confused and in need of rectification—an elucidation of those texts is secondary to my main objective. Hobbes's writings on liberty are immensely valuable both as targets of criticism and as sources of insights; but the success or failure of my efforts to explicate those writings does not have any bearing on the success or failure of my general philosophical project of conceptual clarification.

In line with what was mentioned earlier, the conclusion of this subsection has in some respects been a slightly backhanded tribute to Skinner. Although his interpretation of Hobbes is questionable, it is questionable precisely because it delineates a conception of liberty more robust than the conception that is present in Hobbes's works. If Skinner has gone astray exegetically to some extent, he has done so in a manner that redounds to his credit philosophically. Still, the enhanced doctrine which he imputes to Hobbes is philosophically inadequate in a number of ways. It distinguishes between 'not free' and 'unfree' on the basis of the internal/external dichotomy rather than on the basis of causal enquiries; it holds that the existence of any freedom is desire-dependent; it submits that the question of a man's liberty to perform acts beyond his capacities does not arise (as if we could not determinately answer that apt question by affirming that the man lacks the liberty to perform those acts); and it does not sufficiently disentangle normative freedom and non-normative freedom. Having explored each of these shortcomings to some degree already, we shall now look again at the normative/non-normative conflation.

1.4. Freedom as Normative Condition and Freedom as Physical Fact

1.4.1. Some General Philosophical Observations   In the F Postulate and the U Postulate with which this book has sought to encapsulate the conditions for the existence of particular freedoms and unfreedoms, the central points of reference are the modal categories of possibility and impossibility. By contrast, the deontic categories of permissibility and impermissibility do not figure at all. As should be quite plain, then, the states of freedom and unfreedom on which this book principally concentrates are non-normative. A person P is non-normatively free-to-φ if and only if he is physically unprevented from φ-ing. P is non-normatively unfree-to-φ if and only if he is physically unable-to-φ as a result of some action(s) by some other person(s). (In these statements, the word 'physically' is not to be construed in contrast with 'mentally' or 'psychologically'. We do not have to delve very deeply into the mind–body relationship to realize that somebody mentally or psychologically precluded from φ-ing is likewise physically precluded from φ-ing. If the physical preclusion did not obtain, then the psychological preclusion would not genuinely consist in preventedness. A person is mentally incapacitated from learning how to read, for example, only if it is not possible for him to undertake and undergo the full set of physical processes—chiefly cerebral processes—that would constitute his learning how to read. In sum, regardless of how one perceives the mind–body relationship, one should recognize that psychological impossibility and physical impossibility are both indeed conditions of sheer preventedness. Precisely that common characteristic is what separates them from normative impermissibility, which consists in forbiddenness rather than in precludedness. Instead of being implicitly contrasted with 'mentally,' then, the word 'physically' throughout this subsection is to be construed in opposition to 'normatively'.)

Normative liberty consists not in the physical fact of unpreventedness, but in a state of permittedness that is implicitly or explicitly established by authoritative norms such as laws or moral precepts or institutional rules. Any action which those norms allow is something which a person is normatively free to do. Contrariwise, any action which those norms forbid is something which a person is normatively unfree to do. When we are enquiring into someone's normative freedom or unfreedom, the categories that inform our investigation are deontic rather than modal. That is, we are asking whether particular modes of conduct are unprohibited or prohibited, rather than whether they are possible or infeasible. We are seeking to discover not whether a person is *capable* of doing certain things, but whether he is *entitled* to do them.

Normative freedom as a state of permittedness and normative unfreedom as a state of forbiddenness are different in crucial respects from non-normative freedom and unfreedom. For one thing, 'free' and 'unfree' in their normative senses are bivalent; 'normatively not free' is equivalent to 'normatively unfree', and 'normatively not unfree' is equivalent to 'normatively free'. A person P is normatively at liberty to φ—for instance, morally or legally at liberty to φ—if and only if he is not prohibited from φ-ing by any authoritative norms such as moral precepts or laws. P is normatively unfree-to-φ if and only if he is prohibited from φ-ing by some authoritative norm(s). When our focus is on normative states of affairs, no gap obtains between 'unfree' and 'not free'. Of course, there are different varieties of authoritative normativity. P can be morally free-to-φ while being legally unfree-to-φ, and vice versa. Nevertheless, so long as we are talking about authoritative normativity generally or about a single variety of such normativity, any application of the predicate 'not free' is equivalent to an application of the predicate 'unfree'. Likewise, any application of the predicate 'not unfree' is equivalent to an application of the predicate 'free'.

Perhaps even more important than the foregoing difference between non-normative liberty and normative liberty is the difference between them as a state of unpreventedness and a state of unforbiddenness respectively. Equally significant, of course, is the difference between non-normative unfreedom as a state of preventedness and normative unfreedom as a state of forbiddenness. Whenever someone is non-normatively free to do *A*, she is able to do it—irrespective of whether she is permitted to do it. She *can* do it, whether or not she *may* do it (that is, whether or not she can do it legitimately). She might be transgressing moral or legal norms in the process, but she is non-normatively at-liberty-to-do-*A* inasmuch as she is unprecluded from doing it. Ability, not permissibility, is the key category for non-normative freedom. Quite the reverse is true for normative freedom. Whenever somebody is normatively free to do *A*, she is allowed to do it by any authoritative norms that might be applicable. If none of those norms imposes on her a duty to abstain from doing *A* or to abstain from doing something that would be indispensable for the doing of *A*, then the performance of *A* is something which she is normatively free to undertake. She enjoys normative freedom in respect of *A* inasmuch as she is not required by any authoritative norms to forgo *A*. However, her normative latitude to carry out *A* will not necessarily be accompanied by any non-normative freedom to do it. She might be wholly unable to perform *A*, either because of her own incapacities or because of some external preventive factor. For example, while not being under any legal or moral duty to refrain from running a mile in less than four minutes, and while likewise not being under any duty to refrain from engaging in some activity (such as regular practice) that would be indispensable for the performance of such a feat, Mary is utterly unable to run a mile so swiftly. Though she is normatively at liberty to run a mile in less than four minutes, she lacks the capacity to do so, and therefore she does not enjoy any non-normative liberty to run with such celerity.

Whenever someone is non-normatively unfree to do *A*, he is unable to do it, and his inability has been caused by some action(s) of some other person(s). He might be perfectly entitled to do *A*—that is, he might be normatively at liberty to do it—but at least one action by some other person(s) has physically prevented him from doing it. In other words, even if he enjoys the normative freedom to do *A*, the actions or dispositions of some other person(s) have made him unable to exercise that freedom (whether or not he endeavours to exercise it). Permissibility and impossibility can coincide. Much the same can be said, conversely, about the potential coincidence of possibility and impermissibility. Whenever somebody is normatively unfree to do A, he is prohibited from doing it by some authoritative norm that imposes a duty on him to eschew A or to eschew some action(s) that would be indispensable for his performance of A. Because of the forbiddenness of A or the forbiddenness of an essential prerequisite thereof, he cannot perform A without disobeying the requirements of some moral or legal or other authoritative norms. Nonetheless, although he cannot perform A without disobeying those requirements, he might be able to perform it with ease. There need not be and frequently will not be a convergence between what is barred by legal or moral mandates and what is rendered impossible by the physical facts of a situation. Those facts frequently enable occurrences which the prevailing legal or moral norms prohibit. As was noted earlier, even the regular enforcement of legal mandates will seldom preclude violations of their requirements. That enforcement is usually *post hoc* rather than anticipatory. In short, impermissibility and possibility very frequently coincide—which means, of course, that the normative unfreedom-to-φ and the non-normative freedom-to-φ very frequently coincide. We have seen above that there is no necessary correlation between instances of normative freedom and instances of non-normative freedom, and we have seen here that a similar point obtains in regard to normative and non-normative *un*freedom.

Another dissimilarity between normative freedom or unfreedom and non-normative freedom or unfreedom pertains to the isolability of actions that are proscribed or precluded. The removal of someone's non-normative freedom-to-do-X will sometimes require the removal of his non-normative freedom-to-do-things-that-are-crucially-pre-requisite-to-his-performance-of-X, whereas a prohibition on his doing X (that is, the removal of his normative liberty-to-do-X) will never require the prohibition of any prerequisite actions that are logically distinct from his doing X. If somebody retains the non-normative freedom to take steps that are immediately antecedent to his performance of X, then the prevention of his doing X—that is, the removal of his non-normative liberty-to-do-X—will typically depend on monitoring and rapid interventions by other people to an extent that will sometimes not be feasible. To be sure, such monitoring and interventions will often be feasible, in connection with many activities. For example, just as King Uzziah was about to offer incense on the altar of the ancient temple of Judah, dozens of priests interposed themselves between him and the altar, and they thrust him away.[61] In some circumstances, however, last-minute preventive intrusions of this sort are not realistically possible. An intervention at an earlier stage will sometimes be essential if a person's non-normative liberty-to-do-X is genuinely to be eliminated. Nothing similar is ever essential for the removal of someone's normative liberty-to-do-X. Suppose, for illustration, that somebody in a queue for a bus has assaulted somebody else in the queue. The assault was legally and morally forbidden, even though the close physical proximity of the two people in the queue—essential for the perpetration of the assault—was not itself illegal or immoral. That is, the assailant had no normative liberty to commit the assault, even though he did enjoy normative liberty (as well as non-normative liberty) to do virtually everything prerequisite to his commission of the assault. Precisely because the elimination of any person's normative liberty-to-do-X concerns what is impermissible rather than what is impossible, that elimination is always perfectly consistent with the fact that the person retains the normative liberty to do just about everything that is physically indispensable for his undertaking of X. (Of course, sometimes a person will not enjoy the normative liberty to take steps that immediately lead up to his proscribed performance of X. What I have argued here is simply that the absence of his normative liberty to take those steps is never necessary for the absence of his normative liberty to perform X itself.)

Still another divergence between normative unfreedom and non-normative unfreedom is evident from the first chief subsection of this chapter. As was argued there, a person whose mind has not been completely taken over by someone else or by a severe mental illness will retain the non-normative freedom to eschew any particular action. At the very least, such a person will always have the option of surrendering in a wholly passive manner to the operations of external forces. In other words, there is no such thing as a physically unavoidable action. When we cross from the realm of the non-normative to the realm of the normative, we encounter a very different situation. Any person P can be normatively unfree to forgo certain instances of conduct. For example, every person whose income is subject to taxation will be legally unfree—and perhaps morally unfree—to abstain from doing what is necessary in order to pay any taxes that are owed. Though P is always physically free (albeit perhaps at great cost) to refrain from signing the requisite forms and cheques for the payment

---

[61] II Chronicles 19:16–20.

of his taxes in a timely fashion, he is normatively unfree to hold back in that manner. He is legally obligated and perhaps morally obligated to sign the relevant documents. A moral or legal obligation can render the doing of *A* normatively mandatory, by rendering impermissible a failure to do *A*. In that respect, as well as in other respects, the mandatoriness created by legal or moral requirements is distinguishable from the necessity created by physical constraints.

In a chapter aimed at repelling Skinner's challenges to the modern conception of negative liberty, the differences between normative freedom or unfreedom and non-normative freedom or unfreedom are of considerable importance (as we shall shortly behold). Before leaving behind these general observations concerning the normative/non-normative dichotomy, however, we should note fleetingly that some subtle aspects of freedom cut across that dichotomy. Divergent though normative liberty and non-normative liberty are, they exhibit some affinities that are far from inconsequential. Let us glance at two of those affinities, before moving on. First, in certain circumstances, two or more people can each be free to occupy exactly the same place at the same time—even though their joint occupation of exactly the same place at the same time is of course impossible. This counter-intuitive state of affairs is possible (under certain circumstances) both in connection with normative liberty and in connection with non-normative liberty. Less strikingly counter-intuitive but often overlooked is a second point that applies to both sides of the normative/non-normative divide: the fact that the freedom-to-φ is often considerably more valuable than φ-ing itself. People who set very little store indeed by some activity might nonetheless bridle if their freedom to pursue that activity were removed. Each of these two characteristics possessed by both normative freedom and non-normative freedom will receive careful attention in my next chapter. Thus, as we turn to concentrate now on some conflations of the normative and the non-normative, we should remain aware that my disentangling of those categories is fully consistent with their sharing of some noteworthy properties.

1.4.2. Skinner and the Normative/Non-normative Diremption   As we saw at the end of the first major subsection of this chapter, Skinner sometimes aptly separates the normative and non-normative dimensions of freedom. At other times, however, he runs those dimensions together. Having observed a few instances of this conflation already, we shall look at two further—and somewhat more compli-cated—examples here.

1. Let us begin by returning to Skinner's discussion of Hobbes, where an instance of the aforementioned conflation occurs while Skinner is seeking to warn against that very sort of mistake:

[Hobbes] does not contradict himself by first saying that liberty can only be constrained by external impediments and later that it can also be constrained by laws. Rather one can summarise his argument by observing that liberty on the one hand, and civil law on the other, belong for Hobbes to different spheres. Liberty belongs to the sphere of nature, the sphere in which everyone has an equal right, and thus a liberty, 'to use his own power, as he will himselfe, for the preservation of his own Nature'. This liberty can only be constrained by ties or bonds which are themselves natural—that is, physical—in character.[62]

Before focusing on the normative/non-normative conflation in this passage, we should glimpse at a partly related problem that will emerge saliently in the second half of this chapter. The word 'laws' in the first sentence of this extract needs to be elucidated. If the word denotes the sheer formulations of legal requirements (and other legal positions) in abstraction from any processes of effectuating those requirements, then obviously laws do not limit anyone's non-normative freedom at all. Considered in strict isolation from all mechanisms and operations of enforcement, legal norms do not encroach even slightly on any-body's physical ability to φ. Alternatively, however, the word 'laws' can refer not only to the abstract formulations of legal requirements (and other legal positions), but also to the various means by which those requirements are applied and implemented. When the term is construed in this fashion—as it frequently is, in this book and else-where—we should grasp that the existence of well-enforced laws does impinge on people's non-normative liberty.

To be sure, even when we do thoroughly take account of the imple-mentation of legal norms, we should acknowledge that the existence of regularly enforced laws does not usually render impossible the perpet-ration of any acts which the terms of those laws proscribe. As has been stated more than once already, the typical means of giving effect to legal obligations are after-the-fact punishments and compensatory/restitutionary orders (which are themselves backed up by punishments or by seizures of assets). Normally, the existence of a well-enforced legal prohibition on doing A will not scotch anyone's non-normative liberty-to-do-A. However, as applied to each person, it will *pro tanto*

[62] Skinner, 'Signification', 138, footnote deleted.

reduce his or her overall non-normative freedom by eliminating the performability of certain combinations of actions. We have perceived as much in some earlier subsections of this chapter. In respect of overall freedom, then, a network of regularly enforced laws as applied to each person is *pro tanto* an array of 'external impediments'. By doing away with the conjunctive exercisability of sundry options that would otherwise be conjunctively exercisable, such laws *pro tanto* reduce each person's overall liberty—even though most of the acts forbidden by the terms of those laws are still separately possible for most people. Skinner or Hobbes tends to obscure this point about overall freedom by contending that 'the laws of the Commonwealth...leave entirely unimpaired our natural liberty to make use of our powers'.[63] (N.B. As is suggested by the several appearances of the phrase '*pro tanto*' above, this paragraph has certainly not sought to indicate that the general implementation of a well-enforced legal mandate will have produced an all-things-considered reduction in the non-normative liberty of each person. On the contrary, virtually any sensible legal mandate that is regularly enforced will have increased almost everyone's overall non-normative liberty by discouraging certain forms of liberty-curtailing behaviour that might otherwise take place. Because the well-enforced mandate will have led the large majority of people to be uninclined to engage in those forms of behaviour, each person is unlikely to encounter such behaviour on the part of other people, and each therefore enjoys a greater degree of non-normative latitude than he or she would enjoy in the absence of the mandate. Such a conclusion, which will surface again shortly in a different context, is perfectly consistent with the point made in this paragraph. Here my point has simply been that, when we consider the application of a well-enforced legal mandate to any person in isolation—and when we therefore put aside the fact that the mandate gets applied to everyone else as well—the upshot is a *pro-tanto* diminution of the person's overall non-normative freedom.)

In the long passage quoted above, the principal conflation of the normative dimension and the non-normative dimension occurs in the sentence which asserts that liberty 'belongs to the sphere of nature, the sphere in which everyone has an equal right, and thus a liberty [to endeavour to sustain himself]'. Contrary to what Skinner proclaims in the rest of the extract, the 'equal right' in the Hobbesian State of Nature is in fact an equal *normative* liberty. It consists in the absence of any *normative* restrictions or obligations that would render impermissible

---

[63] Ibid.

the efforts of a person to ensure his own survival and basic comfort. In other words, the distinction that must be drawn in order to make sense of Hobbes's seemingly inconsistent claims is not the distinction that Skinner draws between liberty and civil law. Rather, the relevant distinction is between two types of liberty, normative and non-normative.[64]

Non-normative liberty for some person *P*, as has been argued throughout this chapter, consists in the absence of any preventive factors that would exclude the physical possibility of *P*'s φ-ing. Moral norms in themselves do not constrict anybody's non-normative liberty at all. Legal norms in isolation from mechanisms of law-enforcement are likewise devoid of any restrictive impact on the non-normative liberty of each person.[65] Only constraints that engender impossibility as opposed to impermissibility—or in addition to impermissibility—are constraints on non-normative freedom.

An inverse situation obtains, of course, with regard to normative freedom. Physical barriers and restraints in themselves do not impair anybody's normative liberty at all. They can make things impossible, but they never in themselves render anything impermissible. Of course, *in combination with authoritative norms*, physical obstacles and trammels can affect the normative liberty of each person. For example, suppose that a law *L* prohibits people from walking on

---

[64] In distinguishing between two types of liberty for the purpose of understanding the ostensibly inconsistent claims which Skinner mentions, my analysis is broadly similar to that in Annabel Brett, *Liberty, Right, and Nature* (Cambridge: Cambridge University Press, 1997), Ch. 6. However, the non-normative/normative dichotomy which I invoke is very different from the physical/deliberative dichotomy which Brett highlights. She relies on a division between the physical liberty of movement and the deliberative liberty of pondering and reaching decisions. The essence of the position which she attributes to Hobbes is that 'civil law, the constraint on the will, restrains natural liberty in the sense of the liberty of deliberation' (*Liberty, Right, and Nature*, 231). Although Brett's exposition is careful and learned and in many respects illuminating, its obfuscation of the non-normative/normative distinction is deeply regrettable on both philosophical and exegetical grounds. (For another quite perceptive analysis of Hobbes's conception of liberty that is even more seriously marred by a failure to attend to the normative/non-normative distinction, see Wolfgang von Leyden, *Hobbes and Locke* [London: Macmillan, 1982], 10–12. See also Flathman, *Freedom*, 23.)

[65] Hence the following statements, made in connection with non-normative freedom, are not sustainable: '[A] law against doing *x* makes us unfree to do *x*, however "weak" the threatened sanction is, or however unlikely it is that we will be caught... [I]f there is a ban on speeding... then I am not free to speed... however likely or unlikely it is that this regulation will be enforced' (Kristjánsson, *Social Freedom*, 46, 47).

plots of land that are enclosed by fences but allows them to walk on any plots of land that are not so enclosed. If Joe puts up a fence around his field, he will thereby have reduced the normative freedom (the legal freedom and perhaps also the moral freedom) of each of his fellows. Nevertheless, the fence in itself—the fence in detachment from any legal or moral norms—does not bring about the reduction. Instead, the erection of the fence triggers the applicability of *L*'s ban to Joe's estate. If *L* did not exist, and if the prevailing legal and moral norms did not forbid the activity of walking on other people's land and did not forbid the surmounting or damaging of other people's fences, the construction of the fence by Joe would not impair anybody's normative liberty at all. It would not disallow anything that had thitherto been permitted. Only through the obligation-imposing force of legal or moral or other authoritative mandates does anything become disallowed.

When Hobbes wrote about the so-called right of nature to which Skinner refers, he was maintaining that every person enjoys full normative liberty to take any steps which he or she deems necessary for survival.[66] No moral norms or other authoritative norms—not even the legal norms of the Hobbesian sovereign—will ever constrict that liberty at all. Hobbes was not making a claim about non-normative freedom when he insisted on this point. After all, from his premise about the irreducible liberty of every person to strive for survival, he derived the thesis that in the State of Nature 'every man has a right to every thing; even to one another's body'.[67] By 'right' he again clearly meant 'liberty', and equally clearly he was making a pronouncement about normative rather than non-normative liberty. Had he instead been adverting to non-normative freedom, he would have been taking the preposterous view that every person in the State of Nature possesses a comprehensive and irreducible physical ability to make use of all requisite life-sustaining resources including every other person's body. Indeed, such a view is not only preposterous but incoherent. To avoid the conclusion that Hobbes was putting forth arrant nonsense, then, we must infer that his comments on the so-called right of nature (and its derivatives) were about permittedness rather than about capability. When those comments are understood as claims about normative legitimacy—that is, when they are understood as claims about the non-existence of any veritable obligations that would prohibit each person's pursuit of his or her own survival—the preposterousness and incoherence of Hobbes's position disappear.

---

[66] Hobbes, *Leviathan*, 86 (Ch. 14, para. 1).
[67] Hobbes, *Leviathan*, 86–7 (Ch. 14, para. 4).

Though to some degree his discussions do veer quite confusingly between a focus on normative freedom and a focus on non-normative freedom, the chief strands of the discussions can be suitably disentangled.

Hence, Skinner (in the lengthy extract above) has reversed the true scheme of things when he declares that the so-called right of nature 'can only be constrained by ties or bonds which are themselves natural—that is, physical—in character'. The right of nature is a normative liberty, a comprehensive normative liberty, that is wholly unconstrainable. Were it subject to being curbed, any curbs would have to arise through authoritative norms. If physical impediments contribute at all to the curtailment of anybody's normative liberty, they do so only by triggering the applicability of some authoritative norms such as those involved in the scenario of Joe and his fence. Far from being the exclusive sources of restrictions on each person's normative liberty, physical constraints are derivative sources at most. Normative constraints in the form of authoritative mandates are indispensable for any limitations on the permissibility of various actions.

2. A second noteworthy conflation of the normative and the non-normative occurs at the end of a fairly early article in which Skinner contrasts the modern understanding of liberty with the civic-republican understanding. He submits that Machiavelli's recommendations concerning the sustainment of individual and collective freedom 'may thus be said to reverse the usual relationship between liberty and the law...expressed in most contemporary theories of liberty'. Skinner expands on this assertion as follows:

Among contemporary theorists, the coercive apparatus of the law is generally pictured as an obvious affront to individual freedom. The power of the law to constrain us is only held to be justified if, in diminishing the extent of our natural liberty, it serves at the same time to assure more effectively our capacity to exercise the freedom that remains to us. The proper relationship between the law and liberty is thus held to be expressed by saying that—as Isaiah Berlin puts it—the law should create a framework within which 'as many individuals as possible can realize as many of their ends as possible, without assessment of the value of these ends as such, save in so far as they may frustrate the purposes of others'.

For Machiavelli, by contrast, the law is in part justified because it ensures a degree of personal freedom which, in its absence, would altogether collapse. If the coercive apparatus of the law were withdrawn, there would not be a greater degree of personal liberty with a diminished capacity to enjoy it without risk; due to our self-destructive natures, there would rather be a diminution of personal liberty, a rapid slide towards a condition of complete servitude.[68]

This passage contains two closely connected misrepresentations. First, Skinner errs in contending that all or nearly all present-day liberals espouse the view that restrictions on liberty are justified only when those restrictions strengthen the capacity of each individual—or of individuals generally—to enjoy the liberty that remains. Instead, many liberals maintain that any particular restriction on freedom is justified only when it serves to increase freedom overall for each individual or for individuals collectively. Second, also mistaken is the suggestion that liberals would perceive the removal of all governmental controls as a means of augmenting everyone's liberty while reducing the capacity of each person to avail herself of the more expansive liberty without risk. Rather, liberals as opposed to anarchists would regard the elimination of all governmental controls as a development certain to reduce sharply the overall freedom of virtually everyone.[69]

In the second half of this chapter, we shall more lengthily examine Skinner's efforts to raise republican queries about liberal attitudes toward the relationship between law and liberty. What is of most importance here is the normative/non-normative conflation that underlies the two misrepresentations just described. On the one hand, Skinner is referring primarily or exclusively to non-normative freedom in the passage excerpted above. Within that passage, his orientation is most directly evident from his quotation of the remark by Isaiah Berlin about the latitude of individuals to realize their ends. That remark is entirely focused on individuals' abilities and thus on

---

[68] Skinner, 'Maintenance', 12–13, footnotes deleted, quoting from Berlin, *Four Essays*, 153 n. 1.

[69] Skinner has probably committed much the same misstep as Ronald Dworkin, who erroneously assumes that the only constraints-on-freedom recognized by theorists of negative liberty are those imposed by governments. See Ronald Dworkin, *Taking Rights Seriously* (Cambridge, MA: Harvard University Press, 1977), Ch. 12; Ronald Dworkin, 'Do Liberal Values Conflict?', in Mark Lilla, Ronald Dworkin, and Robert Silvers (eds), *The Legacy of Isaiah Berlin* (New York: New York Review Books, 2001), 73, 83–90. Cf. Raymond Geuss, *History and Illusion in Politics* (Cambridge: Cambridge University Press, 2001) [Geuss, *History*], 93, 94–5; Alan Ryan, 'Freedom', 40 *Philosophy* 93, 110 (1965) [Ryan, 'Freedom']. Even more plainly misguided is Dworkin's suggestion that negative liberty can adequately be characterized as 'freedom from legal constraint'. Ronald Dworkin, *Sovereign Virtue* (Cambridge, MA: Harvard University Press, 2000), 120. Such a suggestion combines the misstep mentioned above with the equally erroneous notion that negative liberty is exclusively or primarily normative rather than non-normative.

their non-normative freedoms. Moreover, Skinner throughout his art-icle—and indeed in all of his writings on liberty until the late 1990s—accepts the negative-liberty theorists' conception of non-normative freedom as the 'absence of constraint'.[70] His aim has not been to replace their conception with a definition of normative liberty or with a 'positive' understanding of freedom; instead, his aim has been to show that republican views about the proper uses of law are thor-oughly compatible with the negative-liberty theorists' conception.

On the other hand, although Skinner is endeavouring to contest a thesis about non-normative liberty (specifically, a thesis about the relationship between such liberty and the law), his ripostes to that thesis rely on a dichotomy that is pertinent only in connection with normative liberty: namely, a dichotomy between freedom and the conditions or capacities for the exercise of freedom. Such a distinction does make sense in regard to the normative variety of liberty, but it is untenable in regard to the non-normative variety.

When we affirm that some person P is normatively free to φ, we can further affirm with perfect consistency that P is unable to φ and that his inability stems either from his lack of the capacity-to-φ or from the presence of social conditions or natural conditions which block the exercise of that capacity. An ascription of normative liberty in itself pertains only to what is *permissible* for a person, and not necessarily to what is *feasible* for him or her. Accordingly, the distinction between freedom and the conditions or capacities for the exercise of freedom is fully germane. For example, whereas everyone in the Hobbesian State of Nature is normatively at liberty to do anything whatsoever, each person's attempts to make use of that liberty in sundry ways will very often be frustrated by the aggressively fearful behaviour of his fellows. Hence, each person in such a predicament is well advised to relinquish many of his particular normative liberties in order to bring about the governmentally enforced conditions of security that will enable the efficacious exercise of his remaining normative freedoms. The range of his normative liberties will have diminished, but his ability to avail himself of his unsurrendered normative liberties will have been greatly enhanced. In short, if our focus is on normative freedom, then Skin-ner's comments on the trade-off between freedoms and the capacity for exercising freedoms are unexceptionable. Even if we do not assume that the situation of people outside any society would be normatively akin in all respects to the Hobbesian State of Nature, the general point about the aforementioned trade-off will withstand scrutiny.

[70] Skinner, 'Maintenance', 10.

However, a decidedly different conclusion is warranted if our focus lies instead on non-normative liberty. Given such a focus, there is no room for a distinction of the sort that Skinner draws. If a person P is non-normatively free to φ, then she is able to φ—which means, among other things, that she possesses the capacity to φ. Thus, when P agrees to trade off some of her current non-normative freedoms in return for her gaining of new unimpeded capacities or in return for the lifting of obstacles to the exercise of some of her current capacities, she is trading freedoms for freedoms. When she surrenders some of her non-normative liberties for the sake of increasing the security of her other non-normative liberties, she again is trading freedoms for freedoms. After all, the increased security consists in the fact that certain types of actions or circumstances are now regularly available to her whereas previously they were sometimes or always closed off to her. Various instances of those types of actions or circumstances are now within the range of things which she is able to achieve, whereas some or all of those instances would have fallen outside that range if she had not engaged in her trade-off. Expanded security is expanded ability and is therefore expanded freedom. In the exchanges which Skinner depicts, people do cede some of their non-normative liberties but only in order to attain other such liberties. Furthermore, there is no reason to believe that the ceded liberties will inevitably surpass the attained liberties on any relevant scale, and there are ample reasons for believing that the latter will typically surpass the former. Therefore, Skinner has once again reversed the true scheme of things when he contends that liberal theorists would look upon the absence of any governmental institutions as a situation of uncurbed freedom. Though such an absence would of course involve uncurbed *legal* freedom, it would involve a myriad of unpleasant constraints on just about everyone's *non-normative* freedom—constraints that could be largely removed through the less numerous and less disagreeable constraints imposed by decent governmental institutions.

In fairness to Skinner, we should note that a similar normative/non-normative conflation has beguiled some of the modern theorists whom he takes as his targets. Most notable among those who have stumbled in this manner is Berlin himself. Let us examine the following passage:

It is important to discriminate between liberty and the conditions of its exercise. If a man is too poor or too ignorant or too feeble to make use of his legal rights, the liberty that these rights confer upon him is nothing to him, but it is not thereby annihilated. The obligation to promote education, health, justice, to raise standards of living, to provide opportunity for the growth of the arts and the sciences, to prevent reactionary political or social or legal policies or arbitrary inequalities, is not made less stringent because it is not necessarily directed to the promotion of liberty itself, but to conditions in which alone its possession is of value, or to values which may be independent of it. And still, liberty is one thing, and the conditions for it are another.[71]

Admittedly, it is not inconceivable that Berlin used 'liberty' throughout this passage to denote normative freedom alone. On the following page, after all, he wrote of 'the need to create conditions in which those who lack them will be provided with opportunities to exercise those rights (freedom to choose) which they legally possess, but cannot, without such opportunities, put to use. Useless freedoms should be made usable, but they are not identical with the conditions indispensable for their utility'.[72] In this latter comment, the word 'freedoms' and also the word 'rights' undoubtedly denote *legal* liberties. Nevertheless, it is highly unlikely that a similar pattern of usage obtains throughout the longer passage above. The statements in that extended extract occur within a general discussion that is oriented primarily toward non-normative freedom. Such an orientation is patent at virtually every juncture. For example, just a couple of pages after the observation about '[u]seless freedoms', Berlin reaffirmed that '[t]he fundamental sense of freedom is freedom from chains, from imprisonment, from enslavement by others. The rest is extension of this sense, or else metaphor'.[73] In any event, we do not have to speculate prolongedly about the non-normative or normative tenor of the term 'liberty' on its several appearances in the lengthy passage above. At a slightly earlier stage of his discussion where he was manifestly adverting to non-normative freedom, Berlin drew precisely the same distinction between liberty and the conditions for the exercise of liberty: 'Failure to discriminate between human and non-human obstacles to freedom seems to me to mark the beginning of the great confusion of types of freedom, and of the no less fatal identification of conditions of freedom with freedom itself, which is at the root of some of the fallacies with which I am concerned.'[74]

In sum, at least on some occasions and probably on most occasions when Berlin differentiated between freedom and the conditions for the exercise thereof, he had in mind non-normative freedom. He thereby committed the misstep to which Skinner has likewise fallen prey. Had

[71] Berlin, *Four Essays*, liii.
[72] Berlin, *Four Essays*, liv.
[73] Berlin, *Four Essays*, lvi.
[74] Berlin, *Four Essays*, xlix.

he been concentrating instead on normative liberty, his freedom/conditions dichotomy would have been apt and sustainable. If a person P is too weak or too ignorant or too ill to take advantage of many of his legal and moral liberties, those liberties are not thereby negated and transformed into obligations. P is still morally and legally permitted to do whatever those liberties allow him to do, even though his ignorance or weakness or illness means that the *permissibility* of those actions is not accompanied by their *feasibility*. Likewise, if a person Q is too indigent to acquire land and appurtenant resources which she is nonetheless morally at liberty to use (even non-consensually through a forcible entry), the formidable fences and other barriers that prevent her from gaining access to the land have affected what is *possible* for her rather than what is morally *legitimate*. She retains her moral liberties despite her inability to take advantage of them. In these situations and in myriad other situations that can be imagined, people's efforts to exercise moral or legal liberties are thwarted by an absence of the conditions that are essential for the success of such efforts. If we want people to enjoy those liberties effectively rather than merely formally, we shall have to strive to bring about the aforementioned conditions.

Apposite and illuminating though the freedom/conditions distinction is when invoked in respect of moral or legal liberty, it is wholly inapposite in respect of non-normative liberty. Berlin went astray in presuming otherwise. As has been indicated in my response to Skinner, an absence of conditions that are necessary for the exercise of non-normative freedoms is an absence of those freedoms *tout court*. Unlike a normative liberty-to-φ, a non-normative liberty-to-φ is an ability rather than a permission; consequently, when a lack of certain conditions has precluded some person P from φ-ing, P's non-normative liberty-to-φ has ceased to exist (or has never come into existence). Whereas P's permission-to-φ can abide in the absence of the conditions that would enable P to φ, P's ability-to-φ cannot similarly obtain in the absence of those conditions. Hence, any distinction between a non-normative freedom and the conditions for the exercise of that freedom is a non-starter. Both the critics and the proponents of modern doctrines of negative liberty have sometimes failed to attend to this point.[75]

---

[75] See for example Ryan, 'Freedom', 108–10. Of course, some proponents have indeed attended to this point (in terms rather different from my own). See for example Carter, *Measure*, 234–5; G. A. Cohen, *Self-Ownership, Freedom, and Equality* (Cambridge: Cambridge University Press, 1995) [Cohen,

1.5. A Matter of Time

1.5.1. Some General Reflections In this final principal subsection of the first half of this chapter, my rejoinder in defence of negative-liberty theories will be aimed at one of Skinner's critics rather than at Skinner himself. That rejoinder will emerge from some reflections on the role of temporality in attributions of freedom. Any ascription of freedom to someone must implicitly or explicitly contain at least two temporal indexes: one pertaining to the time(s) at which the ascribed freedom exists, and the other pertaining to the time(s) at which the action or event covered by the freedom is to

---

Self-Ownership], 57–9. Cf. Lawrence Crocker, *Positive Liberty*, 86–92; van Parijs, *Real Freedom*, 23–4. For a straightforward endorsement of Berlin's freedom/conditions distinction, see John Gray, 'On Negative and Positive Liberty', in *Liberalisms: Essays in Political Philosophy* (London: Routledge, 1989), 45, 55. See also Benn, *Theory*, 139–40. In an unpublished typescript, 'Freedom and Money', G. A. Cohen has trenchantly attacked Berlin's distinction. When Cohen extends his attack to John Rawls, however, he is to some degree failing to disentangle non-normative liberty and normative liberty.

I should here acknowledge that Berlin's conception of negative liberty differs from mine, and that the freedom/conditions dichotomy does make sense under his conception. Berlin classified mere inabilities as instances of freedom: 'You lack political liberty or freedom only if you are prevented from attaining a goal by human beings. Mere incapacity to attain a goal is not lack of political freedom' (Berlin, *Four Essays*, 122, footnotes omitted). For some similar views, see S. I. Benn and R. S. Peters, *Social Principles and the Democratic State* (London: Allen & Unwin, 1959), 212–13; J. Pennock, *Democratic*, 24–7; Weinstein, 'Concept', 150–4, 159–60. Cf. Geuss, *History*, 87, 97; H. J. McCloskey, 'A Critique of the Ideals of Liberty', 74 *Mind* 483, 486–94 (1965). For two reasons, however, my present discussion has accused Berlin of confusion in connection with his invocation of the freedom/conditions distinction. First, the classification of mere inabilities as instances of freedom has already been rejected in this chapter, on independent grounds. (One of those grounds is that such a classification would undermine every attempt to gauge the extent of anyone's overall freedom or to compare that extent with the level of anyone else's overall freedom. Another ground for rejecting Berlin's treatment of mere inabilities is the unworkableness of the distinction on which his analysis relies. If a man is unable to escape from the prison cell in which he has been detained, is the curtailment of his opportunities attributable to the actions of other people in jailing him or to his own natural strength which is insufficient for him to break down the walls and bars that confine him?) Second, at least in some of the situations which Berlin mentioned when asserting that freedoms can be uncombined with the conditions for the exercise of those freedoms, the conditions-for-exercise are missing because of the actions of other human beings. In regard to those situations, then, Berlin's own conception of liberty does not leave room for a freedom/conditions distinction.

occur.[76] Although those two temporal foci can of course converge, they can likewise be quite distinct.

If a person P is currently free to φ at some subsequent time t, then at least one way (and perhaps many ways) in which he can behave between now and t will lead at t both to his having the capacity-to-φ and to the unpreventedness of his exercising that capacity. Of course, between now and t, P might choose to behave in some alternative manner that will close off the option of φ-ing at t. Nevertheless, provided that there is currently at least one course of conduct available to him that would result in his being able to φ at t, he is now free to φ then. He can be free in this respect regardless of whether he is now also free to φ at present.

Suppose that Jim is waiting for the arrival of a train on which his father is a passenger. When the train arrives in a few hours, and when the passengers disembark shortly thereafter, Jim will be able and thus free to see his father. Let us designate as 't' the first moment at which Jim can behold his father. We can correctly say that Jim is currently free to see his father at t. He is not now free to see his father at present, but he is now free to see his father in a few hours. At least one course of conduct is open to him that will enable him to catch sight of his father at t. There are indeed many such courses of conduct, all of which involve his being in the appropriate area of the railway station at t. Of course, there are also numerous modes of behaviour available to Jim between now and t that would prevent him from seeing his father at that time. Jim might go away from the relevant portion of the railway station—or might stay away therefrom, if he is not there at present. He might gouge his own eyes out, or he might become embroiled in an altercation that results in his suffering from blindness, or he might drink himself into a stupor. And so forth. In any number of ways during the period that eventuates in the disembarkation of the passengers, Jim might do something or be somewhere as a consequence of which he will not be able to see his father at t. Notwithstanding, those numerous potential freedom-extinguishing developments can all remain unactualized. Open to Jim at present are multitudinous avenues

---

[76] For some brief but important pioneering work in this area, see G. A. Cohen, 'Capitalism, Freedom and the Proletariat', in Alan Ryan (ed.), *The Idea of Freedom* (Oxford: Oxford University Press, 1979) [Cohen, 'Capitalism'], 9, 20–1; Cohen, *History*, 259–61. My present topic is related, albeit tenuously, to the ancient problem of the logical status of propositions about future contingencies. For a pithy discussion of that problem, see P. T. Geach, *Logic Matters* (Berkeley: University of California Press, 1980), 81.

of behaviour that will leave him free at t to see his father then. If he opts for any of those avenues, his current freedom to see his father at t will be matched by a similar freedom at t itself.

Let us glance at a slightly more complicated example. Suppose that Ken at noontime has locked a magnificent painting in a vault, along with an explosive device that will destroy the painting—and everything else in its vicinity—in two hours (that is, at 2.00 p.m.). The vault is formidably impregnable to anyone who does not know the 20-digit combination number that will release its lock, a number known only to Ken. However, if the vault is indeed opened, the bomb inside can easily be rendered inoperative. Is the painting's owner, Oscar, currently free to look admiringly at his work of art in two hours? Suppose that, just after Ken has locked away the painting and the bomb, Oscar captures him. Ken is a tough-minded person, and he will resist most blandishments and most forms of coercion that are aimed at inducing him to release the painting. If Oscar resorts to such inveiglements or to such coercive tactics, he will fail to open the vault and will therefore not be free at 2.00 p.m. to view the painting at that time. However, within Oscar's capabilities there are certain routes of persuasion or certain varieties of torture that will indeed impel Ken to surrender the painting before the expiration of the two-hour period culminating in an explosion. If Oscar adopts one of those lines of persuasion or methods of torture, he will save the painting and thereby enable himself to stare at it in two hours, at 2.00 p.m. Consequently, he is now free to view and touch the painting at 2.00 p.m. Whether he will still be free at 2.00 p.m. to view and touch the painting at that time is a question to which the answer will hinge on his interaction with Ken between now and then.

This scenario of Ken and Oscar brings out several complexities in the temporal aspects of liberty. First, the freedom of Oscar at noontime to view the painting at 2.00 p.m. is not undermined by the fact that his access to the painting at that time will depend on a decision by somebody else—Ken—to give him such access. To be sure, in so far as Oscar can do anything to rescue the painting, he has to operate by bringing exhortative or coercive pressure to bear on Ken. He cannot gain entry to the vault through sheer physical strength, and he lacks the time to get the degree of assistance that would enable him to undo the lock without the cooperation of Ken. Nonetheless, his reliance on Ken in this respect is not fundamentally different from the reliance of Jim on the performance of the railway crew in driving the train with his father. Though Oscar's ability to behold his painting at 2.00 p.m. is partly dependent on the decisions and actions of someone else, much the same can be said about Jim's ability to see his father at t. Of course, the specific nature of the dependence in the one case is different from that in the other. Jim does not have to rely on expostulations or savage tortures in order to be able to catch sight of his father (though such tactics might be advisable in dealing with certain railway companies). Still, in each situation the conscious choices of at least one person other than Jim or Oscar are indispensable for the existence of the relevant ability at t or at 2.00 p.m.

Second, while the differences just discussed are not fundamental, they are indeed important. They bear most notably on the likelihood that a reasonable observer can know whether someone is now free to do something at some later time. In Jim's situation, the chief factors on which his father's timely arrival depends are not guaranteed to function perfectly—as anyone who travels frequently by rail will know—but they are not wildly unpredictable, either. If we construe 't' as ranging over a period of time (perhaps a period of two or three hours) rather than as designating a particular moment, then a reasonable observer will very likely be able to know whether Jim is now free to see his father at t. By contrast, a reasonable observer will probably be in a much less advantageous epistemic position when seeking to determine whether Oscar is now free to view and touch his painting at 2.00 p.m. Gauging the extent of Ken's recalcitrant and evil fortitude is undoubtedly no mean feat. Hence, daunting indeed are the difficulties in arriving at the correct answer to the question about Oscar's freedom, and even more daunting are the difficulties in arriving at that answer for reasons that are an adequate justification of one's claim to knowledge. Jim's situation, by comparison, is considerably more straightforward for the observer (and for Jim himself!).

This point concerning the relative knowability of states of freedom will apply when one's orientation is retrodictive as well as when it is predictive. A predictive or prospective outlook is what we have just been pondering. If one is currently endeavouring to determine whether some person P is now free to φ at some juncture in the future, both the likelihood of the truth of one's determination and the likelihood of the adequacy of one's epistemic justification for arriving at that determination will vary in accordance with the nature of P's circumstances. A situation like that of Jim and his father, or any other situation that is comparably routine, will be much more conducive to one's knowledge of current freedoms or unfreedoms than will a situation like that of Oscar and Ken (or any other situation that is comparably fraught with uncertainty). Much the same can be said, *mutatis mutandis*, when we are peering back into the past rather than ahead into the future. To be sure, in one salient respect the unclarity that might hinder a prediction will have disappeared when we look backward. If P has indeed φ-ed at the relevant juncture t or has manifestly been able to φ at that time, then we can state with full confidence that in the past he was free to φ at t. Irrespective of the obstacles that may have prevented his φ-ing at some juncture in the past—a juncture henceforth designated as 'tE'—he managed to adopt a course of conduct that led to his being able to φ at t. At that past juncture tE, therefore, he was free to φ at t. (Perhaps the pertinent course of conduct by P consisted in little more than his forbearance from hampering or antagonizing somebody else who removed the obstacles to P's φ-ing.) A retrospective ascription of freedom or unfreedom is much less easy when P has not φ-ed at t and has not been able to φ then. Given such an eventuality, we have to try to discern whether some alternative course of conduct by P between tE and t would have enabled P to φ at t. If there was such a possible course of conduct, then P at tE was free to φ at t; contrariwise, if no such course of conduct was possible, then P at tE was not free to φ at t. Although this test for the existence or non-existence of past freedoms is perfectly straightforward when expressed in the abstract, the application of that test in practice can prove fiendishly intricate. Many retrospective ascriptions of freedom will be no less conjectural than many prospective ascriptions.

A further noteworthy point about the temporal aspects of liberty pertains to the distinction between particular freedoms and overall freedom. When we ask whether P at tE is free to φ at t, our answer should not be affected by the number of possible courses of conduct between tE and t that will enable P to φ at t. Although *pro tanto* P's overall liberty will be greater or lesser in proportion to the numerousness or fewness of the feasible alternative patterns of behaviour that can result in his being able at t to φ at t, the question whether at tE he is free-to-φ-at-t will not hinge on the numerousness of those patterns. The existence or inexistence of P's particular freedom to φ at t is a matter separate from that of the extent of his overall liberty.

Still, enormously important though the distinction between the existence of particular freedoms and the extent of overall freedom is, it should not induce us to think that overwhelmingly difficult accomplishments can never rightly be classified as impossible (with merely implicit qualifications). Let us investigate the following scenario. Bob immures Dave in a cell whose door is fastened by a computerized lock that forms an irrefrangible seal. No one can release the lock from the inside except by typing into the computerized device a number composed of 200 digits that are arranged in a random sequence which is unknown to Dave. Now, clearly, the unfreedom of Dave to leave the room will last at least as long as it takes for him to type 200 digits. After all, even if he had the full number printed in front of him, he would have to expend some time on the task of typing it all in. Let us designate the end-point of that amount of time as 't'. Once the requisite period of time has elapsed and t has arrived, there is a non-zero probability that Dave will have liberated himself from the room. Notwithstanding that he has never been apprised of the number that will undo the lock's seal, he might miraculously type all 200 digits correctly on his first attempt. Nevertheless, the adverb 'miraculously' in the preceding sentence aptly signals the nearly unimaginable tininess of the likelihood that Dave will succeed on his first attempt or indeed on any of his attempts. For all practical purposes, his chances of freeing himself from the room are no greater in the presence of the computerized device than in its absence. Were we to describe him without qualification as currently free to walk out of his cell at t, we would be distorting his plight beyond recognition. For all practical purposes, he is currently just as starkly unfree to depart from the cell at t as he will be at t itself—when he has failed to disengage the lock. Although our prospective attribution of unfreedom to him is probabilistic, the probability involved is so overwhelmingly high that it can almost always go unmentioned when we state the attribution.

Before drawing any general conclusions from the scenario of Bob and Dave, we should ponder a variant of that scenario. Suppose that Dave's cell—a cavernously spacious cell—contains several million books. Suppose further that, to a page in one of those books, Bob has deliberately or inadvertently affixed a card that will deactivate the computerized lock and enable Dave to depart. During the several minutes required to fetch the book and the card, Dave will be unfree to exit the dungeon; even if he were told the exact location of the relevant book, his retrieval and use of the card would take up a certain amount of time. Let us designate the endpoint of that length of time as 't'. Should we say that, at the point of initial imprisonment, Dave is free to leave the dungeon at t? Once again, an affirmative answer without any qualification would distort rather than illuminate the situation that we are examining. Since Dave does not even know about the card at all—much less about its precise location—the probability of his finding and using it at t is extravagantly low. For all practical purposes, that probability is nil. For all practical purposes, Dave is no more likely free at present to depart from his cell at t than he would be if Bob had never attached any card to a page of some book. In just about every context, an ascription of unfreedom to Dave need not take explicit account of the preposterously remote chance that he will happen to pick up the correct book and grasp the significance of the card therein. In just about every context, then, we can describe him without any overt qualification as currently unfree-to-leave-at-t.

These scenarios involving the imprisonment of Dave by Bob can serve to highlight some key respects in which the dimension of temporality and the role of probabilities bear on the existence of freedoms. Perhaps the most significant point concerns the distinction that was re-emphasized three paragraphs ago, between particular freedoms and overall freedom. As was stated there with reference to the possible courses of conduct between an earlier time tE and a later time t that will enable P to φ at t, the breadth or narrowness of the range of those courses of conduct is of relevance to P's overall freedom but not to the existence at tE of his freedom-to-φ-at-t—so long as at least one enabling path of behaviour is indeed available. Now, despite any appearances to the contrary, such a contention is fully consistent with the chief conclusions derivable from the scenarios of Dave and Bob. Let us first take note of the appearances to the contrary. In each of the scenarios just broached, only a single course of conduct by Dave (with room for any number of trifling variations in the movements of his body) can enable him to escape his cell at t; in the first situation he has to punch the correct sequence of 200 digits into the locking mechanism, and in the second situation he has to fetch the correct book and make use of the card that has been placed in it. Moreover, in regard to each of those scenarios, the correct conclusion about the current freedom of Dave to escape at t is that for all practical purposes he does not enjoy any such freedom. Accordingly, there might appear to be a tension between the message of those scenarios and the claim made three paragraphs ago on the basis of the distinction between overall liberty and particular liberties. That is, the message of the scenarios involving Dave and Bob might seem to be as follows: precisely because of the severe fewness of the possible courses of conduct at tE that will enable Dave to depart at t, his particular freedom-at-tE-to-depart-at-t is non-existent for all practical purposes.

A tension of the sort described in my last paragraph is illusive. In the scenarios of Dave and Bob, the *fewness* of the escape-enabling courses of conduct is in itself largely beside the point; what is of consequence is the overwhelming *improbability* that any such course of conduct will be discerned. Suppose for a moment that Bob had provided Dave with a neatly printed rendering of the sequence of 200 digits that will release the lock. Or, in the second scenario, suppose that Bob had specified to Dave (perhaps ostensively) the exact whereabouts of the book with the lock-disengaging card. Though Dave could then effect a ready departure from the cell because he would possess all the information necessary for that purpose, there would still be only one available course of conduct for him in each scenario that could lead to his being free to depart at t. The range of escape-enabling options would not be expanded at all. What *would* of course be expanded—hugely—is the likelihood that the lone feasible escape-enabling option will be perceived by Dave. That likelihood would increase immensely because of the removal of his ignorance rather than because of any change in his physical surroundings or capacities. Only on account of that erstwhile ignorance has his confinement ever been properly classifiable as a situation of unfreedom-to-leave-the-cell-at-t. Were that ignorance to be dispelled, and were there thus a dramatic rise in the probability of his recognizing the sole available means of exit, we could accurately say that at tE he is free to depart from his cell at t. His freedom to depart in those circumstances would not in any way be negated by the fact that the aforementioned means of exit is indeed the only such means available.

In Dave's predicaments, as in countless other situations, ignorance is itself a disabling factor. The elimination of his ignorance would change his status from currently unfree-to-leave-the-cell-at-t to currently free-to-leave-the-cell-at-t. Such a transformation would occur because of the enormous enhancement of his ability to perceive the correct route for departing, and thus because of the enormous enhancement of his ability to pursue that route. What should be acknowledged, however, is that Dave might somehow incredibly pursue the correct route even if he has not been supplied with any information by Bob. As has been observed, although it is staggeringly unlikely that he will succeed in escaping without having been given such information, it is not strictly impossible.

Nevertheless, if the pertinent information has not in fact been provided to Dave, we are generally warranted in saying that at tE he is unfree to walk out of his cell at t. For the purpose of attributing unfreedom to him, in other words, we are almost always warranted in characterizing an overwhelming improbability as an impossibility. If we declined to adopt such a tack and insisted on construing the wispiest probability as a live possibility, and if we therefore held without any qualification that Dave at tE is free to escape at t even in the absence of any information from Bob, we would be committing ourselves to the view that no one is ever currently unfree to do anything at some non-imminent future point. After all, in connection with any set of circumstances in human affairs during any period, there will always be some probability—no matter how vanishingly minute—that the humanly imposed constraints which at present thwart certain achievements will be lifted or overcome before some non-imminent future juncture. Suppose, for the sake of an illustration, that the computerized lock on Dave's cell cannot be operated or manipulated at all from the inside. In that event, his chances of escaping by typing in the correct sequence of digits have gone from practically nil to absolutely nil. Does such a modification in the scenario mean that the current likelihood of his being able to leave the cell at t is absolutely nil (as opposed to merely nil for all practical purposes)? The correct answer to this question is negative, for there will always be some probability—albeit perhaps an almost infinitesimally small probability—that the present barriers to Dave's exit at t will have been removed by then because of some natural force such as an earthquake or a thunderbolt or because of some change of mind on the part of Bob. However formidably remote the prospect of these contingencies is, there will be a non-zero chance (just barely a non-zero chance, admittedly) of their occurrence between now and t. When in virtually any context we nonetheless maintain that Dave is currently unfree to depart from his dungeon tomorrow, we can usually refrain from expressly adverting to those exceedingly remote possibilities. Unless the chance of some escape-enabling development is greater than the shuddersomely minute chance that any of the aforementioned possibilities will be actualized, our ascription of unfreedom to Dave without any overt qualification is not even slightly misleading in most contexts.

In short, we should accept that our attributions of unfreedom can construe staggeringly slight probabilities as impossibilities (with only tacit qualifications), if we are to avoid ruling out all attributions of current unfreedom in connection with non-imminent future endeavours and achievements. If we are to accept as much, however, we should also realize that in respect of such attributions the dichotomy between freedom and an absence of freedom is characterized to some extent by probabilistic gradations. That is, we encounter here a complexity partly resembling the ancient sorites problem, whereby starkly contrary categories shade into each other through imperceptibly fine differentiations. Let us briefly contemplate afresh the situation in which Dave's only means of escape from his dungeon is the typing of an undisclosed 200-digit number. Suppose that the situation were altered to involve a number with 199 digits rather than 200. Since the chances of Dave's coming up with the correct number in the absence of any information from Bob are still nil for all practical purposes, the one-digit reduction does not perceptibly affect Dave's status as a man currently unfree to depart from his cell at t. If the situation is sufficiently altered, however, his status will indeed have changed markedly; for example, if Dave needs to type only one digit in order to release himself, we can and should conclude that he is now free to escape from his cell at *t*. Somewhere between 200 digits and one digit, then, the virtually certain existence of his present unfreedom-to-depart-at-*t* would shade—on a spectrum of probabilistic calibrations—into the virtually certain existence of his present freedom-to-depart-at-*t*.

Many attributions of current freedom or unfreedom pertaining to non-imminent future activities or achievements will be clear-cut, like our attribution to Dave of the unfreedom-to-depart-at-*t* when his only means of escape is his accurate typing of an unknown sequence of 200 digits. In most contexts, such attributions will not have to be accompanied by explicit probabilistic qualifications. However, other circumstances may arise in which neither an ascription of current freedom nor an ascription of a current lack of freedom (relating to some non-imminent future activities or achievements) will be straightforward. In coming to grips with this grey area of vagueness—including some second-order vagueness concerning where the grey area begins and ends—we are best advised to adopt either or both of two main tacks.

One of those tacks has already been obliquely broached, in my discussion of Jim's wait for the arrival of his father on a train. There it was suggested that the relevant time *t* could be construed as ranging over a certain period rather than as being confined to a particular moment. Some equivocal cases of present freedom or unfreedom are doubtless best handled in this manner. Suppose for instance that, instead of having to type an unknown number with 200 digits, Dave has to type an unknown number with three digits. On the one hand, if '*t*' is taken to represent the moment at which enough time has passed for the typing of any three digits (which, of course, might be the correct digits in the correct sequence), then an ascription to Dave of the current freedom-to-leave-his-cell-at-*t* without any overt qualification will be highly misleading. On the other hand, if '*t*' is instead taken to represent a certain period—perhaps the 30 or 40 minutes following the amount of time needed for Dave to type any three digits—then the probability of his being able to liberate himself from his cell during *t* may well be sufficiently high to warrant an ascription to him of the present freedom-to-leave-the-cell-at-some-point-in-*t* without any explicit qualification. Such an ascription, if stated at the time of the events in question, would most naturally be expressed as a claim that Dave is now free to liberate himself within the next 30 or 40 minutes.

Another approach to this matter is to eschew a merely implicit qualification for one's ascription of current freedom/unfreedom and to opt for an overtly probabilistic formulation.[77] Rather than saying flatly that P is now free (or unfree) to φ at some future juncture t, we can submit that there obtains such-and-such a likelihood that P is now free (or unfree) in the respect just mentioned. Let us return to the situation in which Dave has to type an unknown three-digit number in order to escape from the dungeon. Instead of extending 't' as much as was suggested above, we might opt to extend it only slightly—say, to range over a period of two or three minutes after the amount of time needed for typing any three digits. We could then say that there is such-and-such a probability that Dave is currently free to escape from his cell at some or another point within t. Indeed, we could adopt this approach even if we were inclined to let 't' represent the particular moment at which Dave will have had enough time to type any three digits. Both this overtly probabilistic formulation and a formulation that extends 't' along the lines delineated in my last paragraph are ways of acknowledging that there is no unequivocally ascertainable answer to the question which those formulations are at once tackling and circumventing: the question of Dave's present freedom to escape as soon as enough time has elapsed for the typing of any three digits. The aforementioned formulations seek to take due account of both the physical possibility of Dave's escaping at that moment and the disabling effects of ignorance which, despite his best efforts, will very likely prevent the actualization of such a possibility.

Finally, these reflections on the various scenarios involving Dave and Bob are akin to my previous reflections on the examples involving Jim and Ken and Oscar, in that they apply to a retrodictive orientation as well as to a predictive orientation. Regardless of whether one's standpoint is prospective or retrospective, the issues analysed here will arise in relation to any claim that a person P at some moment tE

---

[77] For some perceptive expositions of an approach broadly along these lines—which will be discussed at much greater length in my final chapter—see Carter, *Measure*, 189–91, 233–4. Note that the probabilistic qualifications attach to ascriptions of particular freedoms rather than to predictions about the occurrence of the actions to which those freedoms pertain. Note moreover that any particular freedom, in contrast with the overall freedom of each person and in contrast with properties such as fragility and difficulty, is non-scalar. That is, as I argue in Chapter 3, each particular freedom is insusceptible to gradations; the existence of any particular freedom is an all-or-nothing state, rather than a matter of differing degrees. Hence, when we express P's freedom-to-φ in the proposition 'P will φ if he endeavours (without any blunders) to do so', any probabilistic qualification attaches to the whole of that conditional statement and not just to its consequent.

is free (or unfree) to φ at some subsequent moment t. Again, however, the points raised about prospective attributions of freedom (or unfreedom) are only partially transferable to retrospective attributions. Those points will not be transferable if P has φ-ed at t or has manifestly been able to φ at t. In such an event, we from our retrospective vantage will know that P at tE was free to φ at t. We do not need to extend the range of 't' beyond the particular moment in question, nor do we need to attach any overt probabilistic qualifications when we ascribe to P the particular freedom. If P has not φ-ed at t and has not been unmistakably capable of φ-ing at t, by contrast, the same basic complications that have been explored here in regard to predictions will also emerge in regard to our retrodictions. A look backward will be no less problematic than a look ahead. The suitable analytical approach to be adopted will then depend on the circumstances that we are investigating. Those circumstances may be such that we can arrive at a clear-cut verdict to the effect that P at tE was (or was not) free to φ at t. Alternatively, the circumstances may be such that we have to arrive at an equivocal verdict—either by extending the range of 't' or by delivering our verdict in an expressly probabilistic manner.

1.5.2. General Considerations Applied   As has just been argued, any attribution of freedom involves two temporal indexes. As will be apparent to any reader of the foregoing discussion, however, the explicit articulation of both of those indexes in a claim about somebody's freedom (or unfreedom) tends to be stylistically inelegant and ponderous. Fortunately, it is often the case that one or both of the pertinent indexes can remain implicit; frequently the context of an ascription of liberty will make clear the temporal bearings thereof. Nevertheless, although we often can safely avoid stylistic clumsiness by leaving implicit at least one of the two temporal references in this or that statement about someone's liberty, we should never lose sight of those references altogether. Confusion can too easily ensue when the temporal aspects of freedom and unfreedom are obscured.

For an illustration of the pitfalls that await anyone who neglects the temporality of freedom, we shall scrutinize an argument mounted against Skinner by John Charvet.[78] Because Charvet's argument

---

[78] The argument is contained in John Charvet, 'Quentin Skinner on the Idea of Freedom', 2 *Studies in Political Thought* 5 (1993) [Charvet, 'Idea of Freedom'].

objects to Skinner's treatment of positive liberty (as distinguished from negative liberty), it will serve as a useful transition to the second half of this chapter—which will begin with an examination of that very topic. Charvet complains that Skinner misrepresents the doctrine of positive freedom, and as a corrective Charvet endeavours to distil the central ideas of that doctrine. We shall not explore here his criticism of Skinner or the details of his own account of positive liberty. What instead should attract our attention in the present subsection is Charvet's attempt to bolster the idea of positive freedom by exposing the alleged absurdity of the idea of negative freedom:

[W]hat is at the very centre of the positive idea...is that freedom is an attribute of acts, and that the negative concept, when understood as an opportunity concept and taken on its own, cannot explain how a *free act* is possible. The negative concept is the idea of an opportunity present to an agent to do *x* or *y*. Whether he does *x* or *y* is a matter for his determination. So the agent must be understood as having the power to choose whether the world will be *x* or *y* and to give effect to his choice in the appropriate act. However, on the negative understanding of freedom one can be said to be free only insofar as one *does not act*. For freedom is defined in terms of the presence of an opportunity. Once the opportunity is seized and the agent acts, he loses his freedom in the moment of exercising it. In determining that the world shall be *x* rather than *y*, he no longer has the opportunity to make it *x* or *y*. But it is surely absurd to say that we are free only insofar as we do not act.[79]

In this extract is the entirety of Charvet's critique of negative liberty, which forms the point of departure for his championing of a Hegelian conception of freedom. Though we shall not here grapple directly at all with his Hegelian stance, the critique that underlies it must come into question. A focus on the temporal bearings of freedom can reveal that the doctrine of negative liberty is unscathed by Charvet's attack.

Before considering the way in which Charvet's critique unravels as a result of his unmindfulness of freedom's temporality, we should note his claim that negative-liberty theorists cannot explain how a free act is possible. The precise tenor of his allegation emerges in the rest of the passage, but we should pause briefly to ponder that allegation on the negative-liberty theorists' own terms. As applied to acts, the predicate 'free' would normally be understood by a negative-liberty theorist as synonymous with 'uncoerced' or 'voluntary'. In other words, such a theorist would apply that predicate to acts which are undertaken for reasons other than the sheer absence of decently palatable alternatives.

[79] Charvet, 'Idea of Freedom', 7, emphases in original.

In a different vein, 'free' could simply mean 'unprevented'. So construed, the term would apply to all acts that are actually undertaken and to all acts that could have been undertaken. At any rate, in either of these senses, the predicate 'free' is straightforwardly applicable to some or all acts that do in fact occur. Consequently, notwithstanding Charvet's assertion to the contrary, a negative-liberty theorist encounters no difficulties whatsoever in explaining how free acts are possible. Such a theorist certainly should not baulk at the notion that freedom—or freeness—can be predicated of actions.

Charvet endeavours to substantiate his assertion with the line of reasoning set forth in the passage quoted above. Unfortunately for him, that line of reasoning suffers from two major shortcomings. First, he errs in assuming that every act of choosing between x and y will have closed off all opportunities for choosing between x and y afresh. Although some specifications of the 'x' and 'y' variables would fit with Charvet's assumption, many more such specifications would not. For example, suppose that I choose between holding my right hand at my side and holding my right hand above my head. Except in unusual circumstances, my choosing one way or the other will leave me with the opportunity to choose again—and again—between precisely the same alternatives. If I determine that the world shall be a place in which I am holding my right hand above my head, I still have the opportunity to make it either a place in which I am holding my right hand above my head or a place in which I am holding my right hand at my side. My abiding opportunity to select between those alternatives has not been foreclosed. Charvet has therefore gone astray when he declares (in the extract above) that '[i]n determining that the world shall be x rather than y, [an agent] no longer has the opportunity to make it x or y'.

A second problem in Charvet's reasoning—a problem more directly connected to the topic of this subsection—arises from the most evident way of addressing the shortcoming that has just been highlighted. In order to deal with the point made by my preceding paragraph, Charvet might submit that the 'x' and 'y' variables must be specified by reference to a particular moment in time. For example, instead of accepting a specification of 'x' as 'holding my right hand at my side' and a specification of 'y' as 'holding my right hand above my head', he might insist that the former has to be 'holding my right hand at my side at t' and that the latter correspondingly has to be 'holding my right hand above my head at t'. In each case, 't' designates some particular instant in time. Now, although such a move in itself is plainly unexceptionable, it does not go any way toward supporting Charvet's line of argument. If the temporal index of each act (that is, of x and of y) is rendered definite rather than left indefinite when 'x' and 'y' are specified, then so too the temporal index of any freedom-to-choose-between-x-and-y must be rendered definite—sufficiently definite, at any rate, to avoid the positing of absurdities such as freedom in the present to perform some action in the past. However, once we fix the temporal bearings of the freedom-to-choose-between-x-and-y, we can see that Charvet's argument does not tell at all against the doctrine of negative liberty.

Once again, let 'tE' designate some moment earlier than t. We shall assume that at tE I am free to hold my right hand at my side at t, and that I am also free at tE to hold my right hand above my head at t. I remain free to choose either of those two temporally specified actions—designated as 'x' and 'y'—until t itself (or until a split-second before t), when I will have chosen one or neither of those options. At t, my erstwhile freedom-to-choose-either-x-or-y will have come to an end and will have culminated in my performing one or neither of those possible actions. If I perform x, then at t I am free to perform x but am no longer free to perform y; conversely, if I perform y, then at t I am free to perform y but am no longer free to perform x. Plainly, at t I cannot hold both of the twofold freedoms—the freedom to do x and the freedom to do y—which I held at tE. Since doing x precludes doing y and vice versa, I cannot opt for both of those temporally defined actions and must therefore opt for only one or neither of them. At t, then, I shall have retained at most only one of the aforementioned twofold freedoms. This evolution, whereby the dual freedoms at tE have given way to one or neither freedom at t, is not at all mysterious or absurd. Rather, it simply follows from the passing of time and from the impossibility of the joint occurrence of certain temporally specified actions.

As should be apparent from what has just been said, Charvet introduces a red herring when he suggests that negative liberty consists in one's preservation of one's opportunities by not acting. Passivity is itself a way of losing one's temporally specified opportunities, just as much as is acting. Suppose that at tE I am sitting at my desk with my right arm resting thereon. Once again, 'x' will designate my holding my right hand at my side at t, and 'y' will designate my holding my right hand above my head at t. At tE I am free to do x and am also free to do y, because there is enough time between tE and t for me to move my hand either to my side or above my head. If I elect to do x, then at t I shall be free to do x but no longer free to do y; conversely, of course, if I elect to do y, then at t I shall be free to do y but no longer free to do *x*. We have seen as much in the preceding paragraph. However, let us now consider a third option for the period between *tE* and *t*, the option of staying inert. If I follow this third course, then the position of my arm at *tE* will remain unchanged at *t*. Let us designate as 'z' this option of leaving my arm on my desk at *t*. At *t*, if I indeed have opted for *z*, I will have lost both my freedom to do *x* and my freedom to do *y*. I shall manifestly have retained my freedom to choose *z*, but I will have lost both of the other freedoms. Far from preserving my opportunity to select between *x* and *y*, my inaction has irrevocably ruled out my taking either of those temporally specified options.

In short, whether Charvet ties *x* and *y* to a particular moment or whether he instead leaves indefinite the temporal bearings of each of those actions, his critique of the doctrine of negative liberty cannot succeed. If the temporal index of each action is left indefinite, then the '*x*' and '*y*' variables can be specified in myriad ways that keep open the possibility of my choosing between *x* and *y* (again and again) even after I have opted for one or the other of those actions. Every such possibility belies the assertion by Charvet in the extract above that '[o]nce the opportunity [to choose between *x* and *y*] is seized and the agent acts, he loses his freedom in the moment of exercising it'. Should Charvet seek to dodge this pitfall by pinning down a definite time at which *x* or *y* will occur if either of them does occur, he must likewise pin down the temporal index of the freedom-to-do-*x* and the freedom-to-do-*y*. When the variables are construed in this fashion, the statement just quoted is no longer false but is utterly harmless. Obviously some temporally indexed freedoms to commit some temporally indexed acts will cease to exist as soon as the moment for those acts has passed. So what? In other words, to the extent that Charvet's remarks about negative liberty are sustainable, they are not even slightly damaging. Only an inattentiveness to the temporal bearings of freedom would lead anyone to think otherwise.

2. A Distinct Understanding of Liberty?

The first half of this chapter has explicated some facets of the concepts of freedom and unfreedom, and has sought to develop the explications in part by lodging objections to a number of stances which Skinner has taken. Heretofore, however, my critical assessments of his positions have not extended to the two or three most prominent lines of reasoning in his writings on liberty. My sundry discussions below will all concentrate on those central lines of reasoning. At the same time, these discussions will amplify my analyses of the concepts of freedom and unfreedom, and will further unfold some of the ideas propounded already; most notably, this chapter will now devote considerably more scrutiny than hitherto to the distinction between particular freedoms and overall freedom. As will be seen, an alertness to that distinction can reveal some significant weaknesses in Skinner's attempts to favour his own conception of freedom over that of the negative-liberty theorists.

This half of the chapter will be divided into three main subsections. In the first and shortest of those subsections, we shall look at Skinner's rather fleeting pronouncements on the ideal of positive liberty. Throughout his work on freedom, Skinner has sedulously refrained from endorsing any such 'positive' ideal; but he has quite sympathetically defended it against criticisms from negative-liberty theorists. His terse treatments of the topic deserve some wary investigation. In the second principal subsection below, we shall consider the many passages where Skinner argues that negative-liberty theorists have overlooked some crucial civic-republican insights into the connection between public virtue and negative freedom itself. As will be maintained, those republican insights consist in theses that can be readily acknowledged—and have been readily acknowledged—by the proponents of a negative understanding of liberty. A key element in my riposte is the distinction between particular freedoms and overall freedom. That distinction also figures conspicuously in the final major subsection of the chapter, where we shall explore Skinner's most recent efforts to distance his republican conception of freedom from the negative-liberty theorists' conception. Although Skinner disparages the latter conception as unduly narrow, it will prove to be more capacious than the republican approach which he esteems.

2.1. On Positive Liberty

As was noted in the preceding paragraph, Skinner has never bestowed his outright approval on the ideal of positive liberty. His own republican conception of freedom, as we shall see, is a variant of the 'negative' approach to the topic. Nevertheless, he endeavours to counter the negative-liberty theorists' challenges to the doctrine of positive freedom. Without ever embracing that doctrine, he has sought to gain a highly receptive hearing for it.[80]

---

[80] Skinner, 'Idea', 195–7; Skinner, 'Paradoxes', 232–5; Skinner, 'Republican', 295–8; Skinner, *Liberty*, 114 n. 22.

Skinner's basic description of the ideal of positive liberty will go largely uncontested here. Indeed, except for his disregard of procedural or content-neutral versions of positive-liberty doctrines,[81] his account serves as a useful backdrop for pinpointing the differences between negative and positive understandings of liberty—and also for oppugning his own characterization of those differences. In line with what Skinner maintains, the doctrine of positive liberty rests on the premise that the attainment of certain goals or the carrying on of certain activities or the following of certain procedures is essential for the full realization of each person's potential as a human being. Only by exercising some worthy faculties or by achieving some worthy aims or by performing some worthy activities or by basing projects and decisions on autonomously formed objectives, can human beings give effect to their deepest ends. Should a person neglect such endeavours, he will have failed to act in accordance with his underlying human nature and will have failed to accomplish the grandest purposes that attach to him as the possessor of such a nature. Thus, only by acting or deciding in the appropriate manner can anybody become truly free. That is, each person's consummate freedom resides in the patterns of behaviour or decision-making that constitute his maximal flourishing as a rational human agent. So argue the champions of the ideal of positive liberty.

Before we consider the chief divergences between negative freedom and positive freedom, we should probe two of Skinner's pronouncements concerning where those divergences lie. In one of his earliest writings on the topic, Skinner contends that the debate between negative-liberty theorists and positive-liberty theorists is fundamentally a disagreement over the existence of an underlying human nature:

Much of the debate between those who think of social freedom as a negative opportunity concept and those who think of it as a positive exercise concept may thus be said to stem from a deeper dispute about human nature. The argument is *au fond* about whether we can hope to distinguish an objective notion of *eudaimonia* or human flourishing. Those who dismiss this hope as illusory—such as Berlin and his many sympathizers—conclude that this makes it a dangerous error to connect individual liberty with the ideals of virtue and public service.[82]

---

[81] For such a version of the doctrine of positive liberty, see Christman, 'Liberalism'. Cf. Gerald Dworkin, *The Theory and Practice of Autonomy* (Cambridge: Cambridge University Press, 1988), Chs 1–2.
[82] Skinner, 'Idea', 197, footnote omitted.

To be sure, Berlin did indeed take strong exception to the idea of an essential human nature, and his hostility toward such an idea was largely (though not exclusively) the impetus behind his opposition to the claims of positive-liberty theorists. Skinner is correct to observe as much. However, the passage above goes too far in suggesting that the controversy over negative liberty versus positive liberty is *au fond* a dispute over the existence of a determinate human nature. As will become evident shortly, neither of my major objections to the doctrine of positive liberty has anything to do with the existence or non-existence of a human essence. Furthermore, the notion of an objective human nature with highly laudable capacities can commend itself to negative-liberty theorists. Theorists who take such a view will perceive the exercise of those capacities as the means whereby each human agent can achieve self-fulfilment or self-mastery. Those theorists might even value negative liberty primarily or exclusively in so far as it is conducive to such self-fulfilment. They can adopt these positions while remaining diehard negative-liberty theorists, precisely because their opposition to the doctrine of positive liberty is a stance concerning the nature of liberty rather than the nature of human beings. What they reject is not an Aristotelian vision of human self-realization, but the thesis that such a vision is an account of freedom rather than of some other value (perhaps at least as admirable as freedom).

Also by and large misdirected is Skinner's repeated assertion that the staunch defenders of negative liberty have insisted that their own way of explicating the concept of freedom is the uniquely coherent analysis of that concept.[83] All other understandings of that concept and all other definitions of the word 'freedom' or 'liberty' are allegedly said to be unintelligible or flatly self-contradictory. Skinner concedes that many proponents of the doctrine of negative liberty have been 'moderate' and 'fairminded', but he declares that 'by no means all have been so fairminded'.[84] Now, on the one hand, there have indeed been some theorists within the broad negative-liberty tradition who have taken the aridly stipulative view which Skinner disapprovingly attributes to them. Those theorists deserve his censure. On the other hand, the people who subscribe to that arid view are *not* strict defenders of the doctrine of negative liberty. Each of the people whom Skinner correctly singles out—J. P. Day, Antony Flew, William Parent[85]—has

---

[83] Skinner, 'Idea', 194–6; Skinner, 'Paradoxes', 230–1, 233; Skinner, 'Republican', 295–7.

[84] Skinner, 'Idea', 196 n. 8.

[85] Skinner, 'Idea', 196 n. 8, 199.

attached numerous qualifications to the idea of freedom that are un-acceptable to anyone who favours an austerely negative account of liberty. Flew, for example, adheres to one of the moralized conceptions of freedom that will be criticized later in this subsection.[86] By contrast, those philosophers who unflinchingly uphold the doctrine of negative liberty, such as Hillel Steiner and G. A. Cohen and Ian Carter, have never maintained that positive conceptions of freedom are incoherent or semantically illicit. Skinner oddly ascribes to Steiner the same sterile view which he accurately ascribes to Day.[87] In fact, however, Steiner has never contended that any positive understanding of liberty is to be ruled out on account of its incoherence or semantic illegitimacy. On the contrary, he has emphasized the open-endedness and variegated-ness of ordinary language, and has firmly counselled against thinking that controversies over the delimitation of the concept of freedom can be resolved through appeals to semantic intuitions.[88] He fully recog-nizes that those controversies cannot be fruitfully carried on except through substantive argumentation that reveals the implications (be they commendable or unacceptable) of various positions. Analyt-ical sharpness and comprehensiveness, which go well beyond bare coherence and semantic propriety, are the chief touchstones in such argumentation. In insisting as much, Steiner is resolutely at one with the other principal writers who have embraced an uncompromising version of the doctrine of negative liberty.

Although the coherence and semantic legitimacy of 'positive' accounts of liberty are not in doubt here at all, the illuminatingness and sharpness of their categories are indeed open to question. Here we come to the first main complaint by negative-liberty theorists against the doctrines of positive liberty. Whereas the phenomenon which the negative-liberty theorists designate as 'freedom' cannot readily be re-characterized in an equally illuminating fashion, there are numerous more precise designations for the phenomena which positive-liberty theorists label as 'freedom'. To denote the condition of negative liberty, some rather awkward and uncommon terms such as 'unpreventedness' and 'unprecludedness' would be necessary as replacements for 'free-dom' and 'liberty' themselves. The only adequate common substitute

---

[86] For some criticism of Flew on this score, see Cohen, 'Illusions', 226–9; Cohen, *History*, 292–6; Kymlicka, *Contemporary*, 146–51.

[87] Skinner, 'Idea', 196 n. 8.

[88] See Steiner, *Essay*, 6–9. On this particular point, Philip Pettit is broadly in agreement with Steiner. See for example Philip Pettit, 'Comment on Kristjánsson: Actions, Persons and Freedom as Nondomination', 10 *Journal of Theoretical Politics* 275, 277–9 (1998).

would be 'ability', which is less effective than 'liberty' or 'freedom' in highlighting the relational character of the designated phenomenon (that is, the fact that the designated phenomenon consists not only in a person's possession of capacities but also in his being unprevented from exercising those capacities). For discussions focused on the conceptual space carved out by the negative-liberty theorists, the language of 'liberty' and 'freedom' is singularly apposite. A very different situation obtains when we turn our attention to positive liberty. While the sundry versions of the positive-liberty ideal will warrant the application of a variety of terms—most of which will be appropriate for only some of those versions—there are indeed many pertinent designations available. Terms and phrases such as 'self-fulfilment', 'self-realization', 'self-expression', 'self-mastery', 'autonomy', 'self-reliance', 'self-control', 'self-determination', 'self-development', 'flourishing', 'self-direction', 'political participation', and 'active citizenship' can each figure saliently in one or more of the major positive-liberty credos. Moreover, when wielded aptly, each of those terms and phrases will typically be much more exact—and probably more vivid—than 'freedom' or 'liberty' as a means of pinpointing the state or process that is posited as a fundamental human desideratum. Hence, not only will little or nothing be lost if the positive uses of 'freedom' and 'liberty' are eschewed, but in addition an avoidance of those terms as designations for the positive-liberty theorists' objectives will promote analytical precision. 'Freedom' and 'liberty' in their positive senses are superfluous, since the potential replacements for them are myriad; and those replacements are generally superior in denoting the specificities of the ideals which the positive-liberty theorists extol.

An even more important reason for looking askance at a positive account of freedom is that any such account generates an unacceptable conclusion (whether explicitly drawn or not)—the conclusion that the prevention of numerous actions and omissions does not restrict freedom in any way if the prevention is in furtherance of the ideal upheld by the account. Such a conclusion compares unfavourably with the negative-liberty theorist's sensible view that certain freedoms or the conjunctive exercisability of certain freedoms will have to be eliminated if overall liberty is to be maximized. Although many negative-liberty theorists will normally regard the sacrifice of certain freedoms (or the sacrifice of the conjunctive exercisability of certain freedoms) as a price worth paying in order to expand the overall liberty of each person or of a society, they will recognize that those freedoms are indeed freedoms that are being sacrificed. By contrast, somebody who espouses the ideal of positive liberty is thereby logically committed to the view that freedom-promoting constraints do not eliminate any instances of liberty at all. If freedom consists in undertaking some specified activities or in following some specified procedures—as the positive-liberty theorists submit—then we do not limit any freedoms whatsoever when we preclude conduct that is contrary to those activities or procedures. Far from cutting off any liberties, our prevention of the disfavoured conduct merely cuts off opportunities that are antithetical to true liberties.

Let us suppose that some positive-liberty doctrine *PLD* declares that genuine freedom resides in the greatest possible development of each person's most prominent aesthetic talents. Let us suppose further that Alice is a highly gifted piano player whose tendency to become distracted by non-aesthetic activities will lead her to neglect her piano-playing unless she is chained to her immobile instrument for several hours each day. Now, for the proponent of *PLD*, any opportunities that do not facilitate the greatest possible development of one's paramount aesthetic talents are not freedoms at all. Hence, the countless opportunities denied to Alice by her shackles are not freedoms of which she has been deprived; they are not freedoms, period. Instead, they are obstacles to the realization of her true freedom—obstacles from which her chains liberate her. Her shackles will effectively have set her free without causing her to lose even the slightest instance of liberty. In other words, the augmentation of her positive liberty through the curbs on her mobility will involve no sacrifices of any of her particular freedoms. She has not been rendered unfree in any respect.

The conception of freedom expressed in *PLD* is not starkly incoherent or semantically unintelligible, but it is strange indeed. Though perhaps the labelling of self-fulfilment or self-expression as 'freedom' is too common in the history of political theory to seem joltingly inapposite in itself, the implications of such a designation are much more troublesome. While the scenario of Alice and her piano is contrivedly vivid, the unacceptable conclusions arising therefrom are derivable—*mutatis mutandis*, and in less striking forms—from any positive-liberty credo. Every such credo, which proclaims that freedom amounts to the exertion of certain faculties or the performance of certain acts or the following of certain procedures, will commit its advocates to the view that opportunities inconsistent with the relevant exertions or performances or procedures can be removed wholesale with no loss of any particular freedoms. Instead of being able to represent the closing off of those opportunities as the removal of some of a person's liberties for the sake of increasing her overall liberty, theorists stoutly upholding a positive account of freedom must contend that no removal of liberties is involved at all. A claim along those lines is not self-contradictory or meaningless, but it is decidedly odd. That such a claim follows as a corollary from every positive conception of freedom is a good reason for rejecting that conception.

A corollary of that sort does indeed follow from every 'positive' account of liberty. An argument to the contrary has been put forward by Tom Baldwin, whose approach to positive freedom has quite heavily influenced that of Skinner. In a discussion of T. H. Green, Baldwin maintains that Green's positive conception of liberty does not run afoul of the problem highlighted here, since the specific tenor of his conception rules out the possibility that the elimination of opportunities will in some circumstances not scotch any liberties: 'Green makes it very clear (expressly invoking Kant) that [positive] freedom can only be attained where an agent acts virtuously for the sake of the virtue of his actions. It cannot therefore be attained simply through coercion, which is indeed liable to obstruct it by interfering with the motive of virtue for its own sake.'[89] Baldwin reasons that, although coercive measures can induce a person to undertake virtuous acts, they cannot induce him or her to act for virtue's sake. Such measures will indeed be counter-productive. Consequently, Green's account of positive freedom—which affirms that liberty resides in acting for virtue's sake—will not give rise to the problem of the unclassifiability of squelched opportunities as lost freedoms. Since the removal of various opportunities will do nothing to promote the attainment of freedom (when freedom is understood as acting for the sake of virtue), and since every removed opportunity is a chance to act virtuously for virtue's sake, the elimination of anyone's opportunities is straightforwardly classifiable as freedom-impairing. Hence, nothing akin to the strange conclusions engendered by the application of *PLD* to Alice will here emerge. So, in effect, Baldwin argues.

The basic snag in Baldwin's line of reasoning is the falsity of his premise that coercive measures cannot prod people to act for the sake of virtue. On the one hand, such measures will indeed often fail to generate the desired result and may in fact set back the objective which they are meant to further. On the other hand, the failure is not inevitable in all contexts. Sometimes the administration of outright force in order to shape people's outlooks and motives will yield the intended

---

[89] Tom Baldwin, 'MacCallum and the Two Concepts of Freedom', 26 *Ratio* 125, 137 (1984).

effects, as St Augustine grasped when he chillingly supported the persecution of heretics:

If anyone were to see an enemy, delirious with dangerous fever, running headlong, would he not be returning evil for evil if he let him go, rather than if he took means to have him picked up and restrained? Yet he would then seem to the man himself most hateful and most hostile when he had proved himself most helpful and most considerate. But, when [the delirious man] recovered his health, his thanks would be lavish in proportion to his former feeling of injury at not being let alone ... And what of that other kind of deadly illness which afflicts those who had no impulse to make trouble, but who sank down, under the weight of long inertness, saying to us: 'What you say is true; we have no answer for it; but it is hard for us to leave the way of life of our forefathers'? Should they not, for their own good, be roused by a set of temporal penalties, so as to make them come out of their lethargic sleep and awake to the health of unity? How many of these, too, who now rejoice with us, blame the former weight of their deadly custom, and confess that it was right for us to disturb them and so prevent them from perishing in that sleep of seeming death and that disease of long-standing habit ...

You see now, I think, that the point to be considered is not whether anyone is being forced to do something, but what sort of thing he is being forced to do, whether it is good or bad. Not that anyone can be good against his will, but, by fear of enduring what he does not want, he either gives up the hatred that stands in his way, or he is compelled to recognize the truth he did not know. So, through fear, he repudiates the false doctrine that he formerly defended, or he seeks the truth which he did not know, and he willingly holds now what he formerly denied.[90]

Loathsome though Augustine's fervent approval of repression and compulsion may have been, it was not entirely naive or obtuse psychologically. When Augustine went on to recount numerous sincere recantations of heterodoxy that attested to the effectiveness of the use of force for achieving a virtuous state of purity, he was not engaged merely in wishful thinking. Although violent and restrictive measures are undoubtedly often counter-productive if the aim is to impel people to act for the sake of virtue, such measures can sometimes further precisely that aim. A person who is coerced into adopting certain patterns of behaviour might eventually come to see those modes of behaviour as intrinsically worthy and might then strive to adhere to them for their own sake. To be sure, because compulsion tends to engender resentment, these sincere conversions are rare. Nevertheless, they are always possible and sometimes actual.

[90] St Augustine, 'Letter 93: To his beloved brother, Vincent', in *Letters*, ii, trans. Wilfrid Parsons (New York: Fathers of the Church, 1953), 56, 58–9, 72.

In so far as constraints are applied with sufficient cleverness and tenacity to induce some reprobate people to begin acting virtuously for the sake of so acting, those constraints are promotive of the condition which Green designated as 'freedom'. Opportunities eliminated by those constraints are not classifiable (by followers of Green) as lost freedoms at all, since those eradicated opportunities would have been impediments to freedom if they had been left in place. Thus, the restrictive measures that close off those opportunities—measures that might be highly restrictive indeed, including imprisonment and shackles—have thereby promoted liberty without sacrificing any particular liberties whatsoever. In other words, just as an unacceptable corollary follows from *PLD* when applied to the scenario of Alice and her piano, a fundamentally cognate corollary follows from Green's positive conception of liberty when applied to situations of sincere moral conversions that have been brought about by force. Every positive-liberty theory yields some variant of that corollary, and is objectionable *pro tanto*.

Of course, such a theory might be combined with a negative account of liberty to forestall the derivation of any corollary akin to those just discussed. A hybrid approach of that sort would explicate the concept of freedom in a positive fashion for some purposes and in a negative fashion for other purposes. A move along those lines would not be illegitimate or self-contradictory, of course, but it would amount to an acknowledgment of the inadequacy of positive-liberty doctrines. After all, a negative-liberty theory does not similarly have to fall back upon a positive account of freedom in order to ward off preposterous implications that would otherwise follow from its central thesis. With regard to a negative conception of liberty, there is no danger of such implications; hence, they need not be averted through a desperate resort to an alternative understanding of freedom. A hybrid approach, which invites confusion, can and should be eschewed in favour of the univocal rigour of a negative approach.

In respects relevant to this discussion—though not necessarily in other respects—positive-liberty doctrines are closely similar to moralized conceptions of freedom. Albeit a moralized conception of freedom need not be teleological, every such conception affirms one or both of the following two theses: (1) the prevention of some action or state of affairs does not eliminate any particular freedoms unless the prevention is wrongful, or (2) the prevention does not eliminate any particular freedoms unless the stymied action or state of affairs would have been legitimate. Under the first of these theses, the preclusion of a person from φ-ing will count as a *pro-tanto* curb on his freedom only if he had a moral right against the sort of interference that thwarted him from φ-ing. Under the second thesis, the preclusion of a person from φ-ing will count as a *pro-tanto* curb on his freedom only if he had no moral obligation to refrain from φ-ing. In either case, a moralized conception of freedom will decline to classify some eliminated liberties as eliminated liberties.

Thus, for example, if Alec's prevention of Susan from wantonly setting fire to a neighbour's house is morally legitimate, then Alec does not deprive Susan of any freedoms at all when he manages to avert the arson by grabbing and restraining her. If she struggles to reach the neighbour's premises so fiercely that he has to pin her to the ground and even bind her hands and feet, she will still not have been deprived of any freedoms. Such, at least, is the view taken by the proponents of moralized conceptions of freedom. Whereas my F Postulate and U Postulate explicate the concepts of freedom and unfreedom by reference to one's abilities and to the causes of one's inabilities, a moralized approach explicates those concepts by reference to *the moral status* of the causes of one's inabilities or to *the moral status* of one's exertions of one's abilities—that is, the moral legitimacy or illegitimacy of the causes of one's inabilities, or the moral legitimacy or illegitimacy of one's exertions of one's abilities.

Moralized conceptions of freedom, from which Skinner has always wisely distanced himself, are vulnerable to major criticisms.[91] One of the foremost criticisms should be evident from the scenario of Alec and the aspiring arsonist Susan. That is, every moralized account of freedom insists that even the severest constraints on a person's latitude

---

[91] For Skinner's rejection of a moralized approach to liberty, see for example, *Liberty*, 83 n. 54. Skinner's stance on this point is strikingly different from that of Philip Pettit, with whom Skinner agrees on most other issues relating to freedom. For a rather startling expression of Pettit's position, see his *Republicanism: A Theory of Freedom and Government* (Oxford: Oxford University Press, 1997) [Pettit, *Republicanism*], 56 n. 3: '(U)nder a conception of freedom as non-domination... neither a tax levy, nor even a term of imprisonment, need take away someone's freedom.' See also Philip Pettit, *A Theory of Freedom* (Cambridge: Polity Press, 2001) [Pettit, *Theory*], 75–7, 134–5. For largely similar views, see Ronald Dworkin, 'Thirty Years On', 115 *Harvard Law Review* 1655, 1667–8 (2002); Allen Wood, *Hegel's Ethical Thought* (Cambridge: Cambridge University Press, 1990), 40–1. For some criticisms of moralized theories of freedom, see Carter, *Measure*, 69–72; Cohen, 'Capitalism', 11–13; Cohen, 'Illusions', 226–9; Cohen, *Self-Ownership*, 35–7, 53–65; Cohen, *History*, 251–3, 256, 292–6; Kymlicka, *Contemporary*, 138, 145–51; Kristján Kristjánsson, 'Is There Something Wrong with "Free Action"?', 10 *Journal of Theoretical Politics* 259, 268–9 (1998) [Kristjánsson, 'Free Action']; Kristján Kristjánsson, 'Reply to Pettit and

might not remove any of a person's liberties. No such removal will have taken place unless the constraints are wrongful or unless the prevented conduct would have been legitimate. Consequently, if the placement of a highly dangerous man in chains or a straitjacket is legitimate because of his uncontrollably violent behaviour, neither of those means of immobilization will deprive him of any liberties. A theory that generates such a conclusion can hardly claim to be cogently illuminating.

Moreover, with reference to any situation in which some person P has been deprived of the freedom-to-φ, a moralized conception of freedom must submit either that any questions about the illegitimacy of the deprivation are pointlessly pleonastic or that any questions about the legitimacy of P's φ-ing are pointlessly pleonastic. If the restrictions on P's φ-ing are indeed restrictions on his liberty, so we are told, then either *ipso facto* they are illegitimate or *ipso facto* his φ-ing would have been legitimate. In other words, any moralized approach to freedom whisks out of existence an array of perfectly ordinary inquiries. Perhaps even more unsettling is that, when such an approach is focused on the illegitimacy of preventive constraints, it strips freedom of any independence as a factor that can militate either in favour of various socio-political arrangements or against them. Because the only constraints on human conduct that will count as limitations on liberty are unjust constraints, a denunciation of certain institutions as restrictive of liberty will add nothing to a denunciation of them as unjust. Likewise, because such a moralized theory construes freedom as nothing more than the absence of *illegitimate* constraints, a commendation of certain institutions as promotive of freedom will add nothing to a commendation of them as legitimate and fair. In short, the fostering or impairing of freedom (as understood by a moralized theory of this type) will have ceased to be a consideration that might carry some independent justificatory or condemnatory weight. The redundancy of that fostering or impairing as a justificatory or condemnatory factor stems from the status of freedom as a mere facet of some substantive moral ideal—an ideal on which the whole burden of justification or condemnation rests. Though moralized approaches to liberty that are focused on the illegitimacy of obstacles might seem to

Norman', 10 *Journal of Theoretical Politics* 291, 294 (1998); van Parijs, *Real Freedom*, 15. Cf. Serena Olsaretti, 'Freedom, Force, and Choice: Against the Rights-Based Definition of Voluntariness', 6 *Journal of Political Philosophy* 53 (1998); David Zimmerman, 'Coercive Wage Offers', 10 *Philosophy and Public Affairs* 121 (1981).

elevate the status of liberty by imbuing it with a morally favourable tenor, they in fact eliminate liberty as an independent category by reducing all questions of greater or lesser freedom to questions of greater or lesser rectitude. For anyone who wishes to appraise socio-political arrangements not only on the basis of their justice or injustice but also (separately) on the basis of their conduciveness or inconduciveness to high levels of overall liberty, a moralized conception of freedom should be forsworn. For anyone who believes that liberty and justice can sometimes conflict—in a clash between liberty and equality, for example—a moralized conception of freedom should be forsworn.

This discussion should close with two caveats or clarifications. First, although this subsection has advanced some strong reasons for rejecting moralized understandings of liberty, it has not shown and has not endeavoured to show that a full explication of the concept of liberty can completely forgo any reliance on moral judgements and categories. Even if we leave aside the problems of measuring the extent of each person's overall freedom, and thus even if we concentrate exclusively on questions relating to the existence of particular freedoms and unfreedoms, we cannot simply take for granted the forgoability of moral appraisals. Instead, an insistence on the dispensability of such appraisals must be backed up with arguments. To that end, my subsequent chapters will present a number of pertinent lines of reasoning. The marshalling of those arguments is crucial for my full-scale theory of freedom, because some aspects of that theory might initially appear to implicate moral considerations. Most notably, some readers might presume that the causal attributions which operationalize the distinction between 'not free' and 'unfree' must involve moral judgements. In order to deny that such judgements are necessary, my fourth chapter will set forth appropriate causal criteria that do not invoke moral touchstones.[92] Although that task will not be undertaken until then, the need for it indicates that the current subsection has not per se supplied comprehensive grounds for thinking that the

---

[92] For a sophisticated variant of the position which I shall be opposing—a variant with specific reference to attributions of freedom—see David Miller, 'Constraints on Freedom', 94 *Ethics* 66 (1983). See also Kristján Kristjánsson, 'For a *Concept* of Negative Liberty—but which *Conception*?', 9 *Journal of Applied Philosophy* 221 (1992); Kristján Kristjánsson, 'Social Freedom and the Test of Moral Responsibility', 103 *Ethics* 104 (1992); Kristjánsson, *Social Freedom*. Cf. Robert Nozick, *Anarchy, State, and Utopia* (New York: Basic Books, 1974), 191–2.

ascertainment of particular freedoms and unfreedoms can proceed without any reliance on moral assessments.

A second caveat for the close of this discussion pertains to the nature of my admonitions regarding the appropriate senses of the terms 'freedom' and 'liberty'. All of the arguments in this subsection which prescribe certain uses for those terms and which frown upon other uses are concerned with the employment of the language of 'freedom' in the rigorous theorizing that constitutes political philosophy. Nothing said in this book is aimed at regimenting the multifarious patterns of usage that occur in the much less rigorous discourses of everyday life. In many of those discourses, where consistency and subtlety and clarity and precision are of far less importance than in philosophical writing, one's designation of self-fulfilment as the attainment of 'freedom' might be perfectly apt. Plainly, as has been repeatedly acknowledged in this subsection, there is nothing semantically illicit about such a designation. Given that the language of 'freedom' will be intelligible and coherent, and given that the inexactitude of its application will not greatly matter in the to-and-fro of mundane deliberations and exhortations, we should not feel inclined to rein in the multiple senses that might attach to 'freedom' and 'liberty' in a host of ordinary contexts. Such an endeavour would be patently futile in any event.

Not at all futile or ridiculous, however, is an effort to enhance the rigour and precision of philosophical thinking about freedom. If the aim is to come up with a theory that carefully distinguishes the concept of freedom from other concepts while capturing its myriad complexities, then some degree of terminological regimentation is inevitable. Some uses of 'freedom' and 'liberty' countenanced in day-to-day parlance have to fall by the wayside when a painstaking philosophical investigation of freedom seeks to elaborate the necessary and sufficient conditions for the truth of any proposition 'P is free to φ'. For the purposes of such an investigation, we are warranted in disapproving of the inexactitude and misleadingness and inconsistency of many of those ordinary uses. Philosophical analysis proceeds by clarifying and refining the concepts that are invoked in relatively unreflective modes of thought and discourse, as it aspires to transcend the murkiness and looseness of those familiar modes of speaking. The tasks of conceptual clarification and purification can scarcely go ahead without some notable tightening of everyday terminology. To insist as much, however, is not at all to insist that a similar tightening is advisable or even feasible in everyday discourses themselves.

2.2. Civic Virtue and the Promotion of Freedom

At least until very recently, the most conspicuous strand of argument in Skinner's writings on liberty has concerned the instrumental connection between people's compliance with duties of civic virtue and their enjoyment of negative freedom. Skinner has repeatedly proclaimed that that connection is overlooked by the modern exponents of the concept of negative liberty, who are therefore blind to the straightforward ways in which people must sometimes be forced to be free. Writers in the civic-republican tradition, by contrast, always laid stress on the essential role of civic virtue in securing the flourishing of liberty. Skinner submits that those writers adhered to the very same conception of freedom that is upheld by contemporary negative-liberty theorists. (His position on this particular point has slightly changed during the past few years, as we shall see later.) Yet, while sharing a negative conception of freedom with present-day theorists, the civic-republican writers ostensibly differed from those theorists in setting great store by the common good—because the civic republicans unflinchingly understood that the promotion of the common good is a sine qua non for the preservation of individual liberty.

Skinner affirms that an examination of the civic-republican heritage can reveal the potential truth of two propositions that are supposedly scorned by present-day exponents of the doctrine of negative liberty.[93] The first of these propositions is that liberty cannot be securely enjoyed except in societies where citizens participate actively in the chores and responsibilities of public service. Unless people are extensively involved in running and shaping the system that governs them, their freedom will be imperilled. The second of the propositions which Skinner hopes to vindicate is that people sometimes must be forced to be free. Specifically, because of the tendency of individuals to become preoccupied with their private concerns and projects, they need to be prodded to carry out the civic duties and offices through which they ensure the continuation of their liberties. Were citizens not roused out of their self-absorbed disinclination to engage in public service, their indifference to the common good would undermine the very array of freedoms which all of them prize.

According to the civic-republican thinkers—as described by Skinner, whose accuracy in recounting their views is not under challenge here at all—the populace of any society can be divided into two broad

[93] Skinner, 'Paradoxes', 229–30; Skinner, 'Republican', 294–5.

groups: the powerful, who strive for glory and conquest and dominance; and the ordinary citizens, who want chiefly to be secure from interference with their private projects. If we leave aside the dangers posed by external nations, the paramount threats to individuals' liberties arise from the ambitions of the powerful. Although those ambitions can redound to the benefit of the common weal in quite a few contexts, they can on other occasions lead to the overriding of basic freedoms and the imposition of a despotic sway. Hence, if citizens' liberties are to be held securely, the taming of the powerful and the channelling of their ambitions into worthy routes will be essential. A structure of governance should be designed to steer the aspirations of those mighty people into just such routes. Yet, the civic republicans argued, the only structure of governance which can achieve that salutary effect is a regime in which all citizens (both the powerful and the ordinary) participate extensively in the formation and implementation of policies. Even if people remain absorbed by their own affairs to a large extent, their behaviour within the institutions of civil governance must be the sort of behaviour that would be exhibited by truly public-spirited citizens. Without such conduct on the part of virtually everyone, the nobles will be able to pursue their power-hungry aims to the detriment of everyone else's liberty. Political participation and the fulfilment of duties of civic virtue, then, are vital for the preservation of liberty. Rather than perceiving the political sphere as something that must be kept at a distance in order to safeguard individual freedom, the civic republicans insisted that such freedom can never be soundly protected unless citizens enter the political sphere actively and frequently.

At a few junctures, Skinner's account of the civic-republican writers comes close to suggesting that they took a robustly optimistic view of the potential for selfless behaviour among citizens. We are told, for example, that those writers insisted that citizens 'must all cultivate the political virtues and devote [themselves] whole-heartedly to a life of public service'.[94] For the most part, however, Skinner rightly emphasizes the bleak view of human nature to which Machiavelli and some other civic republicans wisely subscribed. Machiavelli was keenly aware that most people act in furtherance of their own selfish interests and that they often do so short-sightedly. He accordingly recognized that the institutions of civic governance—and kindred institutions such as that of religion—must be arranged in ways that effect a conver-

---

[94] Skinner, 'Paradoxes', 243.

gence between each individual's interest and the common interest. By being steered in this manner toward working for the public good, each individual will likewise be steered toward working for his own long-term interest in the preservation of his individual freedom. As Skinner contends:

What the law can hope to achieve in the face of [the tendency of people to seek short-sightedly to advance their own selfish interests], Machiavelli suggests, is to coerce and direct us in just such a way that, even if we continue to act solely out of a corrupt desire to further our own individual or factional advantage, our motivations may nonetheless be capable of being harnessed to serve the public interest, although the outcome of precisely the same motivations, in the absence of any such coercion, would have been destructive not merely of the public interest, but also—and in consequence—of our own individual liberty at the same time.

This process is not envisaged as one in which the agent is made to bring his desires in line with those of a 'higher self'. On the contrary, he retains his selfish patterns of motivation and in consequence his self-destructive proclivities. All that happens is that the law operates to channel his behaviour in such a way that, although his reasons for action remain self-interested, his actions have consequences which, although not intended, are such as to promote the public interest, and hence his own individual liberty. The agent is thus enabled, by means of the coercive powers of the law, to attain the freedom he actually desires, and to avoid the servitude his unconstrained behaviour would otherwise have produced.[95]

As Skinner pithily summarizes the matter in a different passage, a prudent regime of law will ensure that citizens are 'given selfish reasons for behaving virtuously'.[96]

These and many other passages in Skinner's essays make clear that civic republicanism requires only virtuously communitarian conduct as opposed to virtuously public-spirited motives. Although such motives are undoubtedly salutary when they are present, they are too rare to serve as a reliable basis for the enterprise of securing individual liberty. In lieu of such motives, virtuous conduct impelled by largely selfish considerations will be admirably serviceable for that enterprise. What is crucial for the success of a civic-republican regime is that its legal framework and its other mechanisms are arranged to ensure that myopically selfish promptings are indeed channelled into the furtherance of the public weal and thus into the furtherance of individual freedom. (With great ingenuity and with a learned knowledge of

[95] Skinner, 'Maintenance', 10.
[96] Skinner, 'Idea', 219.

Roman history, Machiavelli explained at length how a suitable scheme of governance might be designed. His proposals, some of which are lucidly and informatively recounted by Skinner, cannot be explored here.) By accepting and indeed emphasizing that the motives for virtuous participation in a properly devised structure of governance will typically be short-sighted and selfish, the civic republicans went quite a long way toward overcoming a major set of difficulties that would otherwise have plagued their theory: the difficulties posed by free-rider problems and other collective-action problems.[97]

If the republicans had hoped to ground the security of liberty on the widespread occurrence of altruistic behaviour or even on the widespread pursuit of enlightened self-interest, they would have left themselves highly vulnerable indeed. Visions of pervasive altruism are too fanciful to be taken seriously, and even a theory which ascribes to all or most members of the populace a substantial degree of far-sightedness in their pursuit of their own interests will confront severe motivational problems. After all, notwithstanding that each person might be able to discern the link between general political participation and the preservation of individual freedom, he might believe that his own interest in the preservation of freedom will be sufficiently upheld by the participatory activities of his fellow citizens. Or, slightly more subtly and accurately, he might believe that his own abstention from the shouldering of public responsibilities will make little or no difference to the success or failure of his fellows in shouldering those responsibilities and in thus safeguarding everyone's freedom. If this desire to take a 'free ride' on the striving of others is widely harboured—as it almost certainly will be, if the only incentives for participation reside in appeals to enlightened self-interest—then a liberty-preserving regime of civic virtue will not emerge or will not endure. Basically similar problems are bound to arise if each citizen believes that his fellows will be remiss in carrying out their civic responsibilities. Though each person might well grasp the connection between the general fulfilment of such responsibilities and the sustainment of individual freedom, each might feel that the accidie of other citizens will render his own efforts unavailing. Again, if such an outlook is widely held, a

---

[97] Curiously, Skinner does not take account of these problems. He is aptly criticized on this point in Patten, 'Critique', 29. (More broadly, Patten's essay is an excellent critique of Skinner's general doctrine of instrumental republicanism, which I am exploring throughout this subsection.) For a classic, highly readable exposition of the sorts of collective-action difficulties that have to be addressed by civic republicans, see Mancur Olson, *The Logic of Collective Action* (Cambridge, MA: Harvard University Press, 1971).

liberty-preserving regime of civic virtue will be doomed to failure. No one will opt to engage in what he perceives as a wholly futile endeavour. These difficulties and myriad other difficulties pertaining to collective action would afflict civic republicanism severely indeed if the proponents of that doctrine had relied on enlightened self-interest as the sole motivating force for virtuous conduct. In fact, however, as we have observed, the civic republicans in the tradition of Machiavelli were perspicaciously alert to the uncooperatively self-seeking tendencies in most people's characters. They knew that, even if each person is sufficiently astute to grasp the importance of popular political participation for the advancement of his or her long-term interest in the preservation of liberty, short-term interests will often impel him or her away from participation. Those short-term interests themselves must be enlisted in the cause of civic virtue if such virtue is to be realizable and durable. Though the civic republicans did not discern the array of collective-action problems to which modern social-choice theorists and game theorists have sophisticatedly drawn attention, their unromanticized view of human nature led them to propose political arrangements that alleviate those problems to quite an extent.

While civic republicans' tough-mindedness about human nature was one great strength of their theorizing, another such strength lay in their adherence to a negative conception of liberty. Although in the past few years Skinner has partly renounced the view that the republican and liberal conceptions of freedom are indistinguishable, he has continued to affirm that the republicans subscribed to a negative understanding of freedom. They did not suggest that liberty consists in the performance of certain activities or the exertion of certain capacities or the following of certain procedures. Specifically, unlike some writers in the Aristotelian tradition, they did not submit that the fulfilment of duties of civic virtue through political participation is itself the attainment of freedom. Although participation presupposes the liberty-to-participate, and although it may well help to secure other liberties, neither it nor any other activity is itself liberty. Rather, as the civic republicans maintained, the freedom of a person amounts to his being unprevented from doing or becoming or remaining whatever he is capable of doing or becoming or remaining.

While eschewing a positive conception of freedom, the civic-republican writers nonetheless endorsed the two propositions (mentioned earlier herein) that are singled out by Skinner as objects of contemporary negative-liberty theorists' disdain. In the first place, the republicans clearly contended that individual liberty will not be secure unless citizens engage vigorously and regularly in public service. A solid instrumental connection obtains between the wide-spread fulfilment of duties of civic virtue and the retention of individual freedoms. Under a regime where popular participation in government is largely non-existent, the liberty of each citizen will be dauntingly precarious because the ambitions of the powerful will be largely unchecked. Moreover, precisely on account of the hazards to liberty that stem from the meagreness of popular participation, civic republicans endorsed the second of Skinner's propositions—the proposition that people might have to be forced to be free. Political and legal arrangements should be such that people cannot enjoy with impunity the highly dangerous luxury of remaining disengaged. Whether or not citizens are naturally inclined to protect their liberties over the longer term by involving themselves persistently in public service, they should be required to undertake just such service. If their natural inclinations render them neglectful of their freedoms, their scheme of governance should lift them out of their liberty-imperilling remissness by bringing to bear a number of pressures designed to induce them to behave virtuously.

Now, given that the civic-republican writers subscribed to a commendably realistic view of human nature that went quite a way toward compensating for their unacquaintance with modern analyses of collective-action problems, and given that those writers adhered to a strictly negative conception of freedom, why should their acceptance of Skinner's two propositions be problematic at all in the eyes of modern negative-liberty theorists? Skinner plainly feels that the civic republicans came up with insights that are at odds with the positions of the modern theorists. Indeed, his cardinal purpose in unearthing the republicans' treatment of liberty is to highlight the blinkeredness of the modern theorists' approach to the topic. If that purpose is to be achieved, there must be something in the civic-republican writers' ideas which differs significantly from contemporary negative-liberty doctrines and which therefore cannot be accommodated within those doctrines. But why should we think that there is any divergence at all? Save for the inadequacy of the republicans' apprehension of collective-action problems, everything in their proposals for the preservation of individual freedom would appear to be straightforwardly consistent with the stances of present-day exponents of negative liberty. Is there any reason to doubt this appearance of manifest consistency?

Certainly, the notion of an instrumental link between extensive popular political participation and the safeguarding of individual liberty does not serve to distinguish the civic republicans' positions from those of the modern negative-liberty theorists. What would of course form a point of contrast between those two sets of positions is a claim by the civic republicans that the fulfilment of duties of civic virtue through political participation is itself freedom. Rather than simply maintaining that the activity of participation presupposes the freedom-to-participate and that it may be instrumental in solidifying the exist-ence of other freedoms, a claim of the sort just mentioned would assert a relationship of equivalence between virtuous participation and free-dom. Such a claim would be one of the standard statements of the ideal of positive liberty and would accordingly be inconsistent with nega-tive-liberty doctrines in most respects. We have looked at the numer-ous points of inconsistency in my last subsection. At this stage, let it suffice for us to recall that a positive-liberty position along those lines must affirm that any squelching of opportunities which promotes political participation is not a removal of particular freedoms at all. Not only is that squelching of opportunities a means of maximizing the overall freedom of each person or of a society; what is more, it does not involve the slightest loss of any instances of freedom. After all, the only opportunities cut off are those that are incompatible with the full realization of civic virtue, which is itself equated with freedom by the positive-liberty approach. Now, as has been argued in my last subsec-tion, this contention that opportunities can be eliminated without any elimination of freedoms—a contention entailed by any positive-liberty theory—is unacceptable. It is flatly irreconcilable with any negative-liberty credo. Had the civic republicans relied on a positive conception of freedom, then, they would have been espousing theses that cannot be taken on board at all by a negative account of freedom. Yet, as Skinner himself duly emphasizes, the civic-republican writers (at any rate, those whom he discusses) did not adopt a positive-liberty stance. When proclaiming an instrumental connection between the political engagedness of citizens and the security of individual freedoms, they were propounding a thesis about negative liberty rather than about positive liberty. Exactly why Skinner expects us to view that thesis as an anathema to negative-liberty theorists is consequently quite puzzling.

Far from breaking upon the present-day scene as a revelatory thun-derbolt, the civic-republican thesis in its broad outlines is a common-place in much of contemporary political thought. Let us here pretermit the collective-action problems that are raised by the republican pos-ition. In that event, the central message of the republican credo in the context of modern political thinking is more platitudinous than unset-tling or innovative. The extent to which that message has long figured in ordinary political discourse is perhaps nowhere more evident than in connection with the United States, a country designated by its own national anthem as the land of the free and the home of the brave. In light of that emphasis both on freedom and on republican virtues such as bravery, we should not be surprised that one of the most self-indulgent libertines ever to hold the office of President of the United States would stirringly adjure his compatriots to ask not what their country could do for them but what they could do for their country. Nor should we be surprised that the apothegm 'Eternal vigilance is the price of liberty'—an apothegm quoted in its original form by Skinner[98]—is one of the ubiquitous clichés of American political discourse, not only in application to foreign foes but also in application to the aggrandizement of the federal government. Equally in keeping with the liberal republicanism or republican liberalism of the United States is the frequent bandying about of Thomas Jefferson's famous pronouncement that the tree of liberty must be refreshed from time to time with the blood of patriots and tyrants. Possibly the most striking manifestation of the American orientation toward civic virtue in the cause of freedom is the practice of having schoolchildren in the United States recite the Pledge of Allegiance each day. As the children vow their loyalty to their republic—admittedly, often in a highly perfunctory manner—they laud that republic as a nation with liberty for all. In these respects and in many other respects, a connection between public service and individual freedom is routinely recognized in the political life and culture of the United States. At least within an American setting, the civic-republican insights concerning the promotion of liberty through the exercise of civic virtue are so familiar as to be hackneyed. (Of course, nothing said in this paragraph has been meant to suggest that the civic-republican position is so obviously correct as to be beyond contestation in every detail. Even if we leave aside the problems of collective action, the republican position can never be *categorically* correct. A tenable thesis about an instrumental connection, however plainly sound it may be on the whole, is typically rather than invariably true. Even in the United States, for example, the link between popular political participation and the upholding of individual freedom does not obtain across the board. Undemocratic judicial institutions in the United States, largely shielded from the pressures of popular participation, have at times played a major role in the safeguarding of various civil liberties. Judicial elites, construing the limitations on public legislative-administrative power that have been placed virtually beyond the reach of democratic majorities

---

[98] Skinner, 'Justice', 219.

through a number of constitutional provisions and amendments, are quite frequently more solicitous of the aforementioned liberties than are the democratically accountable branches of the American government.)

In short, the civic-republican writers' insistence on an instrumental connection between the active political involvement of citizens and the continuation of the citizens' freedoms is a well-established component of the intellectual and political culture of liberal-democratic societies. Though the details of the republicans' institutional prescriptions are somewhat different from those that have gained favour in liberal democracies, the general notion of a link between civic virtue and the preservation of individual liberties is far from unfamiliar. Why, then, does Skinner think that contemporary negative-liberty theorists will be taken aback by such a notion? After all, those theorists live and work in liberal democracies. Have they really been so blind to the assumptions that imbue many of the discourses and practices in their societies?

Skinner offers a number of reasons for thinking that his excavation of the civic-republican position should indeed be unsettling for the modern proponents of the doctrine of negative liberty. Foremost among those reasons is the purported fact that some of the negative-liberty theorists have rejected and derided the two basic propositions which he presents as the core of the civic republicans' message— namely, the proposition that the flourishing of liberty requires the extensive involvement of citizens in public service, and the proposition that people must sometimes be forced to be free. Are these propositions, as understood by Skinner, really disdained by the philosophers who have expounded the concept of negative liberty?

Skinner adduces a passage from Hobbes in relation to the first of the two propositions.[99] In fact, however, the passage in question occurs at the end of a paragraph in *Leviathan* that is concerned with distinguishing between the liberty or autonomy of commonwealths and the liberty of individuals. Let us look at that paragraph's closing portion, to which Skinner adverts: 'There is written on the turrets of the city of Lucca in great characters at this day, the word LIBERTAS; yet no man can thence infer, that a particular man has more liberty, or immunity from the service of the commonwealth there, than in Constantinople. Whether a commonwealth be monarchical, or popular, the freedom is still the same.'[100] Only the laconic phrase 'or immunity from the

---

[99] Skinner, 'Idea', 196; Skinner, 'Paradoxes', 230–1; Skinner, 'Maintenance', 295.
[100] Hobbes, *Leviathan*, 143 (Ch. 21, para. 8), capitalization in original.

service of the commonwealth' is of any relevance to the thesis which Skinner tries to distil from this passage. Whether that phrase should be construed as appositive or as genuinely disjunctive is not clear. That is, we cannot be certain whether Hobbes introduced that wording as a mere explanatory gloss on 'liberty' or whether he instead used it to designate a condition which he perceived as not equivalent to liberty (though undoubtedly overlapping with it). At any rate, the whole of the quoted passage—like the paragraph whence it comes—is focused on the distinction between national independence and individual liberty. Hobbes interpreted the inscription on the turrets as a reference to the independence of Lucca, and he accordingly warned that no conclusions could be drawn therefrom about the liberty of individual Luccans. The freedom mentioned in the final sentence of the passage is predicated of commonwealths rather than of individuals. Hobbes had undertaken a similar predication in the sentence that immediately precedes the pronouncement quoted by Skinner: 'The Athenians, and Romans were free; that is, free commonwealths: not that any particular men had the liberty to resist their own representative; but that their representative had the liberty to resist, or invade other people.'[101] Hobbes's point at the end of the passage quoted by Skinner, in other words, was to stress that national autonomy is national autonomy regardless of the character of the regime involved. Such a point is manifestly compatible with his underscoring of the divide between the level of the nation and the level of the individual.

In contrast with the straightforward interpretation just offered, Skinner detects some boldly sardonic assertions in the portion of *Leviathan* which we have been examining. According to him, Hobbes 'insist[ed] that, since the liberty of subjects must involve "immunity from the service of the commonwealth", any suggestion that freedom involves the performance of such services, and the cultivation of the virtues necessary to perform them, must be totally confused'.[102] This comment is dubious both on exegetical grounds and on philosophical grounds. It is exegetically suspect because the only citation advanced in support of it is to the passage on Lucca quoted above, which does not discuss or dismiss any suggestion of the kind that Skinner describes. His remark is likewise philosophically weak, because it fails to distinguish adequately between particular freedoms and overall freedom. Since any effort to maximize the overall liberty of each individual or of a society will involve some sacrifices of particular liberties—sacrifices

---

[101] Ibid.
[102] Skinner, 'Idea', 196.

that are desirable because they enable the generation or consolidation of more substantial liberties—the conclusion ascribed to Hobbes would not follow from the premise ascribed to him. Even if he perceived every instance of freedom as involving immunity from the service of the commonwealth, he could still claim (with perfect consistency) that the maximization of everyone's overall freedom will involve quite a bit of mandatory service for the commonwealth by each person.

Still more questionable is the slightly later interpretation of the passage from *Leviathan* which Skinner presents in two of his essays:

[Hobbes] tells us with scorn about the Lucchese, who have 'written on the turrets of the city of Lucca in great characters, at this day, the word LIBER-TAS', in spite of the fact that the constitution of their small-scale city-republic placed heavy demands upon their public-spiritedness. To Hobbes, for whom liberty (as we have seen) simply means absence of interference, it seems obvious that the maximising of our social freedom must depend upon our capacity to maximise the area within which we can claim 'immunity from the service of the commonwealth'. So it seems to him merely absurd of the Lucchese to proclaim their liberty in circumstances in which such services are so stringently exacted.[103]

Hobbes unmistakably preferred monarchies to republics, and thus he probably did harbour a rather scornful attitude toward the republic of Lucca. Nevertheless, in the relevant passage from *Leviathan*, he was simply highlighting the difference between national autonomy and individual freedom. He gave no indication whatsoever that the Lucchese proclamation of liberty—a proclamation of national autonomy—was absurd. Instead, he merely sought to emphasize that that accurate proclamation did not enable anybody to draw conclusions about the extent of the liberty enjoyed by each person in Lucca. Though national independence and the flourishing of individual freedom are hardly incompatible, the former does not entail the latter; hence, from the existence of the former we cannot *sans plus* infer the existence of the latter. All the same, an expression of caution about a modus-ponens inference is not tantamount to an assertion of the meagreness of individual liberty in Lucca. Contrary to what Skinner declares, Hobbes (in the passage under consideration) took no position one way or the other on the extent of that liberty. He left the matter an open question.

Nonetheless, for the sake of argument, let us grant that Skinner's embellishment of Hobbes's statements is an accurate reading thereof.

---

[103] Skinner, 'Paradoxes', 230–1; Skinner, 'Republican', 295, footnotes deleted.

Why should we think that an excerpt from Hobbes has any bearing on the present-day debates that are Skinner's prime concern? After all, neither Hobbes's conception of freedom nor his general conception of politics is very close to the views held by modern negative-liberty theorists. Nearly all such theorists would bridle at his belief that the existence of any freedom is desire-dependent, and many of them—including me—would object to his failure to recognize the capacity-dependence of any freedom. In the matter of political orientation, the contemporary negative-liberty theorists are even more strikingly distant from Hobbes. Few if any of them share his dislike of the separation of governmental powers or his aversion to the jockeying of widespread political contestation, for example. Hence, if Skinner is to be persuasive in claiming that the negative-liberty theorists have scorned his proposition about the shoring up of individual liberty through public service, he must go beyond Hobbes to the texts of the present-day theorists themselves.

When moving to those present-day texts, however, Skinner furnishes arrestingly little evidence for his allegation. Apart from quoting some fleeting remarks by Felix Oppenheim that are not really germane when read in their original contexts,[104] Skinner resorts chiefly to a quite tendentious characterization of a comment by Isaiah Berlin. In the course of advocating a pluralistic approach to political values, Berlin delivered a scathing indictment of grand visions that close off the process of normative deliberation: 'To say that in some ultimate, all-reconciling, yet realizable synthesis, duty *is* interest, or individual freedom *is* pure democracy or an authoritarian state, is to throw a metaphysical blanket over either self-deceit or deliberate hypocrisy.'[105] This comment, so clearly directed against utopian striving for the reconciliation of all differences, is described by Skinner as follows: 'Isaiah Berlin remarks... that to speak of rendering myself free by virtuously performing my social duties, thereby equating duty with interest, is simply "to throw a metaphysical blanket over either self-deceit or deliberate hypocrisy"'.[106] Berlin's warning against the repressiveness of millenarian dreams of unity is here transformed into a rejection of the notion that the virtuous performance of social duties can ever promote freedom. Berlin, at the stage in his argument where the quoted remark occurs, was not in any way addressing the type of connection between public service and individual liberty on which

---

[104] Skinner, 'Paradoxes', 231; Skinner, 'Republican', 295–6.
[105] Berlin, *Four Essays*, 171, emphases in original.
[106] Skinner, 'Idea', 196.

Skinner is concentrating. His focus was markedly different. Instead of foolishly maintaining that duties of civic virtue can never further the cause of freedom, he was laying stress on the illusiveness and extreme dangers of all hopes for a climactic synthesis of values—a synthesis that will somehow give rise to a perfect harmony between the individual and the collective. An admonition of this sort is fully consistent with Skinner's civic-republican thesis about an instrumental connection between popular political participation and the secureness of individual freedom. Berlin cannot fairly be said to have denied that civic-republican thesis.

Even if we put aside the misleadingness of Skinner's reconstruction of Berlin's exhortation, moreover, there is a revealing ambiguity in the observation by Skinner. The words 'rendering myself free' in his phrase 'rendering myself free by virtuously performing my social duties' can be understood in either of two principal ways. On the one hand, that wording might mean 'contributing to the greater security of my freedom'. So construed, the words in question would suggest an instrumental link between the performance of social duties and the solidity of individual liberty. On the other hand, 'rendering myself free' might mean 'achieving a state of freedom that consists in adopting certain modes of conduct'. So construed, those words would suggest a constitutive relationship or a relationship of equivalence between performing certain actions and becoming free. Now, under the first of these construals Skinner would be portraying Berlin as an opponent of the theses of civic republicanism, whereas under the second construal he would be portraying Berlin as an opponent of the claims of positive-liberty theorists. Under the second interpretation, then, Skinner's observation would be essentially accurate and uncontroversial; Berlin and other negative-liberty theorists have indeed implacably oppugned the doctrines of positive liberty. However, only under the first interpretation—whereby Berlin is depicted as a foe of civic republicanism—would Skinner's observation, if correct, have any real force and pertinence. After all, the republican thesis about an instrumental connection between civic virtue and individual freedom is the thesis which Skinner himself defends. He refrains from any endorsement of positive-liberty doctrines, as was noted in my last subsection. When he vindicates his first basic proposition about the link between public service and the preservation of freedom, he does so along republican lines rather than along positive-liberty lines. Hence, only if Berlin and other negative-liberty theorists were opposed not solely to the doctrine of positive liberty but also to the insights of civic republicanism, would they be taking a stance that is potentially vulnerable to Skinner's republican retorts. Yet, in fact, neither Berlin nor any other major negative-liberty theorist has ever assailed the civic-republican position. If anyone in the negative-liberty camp has indeed challenged that position, the challenge has certainly not stemmed from the fundamental tenets of the negative conception of liberty (in distinction from some obtrusively right-wing principles that might be combined with those tenets in the writings of a few theorists).

What makes the civic-republican credo acceptable and the positive-liberty credo unacceptable is that the former does acknowledge and the latter does not acknowledge the need for a variety of trade-offs between overall freedom and some particular freedoms. Civic republicans endeavoured to specify the conditions for the maximal solidity and expansiveness of individual liberty. Within their proposals, certain freedoms for virtually everyone have to be sacrificed in order to reinforce the overall freedom of virtually everyone. Civic republicans did not maintain that no instances of freedom will be lost in the process of securing and augmenting each person's overall liberty; on the contrary, they insisted that that process will inevitably involve the elimination of particular freedoms (or, at the very least, the elimination of the conjunctive exercisability of certain freedoms). Positive-liberty theorists, by contrast, submit that the consummate realization of freedom for each person will involve no losses of particular freedoms—since those theorists define particular freedoms as the instances of conduct that constitute or foster the realization of some championed objective, which they characterize as true liberty. Opportunities to engage in other modes of conduct do not count as freedoms, and thus any losses of those opportunities do not count as removals of particular freedoms. This implication of the positive conception of freedom is rightly and firmly resisted by negative-liberty theorists.

When the first of Skinner's propositions (his proposition about the ties between public service and individual freedom) is developed as a positive-liberty thesis, it cannot be squared with any negative-liberty doctrine. No negative-liberty theorist can accept that a person's public service through the fulfilment of duties of civic virtue is itself the attainment of freedom. However, when Skinner's first proposition is developed as a civic-republican thesis—the only version of the proposition which Skinner himself upholds—it asserts nothing that is at odds with the doctrine of negative liberty. Exponents of the negative-liberty doctrine can and do apprehend the instrumental role of popular political participation in preserving and bolstering the overall freedom of individuals. They can and do fathom that role, which is so pervasively recognized within the liberal-democratic societies in which they live.

Negative-liberty theorists subscribe to the first of Skinner's propositions in its civic-republican form. Do they have any reason to baulk at the second of his propositions, which affirms that people must sometimes be forced to be free? Again, everything will hinge here on the way in which we construe the proposition. If we understand it as a positive-liberty thesis about the need to eliminate various opportunities that divert people from the performance of certain activities or the attainment of certain objectives or the following of certain procedures, then the proposition is unacceptable. Such a thesis would equate the favoured performance or procedure or attainment with freedom itself, and would not classify the eliminated opportunities as sacrificed freedoms at all. Neither of those points is reconcilable with the doctrine of negative liberty. Although each person's performance or attainment of X will presuppose his liberty to perform or attain X, and although it may well be serviceable for the promotion of his overall freedom or the engendering of certain particular freedoms of his, it does not itself amount to freedom. For the negative-liberty theorist, freedom consists in unpreventedness—both with regard to capacities and with regard to external obstacles—rather than in any of the endeavours or accomplishments that are unprevented. Even more plainly, negative-liberty theorists cannot countenance any failure to classify suppressed opportunities as lost freedoms. For the proponent of positive liberty, those opportunities are hindrances to freedom; hence, the removal of them unequivocally furthers liberty and does not involve any trade-offs or sacrifices of particular freedoms. When one is forced to be free, one is not thereby deprived of any instances of freedom whatsoever. Or so we are asked to think. Negative-liberty theorists reach a very different verdict. As has been underlined by my last subsection, the closing off of opportunities does consist in restrictions on freedom—even when those restrictions contribute to the maximizing of the overall liberty of each person who is affected by them.

Construed as a positive-liberty thesis, Skinner's second proposition is starkly in conflict with the doctrine of negative liberty. However, it should come as no surprise that that proposition tallies with that doctrine if we construe the proposition as a civic-republican thesis. Indeed, so construed, the proposition once again becomes not much more than a bromide. Given the hardly unfamiliar fact that steadfast vigilance is the price of liberty, and given the equally evident fact that most people cannot be relied upon to sustain a proper level of vigilance in the absence of some well-enforced legal requirements and other pressures, the shoring up of each person's overall freedom must derive in part from the imposition of just such requirements. A scheme of governance that does not place people under any legal duties of civic virtue will thereby weaken rather than strengthen their overall liberty, since it will increase the likelihood of the emergence of a despotic regime. Although the imposition of those duties will undo the conjunctive exercisability of many liberties, the freedom-constricting effects will be more than offset by the freedom-enhancing role of those duties as a bulwark against despotism. Such, at least, is the plausible claim put forward by the civic-republican version of the 'forced to be free' proposition.

Of course, nothing said herein should lead anyone to conclude that negative-liberty theorists *have* to endorse civic-republican claims. Those claims arise from disputable empirical assumptions, and are consequently themselves disputable. As Skinner himself avows, the civic-republican writers may have been 'unduly pessimistic' in their insistence that all or nearly all citizens must show public-spiritedness if each individual's liberty is to be suitably secure.[107] In the context of a large nation-state with modern communications and high levels of education among the populace, rivalries among an array of elites may oft-times be sufficient to safeguard individual freedom without necessitating much political participation on the part of ordinary people. In such a context, the civic-republican message can appear quite overstated. The fact that that message has been encapsulated in some of the clichés of liberal-democratic politics does not in itself serve to establish the message's warrantedness and accuracy. Platitudes can be false or—more often—excessively sweeping. Still, there are some countervailing considerations which give us grounds for thinking that the civic-republican stance might be especially pertinent in the present era. Most notably, inasmuch as the civic-republican writers failed to anticipate modern analyses of collective-action problems, they did not draw upon some powerful lines of argument that could support their basic position on the need to make public service legally obligatory. More clearly than those writers, we are able to see that the carrying out of such service cannot be left to the enlightened self-interest of each individual (which, even if it is the chief determinant of his or her actions, will tend to militate against his or her voluntary shouldering of the burdens of political involvement). Consequently, in so far as public service on a broad scale is indeed crucial for the maximizing of the liberty of individuals, the modern observer is especially justified in concluding that people must in some respects be forced to be free.

---

[107] Skinner, 'Paradoxes', 250; Skinner, 'Republican', 309.

In any event, regardless of whether the civic-republican position is indeed overstated and in need of tempering, the key point here is that that position is fully consistent with the doctrine of negative liberty. Both of Skinner's two basic propositions are smoothly compatible with that doctrine when they are explicated along republican lines. In one sense, of course, Skinner himself would heartily agree with this point. He does, after all, repeatedly declare that the civic republicans subscribed to a negative conception of freedom. Nevertheless, he also repeatedly declares that the modern exponents of the negative conception of liberty have overlooked the insights of the republicans and have thus blinded themselves to the tenable versions of his two propositions. His expositions of the civic-republican understanding of liberty have been meant to rectify this oversight which he attributes to contemporary negative-liberty theorists. My current subsection has aimed to cast doubt on the actuality of such an oversight. Although the civic-republican writers' institutional programmes might not commend themselves to present-day theorists of negative liberty, the general civic-republican thesis of a connection between the widespread political involvement of citizens and the safeguarding of freedom would not strike most negative-liberty theorists as novel or unappealing. As has been pointed out, that connection is expressed in some of the shop-worn slogans of the political culture within which those theorists work. They can hardly have failed to take some notice of it. Moreover, so long as those theorists distinguish appropriately between the overall freedom and the particular freedoms of each person, they can firmly grasp how the link between mandatory political engagement and individual freedom operates in accordance with their own conception of liberty. They can recognize, in other words, that that link operates through the sacrifice of some particular freedoms—or, more likely, through the sacrifice of the conjunctive exercisability of some particular freedoms—for the sake of increasing each person's overall freedom. Those theorists will thus join Skinner in insisting that his two basic propositions can 'be accommodated within an ordinary negative analysis of political liberty'.[108] They should simply add that he is not really telling them anything new, at least in the general drift of his message.

To be sure, we should not go so far as to think that there are no important differences between civic republicanism and the political views held by most theorists of negative liberty. As has already been remarked, the concrete institutional proposals advanced by modern

[108] Skinner, 'Paradoxes', 248; Skinner, 'Republican', 307.

theorists are bound to be different from those propounded by Renaissance republicans. Still more significant is a divergence pertaining to the relationship between the individual and the community.

Now, before exploring the divergence just mentioned, we should briefly note that the negative conception of liberty does not in itself commit its proponents to any particular political views, liberal or otherwise. A negative account of liberty is per se an analytical exposition of the nature of freedom rather than a prescriptive theory about the best ways of distributing or preserving freedom. As should be clear from my F Postulate and U Postulate, my analyses of the concepts of freedom and unfreedom do not in themselves yield or contain any political recommendations. Although Skinner and others have often appeared to assume that the doctrine of negative liberty is indissolubly tied to liberalism,[109] any nexus between the two is in fact contingent. Nonetheless, contingent though the combination of the two may be, it is certainly true that most exponents of the doctrine of negative liberty are liberals (of varying persuasions). We are therefore justified in glancing here at an important divergence between civic republicanism and many strands of liberal political philosophy.

As Skinner aptly recounts, the civic republicans were concerned primarily with the freedom of the overarching community—that is, with national independence or autonomy.[110] Although they repeatedly stressed that one major reason for treasuring national independence is that individual liberty can scarcely flourish under conditions of conquest and resultant servitude, their top priority was the glorious self-determination of the national community as a whole. They did set considerable store by individual freedom, but the bolstering of that freedom was secondary in their eyes to the flourishing and independence of the commonwealth. As Skinner comments:

Classical republican theorists generally place less emphasis than contractarian [liberal] writers on individual liberties. And even when they connect the maintenance of such liberties with the pursuit of the common good, they

---

[109] Humorous effects sometimes ensue. For example, the Marxist G. A. Cohen understandably takes umbrage when his negative conception of liberty is designated by John Gray as 'the liberal view'. See Cohen, *Self-Ownership*, 62 n. 27. The application of the label is especially odd because Gray himself has elsewhere taken the view that the standard liberal conception of freedom is not robustly negative. See John Gray, 'On Negative and Positive Liberty', in *Liberalisms: Essays in Political Philosophy* (London: Routledge, 1989), 45, 62–4.

[110] Skinner, 'Paradoxes', 237–41; Skinner, 'Republican', 300–3; Skinner, 'Justice', 215–21.

make it clear that this is not their principal reason for insisting that the common good should be pursued. Instead they argue, as we have seen, that the pursuit of the common good is mainly to be valued as the indispensable means of upholding the ideal of 'free government'.[111]

According to civic republicanism, then, sacrifices of particular freedoms—or of the conjunctive exercisability of particular freedoms—are justified primarily in so far as they strengthen the autonomy and greatness of a nation, and only derivatively in so far as they enhance the overall freedom of each individual.

Many varieties of liberalism reverse the republican pattern of prioritization and subordination. For numerous liberals, the furtherance of individual liberty is the paramount consideration in determining the warrantedness or unwarrantedness of the imposition of any legal requirement. Legal duties that promote the overall freedom of individuals are justified chiefly by dint of that very effect, and only secondarily by dint of the likelihood that they will reinforce the autonomy of a commonwealth. Though the immense importance of national independence can of course be recognized within liberalism, that importance is regarded (by many liberals) as largely epiphenomenal or ancillary. In other words, a lot of liberals tend to advocate the warding off of threats to national autonomy precisely because the relinquishment of such autonomy is in most contexts strongly unconducive rather than conducive to the sustainment of high levels of individual liberty. In the exceedingly unusual circumstances where a loss of national independence will significantly expand the freedom of nearly all individuals, quite a few liberals would perceive such a loss as salutary. More broadly, legal duties that do not redound at least indirectly to the benefit of individual liberty are sacrifices of freedoms (or, usually, of the conjunctive exercisability of freedoms) that will not be countenanced by many liberal theories. If any such sacrifices are to be endorsed, they must be ultimately justifiable by reference to their role in the fostering of liberty. Notwithstanding that national self-determination and other desiderata such as equality and sociability receive ample esteem from most liberals, those values typically remain subordinate to the cardinal value of freedom.[112]

---

[111] Skinner, 'Justice', 220.

[112] In this discussion I shall henceforth drop phrases such as 'many liberals' and 'quite a few liberals', in favour of the unqualified term 'liberals'; but I shall do so only out of a stylistic concern to avoid cumbersome prose. I certainly do not mean to imply that the views designated herein as 'liberal' would be accepted by everyone to whom that label can plausibly be applied.

In sum, there is an abiding difference between liberalism's ultimate focus on the individual and civic republicanism's ultimate focus on the community. Nevertheless, we should refrain from overestimating the practical implications of that difference. Specifically, we should beware of thinking that the individualistic underpinnings of liberalism preclude it from bestowing approval on the duties of civic virtue that are associated with civic republicanism.[113] Skinner often appears to embrace such an erroneous view, as he draws a stark distinction between the liberal insistence on the 'priority [of liberty] over any calls of social duty' and the republican insistence 'that we can only hope to enjoy a maximum of our own individual liberty if we do not place that value above the pursuit of the common good'.[114] As my last few paragraphs have in effect acknowledged, this liberal/republican contrast posed by Skinner is not *entirely* baseless. Nonetheless, it is extremely misleading as stated, for it suggests that liberals cannot plump for the duties of public service which the civic-republican writers favoured. On the contrary, liberals can readily argue for the imposition of just such duties—if they join the civic republicans in believing that those duties are crucial for the maximizing of each individual's freedom. Indeed, in so far as liberals do join the civic republicans in that belief, and in so far as they adhere to theories of justice that call for the maximization of each individual's freedom, they will *insist* on the establishment of duties of civic virtue. Such an insistence is in no way ruled out by the liberal prioritization of the individual over the community, and is in fact required by it. What *is* ruled out for liberals (on grounds of inconsistency), plainly, is a demand by them for duties of civic virtue that cannot ultimately be justified by reference to the furtherance of individual freedom. Only if no such duties could be so justified, would liberals have to reject altogether the civic-republican versions of Skinner's two basic propositions. Of course, in those circumstances—prodigiously unlikely circumstances—Skinner himself would have to reject his two propositions. If he can instead endorse those propositions by pointing to credible connections between various duties of public service and the sustainment of individual freedom, then liberals can do exactly the same.

---

[113] For some especially good criticisms of Skinner on this point, see Patten, 'Critique', 32–4.

[114] Skinner, 'Paradoxes', 248; Skinner, 'Justice', 221.

2.3. Liberty and Dependence

Throughout the preceding subsection, we have beheld the importance of the distinction between the particular freedoms and the overall freedom of each person. That distinction figures saliently as well in this final main portion of the present chapter, where we scrutinize the latest developments in Skinner's theory of liberty. Until his 1998 book *Liberty Before Liberalism*, Skinner always contended that the civic-republican conception of freedom is the same as the conception espoused by modern negative-liberty theorists. He criticized those present-day theorists for their supposed inattentiveness to the connections between the good of the public and the preservation of individual liberty, but he sided with them in their 'negative' understanding of freedom. What he has endeavoured to show, in other words, is that the doctrine of negative liberty is perfectly compatible with a political credo that adjures people to devote themselves to the common weal. Until 1998 he never assailed the negative-liberty stance itself, as opposed to the ostensibly inadequate way in which it has been developed by its modern votaries.

Skinner has recently altered his position and has now submitted that the fundamental conception of freedom upheld by the civic-republican writers is more subtle and capacious than that championed by the negative-liberty theorists. On the one hand, he continues to maintain that the civic-republican writers adhered to a negative rather than positive account of freedom. That is, he still affirms that liberty does not amount to the performance of certain actions or the exercise of certain faculties or the following of certain procedures. On the other hand, he declares that the republicans were more perceptive in apprehending the sources of unfreedom than are the modern exponents of the idea of negative liberty. According to Skinner, unfreedom arises not merely when somebody is prevented from φ-ing by someone else, but also when somebody is dominated by someone else. Domination consists in a state of subordination or subjugation, whereby somebody's latitude-to-φ is dependent on the tolerance or leniency of someone else. When somebody P is in such a state of dependence with regard to φ-ing, his ability to φ is not sufficient to render him free-to-φ. In other words, if his being unprevented from φ-ing is at the whim of someone else who enjoys a position of dominance over him, we cannot correctly attribute to P the freedom-to-φ. Or so we are now told, in *Liberty Before Liberalism*.

Skinner believes that the civic-republican conception of freedom, as he newly recounts it, is significantly different from the negative-liberty theorists' conception. My terse rehearsal of his new position has so far accentuated the apparent divergence between the republican conception and the modern negative conception, by focusing on particular freedoms (that is, on each freedom-to-φ). That focus does create the appearance that 'free' and 'freedom' as used by civic republicans are quite different in meaning from those terms as used by negative-liberty theorists. However, as will be seen shortly, Skinner himself does not elaborate his new stance with reference to particular liberties; he concentrates instead on conditions of overall dominatedness and overall liberty. Given such a focus, his attempt to distinguish his republican understanding of freedom from the negative-liberty theorists' understanding is more straightforwardly rebuttable than it otherwise would be. At any rate, even if Skinner were to develop his position in the direction sketched by my last paragraph, it would prove unsustainable as a conception of freedom that is distinct from the negative-liberty theorists' conception.

In order to unpack Skinner's new doctrine, my critique will have to draw on some of the ideas already broached in this chapter. We shall have to be especially alert to the twofold temporal indexes of each freedom, the role of probability in ascriptions of freedoms, and the gap between particular liberties and overall liberty. Once we have taken those factors duly into account, we shall find that Skinner's new approach is no more successful than his erstwhile approach in showing that modern theories of negative liberty can somehow be exposed as inadequate when they are compared with civic republicanism.[115]

Central to Skinner's discussion in *Liberty Before Liberalism* is a distinction between two ways in which a person can be made unfree: force or the coercive threat of force, and domination. When a person is prevented by someone else from engaging in certain activities or combinations of activities, then she has obviously been made unfree *pro tanto*. Like the negative-liberty theorists, Skinner accepts as much and indeed insists as much. However, he also insists that dependence is a

---

[115] For an excellent critique of Philip Pettit that bears several resemblances to my critique of Skinner in this subsection, see Carter, *Measure*, 237–45. See also Kristjánsson, 'Free Action', at 267–9. Skinner has recently expanded on the position which he and Pettit share, in 'Against Servitude', 7/2 *Centre for the Study of Democracy Bulletin* 10 (2000). That position also informs his 'John Milton and the Politics of Slavery', 23 *Prose Studies* 1 (2000). See also his 'A Third Concept of Liberty', 24/7 *London Review of Books* 16 (2002).

separate mode or source of unfreedom, and he maintains that it is overlooked by the aforementioned theorists. Dependence, the product of domination, gives rise to a situation of unfreedom because it renders a person's latitude precariously contingent on the forbearance of a dominant person. Somebody in a position of dependence cannot afford to ignore or flout the wishes of the person to whom she is subordinate. Hence, even if the dominant party is uninclined to interfere much at all with the leeway of the dependent person, the relationship between them is not unconstrained. So long as the situation of domination persists, that relationship is marked overtly or implicitly by the dependent person's need to seek or retain the good grace of the other party.

Skinner contends that the negative-liberty theorists and their intellectual precursors have declined to acknowledge the character of dependence as a state or source of unfreedom. He suggests that they distinguish between freedom and the security of freedom, and that they do not classify encroachments on the latter as restrictions on the former.[116] Thus, because a posture of dependence impairs only the security of one's freedom without necessarily reducing the extent of that freedom in any way, it should not be viewed as a species of unfreedom at all. Such is the claim which Skinner ascribes to the modern negative-liberty theorists and their forebears (such as Hobbes and William Paley).

Now, the current subsection will not engage in any exegetical jousting. Partly because Skinner in *Liberty Before Liberalism* does not discuss any present-day proponents of the doctrine of negative liberty other than Isaiah Berlin, and partly because he does draw attention to some inadvisable or misleading passages in the writings by Berlin and Paley which he examines, the points of contention here are not cruxes of interpretation. Instead, the key point is whether the doctrine of negative liberty—the doctrine encapsulated in my F Postulate and U Postulate—entails the theses which Skinner associates therewith. As will be seen, people on both sides of the debate charted by Skinner are confused. Civic republicans and some negative-liberty theorists alike have erred in overstating the difference between the dependence of a dominated person and the confinedness of a person who is thwarted from φ-ing. What the civic republicans have regarded as two varieties of unfreedom will turn out to be two aspects of a single type of unfreedom. Likewise, what some negative-liberty theorists

---

[116] Skinner, *Liberty*, 80.

have perceived as a divide between unfreedom and insecurity will turn out to dissolve into a single complicated condition of unfreedom. To arrive at these conclusions, we shall have to keep in mind the chief factors that were singled out three paragraphs ago: temporality, probability, and the particular/overall dichotomy. Let us begin with the last of these factors.

2.3.1. The Restrictive Effects of Domination   As has already been indicated in the first half of this chapter, the overall freedom of each person P is largely determined by the range of the combinations of conjunctively exercisable opportunities that are available to him. If P is free to φ, but if his φ-ing will sharply reduce his future opportunities, then his freedom-to-φ does not add much to his overall liberty (since only a small number of the combinations of conjunctively exercisable freedoms that make up his overall liberty will each include his freedom-to-φ as an item). If most of the opportunities available to P at any given time are similarly hemmed in—perhaps because most activities are forbidden by severe and well-enforced laws—then his overall liberty is highly straitened, notwithstanding that his particular liberties at the time might be numerous. Thus, if a situation of domination eliminates some of P's combinations of conjunctively exercisable freedoms, it curtails his overall liberty. If the eliminated range is substantial, then so too is the curtailment. Consequently, in so far as we have good grounds for thinking that a relationship of domination will indeed produce an effect of that sort, we *ipso facto* have good grounds for deeming such a relationship to be inimical to freedom. That verdict follows straightforwardly from the doctrine of negative liberty; there is certainly no need to augment or modify that doctrine in order to reach such a verdict.

On the basis of Skinner's expositions of civic-republican worries about domination, we have ample reasons indeed for believing that the dependence of a dominated person will impair her freedom in the way just described. Though her state of dependence might eliminate very few of her particular freedoms, it will eliminate the conjunctive exercisability of many such freedoms and will thereby significantly reduce her overall liberty. Specifically, the combinations of conjunctively exercisable liberties that will typically be removed are those which include freedoms to engage in patterns of behaviour that are not suitably deferential toward the dominant party. Because somebody who makes use of such freedoms will arouse the ire of the dominant party and will thereby trigger harsh penalties, those freedoms are not exercisable conjunctively with any freedoms that would be scotched by the penalties. Myriad combinations-of-liberties, every one of which would be a conjunctively exercisable set in the absence of domination, will each contain liberties that are not conjunctively exercisable in the presence of domination. As a consequence, the dependent person's overall liberty is seriously constricted. We can discern as much on the basis of my negative theory of liberty alone, without any need for the putatively supplementary theses of civic republicanism.

Skinner repeatedly makes clear that a relationship of dominance and dependence does indeed cabin freedom in the manner outlined by my last paragraph. As he writes, for example, when summarizing James Harrington's remarks on the autocratic regime in Constantinople: 'If you are a subject of the sultan... your freedom in Constantinople, however great in extent, will remain wholly dependent on the sultan's goodwill... You will find yourself constrained in what you can say and do by the reflection that, as Harrington brutally puts it, even the greatest bashaw in Constantinople is merely a tenant of his head, liable to lose it as soon as he speaks or acts in such a way as to cause the sultan offence.'[117] Skinner quotes and paraphrases many similar statements propounded by other civic-republican writers. We shall look here at only a couple of the germane passages. When synopsizing the views of Algernon Sidney concerning despotic regimes (such as that of Charles II), Skinner declares that 'Sidney... emphasises the life of extreme precariousness that everyone is made to suffer under such forms of government... The outcome of living under such a regime... is that everyone lives in continual fear and danger of incurring the tyrant's displeasure. It becomes everyone's chief preoccupation "to avoid the effects of his rage"'.[118] Skinner offers a cognate observation when recounting the attitude of civic republicans toward the untrammelled discretion of tyrants: '[I]f you live under any form of government that allows for the exercise of prerogative or discretionary powers outside the law, you will already be living as a slave... The very fact... that your rulers possess such arbitrary powers means that the continued enjoyment of your civil liberty remains at all times dependent on their goodwill. But this is to say that you remain subject or liable to having your rights of action curtailed or withdrawn at any time.'[119]

As has been argued, the freedom-corroding effects of domination are readily explicable within my theory of negative liberty. When the

[117] Skinner, *Liberty*, 86.
[118] Skinner, *Liberty*, 91–2.
[119] Skinner, *Liberty*, 70.

civic-republican writers attacked despotic and autocratic regimes, they nicely captured the ways in which those regimes cut off the conjunctive exercisability of various liberties. When a ruler wields tyrannical power, many of the freedoms of citizens to engage in non-obsequious patterns of behaviour will no longer be exercisable conjunctively with their freedoms to engage in any modes of conduct that would be prevented by the tyrant's penalties for insufficient deference. There is no need whatsoever to go beyond a theory of negative liberty for this important insight into the workings of despotism. Nonetheless, Skinner resolutely endeavours to put some distance between the civic-republican approach and that of the negative-liberty theorists by stressing that the republican campaign against tyranny was informed by a more expansive sense of the nature of unfreedom.

Skinner sounds this theme at a number of junctures, such as the following: 'The thesis on which the [civic-republican] writers chiefly insist, however, is that it is never necessary to suffer...overt coercion in order to forfeit your civil liberty. You will also be rendered unfree if you merely fall into a condition of political subjection or dependence, thereby leaving yourself open to the danger of being forcibly or coercively deprived by your government of your life, liberty or estates.'[120] A similar message emerges in the course of Skinner's discussion of Sidney: 'As Sidney makes clear, it is the mere possibility of your being subjected with impunity to arbitrary coercion, not the fact of your being coerced, that takes away your liberty and reduces you to the condition of a slave.'[121] A host of other statements along the same lines bestrew Skinner's account of seventeenth-century republicanism. His reason for insisting on the point is most directly expressed in the following passage:

What the [civic-republican] writers repudiate *avant la lettre* is the key assumption of classical liberalism to the effect that force or the coercive threat of it constitute the only forms of constraint that interfere with individual liberty. The [civic-republican] writers insist, by contrast, that to live in a condition of dependence is in itself a source and a form of constraint. As soon as you recognise that you are living in such a condition, this will serve in itself to constrain you from exercising a number of your civil rights. This is why they insist...that to live in such a condition is to suffer a diminution not merely of security for your liberty but of liberty itself.[122]

---

[120] Skinner, *Liberty*, 69–70.
[121] Skinner, *Liberty*, 72.
[122] Skinner, *Liberty*, 84, footnotes deleted.

Skinner's attempt to stake out the distinctiveness of the civic-republican understanding of freedom and unfreedom is unsuccessful. His expositions make clear that the republican analyses do not advance at all beyond a theory of negative liberty which properly distinguishes between particular freedoms and overall freedom. Indeed, in two important respects (which will be specified shortly), the civic-republican conception of liberty and unfreedom—at least as described by Skinner—is unduly narrow rather than commendably wide-ranging.

My U Postulate refers to other people's actions (whether actual or potential) as preventive factors that give rise to unfreedom. There is no suggestion whatsoever that the unfreedom-engendering conduct must occur by certain routes, such as the actual application or coercive threat of force. The freedom-reducing effects of domination occur so long as some people are at the mercy of others and are therefore obliged to propitiate those others in order to escape their wrath. If the dependent people give offence to the dominant parties, they will suffer fierce retaliation. In those circumstances, freedoms to engage in non-deferential patterns of behaviour are no longer exercisable conjunct-ively with freedoms to engage in any patterns of behaviour that would be precluded by the retaliatory measures which the insufficient defer-ence will trigger. In this manner, the situation of domination impairs the overall liberty of each dependent person. In connection with this point, the exact nature of the techniques by which the dominant parties exert their ascendancy is almost wholly immaterial. Whether those parties impose their sway through the frequent application of violence and the issuance of overt threats, or whether they impose it instead more subtly by constantly displaying their superiority in ways that render largely superfluous the use of outright threats and force, their dominance means that certain combinations-of-liberties which would otherwise each be conjunctively exercisable are not so. When a nega-tive-liberty theorist recognizes that the conjunctive exercisability of each of those combinations has been removed, he is not automatically presuming that the removal must have been due to the actual wielding of violence or explicit threats. After all, my U Postulate affirms that unfreedom obtains whenever some person P would be prevented from φ-ing by somebody else's actions if P were to endeavour to φ. In other words, the existence of unfreedom does not necessarily involve any actual endeavour and thus does not necessarily involve any actual obstruction; the endeavour and the obstruction can remain hypothet-ical. If the only door to a room would be locked if a man inside were to attempt to leave, then he is unfree-to-leave regardless of whether the

attempt and the locking ever actually take place. Given that the existence of unfreedom does not perforce presuppose the actual occurrence
of preventive steps, it obviously does not perforce presuppose the actual
occurrence of preventive steps of certain specified types. Hence, Skinner goes astray when he repeatedly declares that negative-liberty theorists acknowledge only force and threats as sources of unfreedom.

In two respects, as has been stated, Skinner's civic-republican
account of freedom and unfreedom is narrower—not broader—than
the negative-liberty account. First, in the final passage quoted above,
Skinner implies that unfreedom arises only '[a]s soon as you recognize
that you are living in such a condition'. By contrast, my theory of
negative liberty does not set any such limitation on the emergence of
unfreedom. If a man is in a room where the only door has been firmly
locked by someone else, then he is unfree-to-depart irrespective of
whether he knows that the door cannot be opened. Of course, he will
not *feel* unfree unless he does apprehend that he is confined to the
room; but he will *be* unfree even if he remains ignorant of his plight.
Much the same can be said with reference to a relationship of domination. A dependent person might never become aware of her position
as such. That is, she might fail to grasp that her combinations of
conjunctively exercisable opportunities are diminished by the dominance of someone else, who will punish her severely if she engages in
behaviour that displeases him. If she fortuitously avoids such behaviour, and if she does not otherwise become aware of her subordination,
then she will not *feel* unfree in her position of dependence. As a result,
she will probably not adopt the sycophantic mien of a knowingly
subjugated person. Nonetheless, she will *be* unfree in many respects
so long as the dominant person's ascendancy decreases the range of her
combinations of conjunctively exercisable liberties. Her unfreedom is
independent of her knowledge of her unfreedom. (Of course, nothing
said here has been meant to suggest that a dependent person is very
likely to remain ignorant of the lowliness and precariousness of her
condition. As Philip Pettit has argued, a situation of dominance and
subjection will typically impress itself upon the consciousness of each
party involved, who will also grasp that the other party harbours a
corresponding awareness of their relationship.[123] Nevertheless, even in
the unusual circumstances where this typical situation of common
knowledge does not obtain, the structure of mastery and subordination restricts the overall liberty of the person who occupies the inferior position in the structure.)

[123] Pettit, *Republicanism*, 58–61.

A second inadvisably cramping feature of civic republicanism is its apparent assumption that unfreedom comes about only by way of conduct that is *intended* to cause such an effect. Although the civic republicans correctly perceived that deliberate violence and threats are not the only sources of unfreedom, they unwisely adduced only one further source: domination. Like the wielding of force and threats, the exercise or sustainment of domination is intentional rather than inadvertent. It is thus the sort of activity which the civic republicans would recognize as generative of unfreedom. The importance of intentionality or deliberateness in the conduct that produces unfreedom is manifest within the work of the present-day republican writer Pettit, who explicitly excludes 'non-intentional obstruction' from the set of factors that give rise to unfreedom.[124] Pettit explains his position on this matter as follows: 'Were non-intentional forms of obstruction also to count as interference, that would be to lose the distinction between securing people against the natural effects of chance and incapacity and scarcity and securing them against the things that they may try to do to one another. This distinction is of the first importance in political philosophy, and almost all traditions have marked it by associating a person's freedom with constraints only on more or less intentional interventions by others.'[125] Pettit's explanation does not support our limiting of the sources of unfreedom to intentional obstructions or interventions. Instead, it supports our limiting of those sources to any obstructions or restraints that have been imposed on some person(s) by the actions of some other person(s), whether the effects of the actions are intentional or unwitting. Causal attributability along those lines, of course, is precisely what my U Postulate specifies as the key requirement that must be satisfied if a constraint on freedom is to count as an instance of unfreedom.

To be sure, Pettit's category of 'intentional interventions' is more expansive than would normally be true of a category so labelled. It apparently includes 'the sort of action in the doing of which we can sensibly allege negligence'.[126] Exactly why Pettit designates negligently produced results as 'intentional' is far from clear; at any rate, his somewhat idiosyncratic classification renders less objectionable his insistence that unfreedom must be due to intentional obstructions. Still, even though negligent actions are comprehended within his array of unfreedom-engendering factors, his account remains too

---

[124] Pettit, *Republicanism*, 26.
[125] Pettit, *Republicanism*, 52–3.
[126] Pettit, *Republicanism*, 52.

narrow. It should encompass all types of human actions rather than only some types. Among the potential sources of unfreedom, the sundry unintentional effects of other people's actions should be included—even if the occurrence of those inadvertent effects is not due to negligence at all. Given Pettit's desire to distinguish between the results of sheer chance or incapacity or scarcity and the results of other people's endeavours, we should mark the divide between 'not free' and 'unfree' by differentiating between states of preventedness that are not causally ascribable to other people's actions and states of preventedness that are so ascribable. Such a differentiation will have placed the unintentional effects of non-negligent actions among the possible sources of unfreedom.

Before we move on, we should glance at an example that helps to underscore the drawbacks of distinguishing between the intentional effects and the unintentional effects of human actions, for the purpose of ascertaining whether someone has been made unfree.[127] Suppose that Mark and Molly are both in a room, and that they are endowed with roughly equal strength. Simon shuts and locks the only means of exit from the room. Knowing that Molly is inside, Simon has locked the door because he wants to confine her there. Simon knows nothing of Mark's presence in the room—either because Simon has been negligent or because there were no reasonable grounds for him to be aware of Mark's location. (Mark may have been hidden from view, such that even a careful and attentive person would not have been able to espy him.) If we correlate the 'intentional'/'unintentional' dichotomy with the distinction between 'unfree' and 'not free', we shall have to conclude that Simon's act of locking the door has made Molly unfree-to-leave but has made Mark merely not-free-to-leave. In other words, we arrive at the verdict that a single human act which imposes exactly the same physical constraints on two people of similar capacities has affected their unfreedom in markedly different ways. Such a verdict is unacceptable for any non-moralized account of freedom and unfreedom. We can and should acknowledge that Molly has been wronged to a greater degree than Mark, but we should not accept that the severity of the wrong bears even tenuously on the question whether Mark has been rendered unfree-to-leave-the-room by Simon. That question is a factual inquiry about one of Mark's inabilities and about the causes thereof, rather than an inquiry about the morality of Simon's action or

[127] My example builds on a laconic remark in William Parent, 'Some Recent Work on the Concept of Liberty', 11 *American Philosophical Quarterly* 149, 159 (1974).

about anyone's intentions. Certainly if we aim to give due heed to the distinction which Pettit highlights—the distinction between the results of natural incapacity or chance or scarcity and the results of human activity—we should conclude that both Molly and Mark have become unfree-to-leave as a consequence of Simon's locking of the door.

2.3.2. The Gentle Giant   Skinner and especially Pettit broach the possibility of a relationship of dominance and dependence that eliminates very few of the dependent person's combinations of conjunctively exercisable freedoms. If the ascendant party in the relationship is sufficiently tolerant and undemanding, then his tendency to retaliate in the event of contumacious behaviour by the subordinate party might be extremely slight—so slight as to constitute virtually no impingement on the subordinate party's overall freedom. In so far as we assess this situation by reference to the doctrine of negative liberty, then, we shall have to conclude that the indulgent dominator's sway has no significant impact on the freedom of the dominated person. Indeed, the dominator might not reduce the inferior person's overall freedom to any greater extent than would the presence of someone else who lacks a position of dominance altogether. In the eyes of the negative-liberty theorists, accordingly, the soft-hearted dominator's superiority is not in itself a source of unfreedom; everything hinges on what the dominator does with his superiority. In any case, such is the view ascribed to the negative-liberty theorists by Skinner and Pettit. For the proponents of the civic-republican conception of freedom, by contrast, the superiority of the dominator is in itself a source of unfreedom. Though the ascendant person might not interfere with any of the subordinate person's projects and activities, the very structure of their relationship—a relationship of outright superiority and inferiority, in which the former party is sufficiently powerful to impose his will on the latter party if he chooses—is a situation of dependence and thus of unfreedom. Whenever the sustainment of someone's overall liberty hinges on the good will of other people—who might be impeccably benevolent indeed—his liberty has thereby been curtailed.

Skinner suggests this line of thought at several junctures, most directly in the following passage (part of which was quoted earlier):

[I]f you live under any form of government that allows for the exercise of prerogative or discretionary powers outside the law, you will already be living as a slave. Your rulers may choose not to exercise these powers, or may exercise them only with the tenderest regard for your individual liberties. So you may in practice continue to enjoy the full range of your civil rights. The very fact, however, that your rulers possess such arbitrary powers means that the continued enjoyment of your civil liberty remains at all times dependent on their goodwill.[128]

Pettit has more insistently sounded this theme, as he seeks to accentuate the ostensible divergences between his own conception of freedom and the conception put forward by the negative-liberty theorists. He repeatedly adverts to the possibility of dominators whose benignly uninterfering obligingness ensures that their power does not cause any significant loss of day-to-day latitude for the people under their sway. For example, near the outset of his discussion of the contrasts between the republican account and the negative account of freedom, he submits that 'I may be dominated by another—for example, to go to the extreme case, I may be the slave of another—without actually being interfered with in any of my choices. It may just happen that my master is of a kindly and non-interfering disposition'.[129] Pettit persistently harks back to this example of the indulgent master in order to emphasize that a structure of domination does not necessarily remove particular freedoms or impair overall freedom as defined by the negative-liberty theorists. The example illustrates his general thesis that the unfreedom of domination exists whenever powerful people *can* inflict oppression, rather than only when they *do* inflict oppression. 'Domination can occur without interference, because it requires only that someone have the capacity to interfere arbitrarily in your affairs; no one need actually interfere.'[130] Accordingly, an absence of domination consists in the absence of anyone's ability to exploit others for his or her own gain.

Pettit recurrently maintains that the negative conception of liberty contrasts sharply with his own conception. We are told again and again that negative-liberty theorists feel that no unfreedom is engendered when 'some people hav[e] dominating power over others, provided they do not exercise that power and are not likely to exercise it'.[131] Now, before we continue to explore the possibility of an indulgently uninterfering dominator, we should note that Pettit frequently has some quite different possibilities in mind when he writes about the unlikelihood of a dominator's interference. Often, what he means

[128] Skinner, *Liberty*, 70.
[129] Pettit, *Republicanism*, 22.
[130] Pettit, *Republicanism*, 23.
[131] Pettit, *Republicanism*, 9.

when he talks about the improbability of interference is that the subordinate person in a hierarchical relationship can behave with enough sycophancy or cunning to forestall any angry exertions of force by the ascendant person. Through sufficient grovelling or sufficient furtiveness and shrewdness, a subjugated person can guard against triggering the wrath of her master and can thereby save herself from being physically battered or trammelled. On the many occasions when Pettit refers to toadying and stealthiness as patterns of conduct that can make the interference of a dominator unlikely, he is committing an error which I have already criticized at length.[132] He is failing to recognize that the overall freedom of each person is largely determined by the range of the combinations-of-conjunctively-exercisable-liberties available to her. Inasmuch as we do grasp that point, we can see that the overall freedom of a subordinate person *P* is significantly impaired when she has to resort to obsequiousness or unobtrusiveness in order to stave off a dominant person's punitive measures. Far from being a situation wherein interference is unlikely, *P*'s plight is a situation wherein interference is occurring extensively. That interference does not come about through the actual application of violence (*ex hypothesi*), but it consists in the undoing of the conjunctive exercisability of many opportunities—opportunities that could have been exercised conjunctively in the absence of the dominant party's sway. In the presence of that sway, if *P* acts in any manner that is insufficiently humble or furtive, she will not also be able to act in any manner precluded by the retaliation that will be undertaken against her as a response to her perceived audacity. Her freedom to act in the former manner is not exercisable conjunctively with her freedom to act in the latter manner, because of the dominant party's preparedness to remove the latter freedom if the former freedom is acted upon. Hence, under any tenable account of negative liberty, we must conclude that *P*'s overall freedom is substantially reduced by her subjection to the dominant party. Contrary to what Pettit contends, the dominance of that party is indeed being exerted—not through the actual infliction of violence (which is unnecessary in the circumstances), but through the party's readiness to inflict violence. That very readiness eliminates many combinations-of-conjunctively-exercisable-freedoms for *P*.

In short, if Pettit's remarks about the unlikelihood of a dominator's interference are to stand any chance of going beyond arguments that have already been rebutted in this chapter, they will have to be

---

[132] Pettit continues to commit this error in his most recent reflections on the topic. See Pettit, *Theory*, 136–8.

construed as pertaining only to contexts in which the ascendant parties are too obliging or uninterested to obstruct the activities of the inferior parties. To drive home his point with reference to such contexts, Pettit distinguishes between the mere *improbability* of domination and the *infeasibility* thereof. Whereas the uninterfering disposition of a master can render highly unlikely the application of physical force, the only veritable guarantee against the wielding of such force is the dismantling of the whole structure of mastery and subjugation. As Pettit writes:

> Seeing an option as an improbable choice for an agent, even as a vanishingly improbable choice, is different from seeing it as a choice that is not accessible to the agent: seeing it as a choice that is not within the agent's power. Thus the fact that another person is unlikely to interfere with me, just because they happen to have no interest in interfering, is consistent with their retaining access to the option of interfering with me . . . And so it is quite possible for me to be forced to think of myself as subordinate to someone who is no more likely to interfere with me than I am to interfere with them.[133]

This distinction between the mere unlikelihood and the impossibility of oppression is crucial for Pettit's republican position. We should therefore note an array of objections to his use of that distinction—objections that are cumulatively fatal to his insistence on the distinctiveness of the republican conception of freedom and unfreedom.

First, when Pettit repeatedly relies on a dichotomy between not being endowed with sufficient strength for the exploitation of others and not being inclined to avail oneself of that strength, he is doing so in order to differentiate between a situation where dominating interference is impossible and a situation where such interference is merely improbable. 'The point is not just to make arbitrary interference improbable; the point is to make it inaccessible.'[134] This impossibility/improbability distinction is deeply problematic, since the availability or unavailability of resources essential for domination is always itself a matter of greater or lesser probability. Only in a utopian fantasy can the emergence of domination and its effects be strictly ruled out. In any possible world outside such a fantasy, the most that can be done is to render domination highly unlikely.

To be sure, the focus of the probabilistic calculations will not always be the same for Pettit as for the opponents whom he strives to counter. Someone adopting Pettit's position has to inquire about the likelihood that any person or group of people will be able to gain access to means

---

[133] Pettit, *Republicanism*, 88.
[134] Pettit, *Republicanism*, 74.

of oppressive power. Pettit's opponents, by contrast, have to inquire about the likelihood that any person or group capable of wielding oppressive power will choose to make use of that capability. Now, Pettit's republican institutional proposals will aim to minimize the first of these probabilities—the probability that people will become capable of acting as dominators—but will never reduce it to zero. Were anyone to think that that risk can indeed be altogether removed, he or she would be indulging in irresponsibly wishful dreaming; such dreaming may be suitable for the conclusion of a fairy tale, but it should not enter into political philosophy. Within the domain of political philosophy, both the inquiry associated with Pettit's stance and the inquiry associated with his opponents' stance are about contingencies that can never be ruled out categorically for the future. Instead of a sharp division between a quest for the infeasibility of oppression and a quest for the mere unlikelihood thereof, the split between Pettit and his opponents is nothing more than a matter of alternative foci concerning the ineliminable risk of the onset of domination. Pettit concentrates on minimizing the chance that anyone will come to occupy a position of ascendancy, while his opponents concentrate on minimizing the chance that the powers of any such position will be exerted. In each case, the goal pursued is improbability rather than strict impossibility.

A second objection to Pettit's argument goes together well with the first. Not only are both sides of the debate between Pettit and his opponents focused on probabilities, but furthermore they will very often be focused on the same set of probabilities. For anyone who desires to minimize the likelihood of the exercise of oppressive powers, the best route will typically be to minimize the accumulation of such powers in the first place. Once those powers have been amassed by some person or group of people, the chance of their being exerted is typically extremely high; almost always, then, the freedom-constricting consequences of relationships of domination can most effectively be averted if the relationships themselves are nipped in the bud. A reliance on the sheer benevolence or indifference of people in positions of dominance is a far, far less effective tack. Skinner and Pettit quote a myriad of thunderous declamations by republicans who warned of the corruptions and temptations to which the holders of autocratic power are prone. We have no reason whatsoever to doubt the pertinence of those warnings. Indeed, Pettit's acute awareness of the tendency of powerful people to make use of their dominance is precisely what lies behind his assumption that subordinate people must normally resort to flattery or diffidence in order to stave off harsh penalties. Tyrants and masters and other power-holders usually take advantage of their superiority in any number of ways that impair the overall liberty of their underlings to varying extents. Thus, if one's aim is to lower the probability of impairments of each person's liberty as much as possible, one should generally resist the establishment of positions of dominance—even if one believes that some specific occupants of those positions will be scrupulously unassertive in the exercise of their powers. Such forbearance (whether due to benignity or to indifference) is very seldom to be found among power-holders, as the civic republicans themselves would heartily agree. It should hardly ever be counted on.

A third objection pertains to the rare circumstances in which people capable of systematically exploiting and mistreating others are wholly uninclined to do so. In any such set of circumstances, where the probability of serious encroachments by a dominant person on the overall liberty of his or her contemporaries is practically nil, we should acknowledge as much in our measurements of freedom. That is, we should acknowledge that the redoubtable might of the person does not lessen anyone else's overall liberty significantly. A rather far-fetched example should illuminate this point. Suppose that, in a community not far from some hills, a gigantic person G is born. From adolescence onward, G is far larger and stronger and swifter and more intelligent than any of his compatriots. If he wished, he could arrogate to himself an autocratic sway over his community by threatening to engage in rampages and by coercing some of the residents into serving as his henchmen. Were G so inclined, no one would dare to resist his bidding. He is well aware of this state of affairs. Ergo, as a matter of sheer capability—which, as has already been mentioned, is the determinative factor for someone's status as a dominator[135]—G clearly occupies a position of dominating ascendancy. In fact, however, he loathes the idea of becoming a tyrant; his principal desire is to seclude himself altogether from his community. He does indeed depart therefrom in order to reside in a cave among the nearby hills where he contentedly feeds off natural fruits and wildlife and where he spends his time in solitary reflection and meditation and exercise. In these circumstances G is a dominator (according to Pettit's criteria for that status), but he is not significantly reducing the overall liberty of anyone else. Given his formidable strength and size, he could impose his will on others if he so chose. However, given his inclinations and self-sufficiency, there is no prospect of his doing so. Because of his reclusive

---

[135] Pettit, *Republicanism*, 23, 52, 54–5.

disposition, the likelihood of his expunging many liberties of his contemporaries—or many of their combinations of conjunctively exercisable liberties—is effectively zero. His abstention from exerting his formidable powers against his fellows is a product of inveterate traits of his personality, and is thus not something that is liable to change. Those ingrained features of his character are as much facts of his existence as are his size and physical strength. If we described him as rendering his contemporaries unfree in many respects simply by dint of his dominating capacity, we would be misrepresenting his situation rather than elucidating it.[136] His withdrawal from his community to the cave reveals the potential gap between dominance and the engendering of unfreedom. Though that gap is prodigiously uncommon, it is certainly possible.

This point becomes even more palpable when we consider an example of a dominator who is subordinated by someone whom he himself could oppress. Let us ponder a scenario involving Lennie and George (who bear a considerable resemblance, though not a perfect resemblance, to their namesakes in John Steinbeck's *Of Mice and Men*). Lennie is nearly as strong and large and swift-footed as G in my previous example, but he is less intelligent and free-spirited. George is much smaller and weaker than Lennie, but his domineering tough-mindedness offsets his physical deficiencies. Although Lennie is physically much more powerful than George, and although the intellectual disparity between the two men is not vast, the differences between their temperaments eventuate in the wholesale domination of the more brawny man by the more diminutive. George continually browbeats Lennie into performing countless menial tasks that serve George's needs and comfort, and he insists on getting his way whenever Lennie forms intentions that are at odds with his own. He terrorizes Lennie with his fits of temper and his piercing insults; Lennie, thoroughly overmastered and intimidated by George, is his dutiful servant. Now, even if this scenario were to be moderated by the addition of some ties of friendship and protection between the two men, the basic point illustrated by it would remain prominent. Somebody fully capable of dominating another person—somebody whom Pettit's analysis will therefore classify as a dominator—can turn out to be exploited and bullied by that other person. If we were to describe George as having been made unfree by Lennie's dominating strength, we would be distorting his situation even more markedly than a

---

[136] Pettit himself occasionally offers analyses that are roughly in accordance with what I am claiming here. See especially *Republicanism*, 64, 262, 266–7.

cognate description of *G*'s compatriots in my previous example would distort *their* situation.

Admittedly, it might be that George's irascible and imperious behaviour is itself necessary to ward off domination by Lennie. If George's aggressively tyrannical conduct is indeed a means of defending his own overall liberty, then that liberty has been diminished by Lennie's daunting presence. After all, were George to abstain from his domineering surliness under such circumstances, he would very quickly render himself unfree to undertake any projects or activities that will have been precluded by Lennie's assumption of the ascendant posture in their relationship. Under such circumstances, that is, Lennie's latent disposition to exert his might has extinguished the conjunctive exercisability of many of George's liberties. Nonetheless, this feature of the situation is purely contingent. We can just as easily imagine that a softening of George's demeanour would produce less dramatic effects. Perhaps it would not induce any substantial changes at all in the subordinate posture of Lennie, who might be unshakeably habituated to George's dominance. Or, what is slightly more plausible, the growing emollience of George might simply induce Lennie to become less dutiful and subservient without actually prompting him to act despotically toward George. Instead of inverting the previous relationship of mastery and submission, Lennie might simply opt to live alongside George as an equal. Or perhaps he would separate from George and go his own way. Whatever might be the precise outcome of a marked alteration in George's authoritarian mien, it would not necessarily involve any significant loss of liberty for George himself (especially if the baseline for measuring the loss is a situation in which neither of the two men dominates the other). In that case, his currently overbearing behaviour is not a means of safeguarding his own freedom against the potential dominance of Lennie, but is straightforwardly a means of coercing and manipulating the bulkier man. Such a state of affairs can obtain even though Pettit's analysis of domination clearly generates the conclusion that Lennie is a dominator. Someone can qualify as a possessor of that status—as defined by Pettit—without significantly impairing the overall freedom of anyone else.

In short, in the rare circumstances where relationships of domination genuinely involve extremely low probabilities of non-trivial encroachments on the freedom of subordinate people, we should not characterize the state of subordination as a state of unfreedom. When we examine the posture of the gigantic recluse *G* as a dominator vis-à-vis the other members of his community, and when we examine the posture of Lennie as a dominator vis-à-vis George, we shall be misunderstanding those situations if we maintain that G and Lennie have significantly abridged the overall freedom of the people to whom they are hugely superior physically. Pettit's republican inclination to equate domination and unfreedom does not illuminate such situations.

Before we move on from this discussion of probability, we should very briefly note that most of the principal contentions herein about the curtailment or non-curtailment of overall freedom are applicable *mutatis mutandis* to the inexistence or existence of particular freedoms. If it is virtually certain that somebody in a dominant position will use his ascendancy to prevent a subordinate person S from φ-ing in the event that S endeavours to φ, then we are warranted in saying that S is unfree to φ. We can for most purposes leave implicit any probabilistic qualifications. By contrast, if the likelihood of the powerful person's prevention of S from φ-ing (in the event of S's endeavouring to φ) is lower but still non-trivial, then our statements about S's unfreedom-to-φ should be overtly probabilistic. Finally, if the likelihood of the powerful person's prevention of S from φ-ing in the event of S's endeavouring to φ is exceedingly small—as it clearly is in the case of G or Lennie above, for most specifications of the 'φ' variable—we shall be amply warranted in affirming that S is free to φ (vis-à-vis the powerful person). Once again, any probabilistic qualifications can for most purposes be left implicit. In other words, with regard to the reduction or non-reduction of a person's overall freedom, and with regard to the inexistence or existence of any of a person's particular freedoms, our basic focus in a context of domination should be the same. The crucial consideration in such a context is not the sheer fact of the domination, but the probability that that fact will result in the prevention of certain actions or combinations of actions.

2.3.3. Time for a Change The last paragraph's terse remarks on particular freedoms can serve well as a transition to the focus of this closing discussion, where we look at the impact of domination on a subordinate person's ability to perform particular actions at specified times. As has been observed, Skinner and Pettit and other republicans have generally expounded their doctrine with reference to overall freedom and unfreedom rather than with reference to particular liberties. However, a shift of orientation from the former to the latter will enable us to detect some further complexities in republican ascriptions of freedom and unfreedom. Specifically, we shall explore here afresh some of the difficulties relating to time that have been investigated in the first half of this chapter.

Let us concentrate on a scenario involving a huge bully Barry and a much smaller lad Ernest. Ernest keenly desires to eat a russet apple that is on a table very close to the spot where Barry is now standing. Barry indicates loudly and unmistakably that he will prevent Ernest from eating or even touching the apple if the smaller boy attempts to gain possession of it. He positions himself squarely between Ernest and the apple, and thereby blocks off the only route of access to the piece of fruit. A relationship of domination clearly obtains between the two boys. Feeling famished, and avidly enthusiastic about russet apples in any event, Ernest becomes despondent and desperate. He pleads with Barry to step aside, but the bully is unyielding. Ernest falls to his knees and grovels, and he even kisses Barry's feet while exhorting the brawny boy to desist from preventing his consumption of the apple. Barry, delighted by this confirmation of his extravagant sense of his own worth, eventually relents and moves away in order to give Ernest access to the table. While Barry watches from a short distance, Ernest joyously grabs the apple and consumes it with gusto.

Let us designate as 't_6' the time at which Ernest takes hold of the russet apple. Manifestly he is free at t_6 to clutch the apple at t_6, since necessarily he is able to perform an action which he in fact does perform. Somewhat less obviously, he has also been free at each earlier juncture to grab the apple at t_6. Let us designate the earliest relevant juncture—say, the point at which Barry initially decides to prevent Ernest from getting hold of the apple—as 't_1'. We may designate some of the intervening moments as 't_2', 't_3', 't_4', and 't_5'. Ernest at t_1 (and at every subsequent stage) is free to gain possession of the apple at t_6, for there is at least one course of conduct open to him at t_1 that will enable him to acquire the apple at t_6. Retrodictively we can easily know as much, because Ernest in fact does acquire the apple at t_6. Quite a different matter is our knowing at t_1 whether Ernest is free at that very moment to clutch the apple at t_6. At any rate, either retrospectively or prospectively, we can correctly ascribe to Ernest just such a freedom.

Now, this analysis of the situation may seem insensitive to the harsh and dispiriting constraints imposed by domination. After all, my account maintains that Ernest is free at every stage—t_1, t_2, ... t_6—to grab the apple at t_6. Yet, as we have been told, he manages to get the apple at that time only by having resorted to a series of self-abasing manoeuvres of the most humiliating sort. Operating within the severe confines established by Barry's powerful presence, Ernest has had to undergo considerable anguish and ignominy in the struggle to achieve his objective. Yet my ascription to him of freedom at every stage might appear to suggest that his plight has not been significantly different from a situation in which his access to the apple is never obstructed at all. If the need for arduous efforts of cajolery by him is deemed to be fully consistent with his constant possession of the freedom-to-clutch-the-apple-at-t_6, then my exposition might seem to be portraying those efforts as largely indistinguishable from his simply walking up and snatching the apple without any opposition. Given that the particular freedom (Ernest's freedom-to-clutch-the-apple-at-t_6) is said to exist at every juncture in the face of Barry's pugnacity, the contrast between a stifling ordeal of domination and a refreshing lack of domination may appear to be disregarded by my analysis. Were that contrast indeed slighted by a negative-liberty approach, the republican criticisms of such an approach could have a new lease on life.

In fact, however, the gap between the presence and the absence of domination can be charted precisely and illuminatingly within a negative-liberty account. Three chief points should be emphasized. First, as has already been intimated, any prospective attribution to Ernest of the freedom-at-t_1-to-hold-the-apple-at-t_6 will be fiendishly problematic indeed. Because of Barry's bulk and temperament, the chances of Ernest's becoming able to gain access to the russet apple at t_6 are shuddersomely slim at t_1 (and at t_2 and t_3). In light of the meagreness of those chances, any apposite prospective attribution of unfreedom—any apposite claim at t_1 that Ernest at t_1 is unfree to acquire the apple at t_6—will be subject to only a light probabilistic qualification. When somebody propounds such an attribution, she submits that Ernest despite his best efforts will be unfree at t_6 to hold the russet apple at that time, but she adds that at t_1 there is a small chance that her prediction of unfreedom-at-t_6 will turn out to be false. Conversely, any apposite prospective attribution to Ernest of the freedom-at-t_1-to-grab-the-apple-at-t_6 will be subject to a stringent probabilistic qualification. If the probability is specified accurately, then a claim of this type will exactly correspond (in content) to an accurate retrospective account of Ernest's situation at t_1. In any accurate predictive statement at t_1 about the possible success of Ernest's persistent endeavours to become free at t_6 to clutch the apple at t_6, and in any accurate retrodictive statement made later, an ascription of freedom will be accompanied by an acknowledgment of the unlikelihood of his success. Both the heavily qualified prospective ascription of freedom and the heavily qualified retrospective ascription will have drawn due attention to the repressiveness of domination. In each case, the emphasis lies on the preventive force of Barry's minatory presence and on the consequent cabinedness of Ernest's ability at t_1 to grab the apple at t_6. Stringent probabilistic qualifications underline the narrowness of Ernest's room for manoeuvre. (Those qualifications from a retrodictive vantage point do not, of course, pertain to the likelihood after t_6 that Ernest was free at t_1 to grip the apple at t_6. From such a vantage point, we can know with certainty that he was so free. Instead, the probabilistic qualifications pertain to the likelihood at t_1 of Ernest's being free at that time to grab the apple at t_6.)

In short, any accurate ascription to Ernest of the freedom-at-t_1-to-get-the-apple-at-t_6 will be no more neglectful of his dominated abjection than will an accurate ascription to him of the unfreedom-at-t_1-to-get-the-apple-at-t_6. A severe probabilistic qualification attached to the former ascription or a light probabilistic qualification attached to the latter ascription will equally well indicate the likelihood at t_1 of Ernest's being unfree to clutch the apple at t_6. Here the effect of the probabilistic caveats, in other words, is to highlight the misery of his plight. They enable us to be aware of the grim efforts by Ernest that were essential for the realization of his liberty-at-t_6-to-grip-the-apple-at-t_6. Qualified by such caveats, prospective or retrospective claims about Ernest's freedom-at-t_1 can fully take into account the oppressiveness of Barry's dominance at that time.

As we gauge the pertinence of the doctrine of negative liberty in coming to grips with domination, then, one key point to be noted is the probabilistic character of nearly all retrospective and prospective attributions of freedom. When the probabilistic aspect of any such attribution is expressed overtly—as it very frequently should be—the limitedness of the freedom enjoyed under conditions of oppressive power is readily apparent. A second principal point deserving attention here is the revealingness of any accurate accounts of Ernest's situation at t_1 (or at t_2 or at t_3) that are neither predictive nor retrodictive. When the topic under consideration is Ernest's freedom-at-t_1-to-grab-the-apple-at-t_1, a negative reply is clearly in order. At t_1, Ernest is unfree to clutch the apple at t_1. Hence, whatever freedom he may have at that moment in connection with clutching the apple at t_6 is not paralleled by any comparable freedom in connection with clutching the apple at t_1 itself. Much the same can be said about his posture at t_2 and t_3. He at t_2 is unfree to hold the apple at t_2, and he at t_3 is unfree to hold the apple at t_3. When the two temporal indexes in each attribution of freedom or unfreedom are simultaneous, what becomes plain is that Ernest's freedom at t_1 (or t_2 or t_3) concerning the grabbing of the apple in the future is conjoined with his *un*freedom at t_1 (or t_2 or t_3) concerning the grabbing of the apple in the present. In other words, although the apple might become available to Ernest hereafter—as it in fact does, through his genuflections—it is currently unavailable to him because of Barry's obstruction. Thus, when we ascribe to Ernest the freedom-at-t_1-to-seize-the-apple-at-t_6, we do not have to rely solely on probabilistic qualifications in order to capture the bleakness of his plight. We can and should also stress that his freedom pertaining to a future act of seizure is combined with his unfreedom pertaining to a current act of seizure. That unfreedom does not negate that instance of freedom, of course, but it does hem in that instance of freedom quite severely. By highlighting what Ernest cannot now do, we place in context the fact that he might be able to perform a certain action subsequently. Even if the likelihood of his future ability were greater than it is, it would be tempered by his present inability.

To perceive a third way in which a negative-liberty analysis can pinpoint the divergences between the presence and the absence of domination, we should suppose that t_4 is the moment at which Barry relents and decides to let Ernest have the apple. We should furthermore suppose that t_5 is the moment at which Barry becomes unable to prevent Ernest from clutching the apple. (At that moment—presumably, only a split-second before t_6—Barry is no longer able to reach Ernest in time to avert the clutching.) At t_4, the probability of Ernest's being free at t_6 to grab the apple at t_6 will have increased dramatically, and that probability at t_5 will have become 100 per cent or virtually 100 per cent. Even more important for our present focus is the change in Barry's position. At t_1, t_2, and t_3, Barry is able and therefore free to obstruct Ernest from getting hold of the apple. At t_5 he is no longer able, as has been stipulated. At t_4, and at each moment between t_4 and t_5, the situation is somewhat more complicated. On the one hand, as has been stated, the probability of Barry's continuation of his obstruction diminishes greatly at t_4. On the other hand, his ability to preclude Ernest from snatching the apple will continue until t_5. That is, the state of affairs in the interval between t_4 and t_5 is plainly a situation that would be characterized by Skinner and Pettit as domination without interference. An analysis of the sort carried out here can illuminate the precise structure of non-interfering dominance in the interaction between Barry and Ernest.

Of course, a full examination of this matter requires us to look beyond Barry's particular freedom-to-stop-Ernest-from-grabbing-the-apple-between-t_4-and-t_5. We have to inquire whether Barry's exercise of that freedom would detrimentally affect his subsequent freedoms. In other words, we have to investigate the combinations-of-conjunctively-exercisable-liberties that constitute his overall freedom. If Barry can thwart Ernest's efforts with impunity—as my scenario has implicitly assumed—then his exercise of his freedom to block those efforts would not occasion the elimination of any of his own subsequent liberties. In such circumstances, we should designate Barry as a dominator even if he is not disposed to interfere with Ernest (as is true after t_4). That same designation will be pertinent if Barry's exercise of his freedom would have only a small negative effect on his other liberties. By contrast, if a lot of his subsequent freedoms would be negated by dint of his exercising his liberty to thwart Ernest's striving, Barry is not appropriately characterized as a dominator; or, at any rate, he is not appropriately characterized as a dominator simply because he can prevent Ernest from getting the apple. Suppose, for example, that his prevention of Ernest from clutching the apple would lead to the levying of serious penalties on himself. In that event, at least with regard to the modes of behaviour under consideration here, Barry is not a dominator vis-à-vis Ernest. His ability to interfere is not a product of a clear ascendancy.

In any case, whether or not a full exploration of Barry's position would yield the conclusion that his ability to obstruct Ernest is indicative of domination, an analysis in line with the doctrine of negative liberty enables us to specify quite exactly the nature of non-interfering dominance. If the following four conditions obtain, then the relationship between any two people X and Y in connection with any activity A is *pro tanto* a relationship of domination without interference: (1) X will not seek to prevent Y's performance of A and will not in fact prevent it; (2) X is able to prevent Y from performing A; (3) X would not suffer any significant adverse consequences if he availed himself of his ability to prevent Y from performing A; (4) Y is not able to prevent X from performing A, or would suffer significant adverse consequences if he did prevent X from performing A. These four conditions can of course obtain when Y is free at some time t to do A at some time later than t. We have seen as much in the scenario of Barry and Ernest. Hence, an ascription to Ernest of the freedom-at-t_4-to-gain-hold-of-the-apple-at-t_6 is entirely consistent with the proposition that Ernest at t_4 is still under the dominance of Barry. Furthermore, an ascription to Ernest of the freedom-at-t_1-to-grab-the-apple-at-t_6 is fully consistent with the proposition that until t_4 the domination of him at the hands of Barry (in respect of the apple) is marked by interference rather than by non-interference. Though Ernest cannot be endowed with the freedom-at-t_1-to-gain-hold-of-the-apple-at-t_1 unless Barry's domination at that time (in respect of the apple) is marked by non-interference, he can perfectly well be free-at-t_1-to-gain-hold-of-the-apple-at-t_6 even if Barry's domination at t_1 is actively obstructive.

3. A Pithy Conclusion

This chapter at a number of junctures has pointed to topics that will receive far more sustained scrutiny in my subsequent chapters. Much remains to be said about many aspects of the concept of freedom, some of which have not even been mentioned (still less pondered carefully) in the present chapter's discussions. All the same, while numerous important lines of enquiry and analysis have yet to be pursued, the foregoing arguments suffice to indicate that Skinner's doubts about the modern doctrine of negative liberty are unfounded. Though not every variant of that doctrine is unexceptionable, a suitable formulation of it can withstand all of Skinner's criticisms and accommodate all of his insights. As has been seen in the second half of this chapter, his efforts to commend a peculiarly republican theory of liberty come to nought. The civic-republican thesis concerning an instrumental connection between popular political participation and the preservation of individual freedom is scarcely something that will strike negative-liberty theorists as a joltingly unfamiliar observation. Equally inadequate as a basis for a distinctively republican understanding of freedom and unfreedom is a focus on domination; conclusions arising from that focus can be elaborated rigorously with the categories and techniques of a modern negative-liberty theory. Although civic republicanism as a general political doctrine can perhaps lay claim to distinctiveness, it does not provide an analysis of the concept of freedom that goes beyond the negative-liberty approach in any valuable way. When subtleties and fine distinctions are duly taken into account, the modern exponents of negative liberty can fare very well indeed in a confrontation—and a reconciliation—with their civic-republican counterparts.

3

Instances of Freedom

While the preceding chapter's rejoinders to Quentin Skinner have been in part a ground-clearing endeavour, they have also introduced a lot of the basic features of my negative conception of liberty (albeit some of them only fleetingly). The rest of this book will refine and amplify that conception by fleshing out some of the ideas already broached and by pursuing many new lines of enquiry. Unlike Chapter 2, the remaining chapters will not focus sustainedly on any single theorist or set of theorists. Though this book will continue to engage with the ideas of other writers on the topic—for purposes of commendation or of contestation—my primary ambition will be to present a systematic account of social and political freedom, through explorations of the manifold complexities and cruxes that confront any such account. In furtherance of that ambition, the philosophical analyses begun in Chapter 2 will hereafter come to the fore; they will be developed and expanded without additional bouts of exegetical disputation.

In the present chapter, we shall investigate a number of the complicated issues that arise in connection with the existence of particular freedoms and unfreedoms. Some of those issues have surfaced (at least passingly) in the preceding chapter, whereas other difficulties addressed herein have not previously been touched upon. The most formidable set of complexities surrounding the existence of particular unfreedoms will not receive attention until the next chapter, however. There we shall tackle the knotty causal questions that are raised by any attempt to specify the conditions under which the inexistence of a particular freedom is an instance of unfreedom. As has been noted in Chapter 1, such a task requires us to distinguish between a lack of freedom that is due partly to the actions of other people and a lack of freedom that is due solely to natural forces or to one's own conduct. To enable the drawing of such a distinction with adequate consistency and rigour in myriad contexts, this book will have to elaborate some appropriate causal criteria.

Coming up with those criteria is important in itself, of course, but it is especially important for the enterprise of measuring everyone's overall freedom. As Chapter 2 has observed, such an enterprise must take account both of particular freedoms and of particular unfreedoms; it therefore cannot get off the ground unless we have pinned down the necessary and sufficient conditions for the existence of unfreedoms. Once those conditions have been suitably articulated, the final chapter of this book will look at many other problems relating to the measurement of everybody's overall liberty. As will be contended, the extent of each person's overall freedom is something that cannot be ascertained entirely in the absence of evaluative assumptions. By contrast, the existence of any particular freedom or unfreedom—the matter on which the present chapter concentrates—is a strictly factual state of affairs. If we wish to determine whether some particular freedom or unfreedom exists, we need not have recourse to any evaluative or normative assumptions. Still, while the existence of any particular instance of liberty or unfreedom is indeed strictly a matter of fact, it can sometimes be far from straightforwardly ascertainable. The current chapter will endeavour to come to grips with some of the more elusive aspects of the topic, and with some of the tricky situations in regard to which we cannot readily say whether certain particular freedoms and unfreedoms exist or not.

Important and far-reaching though the distinction between one's particular liberties and one's overall liberty is, we ought not to infer that the sets of issues surrounding the two sides of that distinction can or should be isolated from each other sharply. I have not meant to convey such an impression in the last couple of paragraphs. In fact, although the two sets of issues are hardly identical, they do overlap at a number of points. As will be seen in this chapter, some of the potential pitfalls confronting any effort to delineate the necessary and sufficient conditions for the existence of particular freedoms/unfreedoms are problems that can best be addressed in light of their implications for the measurement of everyone's overall freedom. To be sure, questions relating to particular liberties and unfreedoms are to the fore throughout this chapter. Nonetheless, my grappling with those questions will often explicitly prepare the way for my later reflections on how we can best gauge the overall liberty of any individual or society.

Before we move on to consider some of the principal snags and subtleties concerning particular freedoms and unfreedoms, a few methodological remarks are in order. As should be clear from Chapter 1, the methodological posture of this book is austere. My efforts to explicate the concept of freedom are not driven or shaped by a political vision that might be distinctively served by those efforts. Instead, the objective herein is to elucidate and hone an array of concepts that will enable greater rigour in the discussion of political affairs, whatever one's stances in respect of those affairs might be. That is, although a key part of the impetus for this project is ultimately practical in a general sense—and is therefore something that goes beyond the purely theoretical aim of conceptual clarification for its own sake—the sense in which the orientation of this book can be designated as practical is highly general indeed. My analyses are certainly not tied to any specific cluster of political aspirations. Exactly because they are not so tied, those analyses can enhance the clarity and precision of the overarching debates in which sundry sets of political aspirations vie. Divergent political theories can avail themselves profitably of a sharpened understanding of freedom, which can be put to use for any number of substantive purposes.

At least superficially, this methodological austerity is at odds with the approaches favoured by some other writers on liberty. John Gray, for example, has declared: 'The task of a theory of freedom is to give freedom a definite content by reference to a larger moral and political theory...This task is not advanced by a bankrupt philosophical method in which descriptions of local linguistic behaviors masquerade as fundamental truths of moral and political life.'[1] The first sentence in this quotation is a sheer assertion, which depends on the second sentence for support. That is, Gray could not be justified in ruling out a politically neutral conceptual analysis of liberty unless he could adduce grounds for thinking that any such analysis must be untenable. Along with some accompanying remarks to the same effect, the second sen-

---

[1] John Gray, 'Against Cohen on Proletarian Unfreedom', 6 *Social Philosophy & Policy* 77, 103 (1988) [hereinafter cited as Gray, 'Unfreedom']. A slightly milder version of the same position pervades William Connolly, *The Terms of Political Discourse*, 2nd edn (Princeton: Princeton University Press, 1983) [Connolly, *Terms*], Ch. 4. See also John Gray, 'On Negative and Positive Liberty', in *Liberalisms: Essays in Political Philosophy* (London: Routledge, 1989) [Gray, 'Negative'], 45–6, 64. In the latter essay Gray suggests that the lone alternative to his own methodological stance is the daft thesis that 'it must in principle be possible to elaborate a preferred view of freedom against the background of an authoritative elucidation of the concept of freedom, so that the resultant theory of freedom will commend itself to all reasonable men' (Gray, 'Negative', 45). For an analysis of freedom that is occasionally deserving of Gray's overheated strictures, see John Plamenatz, *Consent, Freedom, and Political Obligation* (London: Oxford University Press, 1938), Ch. 5.

tence in the quotation maintains that conceptual analyses are unacceptably parochial because they simply chart the ways in which certain speakers ordinarily use the language of 'freedom'. Yet, as should be evident from some of my comments in the first two chapters, Gray is misrepresenting the project of conceptual explication. Among the prominent contemporary theorists of negative liberty who engage in such a project—Hillel Steiner, Ian Carter, G. A. Cohen, Martin van Hees, and others—no one believes that the task of tracing the implications of a concept consists in mapping ordinary patterns of usage. (Nor does anyone among them believe that that task is to be carried out through etymological speculations).[2] Everyone recognizes the truth of Gray's contention that '[a]mong us, at any rate, there is no clear uniformity of usage in respect of the key terms of moral and political discourse'.[3] Instead of seeking in a futile and blinkered manner to discover a univocal pattern of usage where none is present, the contemporary negative-liberty theorists who undertake conceptual analyses are embarked on an enterprise which Gray himself lauds: 'As its most sophisticated exponents have long recognized, a neutral or value-free definition of liberty is a term of art, a technical expression developed as part of a reconstruction by stipulation of the terms of ordinary discourse.'[4] Although any plausible account of freedom must have its roots in some of the channels of ordinary usage, those channels exist alongside conflicting patterns of usage and are therefore merely some starting places rather than a definitive template. A rigorous exposition of the concept of liberty must inevitably involve stipulations which highlight only certain elements of ordinary discourse and which reject or de-emphasize alternative elements. A rational reconstruction along the lines envisaged by Gray cannot proceed in any other manner. What is crucial is to explore thoroughly the various implications of the favoured characterization(s) of freedom. What is neither essential nor feasible, by contrast, is to incorporate into one's account all the clashing characterizations that might be found in day-to-day speech.

Of course, one should hardly infer that every set of starting places in ordinary discourse will be as good as every other. While the keystone of any conceptual analysis is a careful investigation of the implications

---

[2] For an essay that relies inordinately on etymological speculations, see Gary Frank Reed, 'Berlin and the Division of Liberty', 8 *Political Theory* 365, 370–6 (1980). See also Bernard Crick, 'Freedom as Politics', in Peter Laslett & W. G. Runciman (eds), *Philosophy, Politics, and Society: Third Series* (Oxford: Blackwell, 1967), 194, 201–2. Cf. Hanna Pitkin, 'Are Freedom and Liberty Twins?', 16 *Political Theory* 523 (1988).

[3] Gray, 'Unfreedom', 102.   [4] Gray, 'Unfreedom', 102, footnote omitted.

of one's premises, such an investigation may lead to the verdict that the premises are unfruitful and that they should consequently be abandoned. Hence, analytical meticulousness is insufficient (though necessary) for a solid theory of liberty; in addition, plainly, the starting points of the theory must be properly chosen. A host of factors bear on the appropriateness of those starting points. We have seen as much already, in some of Chapter 2's discussions. For instance, any conception of the predicates 'free' and 'unfree' as bivalent has been rejected because it is incompatible with the measurability of overall freedom. Likewise, all moralized accounts of freedom and any accounts of the existence of freedoms or unfreedoms as desire-dependent have been repudiated because such accounts yield unacceptably outlandish conclusions. An equally important consideration in the selection of the premises for one's exposition of freedom is the extent to which those premises foster clarity and exactitude. As Gray himself notes, any theorizing about freedom 'should be conducted with as much clarity as we can achieve'.[5] One of the great virtues of the robustly negative conception of liberty as unpreventedness is indeed its tendency to promote clarity and precision.[6]

To be sure, clarity and precision are politically protean. A negative-liberty theory which takes those desiderata as its lodestars will not *sans plus* have answered any questions about the substance of the freedoms that people ought to have, or about the suitableness of various principles for distributing those freedoms (or for distributing freedom generally). Gray submits that the political open-endedness of the conceptual analyses undertaken by negative-liberty theorists is a shortcoming, as he complains that those analyses 'encompass ... a dis-severation of concepts from theories and theories from values in political thought'.[7] A position broadly similar to Gray's has been taken by Joseph Raz, who contends that the undoubted virtues of conceptual sharpness and rigour are themselves inadequate for the purposes of political philosophy. 'Neither a definition nor a conceptual analysis of

---

[5] Gray, 'Unfreedom', 103.

[6] 'Not only is [the negative conception of liberty], in my view, the only clearly defined notion of liberty; it is also the only account which does not conflate several different ideas, some of them opaque and indistinct, which it is useful and fruitful to separate.' Michael Taylor, *Community, Anarchy, and Liberty* (Cambridge: Cambridge University Press, 1982) [Taylor, *Community*], 142. See also Keith Dixon, *Freedom and Equality* (London: Routledge & Kegan Paul, 1986), 23: 'The stark version of negative freedom serves both intellectual and political purposes. It enhances clarity of discussion and simultaneously allows us to argue for the possibility of valuing freedom as absence of constraint as an end-in-itself.'

[7] Gray, 'Unfreedom', 103.

"freedom" can solve our problems... What we need is not a definition nor mere conceptual clarity. Useful as these always are they will not solve our problems. What we require are moral principles and arguments to support them.' Contrasting his own approach with that of theorists who engage in stark conceptual analyses, Raz elaborates: 'One may... say that the whole purpose of [*The Morality of Freedom*] is to defend a concept of political freedom. It is only important to remember that that concept is a product of a theory or a doctrine consisting of moral principles for the guidance and evaluation of political actions and institutions. One can derive a concept from a theory but not the other way round.'[8]

Now, Raz is of course correct when he asserts that conceptual clarification by itself does not suffice to generate the morally laden prescriptions and evaluations that figure saliently in political philosophy. It is indeed true that a full-blown political doctrine cannot be derived from a concept, even a carefully refined concept. However, far from throwing doubt on the importance of the theory of freedom advanced herein, Raz's observations tend to underline the usefulness of the conceptual analyses put forward by this book. Exactly because a doctrine cannot be derived from a concept, my analyses are not linked to this or that political credo; their results can be drawn upon by exponents of virtually any such credo. Although a political doctrine surely cannot be *derived* from a concept, it can be *built on* or *with* a concept.[9] Given that this book's exposition of the concept of freedom is meant to provide some materials for the development of political prescriptions, and given that it is not meant to yield such prescriptions on its own, the political neutrality of the exposition is manifestly a strength rather than a weakness. Because of that neutrality, the gist of the conclusions reached in my exposition can be taken on board by theorists whose political allegiances diverge markedly. Unconfined to any particular political creed, my demarcation of the concept of liberty can strengthen the argumentative rigour of political philosophy generally.

[8] Joseph Raz, *The Morality of Freedom* (Oxford: Clarendon Press, 1986), 14, 15, 16.

[9] If the conceptual analyses are indeed politically neutral, then the devising of a political doctrine cannot properly occur through some process of reciprocal adjustments that will result in an equilibrium between the intellectual demands of one's political aspirations and the details of one's conceptual building blocks. Any such process of adjustments, even if confined to modest tinkering, would cut against the very neutrality for which I am striving. It would amount to a partial abandonment of my conceptual analyses. I therefore disagree with the position taken in Ian Carter, *A Measure of Freedom* (Oxford: Oxford University Press, 1999) [Carter, *Measure*], Ch. 4.

Of course, it is true that the present book does not go on to combine its conceptual analyses with the prescriptive and evaluative theorizing for which Gray and Raz have called. In that respect, my project remains politically disengaged. Nonetheless, such disengagement could rightly be reproached only if the task of conceptual delimitation and clarification were not itself a major endeavour. If that task were indeed triflingly straightforward, then the account of freedom offered in this book could aptly be criticized as truncated and meagre. However, as has been remarked already, any serious attempt to explicate the concept of liberty is hardly an unproblematic exercise that can be dispatched briskly. It is an undertaking worthy of a lengthy book; it is an undertaking worthy of the multitudinous writings that have been devoted to it. Its complexities warrant no less. Moreover, in addition to being a formidably challenging venture that must confront countless intricacies, it is of crucial importance for any of the prescriptive/evaluative theories that can benefit from it. After all, unless the concept of liberty has been pertinently honed, those theories are in danger of falling into muddles. Whatever may be a political doctrine's substantive prescriptions and evaluations concerning freedom or particular freedoms, its intellectual merits can be improved through an avoidance of the fallacies against which this book strives to warn. Erroneous assumptions about the implications of a negative conception of liberty will detract from any theory that deals with the matter of liberty at all. Even if some scholars decide to champion a positive conception of freedom in preference to a negative conception, they will do well indeed to have an accurate sense of the position which they are eschewing. They should apprehend that position's strengths and advantages before they opt for an alternative. In short, though Raz is on solid ground when proclaiming that austere analyses of the concept of liberty 'will not solve our [normative and evaluative] problems' in the absence of substantive moral/political reflections, those analyses are vital for the successful tackling of such problems. To say that the analyses in themselves do not furnish solutions—as they clearly do not—is fully compatible with insisting that they will play an indispensable role in any worthwhile efforts to arrive at solutions.

1. To What Does Freedom Pertain?

As has been made clear in some earlier parts of this book, the type of freedom principally examined in each of my chapters is social and political liberty of the non-normative variety. Because of this focus, some aspects of my theory can readily be surmised. For example, the beings to whom we can appositely ascribe freedom or unfreedom are live human beings. (Of course, when 'free' and 'unfree' are used somewhat loosely as synonyms for 'voluntary' and 'involuntary', we can attribute freedom or unfreedom to human actions and decisions.) Unlike Hobbes, we are not dealing here with the freedom of corpses or other inanimate things to move around—or remain stationary—in various ways. Nor are we dealing with the freedom of animals to perform sundry actions or undergo sundry processes. Although the liberty of such creatures could be expounded and analysed in a manner basically similar to that of the present book's investigations, and although their liberty is of course an important and perfectly respectable object of study, it is not encompassed by the enquiries undertaken here. Just as people distinctively affect the overall socio-political freedom of one another by giving rise to unfreedoms—and also by giving rise to a lot of the freedoms enjoyed by one another—they are the beings to whom our ascriptions of freedom and unfreedom uniquely apply. Only people can be the subjects of such ascriptions, since only they form the social and political relations that are of paramount interest throughout this book. A wider focus for my enquiries would not have been illegitimate, but my chosen focus is more in keeping with this book's political-philosophical orientation. (For the slightly different purpose of distinguishing mere inabilities from unfreedoms, Chapter 2 has emphasized the interpersonal character of socio-political freedom and unfreedom. For that same purpose, we in Chapter 4 shall look further at the causal problems surrounding the interpersonal nature of unfreedom.)

More tricky than pinning down the subjects of our attributions of freedom and unfreedom is pinning down the contents thereof—that is, the sorts of things that can be covered by such attributions. With reference to the notation introduced in Chapter 1, this crux can be described as a matter of determining what sorts of things are covered by the 'φ' symbol in my F Postulate and U Postulate. Ian Carter has argued that the 'φ' variable does not range over anything other than actions. When somebody is free to φ, it is always the case—according to Carter—that he or she is free to *do* something. As Carter observes, his explication of the concept of freedom 'refers only to possible actions, and not also ... to possible "becomings". I make no apology for this restriction of the concept of freedom, the justification of which is simply that my starting point is a *liberal* concept. When liberals talk about freedom, they do not normally refer to possible "becomings"—

only to possible "doings".[10] He contrasts his position with that of some Marxists, who believe that 'communism offers the possibility of attaining a "higher" kind of freedom, where man is no longer "alien-ated", but becomes a "species being"'.[11]

As Carter explicitly recognizes, his stance on this matter constitutes a departure from the renowned exposition of freedom propounded by Gerald MacCallum. MacCallum maintained that a state of freedom can pertain to 'doing, not doing, becoming, or not becoming something'.[12] As should be evident from my second chapter, this book takes an even more expansive view than that favoured by MacCallum. Not only can a person be free to do or become or remain something, but she can also be free to undergo something. Plainly, my expansive approach to this topic stands in need of some defence against Carter's contrary position.

Let us begin with two partial concessions, very readily granted. First, it is indeed true that most writings about negative liberty have trained their scrutiny exclusively or almost exclusively on freedoms-to-perform-actions. For example, virtually all of the scenarios probed in my second chapter are concerned with clear-cut actions. Carter's description of theorists' priorities is certainly not incorrect. Second, if the term 'action' (or the concept of action) were to be construed in an extravagantly broad fashion, then the current point of dispute would largely or wholly disappear. However, Carter wisely forbears from adopting such a misleading tack. When he submits that freedoms pertain only to actions, he is indeed plumping for a relatively narrow conception of liberty—a conception narrower than the one espoused here. The disagreement between his position and mine is genuine, rather than an instance of people talking past each other.

What, then, can be said against Carter's position and in favour of my own? In the first place, the principal factor cited by Carter in support of his view is not a consideration that carries weight within my meth-odologically austere approach to the issue. As has been remarked briefly in Chapter 2, the association between negative-liberty theories and liberal political doctrines—though strong and conspicuous—is contingent. Nothing in the negative conception of freedom inherently renders it palatable only to liberals. Indeed, one of the foremost theor-ists of negative liberty in recent decades, G. A. Cohen, has written as a

---

[10] Carter, *Measure*, 16, emphasis in original. [11] Carter, *Measure*, 17.

[12] Gerald MacCallum, Jr, 'Negative and Positive Freedom', 76 *Philosophical Review* 312, 314 (1967). The aspect of MacCallum's formulation which I highlight here is elided in Kristján Kristjánsson, 'Is There Something Wrong with "Free Action"?', 10 *Journal of Theoretical Politics* 259, 261 (1998).

Marxist. Even among scholars (including some liberals) who uphold values such as equality and community in preference to liberty, a negative account of freedom can commend itself. After all, with perfect consistency somebody can endorse the analytical theses advanced in this book while contending that the condition of freedom staked out by those theses is not a property that should be greatly cherished. Although several of the arguments in this book do presuppose that virtually every instance of negative freedom has *some* value for the person who is free, the sizeableness of that value—with regard to any particular instance or to negative liberty generally—is not something on which this book needs to take a firm stand. Even less is there a need for me to take a firm stand on the sizeableness of the value of any particular freedom (or type of freedom) for a society as a whole. Likewise, as has already been noted, this book does not enter at all into the debates over the proper principles for the distribution of various liberties. Certainly, none of the arguments in this volume must appeal to moral/political premises that are acceptable uniquely to liberals. Indeed, as this chapter has already indicated, the political inscrutability of my arguments is one of their strengths. Hence, this book does not follow Carter in tailoring the narrowness or breadth of its conception of freedom to the characteristics of one political tradition, however admirable and rich that tradition surely is.

Of course, nothing just said should be taken as a defence of Marxist understandings of freedom. Many versions of Marxism have embraced a positive conception of liberty, affirming that the attainment of 'true' freedom resides in some grand feat of self-fulfilment for the human species and for each member of that species. Every such version of Marxism is vulnerable to all the criticisms which my second chapter has posed against positive-liberty doctrines. Moreover, the Marxist credo is distinctively vulnerable in two further respects: it is incoherent, and it is pernicious. The most salient Marxist vision of communism portrays it as a utopia of completely transparent social relations, where people are no longer estranged from one another and themselves. Such a vision is not just fanciful but also unintelligible, since it purports to delineate future social relations while maintaining that they lack the very feature (namely, some degree of opacity) which marks them out as relations rather than as a simple unity.[13] Furthermore, the Marxist

---

[13] See Matthew H. Kramer, *Legal Theory, Political Theory, and Deconstruction: Against Rhadamanthus* (Bloomington: Indiana University Press, 1991), 209–10. Cf. Nigel Simmonds, 'Bringing the Outside In', 13 *Oxford Journal of Legal Studies* 147, 158–60 (1993).

vision is repulsive as well as incoherent, for it has inspired some of the twentieth century's most heinous regimes to impose their designs remorselessly on the hapless people who have suffered under their sway. Still, the evils of Marxism as a ruling ideology should be deplored and combated as such, and should not be seen as products of the sheer fact that Marxist explications of the concept of liberty have classified 'becomings' along with 'doings' as occurrences on which people's freedoms can centre. Instead of focusing our denunciations on the proposition that each person can be free to become something as well as to do something, we should focus on the hideous utopian folly of Marxist claims about the capacity of people to become seamlessly integrated into some higher society. (Carter, it should be mentioned, never suggests that the wickedness of Marxist regimes has in any way been due to the mere placing together of 'becomings' and 'doings' within most Marxist accounts of freedom.)

To discern some more substantive points that tell against Carter's narrowing of the concept of freedom, we should think about the occasions on which people become certain things or undergo certain processes without engaging in actions or in bodily movements that could be actions. Now, before proceeding, we should note the significance of the final eight words in the foregoing sentence. Those words are important because Carter makes clear that his analysis of freedom encompasses not only all volitional bodily movements—actions—but also every bodily movement that could have been volitional if the moving person had had some reason to perform it.[14] For Carter, freedom consists in the availability of any potential actions rather than just in the availability of actions which people actually have reasons to undertake. Thus, when oppugning the Carterian view that the 'φ' variable in my F Postulate and U Postulate will range only over actions, I cannot successfully retort by pointing out that manifold non-volitional bodily movements (such as inadvertently stumbling and falling onto the ground) are not actions and are nonetheless covered by 'φ'. Any retort along those lines would be otiose against Carter—who unmistakably submits that freedoms pertain to any bodily movements that *could* be actions, rather than only to bodily movements that actually are actions if they occur. As he argues:

It is true that any number of *actual* bodily movements fail to qualify as actions, but it does not follow from this that an agent's *available* (*unprevented*) bodily movements do not all qualify as *available* (*unprevented*)

---

[14] On this point, Carter is in full agreement with Hillel Steiner, *An Essay on Rights* (Oxford: Blackwell, 1994) [Steiner, *Essay*], 16–21.

actions. Actions are normally distinguished from 'mere behaviour' by saying that the former are carried out for some *reason*...However,...all that is needed for an *available* piece of behaviour to count as an *available* action is that the agent *could conceivably* have a reason to carry it out (even though she might not *actually* have a reason to carry it out)... [F]reedom...includes the possibility of performing actions that one could conceivably (but does not actually) have a reason to perform.[15]

In sum, Carter is well aware that people can be free to move non-volitionally. When he insists that freedoms pertain only to actions, he is referring to any bodily movements that could be volitional (whether or not they are volitional if they actually occur). No criticism of him should imply that he has neglected this point.

Nevertheless, although Carter is not vulnerable on the count just mentioned, his stance can be impugned from a couple of other directions—even if we were to condone his grounding of that stance on a particular political outlook. First, it is almost certainly the case that some bodily movements are never volitional and are therefore not potential actions. In pondering this possibility, we should notice that the non-volitional bodily movement to which Carter adverts (that is, a person's headlong tumble onto the floor) is something which a person could do on her own if she undertook it as a deliberate action. Markedly different, then, are some other bodily movements which the people involved could never do on their own. Let us consider an example, which received a little bit of attention from a slightly different angle in Chapter 2.

Recall the scenario of Dorothy caught up in a whirlwind that carries her along irresistibly over quite a lengthy distance. If Dorothy remains alive throughout the period when she is impelled forward, she will have been free to soar along the trajectory of her flight—in the presence of the whirlwind. Is her hurtling through the air a potential action? This question should plainly be answered in the negative. On the one hand, as was suggested in Chapter 2, the resistless hurtling might sometimes be attributable to Dorothy as an element of her conduct. In circumstances where she has deliberately placed herself in the path of the whirlwind in order to enjoy a ride thereon, we may well be warranted in classifying that ride as part of an elaborate action which she has undertaken. If such a classification is correct, then her soaring through the air does constitute part of a potential action (and also part of an actual action, in the posited circumstances). On the other hand, however, the aforementioned classification is pertinent only in

---

[15] Carter, *Measure*, 213, emphases in original.

circumstances where Dorothy's flight is preceded by her efforts to get driven along by the whirlwind. In circumstances where such endeavours by Dorothy are absent, her being whisked away by the whirlwind is not ascribable to her as a component of her conduct.

Still, as has been stated, the flight of Dorothy may well be classifiable as an element of her conduct when it is anteceded by some attempt of hers to get caught up in the whirlwind. If such a classification is apposite, does it suffice to vindicate the view that her flight is a potential action? A negative answer is appropriate here, since (in line with what my last paragraph has asserted) the flight is only *part* of a potential action. Without some initial endeavour by Dorothy to place herself in the grip of the whirlwind, her falling into that grip is not ascribable to her at all as a constituent of her conduct. Her flight cannot stand on its own as a potential action, since her flight in isolation from the conduct that triggers it is never an actual action and is consequently not a potential action. Only in combination with a certain mode of conduct that precedes it—a mode of conduct involving some deliberate effort by Dorothy to place herself at the disposal of the whirlwind—is her flight ever attributable to her as a component or facet of something that she has done. Hence, under any tenable criteria for the individuation of actions, we shall have to conclude that her hurtling through the air is at most a *part* of a potential action and is not itself such an action. Any suitable individuating criteria should steer us away from thinking that somebody can perform a complete action during a period when his or her volitions are utterly devoid of causal efficacy. The hurtling of Dorothy is not a potential action, then, since it can never per se be a complete action. Yet that hurtling is undoubtedly covered by the 'φ' variable in my F and U Postulates; because Dorothy is unprevented from soaring through the air in the presence of the whirlwind, she is free to soar. We can know that she is free to move along the trajectory of her flight, since she in fact does move along it. Any difficulties faced by Carter in accommodating this point can easily be overcome or circumvented if we accept that the 'φ' variable comprehends the undergoing of processes as well as the performance of actions.

At first glance, these remarks about the inescapable undergoing of processes might seem to be of minor importance. After all, the freedom to be pushed along irresistibly by some overpowering force such as a tornado might not initially strike many people as a very interesting and valuable freedom. Nonetheless, the point made in my last paragraph is applicable to any number of situations involving freedoms that are plainly more significant. For example, suppose that Dorothy is not being hurled about by a whirlwind but is instead being carried by an aeroplane that transports her from London to New York. If she were derangedly rash enough to attempt to stop the plane—or to try to escape from its confines by smashing open an exit—the crew and the other passengers would prevent her from doing so. Likewise, if she feigned illness, she would not induce the pilot and the crew to deviate from the path of their journey. (They have ample medical supplies aboard.) Thus, although she can move in various ways within the aeroplane of her own volition, and although she is therefore not completely overpowered from acting, she throughout her flight is unfree to avoid undergoing the process of being transported from London to New York. That unfreedom is of course fully consistent with her freedom to undergo the specified process, and indeed the former property entails the latter. A freedom of that type is generally valuable and important, notwithstanding her inability to refrain from exercising it once the plane has taken off. Many other scenarios involving similarly significant freedoms could be adduced. (Not all of those scenarios would centre on large-scale movements of a person's body. For example, the freedom of Odysseus to hear the song of the Sirens was something which he keenly desired, even though he could not abstain from exercising that freedom after he had been tightly bound and the ears of his crew had been stopped up. His body was being carried over the water by his ship at the time of the Sirens' allurements, but the only bodily movements that constituted his exercise of his freedom-to-hear-the-Sirens were the vibrations in his ears and the associated activity in his nervous system.)

Now, as we have just seen, one drawback of Carter's position is its neglect of the fact that not all the movements of a person's body are potential actions. A second problem resides in his position's neglect of the fact that not everything covered by the 'φ' variable must involve some external bodily movements. Indeed, not all potential actions or actual actions involve external bodily movements. Carter pointedly asserts a contrary view: '[A]ll (non-mental) acts are, *inter alia*, the bringing about of some physical movement...[A]ll actions involve, *inter alia*, physical movement.'[16] Although my principal focus at present lies elsewhere, we can pause for a moment to wonder why someone who defiantly stands still after being ordered to move along is not performing an action. If a black person is told to relinquish her seat on a bus to a white person, and if she resolutely continues to sit instead of moving at all, is she not engaging in an action? Likewise, we can feel puzzled at the notion that a man is not performing an action when he

[16] Carter, *Measure*, 212.

remains firmly stationary for a long period as he presses a board against a hole in the side of a tank so as to prevent the spilling out of water through the hole. Many other comparable scenarios could be imagined. Let us note that, on this specific point about actions and movements, Carter diverges from the stance taken by Hillel Steiner—who is otherwise generally in agreement with Carter about the limitation of the 'φ' variable to actions. Steiner expresses his disapproval of a 'reference exclusively to movement', and he submits that '[p]ure negative freedom is equally concerned with impediments to, or preventions of, a person remaining or being stationary'.[17] In the light of Steiner's observation, let us recall my second chapter's discussion of a man in a room with walls that move slowly inward. At some juncture, the man is no longer able to stay on the portion of the floor where he has been standing. He must either retreat from the oncoming wall or else allow himself to be pushed along by it. If Carter's remarks about actions and movements were correct, and if his insistence on confining the U Postulate's 'φ' variable to actions were also correct, then we could not rightly say that the man in the room is unfree to remain stationary.

However unpalatable are several of the conclusions generated by Carter's claim that all actions involve bodily movements, a somewhat different aspect or corollary of his position is more directly relevant to my current discussion. Instead of venturing to show that some instances of stationariness are actions, one can avouch that some such instances are not actions, and one can nonetheless contend that some of those non-actions are encompassed by the 'φ' variable in my F and U Postulates. Whereas my earlier investigation of Dorothy's ride on the whirlwind has indicated that the undergoing of processes is covered by the aforementioned variable, an analysis of a scenario illustrating this present point about non-actions will indicate that 'becomings' are comprehended by that variable along with 'doings' and 'undergoings'.

Affirming both that all actions consist partly in bodily movements and that actions are the only occurrences to which freedoms and unfreedoms pertain, Carter has to deny that anyone can be free/unfree to become angry or happy or sad in circumstances where becoming angry or happy or sad does not involve any bodily movement. Let us ponder an admittedly contrived example that will bring out starkly the unacceptable conclusions to which Carter's position leads. Suppose that Hilda is physically incapacitated from her head to her feet, either because of some natural malady or because of the administration of a drug to her by her fiendish captors. She cannot even move her eyes or

---

[17] Steiner, *Essay*, 16–17 n. 22.

her mouth, much less any other part of her body. She is fully conscious, however, and she can experience the full range of emotions that she would ordinarily be able to feel. Naturally, she is both despondent and furious about her plight; her rage knows no bounds. Now suppose that the technology for controlling people's brains has advanced to a point where her captors can regulate her moods in minute detail without depriving her of her own consciousness altogether. Through the implantation of some device or the transmission of electromagnetic impulses or the administration of yet another drug, they now prevent Hilda from becoming angry. In other respects, her mind remains her own. In these circumstances, her inability to become angry does not affect the range of the physical movements available to her. *Ex hypothesi* she cannot move any part of her body, and accordingly the elimination of her capacity for anger does not reduce by one whit the scope of the physical activity of which she is capable. Hence, Carter is logically committed to the view that the captors' preclusion of Hilda's anger does not impair her freedom in any way. Carter has to deny that Hilda is unfree-to-become-angry, since he denies that freedoms and unfreedoms pertain to 'becomings' that are not 'doings'. In sum, he has to deny that her freedom or unfreedom is even slightly affected when her abductors deprive her of her ability to become angry. (Let it not be thought that the cerebral and neural processes which constitute Hilda's anger are themselves physical movements that would be classified by Carter as the contents of some freedoms and unfreedoms. He explicitly abjures such a classification: 'Mental acts cannot themselves be members of the set of acts that are taken into account by measurements of overall empirical freedom: even where such acts are conceived in physical terms, their "extensiveness" will be trivial.'[18])

If we reject Carter's position and accept that people can be free/ unfree to become angry or sad or happy or enthusiastic—even when their 'becomings' are not connected to any 'doings'—then we can readily conclude that Hilda is rendered unfree to become angry when her capacity for anger has been extinguished by her abductors. With such a conclusion we can adequately recognize that her new inability is indeed an inability caused by other people, and that it should conse- quently figure among her unfreedoms. Indeed, a similar conclusion beckons even if the scenario of her ordeal is rendered more realistic by the modification of some of its details. Let us progressively relax a couple of the scenario's fanciful stipulations, in order to perceive that an ascription to Hilda of the unfreedom-to-become-angry will still be

---

[18] Carter, *Measure*, 206.

germane. First, while continuing for the moment to assume that her experiencing of anger would not enable her to adopt any modes of conduct that she is otherwise unable to adopt, we can dispense with the premise that she is totally paralysed. All we need to assume is that her anger could never reach a pitch of intensity that would trigger adrenal surges which would enable her to perform feats beyond her normal strength. Perhaps her long-standing incapacity to feel truly irate is due to weakness and diffidence, or maybe it is due to otherworldliness or a magnanimously equable personality. Whatever may be the reason for the fact that she is incapable of becoming utterly incensed, we can be sure that the removal of her capacity for anger in such circumstances does not in effect take away her ability to carry out certain actions. As has been suggested, the removal of her capacity for anger *would* have such a freedom-impairing effect if she had previously been capable of becoming enraged to such an extent as to gain considerable strength during her fury from her stimulated flows of adrenalin. In regard to the situation of Hilda as described immediately above, however, we can know that there is no such freedom-impairing effect—because we know that she has not theretofore been capable of becoming so enraged. Hence, the extirpation of her capacity for anger does not decrease her freedom (or increase her unfreedom) to engage in various actions. Nevertheless, it renders her unfree to become angry.

Let us now go a step further in moderating the far-fetched features of Hilda's plight. We may henceforth assume that, on any appropriate occasion, Hilda is indeed ordinarily capable of experiencing a degree of fury that substantially enhances her strength by triggering surges of adrenalin. We should therefore now readily accept that the elimination of her capacity for anger will have made her unfree to carry out the actions of which she is capable only when infuriated. On that point, of course, Carter would agree. However, he cannot acknowledge that—in addition to being rendered unfree in the respect just mentioned—Hilda has been rendered unfree to become angry. For Carter, becoming angry is not something to which any freedom or unfreedom pertains. On this latter point, we should eschew Carter's position and should impute to Hilda the unfreedom-to-become-angry. Quite apart from any actions that are newly unavailable to her by dint of the eradication or suspension of her capacity for rage, the very process of becoming angry is newly unavailable to her. We should reflect that fact in our analysis of her situation, by ascribing to her the unfreedom to go through that process (as well as the unfreedoms to carry out any actions that would be feasible for her if and only if she were able to go through that process).

Since an ascription of unfreedom along those lines is analytically impeccable and is in harmony with ordinary linguistic/conceptual patterns, we should ask why Carter has felt a need to rule out any such ascription. My most recent quotation from his book, three paragraphs ago, supplies the answer to this question. Although Carter initially explains his exclusion of 'becomings' from the domain of freedom by invoking liberal political theory—in a passage which we have examined—his chief concern throughout is to come up with a conception of freedom that will facilitate his project of measuring the overall liberty of each person. By holding that actions are the only contents of freedoms and unfreedoms, and by holding that all actions involve physical movements, he has staked out a conception of freedoms and unfreedoms that is apparently most conducive to the task of measurement.

Tailoring one's conception of freedoms and unfreedoms to the requirements of one's general theory—the theory within which that conception gains its form—is of course both legitimate and essential. Indeed, my own denial of the bivalence of 'free' and 'unfree' has stemmed principally from the same concern that looms at the forefront of Carter's mind: a concern to ensure the measurability of overall liberty. However, given the strongly counter-intuitive implications of Carter's insistence that the only contents of freedoms and unfreedoms are potential actions, we should query whether that insistence is really necessary for his purpose. If his view on this matter can be abandoned without damage to his fundamental objective of securing the measurability of each person's overall freedom, then an abandonment of that view is advisable. We can thereby pursue his underlying objective while recognizing that freedoms pertain not only to actions but also to some bodily movements that are not potential actions and to sundry 'becomings' and 'remainings' that do not unfold via bodily movements.

Chapter 5 will elaborate my approach to the measurement of overall liberty. Not until that chapter will it become evident that a successful project of measurement can indeed allow that 'undergoings' and 'becomings' and 'remainings' as well as 'doings' are contents of freedoms and unfreedoms. At this juncture, one or two exceedingly terse anticipatory remarks must suffice. Before those fleeting remarks, however, let us straightaway note that my rejection of Carter's exclusive focus on actions will be of fairly limited importance at the extensional or practical level. The large majority of bodily movements are undoubtedly potential actions, and most 'becomings' and 'remainings' are undoubtedly aspects of 'doings' or of sets of 'doings'. Of greater significance, to be sure, is the fact that not all actions involve external bodily movements. Still, although the theoretical differences between my position and that of Carter are sizeable, and although the practical differences are not altogether to be discounted, we should be careful about overestimating those practical divergences.

How, then, can instances of stationariness—some of which are most suitably classed as actions, and some of which are mere 'becomings' or 'remainings'—be taken duly into account when we seek to measure anyone's overall liberty? Not even an outline of a full answer to this question can be provided here, since it would have to be prefaced by many of the arguments that will emerge in Chapter 5. One observation may serve in lieu of such an outline. Every exercise of a freedom involves the use or positioning of some object(s)—such as the human body—and the occupation of space.[19] This proposition about the exercise of any freedom applies to instances of stationariness as well as to actions that consist in bodily movements. As G. A. Cohen has remarked, '[e]ven the mental activity of an immobile agent requires the space he occupies'.[20] Hence, what our techniques for measurement must adequately gauge is not only the potential movements of each human body, but more broadly the potential uses or positionings thereof. Most of the uses of anyone's body (and other objects) involve external movements, but some important uses do not. In sum, while endeavouring to delineate a system of measurement that is sensitive to the physicality of the exercise of any liberties, this book maintains that that inevitable physicality resides not perforce in external motions but in the positioning of objects and the occupation of space; consequently, I can repudiate Carter's premise that every exercise of a liberty must consist partly in some external bodily movement(s). The outlandish corollaries of his premise can be avoided without any jeopardy to his

---

[19] This observation has been most forcefully and prominently advanced by Hillel Steiner. See for example Steiner, *Essay*, 35–41; Hillel Steiner, 'Individual Liberty', in David Miller (ed.), *Liberty* (Oxford: Oxford University Press, 1991) [Steiner, 'Liberty'], 123, 137–9; Hillel Steiner, 'How Free: Computing Personal Liberty', in A. Phillips Griffiths (ed.), *Of Liberty* (Cambridge: Cambridge University Press, 1983) [Steiner, 'Computing'], 73, 86. However, some of the specific formulations of this point by Steiner have left him gratuitously vulnerable to the criticism levelled against him by G. A. Cohen, 'Illusions about Private Property and Freedom', in John Mepham and David-Hillel Ruben (eds), *Issues in Marxist Philosophy: Volume IV, Social and Political Philosophy* (Sussex: Harvester Press, 1981) [Cohen, 'Illusions'], 223, 237–8, 241 n. 21. See also G. A. Cohen, *Self-Ownership, Freedom, and Equality* (Cambridge: Cambridge University Press, 1995) [Cohen, *Self-Ownership*], 98 n. 7.

[20] Cohen, *Self-Ownership*, 98.

aim of ensuring that—at least in principle—each person's overall liberty is rigorously measurable.

Before we leave this topic, one caveat should be entered in connection with the preceding paragraph. Although the term 'exercise' may suggest an exertion that would qualify as an action in Carter's sense, the term has clearly been used here more expansively. An exercise of a freedom by some person P is the actualization of any possibility that has been open to P, whether or not the actualization occurs through some action of hers. Because theorists who write about liberty (including me) so often concentrate their attention on potential actions, we can safely think of actions as the paradigmatic exercises of liberties. Nonetheless, in light of the arguments in this section, we should grasp that 'undergoings' and 'becomings' and 'remainings' are also exercises of liberties. Regardless of whether some specific undergoings and becomings and remainings are potential actions, they are routes by which various possibilities available to people can be realized. That is, they are ways in which freedoms can be exercised. If the actions of other people prevent for some person P the realization of possibilities that could have been actualized through processes of undergoing or becoming, then P has been made unfree in those respects—just as she would be if the blocked modes of actualization, the blocked exercises of freedoms, were potential actions.

2. *Not by Degrees*

Many portions of Chapter 2 have highlighted the distinction between overall freedom and particular freedoms. Overall liberty is plainly a scalar or partitive property that exists in different degrees.[21] Whether the overall liberty is of an individual or of a society, it will be present to a greater or a lesser extent in comparison with the overall liberty of some other individual or society. Indeed, precisely because overall freedom can exist in differing degrees, it lends itself to measurement and comparisons. If in principle as well as in practice it could not ever vary at all in its extent, the project of gauging its proportions would be utterly futile. Measurements presuppose the possibility of discovering more or less of the investigated property than is actually discovered. If that property were insusceptible to quantitative variations and if it thus

[21] By 'scalar' I do not mean 'susceptible to cardinal measurements'. Rather, I mean 'susceptible at least to ordinal comparisons and perhaps also to cardinal measurements'.

existed in an all-or-nothing fashion, then it could never be measured but could only be deemed present or absent.

Are particular liberties similar to overall liberty in being scalar or partitive? In other words, can each particular freedom exist to varying extents? Can somebody be free-to-φ to a certain degree, and be less free-to-φ or more free-to-φ than somebody else? With only one trifling qualification, the current section of this chapter will maintain that the answers to these questions are negative. The existence of any particular liberty, as opposed to the extent of anybody's overall liberty, cannot vary cardinally or ordinally. Having disagreed with Carter about the range of things to which freedoms can pertain, this book sides firmly with him on the present issue. He writes that '[t]he freedom to do x is not a matter of degree; one either is or is not free to do x', and he oppugns 'the claim that specific freedoms are a matter of degree (i.e., that one can be more or less free *to do x*)'.[22] Steiner aptly espouses a similar view: 'The notion of degrees of freedom to do an action is superfluous, misleading and descriptively imprecise.'[23]

Like Carter and Steiner, this book contends that the freedom-to-φ of any person P consists in the possibility or unpreventedness of P's φ-ing. The lack of such a freedom, therefore, consists in the impossibility or preventedness of P's φ-ing. (An unfreedom exists when the impossibility or preventedness is due to the actions of some person or set of persons other than P.) What is crucial here is that the germane categories for the analysis of particular freedoms are the stark alternatives of possibility and impossibility, or unpreventedness and preventedness. The difficulty or easiness of P's φ-ing, which of course exists in degrees, is irrelevant to the question whether P is free to φ. Either P's φ-ing is possible, and P is thus free to φ; or P's φ-ing is impossible, and P is therefore not free to φ (and is perhaps unfree to φ).

Although my book's stance on the current topic is in accordance with the positions taken by Carter and Steiner, it clashes with the views put forward by quite a few other theorists.[24] Hence, we ought to ponder why a number of other theorists would be attracted to the thesis that P's freedom-to-φ will wane or wax in proportion to the difficulty or easiness of P's φ-ing. If we can eschew that thesis

---

[22] Carter, *Measure*, 228, 233, emphasis in original.

[23] Steiner, 'Computing', 78.

[24] See for example Cohen, 'Illusions', 230–1; G. A. Cohen, *History, Labour, and Freedom* (Oxford: Clarendon Press, 1988) [Cohen, *History*], 246 n. 12, 270; Lawrence Crocker, *Positive Liberty* (The Hague: Martinus Nijhoff, 1980), 18–22 *et passim*; Joel Feinberg, *Social Philosophy* (Englewood Cliffs: Prentice-Hall,

while coming up with an analysis of freedoms that does not at all neglect the importance of the difficulty or easiness of P's φ-ing, then we ought indeed to insist that the existence of any particular freedom is an all-or-nothing affair. That is, we should adopt the view that each such freedom is either present or absent, and that its presence or absence is never a matter of degree. Any contrary view tends to diminish the clarity and precision of one's analysis, as is rightly suggested in the quotation from Steiner above. My discussion in this section will seek to substantiate his allegation.

2.1. Overall Liberty versus Particular Liberties

Probably the most common source of the inclination of theorists to perceive particular liberties as scalar is a failure to distinguish sufficiently between those liberties and overall liberty. Such a failure has been repeatedly criticized in Chapter 2, of course, in other contexts. Here it manifests itself in the tendency of many analysts to presume that the costliness or difficulty of exercising a freedom-to-φ will diminish the extent of that freedom rather than simply diminishing the range of the combinations of conjunctively exercisable liberties in which that freedom is a member. In fact, however, that range is exactly where the costliness or difficulty of exercising the particular freedom will have its effect. To discern as much, let us consider the sort of situation which many theorists have in mind when writing about this matter.

Suppose that a government imposes a rigorously enforced tax or penalty on the carrying out of some activity X. Or suppose that the government bestows access to the means for performing X only on people who have complied with numerous bureaucratic requirements such as the filling out of forms. In each case, one's exercise of the freedom to engage in X at any particular place and time has been made more costly or difficult. When the well-enforced tax or penalty

1973), 8; Joel Feinberg, *Rights, Justice, and the Bounds of Liberty* (Princeton: Princeton University Press, 1980), 8; Felix Oppenheim, *Dimensions of Freedom* (New York: St Martin's Press, 1961), Ch. 8; Christine Swanton, 'The Concept of Overall Freedom', 57 *Australasian Journal of Philosophy* 337, 343–5 (1979) [Swanton, 'Concept']; D. M. White, 'Negative Liberty', 80 *Ethics* 185, 187 (1969–70). Cf. Tim Gray, *Freedom* (London: Macmillan, 1991) [T. Gray, *Freedom*], 133–6. For an outstanding discussion of the topics addressed in this section of the current chapter, see Carter, *Measure*, Ch. 8. See also Ian Carter, 'Freedom and Its Specificity: A Reply', 57 *Politeia* 35, 36, 37–9 (2000) [Carter, 'Specificity']. For another important treatment, see Steiner, 'Computing', 76–9.

has been introduced, the heightened costliness of exercising the free-
dom-to-do-X for a person P resides in his having to bear the untoward
consequences that will ensue from his availing himself of that freedom.
Even more plainly is the difficulty of his exercising that freedom
increased when he has to comply with numerous bureaucratic requirements before governmental officials will provide him with the means
of performing X. Satisfying the demands of cavalier functionaries can
be extremely irksome and time-consuming.

In either of the scenarios just broached, P will encounter some costs
or difficulties if he attempts to engage in the activity X at some time t.
Should we therefore conclude that his freedom-to-engage-in-X-at-t is
less than it would be if the aforementioned costs or difficulties did not
loom? The answer to this question is negative, for two reasons. First, as
will be discussed in my next subsection, what is lower—as a result of
the penalties or the bureaucratic hurdles—is not the freedom-to-
perform-X-at-t but the likelihood that that freedom exists. Second is
a point on which we are focused in the current subsection. Although
the particular liberty of P to perform X at t is not lowered by sanctions
or bureaucratic obstacles, the overall liberty of P is indeed lowered. If P
will be punished whenever he does X, then his freedom-to-do-X-at-t is
not lessened; but the range of his combinations-of-conjunctively-
exercisable-liberties which each include that freedom is indeed
reduced. He cannot now exercise that particular freedom in conjunction with liberties to engage in any activities that will be ruled out by
the sanctions imposed for his doing of X at t. Much the same can be
said, *mutatis mutandis*, about a situation in which P has to jump
through bureaucratic hoops in order to gain access to the means of
engaging in X at t. Again the range of his combinations of conjunctively exercisable freedoms is diminished, as that range now does not
encompass any combination that includes both the liberty to abstain
from jumping through any of the requisite hoops and the liberty to
engage in X at t. Those hoops do impair P's freedom significantly, but
the freedom impaired is his overall liberty rather than his particular
liberty-to-perform-X-at-t.

Why, however, should we not accept that the particular freedom of P
to carry out X at t has been reduced by the penalties or the bureaucratic
hurdles? Let us take the scenarios in turn. If the punishments to be
inflicted on P for his doing of X at t are purely *post hoc* (as I have been
assuming), then they do not preclude him in any way from actually
doing X at t. They merely preclude him from doing certain other things
in the aftermath of his performance of X at t. Thus, since someone is
free to do whatever he is unprevented from doing—unprevented by

external constraints and by internal incapacities—*P* is straightforwardly free to engage in *X* at *t*. Of course, if the sanctions for performing *X* are severe, he might not *feel* free to do *X* at *t*; but his freedom-to-do-*X*-at-*t* obtains as a state of unpreventedness, whose existence as such is unaffected by *P*'s attitude toward that state.

Suppose now that the steps taken by the government against *P*'s engaging in *X* at *t* are not purely *post hoc*. Suppose that among those steps are some anticipatory preventive measures. If those measures succeed, then obviously they will have closed off the option of his performing *X* at *t*. However, their effect in that event is not to *reduce* the freedom of *P* to do *X* at *t*; their effect, rather, is to *eliminate* that particular freedom altogether. If *P* is not able to do *X* at *t*, he is not free to do it then, and indeed in the posited circumstances he is unfree to do it then. Instead of being less free to perform *X* at *t*, he no longer has that particular freedom at all. By contrast, if the anticipatory preventive measures do not succeed, then *P* is indeed able to perform *X* at *t*, and thus he is free to perform it at that time. Instead of being wholly absent—as would have been the case if the preventive steps had not failed to achieve their aim—his freedom to carry out *X* at *t* is wholly present.

Let us turn to the other scenario, in which the government lays down bureaucratic procedures that must be followed by anyone who wishes to gain access to the means of doing *X*. If *P* has abided by the requisite procedures to the satisfaction of the officials involved (who accordingly provide him with the means of performing *X*), and if his compliance with those procedures has occurred ahead of *t*, then he is able to do *X* at *t*. That is, he enjoys the freedom to do *X* at *t*. The government's bureaucratic requirements have made it more difficult for him to secure that particular freedom for himself, but his timely fulfilment of those requirements has endowed him with precisely that freedom. Though his overall liberty has been diminished by those requirements—as has been explained above—his particular freedom-to-perform-*X*-at-*t* has not been diminished even slightly. We should not make the mistake of thinking that the impairment of his overall freedom is paralleled by an impairment of the particular freedom. What has been reduced is not that particular freedom's existence or intensity, but the frequency of its inclusion in the combinations-of-conjunctively-exercisable-liberties that are available to *P*. Because the particular freedom amounts to nothing more and nothing less than the ability of *P* to perform *X* at *t*, and because (*ex hypothesi*) he possesses that ability, his freedom-to-perform-*X*-at-*t* is straightforwardly present.

Of course, if *P* has not managed to conform with the government's requirements in a timely fashion—to the satisfaction of the relevant officials—then he will be unable to do X at t. In those circumstances, in other words, his freedom-to-perform-X-at-t will not exist at t. Once again, however, we cannot correctly say that that particular freedom has been impaired or reduced. Rather, it has been altogether negated. Just as it is fully present whenever it is present, it is fully absent whenever it is absent. Because it is not contained in any of P's combinations-of-conjunctively-exercisable-liberties that include the liberty to abstain from conforming in a timely fashion with the government's bureaucratic procedures, it will be eliminated by his exercise of the latter liberty. After all, when the latter liberty is exercised by P, his freedom-to-perform-X-at-t cannot be exercised; and a non-normative liberty that cannot be exercised is no non-normative liberty at all.

In sum, when we carefully distinguish between overall freedom and particular freedoms, we shall not be prone to think that any particular freedom exists to varying degrees. Among the considerations that impel people to embrace the varying-degrees position, one of the most powerful is the fact that anybody who does encounter or would encounter burdens in exercising the freedom-to-perform-X-at-t is *pro tanto* less free than somebody who does not or would not encounter such burdens. As we have seen, that fact about the diminution of liberty can be readily acknowledged within a theory that rejects the varying-degrees position, because the fact in question pertains to a person's overall liberty rather than to the existence of a particular freedom. When impediments render more onerous for P the exercise of some particular liberty, his freedom has decreased. Any tenable theory of freedom has to be alert to that decrease. While being duly alert, however, one should recognize that the decrease is not in the existence of the particular liberty but in the extent of P's overall freedom. A full awareness of the reduction in the overall posture can keep us from mistakenly characterizing it as a reduction in the particular freedom's intensity or scope.

2.2. *Probability Revisited*

What has been said in the preceding subsection about the overall/particular distinction might not entirely put to rest the temptation to think of particular freedoms as scalar. Another source of that temptation has been fleetingly broached in the preceding discussion, and will now be squarely addressed. As has been argued in Chapter 2, most ascriptions of freedom and unfreedom are explicitly or implicitly probabilistic. When some person P has to surmount numerous bureaucratic hurdles in order to gain access to the means of doing X at some time t, the likelihood of his being free at t to do X at t might be slim. (Throughout the present discussion, purely for ease of exposition, I shall assume that P will do his best to enable himself to perform X at t. Accordingly, the only factor bearing on the probability of his being endowed at t with the freedom-to-perform-X-at-t is the difficulty or easiness of his acquiring that particular freedom. We need not here take into account any complexities posed by the possibility of his being uninclined to try to become free-at-t-to-perform-X-at-t.) Hence, if well ahead of t we are asked to determine whether P at t will be free to do X at t, our ascription to him of the freedom-at-t-to-do-X-at-t should expressly carry a probabilistic qualification indicating that the chances of his enjoying that particular freedom are fairly small. The greater the number and severity of the bureaucratic hurdles, the smaller are his chances of being endowed with that particular freedom. An accurate description of his situation will explicitly reflect that lowered probability.

Plainly, then, any non-trivial difficulties faced by P in gaining and exercising a particular freedom will reduce the likelihood of his having that freedom at all. Any diminution of that likelihood will be in proportion to the arduousness of the difficulties that confront P. What is of central importance here, however, is that the diminution pertains to the likelihood of the particular freedom's emergence rather than to that freedom itself. The particular freedom itself is not lessened in any sense by the lessening of the probability of its obtaining. If P's freedom-to-perform-X-at-t does exist at t, then it exists in full—regardless of whether the chances of its emergence were low or high. Conversely, if that particular freedom does not exist at t, then it does not exist at all. Its existence and non-existence are starkly dichotomous, even though the probability of its existence or non-existence can vary over countless different degrees.

Suppose that 25 men are in a room and that one of them is my twin brother. I know as much, though I cannot see any of the men. Suppose further that one man in the room is mentioned with reference to some characteristic—for example, his proximity to a certain painting on the wall—that does not bear at all on the likelihood that he is my twin brother. I therefore know that there is a 4 per cent chance that the specified person will turn out to be my twin brother. In articulating that probabilistic judgement, I am clearly not suggesting that the person singled out is 4 per cent my twin brother and 96 per cent somebody else. That person is either my twin brother *tout court* or someone else *tout court*; my current uncertainty about his identity has not impinged on his existence or character or status as the person he is. Now suppose that I am informed that the man in question has blue eyes. I know that exactly ten of the men in the room have blue eyes, and that my twin brother is one of them. Ergo, I know that there is a 10 per cent chance that the specified person will turn out to be my twin brother. Obviously, the increase in the information available to me has augmented the probability which I can attach to my judgement that the person who has been singled out is indeed my twin brother. However, that increase has not in any way affected the identity or personality or existence of that person. It has manifestly not caused him to take on more of the identity of my twin brother and less of the identity of someone else. Either he is my twin brother and nobody else, or he is not my twin brother at all. My probabilistic judgements concern an all-or-nothing matter.

In that key respect, those judgements resemble our ascriptions of particular freedoms and unfreedoms. If a person P will encounter very few difficulties in attaining the particular freedom-at-t-to-perform-X-at-t, and if we have an accurate sense of his situation, then we can ascribe to him the freedom-to-perform-X-at-t with a very high degree of probability. In other words, we can predict with a very high degree of confidence that, if P endeavours (without any blunders) to attain and exercise the freedom-at-t-to-perform-X-at-t, he will succeed in doing so. If by contrast there are some formidable difficulties confronting P in any efforts that he might make to attain the freedom-at-t-to-perform-X-at-t, we have to attach a much lower probability when we attribute to him now the freedom-to-perform-X-at-t. That is, we can predict with only a slim degree of confidence that he will attain the liberty-at-t-to-perform-X-at-t if he endeavours to do so. Between the situation of no serious obstacles and the situation of very serious obstacles, then, the probability of P's being able to acquire the particular liberty-at-t-to-perform-X-at-t will have declined. The overall freedom of P will also have declined, in the manner expounded by my last subsection. Both his overall liberty and the *probability* of the existence of his particular liberty are matters of degree. What is not in any way a matter of degree, however, is the existence of the particular liberty itself. Either P at t is free to carry out X at t, or he is not. When we say that the probability of his being thus free is lower in the situation of very serious obstacles than in the situation of no serious obstacles, we are not saying that the scope or intensity or character of the freedom-to-carry-out-X-at-t will have fallen to a lower level. It is not the case that P in the situation of very serious obstacles is only somewhat free-at-t-to-perform-X-at-t. Either he is endowed in full with that particular freedom, or he is not endowed with it at all. When we affirm that there is a lowered probability of his being endowed with that particular freedom, we are affirming that there is a lowered probability of his being endowed with it in full. We are *ipso facto* affirming that there is an increased probability of his not being endowed with that particular freedom at all. Should things come to pass in accordance with that increased probability, *P*'s freedom-to-perform-*X*-at-*t* will not have been *diminished* but will instead have been *scotched* altogether.

Of course, the fact that *P* lacks some particular liberty *L* is perfectly consistent with his possession of some other particular liberty that has a content amounting to part of the content of *L*. Let us suppose, for example, that the particular freedom which *P* lacks is the freedom to walk at least two miles in an easterly direction on a certain road between 11.00 a.m. and 11.30 a.m. on a specified day. Perhaps because he is not physically fit, or perhaps because the condition of the road or of the weather is obstructive, or maybe because other people will forcibly stop him after a certain point, he cannot walk two miles within the allotted period of time. He can, however, walk any distance up to one mile in an easterly direction along the road during that period. He is therefore free to do exactly that; neither his own incapacities nor any external constraints prevent him. Now, from the fact that he is free to walk one mile, we should not infer that he is partly or somewhat free to walk two miles. Nor should we infer that he possesses a particular freedom-to-walk-two-miles-during-the-stipulated-period that is less intense or more limited in scope than would be true if he could actually walk two miles. Equally misconceived is the view that that ostensible freedom of his to walk two miles is existent at a reduced level. Rather, given that he is unable (for whatever reason) to walk more than a mile during the 30-minute span, he altogether lacks the freedom to walk two miles during that span. In application to him, that particular freedom does not exist at all. The ability which is indispensable for the existence of that freedom—the ability of *P* to walk at least two miles during the 30 minutes—is absent. If we were to endorse the claim that his particular liberty-to-walk-two-miles exists at a reduced level when he can walk only one mile, we ought also to endorse the preposterous claim that a fully grown man who stands six feet in height is a seven-foot man existing at a reduced level.

In one important sense, to be sure, *P* is less free in the situation just posited than in a situation where he is capable of walking at least two miles. *Pro tanto*, his overall freedom is lower in the former situation than in the latter. As has been readily acknowledged and indeed emphasized herein, the overall liberty of each person—or of a society—can obtain in many different degrees at different times. Nevertheless, the scalar character of overall freedom is inconsequential here. My arguments have hardly been directed against the thesis that one person can be less free overall than some other person (or than himself at some other time). Instead, my attack has been directed against the thesis that one person can be less free-to-do-X-at-t than some other person (or than himself at some other time). The extent of anyone's overall liberty is scalar, but the existence of any particular liberty is not. A particular liberty is always present *tout court* or absent *tout court*. Thus, with reference to circumstances along the lines depicted in my last paragraph, we should not designate P as less free-to-walk-two-miles-along-the-road-between-11.00-a.m.-and-11.30-a.m. than somebody who is capable of walking the distance of two miles within the specified period. P is less free overall (*pro tanto*) than is the more capable walker, but no ordinal comparison between them is appropriate in respect of the particular freedom-to-walk-two-miles-along-the-road. Whereas the more capable walker enjoys that particular freedom fully, P enjoys it not at all. Any comparison between them in regard to that particular freedom is a matter of all or nothing, rather than a matter of more or less.

2.3. *Types and Tokens*

In adducing the example of P's journey on foot along the road, the last subsection specified quite precisely the content of the particular freedom under investigation (though a great deal of further precision—extremely tedious further precision—would have been possible, of course). Because the 'X' and 't' variables in the formulation 'liberty-to-do-X-at-t' are fixed with quite a high degree of specificity in the scenario of P's ambling, the discussion of that scenario has perhaps left unaddressed a further source of the temptation to perceive particular liberties as scalar. We shall here examine that source by pondering the distinction between act-types and act-tokens.[25] This subsection will reaffirm what has been argued so far, while offering one very small qualification along the way.

An act-type is a distinctive feature or set of features common to all members—if any—of a class of actions. An act-token is an instance of an act-type; in other words, it is an action which partakes of the feature or set of features whose presence is sufficient to qualify an action as

---

[25] This distinction, of fundamental importance in the philosophy of action, is highlighted for slightly different purposes in Steiner, *Essay*, 33–7; Carter, *Measure*, Ch. 7.

belonging to a certain act-type. What is of central importance here is that act-types can be specified with differing degrees of vagueness or precision. Walking is an act-type, as is walking along a road, as is walking along a road on a Tuesday, as is walking along a road on a Tuesday morning, and so forth. Any number of levels of abstraction will be available when we choose among act-type descriptions for the actions that we or other people carry out. (In addition, of course, descriptions at roughly similar levels of abstraction are themselves multifarious. For example, an action describable as 'walking along the road' might also be correctly describable as 'going to work' or 'going to school' or 'returning home from the house of one's friend'.)

When people refer to their own actions and the actions of others, they almost invariably use act-type designations. Hardly ever do they specify the space-time coordinates of those actions with great precision, at least in quotidian discourse and indeed in virtually all non-scientific intellectual discourse. Every characterization of an action within this chapter, even the characterization of *P*'s sauntering along the road during a carefully demarcated 30-minute period, has made use of act-type formulations. Were such formulations to be eschewed in ordinary contexts, our accounts of actions would become unmanageably tedious and cumbersome. Any drawbacks associated with the imprecision of act-type designations are costs well worth paying for the flexibility and workability that those designations provide.

Hence, on almost every occasion when we elaborate the content of this or that particular freedom, we use the language of act-types. Obviously, then, the divide between particular liberties and overall liberty does not correlate—except in a highly imperfect fashion—with the dichotomy between act-tokens and act-types. Rather, the particular/overall split is a divide between any state of unpreventedness with a distinctive content and a quantification over all such states. What is meant by 'distinctive' here is simply that the content of each particular freedom differentiates it from every other particular freedom (including any particular freedom whose more concrete content is subsumable within its own). Any particular freedom is what it is by dint of its content—that is, by dint of its pertaining to some specific type or instance of human conduct, which is different from the type or instance of human conduct to which any other particular freedom pertains. (For present purposes, we may overlook freedoms that pertain to the undergoing of irresistible processes. Taking them into account would introduce stylistic gnarls and would not change my basic substantive points at all.)

Now, because the content of any particular liberty is what distinguishes or defines it as that particular liberty, and because any such content is nearly always articulated as an act-type rather than as an act-token, we identify each particular freedom as something that potentially comprehends many other particular freedoms with more concrete contents. Here we come to the source of the temptation to think that particular liberties are scalar. Given the existence of any particular freedom whose content potentially encompasses the contents of countless other particular freedoms, some of those more concrete freedoms may well be absent even though the freedom whose content potentially encompasses theirs is robustly present. Consider, for example, the liberty to traverse on foot the full length of Grange Road in Cambridge, England. Let us suppose that Joe enjoys that particular liberty, in that he is able to walk from one end of Grange Road to the other on many occasions. Perhaps, however, he is not free to walk there on any of the days when repairs are being carried out. On those days, the formidable barriers and the preparedness of workmen to exclude him if necessary are sufficient to prevent Joe from traversing the full length of the road. Thus, although his liberty to walk from one end of the road to the other could potentially be instantiated by his liberty to do so on any given day when repairs are carried out, the latter liberty does not in fact exist. A potential instance of the more abstract liberty is absent, as are some other potential instances thereof. Nonetheless, the more abstract liberty itself can perfectly well exist, so long as some of its potential instances—such as Joe's freedom to traverse the length of Grange Road on this or that day when repairs are not being carried out—do in fact exist. We can then correctly say that as a general matter Joe is free to walk from one end of Grange Road to the other, even though occasionally he is blocked from doing so. The existence of a liberty with a relatively abstract content does not depend on the existence of *every* potential instance of that liberty, so long as *some* of the potential instances are actual.

Precisely because a particular freedom with a relatively abstract content can exist even if quite a few of the freedoms that would instantiate it are non-existent, the view of particular freedoms as scalar can seem quite apposite. To see this point, let us look again at the example of Joe's strolling on Grange Road. Suppose initially that, on every single day when repairs are undertaken, Joe is unable to walk along Grange Road. Now suppose that the workmen become a bit less surly and a bit more accommodating. Carrying out repairs no more often than previously—say, five days each year—they now sometimes leave a path open for pedestrians. Whenever the workmen do clear such a path, Joe is able to traverse the length of Grange Road. Hence, he is now able to perform such a feat more frequently than he could heretofore. An observer may therefore be inclined to conclude that Joe is now freer than before to walk from one end of Grange Road to the other. His particular freedom to engage in such a walk has increased in its extent, or so it may seem.

Although this subsection will argue against the inference broached at the end of the last paragraph, a minor qualification or concession is in order first. If people wish to say that somebody P is 'freer to do X than before' when they mean that P is now free to do more of the actions that instantiate X than he could do before, then such a pattern of usage—though highly misleading and inexact—is quite understandable. In ordinary discourse, as opposed to the much more careful argumentation of political philosophy, the aforesaid pattern of usage is very likely irrepressible. After all, in the circumstances just mentioned concerning P, he has gained some particular liberties to perform certain actions that are instances of X. Many observers will doubtless feel tempted to claim that P has thereby enlarged his freedom-to-do-X.

Nevertheless, as has been indicated, any such temptation should be resisted. The key to mounting a stalwart resistance is a point already adumbrated in this subsection. If any of the potential instances of the freedom-to-do-X are actual, then the freedom-to-do-X itself is actual; the existence of any instance of a particular liberty entails the existence of the liberty that is instantiated. In illustration of this point, let us ponder a variant of the scenario involving Joe on Grange Road. Suppose that Joe is able to traverse the length of Grange Road on one of its sides but not on the other. For whatever reason, the left-hand side of the road (facing northward) is wholly unusable for pedestrian traffic. Perhaps it is insurmountably closed off by barriers, or maybe its surface has the consistency of quicksand, or perhaps workmen are constantly labouring on that side and are undisposed to let anyone else trudge along it. By contrast, the right-hand side of the road (facing northward) can be walked upon straightforwardly by Joe and other pedestrians. Joe is thus endowed with the particular liberty to walk the full length of Grange Road on the right-hand side, even though he cannot proceed at all on the left-hand side. His possession of that particular liberty entails his possession of the liberty to walk the full length of Grange Road. One cannot be free to perform an action of a certain type in some specific manner or in some specific location without being free to perform an action of that type. If I am free to walk briskly, then I am free to walk—irrespective of whether I am also free to walk slowly. Likewise, if I am free to walk slowly, I am free to walk—irrespective of whether I am also free to walk briskly. The existence of any particular liberty that instantiates a liberty with a more abstract content will entail the existence of that latter liberty.

Let us pause for a moment to glance at the difference between abstraction and inclusiveness, and between instances and corollaries. Consider the following three particular freedoms: (A) the liberty to traverse the full length of Grange Road; (B) the liberty to traverse the full length of Grange Road every day of every week; and (C) the liberty to traverse the full length of Grange Road every Tuesday. In comparison with the content of C, the content of A is abstract whereas the content of B is inclusive or expansive. Let us henceforth designate those contents as 'A_c', 'B_c', and 'C_c'. A_c is abstract because it leaves undetermined a myriad of details, one of which is settled by the relatively concrete content of C. B_c, on the other hand, is at least as concrete as C_c, for it leaves nothing undetermined that is settled by C_c. Nonetheless, while no more abstract than C_c, B_c is manifestly more expansive or inclusive. It includes C_c, but it extends more broadly in its affirmative settling of details that are left undetermined by A_c. In sum, A_c is more abstract than C_c, whereas B_c is more inclusive or expansive than C_c. Note that, because of the non-equivalence between the abstraction/concreteness relationship and the inclusiveness/narrowness relationship, the logical ties between liberties A and C are very different from the logical ties between liberties B and C. As C is one of the instances of A, the existence of C entails the existence of A but not vice versa. By contrast, as C is one of the corollaries of B, the existence of B entails the existence of C but not vice versa. Throughout this subsection I am focusing chiefly on the abstraction/concreteness relationship and thus on instances, rather than on the inclusiveness/narrowness relationship and on corollaries.

Now, because the existence of any particular liberty that instantiates a liberty with a more abstract content will entail the existence of the latter liberty, the liberty with the more abstract content will exist whenever some of its instances do. Its existence is an all-or-nothing matter. If none of its potential instances is actual, then it itself altogether lacks actuality; contrariwise, if at least one of its potential instances is actual, then it itself actually obtains. We would consequently be misguided if we yielded to the temptation to describe somebody as 'more free-to-do-X' when she becomes free to do X in some additional way(s). So long as she has already been free to do X in some way(s), she has been free to do X. Newly engendered instances of her particular freedom-to-do-X will not augment the scope of that freedom, since it has all along been broad enough to encompass the new instances even before they have arisen.

What, then, are the general effects of any additional instances of a person's freedom-to-do-X? An exploration of those effects may help to explain why the advent of such instances can tempt us to say that the person in question has become more free-to-do-X (or that the person's freedom-to-do-X has increased). An exploration of those effects should also help to allay that temptation.

First, and most evident, the new instances of a particular liberty are themselves particular liberties which a person has gained. Exactly because the instances of a particular liberty are not entailed by that which they instantiate, they are genuinely new or restored freedoms when they emerge. Second, the emergence of those particular freedoms will have expanded the overall liberty of the person P who has come to be endowed with them. Because they are genuinely new or restored freedoms, they expand the range of P's combinations of conjunctively exercisable freedoms, and thus they enlarge his overall liberty. There is no doubt that P is freer than before; but, as has already been stressed, he is freer in respect of his overall standing rather than in respect of one of his already existent liberties. Third, and most important for our present purposes, the advent of additional instances of P's freedom-to-do-X will indeed have an impact on that particular freedom itself. However, the impact will consist not in the augmentation of the scope of that freedom, but in the shoring up of its secureness. What is enlarged, in other words, is the probability that P's freedom-to-do-X will persist. That is, the key issues raised by the engendering of the further instances of P's freedom-to-do-X—more precisely, the key issues as far as the present subsection of this chapter is concerned—are basically similar to the issues that have been probed in my last subsection.

In two main respects, new instances of P's freedom-to-do-X will generally increase the probability of P's enjoying that particular freedom. First, and less important, is a purely epistemic point relating to our ascriptions of freedom and unfreedom when our knowledge of P's more concrete liberties is quite limited. If we have good grounds for believing that P can exercise his freedom-to-do-X in a host of significantly different ways—that is, if we have good grounds for believing that P is endowed with sundry instances of the freedom-to-do-X—we can attach high probabilities to our statements of P's freedom-to-do-X in various sets of circumstances, notwithstanding that we do not know in exactly which sets of circumstances he does normally enjoy that particular freedom. Accordingly, if we have good grounds for believing that the ways in which P can exercise his freedom-to-do-X have increased (without our knowing exactly where the increases have occurred), we can attach even higher probabilities to our statements of his freedom-to-do-X in various sets of circumstances.

More important is a second respect in which the new instances of P's freedom-to-do-X will typically have raised the probability of his possessing that particular freedom. The emergence of the further instances of that freedom will tend to reduce the likelihood that his possession of the freedom-to-do-X will cease in the future, since the termination of that freedom would now involve the shutting down of additional options that have become open. If P can do X in multitudinous ways that are significantly different from one another, then the chances of the continuation of his ability to do X are normally higher than if he can do it in only one way or a few ways. Hence, a growth in the number of those ways will normally render that continuation more likely. Crucial here is that what will have undergone an increase is not the freedom-to-do-X but the security of that particular freedom—that is, the likelihood of its being sustained.

In short, once we duly distinguish between any particular freedom and the secureness of that freedom, we can see that new instances of the freedom tend to augment its secureness rather than its reach. Not only is a description of somebody as 'more free-to-perform-X' quite inapposite, but it also obfuscates the precise effects of additional instances of the freedom-to-perform-X. Similarly, once we duly distinguish between overall liberty and each particular liberty, we can see that only the former is scalar. In being non-scalar, 'free' and 'unfree' in discussions of particular actions and types of actions are on a par with 'possible' and 'impossible' (though the latter two predicates, unlike the former two, are bivalent). When P has been able to perform X and has now become able to perform X in some novel manner, we cannot correctly state that his performance of X is now more possible than before. 'Possible' applies in an all-or-nothing fashion, as does 'impossible'. Instead of declaring that the performance of X by P is now more possible than previously, we ought to declare that the performance of X by P is now possible in more ways than previously. A parallel pattern of usage is necessary when we are speaking of particular freedoms. Rather than maintaining that P has become more free-to-perform-X than he was before, we ought to maintain that P is now free-to-perform-X in more ways than before. (And, we can add, P has therefore become more free overall.) As Steiner has suggested in the pronouncement quoted earlier, the characterization of any particular liberty as scalar is superfluous, misleading, and inexact.

3. *Counter-factuals and Conservation*

This chapter has hitherto sided with Steiner on each of the topics that it has addressed. In the present section, however, Steiner figures as the principal target of several of my arguments. My discussions will seek to investigate the implications of the counter-factual aspect of freedom and unfreedom. That is, we shall explore how everyone's freedom and unfreedom are partly determined by potential events which do not occur but which could have occurred.

The counter-factual aspect of unfreedom is made explicit in my U Postulate, the second prong of which affirms—in part—that a person P capable of φ-ing is unfree-to-φ if an endeavour by him to φ would have been thwarted by some action(s) of some other person(s). As is evident from the wording in that portion of the U Postulate, with its reference to dispositions as well as to actions, the actual occurrence of some preventive step(s) by some other person(s) is inessential for the existence of unfreedom. So long as some such step(s) would have been undertaken by some other person(s) if P had attempted to φ, and so long as the step(s) would have foiled any such attempt by him, he is unfree to φ. Equally important is the counter-factual aspect of *freedom*, though the F Postulate does not state this matter directly and expressly along the lines of the U Postulate. The counter-factual aspect of freedom is instead implicit in the F Postulate's equation of the freedom-to-φ and the ability-to-φ, since people are generally able to perform any number of actions which they do not actually perform. The measure of the freedom of each person is defined by what he or she could have done, as well as by what he or she does. An action or a process can be unprevented without actually taking place.

Given that freedom and unfreedom each contain a counter-factual element, the dispositions of people affect the freedom and unfreedom of other people. Each person's freedom or unfreedom is affected not only by what others in fact do, but also by what they are disposed to do. What other people are disposed to do (and capable of doing) is what they will indeed do if certain circumstances arise; if those circumstances do not materialize at a given juncture, then what other people were disposed to do (and capable of doing) at that juncture is what they would have done if the circumstances had arisen. Their dispositions crucially bear on the freedom and unfreedom of each person, since those dispositions play a key role in determining whether the abilities and inabilities of each person would continue as such if the person's conduct or situation were altered in various respects. Only by asking how far those abilities and inabilities reach—past actual events into counter-factual events—can we ascertain the extent of each person's overall liberty and the existence of many of his particular liberties. Until we know whether people would or would not have acted in certain ways if a given person had sought to do something, we cannot know whether that person was free to do that thing. Nor can we know whether the person was free to perform that action in combination with manifold subsequent actions. Thus, whether overt or implicit, counter-factual scenarios are indispensable for any enquiry into a person's liberty. By relying tacitly if not explicitly on such scenarios, which trace how people are disposed to act vis-à-vis one another, we take account of the central role of unmanifested dispositions in setting the bounds of people's freedom.

Before proceeding, we should momentarily pause for three clarificatory caveats that ought to be entered at the outset of this long section on the counter-factual dimension of negative liberty. *First*, the terms 'disposition' and 'inclination' are used interchangeably herein, as are 'disposed' and 'inclined'. *Second*, when discussing what people are disposed to do, this section will always be concentrating on what they are disposed to do *and are capable of doing*. If a person *P* is disposed to do *x* but is unable to do *x*, that disposition will not impinge on anyone else's freedoms or unfreedoms at all—save in so far as it would lead *P* to perform some other freedom-constraining or freedom-expanding action *y*, in which case we should construe his disposition as a disposition to do *y*. Hence, my references to dispositions are always references to dispositions-accompanied-by-abilities, even if the abilities are not expressly mentioned. Purely mental dispositions, with no efficacious connections to potential actions, are not the object of my attention in this section. *Third*, my references to dispositions are references to all-things-considered dispositions. That is, the inclinations on which this section focuses are not desires that may get outweighed or overridden by other desires. Rather, a disposition is a preparedness-to-act-in-a-certain-fashion that emerges from the various possibly conflicting desires harboured by a person. When my discussions indicate that somebody is inclined to act in a certain fashion in circumstances of some type *Q*, what is meant is that the person will indeed act in that fashion if *Q*-type circumstances arise. Thus, if something that would be a disposition is in fact outweighed by a more powerful countervailing impulse, it is not a disposition at all for the purposes of my discussions.

3.1. An Ostensible Difficulty

Martin van Hees has queried whether negative-liberty theorists can properly allow that the freedom and unfreedom of each person are substantially affected by the dispositions of other people. Van Hees suggests that such a thesis about people's dispositions is at odds with the view that the existence of any particular freedom or unfreedom is desire-independent. The latter view has been expounded in my second chapter and has been endorsed there as a central tenet of any acceptable negative-liberty doctrine. Hence, if van Hees's uneasiness were well-founded, we would have to rethink some of the fundaments of the theory which this book aspires to defend.

In support of his worries about a tension between an insistence on the desire-independence of freedoms/unfreedoms and an acknowledgment of the freedom-constraining role of behavioural dispositions, van Hees offers a couple of examples. He conjures up a scenario in which a bottle of beer can be snatched by either of two people. In the initial version of the scenario, one of the people hates alcohol and is not inclined to take the bottle of beer at all. She shudders at the thought of drinking the beer herself, and she has no wish to give it to anyone else. Hence, the other person (who may or may not like alcohol) is free to grab the bottle of beer, with a probability approaching 100 per cent. Van Hees then modifies the example by doing away with the assumption that one of the people is averse to liquor. We may now presume that the quondam hater of beer has developed a taste for alcohol and would be happy to take the bottle in order to quaff its contents. Let us suppose that, perhaps because of an enmity between the two people involved, there is no prospect of their sharing the bottle of beer. One or the other of them will take it. In that event, if the two people are of roughly equal strength and if they enjoy pretty much the same array of opportunities to grab the bottle, the shift in the first person's preferences will have reduced to approximately 50 per cent the probability that the other person will be free to get the beer. (In the circumstances here outlined, that level of probability obtains regardless of whether the other person is enthusiastic about the beer or uninterested in it.) If the first person is stronger than the other, or if she enjoys some especially advantageous opportunities to clutch the bottle of beer, the change in her preferences will have reduced the probability of the other person's liberty-to-snatch-the-bottle to a level below 50 per cent. Indeed, even if the first person is weaker or less agile than the other person, she will stand some chance of grasping the bottle—unless she is wholly incapacitated, of course. Notwithstanding her relative weakness, then, the alteration in her attitude toward the beer will have lowered the probability of the other person's freedom-to-get-the-bottle. Now, since the probabilities attached to our ascriptions of particular liberties will figure saliently in our calculations of each person's overall liberty (in ways intimated by Chapter 2 and more sustainedly expounded in Chapter 5), the transformation here in the first person's desires will be registered by our measurements as a diminution in the overall liberty of the other person. As van Hees writes, 'because of the change in [the first person's] preferences concerning beer, [the second person's] freedom has decreased'.[26] Such a result may seem incompatible with the notion of the desire-independence of freedoms and unfreedoms. Even starker is the putative incompatibility with that notion when a change in someone's inclinations has reduced the probability of some particular liberty of another person to a level closely approximating zero. After all, the upshot of such an eventuality is that a shift in the first person's desires and intentions has not only lessened the second person's overall freedom, but has also virtually eliminated one of that person's particular liberties.

Van Hees himself observes that his scenario recounts a connection between desires and freedoms/unfreedoms that is quite different from the connection posited by some opponents of negative-liberty theories. He recognizes that '[t]his relationship between preferences and freedom is causal and not, as in the case of the preference-based approaches [to the ascertainment of freedoms], conceptual'. Nonetheless, he believes that 'even with such a causal rather than conceptual relationship, some of the counterintuitive conclusions deriving from the preference-based approach may pop up again'. He elaborates: 'For instance, whereas in this example it cannot be said that suppressing a person's own desires can increase the person's freedom, his or her freedom can be increased by eliminating the desires of others'.[27]

Van Hees slightly later offers a somewhat more complicated example—involving a scheme of governmental regulation that will be enforced only if more than a few people engage in the practice proscribed by the scheme[28]—in order to illustrate the same apparent tension between the desire-independence of freedoms and the freedom-delimiting role of behavioural dispositions. However, the basic point illustrated by that example is the same as in the scenario involving the bottle of beer, and thus my riposte will concentrate on the bottle-snatching scenario. Van Hees himself, by distinguishing between causal and conceptual connections, has staked out a suitable line of response to his own argument. Let us begin by briefly recalling what the champions of negative-liberty doctrines are contending when they gainsay the

---

[26] Martin van Hees, *Legal Reductionism and Freedom* (Dordrecht: Kluwer Academic Publishers, 2000) [Van Hees, *Reductionism*], 133.

[27] Van Hees, *Reductionism*, 133, 134.   [28] Van Hees, *Reductionism*, 138–9.

desire-dependence of the existence of freedoms and unfreedoms. (My second chapter has presented a much more ample exposition, of which the next paragraph below is merely a laconic and partial synopsis.)

An affirmation of the desire-independence of the existence of freedoms and unfreedoms is focused above all on the outlook of the person P whose freedoms and unfreedoms are under scrutiny. Negative-liberty theorists submit that the favourableness or unfavourableness of P's attitude toward φ-ing (or towards the freedom-to-φ) has no bearing whatsoever on the correct answer to the question whether P is free-to-φ or not. He can be free to adopt some mode of conduct which he has not the slightest inclination to adopt—since his state of freedom consists in his being *unprevented* from undertaking that mode of conduct, rather than in his being *disposed* to undertake it. Likewise, he can be unfree to adopt some mode of conduct which he has not the faintest desire to adopt, since his aversion towards that mode of conduct is perfectly consistent with his having been precluded from engaging in it by the actions or dispositions-to-perform-actions of some other person(s). P cannot alter his overall liberty or any of his particular liberties by simply altering his preferences. Those preferences might importantly affect whether he *feels* free or unfree in any given situation, but they do not affect whether he *is* free or unfree therein. A prisoner who lacks any desire to leave his cell is just as plainly unfree to leave it as a fellow prisoner who yearns to escape. Conversely, a man who is easily able to purchase and consume radishes is at liberty to consume them even if he views them as rebarbative; he is no less plainly at liberty to consume them than someone else who can equally easily acquire them and who eats them with zest. (Of course, P's sincere or feigned manifestations of his desires can potentially affect his freedoms, by influencing the ways in which other people behave towards him or the ways in which they are disposed to behave towards him. Animals, too, could be influenced by some of those manifestations of his aims and attitudes. Nonetheless, P's desires themselves—as opposed to some manifestations thereof—will have no effect on his freedoms.[29] Moreover, even the manifestations of the desires will not

---

[29] In fanciful circumstances, the manifestations of a person's desires could consist simply in certain patterns of activity within his brain. Suppose that a scientist is monitoring those patterns within my brain, and that he therefore knows at a given time t whether I desire to perform some action X. If at t I do desire to perform X, the scientist will arrange for insurmountable impediments to my carrying out of that action. By contrast, if at t I do not desire to perform X, the scientist will leave open the option of my carrying out that action and will not close it off even if I later change my mind about X. In this situation, then, the

affect his freedoms except by eliciting certain reactions on the part of other people or animals. Any connections between his desires and his freedoms are causal rather than constitutive or conceptual.)

Now, although a negative-liberty theory's claims about the desire-independence of the existence of any freedoms or unfreedoms are focused principally on the sentiments of the person P whose freedoms or unfreedoms are under consideration, those claims are also focused to some degree on the sentiments of other people. Of relevance specifically is the *disengaged* approval or disapproval felt by other people. That is, the thesis of desire-independence pertains to any disapproval or approval by other people which does not lead them to prevent P from engaging in modes of conduct that would otherwise be feasible for him, and which does not lead them to enable P to engage in modes of conduct that would otherwise be infeasible for him. Favourable or hostile feelings wholly detached from any facilitative or preventive measures will have no effect on the liberty of the person(s) to whose behaviour the feelings apply. Other people's attitudes expand or constrict one's liberty only indirectly, through the supportive or obstructive steps which the attitudes impel those other people to take.

Although the disengaged sentiments of other people do not have any impact on the overall freedom or particular freedoms of P, their engaged sentiments have an indirect impact in the manner just suggested. That impact, however, does not perforce depend on the actual manifestation of the engaged sentiments through the occurrence of facilitative or obstructive measures. If no occasion arises that would call for the carrying out of such measures, then they will not be carried out. Nevertheless, if they *would* have been undertaken in the event that such an occasion had arisen, then the freedom or unfreedom created by those measures is already a facet of the relationships of P with the

---

impulses in my brain which reveal my desires to a knowledgeable observer will have a decisive bearing on my subsequent freedom to perform X. We shall reach a similar conclusion if we assume that the scientist will react to my desires in a converse manner. That is, if at t I desire to perform X, he will leave me unobstructed from carrying out that action. By contrast, if at t I do not desire to perform X, he will arrange for insurmountable impediments to my carrying out of that action and will leave those impediments in place even if I later change my mind about X. Thus, once again, the impulses in my brain which evince my desires to a knowledgeable observer will have a decisive bearing on my subsequent freedom to perform X. What is crucial in each of these two situations, however, is that my desires affect my freedom only by being made manifest to someone else who reacts to them. Without the manifestations and reactions, the desires would not impinge on the existence of my freedoms at all.

people around him. Any such freedom or unfreedom can unproblematically be ascribed to *P*.

Suppose, for example, that *P* lives in a well-fortified apartment building in the middle of New York City. Whenever a resident of the building wishes to leave through the front doors—the only set of doors—a security guard has to release the computerized locks. If *P* relaxes lazily one morning and consequently makes no attempt to go out of his building before noon, the security guard during the morning will have no occasion to release the locks for him. Nonetheless, if the guard would have released the locks in the event that *P* had indeed sought to exit from the building, then *P* has been free throughout the morning to leave through the front doors. Because of the guard's preparedness to open those doors if *P* should endeavour to depart, *P* is unprevented from departing. He is free in that respect.

Although the security guard's preparedness to unseal the locks for the residents can stem from any number of motivations, let us presume that it derives chiefly from his perception of the operations of the apartment building as decent and legitimate. That perception underlies the alacrity of his responsiveness to the needs of the residents. Now suppose that the guard undergoes an abrupt change of mind about the legitimacy of the workings of the apartment building. He decides that, throughout his morning on duty, he will refuse to unlock the doors of the building for any resident who wants to leave. (Let us assume that the residents cannot individually or collectively open the doors without the cooperation of the guard—who, sitting behind an impregnable barrier, is physically inaccessible to them—and let us also assume that any 'rescue' of the residents by people from outside the building would succeed only after several hours.) If *P* lounges in bed throughout the morning and does not make any attempt to leave the building, then there will not be any occasion for the guard to decline to release the locks for him. Nevertheless, because the guard would have refused to release the locks if *P* had sought to go outside, *P* has been unfree to depart from his building throughout the morning. He has been prevented from departing, even though the absence of any attempted departures by him has obviated any manifestation of the guard's disposition to thwart all such attempts.

In the scenario just recounted, as in each of van Hees's scenarios, a change in somebody's preferences or attitudes has impaired the overall freedom of somebody else. However, in each case, the shift in the person's attitudes has produced such an effect only indirectly. Solely because the alteration in the security guard's outlook has issued in his preparedness to prevent residents from exiting, does that alteration diminish the residents' liberty. If the guard's feelings about his job had changed without any corresponding transformation in his perform-ance of the job (apart from a bit of sullenness, perhaps), then no resident's freedom would have been affected at all. The guard's feelings in themselves have no impact on what the residents can do or be or become or undergo. If his newly hostile attitudes had remained strictly disengaged—that is, if they had not disposed him to give vent to his hostility by refusing to release the locks on the doors when requested to do so—the shift in his sentiments could have been safely ignored in any calculation of each resident's overall liberty. However, his trans-figured attitudes are engaged; on the basis of those attitudes, he is fully disposed to keep the residents confined by declining to unlock the doors for them. Only because his negative feelings are indeed operative in this manner (or in some cognate manner) do they play any role in limiting people's freedom.

In other words, van Hees's examples and my own example of the guard and the residents do not clash at all with the negative-liberty theorists' insistence on the desire-independence of the existence of freedoms and unfreedoms. None of the aforementioned examples involves a situation in which the existence of anybody's freedoms/unfreedoms or the extent of anybody's overall liberty is directly deter-mined by the desires of some other person(s). Rather, in each scenario the direct determinant is some actual behaviour or some behavioural disposition on the part of the other person (whom I shall designate generically as 'Q'). To be sure, underlying that behaviour or disposition are Q's transformed attitudes. All the same, as is evident in each scenario, those attitudes bear on anyone else's freedom only indirectly by inclin-ing Q to act in liberty-promotive or liberty-restrictive ways. Without that link to some conduct by Q—whether the conduct is actually undertaken or whether instead it would have been undertaken in cir-cumstances that have not materialized—the altered feelings harboured by Q will be of no relevance to anybody else's liberty. In this respect, then, the scenarios presented by van Hees and by me diverge crucially from those assailed by negative-liberty theorists who are underscoring the desire-independence of particular freedoms. Such theorists are reacting to accounts of situations in which freedoms/unfreedoms are supposedly engendered or eliminated by mere changes in people's desires unconnected to any changes in behaviour or behavioural dispos-itions. Negative-liberty theorists are correct to contend that mere atti-tudinal changes of the sort just mentioned cannot affect the particular freedoms/unfreedoms or overall liberty of anyone. For example, a prisoner who has come to relish his state of shackled immobility does not thereby augment his own overall freedom; his newly developed zest does not expand the range of the combinations of actions or processes or states that are available to him. To assert that the prisoner has augmented his freedom is to make the mistake of presuming that somebody can effect an objective change in material features of the world by simply thinking about them differently. In my apartment-building example and in van Hees's bottle-grabbing example, by contrast, the transformations undergone by the security guard and the one-time hater of beer are not merely attitudinal. Neither example portrays a setting in which some-body has simply started to think about things differently. Instead, the transformations extend to the conduct and behavioural dispositions of the guard and the alcohol-hater—conduct and behavioural dispositions which, in the aftermath of the transformations, objectively constrain the freedom of the other people involved. In those examples, in other words, there are indeed objective changes in material features of the world. Alterations in conduct and in behavioural inclinations produce alter-ations in other people's liberty, through the actual or dispositional clamping of curbs on their latitude.

Thus, when van Hees submits (in a statement quoted already) that his example involving a bottle of beer has depicted a structure of interaction in which someone's 'freedom can be increased by eliminating the desires of others', his pronouncement might not be strictly wrong but is at best highly misleading. If we plausibly assume that the person initially averse to beer would not subsequently have sought to snatch the bottle unless his attitude toward the beverage had altered, and if we plausibly assume that the security guard in the apartment building would not have become disposed to immure the residents unless his feelings about his job had shifted, we can endorse a certain version (a harmless version) of the quoted statement. That is, we can accept that the expunction of the guard's newly embittered feelings or of the erstwhile beer-hater's newly acquired fondness for alcohol would increase the freedom of one or more other people. However, we should accept such a claim only because—as we are assuming—the sense of disgruntlement or the hankering for beer is a necessary condition for the occurrence of free-dom-constraining actions or for the emergence of freedom-constrain-ing dispositions. Such actions or dispositions are the direct causes of reductions in the freedom of other people. The removal of those actions or dispositions is what will avert those reductions and is what will thereby effectively increase the freedom of the other people. Any free-dom-expanding importance attached to the elimination of certain desires is due entirely to the role of those desires in impelling the aforementioned actions and dispositions. In themselves, disengaged from the prompting of those actions and dispositions, the desires are of no relevance to other people's freedom. So long as this point about the irrelevance of desires in themselves is recognized, an insistence on the desire-independence of the existence of freedoms and unfreedoms will have been duly upheld.

3.2. Under Threat

One of the most frequently discussed problems relating to the effects of behavioural dispositions on other people's freedom is the nature of threats. When somebody issues a genuine threat, he intends to inflict some untoward consequence on the addressee of the threat if and only if the addressee refuses to comply with the threatener's demands. If the threat is genuine, moreover, the person issuing it is capable of imposing the sanction—or at least part of the sanction—which he has indicated as the penalty for recalcitrance by the addressee. Plainly, then, a threatener will be curtailing the overall liberty of the person who is threatened. Pinning down how and when the curtailment takes place, however, is a task that has generated considerable controversy among political philosophers.[30]

3.2.1. A Focus on Overall Freedom   My approach to this matter should be readily inferable from Chapter 2, which discussed more than once the punishments attached to legal mandates. The gist of that chapter's treatment of legal sanctions can be generalized to situations involving other sorts of threats. Crucial to any adequate analysis

---

[30] For an analysis that powerfully supersedes all previous discussions of this topic, see Carter, *Measure*, 224–32. Quite a few of the treatments of the topic from the third quarter of the twentieth century are cited and assessed in J. P. Day, 'Threats, Offers, Law, Opinion and Liberty', 14 *American Philosophical Quarterly* 257 (1977) [Day, 'Threats']. For some of the treatments from more recent decades, see Joel Feinberg, 'The Interest in Liberty on the Scales', in Alvin Goldman and Jaegwon Kim (eds), *Values and Morals* (Dordrecht: D. Reidel Publishing, 1978) [Feinberg, 'Interest'], 21, 28–9; Gray, 'Negative', 53; T. Gray, *Freedom*, 23–8; Kristján Kristjánsson, 'Freedom, Offers, and Obstacles', 29 *American Philosophical Quarterly* 63 (1992) [Kristjánsson, 'Offers']; Kristján Kristjánsson, *Social Freedom* (Cambridge: Cambridge University Press, 1996) [Kristjánsson, *Freedom*], Ch. 3; J. Roland Pennock, *Democratic Political Theory* (Princeton: Princeton University Press, 1979), 20–3; Steiner, *Essay*, 22–32; Christine Swanton, *Freedom: A Coherence Theory* (Indianapolis: Hackett, 1992), Ch. 8; Taylor, *Community*, 143–7; Albert Weale, *Political Theory and Social Policy* (London: Macmillan, 1983), 51–2.

of such situations—for the purposes of this book—is the distinction between particular freedoms and overall freedom. Usually, an addressee of a threat is able to perform the action which the threatener seeks to discourage. For example, as Chapter 2 several times mentioned, numerous legal requirements (especially in liberal democracies) are enforced through post-violation punishments rather than through anticipatory preventive measures. Many other threats are similar in this respect. Hence, we cannot normally single out the freedom-constricting impact of a threatener's behaviour if we look only at the action or set of actions which the threatener aims to deter. Instead of inquiring whether the recipient of his threat is free to carry out that action or set of actions, we should be inquiring about the range of the recipient's combinations of conjunctively exercisable liberties. That range will be narrowed by the behaviour of someone who issues any genuine threat (not least, of course, when the threatener does take effective anticipatory preventative measures to block the action or set of actions which he wishes to avert).

When we concentrate on the level of overall liberty, we can see that somebody uttering a genuine threat will have precluded his addressee from exercising certain particular freedoms conjunctively. More precisely, the following pair of particular freedoms cannot be exercised conjunctively by the recipient of a genuine threat: the freedom to adopt the mode of conduct which the threatener is trying to discourage, and the freedom to undertake any mode of conduct that will be stymied by the threatener's infliction of a penalty for non-compliance. Manifestly, if the issuer of a threat takes steps to eliminate the recipient's freedom to adopt a certain mode of conduct, then that non-existent freedom cannot be exercised conjunctively with any other freedoms. However, even if (as is typically true) the issuer of a genuine threat does not eradicate the particular liberty which he presses his addressee to forbear from exercising, that liberty cannot be exercised conjunctively with any liberties that will be negated by the sanction imposed on the addressee if she declines to abide by the threatener's wishes. In other words, unlike a focus on the specific action(s) which a threatener aims to discourage his addressee from performing, a focus on the addressee's overall liberty will enable us to analyse the freedom-cabining effects of every situation involving a genuine threat.

3.2.2. Joint Actions and Anomalous Threats Before we ponder exactly when the freedom-impairing effects of a minatory intervention occur, we should consider whether every recipient of *every* genuine threat will have undergone such effects. A genuine threat, let us recall, is issued by someone who intends to bring about (and is capable of bringing about) an undesirable consequence for the recipient of the threat if and only if the recipient does not conform with the threatener's demands. Can there be any genuine threat that carries a penalty which would not affect the overall freedom of the threat's recipient? Ian Carter has suggested that the answer to this question is affirmative, when he mentions the possibility of a threat with an attached sanction that 'involves the punishment of someone other than the agent—presumably of someone about whom the agent cares'. He offers the following example of such a threat: '[G]ive me $1,000 or I'll kill your brother'.[31] Some even more vivid examples of threats along these lines can be imagined. For instance, suppose that John sincerely delivers the following ultimatum to Mary: 'Agree to marry me by the end of this week, or I'll kill myself.' Let us suppose that Mary feels fond of John and that his ultimatum is therefore indeed a threat rather than an unwitting offer. Nevertheless, the implementation of that threat will not inflict bodily injury on Mary and will not deprive her of any resources that are vital for her activities. (We may presume that Mary is not dependent on John for financial support or for the provision of any other resources.) Should we conclude, then, that the effectuation of a genuine threat of this kind will not at all redound to the detriment of the freedom of the threat's addressee?

Carter does draw such a conclusion. With reference to his own example of a threat by someone to kill the brother of someone else, he prescinds from various inessential factors and then arrives at the verdict that (in the absence of those factors) the killing will not impair the overall liberty of the threat's addressee: 'We can assume ... that, despite the agent caring about his brother, the brother never does anything to enhance the agent's freedom—for example, by presenting him with gifts (for this would imply that a threat to kill the agent's brother would refer to at least something of a reduction in the agent's overall freedom). On the above analysis, the threatener does not in such cases reduce the overall freedom of the recipient.' We are told that the situation of the agent 'is one in which the sanction does not involve the removal of any of the agent's own options'.[32] Let us assume with Carter that the brother never provides the agent with any resources that facilitate the performance of various activities. Nonetheless, we should distance ourselves from the conclusion that the

---

[31] Carter, *Measure*, 230.   [32] Ibid.

agent's overall liberty will not in any way be affected by the slaying of the brother. Though the impact on the agent's overall freedom will hardly be the most salient aspect of the harm caused to the agent by his brother's death, such an impact will indeed have occurred. Certain options previously available to the agent will no longer be so, and thus his overall freedom will have been abridged pro tanto. Those options cover the myriad actions which the agent could have undertaken with his brother. He will no longer be free to wrestle with his brother or to attend a baseball game with him or to exchange ideas and banter with him. To be sure, the agent remains free to perform any of those activities with people other than his brother (if he can prevail upon them to join him in those activities). For that matter, he can attend a baseball game by himself. All the same, the options with contents precisely specifiable as instances of those activities undertaken *with his brother* are no longer available to him.

Carter at a later juncture in his book recognizes the importance of what he designates as 'joint actions'. A joint action is something that can be done by two or more people in concert but not by any of them separately. Any liberty-to-perform-a-joint-action will contribute to the overall liberty of each person who can undertake the action with others, by an amount that should be 'represented by the number we assign to the combination of equal spatio-temporally specified event-units that constitute the [action], divided by the number of agents whose basic actions are necessary in order for that [action] to be brought about'.[33] When an agent Alan is threatened with the slaying of his brother if Alan declines to submit to the threatener's demands, the carrying out of the threat will deprive Alan of many opportunities for joint actions. He will no longer be able to wrestle with his brother or to throw around a baseball with him or to converse with him or to trade insults with him, and so forth. Of course, as has been acknowledged, Alan will continue to be free to participate in those activities with other people. But the array of joint actions constituted by his participating *with his brother* in any of those sundry activities will have ceased to be open to him. The closing off of those potential joint actions—which would otherwise be available to him as options—is a major freedom-cabining consequence of the threatener's effectuation of the ultimatum concerning the murder of Alan's brother.

Carter might wish to classify some of those potential paths of conduct by Alan and his brother as separately performable individual actions rather than as joint actions.[34] He would certainly apply such a

---

[33] Carter, *Measure*, 250.   [34] Carter, *Measure*, 254, 257.

classification to the activity of attending a baseball game with a brother, mentioned in my penultimate paragraph. In so doing, he would point to the fact that Alan can perform exactly the same bodily movements with or without his brother's participation. Such a claim is undoubtedly correct in connection with attendance at a baseball game, and is probably correct in connection with some of the other activities mentioned here. Nevertheless, that claim does not warrant the withholding of the 'joint actions' designation. Not all of an agent's actions comprise only his own bodily movements; most such actions comprise the use or positioning of other objects as well. Among those objects can be the bodies of other agents, each of which carries its own spatio-temporally distinct history. Any action carried out by Alan in collaboration with the body and mind of some particular agent *B* is different from a parallel action carried out by Alan in collaboration with the body and mind of some other agent *C*, since the entities that amount to the components of the former action are not the same as the entities that amount to the components of the latter. Equally clearly, the entities that amount to the components of the former action are different from the entities that amount to the components of any action performed by Alan in the presence of nobody other than himself. A conversation or wrestling match with a sibling is not the same as a conversation or wrestling match with a stranger, even if one's own bodily movements are identical between the two. Much the same can be said about a conversation with a sibling versus a conversation with oneself. Thus, an action correctly characterized as something undertaken with one's brother is indeed a joint action in Carter's sense. It is not an action that can be performed by oneself, even if one can engage in all the same movements of one's own body by oneself. To be something undertaken with one's brother, the action must be performed with the specified sibling.

To be sure, the analysis presented in the last few paragraphs has revealed that every death throughout the world should in principle get taken into account when we are seeking to ascertain the overall freedom of Alan or any other individual. If Alan resides and works in Massachusetts, for example, his overall freedom is reduced in some respects when an inhabitant of a remote African village who has never had any contact with him whatsoever is murdered. Alan has lost all opportunities to engage in joint actions with the murdered person. Doubtless, he would never have chosen to avail himself of any of those opportunities, which could not have been taken up without considerable difficulty and cost; but the existence of the opportunities is not dependent on the likelihood of their being pursued.

In principle, then, there is not any line to be drawn between those people whose deaths matter to Alan's overall freedom and those people whose deaths do not so matter. Though the opportunities for his interacting with this or that person P in any remote land will hardly be conspicuous, they do exist—until a juncture not very long before P's death or Alan's death, when the physical possibility of any contact between Alan and P will have come to an end. If P has died naturally, her death bears on the overall freedom of Alan only inasmuch as it definitively puts an end to the opportunities for joint actions carried out by the two of them. Solely the freedoms covered by the F Postulate, and not the unfreedoms covered by the U Postulate, are implicated. If P has instead died as a result of human actions (her own actions or anyone else's), her demise not merely has the opportunity-terminating effects of a natural death but also is creative of unfreedom for Alan. Both the domain of the F Postulate and the domain of the U Postulate are here implicated. Squelched opportunities for joint actions that could have materialized between the time of P's unnatural death and the time of what would have been her natural demise are instances of unfreedom for Alan, since the decisive squelching of those opportunities is due to somebody else's actions (whether those of P herself or of anyone else). To be sure, the negated opportunities would not have figured in many of the combinations-of-conjunctively-exercisable-liberties enjoyed by Alan, since his availing himself of those opportunities would have been inconsistent with his availing himself of most of the other options open to him. Accordingly, the opportunities for interaction with P would have added little to Alan's overall freedom, and any loss of those opportunities through the actions of some other person(s) will have added little to his unfreedom. Nevertheless, tiny though those opportunities' contributions to his overall liberty would have been, they would indeed have amounted to contributions. Thus, we should acknowledge that in principle the demise of each person P in a remote land will impinge on Alan's overall liberty. Any man's death diminishes me.

Of course, the effect of a *brother's* demise on Alan's overall freedom will be much more evident. Even if the brothers do not in fact get together very often, and indeed even if they feel very little affection for each other, the fraternal connection between them ensures that recognizable opportunities for joint actions are present irrespective of whether those opportunities are frequently taken. (Perhaps the sole opportunities taken are those for joint actions which consist in exchanges of taunts and blows.) Their fraternal connection, whether marked by solicitude and affection or not, singles each of them out for the other in a way that sustains distinctive opportunities for their interaction. Hence, the removal of those opportunities is something that must plainly be taken into account when we gauge the extent of Alan's overall freedom. The implementation of a threat to kill the brother is a source of unfreedom for Alan, and is thus an occurrence that impairs his overall liberty *pro tanto*. (Here, as in Chapter 2, the words '*pro tanto*' are important. The death of the brother might produce consequences that expand Alan's overall liberty. We certainly cannot know a priori whether the effectuation of the threat concerning the brother will result in a net increase or a net decrease in Alan's overall freedom. What we can know, however, is that the effectuation will inevitably impinge on the overall freedom of Alan by removing some of the options that would otherwise be available to him. In other words, the key point contested here is Carter's claim—quoted near the outset of this discussion—that 'the sanction does not involve the removal of any of [Alan's] own options'. Whatever may be the net effect on the overall liberty of Alan, the sanction imposed against him for his non-compliance will certainly take away some of his options.)

Let us proceed to ponder other threats that would not similarly eliminate any opportunities for joint actions on the part of the recipient Alan. Consider the following ultimatum, which is decidedly unusual but not utterly unintelligible: 'Give me $1,000, or else my henchman who is currently in a remote African village—and who is reachable through a mobile telephone—will pummel one of the inhabitants there. The beating inflicted on that inhabitant will leave him in pain for a day or two, though it will not incapacitate him.' Many other similar threats can be imagined. Indeed, such threats need not even involve any bodily injury to human beings. For example, an imaginative hoodlum might deliver the following ultimatum to Alan: 'Give me $1,000, or else my henchman will destroy a magnificent painting by Rembrandt to which he has managed to gain access in an institution where the painting is normally closed off to everyone who is not a member of the institution.' Let us presume that, quite independently of the henchman's mischief, Alan will never be able to gain access to the painting himself. And let us presume that his inability to gain such access—his inability to become a member of the institution where the painting hangs in seclusion from public view—is readily ascertainable. Again, many other similar threats can be imagined.

The effectuation of either of the threats posited in my last paragraph will have no impact whatsoever on the range of actions available (now or in the future) to the recipient of each threat, Alan. After all, because the African villager who undergoes the thrashing by the henchman will not be incapacitated by it, any opportunities for joint actions involving the villager and Alan—opportunities that will almost certainly not be taken up—will remain unaffected. Likewise, because Alan will not be able to gain access to the painting by Rembrandt at any future juncture regardless of whether it still exists or not, the destruction of it will not reduce the array of opportunities-for-actions that are open to him. Hence, we here behold some genuine threats that when implemented will not affect the range of actions available to their recipient.

Moreover, we have solid grounds for thinking that the aforementioned threats stand reasonably good chances of being efficacious. If Alan is an ordinarily decent person, he will undoubtedly regard the possibility of averting the infliction of harm on others—or on precious artefacts—as an important reason-for-action. He might decide that the price of complying with the threatener's wishes is too high, but he will not choose lightly to avoid that price. He will weigh it against the moral burden of becoming implicated (however unwillingly) in the perpetration of wrongs against other people. Only if that moral onus is less weighty than the substantial hardships caused by bowing to the threatener's demands, will Alan decline to do what the threatener has directed him to do. Clearly, then, each ultimatum broached in the penultimate paragraph above is potentially efficacious in motivating certain conduct on the part of its addressee. Each ultimatum, undergirded by the threatener's intention and ability to impose the specified penalty for non-compliance, is a genuine threat. Yet, as has been observed, the implementation of either ultimatum will not have any bearing on the range of actions that can be undertaken by Alan. Should we therefore conclude with Carter that some encounters marked by genuine threats do not affect the overall liberty of the threats' addressees?

To see why a negative answer is justified here, we should recollect my earlier rejection of Carter's view that potential actions are the only contents of freedoms and unfreedoms. An affirmative answer to the question just posed would overlook a basic way in which anyone who genuinely threatens to commit harm against some third party in the event of uncooperativeness by the threatener's interlocutor will have constricted the interlocutor's overall liberty *pro tanto*. In respect of the interlocutor—as opposed to the third party—this freedom-constricting impact is the lone freedom-impairing upshot associated with each of the two specific threats that we are now considering. In order to discern it, we have to recall that 'becomings' as well as 'doings' are among the occurrences to which freedoms and unfreedoms can pertain.

As has been suggested, Alan will become implicated in the infliction of harm on a third party (or on a magnificent work of art) if he refuses to give in to the hoodlum's demands. To be sure, his involvement may be fully excusable if his decision against relenting is reasonable. Even if not quite fully excusable, his involvement will obviously not saddle him with the same degree of culpability that attaches to the hoodlum and the henchman. Moreover, Alan is undoubtedly horrified at having been placed in the position of determining whether somebody else will suffer serious harm. Nonetheless, his opting for non-compliance with the threatener's wishes is a necessary condition for the occurrence of that harm. His choice between non-compliance and compliance thus plays a pivotal role in bringing about or forestalling the infliction of the harm. If Alan chooses not to capitulate to the hoodlum's demands, we can correctly ascribe to him responsibility for the resultant harm to the third party—even if his refusal to obey is reasonable, and his responsibility is therefore purely causal rather than moral. (By concentrating on genuine threats, my discussion takes as given that the hoodlum is not bluffing in either of two opposite directions. First, he will indeed order the carrying out of his threat if Alan does not comply with his behest. Second, and more important for the present point, the hoodlum will order the carrying out of the threat *only if* Alan does not comply with the behest. If the henchman would inflict the specified harm on the third party regardless of whether Alan were to heed or flout the hoodlum's dictates, then those dictates would not constitute a genuine threat. They would not articulate any veritable reason for Alan to surrender his money.)

Alan is of course free to avoid becoming partly responsible for injurious measures against the third party. After all, he can relinquish his money to the hoodlum and can thereby avert the undertaking of those measures. The hoodlum's preparedness to follow through on his threat in the event of Alan's unyieldingness does not in any way deprive Alan of his particular freedom-to-avoid-becoming-partly-responsible-for-the-effectuation-of-the-threat. What the preparedness of the hoodlum to follow through on the threat does do, however, is to impinge on Alan's overall liberty by removing some of his combinations of conjunctively exercisable freedoms. No longer a conjunctively exercisable set is any combination that includes both Alan's freedom to retain his money and his freedom not to become partly responsible for a third party's suffering. If Alan exercises the first of those freedoms, the second will have been negated. Because the exercise of the first of those freedoms will now terminate the existence of the second, and because any combination of his particular liberties that encompasses those freedoms is thus no longer a conjunctively exercisable array, Alan has undergone a *pro-tanto* impairment of his overall freedom.

To be sure, the impairment is only a *pro-tanto* reduction. Though any combination of liberties of the sort just mentioned is no longer a conjunctively exercisable set, a host of new combinations of conjunctively exercisable freedoms have become available to Alan. Until the hoodlum and the henchman became inclined to harm a distant third party in the event of Alan's non-compliance with their demands, the option of causing harm to that third party in the near future was not available to Alan. That option is now available to him as an element in many new combinations of conjunctively exercisable freedoms, which are new precisely because of their inclusion of that element. Whereas previously Alan could not have caused harm to the distant third party by retaining his own money, he now faces exactly that opportunity. Repellent though such an opportunity may be, it is indeed a fresh opportunity that constitutes a *pro-tanto* expansion of his overall freedom by providing him with many novel combinations of conjunctively exercisable liberties. Nevertheless, although the *pro-tanto* curtailment of Alan's overall freedom discussed in my last paragraph is accompanied by the *pro-tanto* enlargement discussed here, the key point is that the *pro-tanto* curtailment has indeed occurred. As has already been indicated, the message of the present discussion is not that every encounter involving a genuine threat will have produced a net diminution in the overall liberty of the threat's recipient. Rather, the message is that every such encounter will have removed some of the recipient's combinations of conjunctively exercisable freedoms and will thus have reduced his overall liberty *pro tanto*.

In sum, once we allow that 'becomings' and 'not becomings' (along with 'doings' and 'not doings') are among the contents of freedoms and unfreedoms, we are able to descry two respects in which somebody who issues a genuine threat-to-harm-a-third-party will have curtailed the freedom of the addressee of the threat. In the first place, because there almost certainly exist some opportunities for interaction between the addressee and the endangered third party—even if the likelihood of the pursuit of those opportunities by the people involved is vanishingly minute—any loss of those opportunities occasioned by the infliction of irreversible harm on the third party is itself a *pro-tanto* reduction in the addressee's overall liberty. Of even broader importance is the other way in which the person who issues a genuine threat-to-harm-a-third-party will have abridged the overall freedom of the threat's recipient. Whenever any such ultimatum is advanced, the person wielding it has deprived his addressee of the liberty to defy the threatener's dictates without becoming partly responsible for the mistreatment of a third party. To be sure, as my last paragraph has observed, the abridgement of the addressee's overall freedom is accompanied by the augmentation thereof; some combinations of conjunctively exercisable liberties have been eliminated, but other such combinations have become newly available. All the same, the central point is that some such combinations have indeed been eliminated. Hence, having parted ways with Carter by adopting a more expansive view of the range of possible occurrences and states to which freedoms and unfreedoms can pertain, this book has here parted ways with him again by adopting a more expansive view of the freedom-impairing effects of all situations involving genuine threats.

3.2.3. The Time of Curtailment   We now need to pin down the time at which the freedom-constraining effects of a threatener's conduct occur. Discussions of this topic all too often suggest that those effects begin with the issuance of a genuine threat, or with the addressee's receipt of the threat, or with the threatener's imposition of the announced penalty for the addressee's non-compliance. In fact, however, the matter of timing is more subtle. Although either of the first two junctures just specified can sometimes be the point at which a threatener's conduct begins to constrict the freedom of the recipient of a threat, neither of those junctures is necessarily or invariably that point. The unfreedom of the recipient typically begins somewhat earlier. Though the difference in time is not usually very large, it is important theoretically; by taking account of that difference, we can locate the precise source and character of the recipient's unfreedom.

Let us concentrate here on the situation of someone who is the recipient of a genuine threat and who is not physically prevented from acting at odds with the threatener's behest. Purely for ease of exposition, let us also assume that the threatened penalty for non-compliance is the imposition of an injury or some other hardship on the recipient herself. (The anomalous threats examined in my last subsection could easily be accommodated in my present discussion, but a consideration of them here would introduce gratuitous complexities.) In a situation of the sort here envisaged, the recipient's unfreedom consists in her being unable to perform the following combination(s) of actions: any action(s) that would amount to a defiance of the threatener's dictate, and any action(s) that would be precluded by the threatener's imposition of a sanction for the flouting of his wishes. When does that unfreedom arise? We know from the U Postulate that someone otherwise capable of φ-ing is unfree-to-φ when somebody else's actions or dispositions-to-perform-some-actions prevent him from φ-ing, regardless of whether he endeavours to φ. In the current context, of course, the 'φ' variable designates the threatened person's performance of any combination(s) of actions along the lines stated above. Hence, in inquiring about the emergence of the threatened person's unfreedom, we are asking two conditional questions. If the recipient of the threat defies the threatener's behest, when does the threatener's conduct ensure that the recipient will be unable to perform any action(s) ruled out by the penalty for her recalcitrance? If the recipient does not defy the threatener's behest, when does the threatener's conduct ensure that the recipient would have been unable to perform any actions ruled out by the penalty for her recalcitrance if she had opted to disregard his demand?

While the correct answer to each of the two foregoing queries is of course the same, my preceding paragraph's separation of them enables us immediately to perceive the erroneousness of one of the principal ways in which this matter has sometimes been analysed by other theorists. Specifically, theorists have gone astray in so far as they suggest that the unfreedom created by the issuer of a genuine threat begins with the effectuation of the threat. To maintain that the unfreedom of a genuine threat's addressee begins with the implementation of the threat is to maintain in effect that the addressee has not been made unfree at all if she has chosen to bow to the threatener's dictates; after all, if the addressee has made such a choice, the threat will never be implemented. Such an answer to our bifurcated inquiry about the emergence of the addressee's unfreedom cannot be correct, for the second strand of that inquiry—as formulated in accordance with the U Postulate—presupposes that the addressee has been made unfree even if she does yield to the threatener's behest. Whereas our inquiry is duly attuned to the counter-factual dimension of freedom and unfreedom, an answer focused on the execution of a threat will have elided that dimension entirely. Such an answer mistakenly concentrates only on preventive measures that do actually come about, and it ignores altogether the preventive measures that would have come about if the recipient of the threat had been less cooperative or less craven.

We should therefore train our attention on the other two answers to our inquiry that have frequently been put forward by theorists. Should we accept that the freedom-constricting impact of a threatener's conduct begins either with his issuance of a genuine threat or with the addressee's receipt of such a threat? Though in application to some situations we should answer this latest question affirmatively, an affirmative answer is not generally warranted. The issuance of a genuine threat is typically a means of signalling to the recipient that the threatener has formed an inclination to take certain punitive steps if the recipient does not behave in some specified way(s). What is crucial in the curtailing of the recipient's freedom is the threatener's inclination—an inclination to prevent the recipient from performing any combination(s) of actions of the kind delineated two paragraphs ago. Precisely because the threatener is fully prepared and determined to inflict some sanction(s) if his demands are resisted by his addressee, the addressee's combinations of options have been abridged. The issuance of the genuine threat itself is a means of *manifesting* or *signalling* the threatener's inclination (in order to achieve his aim), but is not usually the event by which the inclination is *generated* or *initiated*.

To be sure, the articulation of a genuine threat can sometimes itself be the originating occasion for the inclination which the threat expresses. Typically, however, the inclination precedes the threat that serves as its vehicle—though the interval between the formation of the one and the delivery of the other is undoubtedly often very brief. In typical circumstances, then, the moment of the issuance of a genuine threat is not the juncture at which the addressee's unfreedom begins. That unfreedom, the addressee's unfreedom to carry out any combination(s) of actions along the lines described three paragraphs ago, has antedated the threat which makes the unfreedom evident.

Of course, the issuance of a genuine threat is more than simply a signal of the threatener's inclination. As such a signal, plainly, it is also a means of inducing the recipient of the threat to act in accordance with the threatener's wishes. If the threat does not succeed in that respect—for whatever reason—the threatener will have failed in his primary objective. Moreover, if the circumstances are such that the threat cannot be communicated or received, the person seeking to issue it might decide not to take any measures against the intended recipient until the threat can be imparted properly. Though such a decision is certainly not inevitable, it will often be sensible; perhaps the threatener will be motivated by a concern for fairness, or perhaps he will simply wish to pursue his primary objective of eliciting the compliance of his addressee with his behest (an objective that might well be set back if the addressee is punished without having been given an opportunity to comply). When a threatener will indeed decline to inflict any sanctions on his intended addressee until he can convey to the addressee his ultimatum, the issuance and receipt of the ultimatum are necessary

conditions for the infliction of the sanctions. They are therefore necessary conditions for the unfreedom of the addressee in the respects that
I have been discussing. Should we accordingly align ourselves with
those theorists who perceive the moment of the issuance of a genuine
threat as the point at which the threat's recipient has been rendered
unfree by the threatener? (In my answer to this question, I shall not
ponder any situation in which a threat is suitably delivered but not
received. My discussion will assume that an ultimatum adequately
issued is an ultimatum absorbed. An examination of circumstances
which are not covered by that assumption would make my analysis
tediously cumbersome and would not raise any new points of theoretical interest.)

As has already been stated, there are indeed some contexts in regard
to which we can correctly maintain that the time of the communication
of a genuine threat is the stage at which the recipient's unfreedom
begins. When a threatener is inclined to suspend any imposition of
penalties until his threat can be communicated, and when an opportunity for sufficient communication arises very unexpectedly, we can
rightly conclude that his seizing of that opportunity is the moment at
which his addressee becomes unfree. On the other hand, there are
numerous contexts in which at least one of the two conditions just
mentioned is absent. In the first place, a threatener need not be inclined
to forbear from acting punitively against his intended addressee in
circumstances where he has not been able to convey his ultimatum
successfully; perhaps the threatener remains unaware that his threat
has not been imparted properly, or perhaps he simply does not care
whether the intended addressee has had an opportunity to comply or
not. Even more important is a second point. Notwithstanding the
preparedness of a threatener to forbear from punitive measures in the
event of his having failed to communicate his ultimatum adequately,
he may correctly anticipate that he will enjoy any number of clear-cut
opportunities for the communication—in which case the unfreedom of
the addressee has begun at the time of the formation of the threatener's
coercive intention, rather than at the time when that intention is voiced
as an ultimatum. For example, if a mother sees that her ten-year-old
son is refusing to eat the vegetables that she has served for dinner, and if
she consequently forms the intention to withhold his dessert from him
if he disregards her behest to consume his carrots and broccoli, she will
know that she can easily articulate her intention to him five seconds
later as an ultimatum. In this scenario, the son's unfreedom consists in
his being unable to perform the following combination of actions:
rejecting the vegetables that have been served, and consuming the

dessert that his mother has prepared. In the circumstances envisaged, his unfreedom arises when his mother forms her conditionally punitive intention—rather than at the slightly later stage when she signals that intention to him as a threat. At that slightly later stage, the son has already become unfree.

Of course, in the example just sketched, the interval between the forming of the intention and the issuance of the ultimatum is extremely short. *Ceteris paribus*, the transitoriness of the interval helps to ensure that the mother when she forms her intention will know that she can easily express it to her son. In many other situations (though certainly not all other situations) where the prospects for forcefully perspicuous communication between threateners and addressees are very good, the corresponding intervals will likewise be brief. In any event, regardless of whether the period between the formation of a threatener's intention and the delivery of his ultimatum is tiny or rather lengthy, the key factor here is the perceptible likelihood (at the point of the formation of the intention) that the ultimatum will be suitably delivered at a time of the threatener's choosing. If that likelihood is very substantial, then we can correctly assert—with some probabilistic qualifications, whether implicit or overt—that the recipient's unfreedom caused by the threatener has begun at the point when the threatener becomes resolutely inclined to give rise to that unfreedom. The unfreedom precedes the ultimatum by which it is manifested to the recipient. We can correctly insist on this point irrespective of whether the threatener would decline to go ahead with the imposition of sanctions if he felt that his ultimatum had not been adequately conveyed. (Obviously, if he would not decline to go ahead, then the likelihood of adequate communication is largely or wholly beside the point. If the non-fulfilment of the threatener's behest will lead to the infliction of penalties willy-nilly—that is, if the penalties will be inflicted even though the reason for the non-fulfilment is plainly that the behest has not been properly communicated—then the unfreedom of the intended addressee will have begun as soon as the threatener adopts an inclination to produce that unfreedom. In such a situation, the actual issuance of the threatening behest has no bearing at all on the emergence of the addressee's unfreedom. His unfreedom clearly obtains already.)

By attending to the frequently small temporal gap between the formation and the enunciation of a threatening intention, we can locate the exact provenance and character of the unfreedom created by the issuer of a genuine threat. That unfreedom derives from the threatener's inclination to behave in ways that block some other person(s) from engaging in some mode(s) of conduct with impunity. The words 'with impunity' are important here because they indicate that the unfreedom of the recipient of a genuine threat usually consists not in his being unable to flout the threatener's wishes, but in his being unable to flout those wishes without losing his ability to perform actions that will be prevented by the penalties imposed for his refractoriness. In other words, the phrase 'with impunity' indicates that combinations of actions—rather than any of those actions considered in isolation—are the contents of the unfreedoms typically signalled by genuine threats. Just as important as that phrase in the second sentence of this paragraph is my reference there to the threatener's inclination. When some person *P* is capable of preventing somebody else's adoption with impunity of a certain mode of conduct *M*, and when *P* has become resolved to prevent exactly that, the other person has become unfree to combine *M* with any actions that will be ruled out by the penalties imposed on her if she persists in opting for *M*. The emergence of this unfreedom can coincide in time with the issuance of a genuine threat, but it can often precede that issuance. Frequently, a threatener's utterance of an ultimatum is correctly classifiable as a means of signalling to an addressee a state of unfreedom that already exists. Though the period between the emergence and the signalling of that state may typically be brief, an alertness to the interposition of that period enables us to recognize clearly the source of the unfreedom involved. That is, such alertness enables us to recognize that the key to the unfreedom created in a situation marked by a genuine ultimatum is not the ultimatum itself but the behavioural disposition of the threatener that has impelled it.

3.3. Steiner's Steady-State Theory

Hillel Steiner is among the leading theorists to draw salutary attention to the counter-factual aspect of freedom and unfreedom. Vitally important though his work is in this respect and in many other respects, however, he markedly underestimates the scope of freedom's counter-factual side. As a consequence, his writings on liberty during the past three decades have repeatedly propounded a thesis that is unsustainable. In this subsection we shall first look at the dubious thesis which Steiner has championed: an insistence on the constancy of the extent of the aggregate freedom among human beings throughout the world. We shall then look at his comments on the counterfactual dimension of freedom and unfreedom. As will be argued, those comments seriously understate the significance of that counter-factual dimension. When the shortcomings in his approach to that matter are remedied, we shall be in a good position to detect the untenability of his thesis concerning the aggregate freedom of human beings—a thesis that will also be assailed from some other angles.

The doctrine under challenge here has appeared at various junctures in Steiner's work on freedom,[35] but we shall investigate it in its most recent guise as the 'Law of Conservation of Liberty'.[36] What Steiner contends is that, because of the very nature of liberty, the aggregate freedom of human beings throughout the world cannot be reduced or expanded. 'Negative liberty is such that it makes no sense to speak of it as being aggregately increased or diminished—much less maximized or minimized—but only as being dispersed or concentrated to some particular extent.' He seeks to substantiate this view by alleging that any gain in freedom for one person must be accompanied by a commensurate loss in freedom for somebody else. To illustrate this ostensibly zero-sum character of liberty, he adduces an example involving the competing entitlements of landowners and ramblers: 'A rule giving ramblers rights of way over agricultural land increases the freedom of ramblers. But it also reduces the liberty of farmers, by mandating the legal prevention of many actions which they might do involving their use of the land over which ramblers enjoy rights of way'.[37] Steiner offers a general explanation of the zero-sum nature of aggregate liberty by reminding his readers that every exercise of freedom involves the use or positioning of material objects and the occupation of space. Precisely because one's exercise of any freedom to make use of a certain thing will entail one's having control over some or all of the aspects of the specified thing, one's loss of that particular freedom will amount to a gain for someone else. Such a loss resides in one's relinquishment of control over the aspects of the thing that have been at one's disposal. Those aspects, Steiner maintains, thereby fall under the actual or hypothetical control of somebody else. Every relinquishment for one person is an acquisition for another, and thus the losses and gains strictly balance each other in an equilibrium that can vary distributively but not aggregatively. As Steiner proclaims:

Being free to do an action is, we've seen, being in (actual or subjunctive) possession of its physical components. And everything is in someone's such possession. What I am free to do is a function of the things possessed by me, and what I am unfree to do is a function of the things possessed by others. My total liberty, the extent of my freedom, is inversely related to theirs. If I lose possession of something, someone else gains it and thereby gains the amount of freedom (whatever it is) which I've lost.

---

[35] Steiner, 'Liberty', 138–40; Steiner, 'Computing', 86–9.
[36] Steiner, *Essay*, 52–4.   [37] Steiner, *Essay*, 54, 53.

Accordingly, Berlin is wrong to claim that there can be social circumstances in which 'an absolute loss of liberty occurs,' and correct to claim that 'Freedom for the pike is death for the minnows; the liberty of some must depend on the restraint of others.'[38]

We shall proceed to ruminate on Steiner's remarks about the counter-factual dimension of freedom in order to get a full sense of the tenets that underlie his Law of Conservation of Liberty. We shall then investigate the fatal difficulties which undermine that putative law. Let us pause for a moment, however, to take note of one obvious difficulty that would arise even if Steiner were correct in presuming that every gain of liberty will be accompanied by a loss and vice versa. Even if his theory were unimpeachable on that point, he would not have provided any grounds for thinking that the gains and losses must match each other in their extent as well as in their number.[39] Indeed, the various examples adduced by him to support his claim that gains must always consort with losses and vice versa—the expanded latitude of ramblers versus the cabined latitude of landowners, the increased liberty of emancipated slaves versus the diminished liberty of the erstwhile owners of those slaves, the enlarged freedom of censors versus the reduced freedom of anyone whose writings or artistic works get banned—are hardly examples that lend credibility to the notion that the extent of each loss matches the extent of each concomitant gain. On the contrary, it seems highly plausible that some of the developments recounted by Steiner will add more to the overall freedom of certain people than will be subtracted from the overall freedom of others.

For instance, suppose that a change of governmental policy eliminates the liberty of a farmer to close off public paths on his land with fences. Because of newly vigilant policing by the relevant officials, any attempt by the farmer to erect a fence that seals off a public path will be quickly thwarted. Every such fence will be dismantled and removed while still in its incipient stages. As a result, countless members of the public—the vast majority of whom could not surmount the fences which the farmer previously maintained—are now able to walk along the public paths, whether or not they choose to do so. Now, even if

---

[38] Steiner, *Essay*, 52, quoting Isaiah Berlin, *Four Essays on Liberty* (Oxford: Oxford University Press, 1969), 125, 124. For a penetrating critique of Steiner's Law of Conservation of Liberty, see Carter, *Measure*, 259–63.

[39] Some other critics of Steiner have fleetingly broached this point. See for example Ian Carter, 'The Measurement of Pure Negative Freedom', 40 *Political Studies* 38, 43 n. 21 (1992); John Gray, 'Marxian Freedom, Individual Liberty, and the End of Alienation', 3/2 *Social Philosophy & Policy* 160, 164 n. 6 (1986) [Gray, 'Alienation']. Cf. T. Gray, *Freedom*, 157, 158.

arguendo (and not very credibly) we concede that the lost freedoms of the landowner and the additional freedoms of the ramblers exactly correspond in number, we should scarcely concede that they coincide in extent. The burden surely lies on Steiner to demonstrate that a coincidence of extent does obtain. In the absence of cogent arguments to that effect, we are justified in thinking that no such coincidence obtains and that a disparity instead prevails. Neither in this example nor in myriad other examples that might be posited, will a reduction in the overall liberty of some people precisely offset an increase in the overall liberty of other people.

In response to the criticism presented in my last two paragraphs, Steiner might seek to have recourse to his analysis of the counter-factual dimension of freedom and unfreedom. At any rate, he will surely seek to have recourse to that analysis in order to defend his view that any augmentation of the overall liberty of some person(s) is always accompanied by a curtailment of the overall liberty of some other person(s) and vice versa. We should therefore train our attention now on what Steiner says about freedom's counter-factual aspect. As will be seen, his remarks on this topic are quite plainly inadequate. An exploration of the shortcomings in those remarks will facilitate our detection of the weaknesses in his Law of Conservation of Liberty.

In *An Essay on Rights*, Steiner begins his discussion of this matter by acknowledging that his earlier analyses of freedom 'erroneously neglected the subjunctive aspect of this conception of liberty'.[40] He accepts that his early position was vulnerable to an objection posed in 1982 by Michael Taylor. Taylor, mounting a sympathetic rejoinder to Steiner's claim that freedom consists in the possession of material objects, argues in part as follows:

It is true that while one individual has possession—enjoys exclusive physical control—of an object, possession during that time is denied to all others. But it does not follow that an individual possesses an object *if* nobody else does. Steiner's error was to assume tacitly that at any moment every object is in *somebody's* possession. An individual (on Steiner's own account) has pure negative freedom with respect to an action just as long as nobody else has possession of the physical components of that action; pure negative freedom does not require that *he* possesses these components.[41]

Steiner allows that Taylor's riposte is well aimed. He observes that, although one's *exercise* of the freedom-to-φ entails one's use or positioning of any material objects necessary for one's φ-ing, one's mere

---

[40] Steiner, *Essay*, 39.   [41] Taylor, *Community*, 153, emphases in original.

endowment with that freedom does not entail one's actual use or positioning of those objects. Instead, one's endowment with the freedom-to-φ entails simply that one will use or position the material object(s) necessary for one's φ-ing *if one endeavours (without any blunders) to do so.*[42] To be sure, if a person P is free to φ, and if P exercises that freedom, then he actually uses or positions the physical ingredients of his φ-ing. On the other hand, if P is free to φ, and if he does not exercise that freedom, then he would have used or positioned the physical ingredients of his φ-ing if he had sought (without any blunders) to do so. That counter-factual dimension of every freedom is what Steiner overlooked in his early work, as he himself avouches:

I was mistaken to suggest that everything must always be in the possession of one person or another. For although our doing actions (which we are *ipso facto* free to do) entails our possessing their components, we can also be free to do actions which we don't do. And thus the components of those unperformed actions may well be things unpossessed by ourselves, as well as being necessarily unpossessed by others. There can, as Taylor insists, be unpossessed things.[43]

Steiner also now explicitly recognizes that any unfreedom, just as much as any freedom, includes a counter-factual dimension. That dimension, of course, is stated expressly in my U Postulate (as has already been noted).

Having conceded so much, however, Steiner tenaciously resists the thesis which Taylor develops in the following passage:

I am free at this moment, and at most times, to perform a variety of acts on the open fields I can see from my window, because neither their legal owner nor any other person has at this moment exclusive physical control of them (of the ground, of the air space directly above them, of the cabbages and corn and other objects on and in them). Of course, if I exercised this freedom—if I actually performed one of the acts I am free to do—then I would be in possession of certain physical objects, so would *then* restrict the pure negative freedom of all other persons. But until I do so, they too have the relevant freedoms.[44]

Before looking at Steiner's retort to Taylor's line of argument, we should briefly consider a misstep in the final sentence of this extract. As should be evident from my preceding subsection, Taylor goes astray in suggesting that the juncture at which other people's freedoms change into unfreedoms is the point at which he performs some act(s)

---

[42] The import of the qualification 'without any blunders' will become clear later in this chapter.

[43] Steiner, *Essay*, 40.   [44] Taylor, *Community*, 153–4, emphasis in original.

in the fields. Rather, the decisive juncture is the point at which he becomes resolutely disposed to perform some act(s) therein. That resolute disposition, in conjunction with the physical capacity to follow through on it—which we may ascribe to Taylor—is what ordains the uses to which certain objects in the fields will be put. By the time Taylor acts, he has already made other people unfree in respect of his uses of those objects. By that time, the answer is already negative to the question whether other people will succeed in gaining possession of those objects if they attempt to do so in ways inconsistent with Taylor's impending uses thereof.

If we put aside the cavil just raised, Taylor's remarks are sound. Taylor is entirely warranted in maintaining that two (or more) people can each be free to occupy exactly the same space at exactly the same time. Of course, the two people can never in fact occupy the same space S at the same time t, but each of them can be free to occupy S at t—if neither of them has any inclination to occupy that space at that time. While the disinclination of each of them does not affect his own freedom-to-occupy-S-at-t, it sustains the corresponding freedom of the other. We shall shortly explore this point further.

Steiner baulks at Taylor's argument, notwithstanding its soundness. A lengthy quotation from Steiner's response is here advisable, since that response encapsulates his understanding—a mistaken understanding—of the counter-factual dimension of freedom and unfreedom. His approach to this matter is what underlies his insistence on the Law of Conservation of Liberty:

Can other persons as well as Taylor be said to have those freedoms [that is, freedoms to perform various actions in the fields visible from Taylor's window]? One such freedom, let's suppose, is Taylor's freedom to throw a particular cabbage fifty feet into the air above the spot where it's growing in two minutes' time. Can it be true as he suggests that, until he actually does this, everyone else is free to do actions involving that same cabbage or space at that same time?

I think not. Taylor's insistence on divorcing freedom from possession rests on the recognition that we can and typically do describe a person as being 'at this moment' free to do a *later* action. We don't say that Taylor is unfree to throw that cabbage in two minutes' time if we believe that he won't be prevented from throwing it then. That's why we can be described as free to do actions whose components are actually unpossessed by us, given (as he says) that they will be possessed by us when we do those actions. But if Taylor is indeed free to do that action in two minutes' time, his neighbour cannot be similarly described as free to do any action then which requires (any of) those same physical components. Her being free to do such an action implies that, were she to attempt it, it would be she who would possess those things at that time. But if that were true, then it cannot be true that Taylor is free to do his throwing action since that implies that those things would be unpossessed by her at that time. Were she, in the event, successfully to attempt to use those components then, we should be bound to regard our earlier judgement—that Taylor is free—as mistaken.[45]

As Ian Carter has suggested,[46] Steiner is here arguing for a claim which would be true about performances of incompatible actions but which is false about freedoms to perform those actions. It is of course true that Taylor cannot throw the cabbage if someone else has performed or is performing an action that precludes his throwing of the cabbage. Two incompatible actions cannot both be performed. Of central interest in Taylor's scenario, however, is not each person's performance of an action but each person's freedom to perform an action. Each person can be free to carry out an action that is incompatible with an action which the other person is free to carry out, even though no more than one of those actions can actually be carried out. This state of affairs can obtain if neither person is inclined to undertake the action which he is free to undertake. If each of them is indeed disinclined to perform any action A_1 that would clash with some action A_2 by the other, then neither of them is preventing the other from acting along those lines. One person's performance of A_1 will not be excluded by the other person's performance of A_2, and the other person's performance of A_2 will not be excluded by the first person's performance of A_1. Hence—unless there have emerged some preventive factors apart from the conduct of each of the two people—one person is free to do A_1, and the other is simultaneously free to do A_2.

Let us re-examine the scenario in which Taylor and someone else, whom we may designate as 'Alice', are each free to throw a specified cabbage into the air at a specified moment t. *Ex hypothesi*, neither of them has the slightest inclination to go into the field in order to throw the cabbage. Likewise, neither of them is inclined to do anything else that would rule out the throwing of the cabbage by the other. Nor, we may assume, are there any other preventive factors that would thwart the throwing of the cabbage by either person at t. If we proceed to ask whether Taylor is now free to throw the cabbage at t, the answer is clearly 'yes'. In this context, such a question is equivalent to the question whether he will throw the cabbage at t if between now and then he does his best to throw it at that time. An affirmative reply to the latter question is clearly appropriate, for there is nothing that would prevent

---

[45] Steiner, *Essay*, 41.   [46] Carter, *Measure*, 261–3.

him from hurling the cabbage then. Alice would not interfere in any way, since she is not disposed at all to throw the cabbage herself or to do anything else that would be inconsistent with Taylor's throwing of the cabbage. Yet, by essentially the same line of reasoning which leads us to perceive that Taylor is now free to throw the cabbage at t, we can perceive that Alice is simultaneously free to throw the cabbage then. If between now and then she endeavours (without any blunders) to carry out such an action at t, nothing will prevent her from doing so. We know that Taylor would not prevent her, for we know that he is not at all disposed to throw the cabbage himself or to do anything else that would stymie her attempt to throw it. In sum, because neither Taylor nor Alice will take any steps to throw the cabbage at t, each of them is now free to throw it then. Given that they share a disinclination to perform that action, neither of them creates any obstacles to the other's performance of it.

The scenario of Taylor and Alice reveals the falsity of Steiner's claim that '[l]ike actual possession, subjunctive possession cannot be ascribed to more than one person for any one time'.[47] Steiner here disregards every situation in which no one will take any steps to do anything that would preclude somebody else's gaining of possession of some specified object(s). Exactly such a situation is portrayed, of course, in the scenario of Taylor and Alice. To ascertain whether someone is in subjunctive possession of something, we inquire whether he or she would possess that thing if he or she endeavoured—without any blunders—to do so. That question, asked about the cabbage, will clearly generate an affirmative answer both in application to Taylor and in application to Alice. Each of them would possess the cabbage if he or she endeavoured (without any blunders) to do so, because the disinclination of the other to gain possession will leave the way clear. Neither of them will do anything that would prevent the other from grabbing and throwing the cabbage, and thus neither of them is in any way prevented by the other from grabbing and throwing it. Each of them is in subjunctive possession of the cabbage, precisely because neither of them is inclined to gain actual possession of it. In light of the possibility of this sort of situation, we can detect a fatal equivocation in Steiner's statement that 'since any conceivable action is one which Taylor is either free or unfree to do—one which, were he to attempt it, would be either unprevented or prevented—it follows that every actually unpossessed component of that action would be possessed either by Taylor or by others'.[48] The equivocation occurs in the final several words of this quotation. Is the disjunction

---

[47] Steiner, *Essay*, 41.   [48] Ibid.

there meant to be exclusive or inclusive? On the one hand, that is, the phrase 'by Taylor or by others' may indicate that each thing is possessed (actually or subjunctively) either by Taylor or by some other person but never both by Taylor and by some other person. Alternatively, that phrase may indicate that each thing is possessed (actually or subjunctively) by Taylor or by some other person(s) or else both by Taylor and by some other person(s). Steiner clearly intends the former of these two interpretations, but only the latter interpretation will save his statement from being falsified outright by the scenario of Taylor and Alice. (As will be argued presently, his statement turns out to be unsustainable even if we construe it in accordance with the latter interpretation.)

The implications of this discussion for Steiner's Law of Conservation of Liberty are far-reaching indeed. We shall first ponder this matter with reference to the situation of Taylor and Alice, and we shall then consider a couple of more complicated examples. Let us suppose that Alice is free to do countless things inside the cabbage fields and is not free to do anything outside them. There is one cabbage in the fields, which she is free to use in various ways (by tossing it around, by consuming it, and so forth). If Taylor now rushes in and grabs the cabbage while Alice is at the far end of the fields, and if he takes the cabbage away from the fields and destroys it, he has reduced Alice's overall freedom without increasing his own overall freedom even slightly. He has not enlarged his own total liberty, because he has all along been free to perform the action which he does perform. (He could have seized the cabbage even in the proximity of Alice, but he has chosen to grab it stealthily in order to prevent her from enjoying any opportunities for joint actions with him.) By taking and destroying the cabbage, he exercises rather than acquires the freedom-to-take-and-destroy-it. At the same time, he has diminished the overall liberty of Alice by removing some of her options without opening up any new options for her. By carrying the cabbage out of the fields, he precludes her from making any further use of it. Had he instead chosen to keep out of the fields, he would not have similarly cabined her options. Thus, in the posited situation, the making and implementation of a decision by Taylor to seize the cabbage from the fields will have reduced Alice's overall freedom without having expanded his own. Instead of the strict conservation of liberty, we encounter here a downright decrease.

We should now consider some examples that cast additional doubt on the Law of Conservation of Liberty by impugning the central claim that is presupposed in the most recently quoted statement from Steiner.

He squarely articulates that claim in his immediately preceding sentence: '[F]or any given time, everything which is not actually possessed is subjunctively possessed [by someone].' As he goes on to declare just a few sentences later: '[A] person actually or subjunctively possesses a thing if nobody else does. For any moment, everything is in someone's actual or subjunctive possession'.[49] To behold the falsity of these assertions, we should turn our attention to the situation of two people who are the sole inhabitants of an island. (Perhaps they live there because of a shipwreck, though we need not concern ourselves with the reasons for their presence there.) Let us suppose that the island contains a steep hill. Each of the two people can climb up part of the hill without any special apparatus or devices, but neither of them is capable of ascending the topmost portion of the hill without such aids. Because of the sheerness and smoothness of the pinnacle, neither of the people stands any chance of scaling it in the absence of some facilitative devices which the two of them have made from the very small supply of wood on the island. Let us now suppose that one of the people—perhaps when intoxicated or angry or simply careless—completely consumes with fire the special climbing devices and all the rest of the wood on the island. There is no other material on the island from which suitable climbing aids can be produced. As a consequence, each of the two people has become unable to ascend the pinnacle. Each of them has lost his former freedom to climb to the top of the hill, and neither of them has gained any freedom that would offset the loss. Options have been closed off without the opening up of any new options. Contrary to what Steiner asserts, then, there can indeed be circumstances in which 'one individual [or, for that matter, more than one individual] can lose freedom without thereby increasing the individual liberty of others'.[50] Equally, this example of the people on the island shows the untenability of Steiner's claim (quoted earlier in this paragraph) that '[f]or any moment, everything is in someone's actual or subjunctive possession'. After the burning of the climbing devices and the wood, no portion of the pinnacle of the hill is in the actual or subjunctive possession of either of the two people who live on the island. It is not the case that either of them is currently astride the pinnacle, and it is not the case that either of them would scale the pinnacle if he endeavoured to do so. The uppermost portion of the hill remains inaccessible to each of them.

Let us now investigate a more complicated variant of the scenario just broached. This variant will pose severe problems specifically for

[49] Ibid.   [50] Steiner, 'Liberty', 140.

Steiner, who not only propounds the Law of Conservation of Liberty but who also maintains that 'free' and 'unfree' are strictly bivalent. Under his theory, which maintains that somebody is free-to-do-X if and only if no one else prevents her from doing X and no one else would prevent her if she endeavoured to do X, technological progress can frequently cause a straightforward diminution of liberty. Let us suppose that Elmer and Emily are the only two inhabitants of an island that contains a steep hill. Each of them is capable of clambering up the lower reaches of the hill, but, because the topmost portion is so shuddersomely steep, neither of them can ascend that part of the hill at all. Within the constraints of their present technology, the pinnacle is wholly inaccessible to each of them. Accordingly, a flat strip of rock at the very top of the mountain is inaccessible to each of them. Now, with reference to these circumstances, someone adhering to Steiner's theory of liberty should conclude that Elmer and Emily are each free to walk along the ridge of rock at the summit of the hill. Elmer is not prevented by Emily from walking on that ridge, and he would not be prevented by her if he attempted to walk thereon. Much the same is true of Emily, who is not prevented by Elmer from traversing the ridge and who would not be prevented by him if she endeavoured to traverse it. Thus, although the peak of the hill is entirely inaccessible to Elmer and Emily, each of them is free to climb that peak and to walk on the strip of rock at the very top. So, at least, the proponent of Steiner's theory of liberty must contend.

Before the factor of technological development is introduced into this example of Elmer and Emily, we should note two important aspects of their situation as described heretofore. First, if we accept the bivalence of 'free' and 'unfree' in the manner of Steiner, we shall have to conclude that Elmer and Emily are each free to walk on exactly the same area of the ridge of rock at exactly the same time. Neither of them will do anything that would obstruct the other from walking on such an area at any time t, and neither of them *would* do anything to obstruct the other in the event that that other tried to walk there at t. Consequently, each of them is free to occupy precisely the same portion of the ridge at precisely the same moment. Such is the conclusion to be drawn from Steiner's conception of freedom as the simple negation of unfreedom. That conception, in other words, generates a conclusion that is inimical to his broader theory. (In my earlier example involving Taylor and Alice, their shared *disinclination* to throw a certain cabbage at a certain time was what accounted for the freedom of each of them to throw the cabbage at that time. In my present example, the key factor is the shared *inability* of Elmer and Emily to walk on the ledge at the top of the hill. Because of this difference between the two examples, only the current one relies on Steiner's conception of freedom and unfreedom as bivalent—a conception which I do not endorse, of course.)

Closely connected is a second important aspect of the scenario of Emily and Elmer as it has been unfolded heretofore. Despite Steiner's repeated assertions that everything is always in the actual or subjunctive possession of somebody, the strip of rock at the top of the hill is not actually or subjunctively possessed by either of the island's two residents. It is not the case that either of them is currently on that strip, and it is not the case that either of them would manage to walk on that strip if he or she essayed to do so. To be sure, someone across the sea with an appropriate aircraft and with other equipment could very likely succeed in gaining access to the ridge of rock if he were to attempt resolutely to do so. In that respect, the ridge can be classified as subjunctively possessed by such a person. However, for at least three reasons, any observation along these lines would be unprofitable for Steiner. In the first place, we can simply assume that the story of Elmer and Emily is set in an era before the development of aeroplanes and helicopters and other equipment that would enable anyone to reach the top of the hill on the island. Furthermore, even in the age of modern technology, any effort by someone across the sea to place himself or herself on the ledge of rock would extend over quite a bit of time. If we suppose that somebody S finally engages in such an effort right now (perhaps in order to rescue Elmer and Emily), and if we suppose that the endpoint of the time involved in mounting this state-of-the-art effort is t, then we can still correctly maintain that until t the ledge is not actually or subjunctively possessed by anyone. After all, nobody can gain access to the ledge any earlier than t—because, *ex hypothesi*, the endeavour by S to gain access to it is the first such endeavour undertaken by anyone with sufficient equipment for success. Moreover, even if we pretermit the difficulties just recounted, Steiner will hardly wish to avail himself of the fact that someone across the sea with adequate technology can be classified as subjunctively in possession of the peak of the hill on the island. After all, there are undoubtedly numerous people with such technology at their disposal. If we classify any one of them as subjunctively in possession of the ridge of rock on the aforementioned peak, we shall have to classify every one of them in that manner. The generalizability of such a classification to every one of them is virtually certain, since it is virtually certain that none of them will be inclined to take actual possession of that ridge (perhaps simply because none of them will be aware of the ridge at all). In other words, if Steiner were to point out that somebody overseas with suitable equipment could reach the acme of the hill, he would unwittingly be suggesting that the story of Emily and Elmer is basically similar in its import to the story of Taylor and Alice. Each story would involve a set of circumstances in which multiple people—Taylor and Alice in one story, the people overseas in the other—will each subjunctively occupy exactly the same place p at exactly the same time t. In each story, such a state of affairs obtains because of the disinclination of every subjunctive occupier to seek to undertake any actual occupation of p at t.

Let us now consider the effect of technological innovation on the situation of Elmer and Emily. Suppose that Elmer eventually invents some contraption that enables a person to scale the pinnacle of the hill and thereby gain access to the ridge of rock at the very top. Because the resources on the island are exiguous, only one of these facilitative devices can be made. Consequently, only one person at a time can now reach the top of the hill; and, at any rate, the ridge of rock is too narrow to be traversed by more than one person at a time. Still, Elmer usually lets Emily borrow the device when she requests it and when he himself does not wish to make use of it. Thus, each of them is frequently free to clamber up the summit of the hill and to walk on the summit's ledge. Now, if Elmer prevents Emily from availing herself of his invention at a given time—either because he is then using the invention for his own purposes or because he simply obstructs her from gaining access to it—he will have made her unfree to scale the hill's pinnacle and to walk on its ledge. Similarly, if Elmer would have prevented Emily from using his device at a certain time had she attempted to use it then, she was unfree to ascend the pinnacle and to walk on the ledge at that time. Conversely, on each occasion when Emily makes use of the contraption, she will have rendered Elmer unfree to walk on the ridge of rock at that time. Her availing herself of the device prevents him from availing himself of it.

Accordingly, if we compare the situation before the invention of the facilitative device with the situation afterward, we shall find that— under Steiner's conception of liberty—there has been a straightforward reduction in each person's overall freedom. Before Elmer's innovation, Elmer and Emily were each free at all times to climb the topmost portion of the hill and to walk along its ledge. Though neither of them could in fact perform such feats at that stage (or, rather, *because* neither of them could perform such feats at that stage), each of them was unprevented by the other from doing so. Each of them was therefore always free to do so, according to Steiner's conception of liberty. Elmer's innovation transforms this situation of unalloyed freedom into a situation of freedom-cum-unfreedom. Elmer is still often free to scale the hill's summit and to walk on the strip of rock at the very top, but is no longer always so. Whenever he lets Emily use his device or is otherwise obstructed by her from using it himself, he is unfree to ascend the summit and to walk thereon. Even more substantially changed is the posture of Emily. Before the invention of the facilitative contraption, she was free at all times to climb the zenith of the hill and to walk at the very top. Afterward, however, she is unfree-to-do-those-things whenever Elmer prevents her from using his device (either because he wishes to use it himself or because he simply does not want her to have it at some particular time).

In sum, under Steiner's conception of liberty, neither Elmer nor Emily has gained any new freedoms in respect of walking on the ridge of rock. Any freedoms of that sort currently enjoyed by either of them are freedoms that pre-existed the advent of Elmer's device. At the same time, as has just been described, Emily and Elmer have each acquired some new unfreedoms in respect of walking on the ridge. Hence, technological progress in the form of Elmer's innovation has brought about a straightforward decrease in the overall liberty of Elmer and Emily. It has not endowed either of them with any new freedoms, and it has removed some of their erstwhile freedoms and replaced them with unfreedoms. This scenario of technological progress thus runs athwart Steiner's attempt to derive a Law of Conservation of Liberty from his conception of freedom.

If the Law of Conservation of Liberty is so plainly untenable—under my own conception of freedom as well as under Steiner's—why has a theorist as sophisticated and astute as Steiner been led to embrace it? Let us briefly ruminate on two possible explanations. First, if we ignore the freedoms that emerge by dint of convergences among people in being disinclined to act in various ways, it is undoubtedly true that most occurrences which in some respects expand overall freedom are also occurrences which in other respects curtail overall freedom. At any rate, this point applies to occurrences that involve the elimination of external obstacles to people's actions. Countless examples could be adduced. One prominent instance received attention at several junctures in Chapter 2: the tendency of duties of civic virtue to enlarge the overall liberty of most people by rendering many of their particular liberties more secure. Those duties produce their freedom-augmenting effects precisely by removing certain freedoms or certain combinations of conjunctively exercisable freedoms. Even more broadly, if basic legal protections against murder and assaults and other serious misdeeds are well enforced, they will tend to expand the overall liberty of each person by restricting what he and everyone else can do. Each person qua potential victim will enjoy a greatly enhanced level of security for his sundry freedoms, but only because each person qua potential perpetrator will be deprived of many combinations of conjunctively exercisable freedoms.

A myriad of more mundane examples can be offered as well. For instance, if stairs are built to enable people to ascend a wall or some other structure, then nobody is now free to occupy any of the space that is taken up by the stairs. Though anyone can run his hand or foot across the surface of each step, he cannot any longer pass his foot or hand through the formerly empty space that has been filled up by the steps. Hence, the liberty-enlarging role of the stairs has been fulfilled only through the elimination of certain liberties—albeit quite trivial liberties. Other examples involve not the removal of existent freedoms but the imposition of limits on new freedoms. Offers, of various kinds, are particularly familiar and significant in this respect. For instance, if somebody offers to sell me a box of apples for five dollars, and if the offer is a firm proposal rather than the first stage of some bargaining, and if the person who advances the offer is sufficiently strong to prevent me from carrying away the apples without paying for them, then his readiness to make the offer will have expanded the range of my options but only by placing definite limits on the expansion. I am not free to gain possession of the apples for any amount of money less than five dollars. Someone presenting an ordinary offer will have widened the recipient's range of possibilities by enabling access to certain goods that would not otherwise be available, but he imposes curbs on the widening by making those goods available only on specified conditions. Indeed, even if the person offering me the apples had proposed to give them to me without any charge, he would thereby have been setting clear bounds on the extent to which he would increase the range of my options. I would not be free to acquire from him gratuitously any number of other assets such as a car or an ocean liner. Only in a myth or a fairy tale where a genie undertakes to grant any three wishes, does the recipient of an offer undergo an unrestricted addition to his liberty.

In short, if we put aside freedoms that arise from the shared disinclination of people to make use of certain resources (such as cabbages for throwing), virtually any expansion of one's overall freedom through the removal of external obstacles will proceed by limiting one's freedom in some new ways: either by removing some of one's existent liberties or by attaching conditions to one's emergent liberties. Obvious though this point may be, it is sometimes obscured in writings on social and political freedom—usually because of a failure to distinguish sufficiently between overall liberty and particular liberties.[51] An alertness to this point may be what has prompted Steiner to espouse his unsustainable doctrine of the Law of Conservation of Liberty. Equally likely, however, is that he has sought to avoid some seemingly counter-intuitive implications of any conception of liberty that duly recognizes the importance of people's behavioural inclinations in the engendering of freedom and unfreedom. We shall finish this section of the present chapter by mulling over some of those implications.

This portion of my discussion builds on G. A. Cohen's seminal work concerning the collective unfreedom of labourers in a capitalist economic system.[52] Cohen has drawn attention to situations in which the opportunities open to everyone are much fewer in number than the people to whom they are open. If everyone or virtually everyone faced with those opportunities is in fact disinclined to avail himself of them, then everyone is free to avail himself of them. In such circumstances, although there are far fewer opportunities than the *potential* takers thereof, there are more opportunities than the *actual* takers thereof. Consequently, everyone who has not seized one of those opportunities (as well as everyone who has, of course) is free to do so.

The basic structure of the situations highlighted by Cohen should be familiar. In its general outlines, it is the structure of conditional freedoms which we have encountered in the opening scenario of Taylor and Alice. Taylor is free to grab the cabbage and throw it, given that Alice is disinclined to do anything that would preclude his grabbing

---

[51] See for example S. I. Benn and W. L. Weinstein, 'Being Free to Act, and Being a Free Man', 80 *Mind* 194, 201–2 (1971) [Benn and Weinstein, 'Being Free']; Stanley Benn, *A Theory of Freedom* (Cambridge: Cambridge University Press, 1988) [Benn, *Theory*], 136–7; John Christman, 'Liberalism and Individual Positive Freedom', 101 *Ethics* 343, 353 (1991); Richard Flathman, *The Philosophy and Politics of Freedom* (Chicago: University of Chicago Press, 1987) [Flathman, *Freedom*], 31–2; Kristjánsson, *Freedom*, 44; H. J. McCloskey, 'A Critique of the Ideals of Liberty', 74 *Mind* 483, 487–8 (1965). For a corrective, see S. I. Benn and R. S. Peters, *Social Principles and the Democratic State* (London: Allen & Unwin, 1959), 213, 215: 'It is the paradox of freedom that we must set a constraint to catch a constraint . . . [T]he condition of [my] being free in some ways is that I should not be free in others.' Cf. Kristjánsson, 'Offers', 64–7.

[52] See G. A. Cohen, 'Capitalism, Freedom and the Proletariat', in Alan Ryan (ed.), *The Idea of Freedom* (Oxford: Oxford University Press, 1979) [Cohen, 'Capitalism'], 9, 20–5; G. A. Cohen, 'Are Workers Forced to Sell Their Labor Power?', 14 *Philosophy & Public Affairs* 99 (1985); Cohen, *History*, at 247–9, 259–85.

and throwing; and Alice is similarly free, given that Taylor is similarly disinclined. Cohen generalizes and complicates this basic structure in some important ways. In line with some of my foregoing analyses, he observes that the structure of conditional freedoms can obtain with regard to any number of agents. If the opening story of Taylor and Alice were broadened to encompass 10 or 20 or 50 other people who would not be inclined to go into the cabbage fields, its underlying point would apply to every one of them. As Cohen writes, 'each is free only on condition that the others do not exercise their similarly conditional freedom'.[53] Moreover, not only can conditional freedoms be held by numerous agents, but in addition those freedoms can pertain to multiple pathways of conduct. Suppose, for example, that the specified action in the scenario of Taylor and Alice and 20 other people is the throwing of any one of three cabbages rather than the throwing of one particular cabbage. If no more than two people are inclined to throw any of the cabbages, and if nobody is inclined to grab and throw more than one cabbage, everyone else will be free to perform the specified action (because at least one cabbage will remain untouched and available). More generally, whenever the opportunities open to some array of people are more numerous than the opportunities that will cumulatively be seized, everyone is free to take advantage of any of the opportunities that remain.

Even when the unseized opportunities are quite numerous, however, the relevant array of people might be far more numerous. Circumstances of this type are precisely what Cohen has in mind when writing about collective unfreedom. Specifically, he has in mind the position of the proletariat within a capitalist country. He maintains that, although there may be quite a few untaken routes out of the proletariat into the ranks of the bourgeoisie, the number of such routes is dwarfed by the total number of proletarians. '[T]here are necessarily only enough petty bourgeois and other non-proletarian positions for a small number of the proletariat to leave that estate.'[54] The potential for a gaping disparity between the opportunities available and the number of people faced with those opportunities is not clearly brought out by the opening scenario of Taylor and Alice (unless that scenario is amplified to comprehend many other people who are not disposed to enter the cabbage fields). Thus, although the situation of Taylor and Alice is *au fond* parallel to that of the proletariat under capitalism, there are some important differences as well. One of the most important

[53] Cohen, *History*, 263, emphases deleted.
[54] Cohen, 'Capitalism', 22.

differences, the potential for a gaping disparity just mentioned, is what leads Cohen to designate the situation of the proletariat as a predicament of collective unfreedom. On the one hand, because some available routes of escape from the proletarian class will almost certainly not be taken up by any members of that class, every such member with a modicum of intelligence and physical stamina is free to escape therefrom. On the other hand, because the available paths of escape are so much fewer than the members of the proletarian class, an accurate ascription of the freedom-to-escape to virtually every member of that class may be somewhat misleading. Such an ascription, though completely accurate, may seem to gloss over the plight of the proletariat in an anodyne fashion. Cohen thus invokes the notion of collective unfreedom in order to supplement his account of the position of each individual proletarian. While still correctly claiming that virtually every member of the proletariat is free to move into the petty bourgeoisie, Cohen combines that claim with the thesis that the proletariat as a whole are an 'imprisoned class'.[55] Members of the proletariat are individually free to transcend their status but are collectively unfree to do so. (To be sure, Cohen defines 'collective unfreedom' with sufficient breadth to encompass any situation in which the number of available opportunities is smaller than the number of the people who are faced with those opportunities, even if the disparity is not large. As he states, 'a group suffers collective unfreedom with respect to a type of action A if and only if performance of A by all members of the group is impossible. Collective unfreedom...is *irreducibly* collective when more can perform A *in sensu diviso* than can perform it *in sensu composito*'.[56] Nonetheless, the impetus for his development of the concept of collective unfreedom has clearly stemmed from his concern with a situation—the plight of the proletariat—in regard to which the aforementioned disparity is huge. As Cohen submits, with reference to the ratio between the number of available opportunities for doing A and the total number of people in a group, 'collective unfreedom matters more the smaller the ratio...is'.[57] When the ratio is nearly one-to-one, an ascription of the conditional freedom-to-do-A to each member of the group is not even superficially misleading.)

What makes the circumstances of the proletariat so problematic for a theory of liberty is that the conditionality of the freedoms involved is unaccompanied by any significant likelihood that all or most of those freedoms will be exercised and thus eliminated. To grasp the signifi-

[55] Cohen, 'Capitalism', 24; Cohen, *History*, 264.
[56] Cohen, *History*, 268–9, emphasis in original.   [57] Cohen, *History*, 269.

cance of this point, we should ponder a situation that contrasts in precisely this respect with the situation of the proletariat. As a pertinent example can reveal, many conditional freedoms are ephemeral in that the prerequisites of their continuation will not be met. Suppose that a professor sincerely announces to her students at her final lecture of the term that the first student to raise his right arm fully extended above his head will receive an excellent mark in her course without having to undergo the examination. At the moment of this announcement, every student in the class is free to attain an excellent mark in this manner, on the condition that no one else will have done so first. Likewise, everybody will continue to be free to attain an excellent mark in this manner, on the condition that no one else exercises that freedom. In these circumstances, the likelihood of the continuation of that freedom for each person is vanishingly small; it is highly likely that at least one student will extend his arm above his head in the requisite fashion. In these circumstances, that is, an accurate ascription to each student of the conditional freedom-to-attain-an-excellent-mark-in-the-specified-manner is an ascription of a freedom heavily qualified with a probabilistic caveat. Such a caveat indicates that the continued existence of the freedom is exceedingly improbable, and it thus indicates that the conditional freedom can perhaps more informatively be designated as a conditional unfreedom. Now, as has been suggested in Chapter 2 and as will be discussed more amply in Chapter 5, the role of probabilities will be fully taken into account by any sound approach to the measurement of overall freedom. When we tally a person's combinations of conjunctively exercisable freedoms in order to calculate his or her overall liberty, we associate every freedom in each such combination with the probability of its existence. Hence, when the conditionality of some particular freedom of a person (such as the freedom of each student to attain an excellent mark by extending his right arm) is accompanied by the improbability of that freedom's continuation, the conditionality will be duly reflected in any measurements of the person's overall liberty. That is, it will be manifested in the smallness of the contribution of that particular freedom to the person's overall liberty.

By contrast, when the conditionality of some particular freedom of a person (such as the freedom of each proletarian to rise above his class) is not accompanied by the improbability of that freedom's continued existence, the conditionality will apparently not be reflected in any calculations of the person's overall liberty. As a consequence, those calculations may seem to be omitting something important. In regard to each member of the proletariat, for example, the calculations fully incorporate his individual freedom to transcend his class, but they apparently disregard his inability to exercise that freedom in tandem with the other members of that class. In other words, the calculations leave out the collective unfreedom in which each proletarian is situated.

In a powerful and perceptive reply to Cohen, Ian Carter has maintained that adequate measurements of each person's overall liberty will capture what is important about the collective unfreedom of people such as proletarians.[58] Carter takes this position, moreover, while submitting that the focus of our measurements can and should lie exclusively on individuals' freedoms/unfreedoms. Collective freedom/unfreedom should not enter our calculations as a separate phenomenon. (Obviously, when gauging the aggregate freedom in a society, we need to arrive at a sum across individuals. What is at issue, however, is whether the sum should involve only *individuals'* combinations of freedoms and unfreedoms, or whether it should also involve *collective* freedom and unfreedom. Carter rightly argues for the former alternative.)

Carter advances several piquant arguments against the idea that collective freedom or unfreedom should be incorporated as a distinct phenomenon into our calculations of the aggregate freedom within a society. Some of those arguments need not be explored in detail here, either because they trade on Cohen's Marxist beliefs—which Carter invokes without endorsing in any way—or because they point to a situation in which collective unfreedom is accompanied by individual unfreedom (that is, a situation where the limited opportunities available to an array of individuals will very likely all be taken up). We are interested here solely in circumstances where collective unfreedom is not so accompanied. Those are the circumstances in which the conditionality of some particular freedom of each person is not conjoined with a high likelihood of the freedom's ceasing to exist.

Let us bestow attention, then, on a different line of reasoning propounded by Carter. He highlights a fact of which Cohen is keenly aware, the fact that an escape from the proletariat into the petty bourgeoisie is usually extremely arduous. Carter contends that Cohen does not sufficiently draw attention to the ways in which the difficulty of transcending the proletarian class will have curtailed each proletarian's overall freedom. Though virtually every proletarian may be free to escape, that freedom cannot be exercised conjunctively with many other freedoms. In other words, though possessed of the par-

[58] Carter, *Measure*, 246–58.

ticular freedom-to-escape, each proletarian cannot avail himself of that freedom unless he forgoes a myriad of actions and states that are incompatible with his availing himself of it. His possession of that freedom does not contribute much to the range of his combinations of conjunctively exercisable liberties. While not entirely devoid of the means of rising above his class, each proletarian is quite tightly hemmed in. As Carter writes, 'if escaping from the proletariat involves saving and working extremely hard, then doing so is impossible in combination with a great many actions which are performable by proletarians who do not try to escape'.[59] While we are warranted in attributing to each proletarian the freedom-to-escape, we should not lose sight of the impairedness of his or her overall liberty. As a consequence of that impairedness, the exercise of the freedom-to-escape entails the relinquishing of manifold other freedoms.

Carter is correct in his observations about the overall position of each member of the proletariat. He is therefore likewise correct in suggesting that, when an ascription of the freedom-to-escape to each proletarian is combined with an adequate account of the limitedness of each proletarian's overall liberty, it is not misleading in the slightest. Measurements of each person's overall freedom will reveal that 'even if proletarians *are* individually free to leave the proletariat, this does not imply that they are individually as free *overall* as non-proletarians'.[60] With reference to the plight of the proletariat—which, of course, is the straitened state on which Cohen principally trains his scrutiny—Carter's riposte is well aimed. Nonetheless, by modifying an example which Cohen offers as an analogy to the situation of the proletariat, we can come up with a scenario of collective unfreedom to which Carter's riposte does not apply. In this scenario, the following three points will obtain: each person's freedom to escape a state of confinement is conditional on the non-exercise of a similar freedom by everyone else; each person's freedom to escape is not associated with a significant likelihood that it will quickly cease to exist; and any person's exercise of his freedom to escape would require very little effort. The third of these points is what differentiates the situation in my scenario from the situation of the proletariat, in a manner that deflects Carter's riposte.

Let us suppose, then, that ten people are locked in a room. They are reliably informed that any one of them can leave at any time, and that not more than one of them can leave. As soon as any one of them has exited, the room will be impregnably sealed in order to render all

---

[59] Carter, *Measure*, 255.   [60] Ibid., emphases in original.

further departures impossible. Perhaps because of a sense of solidarity with one another or maybe because of sheer laziness or perhaps because of a fondness for the room—which is beautifully furnished, we may assume—none of the people has any inclination to leave. There is virtually no likelihood, at least for quite a while, that anyone will choose to be the sole person to exit. Nevertheless, if anyone does eventually so choose, he or she will be able to depart with hardly any effort. As each occupant of the room knows, the first person who extends both of his arms over his head will be whisked out of the room by the captor of the ten people. Nothing more strenuous or time-consuming is required. Notwithstanding, none of the people is at all disposed to undertake the arm-extending gesture as a means of getting out of the room. In these circumstances, accordingly, all three points mentioned in my preceding paragraph are applicable. Most important for our present purposes, anyone's exercise of the freedom-to-escape would not entail the relinquishment of many other liberties. That freedom consequently contributes greatly to the range of each person's combinations of conjunctively exercisable liberties—which means that it contributes greatly to each person's overall freedom. Thus, although no more than one of the ten people in the room can ever leave, the freedom-to-leave enjoyed by each of them is enough to expand the overall liberty of each of them immensely. Every one of the people is free to do a host of things outside the room, even though there is only one opportunity-to-get-outside available to the ten of them.

Many other scenarios with a basically similar structure (though perhaps with less at stake than in a scenario of outright confinement) can be adduced. For example, with a few modifications, the story of the professor and the students will exhibit precisely that structure. Once again, suppose that the professor offers to confer an excellent mark on the first student who fully extends his right arm above his head. Suppose further that every student is wholly uninclined to take up the professor's offer, because each student is keen to ascertain how well he or she can do without any special dispensation. Like someone who wishes to test his own skill in tackling a crossword puzzle without peeking at the answers, each student wants to gauge his or her proficiency in meeting the challenge posed by the examination. Or perhaps some of the students wrongly think that the professor is insincere and that she is trying to make them look foolish. Whatever may be the reason for the shared disinclination of the students to raise their hands, each of them is indeed undisposed to take the small step necessary for the attainment of an excellent mark without having to undergo the examination. In these circumstances, then, the three points recounted in the penultimate paragraph above are all applicable. First, each student's liberty to attain an excellent mark without undergoing the examination is conditional on the abstention of every other student from exercising a similar liberty; second, because every student is uninclined to exercise the aforementioned liberty, the continuation of it for everyone is highly likely (at least for a certain period); third, any one of the students could exercise that particular liberty with very little effort. Because anyone attending the lecture can easily avail himself or herself of the freedom-to-attain-an-excellent-mark-without-undergoing-the-examination, that freedom contributes quite substantially to the range of each student's combinations of conjunctively exercisable freedoms.

Although the foregoing scenarios are somewhat fanciful, some more realistic examples are readily at hand. Let us ponder, for instance, a situation highlighted by John Gray for a somewhat different purpose: the situation of subscribers to a telephone system.[61] Suppose that there are 50 million users of the telephone service, and that there is enough capacity in the system for 20 million people to make use of it simultaneously. (Perhaps on special occasions such as Christmas, the capacity is temporarily increased.) At any given moment, then, each person's freedom to make or receive a telephone call is conditional on the abstention of 30 million or more of the other users from engaging in telephone conversations at that time. We may suppose further that it is extremely unlikely that as many as 20 million users will seek to engage in telephone conversations simultaneously during any ordinary day. As the people who run the telephone company know from past experience, the number of active users at any one time during an ordinary day will almost never exceed 15 million. Hence, only on rare occasions does the sheer number of active users thwart anyone from making or receiving a telephone call. Such occasions, moreover, are transitory. Yet, notwithstanding that there will very seldom be more than 15 million people at any single time availing themselves of the liberty-to-use-the-telephone, the exercise of that liberty is hardly a taxing or time-consuming exploit. It requires not much more effort than the exercise of the liberty-to-attain-an-excellent-mark by any student in my preceding scenario. Thus, once again, we encounter the three elements that together constitute a situation not covered by Carter's riposte to Cohen. Most notably, the third element—the easiness of exercising the conditional freedom under consideration—is what prevents us from invoking here Carter's point about the overall liberty of each proletarian. Whereas Carter can

---

[61] Gray, 'Alienation', 166; Gray, 'Unfreedom', 91.

aptly claim that the exercise by a proletarian of her freedom-to-escape-her-class will entail the elimination of many of her other freedoms along the way, we can scarcely say the same about a person's exercise of her freedom-to-engage-in-a-telephone-conversation. Accordingly, we appear not to have any means of acknowledging the collective unfreedom of the telephone users, when we describe each user's particular liberties and overall liberty.

Should we therefore conclude that situations of collective unfreedom cannot be suitably analysed by my negative-liberty theory, which concentrates on the particular freedoms and overall freedom of each individual, and which gauges the aggregate freedom of a society by adding together the positions of individuals? Must an adequate theory take account of collective unfreedom as an intermediate phenomenon that should get entered into any calculations of the aggregate freedom in a society? Cohen seeks to suggest as much, when commenting on the scenario of the people locked in the room. Presuming that the people are motivated to stay in the room by a sense of solidarity with one another, he writes: '[E]ach [person] remains free to leave. Yet we can envisage members of the group communicating to their gaoler a demand for freedom, to which he could hardly reply that they are free already (even though, individually, they are).'[62] What the members of the group are demanding is an unconditional freedom-to-leave for each of them, whereas the captor is replying that each of them is already conditionally free. We can easily see that his reply is wholly unresponsive to their demand. However, it might appear that his utter unresponsiveness will be overlooked if one's approach to measuring a society's freedom does not take separate account of collective unfreedom. As has been indicated, the approach favoured herein is indeed an approach that does not treat collective unfreedom as a factor to be taken separately into account. When the conditionality of each person's freedom-to-do-X is not associated with a significant likelihood that that freedom will cease to exist (because of someone else's exercise of a parallel freedom), the conditionality will be largely omitted from our calculations. Though Cohen is not focusing on the question of measurement, he in effect seizes on this point. If our efforts to gauge a society's aggregate liberty largely gloss over the fact that the freedom-to-depart of each person in the room is conditional, then we seem to be blinding ourselves to the malicious inappositeness of the captor's reply to the people who demand their freedom. Are we not thereby disregarding something important?

[62] Cohen, *History*, 264.

Two rejoinders are appropriate here, the first of which is of broad applicability, and the second of which is of special pertinence to situations such as that of the people immured in the room. First, any general unease over the omission of collective unfreedom from our calculations of societal liberty is probably attributable—at least in part—to a neglect of the distinction between the freedom to do X and the doing of X. An insufficient attentiveness to this distinction is probably what has led Steiner to the view that each thing must be in the actual or subjunctive possession of one and only one person. If anybody feels disconcerted about maintaining that every one of 50 million users is free to initiate a telephone conversation at virtually any time on a network that can handle only 20 million users simultaneously, she is probably mistaking a proposition about freedoms for a proposition about actions. That is, she is probably mistaking a proposition about potentiality for a proposition about actuality. On the envisaged telephone network, it can never be the case that all 50 million users (or, indeed, any number of users greater than 20 million) actually engage in telephone calls simultaneously. However, in the circumstances specified in my scenario, it can be the case and is the case that every one of the 50 million users is free to engage in a telephone call at each moment. This latter proposition is true exactly because fewer than 20 million of the users at each moment will actually endeavour to avail themselves of the freedom-to-engage-in-a-call that is held by every one of them. The source of that shared freedom—its source in the disinclination of most users to seek to avail themselves of it at any given moment—is fundamentally similar to the source of Taylor's and Alice's shared freedom in the opening scenario of the cabbage fields. Indeed, in any context of irreducibly collective unfreedom, where every one of the people involved is individually free to perform some action A at some time t, that particular freedom of each person obtains precisely because a certain number of the people (all of them, in many contexts) are uninclined to try to exercise it. Thus, our ascription of the freedom-to-perform-A-at-t to each person will presuppose that all or most of the people endowed with such a freedom are not in fact going to endeavour to perform A at t. Consequently, the impossibility of the occurrence of multiple performances of A at t should not lead us to be chary of ascribing to each person the individual freedom to perform that very action at that time.

The foregoing rejoinder is doubtless sufficient to allay any general unease that might be felt about my analysis of collective unfreedom in many contexts. Nevertheless, it is probably not sufficient to quell entirely the unease that might centre on Cohen's scenario of the people in the room who demand their freedom. Merely distinguishing between the freedom to leave the room and the act of leaving the room will not eliminate one's sense that something crucial is being omitted if one's approach to measuring overall liberty cannot reveal the inappositeness of the captor's cynical reply to the people's demand. A further rejoinder is therefore necessary to deal adequately with situations of this sort. Fortunately, a suitable way of proceeding here has been foreshadowed by my earlier discussion of a hoodlum's threats to inflict harm on distant third parties.

Let us consider the key features of the situation of the people in the room. In the first place, of course, that situation exhibits the three main characteristics on which much of this discussion has concentrated. That is, each person in the room enjoys the freedom-to-do-some-action-A, so long as no one else exercises that freedom; and, because of the inclinations of the people involved, there is little or no likelihood that the aforementioned freedom will cease to exist for anyone (by dint of being exercised by somebody else); and, despite the fact that nobody is inclined to exercise the freedom-to-do-A, the steps which anyone would have to take in order to exercise that freedom are neither arduous nor time-consuming. In addition to those three points, however, two other features of the immured people's plight are especially noteworthy. Any person who exercises the freedom-to-leave-the-room will thereby cause everyone else to lose that freedom, and the freedom-to-leave-the-room is of enormous significance for each person's overall liberty. As a consequence of those two factors, anyone exercising that freedom will bear a weighty responsibility—at least a causal responsibility and maybe also a moral responsibility—for sharply cabining the overall liberty of everyone else in the room.

In this central respect, the predicament portrayed by Cohen diverges conspicuously from the other situations of collective unfreedom that we have pondered. Although the scenario of the professor and the students also presents a situation in which any person's exercise of a freedom will deprive everyone else of a homologous freedom, there is considerably less at stake than in the situation of the people confined to a room. To be sure, the prospect of receiving an excellent mark without having to undergo an examination is undoubtedly attractive to all or most of the students. Nevertheless, the elimination of that prospect by somebody else's seizing of the opportunity-to-receive-the-effort-lessly-fine-mark will not normally affect anybody's overall liberty nearly as devastatingly as a loss of the freedom-to-escape-the-room. (Of course, one can imagine circumstances in which the results of an examination will indeed have a profound effect on the future liberty of each person taking the examination. Against the background of such circumstances, the scenario of the professor and the students is closely akin to the scenario of the people locked in the room, at least in respect of students who are unable to attain very high marks through their own endeavours on the examination.) Even more pronounced are the differences between the plight of the people locked in the room and the situation of users on a telephone network. Causal responsibility for any temporary overwhelming of the network's capacity does not rest on a single person or a small group of people, but is very widely diffused. Moreover, except in unusual circumstances, any such overwhelming of the capacity of the system will produce inconvenience and frustration for would-be callers, rather than devastation. Normally, being unable to make a telephone call for a certain period is hardly comparable to being confined in a room indefinitely.

In sum, the ordeal of the people in the room differs saliently from the other settings of collective unfreedom that we have contemplated. It amounts to a situation in which causal responsibility for severely impairing the overall liberty of other people will be clearly attributable to any person who exercises his particular freedom-to-leave-the-room, a freedom which each of the other people also holds. Some degree of moral responsibility may also be attributable to the escaping person, though of course the degree will be less than is attributable to the captor. When explaining why each person in the room is endowed with the freedom-to-leave, Cohen himself intimates that at least a modicum of dishonour may attach to anybody who exercises that freedom: '[I]t remains true of each person that he would suffer no interference if, counterfactually, he sought to [leave] (assume that the others would have contempt for him, but not try to stop him).'[63] At any rate, regardless of whether the situation is such that the ascription of some moral responsibility to the escaping person is appropriate, the causal responsibility is plain.

Why is this point important in the present context? A recognition of it enables us to resuscitate Carter's rejoinder to Cohen in a modified form. That rejoinder, let us recall, maintains that each proletarian can exercise her freedom-to-transcend-her-class only by giving up numerous other freedoms. Her freedom-to-transcend-her-class therefore does not add very substantially to her overall liberty, at least in the short term and medium term. This retort by Carter as it stands cannot be transferred straightforwardly to the scenario of the people locked in the room, since any one of them can exercise the freedom-to-leave

---

[63] Ibid.

without relinquishing many other freedoms. Carter's retort gains new life, however, if we focus it on a different freedom. Here, as in the earlier case of a hoodlum's threat to harm a distant third party, the relevant freedom is the freedom to avoid becoming responsible (causally or morally) for serious harm inflicted on someone else. Unlike the liberty to depart, the liberty to avoid responsibility cannot be exercised by anyone in the room without an abandonment of many other liberties. Precisely in ensuring that the freedom to avoid responsibility is not exercisable conjunctively with countless other freedoms, the captor has gravely restricted the overall liberty of each person in the room. Everyone who might want more ample leeway for his actions than is possible within the confines of a cell will not be able to attain that leeway without becoming partly responsible for the denial of any similar latitude to everyone else. Once we allow that 'becomings' and 'not becomings' can be contents of freedoms along with 'doings' and 'not doings'—or once we construe doings and not-doings sufficiently expansively to encompass the full medley of consequences for which an agent becomes causally responsible during a certain period—we can discern the significant freedom-curtailing effects of the captor's immurement of the ten people. And we can do so without treating their collective unfreedom as a separate item to be entered into our calculations of their aggregate liberty.

On the one hand, as has been observed, my approach to the measurement of overall freedom does not take account of the conditionality of each hostage's liberty-to-leave in circumstances where the conditionality does not involve any perceptible unlikelihood of the continued existence of that particular liberty. On the other hand, my approach to the measurement of overall freedom does indeed take account of each hostage's liberty-to-avoid-responsibility-for-a-severe-diminution-in-everyone-else's-freedom. My approach therefore takes account of the fact that, as a result of the captor's fiendish designs, each hostage's exercise of the liberty-to-avoid-responsibility has been rendered inconsistent with his or her exercise of myriad other liberties. That is, we can recognize that the captor has eliminated many combinations of conjunctively exercisable freedoms that have heretofore been enjoyed by each hostage. Without having to advert to collective unfreedom as a phenomenon intermediate between individual liberty and societal liberty, we can see that the captor has *pro tanto* significantly reduced the overall freedom of each person in the room.

Of course, as was true in my earlier discussion of genuine threats, the phrase '*pro tanto*' is important. The captor has expanded as well as impaired the overall liberty of each hostage. No hostage can exercise both the freedom-to-leave and the freedom-not-to-become-causally-responsible-for-the-permanent-captivity-of-the-other-hostages, but any one of them can exercise both the former freedom and the free-dom-to-cause-the-permanent-captivity-of-the-other-hostages. Since the last-mentioned freedom would almost certainly not be available to any captive in the absence of the kidnapper's evildoing, his evildoing has enlarged as well as diminished the range of the combinations-of-conjunctively-exercisable-liberties available to each captive. A *pro-tanto* reduction is accompanied by a *pro-tanto* increase. Hence, my aim in this discussion is not to establish that the kidnapper has perforce brought about a net decrease—as opposed to a *pro-tanto* decrease—in each hostage's overall liberty. Rather, my aim is to show that he has indeed brought about a *pro-tanto* decrease. My fifth chapter will explain why that *pro-tanto* reduction is in fact also a net reduction.

Having perceived the freedom-constricting effects of the captor's conduct, we can likewise perceive why his cynical reply to the demand of the immured people for freedom is wholly unresponsive and beside the point. Implicit in their demand is that each of them should be able to leave without becoming responsible for the loss of anyone else's freedom to leave. In other words, their demand is (in effect) that each person's freedom-to-leave should be exercisable conjunctively with his or her freedom-to-avoid-becoming-responsible. When the captor replies by declaring in effect that each person in the room is free to leave and that each is also free not to become responsible for a loss of liberty by anyone else, he is omitting to acknowledge that those two freedoms are not conjunctively exercisable. He is thereby omitting to acknowledge that he has *pro tanto* sharply constricted the overall liberty of each of the people in the room. They are calling on him to desist from curtailing the overall liberty of each of them in the way that he has. Because his retort simply ignores the fact that he has indeed *pro tanto* curtailed each person's overall freedom, it is utterly unresponsive to the captives' exhortations. Despite any possible appearances to the contrary, he is sneeringly talking past his captives rather than engaging with them. We can descry as much, on the basis of the categories that inform my approach to measuring any individual's overall liberty and to identifying any individual's particular liberties.

By parting ways with Carter on the matter of identifying particular freedoms, my analysis can satisfactorily handle a situation that remains intensely problematic for him. His own riposte to Cohen is inapplic-able to the circumstances depicted in the scenario of the people locked in the room, and his view that actions are the only contents of free-doms is incompatible with the argument presented in my last several paragraphs—unless he were to define the potential actions of each person very expansively to encompass all the ascertainable causal consequences which those actions would generate during a certain period. Hence, Carter cannot deal adequately with the specified scenario. He cannot explain why the captor's rejoinder to the victims' demand for freedom is inapposite, because he cannot accept that the captor in the stipulated circumstances has significantly impaired the overall liberty of anyone in the room. By contrast, my analysis enables us to pinpoint how a *pro-tanto* reduction in each person's overall liberty has indeed occurred, and it accordingly enables us to understand why the victims can properly feel aggrieved over the reply to their demand. By singling out some prominent features of Cohen's scenario that mark it off from the other portrayals of collective unfreedom which we have contemplated, my discussion has highlighted a key aspect of the overall unfreedom of each person locked in the room. Because we can accurately analyse the ordeal of the people in the room as a situation in which everyone's overall liberty has been significantly abridged *pro tanto*, we do not need to rely on the notion of collective unfreedom in order to come up with a satisfactory account of each person's plight.

Let us close this discussion and indeed this whole section of the present chapter by briefly investigating what may appear to be a conflict or tension between two of my lines of analysis. In my earlier treatment of the hoodlum's threats to inflict serious harm on third parties, opportunities for joint actions figured saliently as elements of any individual's freedom. As was argued there, those opportunities are particular freedoms that contribute to the overall liberty of each individual. In the present discussion, by contrast, one of the chief objectives has been to come up with an account of the immured people's predicament that does not rely on the concept of collective unfreedom. My aim has been to reveal that their plight can perfectly well be characterized as a situation in which the overall freedom of each individual is curtailed in some important respects. Such a characterization obviates the inclusion of collective unfreedom as a separate factor in our calculations of a society's aggregate liberty. Is there any tension between my earlier readiness to invoke the notion of joint actions and my present reluctance to invoke the notion of collective unfreedom?

The answer to this question, of course, is negative. No tension exists, because my previous exposition of joint actions and my current exposition of collective unfreedom have both surfaced in arguments that ascribe particular liberties (and levels of overall liberty) to individuals. My previous remarks concerned the character of some of the actions which individuals are free or not free to do, whereas my current remarks have concerned the character of the beings—individuals separately versus arrays of individuals—to whom certain unfreedoms should be ascribed. My earlier argument did not in any way point to the conclusion that opportunities for joint actions are to be attributed irreducibly to arrays of individuals rather than to individuals separately. On the one hand, any joint action is irreducibly collective in that it cannot take place as such unless certain individuals interact in particular ways. On the other hand, any *opportunities* to engage in joint actions are enjoyed by individuals separately. Similarly, when any such opportunities are denied, they are denied to individuals separately.

To be sure, if an individual X has an opportunity to engage in a joint action with some other individual Y, and if X's willingness to engage in the action is not essential to the performance thereof, it is necessarily the case that Y has an opportunity to engage in that joint action with X. (Were it not the case that Y is free to engage in that action with X, it could not be the case that X is free to engage therein with Y. X cannot be free to do what is impossible, and the joint action with Y would be impossible if Y were not free to do it. After all, given that X's willingness to participate in the joint action is not essential to its occurrence, Y's inability to participate would have to be due to some factor that is not under X's control. That factor would therefore preclude X from undertaking the specified action with Y, just as it would preclude Y from undertaking the action with X.) Conversely, if X has been denied an opportunity to perform a joint action with Y, and if Y's willingness to engage in the action is not prerequisite to its occurrence, then necessarily Y has been denied an opportunity to perform that joint action with X.

Nevertheless, even in a joint-action situation where a relationship of entailment does obtain between the enjoyment (or non-enjoyment) of an opportunity by either potential participant and the enjoyment (or non-enjoyment) of an opportunity by the other potential participant, each opportunity (or the absence of each opportunity) is ascribable to a separate individual and is thus not *irreducibly* ascribable to the pair of potential participants as a unit. Of course, it is fully legitimate to affirm that the pair of them are free (or not free) to engage in the joint action, but it is no less accurate to affirm that each of them is free (or not free) to engage in that action with the other. The irreducibly collective nature of the action does not translate into the irreducibly collective nature of the freedom (or the lack of freedom) to perform it.

In that major respect, anyone's freedom or unfreedom to undertake a joint action is fundamentally different from the collective unfreedom described by Cohen. In contexts of collective unfreedom like those which we have explored, 'there is more freedom for a set of individuals taken individually than for the same individuals when they are taken as members of a group: collective unfreedom, we might say, is *irreducibly* collective when more can perform *A in sensu diviso* than can perform it *in sensu composito*'.[64] To behold the collective unfreedom which Cohen expounds, one has to train one's attention on an array of individuals rather than on the individuals separately. What is collective is the unfreedom itself, as opposed to the action or set of actions to which the unfreedom pertains—or in addition to that action or set of actions.

In short, there is no tension between my earlier focus on joint actions and my current de-emphasizing of collective unfreedom. My approach to the measurement of societal liberty, which proceeds in part by adding together the levels of overall liberty of the myriad individuals in a society, can easily take cognizance of the freedom or unfreedom of each individual to participate in various joint actions. What cannot be taken on board is a state of freedom or unfreedom that is irreducibly collective in being ascribable only to an array of individuals and not to individuals discretely. Fortunately, as has been seen, we can handle Cohen's scenario of the people in the locked room (and other relevantly similar scenarios) in a perfectly satisfactory manner without having to rely on the notion of irreducibly collective unfreedom. Though Cohen is certainly not wrong to have introduced such a notion—which he has defined rigorously and forcefully—an eschewal of it is indispensable for the coherence of my project of measurement. Carter is entirely justified in claiming as much, with reference to his own broadly cognate project. Thus, although the concept of collective unfreedom is quite tenable, and although it is undoubtedly important for many purposes, it is best shunned for the purposes of this book. There are no situations that cannot be analysed adequately without the invocation of that concept, and the avoidance of any such invocation is crucial for the accomplishment of my fundamental project.

4. *Freedoms versus Actions*

In the closing paragraphs of the preceding section, we glanced at the distinction between the collective character of certain actions and the collective character of freedoms or unfreedoms to perform certain actions. The distinction between actions and freedoms—the distinc-

---

[64] Cohen, *History*, 268–9, emphasis in original.

tion between the doing of X and the freedom to do X—is noteworthy in other contexts as well, as we shall see below. My remarks in this section will serve to underscore the importance of distinguishing carefully not only between freedoms and 'doings' but also between freedoms and 'becomings' or between freedoms and 'remainings' or between freedoms and 'undergoings'. For the sake of avoiding unwieldy prose, however, my discussion will concentrate on the freedom/action dichotomy.

Let us begin with a contrast that has often been recognized but also often mishandled or overlooked: the distinction between the value of doing X and the value of the freedom to do X. As can be grasped quite readily, the freedom to perform a certain action will normally be valuable for the person who is endowed with that freedom, even if the action itself would not be valuable for that person or for anyone else. For example, even if somebody would decidedly not value the actual experience of travelling to a place such as North Korea, she might set considerable store by the freedom to travel there. After all, the fact that a person has not been deprived of such a freedom is typically a mark of respect for her autonomy and discretion. She is trusted sufficiently to choose whether to hazard the risks and the moral taint of visiting a land ruled by an odiously repressive regime. As Cohen declares, 'the desire for freedom is not reducible to the desire to do what one would be free to do if one had it. I may resent my lack of freedom to do what I have no wish to do: Soviet citizens who dislike restrictions on foreign travel need not want to go abroad'.[65] In regard to many other endeavours as well that are repellent for the large majority of people, the value of remaining free to pursue such endeavours can be substantial. For example, self-disembowelment is not an action that greatly entices most people. On the contrary, most people would recoil at the thought of performing such an action. All the same, the freedom to engage in self-disembowelment should hardly be dismissed as valueless. To be sure, such a freedom is important partly because any extirpation of it would usually also involve the extirpation of many other freedoms. In addition, however, that freedom is important because the preservation of it is typically an indicator of respect for the rationality and deliberative maturity of each person who is possessed of the freedom. In other words, the preservation of that freedom for any adult of a reasonably sound mind bespeaks the fact that such a person is generally credited with sufficiently good judgement to reach appropriate decisions concerning self-disembowelment as an option. To prevent him from reaching and

[65] Cohen, *History*, 271 n. 23.

implementing perverse decisions on that option would be to evince a lack of trust in his capacity to arrive at suitable decisions. A mentally stable adult deprived of the freedom to undertake self-disembowelment should therefore normally feel aggrieved, notwithstanding that he has no inclination whatsoever to do the suicidal act which he is prevented from doing. He should feel disgruntlement, moreover, even if some sophisticatedly precise electronic means of mind-control has deprived him of the particular freedom-to-engage-in-self-disembowelment without otherwise impinging on his liberty.

While the value of the freedom-to-do-X and the value of doing X are distinct, they are not entirely so. If the latter value is high, then the former value will likewise be large; if someone takes a strongly favourable view of doing X, she will naturally attach considerable importance to being free-to-do-X. The distinctness of the values is operative, then, when the value of doing X is small or negative. When that latter value is indeed minute or negative, the value of being free-to-do-X may nevertheless be substantial (for reasons laconically sketched in the preceding paragraph). In other words, the sizeableness of the value of doing X entails the sizeableness of the value of being free-to-do-X, whereas the sizeableness of the latter value does not entail the sizeableness of the former.

On the basis of the foregoing points, which may in themselves seem fairly evident, we can perceive that some of the most astute contemporary theorists of negative liberty have gone slightly astray when distinguishing between the content-independent value and the content-dependent value of various freedoms. This dichotomy has figured especially prominently in the work of Carter, who designates it as a distinction between the non-specific value and the specific value of freedoms. He draws that distinction along the following lines:

[F]reedom has what I called *non-specific value*. To say that freedom has non-specific value is to say that its value cannot be described wholly in terms of the value of the specific things the agent is free to do...The opposite of non-specific value can be called *specific value*: the specific value of a freedom (which is always either instrumental or constitutive) is its value in terms of the specific thing it is the freedom to do.[66]

As Carter adds slightly later: 'The specific value of freedom varies according to the values of the actions one is free to perform...In contrast, the non-specific value of freedom holds regardless of the differences between one specific freedom and another in terms of

---

[66] Carter, 'Specificity', 40, emphases in original.

the value of the actions the agent is free to perform.'[67] These comments by Carter tally with his manner of drawing the non-specific/specific distinction in his major book, *A Measure of Freedom*. There he contends, for example, that any theories which deny the non-specific value of liberty have reduced 'the value of having a certain measure of freedom to the values of the *specific things* that one is free to do'.[68]

Other important theorists have followed Carter in distinguishing along these lines between the content-independent value and the content-dependent value of any freedom. Martin van Hees, for instance, has submitted that the 'specific value of freedom refers to the value of the things that constitute our freedom. A person's freedom has specific value if at least part of its value derives from the value of the particular things that the person is free to do'. Van Hees reaffirms that the 'specific-instrumental value of your freedom is the value of freedom that can be reduced to the consequences of the things you are free to do'.[69] Serena Olsaretti has adopted a similar stance, as she squarely endorses this aspect of Carter's theory: 'Carter is right, in my view, in suggesting that freedom *as such* has value, or, in other words, that the value of freedom is not exhausted by the value of the things which one is free to do.' Olsaretti repeatedly demarcates the specific from the non-specific in this fashion: 'Freedom has value independently of the value of the specific things that one is free to do, so that our having the freedom to do specific things, such as to move our arms or to practise the religion of our choice, is valuable not only because of the value of doing those specific things, but also because of the fact of our having freedom.'[70] Joel Feinberg, in a well-known essay published two decades earlier, articulates much the same position when he poses a contrast between 'the interest in liberty *as such*' and 'the various interests we have in doing the things we may be free or unfree to do'.[71]

None of these quoted pronouncements is strictly wrong, but each of them is regrettably misleading, for each of them blurs the distinction between the value of doing X and the value of being free to do X. Instead of focusing on a dichotomy between the content-independent value of the freedom-to-do-X and the value of doing X, we should be focusing on a tripartite distinction comprising the content-independent value of

[67] Carter, 'Specificity', 42.   [68] Carter, *Measure*, 127, emphasis in original.
[69] Van Hees, *Reductionism*, 152, 161.
[70] Serena Olsaretti, 'The Value of Freedom and Freedom of Choice', 56 *Notizie di Politeia* 114, 118 (1999), emphasis in original. See also D. D. Raphael, *Problems of Political Philosophy*, 2nd edn (Basingstoke: Macmillan, 1990), 59–60; Alan Ryan, 'Freedom', 40 *Philosophy* 93, 112 (1965).
[71] Feinberg, 'Interest', 27, emphasis in original.

the freedom-to-do-X, the content-dependent value of that freedom, and the value of doing X. The second of these elements, the content-dependent value of a particular freedom, is what each of the quoted comments tends to submerge. Indeed, exactly because the terms 'content-independent' and 'content-dependent' help to keep that second element from being obscured—since they make clear that the designated values pertain to freedoms, which in turn pertain to various actions or processes or states—they are preferable to the terms 'non-specific' and 'specific'.

We should therefore reconstrue the distinction which the theorists quoted above have been invoking. Instead of a contrast between the value of freedom as such and the value of doing some particular thing, the content-independent/content-dependent contrast is as follows: the value of a freedom-to-do-X as a sheer freedom, versus the value of a freedom-to-do-X as a freedom with a particular content. On each side of the dichotomy is the value of the liberty-to-do-X, rather than the value of doing X. On one side is the value of freedom as such, as instantiated in the liberty-to-do-X. On the other side is the value of a freedom with the particular content of the liberty-to-do-X. In other words, the distinction lies between the value of the freedom-to-do-X qua instance of freedom *tout court* and the value of the freedom-to-do-X qua instance of freedom with a specific bearing or orientation. Different from the latter—as well as from the former, of course—is the value of doing X. To be sure, as we have seen, the sizeableness of the value of doing X entails the sizeableness of the value of being free to do X. However, as we have likewise seen, the entailment does not obtain in the opposite direction. Hence, the tripartite distinction delineated here is indeed a genuine departure from the misleading dichotomy expressed in each of the pronouncements quoted above. Neither intensionally nor extensionally is 'value of doing X' equivalent to 'value of being free specifically to do X'. (Similarly, of course, the latter is not equivalent either intensionally or extensionally to 'value of being free'.) Thus, since the objective of each of the theorists quoted above is to distinguish between two ways in which freedoms are valuable—rather than between a way in which freedoms are valuable and the way in which actions are valuable—the appropriate analytical scheme is my tripartite distinction, as opposed to a simple dichotomy that conflates the value of doing X and the content-dependent value of the freedom-to-do-X.

The importance of avoiding such a conflation will become further apparent in Chapter 5, when I contend that evaluative considerations should play a role (albeit a circumscribed role) in any measurements of each person's overall liberty. Some of the arguments that have been mounted against any incorporation of evaluative considerations into such measurements are based on a disregard of the non-equivalence between the value of doing X and the value of being free to do X. Moreover, the distinction between doing X and the freedom-to-do-X is pregnant in other contexts as well—contexts where evaluations of particular freedoms are not at issue. For example, in the preceding section of this chapter we saw that a central reason for the fact that people can each be free to occupy exactly the same place at exactly the same time is that a person's freedom-to-perform-X does not entail his performance of X. At several other junctures in this book we have likewise glimpsed the importance of the distinction between performing and being-free-to-perform, and we shall encounter its importance afresh as we go along. Easily stated in the abstract, that distinction gets overlooked with surprising frequency when theorists grapple with the gnarls and complexities of the idea of negative liberty.

5. Freedom and Force

As should be evident from my discussion of Dorothy and the whirlwind in Chapter 2 and in this chapter, a person who is compelled to φ is free to φ.[72] After all, such a person has φ-ed (*ex hypothesi*), and thus he must have been able to φ. And, given that he has been able to φ, he has been free to φ—since a person is free-to-φ if and only if he is able to φ. In the case of Dorothy, of course, the compulsion exerted on her goes beyond the mere forcing of her to do some action. Instead, she is carried along irresistibly by an impetus that overpowers her from acting. Save in very special circumstances where her ride through the sky can be subsumed under an earlier endeavour of hers to place herself within the sway of the whirlwind, that ride is not correctly classifiable as an element of her conduct at all. It is something that happens to her, rather than something which she performs. It is a process which she undergoes, rather than an action which she undertakes. Nevertheless, she is free to undergo that process, because she is unprevented from undergoing it. Neither an absence of relevant internal capacities nor the presence of any external preventive factors will have precluded her from hurtling through the air, along a trajectory determined by the rush of the whirlwind. Thus, she is free to hurtle along that trajectory. That freedom of hers is of course fully consistent with the fact that she

---

[72] For a very good discussion of this matter, see Cohen, *History*, Ch. 12.

is not free to keep herself from being driven through the air. Her utter lack of alternatives does not in any way negate the possibility of her being impelled by the wind. On the contrary, any physically necessary process is a physically possible process; anything that happens willy-nilly to Dorothy is something that *can* happen to her. She is not free to withstand the surge of the wind, but—because she is wholly unprevented from being carried along by that surge—she is free to be carried along by it.

Even more clear-cut is the situation of a person who is forced to perform some action, as opposed to a person such as Dorothy who is simply shoved around like an object. Here the phrase 'forced to perform some action' applies when a person is led to carry out the specified action only because there is no minimally acceptable alternative to carrying it out. In such circumstances a person acts involuntarily—unfreely—though of course volitionally.[73] (A full-scale theory of voluntariness and coercion would have to qualify my construal of 'forced to perform some action' in certain respects, and would naturally have to explore many subtleties and complications that lurk as potential pitfalls for any such theory. For our present purposes, however, my terse explication is perfectly serviceable.) Some examples of people forced to act in certain ways were offered in Chapter 2, where we pondered the situation of a man who is forced to walk around continuously in a room for a period of two hours. Because the only available alternative to his walking uninterruptedly for that period is his virtually instantaneous death, he will undoubtedly choose to continue walking. Unlike Dorothy in the grip of the whirlwind, the man does have a choice; but the sole option open to him apart from walking is truly shuddersome, and thus he will elect to persist in his perambulations. He is forced to persist. Now, clearly, his being forced to continue his wanderings uninterruptedly is fully consistent with his being free to continue them. Indeed, the former entails the latter, since he cannot do something involuntarily unless he is able to do it. One cannot walk grudgingly unless one can walk—which is to say that one cannot walk grudgingly unless one is free to walk. Being free to do X is a precondition for doing X unfreely.

Of course, when we affirm that the man forced to saunter around the room is free to do so, we are hardly thereby affirming that he enjoys very much liberty overall. He is not free to remain stationary anywhere in the room for more than an instant, for he will immediately be killed

[73] When unfreeness is predicated of actions rather than of actors—as has been noted in Chapter 2—the designated state is that of coercedness rather than of precludedness. An action performed unfreely is performed, however grudgingly, and is thus unprecluded.

if he desists from his trudging. Furthermore, he is not free to leave the room or to do anything outside it, since he is firmly confined therein with impregnable locks. Hence, although he is free to continue walking around the room, and although he is also free to stop his walking (on pain of immediate death), he is unfree to remain stationary and is unfree to go beyond the ambit of the room. Even more meagre is the overall freedom of Dorothy when she is thrust through the air by the whirlwind. Though she is free to be thrust along—since she is unprevented from being thrust along—she is not free to remain standing on the place whence she has been seized by the wind, and she is likewise not free to perform any actions that are inconsistent with her being impelled irresistibly along a trajectory through the air. Indeed, if the whirlwind has completely overpowered her, so that she is temporarily incapable of even shouting or flailing, then she will not be free to perform any actions at all until she has been released from its grip. Her particular freedom to be pushed through the skies by the whirlwind's impetus is accompanied by the severest constriction of her overall liberty. In those circumstances, throughout the period of her ravishment by the whirlwind, her combinations of conjunctively exercisable freedoms are reduced to one.

Now, given that somebody compelled to φ has indeed φ-ed (however resentfully), it should be quite evident that he has been free to φ. Not only is one's being compelled to φ an occurrence fully compatible with one's being free to φ, but the former presupposes the latter. Unless a person is free to do X, she cannot do X unfreely. So much is apparent, or should be apparent. Nevertheless, some estimable negative-liberty theorists have appeared to take a different view. We shall look here at only a few examples.

Contemplating an assertion of the compatibility of liberty and duress, Stanley Benn and William Weinstein suggested that '[t]his looks, to a liberal, wilfully perverse'. They submitted that '[a]ction under coercion or threat is, for the liberal, the very paradigm of unfreedom; the incompatibility of freedom and coercion is, after all, what classical Liberalism is all about'.[74] Benn and Weinstein did not unequivocally endorse the ostensibly liberal view which they outlined, but that view has been wholeheartedly embraced by some other theorists. Joel Feinberg, for example, has adopted just such a stance. He articulates his position in the following argument (which, as other passages in his essay reveal, is focused on non-normative freedom as well as on normative freedom despite being couched exclusively in the language of the latter):

[74] Benn and Weinstein, 'Being Free', 206.

I have an open option with respect to a given act X when I am permitted to do X and I am also permitted to do *not-X* (that is to omit doing X) so that it is up to me entirely whether I do X or not. If I am permitted to do X but not permitted to do *not-X*, I am not in any usual sense at liberty to do X, for if X is the only thing I am permitted to do, it follows that I am compelled to do X, and compulsion, of course, is the plain opposite of liberty.[75]

Construed as pertaining to non-normative liberty, this passage is deeply problematic. We can deal briskly with one difficulty that is obvious in the light of the first principal section of my second chapter. Except in connection with very special circumstances such as thorough mind-control or certain severe mental illnesses, Feinberg is incorrect in thinking that anyone could ever be free-to-do-some-action-X without also being free-to-abstain-from-doing-X. No actions are unavoidable, though some movements of a person's body are (for instance, the movement of Dorothy as she is heaved through the air by the whirlwind). What can often be the case, of course, is that the option of not performing a certain action is exceedingly unattractive. If so, and if the action is itself not so enticing as to be performed for its own sake rather than for the sake of escaping a repellent alternative, then the performance of it is involuntary and forced. The person who engages in it has acted unfreely. Let us assume that Feinberg is adverting to such a state of affairs when he claims that he is compelled to do X. An assumption along these lines is necessary if we are to make sense of his repeated references to the doing of X as opposed to the undergoing of X. Only if the references had been to undergoing rather than to doing, would Feinberg have been correct in declaring that X might be someone's only option. As things stand, however, we have to presume that he does not mean that X might be somebody's sole option; rather, he must mean that it might be somebody's least unappealing option or sole minimally acceptable option.

At any rate, the other major shortcoming in the quoted passage is present as a shortcoming regardless of whether we let 'X' designate an action undertaken or a process undergone. The second sentence in the quotation goes astray in proclaiming that a person is not free to do something which she is compelled to do. Whether the compulsion consists in a truly irresistible impetus such as a whirlwind or whether it instead consists merely in heavy-handed coercion, it does not remove the freedom of the victim to undergo the process or undertake the action which she is compelled to undergo/undertake. On the contrary, the victim's inexorable subjection to the process or her forced performance of the action presupposes that very freedom. Though Feinberg is

---

[75] Feinberg, 'Interest', 27.

correct in suggesting that compulsion involves the negation of freedom, he misidentifies the freedom that is negated.

When Dorothy is irresistibly driven along by the whirlwind, the
freedom of hers that has thereby been negated is not her freedom to be
impelled through the air, but her freedom to do anything that is inconsistent with her soaring through the air. Indeed, if she is completely
overpowered from giving effect to any of her volitions during her flight,
she is not then free to perform any actions at all. Likewise, when the man
in the room has to continue walking in order to stay alive, the liberty of
his that has been negated is not his liberty to continue his perambulations, but his liberty to remain stationary for more than an instant. His
combinations of conjunctively exercisable freedoms have been sharply
curtailed, for any combination that includes momentary stationariness
will include nothing further. Thus, for him as for Dorothy, compulsion
does indeed involve the negation of myriad freedoms and myriad combinations-of-conjunctively-exercisable-freedoms. In each case, however, one liberty clearly not negated is the liberty of Dorothy to be
tossed irresistibly through the air or the liberty of the man to continue
trudging coercedly around the room. When Feinberg submits that
someone who is forced to do X will have lacked the freedom-to-do-X,
he strangely singles out the one freedom that is most clearly not eliminated by the compulsion. Indeed, as has been noted, the existence of that
freedom is a precondition for the success of the compulsion.

Let us now consider another instance of insufficient attentiveness to
the fact that someone compelled to φ is able and therefore free to φ. In
some admirably sophisticated work influenced by game theory, Martin
van Hees and other scholars have contended that somebody faced with
only one opportunity does not enjoy any freedom at all. Following the
lead of Prasanta Pattanaik and Yongsheng Xu,[76] van Hees delineates an
Axiom of Indifference Between No-Choice Situations:

Opportunity sets that each consist of only one alternative will yield the same
amount of freedom of choice.

Van Hees elaborates: 'The underlying intuition is that opportunity sets
consisting of only one element (so-called singleton sets) do not give

[76] Their seminal article is 'On Ranking Opportunity Sets in Terms of Freedom
of Choice', 56 *Recherches Economiques de Louvain* 383 (1990). Their explication
of the Axiom of Indifference Between No-Choice Situations is as follows: '[I]f
neither of two feasible sets [of options] offers the agent any choice in the sense that
both the feasible sets are singletons, then the degrees of freedom offered by the
two feasible sets are identical (being "zero" from an intuitive point of view)' (at
386–7).

any freedom of choice at all. If there is only one alternative available to me, then I am *forced* to choose that option and it is for this reason that one can say that opportunity sets consisting of only one element do not provide any freedom of choice.' As he further states when comparing two singleton opportunity sets, 'my hunch is that the two choice situations provide an equal amount of freedom, namely none. And that is precisely the intuition that the axiom of indifference between no-choice situations captures'.[77] Elsewhere he adds that 'singleton sets do not provide any freedom at all: if you are forced to choose some particular alternative then you cannot be said to be free at all'.[78]

Van Hees's axiom—or his explication of that axiom—bristles with difficulties. We can first question the possibility of singleton sets, since the lone option in each of them as presented by van Hees is an action to be performed rather than an irresistible process or state to be undergone. If the putatively lone option is an action, then there is always at least one other option: the option of not doing that action. As has been argued at length in my second chapter, actions are never strictly unforgoable. To be sure, as the relevant examples in that chapter have underscored, the price of refraining from certain actions can be extremely high. Nonetheless, if we leave aside situations of outright mind-control (which will be pondered in the next section of this chapter), and if we similarly leave aside borderline actions that are largely due to non-volitional reflexes or some serious mental illnesses, we can safely conclude that every instance of volitional behaviour is something that could have been eschewed by the person who engages in that behaviour. Accordingly, an opportunity set containing an action as one of its elements will always contain at least two elements. Nobody is ever free to perform some action without also being free to forgo it, perhaps at a very high price. Only someone in a position comparable to that of Dorothy, who is overpowered by an irresistible force that prevents her for a while from performing any actions, is really confronted with a singleton opportunity set. Only someone in such a position is really without any choices.

---

[77] Van Hees, *Reductionism*, 107, 113, emphasis in original.

[78] Martin van Hees, 'On the Analysis of Negative Freedom', 45 *Theory and Decision* 175, 180–1 (1998). See also Martin van Hees and Marcel Wissenburg, 'Freedom and Opportunity', 47 *Political Studies* 67, 70 (1999) ('[I]n situations of no choice each alternative gives the same "degree" of liberty...i.e., none at all'); Martin van Hees, 'Freedom of Choice and Diversity of Options: Some Difficulties', in H. de Swart (ed.), *Logic, Game Theory, and Social Choice* (Tilburg: Tilburg University Press, 1999), 491 ('[T]wo singleton sets always yield an equal amount of freedom. The underlying idea is that such sets do not offer any freedom of choice at all'). Fully in accordance with van Hees is Connolly, *Terms*, 146, 158.

Van Hees in fact recognizes that the eschewal of an option is itself an option that counts as a member of an opportunity set: 'Note that the option of not choosing an alternative can itself be seen as one of the alternatives.'[79] Given that the possibility of avoiding an action by remaining passive does indeed count as an element of an opportunity set, and given that that possibility is always present when some action is being contemplated, there cannot be any singleton set with an action as its lone unit. To make sense of the Axiom of Indifference Between No-Choice Situations, then, we must assume that (when propounding that axiom) van Hees and other game-theoretical writers do have in mind people like Dorothy who are thoroughly overpowered by some immobilizing constraints or onrushing impetuses. We should therefore now ask why those writers have maintained that the lone element in a singleton set—an element such as being hurled through the air by a whirlwind—does not involve any freedom at all.

In so far as the game-theoretical writers share Carter's view that potential actions are the only contents of freedoms, their stance has already been challenged by my rejoinder to Carter in section 1 of this chapter. In fact, van Hees plumps for a position even more stringent than that of Carter, as will be seen shortly. Whereas Carter submits that the only contents of freedoms are potential actions—which include non-volitional bodily movements that could have been actions—van Hees restricts the domain of such contents to deliberate actions. Let us approach this matter via a slightly circuitous route, by considering the tack which the game-theoretical writers themselves would most likely pursue. They would point out that everybody in a state comparable to that of Dorothy cannot make any choices about the movement and positioning of his or her own body for a certain period. Unlike the man forced to walk around the room, who can always elect to desist from his trudging (on pain of death), Dorothy cannot exercise even that meagre degree of choice. So long as she is in the grip of the whirlwind, she haplessly undergoes what is taking place to her and does not influence the course of her own body's flight in any way. Completely overpowered, she does not have the latitude to choose anything—not even the latitude to choose an alternative as disagreeable as the one that is open to the man in the room. Thus, the game-theoretical writers would submit, Dorothy does not enjoy any *freedom of choice* whatso-ever. She might be free (free, that is, to soar through the air) in some other sense, but the freedom that matters to the game-theoretical

[79] Van Hees, *Reductionism*, 107 n. 3.

writers is the ability to select between alternatives. Devoid of any such ability, she is altogether devoid of any freedom of choice.

In the first of the quotations from van Hees on the Axiom of Indifference Between No-Choice Situations, as well as in that axiom itself, he does indeed refer specifically to freedom of choice. He very likely regards the ability-to-choose as the keystone of liberty, and he is correct to suggest that Dorothy is bereft of any such ability during her ride through the skies when she is wholly at the mercy of the whirlwind's thrust. Throughout that period, the overpowering force of the whirlwind envelops her and prevents her from making any effectual choices. Her ride is something that happens to her willy-nilly. Hence, if van Hees is distinguishing between general freedom and freedom of choice, and if he is contending that only the latter is what Dorothy altogether lacks, his position is unobjectionable. It is indeed the case, *ex hypothesi*, that Dorothy enjoys no freedom of choice while she is tossed around by the whirlwind. She is unprevented from being heaved through the air, but she is prevented from acting on any choices relating to the positioning of her own body during her flight.

In the remaining quotations from van Hees on this topic, however, he shifts from talking about freedom of choice to talking about freedom *simpliciter*. He submits, for example (in one of those quotations), that 'singleton sets do not provide any freedom at all'. In those quotations, then, he has moved from a tenable thesis about the absence of any freedom of choice to an unsustainable thesis about the absence of any freedom at all. Van Hees appears to be unwisely equating freedom of choice and freedom generally. Whereas the former consists in the ability to select between alternatives, the latter consists much more broadly in unpreventedness. The latter, in other words, can obtain in a situation—such as Dorothy's flight through the air—where there are no opportunities for selecting between alternatives. A person is unprevented from undergoing a process that carries her along inexorably.

Now, when presenting his general conception of liberty, van Hees quite plainly advocates a stance that is even more restrictive than that of Carter: 'I adopt the point of view that the freedom of an individual is determined by the person's range of action, and in particular by the absence of external constraints limiting that range of action.' Indeed, when taking up directly the question of the contents of freedoms, van Hees is perfectly explicit: 'I shall assume that ... freedom always refers to *actions* or *decisions*, which can be performed or made by individuals.'[80] Anybody adopting this highly restrictive conception of liberty

[80] Van Hees, *Reductionism*, 98, 96, emphasis in original.

can confidently affirm that the exercise of any freedom must involve a choice, since the performance of any action always proceeds from an implicit or explicit decision against opting for some other mode of conduct. Thus, somebody who limits the contents of liberties to deliberate actions will not really need to distinguish between freedoms generally and freedoms of choice. Given such a limitation on the domain of those contents, every particular freedom is an opportunity for a choice. Nevertheless, not only is such a conception of liberty peculiarly vulnerable to the objections posed against Carter in section 1 of this chapter, but also it disallows any postulation of singleton sets. Under such a conception of liberty, the only contents of particular freedoms are deliberate actions—which means, as we have seen, that every such freedom will always be accompanied by some other freedom(s) pertaining to some alternative mode(s) of conduct. If somebody is free to do some action X, then necessarily he or she is free to abstain from doing X. We have observed as much in Chapter 2. Hence, any ostensible singleton set containing a freedom-to-do-some-action will not in fact be a singleton set. A genuine singleton set comprises as its only element the non-volitional undergoing of an irresistible process or state. An occasion for undergoing such a process or state is not recognized as an opportunity at all, under van Hees's conception of freedom. Under that conception, then, the singleton sets covered by his Axiom of Indifference Between No-Choice Situations are not opportunity sets, despite being labelled as such. Accordingly, we should hardly be surprised that they do not provide—or are deemed not to provide—any freedom.

For anyone adhering to van Hees's restrictive conception of freedom, there is no difference between Dorothy during her flight and a dead person, as far as our ascriptions of freedom are concerned. (There will be a difference in regard to our ascriptions of unfreedom, in circumstances where the complete overpowering of a live person is due not to a natural force such as a whirlwind but to the actions of somebody else.) Both Dorothy while overmastered by the whirlwind and a dead person are endowed with no freedom at all, according to van Hees's conception of liberty. Under my conception, by contrast, the difference between a dead person and an overpowered living person is not effaced. Although the overall liberty of Dorothy during her flight is extremely limited, it is not reduced to zero. Similarly, although the overall liberty of a person who has been completely immobilized is even more severely curtailed than that of Dorothy, it has not been eliminated altogether. Notwithstanding that Dorothy is unable to act upon any choices during her ride through the air, she is unprevented from undergoing that ride; likewise, notwithstanding that an utterly immobilized person is unable to act upon any choices during the time of his incapacitation, he is unprevented from occupying the space which his immobile body takes up. Of course, a corpse can be flung through the air by a whirlwind just as Dorothy can, and a corpse obviously takes up space while lying immobile. Nonetheless, as has been indicated in section 1 of this chapter, the overall freedom of a corpse is nil because a corpse is not someone to whom social and political liberty (or unfreedom) can ever correctly be ascribed. Any living human being, by contrast, is someone to whom freedom and unfreedom can pertinently be attributed. Thus, by recognizing the modicum of liberty involved in the immobility or overpoweredness of a person who is indeed completely immobile or overpowered, we recognize the difference—for the purposes of an analysis of social and political liberty—between the living and the dead.

Having recognized just such a difference and having therefore ascribed some quantity of freedom to any person who faces a singleton opportunity set, we shall have no grounds for thinking that the quantity will be precisely the same from one singleton set to the next. That is, if we take the Axiom of Indifference Between No-Choice Situations to be concerned with irresistible processes or states (in singleton sets), we should reject that axiom's indication of quantitative uniformity among those processes or states. In other words, we should reject the suggestion that the item in each singleton set will provide or presuppose the same quantum of liberty as is provided or presupposed by the item in every other such set. There is no basis for presuming, for example, that the freedom presupposed by Dorothy's flight through the skies and the freedom presupposed by an immobilized person's occupation of space are equivalent in their extent. Any presumption of quantitative equivalence between those two instances of freedom— and between each of those instances and the freedom presupposed by the item in every other singleton set—would stem from mistaken expectations concerning the individuation and measurement of the singleton items. As will become plain in Chapter 5, we have no reason whatsoever to think that our measurements of those singleton items will justify the conclusion that each one involves exactly the same degree of liberty as every other one. We therefore have no reason to suppose that any version of the Axiom of Indifference Between No-Choice Situations is sound. More precisely, we have no reason to think that any version of that axiom is sound when it is applied to freedom as opposed to freedom of choice.

6. *Freedom and Psychological Incapacities*

In this final main section of the present chapter, we shall investigate an array of problems relating to the psychological capacities of various individuals.[81] We need to inquire whether psychological incapacities ever in themselves deprive individuals of liberty; and, if they do, we need to ascertain the conditions under which the freedom-reducing effects occur. A number of difficulties must be skirted or defused if an exposition of negative liberty is to be adequately protected against collapsing into a theory of determinism-versus-free-will or into a positive-liberty doctrine. On the one hand, that is, we have to guard against transforming all questions of social and political freedom into questions of natural or metaphysical freedom. Were we to go down that route, we would very likely arrive at the outlandish conclusion that the only socio-political freedoms in any community are those presupposed by the actions and states and processes which people in the community actually undertake and undergo. At the same time, while seeking not to become embroiled in debates over natural or metaphysical determinism, we must recognize the incapacitating effects of some mental deficiencies—without embracing the sweeping verdict that each person is never free to engage in any of the courses of action which he is not in a position to consider or envisage. That sweeping verdict, though not as far-reaching as the transformation of all questions of social and political liberty into questions of metaphysical liberty, would unduly narrow the range of circumstances in which we can appositely ascribe freedoms to each person. In short, while resolutely acknowledging that some psychological incapacities do destroy freedoms, this final section of Chapter 3 will also aim to cabin that acknowledgement properly.

6.1. *Every Thought Taken Captive*

Among the conditions that will be pondered in our exploration of psychological incapacities, the extreme variety is that of outright mind-control.[82] If somebody's brain has fallen completely under the sway of someone else through surgical or chemical or electronic

---

[81] Among the many treatments of this topic, two of the most suggestive are Flathman, *Freedom*, 40–1, Ch. 4; and Christopher Megone, 'One Concept of Liberty', 35 *Political Studies* 611, 619–22 (1987). Suggestive as well, though markedly different from my own approach, is Philip Pettit, *A Theory of Freedom* (Cambridge: Polity Press, 2001), Chs 2–4.

[82] For some brief treatments of this problem, all very different from my own, see Richard Arneson, 'Freedom and Desire', 15 *Canadian Journal of Philosophy*

means, then the victim has become the living marionette of the controlling person. Every intention harboured by the former is determined fully by the manipulations and designs of the latter. As has been remarked in Chapter 2, there are two principal ways in which such a situation can be analysed. First is an approach not favoured here. Under that approach, a person whose mind has been completely taken over by somebody else is deemed no longer to be anyone to whom freedom or unfreedom can pertinently be ascribed. In other words, the lot of such a victim is assimilated to that of a dead person. In each case, somebody once endowed with sundry freedoms and unfreedoms has ceased to exist in a state that warrants our attributing any freedoms and unfreedoms to her. She has become a mere extension and device of the people who have seized control over her mind. We should not attribute social and political liberty to an ostensible person in that condition, any more than to a mechanical robot that is steered by electrical signals from its owner. That ostensible person is not an agent endowed with freedoms and unfreedoms any more than is a corpse. Like the body of the elderly patriarch Abraham as described by St Paul, she is as good as dead. Such, at any rate, is the conclusion generated by one line of analysis that might be adopted in our efforts to come to grips with the vexed issues surrounding the take-over of anybody's mind.

As has been indicated in Chapter 2, a preferable treatment of this matter proceeds quite differently. Although the person whose mind has been thoroughly taken over is no longer an autonomous agent by any reckoning, such a person is still an agent inasmuch as her dealings with the world are carried on through beliefs and attitudes and intentions. To be sure, in a crucial sense, those beliefs and attitudes and intentions are not her own; they are directly implanted into her by the nefarious manoeuvres of the people who control every aspect of her psyche. Still, while wholly devoid of autonomy, she differs from a robot or any other machine in harbouring beliefs and attitudes and intentions. She interacts with her environment consciously and rationally, even though her consciousness and rationality are piloted by others who shape and channel her thoughts. Because she differs in

425, 432 (1985); Benn and Weinstein, 'Being Free', 210; Day, 'Threats', 263; J. P. Day, 'Individual Liberty', in A. Phillips Griffiths, *Of Liberty* (Cambridge: Cambridge University Press, 1983), 17, 20–1; T. Gray, *Freedom*, 38–40; Steiner, 'Liberty', 139–40; Swanton, 'Concept', 348–9. For a longer treatment, see P. S. Greenspan, 'Behavior Control and Freedom of Action', 87 *Philosophical Review* 225 (1978). Greenspan's analysis is interesting, but it unfortunately runs together the property of being unfree and the property of acting unfreely (that is, coercedly).

this fundamental respect from machines and corpses, she is someone to whom freedom and unfreedom can appositely be attributed.

At the same time, of course, we must take account of the freedom-curtailing character of her condition. Indeed, one of the principal reasons for designating her as someone to whom freedom and unfreedom can be ascribed is that we thus enable ourselves to affirm that she has been made unfree in countless respects by the people who exert dominion over her mind. Were we to rule out attributions of freedom and unfreedom to her, we could not say that her mind's captors are rendering her unfree in any way as they firmly direct her attitudes and beliefs and inclinations. If we instead allow that she is somebody who can be free or unfree in any number of respects, we can chart how the conquest of her mind has affected her freedom and unfreedom—along the lines suggested tersely in my second chapter. On the one hand, that is, we should recognize that she is free to behave in all the ways in which she does behave. Given that everything actual is possible, the modes of conduct in which she actually engages are perforce modes of conduct that are possible for her. She is consequently free to undertake those very modes of conduct. Her freedom to undertake them consists, after all, in nothing more and nothing less than her being unprevented from undertaking them. She obviously *is* unprevented from adopting those modes of behaviour, for she does in fact adopt them. Indeed, even under an unduly narrow conception of liberty as freedom of choice, we would have to conclude that she is free to engage in those modes of conduct. Although her choices to engage in them have been preordained by the people with dominion over her mind, they are nonetheless choices. She is unprevented from choosing what she in fact chooses. Of course, if the control of the brainwashers over their victim's mind is minutely exhaustive, the unpreventedness of her performing the actions which she chooses is accompanied by the preventedness of her performing any other actions. When the masters of her mind pre-decide her in favour of certain paths of conduct, they preclude her from opting for other such paths. Nevertheless, the availability of the chosen paths is evident from the fact that they are indeed pursued.

A victim of mind-control, then, is free to carry out any actions which she in fact carries out. Does she enjoy any other particular freedoms? Two main points are relevant here. First, irrespective of how minutely the brainwashers regulate her thoughts and attitudes, she will be subject to mischances and the vicissitudes of her circumstances. For example, if the brainwashers have prompted her to walk along a certain road, she may stumble and thus depart from the straightforward ambulation which they had envisioned. Such non-volitional movements of her body are events which she is free to undergo, in so far as they happen to her. When she stumbles, her body is unprevented from falling or lurching. No amount of fine-grained control by her mind's captors will be guaranteed to avert such occurrences, and therefore she will be free to undergo any non-volitional bodily movements that are not so averted. Such bodily movements might arise from the complete overpowering of her by some other human being(s) or by a natural force such as a whirlwind. If Dorothy is a victim of thorough mind-control, she will nonetheless be free to soar through the air as she is driven by a whirlwind along a trajectory which the masters of her mind have not anticipated or ordained. She is unprevented from being heaved along that trajectory by the impetus of the wind, notwithstanding that her flight is at odds with the designs of the people who manipulate all her thoughts and intentions.

A second set of particular freedoms that might be enjoyed by a victim of mind-control—apart from her freedoms to perform the actions which she actually performs—will depend on the looseness of that control. On the one hand, the captors of her mind might direct every attitude and belief and intention of hers in the minutest detail. If so, then the only actions which she is free to perform are the actions which she actually performs. (As my last paragraph has indicated, she is also free to undergo any non-volitional processes or states that force themselves upon her.) On the other hand, the brainwashers might exert a more relaxed grip over her mental faculties. They might prevent her from harbouring certain thoughts and forming certain intentions, but they might leave her with some latitude in regard to thoughts and intentions which they have not excluded. In other words, instead of closely regulating every element and impulse of the operations of her mind, they might simply set constraints within which those operations can unfold. Within those constraints, nothing is either preordained or debarred. If the regimen of brainwashing is indeed along these more relaxed lines, then the victim will not only be free to perform whatever actions she in fact does perform; she will in addition be free to perform any of the actions (within her capabilities) that are not excluded by the masters of her mind. In essentially the same way in which a normal person is free to carry out myriad actions which she does not actually carry out, the victim of a relatively lenient system of mind-control will be free to engage in quite a number of actions which she does not actually choose. Furthermore, of course, she will be free to undergo non-volitional processes and states that take hold of her.

More important than the freedom of the victim is her unfreedom. To the extent that the mind-control renders her unfree, it does so only in regard to actions which are not beyond her own capacities and which are not precluded by external impediments or restraints other than the mind-control itself. Many such actions, of course, are not prevented by the mind-control any more than by other potential curbs on her freedom. Hence, the precise set of actions in respect of which the victim has been rendered unfree by the mind-control is the set comprising every action that partakes of the following three characteristics: (1) the action is within the capacities of the victim; (2) it is unprevented by any factors other than the mind-control itself; and (3) it is prevented by the mind-control. That set of actions is what Ian Carter has in mind when he writes that 'if I force you to think certain thoughts, then there are also likely to be many actions that I am preventing you from performing, so that it can at least be said that forcible hypnosis and brainwashing can entail great reductions in freedom'.[83] Plainly, the greater or lesser thoroughness of the mind-control will affect the expansiveness of the set of actions which the victim has been made unfree-to-perform as a result of that control. If the direction of her mind is minutely exhaustive, then the aforementioned set will comprise every action which she does not actually perform and which has not been ruled out by internal or external preventative factors other than the mind-control itself. By contrast, if the regimen of brainwashing is more relaxed, the relevant set will fall short of comprising every not-otherwise-prevented action which the victim does not actually perform. Instead, it comprises only the not-otherwise-prevented actions which the brainwashing has excluded. *Ex hypothesi*, given that the regulation of the mind of the victim is relatively light-handed, that latter set of actions is smaller than the set of not-otherwise-prevented actions which she does not actually perform. As we naturally would expect, a system of mind-control that leaves the victim more latitude in arriving at her intentions and beliefs and attitudes is a system that creates less unfreedom for her.

In short, the taking over of a person's mind by others does not remove her status as someone to whom freedoms and unfreedoms can be imputed. Nor does it deprive the person altogether of her freedom, by any means. She is still unprevented from performing all the actions which she does perform; and, if the regimen of brainwashing is relatively unintrusive, she will likewise be unprevented from performing quite a few other actions. Nevertheless, even a fairly light-handed programme of mind-control imposes constraints on the objectives and intentions that she can form. It therefore imposes limits on the actions which she can carry out. She is unfree to carry out the

---

[83] Carter, *Measure*, 206.

excluded actions. To be sure, the mind-control does not impose limits on non-volitional movements of her body, in the presence of factors that occasion such movements. However, because such factors will often be absent and because when present they will sometimes be evaded by the people who direct her consciousness, the mind-control often renders her unfree to move her body in any ways which those people rule out. By clamping curbs on her thoughts and dispositions, the captors of her mind clamp curbs on her actions and effectively on her bodily movements. They thereby create unfreedom for her.

6.2. *Determinism Defused*

Mind-control qualifies as a source of unfreedom because it operates as a preventive factor whose effects as such are not dependent on the truth of any doctrine of natural or metaphysical determinism. Such a doctrine adverts to the inexorable succession of events in causal chains that are strictly and comprehensively preordained by all the preceding events in the chains and by the applicable laws of nature. A full-blown principle of determinism maintains that the process of inexorable succession just mentioned is characteristic of the unfolding of every event. As Carl Ginet remarks, a theory of 'determinism says that, given the state of the world at any particular time, the laws of nature determine all future developments in the world, down to the last detail'.[84] Let us suppose that some version of such a doctrine is correct. If so, then the character of every occurrence follows perforce from the total array of antecedent occurrences and the applicable laws of nature—which means that the total array of antecedent occurrences and the applicable laws of nature preclude the character of every occurrence from being other than what it is. Within the ineluctable flow of happenings, each thing must emerge with the form and substance that have been predetermined for it by all previous things. Nothing can ever emerge with any form or substance different from that with which it is actually endowed. No event can take any path other than that which it actually takes. Now, if a doctrine of predestination along these lines is correct, there would seem to be no place left for social and political liberty beyond the liberty of each person to behave in exactly the manner in which he or she does behave. After all,

---

[84] Carl Ginet, *On Action* (Cambridge: Cambridge University Press, 1990) [Ginet, *Action*], 92. I do not here need to take any position in debates concerning whether determinism and freedom-of-the-will are compatible or incompatible. Even if compatibilism is correct, it cannot be so in any way that would eliminate the problem which I am addressing in this subsection.

ex hypothesi, each person could not have behaved in any other manner. To presume that he or she could have behaved in other ways is to presume that the events constituting his or her behaviour have not been fully determined by earlier events—which is to depart from the assumption that has been adopted by us *arguendo*, to the effect that determinism prevails. If we cleave to that assumption instead of abandoning it, we shall have to conclude that nobody has ever been able to do anything other than what he or she actually does. Nor has anybody ever been able to undergo any non-volitional bodily movements other than those which he or she actually undergoes. Thus, if socio-political freedoms are understood as abilities—as they clearly are understood within my theory—we apparently have to conclude that people never enjoy socio-political freedoms to perform any acts which they do not perform. Despite appearances to the contrary, no one is ever free to do anything unless he or she actually does it. Must we accept such an unpalatable verdict?

One way of resisting that verdict, of course, is to impugn the doctrine of causal determinism. Somebody can point, for example, to the areas of quantum physics that tend to belie such a doctrine. However, even if we grant that the universe is not thoroughly deterministic, we cannot infer therefrom that the exceptions to strict determinism are of the right sort to enable the occurrence of volitions and actions other than those which actually materialize. As Ginet observes:

[I]f determinism is incompatible with free will . . . then we have the freedom of will we like to think we have only if determinism is false in certain specific ways, only if the laws of nature and the antecedent states of the world leave open all or most of the alternative actions we like to think are open to us. But that determinism is false in all those specific ways does not follow from indeterministic quantum theory. So even if we know that indeterministic quantum theory is true, we cannot know by deduction therefrom that determinism has all the right exceptions. And it is clear that we do not know this in any other way either.[85]

At present, then, the truth-status of deterministic claims about human behaviour remains far from clear. In application to such behaviour, a doctrine of determinism may well be true notwithstanding its apparent falsity in application to the subatomic events studied by quantum physicists. In any case, given that the truth or falsity of that doctrine in application to human actions is currently unresolved and irresolvable, one should not logically commit oneself to an outright rejection

---

[85] Ginet, *Action*, 94.

of determinist theses. If we are to eschew the unpalatable verdict broached in my last paragraph, we should do so on the assumption that determinist claims about human behaviour might be true. Should that assumption ultimately prove to be unfounded, the problem addressed in this subsection will no longer have to be addressed. We cannot at present enjoy the luxury of ignoring that problem, however, and the ultimate resolution of the debates about the truth of determinist doctrines may reveal that we shall never enjoy such a luxury.

How, then, can we avoid the unpalatable verdict delineated two paragraphs ago? A circumvention of that verdict is indeed essential, for otherwise we shall have to accept that all questions of social and political liberty collapse into questions concerning what has happened and what will happen. Political philosophy's treatment of freedom will have been completely displaced by the natural sciences or by predestinarian religion. An exit from this unhappy predicament has been signalled at the outset of this subsection. If mind-control is a source of socio-political unfreedom partly because its status as such does not depend on the truth of determinist doctrines, then a comparable test or criterion should be applied to other preventive factors. Even though we may assume herein that some determinist doctrine is true, we should never rely on the truth of such a doctrine as a reason for classifying anything as a source or manifestation of the impairedness of somebody's socio-political freedom. Thus, for example, if Herbert has just scratched his own nose at some time t, that act will not have betokened a lack of socio-political freedom on his part to abstain from scratching his nose at t. Until the moment for his abstention from scratching at t has passed, Herbert enjoys the socio-political liberty to abstain therefrom at that time. We can know that his scratching of his nose at t does not warrant our inferring that he has theretofore lacked the socio-political freedom to abstain from scratching at that time, since—except in the presence of special circumstances such as thoroughgoing mind-control, which we may assume to be absent— any such inference would have to rely on the truth of a determinist theory. Because we are not allowed to invoke the actuality of determinism as a premise from which to draw conclusions about social and political liberty, we are not allowed to infer that Herbert's scratching of his nose at t is indicative of his having thitherto lacked the social and political liberty to abstain from scratching at t. Instead, we have to infer that Herbert has enjoyed the liberty-to-abstain-from-scratching, and that he has declined to exercise it.

These remarks on Herbert's act of scratching his nose can and should be generalized to other instances of conduct. No such instance should count as a source or manifestation of any limits on someone's socio-political freedom, unless its status as such is independent of the truth of determinist credos. If that status would obtain notwithstanding that all such credos might prove to be false, then the specified instance of conduct can rightly be regarded as promotive or indicative of restrictions on social and political liberty. By contrast, if that status depends on the truth of determinist doctrines, then the specified instance of conduct is not in itself promotive or indicative of any such restrictions.

This test aptly ensures that inquiries about social and political freedom/unfreedom are not collapsed into inquiries about natural or metaphysical determinism. The test does so, moreover, without presuming that any determinist theories are false. It prescinds from the truth-values of the claims of such theories, instead of denying those claims. Nevertheless, the test may strike some readers as question-begging or as suspiciously pat. Does not it presuppose the very distinctness of the two sets of inquiries just mentioned? The answer to this question, of course, is 'yes'. So what? My discussion in this subsection takes as given that an effacement of the distinction between those two sets of inquiries is unacceptable. A thesis about the unacceptability of any such effacement is not a conclusion for which I have sought to argue or for which I should be seeking to argue; rather, it is the central starting point that underlies the devising of this subsection's test. Taking that thesis as given is not an instance of begging the question but is instead a matter of pursuing the question. What is at issue in this subsection is not whether metaphysical and scientific enquiries into the existence of freedom-of-the-will should be separated from political-philosophical enquiries into the existence of anybody's socio-political freedoms or the extent of anybody's socio-political freedom. The need for such a separation is here treated as axiomatic. What is at issue, rather, is whether a suitable test can be devised for effecting that separation. Such a test must satisfy two main requirements. On the one hand, it cannot assume the falsity of determinist theses. As has been noted, a presupposition of the falsity of those theses would not currently be justifiable and might never be justifiable. At the same time, an appropriate test must distinguish between problems of freedom-of-the-will and problems of socio-political freedom in a manner that forestalls any thoroughgoing subsumption of the latter by the former. It must carve out a place for the latter set of problems that will accommodate the array of issues normally addressed by a conception of negative liberty within the domain of political philosophy (by my own conception, for example, as encapsulated in my F Postulate and U Postulate). Both of these requirements for a pertinent test can best be fulfilled by our abstracting from the truth-values of determinist doctrines. While not at all presuming that those doctrines are false, we should not accept any claim about restrictions-on-freedom that indispensably presupposes the truth of those doctrines. By filtering out every such claim, we shall end up with an account of negative liberty that can stand firmly as a theory in political philosophy.

6.3. *Psychological Constraints*

When we defuse determinist doctrines by not allowing them to serve as bases for claims about limits on socio-political liberty, we gain ample leeway to affirm that people are free to do things other than the things which they actually do. We gain such leeway because we prescind from the possibility that people are unable to form intentions and beliefs and attitudes other than those which they actually harbour. Having done as much, we should not hastily conclude that we must forbear from taking any notice of constraints on the formation of intentions and beliefs and attitudes. In my discussion of mind-control, of course, we have already taken notice of one source of such constraints. In this subsection we shall briefly look at some other conditions and afflictions that might qualify as further sources.

Among the conditions and maladies that might seem to curtail the liberty of anybody who suffers therefrom are cowardice, ignorance, phobias, compulsive habits, unintelligence, psychoses, severe depression, schizophrenia, mental retardation, diffidence, shyness, strong enticements, and infatuations. Clearly, a negative-liberty theory as opposed to a positive-liberty theory will decline to classify many of these factors as abridgements of freedom. For example, if cowardice disposes someone to avoid most dangers and ostensible dangers, the person's pusillanimous disposition falls short of an outright inability and thus falls short of an absence of any particular freedoms. Instead of maintaining that a cowardly person lacks the freedom to face certain hazards, we should maintain that he is strongly inclined not to exercise the freedom which he enjoys. Given that we are not allowing determinist theses to serve as bases for claims about curtailments of freedom, we should not accept that a coward is strictly unable and thus unfree to confront various dangers and scary situations which he sedulously avoids. He is free to watch a frightening film, for example, even if he is determinedly disinclined to exercise that freedom. Of course, there are undoubtedly some dangers which he is genuinely unable to handle. For instance, he may be unable to walk on a tightrope suspended between two high points, because he lacks the physical dexterity to do so. In general, however, actions that are physically possible for him are not strictly precluded by his being timorously undisposed to perform them. His cowardice is an aversion to perceived dangers; like other aversions, it should not be taken into account when we ascertain his particular liberties and his overall liberty. A young boy is free to eat broccoli even if he is fiercely uninclined to do so. Similarly, a coward is free to undertake a number of actions from which he shudderingly shrinks. For the purposes of a negative-liberty theory that insists on the desire-independence of the existence of freedoms and unfreedoms, his faint-heartedness is not a factor that should be registered in our enquiries and calculations. Much the same can be said in connection with diffidence and shyness and infatuations and strong enticements, which do not amount to veritable mind-control. Each of those conditions will doubtless make certain modes of conduct (self-assertive conduct or self-restrained conduct) extremely unpleasant, but none of them is a genuinely preventive factor.

Ignorance is a more complicated condition, in the present context. It will often be a straightforwardly disabling factor and will thus impair a person's overall liberty. For instance, if a man has never learned the Italian language, and if he is capable of learning that language through instruction that would have been available to him if he had sought it, his ignorance is what prevents him from reading an Italian newspaper and from understanding an Italian conversation. Were it not for his ignorance, he would enjoy a set of freedoms with which he is not currently endowed. In very different settings as well, ignorance produces freedom-diminishing effects. Let us recall Chapter 2's depiction of Dave who is interned in a cell with only one door, which is sealed with a computerized lock that is formidably unyielding unless Dave manages to type in a 200-digit number correctly. His ignorance of the correct sequence of digits radically lowers the probability of his being able to emerge from the cell, in comparison with a situation in which he has been informed of the exact array of digits that will enable him to escape. Indeed, gauged from any realistic perspective, his chances of typing the correct number and thus of emerging from the cell are effectively nil. With the knowledge of the relevant sequence of digits, Dave would be free to disengage the lock quite soon and would then be free to leave the cell. In the absence of such knowledge, he is almost certainly unfree to disengage the lock and is therefore almost certainly unfree to depart from the dungeon. In this setting, then, ignorance is a severely freedom-constricting and unfreedom-promoting condition.

In other settings, however, ignorance does not affect a person's liberty. Suppose that Bob has abducted Kathy and has placed her in a shed. Inadvertently, he leaves the door to the shed unlocked. A simple turn of the knob by Kathy would open the door and would thus enable her to escape altogether with very little effort. Nonetheless, because Kathy wrongly believes that the door is firmly locked—either because Bob has told her as much, or else because she simply assumes that no kidnapper would be so stupidly remiss as to leave his victim in a wholly unsecured shed—she does not even attempt to open the door, and consequently she does not discover that she can readily escape. Her ignorance in this case does not deprive her of her freedom-to-leave-the-shed; instead, it simply leads her to fail to exercise that freedom. She could very easily have learned of her possession of that freedom and could therefore have easily exercised it. She has neglected to take advantage of an opportunity that has been present all the same. Her situation is markedly different from that of Dave, whose chances of discovering the proper sequence of digits for the computerized lock are practically zero. Unlike Kathy, Dave has not been presented with a significant opportunity which he has neglected to exploit in spite of having been able to exploit it easily. Rather, he has not been presented with any significant opportunity whatsoever.

Ignorance, then, amounts to a freedom-curtailing condition in proportion to the difficulty of its being overcome. When it can be dispelled with hardly any effort, it has no effect or virtually no effect on one's overall freedom. By contrast, when the difficulty of overcoming it is staggeringly formidable—as is true in the situation of Dave in the dungeon—ignorance severely reduces one's overall freedom. These divergences between the effects of ignorance in different situations are, plainly, matters of probability. When one's ignorance can be rectified very easily, there is nearly a 100 per cent probability that one will be able to take advantage of opportunities that would remain unavailable if and only if the ignorance could not be rectified. Whether or not one does take advantage of them, one will almost certainly be *able* to take advantage of them. When one's ignorance is virtually insurmountable, by contrast, there is approximately a 0 per cent probability that one will be able to take advantage of opportunities that would become genuinely available if and only if the ignorance were to be rectified. Countless other settings will involve intermediate levels of difficulty in the overcoming of ignorance. In each case, the probabilistic qualification attached to any ascription of freedom will reflect the likelihood of the dissolution of a person's ignorance if the person were indeed to endeavour (without any blunders) to achieve such a dissolution. When the probabilities are extremely high, we can safely say that a person is free to do whatever his ignorance would prevent him from doing if the ignorance were not susceptible to being dissipated. When the probabilities are almost unimaginably low, we can safely say that for all practical purposes a person is not free to do anything that his undissipated ignorance disenables him from doing—for example, Dave's typing in of the correct sequence of 200 digits. When the probabilities are at intermediate levels, we are best advised to frame our ascriptions of freedom or unfreedom in an overtly probabilistic manner. Hence, whenever the probabilities fall short of being extremely high, ignorance will perceptibly diminish a person's overall liberty. After all, as has been suggested already in this book and as will be explained more lengthily in Chapter 5, the probabilistic qualifications attached to our ascriptions of freedom and unfreedom are entered directly into our measurements of overall liberty. By significantly affecting the probability that a person will be able to perform this or that action, ignorance significantly affects the property which we measure as the person's overall freedom.

Note, incidentally, that the foregoing remarks on ignorance do not imply a relationship of entailment between the following two propositions: (1) 'Subject to some probability p, Charles is free to perform some action A', and (2) 'Subject to some probability p, Charles will perform some action A if he endeavours to do so'. We can fully recognize the disabling effects of ignorance and the empowering effects of knowledge while also recognizing that people sometimes make mistakes which they know how to avoid or which they could very easily have learned how to avoid. Precisely such mistakes have been designated as 'blunders' at the several junctures in this chapter where the parenthetical phrase 'without any blunders' has been included. Because of the abiding possibility of blunders by any human being, the first of the propositions above does not entail the second. By contrast, if the phrase 'do one's best' is stipulatively defined to mean 'endeavour without any blunders', a relationship of entailment does obtain between the following two propositions: (3) 'Subject to some probability p, Charles is free to perform A', and (4) 'Subject to some probability p, Charles will perform A if he does his best to perform it'. In short, because my conception of liberty is focused strictly on abilities rather than on the care or patience with which those abilities are used, it leaves room for a situation in which someone is able and thus free to do something which he tries and fails to do.[86]

---

[86] Accordingly, the following statements by Stanley Benn are too sweeping: 'If Alan is free to φ but does not, then, akrasia apart, it is because he decides not to φ ... A person's power, most generally, is what he could bring about *and therefore would bring about*, given that he had appropriate intentions.' Benn, *Theory*, 126, 140, emphasis added.

Let us move on. Phobias are further potential constraints on any person's liberty. On the one hand, if a phobia amounts simply to a strong fear or dread or revulsion, we should regard it—within our calculations of a person's overall freedom—in much the same way that we regard cowardice and shyness. That is, we should view such a phobia as an aversion that bears on the *palatableness* of options (for the person with the phobia) rather than on the *existence* of those options as such. In other cases, however, phobias can physically restrict people from engaging in various actions. In any such case, a phobia removes some of a person's particular freedoms and thereby reduces his or her overall freedom. Consider, for example, a phobia concerning blood and needles. Such a phobia may go well beyond a strong sense of squeamishness or revulsion, and may lead a person to lose consciousness or to become debilitatingly nauseated in circumstances that activate the phobia. In so far as a phobia does tend to inflict physical incapacitation of this sort on the phobia-sufferer in the aforementioned circumstances, it eliminates some of her particular freedoms and some of her combinations of conjunctively exercisable freedoms. Any such affliction, which effectively immobilizes its victim under certain conditions, will clearly have impaired the victim's overall liberty.

Compulsive habits are likewise potential curbs on freedom. On the one hand, compulsive habits are sometimes merely strong urges that can be treated here as the inverse counterparts of strong aversions. In such forms, compulsive habits do not amount to veritable constraints on what people can do or abstain from doing. Refraining from indulging a strong and inveterate urge may be a highly disagreeable option, but it is indeed an option. On the other hand, compulsive habits sometimes involve considerably more than strong urges. In some cases, compulsively habitual movements of the body are carried out non-volitionally. In any such case, the movement is performed not just inadvertently or unreflectively but without any volition at all. If so, and if the movement cannot always be stifled through conscious efforts to suppress it, then the person plagued by it is not free to keep his body from twitching or contorting (or moving in other ways) quite frequently. In such a situation, of course, the irresistible movement is not an action at all—any more than is a muscular reflex or the trembling of the hands of someone who suffers from Parkinson's disease.

In other contexts as well, compulsive habits are full-fledged limits on people's freedom. Perhaps the most striking cases of freedom-curtailing habits are instances of outright addiction to drugs such as heroin or alcohol. People who have become abjectly dependent on such drugs are not free to desist from them without undergoing a number of physically debilitating effects. Throughout the duration of those effects, a person's ability to undertake many activities will be substantially impaired. Consequently, even if we submit that addicts are typically free to extricate themselves from their state of dependence, we should recognize that the process of extrication will physically incapacitate them (to a greater or a lesser degree) for quite a while. At the very least, in other words, an addict's sorry state removes many of his combinations of conjunctively exercisable freedoms. It thereby reduces his overall liberty quite sharply.

Even when addictive drugs are not involved, a compulsive habit can amount to an encroachment on the overall liberty of a person. When such a habit is a product of a neurosis or some other mental disorder, the eschewal of it can involve debilitation comparable to that undergone by an addicted person who seeks to shake off his dependence on drugs. That is, even when a person's neurotic habit is not strictly non-volitional – in that it can be controlled through conscious efforts to keep it in check – it can eliminate many of the person's combinations of conjunctively exercisable freedoms. The person may be free to restrain his body from moving in its habitual pattern, but the debilitation attendant on that self-restraint will scotch many of his other freedoms for quite some time. In such circumstances, then, his neurotic habit significantly limits his overall liberty.

Most of the remaining conditions and maladies listed near the outset of this subsection can be discussed here very briefly, since they clearly lie outside the control of anybody who is affected by them. An unintelligent person, for example, is different from a merely ignorant person in that the former cannot overcome his condition by applying himself earnestly. He can undoubtedly improve his mind in some respects through painstaking endeavours, but, if he is genuinely unintelligent, he will never be capable of performing the intellectual feats that can be accomplished by someone with a much sharper mind. He is not free to perform such feats. We should note, moreover, that a generally smart person can be afflicted by a paucity of intelligence in some specific area(s). Some people are incapable of learning foreign languages proficiently, for example, regardless of how diligently they try. Other generally intelligent people are incapable of understanding mathematics beyond a fairly elementary level. No matter how carefully they might strive to follow the reasoning and concepts in more advanced mathematics, they remain uncomprehending. They are not free to engage in sophisticated mathematical reasoning, just as the irredeemably monolingual people are not free to speak and write proficiently in foreign languages.

Even more clearly insusceptible to being transcended through persistent efforts is mental retardation or insanity. Although such afflictions can be alleviated in certain respects, and although some types of insanity can be largely or wholly cured over time, no such condition is remediable through sheer exertions of will on the part of the person who suffers from it. Indeed, no such condition is remediable at all in the short term. Throughout the duration of a state of insanity, then, any actions rendered impossible for the insane person by that state will be actions which he is not free to perform. Similarly, throughout the life of a mentally retarded person, any actions or achievements ruled out by his unfortunate condition are things which he is not free to do. Broadly the same can be said about serious mental illnesses such as schizophrenia and severe depression. Notwithstanding that severe depression is typically much more ephemeral than mental retardation or insanity, it incapacitates a person in many respects while it lasts. Likewise, although schizophrenia is often intermittent (with sustained periods of remission) and is sometimes curable, it produces a number of freedom-curtailing effects when it is present. A person afflicted by some strain of the disease cannot keep himself from behaving in ways that are impelled by the disorder of his mind.[87] Whether the schizophrenia is of a kind that induces lethargy or is instead of a kind that inspires strange bursts of energy, it seizes at least partial control of somebody's mind. In that respect—though not necessarily in other respects—it resembles many different psychological incapacities. Like those other incapacities, it diminishes the freedom of anyone who remains within its grip. When psychological afflictions are genuine constraints on freedom, they can be powerful constraints indeed.

In sum, even though full-blown determinist theses cannot serve as bases for claims about restrictions on socio-political liberty, the volition-channelling effects of various psychological maladies are unquestionably to be taken into account when we seek to measure such liberty. We can and should recognize that those maladies circumscribe the range of people's options (often acutely), since our acknowledgement of that point does *not* commit us to an unacceptable reliance on

---

[87] As Stanley Benn remarks with reference to certain severe cases of schizophrenia: 'In certain schizophrenic conditions the subject lacks the self-awareness of an agent...Instead, his consciousness is rather of himself as process or as something to which things happen. In advanced cases he may act out this self-conception in catatonic paralysis, becoming for the world too the mere object he believes himself to be.' Benn, *Theory*, 160.

determinist theses. When we submit that certain well-defined mental conditions and afflictions constrict people's socio-political freedom, we are hardly thereby accepting that every formation of a preference is a limit on such freedom. My observations in this subsection do not go any way toward collapsing all questions about socio-political liberty into metaphysical or scientific questions about the existence of freedom-of-the-will.

7. *Conclusion*

This chapter has sought to pin down some of the more problematic features of particular freedoms and unfreedoms. Along with my next chapter's treatment of causal issues, it forms a bridge between the first two chapters' general conceptions of freedoms/unfreedoms and my final chapter's reflections on the enterprise of measuring the extent of each person's overall liberty. My focus herein on particular freedoms and unfreedoms is crucial for that final chapter because no project of measurement can get under way satisfactorily until we know what we are measuring. Although ascertaining the extent of anybody's overall freedom is an undertaking that raises many distinctive cruxes and complexities—as we shall see—it is also an undertaking that requires clarity and exactitude in the identification of particular freedoms and unfreedoms. Let us remember that the overall liberty of anyone is expressible as a ratio that involves both the range of her combinations-of-conjunctively-exercisable-liberties and the range of her combinations-of-consistent-unfreedoms. Thus, unless we can apprehend quite precisely the states that will count as those liberties or unfreedoms, we shall scarcely make much progress in elaborating the relevant ratio for each person. Consequently, by essaying to outline the necessary and sufficient conditions for the existence of any instance of liberty or unfreedom, the arguments in this chapter (and in Chapters 1, 2, and 4) will have laid the crucial groundwork for this book's ultimate approach to gauging the level of everybody's freedom.

4

Sources of Unfreedom

Since the presentation of the U Postulate in Chapter 1, this book has differentiated between unfreedoms and mere inabilities (that is, the inabilities of any person that are not caused by actions of other people). As has been made clear, such a distinction hinges on the sources of the various constraints that limit the freedom of individuals. Thus, if that distinction is to be incorporated effectively into my general project of determining how to measure the overall liberty of each individual and each society—that is, if it is to serve as an operationalizable component of that project—we shall need some criteria for discriminating germanely among the sources of constraints. Precisely the task of providing such criteria is what the current chapter will aim to carry out.

Let us begin by looking afresh at the U Postulate:

U Postulate: A person is unfree to φ if and only if both of the following conditions obtain: (1) he would be able to φ in the absence of the second of these conditions; and (2) irrespective of whether he actually endeavours to φ, he is directly or indirectly prevented from φ-ing by some action(s) or some disposition(s)-to-perform-some-action(s) on the part of some other person(s).

Whereas my opening chapter's F Postulate equates freedoms with abilities or possibilities, there is no corresponding equation (under the U Postulate) between unfreedoms and inabilities or impossibilities. Every unfreedom is an inability of a person, but not every inability of a person is an unfreedom. In other words, as we have seen, 'free' and 'unfree' are not bivalent. In that respect, those predicates differ fundamentally from 'able' and 'unable' or 'possible' and 'impossible'. In regard to many activities and states and processes, any number of people are neither free nor unfree; instead, in regard to those activities and states and processes, they are simply not free. To lack the freedom-to-φ is not perforce to be unfree-to-φ.

As has been explained in Chapter 2, my reason for insisting on the non-bivalence of 'free' and 'unfree' is that the appropriate formula for measuring each person's overall freedom will prove unworkable unless 'not free' and 'unfree'—and 'not unfree' and 'free'—are distinct. If we count mere inabilities as freedoms, we shall render infinitely large both the numerator and the denominator of the fraction that constitutes the aforementioned formula. If alternatively we count mere inabilities as *un*freedoms, we shall render infinitely large the denominator of that fraction. In either case, the whole enterprise of measuring liberty will have come undone. To sustain that enterprise, then, we have to maintain that not every absence of a particular freedom is an unfreedom. In respect of countless such absences, the predicate 'not free' rather than 'unfree' is applicable to the person involved.

Of course, someone who recognizes the need for a denial of the bivalence of 'free' and 'unfree' might nonetheless contend that my way of drawing the distinction between unfreedoms and mere inabilities is inapposite. Instead of following the U Postulate in singling out other people's actions as the preventive factor that gives rise to instances of unfreedom, someone might argue that the distinctive source of unfreedoms is a preventive factor of a different type. Nothing said in my preceding paragraph has indicated why the U Postulate is correct in its specific focus. Although certain discussions in the past few chapters have gone some way towards justifying that focus, and although some remarks in the present chapter will likewise be suggestive of a justification, a full defence of the U Postulate's explication of unfreedom must await Chapter 5's investigation of the measurement of liberty. This postponement is warranted because my defence of the U Postulate's explication is bound up with my account of the general ratio that defines the extent of each person's overall freedom. In light of the intimate connection between those two matters, a thorough consideration of the former can best emerge in the chapter that concentrates squarely and sustainedly on the latter.

Nevertheless, even if the U Postulate's specific way of distinguishing between unfreedoms and mere inabilities has not yet been fully vindicated, *some* pertinent division between them is essential. Without such a division, the measurement of freedom would be an arrant non-starter not just in practice but also in principle. We shall do well to remember as much throughout this chapter, for certain causal issues can best be addressed by reference to the underlying reasons for discriminating among preventive factors in the first place. As will be observed, the requirements that must be satisfied for the measurability of freedom are a consideration that bears importantly on one's handling of some troublesome causal cruxes.

Equally, throughout this chapter we should keep in mind the precise wording of the U Postulate. As will become apparent, the formulations in the two prongs of that postulate enable us to skirt some formidable problems even while they confront us with an array of other problems. Albeit this chapter will be treating of the nature of causation generally, it will always be concerned with the specific set of difficulties that arise from the U Postulate's stipulations. Knotty though those difficulties may be, they are hardly exhaustive of the range of issues to which a full-scale philosophical theory of causation must address itself. We can safely opt to leave aside some of the complications that preoccupy theorists whose enquiries are not bounded by anything comparable to the U Postulate.

Indeed, the limitedness of my exploration of causality should be emphasized at the outset. One aspect of that limitedness has just been noted: the fact that the U Postulate's formulations enable us to pretermit certain topics that would have to be addressed in a less narrowly focused effort to lay down criteria for arriving at causal judgements. In addition, and even more important, my objective in this chapter is indeed to come up with such criteria rather than to plumb the metaphysical fundaments of causation. Though philosophical issues will of course figure saliently in my discussions, the aim herein is to set forth tests or guidelines that will yield the causal ascriptions which are necessary for discriminating between unfreedoms and mere inabilities. One can accomplish such an aim without investigating in great depth the metaphysical underpinnings of those tests or guidelines.

Thus, for example, we can confine our attention to the actual world and to closely similar worlds. We do not have to try to take account of possible worlds that would be bewilderingly divergent from what is actual: worlds, if any, in which the temporal asymmetries or other elementary features of the actual world would not obtain. Likewise, this chapter for its purposes can legitimately invoke some key notions without attempting to explicate them fully. For instance, while virtually any plausible tests for causal connections must appeal in some way to the existence of causal laws (or laws of nature)—and while my tests are certainly no exception—we shall not have to probe the metaphysical status of those laws. What would have to be pondered in a metaphysical treatise can be left largely unanalysed in a book of political philosophy. Nor will this chapter enter at all into debates between realists and reductionists over the ultimate status of causal relations.

That is, we shall not endeavour to apprehend whether those relations are fundamentally reducible to non-causal states of affairs or not. Central though that question is for any comprehensive philosophical treatment of causation, it does not have a bearing on the topics to which this chapter is addressed.

In short, notwithstanding that this chapter will be tackling philosophical issues and using techniques of philosophical analysis persistently, it will generally remain agnostic on the deep metaphysical problems that pertain to causation. To some extent, its orientation will resemble that of legal theorists who seek to distil general principles of causation in the law. As the footnotes in this chapter will attest, my approach to causation is informed as much by the legal-theoretical literature as by the broader philosophical literature. Like the legal theorists who strive to delineate general causal principles, this chapter takes as its basic aim the elaboration of criteria that can guide causal judgements. Given such an aim, many of the concerns of metaphysicians are quite peripheral. Nevertheless, this point of affinity between the present chapter and the various accounts of causation in the law should not obscure some far-reaching dissimilarities.

Most notable among those dissimilarities is a difference in the upshot or the practical implications. Legal theorists who propound criteria for the resolution of causal problems are engaged in a project with a direct practical import. Those criteria are meant to be accepted not only by other theorists but also by official decision-makers such as judges. The endorsement of any criteria by such people is, of course, more than a scholarly development; it is a development that will palpably affect the outcomes of quite a few cases that come before the courts and agencies on which the decision-makers sit. When officials deem the misconduct of some person *P* to be causally responsible for harm suffered by somebody else, they have taken a crucial step toward holding *P* legally liable for the harm. The tests or guidelines that lead to their determinations on any such causal issues are thus of major practical importance. Exactly because those causal tests are so closely linked to decisions about punishment and compensation, they are typically combined with other criteria which are often designated as 'causal' but which in fact are concerned with questions of morality and political wisdom. For example, even when a court has found that *P*'s misconduct was causally responsible for an injury to someone else, a final judgement against *P* will hinge also on the foreseeability of the type of injury and on the proximity between the misconduct and the harm. Requirements of foreseeability and proximity, which involve considerations of fairness and of public policy rather than of causality, are nonetheless very often designated by courts and commentators as 'causal' requirements (under such labels as 'proximate causation' or 'legal causation'). Hence, the 'causal' determinations in legal cases are usually hybrid, with a focus both on genuine factual issues of causation and on moral-political issues of reasonable accountability.[1]

By contrast, the criteria to be expounded in this chapter are oriented toward strictly factual matters of causation. On the one hand, as has been remarked at the outset of Chapter 3, the basic objective of this book—the objective of clarifying and sharpening the concept of freedom in a manner most conducive to establishing the measurability of each person's overall liberty—is endowed with considerable practical significance. Accordingly the discussions in this chapter, which contribute to the achievement of that underlying objective, are endowed with practical significance. On the other hand, as my third chapter has indicated, the practical significance is at a very high level of generality and abstraction. Whereas the causal standards followed by judges and other officials in their resolutions of legal controversies are directly formative of decisions that weightily impinge on people's lives, the criteria advanced in this chapter are of interest primarily to philosophers. Like this book's general project, these criteria are not meant to favour any specific set of political principles or concrete decisions. They are designed to be serviceable for political disputation generally, without any special benefits for some particular ideological camp. Even more plainly, they are not designed to lead to certain concrete practical decisions within legal or governmental institutions. The judgements which they guide are theoretical judgements that occur in philosophical argumentation. Only in a tenuously indirect and open-ended fashion do my causal tests contribute to the sorts of determinations that are reached by adjudicative officials.

Because of this detachment from pressing practical concerns, the analysis of causation in the present chapter can remain aloof from the moral-political considerations that inflect legal decisions. We can

---

[1] For excellent discussions of the distinction between factual causation and legal causation, see Richard Wright, 'Causation in Tort Law', 73 *California Law Review* 1735, 1741–58 (1985) [hereinafter cited as Wright, 'Causation']; Richard Wright, 'Causation, Responsibility, Risk, Probability, Naked Statistics, and Proof: Pruning the Bramble Bush by Clarifying the Concepts', 73 *Iowa Law Review* 1001, 1011–18 (1988) [Wright, 'Pruning']; Richard Wright, 'Once More into the Bramble Bush: Duty, Causal Contribution, and the Extent of Legal Responsibility', 54 *Vanderbilt Law Review* 1071, 1073–82 (2001) [Wright, 'Duty']. See also the opening several pages of Richard Wright, 'The Efficiency Theory of Causation and Responsibility: Unscientific Formalism and False Semantics', 63 *Chicago-Kent Law Review* 553 (1987).

altogether forgo a striving for fairness, expressed in requirements such as foreseeability and proximity. Any such striving would be out of place in this chapter, since my standards for ascribing causal responsibility will not here be associated with standards for ascribing moral or legal liability. At least for the purposes of this chapter, tracing someone's lack of freedom to the actions of somebody else does not form any part of a process of holding the latter person legally or morally accountable. Therefore, non-causal touchstones apposite for such a legal or moral process of rectification/condemnation will be disregarded here.

In short, although my investigation of causal issues will in some respects resemble the endeavours of metaphysicians and legal theorists to grapple with such issues, it is less abstractly reflective than the metaphysicians' discourses and less engagedly practical than the legal theorists' ventures. The end pursued herein is not that of stark contemplation nor that of institutional guidance, but something in between (albeit closer to stark contemplation). That complex end, indeed, is the lodestar of this book as a whole. Uppermost among the aims of this chapter is the attainment of clarity, precision, and capaciousness in the elaboration of causal criteria that will amount to a key step in the realization of that abiding end.

1. The NESS and But-For Tests

The basic criterion for causal responsibility drawn upon in this chapter is to be found both in the writings of metaphysicians and in the writings of legal theorists.[2] For a careful statement of that criterion, known acronymically as the 'NESS' test (Necessary Element of a Sufficient Set), we may turn to the work of Richard Wright: '[A] condition contributed to some consequence if and only if it was necessary for the sufficiency of a set of existing antecedent conditions that was sufficient for the occurrence of the consequence.'[3] For reasons that will become apparent later, the confines of this chapter will enable

[2] In addition to the articles by Richard Wright cited in note 1 *supra*, see, for example, H. L. A. Hart and Tony Honoré, *Causation in the Law*, 2nd edn (Oxford: Clarendon Press, 1985) [Hart and Honoré, *Causation*], 110–14, 122–5. For some analyses that eventually plump for the but-for criterion after initially upholding the NESS criterion, see John Mackie, 'Causes and Conditions', in Ernest Sosa and Michael Tooley (eds), *Causation* (Oxford: Oxford University Press, 1993) [Mackie, 'Causes'], 33; John Mackie, *The Cement of the Universe* (Oxford: Clarendon Press, 1980) [Mackie, *Cement*], Ch. 3. See also Jonathan Bennett, *The Act Itself* (Oxford: Oxford University Press, 1995) [Bennett, *Act*], 129.

[3] Wright, 'Duty', 1102–3.

and oblige us to simplify the NESS test into what is known among jurists as the 'but-for' test. That is, given the actuality and logical distinctness of two events or states of affairs C and E, we shall have to ask whether the occurrence of C was necessary in the prevailing circumstances for the occurrence of E. Under the prevailing circumstances and the applicable causal laws, would the non-occurrence of C have entailed the non-occurrence of E? Such is the question which the but-for test poses, and such is therefore the question which this chapter will be raising about potential sources of unfreedom. Still, the concept of sufficiency will have figured implicitly in the but-for test as well as explicitly in the NESS test. Furthermore, we need to understand the NESS criterion if we are to grasp why the simpler but-for standard will be a substitute for it in the context of this chapter. Thus, let us initially concentrate at least as much on the NESS test as on the but-for approach.

Both the NESS standard and the but-for standard apply only to events or states of affairs that have in fact come about. Neither test is concerned with gauging the causal efficacy of something that has not arisen, and neither test is concerned with ascertaining the causes of an unactualized effect. The purely hypothetical is not either test's domain; each criterion is designed to determine whether something was a cause of something else, rather than to determine whether something would have been a cause of something else if it had materialized.

Nevertheless, one should not erroneously infer that the NESS and but-for tests will blind us to the causal role of dispositions or inclinations. If such an inference were correct, it would be dismaying. After all, my third chapter has explored at length the ways in which people's dispositions can limit the freedom of other people; hence, if a causal criterion could not take account of dispositions as sources of unfreedom, it would be unacceptably blinkered. (As was remarked in Chapter 3, the term 'disposition' is used narrowly throughout this book. It denotes the all-things-considered preparedness of a person to perform some action under certain circumstances, coupled with the ability to perform that action under those circumstances.) Fortunately, the NESS and but-for tests can perfectly well ascribe causal efficacy to dispositions. Any particular disposition is a property that may or may not be actual. It may or may not be the case that some person is inclined to do X whenever a certain type of situation arises. If an inclination of that sort is actual, then it is something on which the NESS and but-for tests can be brought to bear. It is something to which the status of a cause can be attributed. Of course, what might remain purely hypothetical despite the actuality of a disposition is any manifestation thereof in the form of some action. As was noted in Chapter 3, somebody inclined to behave in a certain fashion might never actually behave in that fashion, if the contexts that confront him do not activate his disposition. All the same, the disposition that he harbours is itself actual—which means that that disposition can qualify as a cause under the NESS criterion or the but-for criterion.

In the quotation from Wright above, we are told that something which causes a consequence is an element in 'a set of existing antecedent conditions that was sufficient for the occurrence of the consequence'. What is the operative conception of sufficiency here? When we say that the occurrence of C in combination with other requisite circumstances was sufficient for the occurrence of E, we are saying that C and the other requisite circumstances in conjunction with the applicable causal laws necessitated the occurrence of E; they made the occurrence of E inevitable. In other words, if it had not been the case that E was going to come about, then C or some other element(s) in each minimally sufficient set of conditions for E would not have come about.[4] (A 'minimally sufficient' set of conditions is a set containing no redundant elements. Every one of those conditions is necessary for the set's sufficiency.)

Although an ascription of causal efficacy to the occurrence of C presupposes the status of C as an element in a set of actual conditions minimally sufficient for the occurrence of E, we very seldom if ever advert to all the conditions in that set when we engage in such an ascription. Typically some of the conditions are unknown and might remain unknown, and even the conditions of which we have knowledge are frequently taken for granted rather than consciously or explicitly noted. Except in a quite unusual situation, for example, a report on the causes of a fire would not make reference to the oxygen in the atmosphere that was essential for the ignition and burning. Nevertheless, although the singling out of C as a cause of E will hardly require an exhaustive specification of the other NESS conditions and the precise causal laws that together with C entail the occurrence of E, it does presuppose the actuality of those conditions and the sway of those laws.

Both the NESS criterion and the but-for test draw our attention to the role of any cause C as a necessary element in a set of conditions sufficient for the occurrence of E. What is the operative conception of necessity invoked by those tests? That conception has been adumbrated by my references to *minimally* sufficient sets of conditions.

---

[4] For a basically similar formulation, see Mackie, *Cement*, 39. See also Wright, 'Pruning', 1021 n. 108; Tony Honoré, 'Necessary and Sufficient Conditions in Tort Law', in David Owen (ed.), *Philosophical Foundations of Tort Law* (Oxford: Clarendon Press, 1995) [Honoré, 'Necessary'], 363, 364–5.

Every element in any such set is necessary for the sufficiency thereof, because such a set contains no redundant elements. If any element C had been removed while everything else was retained, the set of conditions would no longer have been sufficient for the occurrence of E. This conception of necessity as non-redundancy is what underlies each of the two aforementioned tests for causation. If some state of affairs or some event is not an integral part of any set of actual conditions that is minimally sufficient for the occurrence of E, then that state of affairs or event cannot properly be classified as a cause of E. In regard to the bringing about of E, the state of affairs or event is redundant in that its occurrence makes no difference to the occurrence of E. It contributes nothing and is thus devoid of causal efficacy, in respect of E's coming about.

Although causation is best explicated by reference to the concepts of necessity and sufficiency, we should distinguish causal connections from constitutive connections. If a state of affairs S_1 and a state of affairs S_2 are linked constitutively rather than causally, then the very existence of either of them is not logically distinct from the coeval existence of the other. Their relationship thus contrasts with that between any cause and its effect(s), which are linked via laws of nature rather than by dint of instantiation or identity or mereology. For example, consider the fact that I run briskly for 30 minutes every morning and the fact that I exercise vigorously for 30 minutes every morning. These two facts are constitutively rather than causally connected. It is not the case that my running causes my vigorous exercising; rather, the running *is* the vigorous exercising. If a state of affairs S_1 is an instance of a state of affairs S_2, then the connection between them is constitutive rather than causal. As a conceptual matter, rather than merely as a matter of some empirically ascertainable laws of nature, the actuality of S_1 entails the concurrent actuality of S_2. Likewise, if S_1 amounts to S_2, then again the ties between them are constitutive rather than causal. S_1 amounts to S_2 if S_2 is entailed by the combination of S_1 and some aspect(s) of the prevailing circumstances other than any causal laws. Jonathan Bennett offers an apt example in which David extends his arm and in which Betsy has expected David to extend his arm. His stretching out of his arm 'relates non-causally to a state of affairs which it makes obtain, namely the fulfilment of Betsy's expectation. David's extending his arm may have the causal consequence that Betsy thinks he has done what she expected; but the mere fact that her expectation *has* been fulfilled is a non-causal consequence of David's behaviour'.[5]

---

[5] Bennett, *Act*, 38, emphasis in original.

When referring to causal relata—that is, the things between which causal relations obtain—my discussion so far has sometimes designated them as facts or states of affairs and has at other times designated them as events.[6] My subsequent discussions will similarly designate causal relata sometimes as facts and sometimes as events, since the purposes of most of those discussions do not require a rigid adherence to one side or the other of a sharp fact/event demarcation. In the absence of substantive considerations that would call for such an inflexible adherence, my characterizations of causal relata will be determined chiefly by the aim of facilitating the smoothness and clarity of my exposition. What John Mackie stated about his own major study of causation is by and large applicable to my present chapter:

> The distinction between these two kinds of cause [facts and events] is, then, clear and useful. But there are still very close relations between them . . . These close systematic connections between events, their features, event-types, and facts make it legitimate to move freely and without excessive caution between them . . . For some purposes we need to attend to these distinctions, but for most of our investigation of causal regularities and our ways of discovering them we do not.[7]

Nevertheless, we are well advised to note that we can generally attain greater precision when we designate causal relata as facts. When we do so characterize them, we can thereby single out the causally relevant aspects of the events that we are scrutinizing. Quite often, indeed, the sharper focus made available in this fashion is indispensable for the adequacy of a causal explanation or analysis.

Consider, for example, a situation in which a ship's officer navigates his vessel through a body of water despite lacking the formal certificate required by law for anyone who serves as a navigator. During the ship's journey, a collision occurs. If we ask whether the officer's navigation of the vessel was a cause of the collision, the answer is clearly 'yes'. The

---

[6] For a sustained and sophisticated treatment of the distinction between facts and events—along with the bearing of that distinction on causal ascriptions—see Jonathan Bennett, *Events and their Names* (Oxford: Oxford University Press, 1988) [Bennet, *Events*]. For some other important discussions, see Bennett, *Act*, Ch. 2; Hart and Honoré, *Causation*, xxxvii–xxxviii, lviii–lix, 119 n. 11; Mackie, *Cement*, Ch. 10; P. F. Strawson, 'Causation and Explanation', in Bruce Vermazen and Merrill Hintikka (eds), *Essays on Davidson* (Oxford: Clarendon Press, 1985) [Strawson, 'Causation'], 115. As should be plain already, and as will shortly become even more evident, I side with the unifiers in the unifier/multiplier controversy within the philosophy of action. For a very good discussion of that controversy, see Ian Carter, *A Measure of Freedom* (Oxford: Oxford University Press, 1999) [Carter, *Measure*], 175–83.

[7] Mackie, *Cement*, 266–7.

former event (the navigation) was an integral element in a set of actual conditions that was minimally sufficient for the latter event (the collision). What will probably be of greater interest, however, is the role of the officer's lack of a certificate. Yet, if we seek to address that question with event-descriptions, we shall meet with frustration. The question posed with such descriptions would be whether an uncertificated officer's navigation of the ship was a cause of the collision. The answer to that question is plainly affirmative, since the description 'an uncertificated officer's navigation of the ship' will have designated exactly the same event as the description 'the officer's navigation of the ship', even though it highlights different features of that event. Thus, since the causal question articulated with the latter description is clearly to be answered affirmatively, the same must be true for such a question articulated with the former description. Yet, when we inquire about the role of the absence of a certificate, we are almost certainly intending to raise a query to which the answer should not be preordained in this manner. Accordingly, we must reformulate the question with a fact as the relevant relatum. For example, we can ask whether the fact that the officer lacked a certificate was a cause of the collision. That is, we would be asking whether that fact contributed to the collision. Another question with a fact as the antecedent causal relatum—a question subtly different from the one just posed, though manifestly related to it—is whether the fact that an uncertificated officer navigated the ship was a cause of the collision. Did that fact contribute to the collision? Either of these reformulated questions, about the officer's lacking a certificate or about an uncertificated officer's navigating the ship, is undoubtedly of great interest to a legal tribunal; yet neither of those questions can be satisfactorily posed unless we designate the antecedent causal relatum as a fact.

A further distinction of some importance for any study of causation, a distinction mentioned in the quotation from Mackie above, is that between event-types and event-tokens. (We have encountered an offshoot of this distinction in Chapter 3's discussion of act-types and act-tokens. Act-types are a subset of the class of event-types, and act-tokens are a subset of the class of event-tokens.) An event-type is a property or set of properties shared by all the particular occurrences that are comprised by some class of events. An event-token is a particular occurrence that instantiates the property or set of properties by dint of which it is an event of some specific type T. Now, when we apply the NESS criterion or the but-for test, and when we designate the relevant causal relata as events rather than as facts, we are focused on the relationship between two or more event-tokens. We are asking if some actual occurrence was a NESS condition or a but-for condition for some other actual occurrence. Nevertheless, we are asking about those occurrences as events of certain types. We are inquiring about them by seeking to apply causal generalizations—incomplete formulations of causal laws—which fix on causal relations between event-types. When all the types encompassed in such a generalization are instantiated together, and when no special circumstances are present to defeat the inferences that can normally be drawn, the relation between the instances of the generalization's specified preconditions and the instances of the generalization's specified consequences is causal. That relation obtains between event-tokens, but we ascertain it by reference to the types which those tokens instantiate. (In the rigorous and highly self-reflective discourses of law and philosophy, the references to event-types are oft-times explicit. In everyday thought and discourse, the references are usually implicit.) Let us suppose, for example, that we are inquiring whether some damage to a house on a particular occasion was wrought by a fire that was present. Although such a NESS or but-for inquiry is focused on two event-tokens, it is concerned with the general properties which they instantiate. Even if our inquiry adverts to the fire's precise spatio-temporal coordinates and its precise level of intensity, and thus even if we are seeking to determine whether a fire of that precise location and magnitude was causally responsible for the damage to the house, our investigation is governed tacitly or explicitly by some causal generalization concerning the damage-inflicting properties of a fire with that intensity and that position vis-à-vis the damaged area. Usually, of course, our descriptions of event-tokens as causal relata are not so fine-grained; even when they are, however, we are understanding those tokens by reference to some of the types which they instantiate. No application of the NESS test or the but-for criterion can proceed without some such reference, be it express or implicit.

Now, before we go on to explore some complications that must be tackled by any account of causation, we should note that the account provided here has borne out what was said in my opening remarks about the moral-political neutrality of my analyses. The categories that inform the but-for and NESS tests are those of necessity and sufficiency, which can be invoked and applied without any moral judgements. To be sure, the application of either of those tests will require counter-factual judgements whereby we ponder what would have been the case if some element of an actual state of affairs had not obtained. Yet, although the difficulties of pinning down truth-conditions for counter-factuals are well known among philosophers, few people would dispute that myriad counter-factuals (such as those that underlie ordinary causal judgements) are perfectly straightforward. Admittedly, many other counter-factuals are more problematic, and some are deeply conjectural. Still, we scarcely should infer that our causal ascriptions will collapse into moral-political assessments or into dogmatic hand-waving. In the first place, the speculative character of many counter-factuals can be overtly acknowledged and defused through the attachment of probabilistic qualifications to any judgements about their truth-values. Moreover, and perhaps even more important, the vast majority of the causal attributions that distinguish unfreedoms from mere inabilities are gratifyingly straightforward. Most such attributions deal with occurrences whose statuses under the but-for test or the NESS test, in relation to various specified outcomes, are evident and uncontroversial—partly because most occurrences that limit people's freedom can be classified as causes without fiendish snags or complexities, and partly because some patterns of conduct that cannot be so smoothly classified as causes of restrictions on freedom are removed from consideration by my approach to omissions. Furthermore, the causal ascriptions that stake off unfreedoms from mere inabilities are concerned primarily with two broad classes of freedom-constraining factors (the class of those factors that arise from the actions of other people, and the class of those factors that arise from one's own conduct or from natural forces), rather than with the isolation of particular factors within each class. If we can establish that some inability of a person P is directly or indirectly due to the actions of a person or a group of people other than P, we do not have to worry about assigning causal responsibility for the matter to some identified individual(s). The purposes of this chapter and of this book do not require any such identification. Accordingly, when we tacitly or explicitly make the counter-factual judgements which underlie the causal ascriptions that are needed for the fulfilment of this chapter's purposes, we are arriving at judgements that are even more likely to be clear-cut than are counter-factual propositions generally.

2. *Two Complications*

Any plausible theory of causation has to confront two knotty problems: collateral effects and causal priority. The first of these cruxes pertains to the possibility that the NESS and but-for tests will lead us incorrectly to posit a causal connection between two events or facts that are not causally related. The second crux pertains to the possibility that the

NESS and but-for tests will disable us from knowing which of two causal relata is to be classified as a cause and which is to be classified as an effect. Thus, given that this chapter relies on the but-for criterion (and to some degree also on the NESS test) as the core of its approach to causation, we plainly have to grapple with each of these problems.

2.1. The Problem of Collateral Effects

When two events or facts E_1 and E_2 are direct causal products of the same occurrence C, we might be led to conclude that in the prevailing circumstances each of those products was a NESS condition for the emergence of the other. After all, C satisfies the NESS test for each of those effects. What its satisfaction of the NESS test means (in part) is that C in combination with the prevailing circumstances and the applicable laws of nature was sufficient for the emergence of E_1 and E_2—which in turn means that, in the prevailing circumstances, E_1 and E_2 followed ineluctably from the occurrence of C. Hence, we might be tempted to infer, each of those effects was necessary for the other in the wake of C and the prevailing circumstances; in that wake, neither E_1 nor E_2 would have materialized if the other had not materialized. We thus seem to be driven to the conclusion that each of those effects was a cause of the other. Each was a necessary element of a set of actual conditions that was sufficient for the emergence of the other.

Mackie furnished a helpful illustration of the problem of collateral effects: 'Labour's defeat at the election pleases James but saddens John, who, as it happens, are quite unknown to each other. Then James's being pleased does not cause John's being sad, and yet we might well say that in the circumstances John would not have been sad if James had not been pleased.'[8] We can add that likewise, in the circumstances, James would not have been pleased if John had not been sad. Do we have to accept, then, that John's distress was a cause of James's gratification and vice versa?

To overcome the problem of collateral effects, we have to recall with precision the conception of necessity that is operative in the NESS and but-for tests. Nothing ever qualifies as a NESS cause or a but-for cause of some effect E simply by virtue of having followed perforce from the set of actual conditions that was minimally sufficient for the occurrence of E. Rather, the relevant conception of necessity is that of nonredundancy. As Wright pertinently states in his formulation of the NESS criterion that was quoted at the outset of my last section,

[8] Mackie, *Cement*, 33.

something gets classified as a cause of E under the NESS test by virtue of having been *necessary for the sufficiency* of a set of actual conditions that was minimally sufficient for the occurrence of E. That is, if C is a cause of E under the NESS standard, then a set of conditions including C is minimally sufficient for the occurrence of E and would not have been sufficient for that occurrence if C had not been present as an element of that set.

Once we remember that the relevant conception of necessity under the NESS and but-for tests is non-redundancy, we can readily perceive that collateral effects would not qualify (under those tests) as causes of each other. E_1 was not essential for the sufficiency of any set of conditions that was minimally sufficient for the occurrence of E_2, and E_2 was likewise not essential for the sufficiency of any set of conditions that was minimally sufficient for the occurrence of E_1. As Wright has remarked: 'The set of actual antecedent conditions containing the collateral effect is not sufficient for the occurrence of the [other collateral effect] unless the common cause is also included, but if the common cause is included the collateral effect is not necessary for the set's sufficiency.'[9] This point becomes plain when we look again at the example supplied by Mackie. If we altogether leave out of consideration the fact that John was saddened by the defeat of the Labour Party, and if (while disregarding that fact) we ask whether the aforementioned defeat was in the circumstances sufficient to please James, the answer to our question will manifestly be affirmative. The existence or non-existence of John's displeasure had no bearing on the sufficiency of the Labour defeat in the circumstances to produce the effect of pleasing James. Neither the existence nor the non-existence of John's displeasure would contribute anything to the production of that effect, since neither the existence nor the non-existence of his displeasure would render sufficient any set of conditions that was otherwise insufficient for the gratification of James in the circumstances. Much the same can be said (*mutatis mutandis*), of course, if we contemplate the contribution of James's gratification to John's distress. In the circumstances, that gratification was not an element in any set of actual conditions that was minimally sufficient for the occurrence of the distress. To be such an element, the gratification would have had to be necessary for the sufficiency of the set; but in fact it contributed nothing whatsoever to that sufficiency.

In short, the problem of collateral effects does not pose any difficulties at all for my exposition of causal relations. Given that every

---

[9] Wright, 'Pruning', 1041 n. 223.

genuine cause C will have contributed non-redundantly to a set of conditions sufficient for an effect E—that is, given that every C will have been an integral element in some set of conditions minimally sufficient for the emergence of E—the collateral products of a common cause, E_1 and E_2, cannot correctly be classified as causes of each other. Though we can rightly say that in the prevailing circumstances neither E_1 nor E_2 would have occurred if the other had not occurred, we are not thereby saying that either of them was necessary for the other's existence in any way that would qualify it as a cause thereof. The sense of necessity that would be operative in such a statement about E_1 and E_2 is not the sense that would be operative in a causal ascription.

2.2. *Causal Priority*

If something C was a cause of something else E, then C in conjunction with other NESS conditions and the applicable laws of nature was sufficient for the occurrence of E. Given those other NESS conditions, if it had not been the case that E was going to arise, then C would not have arisen. In the presence of those other NESS conditions, that is, the occurrence of E was a necessary condition for the occurrence of C.

If C was a cause of E, then C was an element in a set of conditions that was minimally sufficient for the emergence of E. As an element in a *minimally* sufficient set of conditions, C was necessary for the set's sufficiency. If there were no other sets of actual conditions that were minimally sufficient for the occurrence of E—or if C was an element in every such set—then, in the circumstances, C was necessary for E's occurrence. Accordingly, given the presence of those circumstances, the emergence of E was sufficient for the emergence of C.

Thus, in any situation where some effect E is not overdetermined— that is, in any situation where only one set of actual conditions is minimally sufficient to give rise to E—the occurrence of E is in the circumstances both necessary and sufficient for the occurrence of any of its causes. In other words, the relationship between E and each of its causes in such circumstances would seem to be wholly symmetrical. Each cause C in conjunction with the other causes is necessary and sufficient for the emergence of E, and E in conjunction with those other causes is necessary and sufficient for the emergence of C. (Even if there is more than one set of actual conditions minimally sufficient for the emergence of E, the symmetrical pattern just described will obtain in respect of any cause that is an element of every such set.) In light of this symmetry, how can we distinguish between causes and effects by recourse to the categories of necessity and sufficiency—the central categories in the NESS and but-for tests? Does not a reliance on those categories disable us from telling whether C is a cause of E or whether E is instead a cause of C?

Plainly, we cannot dodge this crux by adverting to the fact that the respective statuses of C and E will be unproblematically ascertainable in any situation where more than one set of conditions is minimally sufficient for the emergence of E and where not every such set contains C as a member. After all, a situation with only one set of actual conditions minimally sufficient for some specified effect is far from uncommon. Moreover, even in a situation with more than one such set, the puzzle outlined here will arise in connection with any cause that is contained in every set. Some causes (such as the continued presence of oxygen in the atmosphere) will very likely be in every such set, at least within the realm of human affairs. Hence, the problem of establishing the priority of a cause over its effect will confront us even in regard to most situations of over-determination.

The most tempting path for someone wrestling with the problem of causal priority is to maintain that every cause temporally antecedes its effect. Someone taking such a position will perceive causal priority as a species of temporal priority. If C in conjunction with all relevant circumstances and applicable laws of nature was necessary and sufficient for E while E was likewise necessary and sufficient for C, we can tell that C was a cause of E (rather than vice versa) if we find that C occurred earlier than E. Such an abrupt and tidy solution to the puzzle of causal priority is obviously enticing, especially since it trades on a common-sense view of causality.

The conception of causal priority as a species of temporal priority should not be dismissed too quickly. After all, countless causes do precede their effects in time. Moreover, some of the stock illustrations of simultaneous causation (that is, temporal simultaneity between causes and their effects) are quite unpersuasive. Consider, for instance, a famous observation by Kant: 'If I view as a cause a ball which impresses a hollow as it lies on a stuffed cushion, the cause is simultaneous with the effect.'[10] Kant's example—like his further example involving a stove that warms a room—is manifestly inapposite. Let us suppose first that the cushion mentioned by Kant is not resilient.

---

[10] Immanuel Kant, *The Critique of Pure Reason*, trans. Norman Kemp Smith (London: Macmillan, 1933), 228 [A203]. My analysis of Kant's example is closely similar to that in D. H. Mellor, *The Facts of Causation* (London: Routledge, 1995) [Mellor, *Causation*], 220–1. (Mellor, however, goes on to reject the possibility of simultaneous causation more sweepingly than I do; Mellor, *Causation*, Ch. 17.) Kant's example is also discussed in Mackie, *Cement*, 109, 161.

That is, if the ball is removed, the surface of the cushion will not spring back to its original position. Instead, the surface will remain in its current position. In that case, the ball's lying on the cushion at some particular moment t_2 is not a cause of the impression-in-the-cushion-at-t_2. Rather, the original placement of the ball on the cushion at an earlier moment t_1 was a cause of the impression-at-t_2. Obviously, that instance of causation involved temporal priority.

Suppose now that the cushion in Kant's scenario is resilient. If the ball is removed, the surface of the cushion will return to its original shape. Nevertheless, it is still not the case that the ball's lying on the cushion at t_3 is a cause of the impression-in-the-cushion-at-t_3. However brief is the span of time during which the surface of the cushion will spring back to its original shape, it is indeed a span of time greater than nothing. Hence, whereas the ball's lying on the cushion at t_3 is not a cause of the indentation-in-the-cushion-at-t_3, the ball's lying on the cushion at a moment t_2 slightly earlier than t_3 was just such a cause. Had the ball been removed from the cushion at t_3, the surface would not have sprung back until a slightly later moment (t_4). By contrast, had the ball been removed at t_2, the cushion would have sprung back by t_3. In sum, the fact that the ball did not get removed from the cushion at t_2 was a cause of the indentation-therein-at-t_3; and the fact that the ball did not get removed at t_3 was not a cause of the indentation-at-t_3, because it made no contribution whatsoever to the indentation-at-that-time—though it did of course make a contribution to the indentation-at-t_4 and was thus a cause thereof. Each of these instances of causation straightforwardly involved temporal priority.

Yet, notwithstanding the unconvincingness of Kant's illustrations, the notion of simultaneous causation is not arrantly unsustainable. Though nothing in my subsequent discussions will presuppose the soundness of that notion, we ought not to presuppose its unsoundness, either. Consider the following example. A slab of wood suitable for a table top is held suspended just slightly above four upright cylinders of wood that would be suitable as legs for a table. The cylinders are positioned under the four corners of the slab, each of which contains a notch on its underside that will smoothly hold the cylinder below it. At some moment t_1 the slab of wood is released from its suspension, and it drops onto the four vertical rods at the slightly later moment t_2. Had the slab not made contact with those four cylinders at that moment, it would have continued to fall. Similarly, if the slab had not dropped onto the cylinders at t_2, then each of them at the next moment t_3 would have begun to fall to the floor; the contact between the four of them and the slab has occurred just in time to prevent each of the cylinders from beginning to topple. We can therefore correctly say that the endowment of the slab with a secure position above the floor at t_2 has been caused by its coming into contact with the four legs at t_2, and we can likewise correctly say that the endowment of each of those legs with a securely upright position at t_2 has been caused by the slab's coming into contact with the four of them at that moment. Both the secure positioning of the table top above the floor and the securely vertical positioning of the four table legs have occurred simultaneously with the legs' arresting of the table top's downward movement. Unlike Kant's scenario, then, this example involves genuine simultaneity between a cause and its effects.

To be sure, some philosophers intent on denying the possibility of simultaneous causation would undoubtedly wish to dispute the conclusion reached in my last paragraph. Moreover, nothing else in this chapter will depend on the truth of that conclusion. All the same, the account of the table top's alighting upon the four legs has presumably revealed that an explication of causal priority should not hinge on the claim that all causes temporally forego their effects. Though the possibility of simultaneous causation is not incontrovertible, it is credible enough to warrant our avoiding any commitment to a denial of it. We shall therefore have to look elsewhere for a means of distinguishing causes from their effects; we cannot safely rely on the view that causes invariably precede their effects in time.

Fortunately, there are other ways of specifying the priority of any cause over its effect.[11] Especially in light of the purposes of this book, the optimal way is to cash out causal priority as explanatory priority. We explain effects by reference to causes, but not causes by reference to effects; something construed as an effect is an *explanandum*, whereas a characterization of something as a cause is an *explanans*. When we wish to elucidate how some state of affairs has come about, we do not adduce the various effects to which it leads. Rather, we single out the salient causes of its emergence. (Of course, as will be discussed presently, a reference to certain effects of some state of affairs S can itself help to clarify the causes thereof, particularly when some of those causes consist in human conduct and motivations. However, such a reference is explanatorily serviceable only in that subordinate status, as an aid to ferreting out the causes of S in which we are interested. Shorn of that facilitative role, a recountal of S's effects would be beside the point in an explanation of how S emerged.)

---

[11] For a valuable discussion, see Mackie, *Cement*, Ch. 7. For my particular focus, see also Mellor, *Causation*, 63–6; Strawson, 'Causation', 133–4.

A cashing out of causal priority as explanatory priority will yield the appropriate result in every context. Any humdrum instance of causation will clearly lend itself to such an analysis. For example, we explain the breaking of a window by reference to the thud of a tree branch against it, whereas we do not explain the thrust of the tree branch by reference to the shattering of the window's panes. More complex situations will likewise prove amenable to such an approach. Let us look again, for instance, at the simultaneous-causation scenario involving the table top and the legs. As has been observed, the contact between the slab of wood and the four legs at t_2 is a key cause of the secure positioning of the slab above the floor at t_2, and is also a key cause of the securely vertical positioning of each leg at t_2. We advert to the occurrence of that contact in order to explain the secureness of the slab's elevated position at t_2, and also in order to explain the secureness of each leg's upright position at t_2. By contrast, we do not advert to either of those states of secureness in order to explain the slab's alighting on the four wooden cylinders. When faced with a situation that is marked by the simultaneity of a cause and its effects, then, we reassuringly find that causal priority tallies with explanatory priority.

A similarly reassuring conclusion awaits us when we turn our attention again to collateral effects. We explain such effects by reference to their common cause, whereas we do not explain the co-occurrence of joint causes or over-determining causes by reference to their common effect. Let us return to Mackie's example of the defeat suffered by the Labour Party that pleases James and saddens John. Whereas we explain James's happiness and John's distress by adverting to the Labour debacle, we hardly explain that debacle by pointing to the feelings of James or John. Nor do we explain James's pleasure by reference to John's consternation, or vice versa; as is indicated by the lack of explanatory connections, neither man's feelings were causally linked to the other's in any way. (Recall that James and John were not familiar with each other at all.) Now suppose that the Labour Party's downfall was due partly to some inspiring speeches by the Conservative leader and partly to the lacklustre performance of the Labour leader—as well as to any number of other factors, of course. We explain the defeat by adducing those joint causes, but we do not explain the inspirational and drab performances by reference to the defeat that was their common effect. In sum, in the presence of joint causes as much as in the presence of collateral effects, causal priority and explanatory priority are at one.

Before moving on, we should probe a bit more deeply into the nature of explanations in order to avert a potential objection to my assimilation of causal priority and explanatory priority. An explanation of something seeks to account for its occurrence or existence by indicating how it came about. An explanation addresses 'how' questions, in that it endeavours to recount some of the chief processes that have led up to something. When one's attention is drawn to the mechanisms or promptings that are revealed by a good explanation of some event or some state of affairs, one gains a better understanding of the array of factors that brought the event or the state of affairs about.

Now, we can endorse the view that an explanation addresses 'why' questions, so long as 'why' is understood as 'by what means' or 'on the basis of what motivations' or 'through what sorts of processes'. We should not endorse that view if 'why' is understood instead as 'towards what end' or 'in furtherance of what significant purpose'. Were we to accept that explanations address 'why' questions of the latter sort, we would jeopardize the congruence between causal priority and explanatory priority; we would be accepting that some *explanantia* consist essentially in statements of effects rather than of causes. Thus, only in so far as 'how' and 'why' are interchangeable, should we allow that explanations are answers to 'why' questions.

Such a restriction, however, may seem at odds with many ordinary patterns of discourse. Quite often we try to shed light on some action or apparatus or state of affairs by focusing on the goal toward which the action or apparatus or state of affairs is oriented.[12] For example, we might attempt to account for the nature of certain institutional arrangements by highlighting the objectives which those arrangements tend to promote. (We might thereby be maintaining that the arrangements were designed to promote those objectives, or we might be maintaining that their possibly undesigned tendency to further those objectives has enabled them to persist and flourish.) In a similar vein, functional accounts of the workings of bodily organs are common. Such an account might illuminate the workings of an animal's heart, for instance, by highlighting the function of the heart in circulating the animal's blood. Even more broadly, a long-standing philosophical tradition—the tradition of teleological explanation, going back at least to Aristotle—would appear to belie my restrictive conception of explanations. For someone working within an Aristotelian framework, the ends toward which substances or activities tend are final causes that become manifest through teleological explanations. Though rather few philosophers and even fewer non-philosophers in the present day would subscribe to Aristotle's metaphysics, the teleo-

---

[12] For a perceptive discussion from which I have benefited, see Mackie, *Cement*, Ch. 11.

logical approach to elucidating the nature and workings of myriad things is robustly present in everyday discourse and in intellectually sophisticated enquiries.

In response to these misgivings, let it be said straightaway that we obviously should not attach any talismanic significance to the word 'explanation' and its cognates. If people wish to employ that word to designate teleological accounts—and if people wish to designate goals as causes ('final causes')—then so be it. There is no point to quarrelling over a label. This subsection's discussion of explanations and explana-tory priority can be rephrased to refer more specifically to etiological explanations and etiological-explanatory priority. Such explanations deal not with teleological 'why' questions but with 'how' questions concerning the means or processes or pathways by which things have come about. (As has been noted, those 'how' questions can be rede-scribed as 'why' questions if 'how' and 'why' are taken to be inter-changeable expressions for posing inquiries about the origins of things.) Instead of adopting a prospective focus on goals and tenden-cies and functions, an etiological explanation adopts a retrospective focus on mechanisms and sources and promptings. So long as it is entirely clear that the earlier portions of this subsection have used the term 'explanation' exclusively in this sense, one scarcely should object to the fact that the term is used more expansively in other settings.

An important point remains to be addressed, however. Can a teleo-logical approach itself be serviceable for etiological purposes? Much depends here on the precise tenor and ambitions of a teleological exposition. If it is a free-standing elaboration of something's role in producing certain consequences, then it will have gone no way toward unearthing and clarifying the origins of that thing. To expound the heart's circulatory function, for example, is not yet to say anything about the processes by which the heart came to be endowed with the capacity to fulfil that function. Likewise, to chart the manifold impli-cations of a military victory in having paved the way for the flourishing of some civilization C is not per se to furnish an account of the means by which the fighting and the victory came about. Someone concen-trating on the aftermath of the military triumph would doubtless be providing an etiological explanation of the flourishing of C, but would not be providing such an explanation of the triumph itself.

However, many teleological accounts are not meant to be free-standing in the way just sketched. Many such accounts play subordin-ate roles in etiological explanations of the phenomena which they elucidate. For example, if we highlight the effects of some action performed by a human being, we may well be dwelling on those effects in order to make clear that she was motivated by a desire to achieve them. We would thus be describing her action teleologically, but we would be doing so exclusively or primarily in order to indicate what led up to it. In a parallel vein, if we highlight the probable results of some kind of endeavour that is frequently carried out by an animal, we might thereby be suggesting that the animal has come to behave in that manner as a result of channelled reinforcement—that is, reinforcement through previous successes in fulfilling its desires by way of just such behaviour. Much the same could be said, *mutatis mutandis*, about the patterns of activity of a sophisticatedly adaptable robot with a feedback mechanism that enables it to 'learn' from its mistakes.

A broadly comparable tack, consisting in a teleological exposition presented for a predominantly etiological purpose, can be pursued in connection with each of the examples mentioned in the penultimate paragraph above. For instance, if an account of the heart's circulatory function is propounded by an evolutionary biologist, he is undoubt-edly offering the account as a component of an etiological explanation of the heart's capacities. Such an explanation combines that functional account with a complicated array of etiological claims focused on genetic mutations, genetic transmissions, and environmental pressures. Conjoined with those claims, the functional account helps to explain how the capacities of the typical heart came to be as they are.

A teleological orientation can likewise be put to etiological uses when someone underscores the importance of a military victory in securing the greatness of the nation that has triumphed. If such an emphasis is combined with the view that a benevolent deity has been guiding the fortunes of that nation, then the person proclaiming the magnificence of the military conquest is thereby indicating (at a gen-eral level) how it came about. Explanations of this sort are not to the liking of secular intellectuals—or anyone else who is sensible—but they continue to appeal to people of a religious bent in many countries. They were even more widespread in the past. The Bible, for example, teems with references to the role of the Lord in ensuring the greatness of His people by fighting on their behalf against their enemies. 'Thy right hand, O Lord, glorious in power, thy right hand, O Lord, shatters the enemy.'[13]

Thus, although a focus on the effects or functions of something will never in itself inform us how the thing came to be as it is, such a focus can prove to be etiologically fruitful when it accompanies some theses

[13] Exodus 15:6.

that posit a link between the origin and the upshot of the thing. The relevant link can take a number of forms—as should be apparent from the several examples mooted in my last few paragraphs—but it always operates through ordinary causation as it forms a bridge between how something emerged and what something does.

At any rate, whether or not some particular etiological explanation includes a teleological component, the key message of this subsection is that causes and effects can be suitably distinguished if we cash out causal priority as etiological-explanatory priority. As has been seen, even a cause that occurs at exactly the same time as its effects is etiologically-explanatorily prior thereto. If we know that two events or states of affairs C and E were causally linked, and if we want to ascertain whether C was a cause of E or vice versa, we must simply determine whether C's coming about is to be explained by reference to E's coming about or vice versa.

3. Over-determination Defused

One of the truly perplexing cruxes for most theories of causation is a matter that can be largely pretermitted by my own theory. In this respect the current section differs from the previous sections of this chapter, which have explicated the concept of causation in a fashion that is not peculiarly a product of my underlying aim to distinguish unfreedoms from mere inabilities. On the one hand, my reflections on causation heretofore in this chapter have been crucial for the accomplishment of that underlying aim; on the other hand, those foregoing reflections are pertinent for any number of projects and are not distinctively tied to the purposes of this book. By contrast, the current section handles the problem of causal over-determination in an unusual manner that is specifically connected with those purposes. More precisely, as we shall discover, the U Postulate—which has given rise to the need for criteria that will distinguish unfreedoms from mere inabilities—enables us to dodge all or most of the difficulties that beset any general analyses of over-determination.

3.1. A Concise Overview of the Problem

To understand why the problem of over-determination can be circumvented in this chapter, we need to grasp exactly what that problem is. We must consider two broad types of over-determination, which Wright has usefully designated as 'duplicative causation' and 'pre-emptive causation'.[14] A situation of duplicative causation obtains when two or more sets of actually occurring conditions are each minimally sufficient for some effect E that actually ensues. Each of those sets on its own would have been enough to bring about E, and therefore no single one of them is necessary for such a result. Of course, some factors, such as the continued presence of oxygen in the atmosphere, will very likely be members of each of the duplicative sets. Any such factors will have been necessary for the occurrence of E. Nevertheless, any factor that is a member of some but not all of the duplicative sets will have been unnecessary for the bringing about of E. Such a factor, which we may label as a 'duplicative cause', does not satisfy the but-for test of causation. (N.B. It is not invariably the case that each duplicative cause is sufficient—in conjunction with the prevailing circumstances apart from the other duplicative cause[s]—to bring about the over-determined effect to which it contributes. So long as the causes are cumulatively more than sufficient to generate that effect, a situation of duplicative causation obtains. For example, if three fires of equal intensity reach a house simultaneously and consume it, and if any two of the fires would together have been sufficient to burn down the house, then we can identify three sets of actual conditions minimally sufficient for the house's destruction. That destruction has been duplicatively caused even though no fire on its own would have been sufficient in the circumstances for such an outcome. Nonetheless, largely for stylistic reasons, nearly every example of duplicative causation in the present section will involve a duplicative cause which—in conjunction with the prevailing

[14] See, for example, Wright, 'Causation', 1775. All of the articles by Wright cited in note 1 *supra* are sustained and highly insightful investigations of the problem of over-determination. See also his 'Actual Causation vs. Probabilistic Linkage: The Bane of Economic Analysis', 14 *Journal of Legal Studies* 435, 446–9 (1985). For some other important discussions, see Hart and Honoré, *Causation*, 235–53; David Lewis, 'Causation', in Ernest Sosa and Michael Tooley (eds), *Causation* (Oxford: Oxford University Press, 1993), 193, 204; David Lewis, 'Postscripts to "Causation"', in *Philosophical Papers*, ii (New York: Oxford University Press, 1986) [Lewis, 'Postscripts'], 172, 193–212; Louis Loeb, 'Causal Theories and Causal Overdetermination', 71 *Journal of Philosophy* 525 (1974); Mackie, 'Causes', 42–4. See also Honoré, 'Necessary', 374–80. Far less persuasive is Martin Bunzl, 'Causal Overdetermination', 76 *Journal of Philosophy* 134 (1979) [Bunzl, 'Overdetermination'], which goes astray not least by failing to recognize that facts as well as events are causal relata. Even less impressive is Peter van Inwagen, 'Ability and Responsibility', 87 *Philosophical Review* 201, 212–20 (1978), which completely overlooks the NESS test as a criterion for the existence of causal relations, and which therefore strangely posits an equivalence between one's causing it to be the case that some person P has died (in a context where the death was over-determined) and one's causing it to be the case that P was mortal.

circumstances apart from the other duplicative cause[s]—is sufficient to produce the over-determined effect to which it contributes.)

Precisely because the but-for criterion does not allow us to recognize duplicative causes as causes, the NESS criterion is a superior test. Though notable instances of duplicative causation are not common, a reliance on the but-for test in one's handling of them would lead to unacceptable conclusions. Suppose, for example, that two terrorists shoot a victim simultaneously. Each bullet reaches the heart of the victim at the same time, and each would have been sufficient on its own to kill him. Under the but-for criterion we would have to conclude that neither gunshot was a cause of the victim's demise. We would thus have to conclude that neither of the terrorists can correctly be said to have committed a slaying, since neither of them was causally responsible for the death. Under the NESS standard, by contrast, each shot was a cause of the death; each terrorist slew the victim.

One can easily imagine many other scenarios of duplicative causation that would reveal the NESS criterion to be preferable to the but-for test. (Indeed, we do not have to imagine them, since several germane examples have become staples of the legal and philosophical literature on causation.) For instance, suppose that an arsonist throws a firebrand onto a pile of dry boards at exactly the same moment that a bolt of lightning strikes the boards. The pile is completely consumed. Each of those incendiary events in isolation from the other was sufficient to ignite a blaze capable of destroying the boards. Accordingly, neither event was necessary for the destruction. Under the but-for standard, then, we have to maintain that the arsonist's action was not a cause of the incineration of the boards; though the culprit can be convicted of the crime of attempted arson, he will have to be exonerated of the crime of arson. He can disclaim causal responsibility for the loss of the boards even though he performed an act that was sufficient—in conjunction with the prevailing circumstances apart from the bolt of lightning—to reduce the boards to ashes. Moreover, he can disavow causal responsibility for the blaze even though (according to the but-for standard) there was no other set of conditions which caused that calamitous event. To avoid this unsatisfactory verdict, theorists should normally resort to the NESS test in lieu of the but-for test as their criterion for attributing causal responsibility.

The NESS standard's superiority over the but-for standard is even more palpable when we encounter situations of pre-emptive causation. In any such situation that is not also marked by duplicative causation, the following two facts obtain: (1) some effect E is brought about by the sole minimally sufficient set of actual conditions C; and

(2) if C had not been present, then E would have been brought about by an alternative set of conditions that would have been minimally sufficient for E in the absence of C. Scenarios involving pre-emptive causation are of two main varieties, V_1 and V_2. In any V_1 situation, an alternative set of conditions actually emerges as such. However, that set reaches its climax as a full sequence slightly later than C and is thus not causally efficacious (since E has already been brought about by C). Its sufficiency is counter-factual rather than actual, because of the actuality of C. In any V_2 situation of pre-emptive causation, an alternative set of conditions does not emerge—precisely because C has emerged.

Countless examples of pre-emptive causation could be adduced. Let us begin with a V_2 scenario. Suppose that the leader of a criminal gang sends one of his followers to purchase narcotics from a supplier. If that particular henchman had not gone to make the purchase, then another member of the gang would have done so. Hence, although the gangster's carrying out of the routine transaction was sufficient in conjunction with the prevailing circumstances to acquire the narcotics for the gang from the supplier, and although the set of conditions that included his carrying out of the transaction was the only set of actual conditions minimally sufficient for the acquisition of the narcotics, his purchase was not a but-for cause of that acquisition. If this particular henchman had refused to comply with his boss's directive, one of his fellow criminals would have acted in his stead. Thus, an application of the but-for test would lead us to the conclusion that the henchman was not causally responsible for the gang's possession of illegal drugs. His transaction with the supplier was not a cause of the acquisition of the drugs, or so we would apparently be asked to believe. By contrast, an application of the NESS test will issue in the conclusion that the aforementioned transaction was indeed a cause of the gang's acquisition of the narcotics. That test allows us to avoid the ridiculous notion that, because every one of the gang-leader's minions was perfectly able and willing to purchase the drugs, anyone among them actually engaging in the purchase would not be causally responsible for it.

The other main kind of pre-emptive causation, V_1, can likewise be illustrated easily. Suppose that two people independently start fires that head towards a large wooden house from different directions. Each fire in isolation from the other is sufficiently large and intense to destroy the house if the house is still standing when the fire reaches it. In fact, however, the blaze approaching the edifice from a northward direction arrives roughly eight hours ahead of the fire that is approaching from a southward direction. By the time that the latter blaze reaches the site, the residence has been reduced to a heap of smouldering ashes. Hence, the fire approaching from the south is not sufficient in conjunction with the prevailing circumstances to burn down the house—since one of those circumstances is the fact that the house has already been consumed. Among the elements in any set of conditions minimally sufficient for the burning down of the residence would be the fact that it has not yet been incinerated. Since that condition does not obtain by the time of the arrival of the second fire, that fire does not qualify as a cause of the house's destruction under either the NESS test or the but-for test. Only the blaze that has approached from the north is a cause of the destruction of the home.

More precisely, that northerly fire qualifies as a cause under the NESS criterion. Its status under the but-for criterion is slightly more ambiguous. For most purposes, one's characterization of the house's destruction will not include a fine-grained temporal index. Whether we opt to characterize that misfortune with an event-description ('the consumption of the house by fire') or with a fact-description ('the fact that the house was consumed by fire'), we shall not usually need to specify with great exactitude the time at which the misfortune occurred. If we apply the but-for test with a description of the house's destruction that does not specify the time of the destruction minutely enough to distinguish between the junctures at which the successive fires arrived, we shall have to conclude that the northerly blaze was no more a cause of the incineration of the house than was the southerly blaze. Neither fire was necessary in the circumstances for the devastation of the house at some point or another during the day on which the devastation occurred. Neither fire was necessary, because the other fire was also present at some point during that day. A different verdict is warranted, however, if we apply the but-for test with a description of the house's destruction that includes quite a precise temporal index—for example, 'consumption of the house by fire no later than 3.00 p.m.'. We shall then conclude that the northerly fire was necessary for the occurrence of that destruction. It was necessary because the southerly fire did not arrive soon enough to produce an effect that would match our temporally indexed description.

Let us consider one further aspect of the situation of the house and the fires. In addition to asking about the incineration of the house (an event that occurs during a certain period of time), we can ask about the house's non-existence or obliteratedness (a state of affairs that ensues from the incineration). Clearly, the southerly fire was neither a NESS cause nor a but-for cause of the house's non-existence. In the prevailing circumstances—which crucially included the presence of the northerly fire—the southerly blaze contributed nothing to the obliteratedness of the residence, which had become obliterated before that blaze ever reached it. What can we say about the northerly fire, then? Under the NESS test, that fire was a key cause of the house's non-existence. Under the but-for test, on the other hand, the northerly fire was a cause of only a short duration of the house's non-existence. That fire was indeed a but-for cause of the obliteratedness of the home between the time of the completion of the actual incineration and the time at which a thorough incineration would have been accomplished by the southerly fire if the home had still been intact when that latter fire arrived. However, the northerly blaze—the first fire on the scene—was not a but-for cause of the home's non-existence for any period after the duration specified in my preceding sentence. If we inquire on the following day whether the house's non-existence at that time is caus-ally attributable to the person who started the northerly blaze that consumed the whole edifice, the but-for criterion will oblige us to answer in the negative. In respect of the house's obliteratedness on that following day and on all subsequent days, neither of the two fires can be correctly classified as a cause under the but-for test.

In short, both with regard to situations of duplicative causation and with regard to situations of pre-emptive causation, the NESS principle avoids the unacceptable verdicts that would be generated by the but-for principle. In application to any context where some effect E has been duplicatively brought about, the NESS standard ascribes the status of a cause to every element in each set of conditions minimally sufficient for E. In application to any context where some effect E has been brought about by some minimally sufficient set of conditions C_1 that pre-empted the operative role of some other set of conditions C_2—a set of conditions that would have been minimally sufficient for E in the absence of C_1—the NESS criterion ascribes the status of a cause to each element in C_1 but not to any element in C_2 that was not also an element in C_1. That criterion deems each element in C_1 to be a cause of E and of everything that has resulted from E.

3.2. Dodging Most Difficulties

Let us recall that the present chapter's exploration of causality has been triggered by the U Postulate's distinction between unfreedoms and mere inabilities. Given the U Postulate's exact formulation of that distinction, however, we can happily circumvent most of the puzzles engendered by situations of over-determination. Were it not for the fact that we can dodge those puzzles, we would manifestly be well advised to favour the NESS test of causation over the but-for test. The preferableness of the former test is encapsulated in the final sentence of the preceding subsection—and in the discussion of the burned-down house's state of obliteratedness, from which that sentence emanates. What makes that particular discussion so important is that the non-existence of the house is relevantly similar to the non-existence of any ability of a human being. Just as the solid edifice of the home has been eliminated by the northerly fire, so too a person's ability-to-φ can be taken away by some occurrence. When a person has been deprived of some ability by duplicative factors, neither the initial deprivation nor the subsequent state of inability will be causally attributable to any of those factors under the but-for criterion. To be sure, when someone has instead been divested of an ability by a *pre-emptive* factor, the initial divestiture will be causally attributable to that factor under the but-for test if our specification of the divestiture includes a precise temporal index and if the pre-empted set of conditions would have taken effect later than the pre-emptive set. Even then, however, nearly the whole of the person's subsequent state of disabledness will not be causally ascribable to either the pre-emptive factor or the pre-empted factor. In respect of any situation of over-determination, in other words, the but-for standard disallows us from causally tracing a persistent lack of freedom to the set of occurrences that brought it about. We should eschew such a ridiculous upshot, especially in light of the importance of causal ascriptions within this book—that is, in light of the central role of those ascriptions in operationalizing the pregnant distinction between unfreedoms and mere inabilities. Consequently, if we had to select between the NESS principle and the but-for principle, we would have very strong reasons indeed for embracing the former and disfavouring the latter.

Fortunately, however, a choice between those two criteria is inessential, since the U Postulate obliges us to resort to the but-for standard whenever that standard clashes with the NESS criterion. We are able to take advantage of the simplicity of the but-for principle without being led astray in regard to situations of over-determination, because such situations are wholly unproblematic under the U Postulate. Far from giving rise to fiendish cruxes, issues relating to over-determined inabilities lend themselves to perfectly straightforward resolutions when they are analysed by reference to that postulate.

Why, then, does the U Postulate defuse all or most of the difficulties associated with over-determination? For one thing, as this chapter has already remarked, the U Postulate trains our attention not so much on specific causal factors as on two broad classes of causal factors (the actions of other people versus one's own conduct or the workings of natural forces). When someone's freedom has been curtailed by the actions of someone else, for example, we are interested not so much in the identity of the other person as in the fact that he or she is indeed another person. Because of our focus on general categories of determinants, we can very easily handle any situation of duplicative causation or pre-emptive causation involving determinants within only one category. Regardless of whether we apply the but-for standard or the NESS standard to any such situation, we shall come up with the same clear-cut answer.

For instance, if two people have simultaneously shot another person, and if each of the gunshots was independently sufficient to incapacitate the victim's left arm, his subsequent inability to move that arm has been over-determined by some actions of other people. One set of actual conditions minimally sufficient for the disabling of the arm included one of the gunshots as an indispensable element, and another such set included the other gunshot. Now, if our focus were not on general classes of causal factors but instead on individual factors within each class, the NESS test and the but-for test would lead here to sharply divergent conclusions. Under the former test, each shot was a cause of the victim's lack of freedom; under the latter test, by contrast, neither shot was a cause. Thus, in regard to this scenario of duplicative causation and in regard to countless other scenarios of over-determination—some of which would be much trickier—a focus on individual causal factors will require us to choose between the NESS criterion and the but-for criterion. (As has been stated, the NESS criterion is manifestly preferable when a choice must be made outside the sway of the U Postulate.) However, no selection between those criteria is required in this context, because our focus lies on broad classes of causal factors when we are analytically separating unfreedoms from mere inabilities. With such a focus, the but-for test and the NESS test here converge. Since every set of actual conditions minimally sufficient for the incapacitation of the victim's left arm included the fact that at least one person other than the victim performed some action, that fact was both a NESS cause and a but-for cause of the victim's incapacity. After all, had it not been the case that at least one person other than the victim shot him in his left arm, he would not in the circumstances have lost the use of that arm; consequently, the but-for test as well as the NESS test will ascribe a causal role to the fact that at least one person other than the victim did indeed shoot him. (A dispensable feature of this example is that each of the attackers injured the victim by the same means. Suppose instead that one of the assailants shot the victim's arm just as the second assailant wounded the arm incapacitatingly with an axe. In that case, the causally relevant fact is that at least one person other than the victim in his immediate proximity performed an injurious action. To that fact both the NESS test and the but-for test will attribute a causal role.)

In short, because the task of staking off unfreedoms from mere inabilities does not oblige us to discriminate among particular causal factors within each of the two general categories of such factors, we can readily come to grips with numerous instances of over-determination. Whenever the over-determining factors all belong to the same broad category, we do not need to inquire further. We do not need to ask, for example, whether those factors were genuinely duplicative contributions or whether instead one was pre-emptive and the other pre-empted. Nor, in connection with a situation of pre-emptive causality, do we need to ask which factor was a pre-emptive contribution and which was pre-empted and was thus not a contribution at all. Of course, such questions are crucial for someone who aims to single out specific factors to which causal responsibility can accurately be ascribed; but those questions are beside the point within the confines of this book, where the U Postulate's concentration on general types of determinants has obviated such detailed probing.

At least as important in defusing all or most problems of over-determination, however, is the first of the two main prongs of the U Postulate (which stipulates that a person's inability-to-φ is a mere inability—rather than an unfreedom—unless the person would be able-to-φ in the absence of the second of the conditions specified by that postulate). The proviso expressed therein spares us from having to ponder the complexities of situations of over-determination that cut across the broad categories of causal factors. Having found already that *intra*-categorial specimens of over-determination are wholly untroubling, we shall now find that much the same is true of *inter*-categorial specimens.

What the first chief prong of the U Postulate establishes is that, when any person *P* lacks some ability-to-φ, the lack is a mere inability rather than an unfreedom unless *every* set of actual or pre-empted conditions minimally sufficient for the non-existence of the specified ability is a set that contains some instance(s) or product(s) of actions performed by some other person(s).[15] If at least one set of actual or pre-empted conditions minimally sufficient for the non-existence of *P*'s ability is a

---

[15] To avoid making the sentences in this paragraph even more ungainly than they are, I have had to use the word 'sufficient' to cover not only actual sufficiency but also the counter-factual sufficiency of any set of conditions that would have been sufficient in the circumstances if some pre-emptive set of actually sufficient conditions had not emerged.

set containing no instances or products of anyone else's actions among its elements, then the inability is a mere inability rather than an unfreedom. It is a mere inability because in those circumstances P would not have been able-to-φ even in the absence of any relevant actions by any other person(s).

Let us notice straightaway that the implications of the U Postulate expounded in the preceding paragraph are applicable to situations of pre-emptive causality as well as to situations of duplicative causality. On the one hand, as was illustrated in my earlier example of the gangster's purchase of narcotics, a pre-empted set of conditions might not ultimately emerge. On the other hand, if such a set containing no instances or products of anyone else's actions would have emerged if some pre-emptive set(s) of conditions had not emerged, then the first prong of the U Postulate has not been satisfied. In those circumstances, it is not the case that P would have been able-to-φ in the absence of any actions by someone else that deprived him of his ability-to-φ. Had those actions not occurred, the pre-empted set of conditions involving no such actions would have occurred and would have deprived P of his ability-to-φ. Thus, even when an over-determining set of conditions does not actually emerge—because it has been obviated by the emergence of an alternative set—it will be taken into account under the first prong of the U Postulate if it is a set comprising no instances or products of anyone else's actions. (One caveat should be entered here. As became clear in my earlier discussion of the obliteratedness of the burned-down house, a situation of pre-emptive causality can be marked by an interval between the time of the actual production of some effect and the time at which the effect would have been produced by the pre-empted set of conditions. If P's ability-to-φ was eliminated at some time t_1 by a pre-emptive cause that directly or indirectly involved somebody else's actions, and if that ability would have been eliminated at a later time t_2 by a pre-empted set of conditions involving no such actions, then P's lack of the ability-to-φ was an unfreedom throughout the interim between t_1 and t_2. At t_2, however, it became a mere inability.)

Before we look at a few examples that will lend some concreteness to the dauntingly abstract discussion in the last couple of paragraphs, one further point should be noted. As was remarked in my initial exposition of duplicative causation, it is not always the case that any duplicative cause of E will be sufficient to bring about E in isolation from the other duplicative cause(s) thereof. Consequently, this subsection's current analysis should lead us to classify impairments of P's freedom as mere inabilities only in some of the situations where the impairments have been duplicatively caused across the U Postulate's broad categories of determinants. That is, the 'mere-inabilities' classification is appropriate only when at least one freedom-impairing set of actual conditions which does not include anyone else's actions is by itself minimally sufficient to produce its freedom-curtailing effects. When instead every such set is sufficient to produce those effects only when it is combined with another set of actual conditions that does include some action(s) of some person(s) other than P, the curtailment of P's liberty will be classifiable as an instance of unfreedom under the U Postulate. Although the causation of that curtailment by the different sets of conditions might be duplicative—since the cumulative causal force of the sets might be greater than is requisite for the curtailment—the situation is not such that P's freedom would have been reduced even in the absence of anyone else's actions.

Let us now consider a few examples that can render this abstract argumentation more concrete. These examples will amount to variations on a basic scenario roughly similar to one which we pondered earlier. Suppose that Albert goes into a cave to explore its interior. Outside the cave at the top of an inclination is his enemy Theodore, who gladly takes advantage of this opportunity to abridge severely the overall liberty of his foe. Theodore gives a shove to a boulder that is precariously perched at the top of the slope on which he is standing. The boulder rolls down and traps Albert in the cave. On the basis of what we have been told so far, we can conclude straightforwardly that the sharp diminution in the overall freedom of Albert has consisted in the creation of commensurate unfreedom for him; his countless new inabilities are unfreedoms rather than mere inabilities. But let us now suppose that, at the exact moment when Theodore pushes against the boulder in order to send it hurtling down the inclination, a very strong gust of wind blows the branch of a tree against the boulder. We should mull over a few versions of this amplified scenario.

Let us initially presume that Theodore's shove and the smash of the branch against the rock were individually sufficient to topple the rock from its position on the slope. Under the first main prong of the U Postulate, then, we should classify the myriad new restrictions on Albert's range of activities as mere inabilities rather than as unfreedoms. It is not the case that, had no actions by anyone else diminished his liberty, Albert would have been able to engage in the activities that are newly closed off to him. Rather, he would have been unable to engage in those activities in any event, since the collision of the branch against the boulder was sufficient in the circumstances to seal him in the cave without any intervention by Theodore. Thus, because a set of actual conditions comprising no instances or products of anyone else's actions was minimally sufficient to trap Albert in the cave, the new curbs on his liberty are mere inabilities even though they were duplicatively caused by a set of conditions that included some of Theodore's actions.

Suppose now that, instead of being an instance of duplicative causation, the events leading up to the immurement of Albert in the cave were an instance of pre-emptive causation. A shove by Theodore sent the boulder rolling toward the mouth of the cave, but shortly after his shove an extremely strong gust of wind propelled a tree branch through the exact region of space that had been occupied by the boulder 20 seconds earlier. Had the boulder still been resting precariously in the position from which Theodore knocked it down, it would have been sent hurtling by the thud of the branch. In the actual circumstances, however, the flight of the branch was pre-empted as a cause of Albert's confinement by Theodore's shove. The sole set of actual conditions minimally sufficient for the confinement was a set that included the shove but excluded the branch's flight. (By contrast, the set of actual conditions that included the flight but excluded the shove was only counter-factually sufficient—rather than actually sufficient—for the confinement of Albert. It would have been sufficient if the shove had not occurred, but it was inefficacious in light of the fact that the shove had already occurred.) Nonetheless, despite the status of Theodore's action as a cause of Albert's entrapment in the cave, and despite the fact that the soaring of the branch was not such a cause, the restrictions imposed on Albert's activities by the entrapment are mere inabilities rather than unfreedoms. To be sure, during the first 20 seconds or so of his entombment, those restrictions were unfreedoms; that period was the interval between the time at which the restrictions were actually imposed and the time at which they would have been imposed if they had been caused by the collision of the branch with the boulder. After that 20-second period had elapsed, however, the limits on Albert's range of activities became mere inabilities. They remain such for as long as Albert continues to be alive and confined in the cave. In sum, for virtually any purpose that might be pursued by an enquiry into the statuses of someone's particular inabilities, the upshot of this example of pre-emptive causation is essentially the same as the upshot of the preceding paragraph's example of duplicative causation. In each case, the first prong of the U Postulate steers us to the verdict that Albert has lost untold freedoms without becoming unfree. Because in each case a set of actual or pre-empted conditions that did not encompass any instances or products of anyone else's actions was minimally sufficient for Albert's loss of those untold freedoms—regardless of whether the sufficiency of each set was actual or counterfactual[16]— we are bound to classify his loss as an array of mere inabilities in essentially the same way for each situation. (The basic point made in this paragraph would be even more evident if the pre-emptive cause of Albert's captivity in the cave had been the striking of the tree branch against the rock. In such a variant of my example, the shoving of the rock by Theodore would have been merely a pre-empted condition rather than a cause. Likewise, the central point made in this paragraph would be underscored if the scenario of pre-emptive causation were altered to remove any interval between the time at which Albert's loss of freedoms actually occurred and the time at which his loss would have occurred if it had been brought about by the pre-empted condition. Moreover, the conclusions reached here would be the same even if the pre-emptive causality were of the V_2 variety rather than of the V_1 variety. In other words, even if there did not materialize any workings of natural forces that would have been sufficient for the entombment of Albert—sufficient, that is, in conjunction with the prevailing circumstances apart from Theodore's actions—the U Postulate will classify the entombment as an array of mere inabilities if the non-occurrence of the workings of those natural forces was due to the pre-emptive occurrence of Theodore's actions.)

We should contemplate one further variation on the story of Albert and Theodore. Heretofore that story both in its duplicative-causation version and in its pre-emptive-causation version has illustrated how the U Postulate enables us to deal handily with situations of inter-categorial over-determination. Whenever a set of actual or pre-empted conditions that does not include any instance or product of anybody else's actions is minimally sufficient for the deprivation of someone's liberty-to-φ—that is, sufficient actually or counter-factually—the deprivation of that liberty constitutes a mere inability rather than an unfreedom. A new variation on the story of Albert and Theodore can show that, in accordance with remarks made four paragraphs ago, some situations of duplicative causation have to be handled in a converse though equally straightforward manner. Let us presume that the thud of the branch against the boulder was not quite sufficient on its own to send the boulder rolling toward the mouth of the cave. Only in

---

[16] I have already sought to make clear what is meant by my references to counter-factual sufficiency. If C_2 has been pre-empted by C_1 as the set of conditions that caused E, then C_2 would have been sufficient for E if C_1 had not already brought E about. That 'would-have-been' sufficiency in a context of pre-emptive causation is what I designate here as counter-factual sufficiency.

combination with Theodore's simultaneous pushing was the collision of the branch capable of producing such an effect. Perhaps Theodore's pushing was sufficient to produce such an effect without any assistance from the thud of the branch, or perhaps it was sufficient only in combination with that thud. Regardless of whether Theodore's action was enough by itself to topple the boulder in the prevailing circumstances, we may suppose that in combination with the collision of the branch it was more than sufficiently forceful to send the boulder hurtling down the slope. Duplicative causation, rather than simply joint causation (where the two causes would together be just enough to produce their common effect), was thus at work in the events that led to the entombment of Albert in the cave. Nevertheless, the U Postulate does not lead us to classify Albert's loss of various freedoms as an array of mere inabilities. Instead, that loss consists in an array of unfreedoms. Because no set of actual conditions minimally sufficient for the confinement of Albert was a set that did not contain any instances or products of somebody else's actions, Albert would have retained his freedoms if the specified actions—namely, Theodore's shoving—had not occurred. Therefore, the first prong of the U Postulate has been satisfied, and the second prong is dispositively applicable.

At any rate, whether a situation of over-determination is one of duplicative causality or of pre-emptive causality, and whether it cuts across our two major categories of causal factors or remains within a single category, and whether duplicative causes (in a situation of duplicative causality) are individually sufficient for their common effect or not, the fundamental message of this section is that the U Postulate averts any difficulties that might otherwise plague us when we have to take account of over-determined inabilities. When the over-determination of some inability of a person has occurred within only one of the two classes of causal factors, we need not enquire any further. If the over-determining factors were all instances or products of other people's actions, then the resultant inability is an unfreedom; if instead those factors were all instances of the person's own conduct or of the workings of natural forces, the resultant inability is a mere inability. When the *duplicative causation* of some inability of a person has occurred across the two categories of causal factors, the key question to be asked is whether any set of actual conditions minimally sufficient for that inability was a set containing no instances or products of anyone else's actions. If the answer to that question is affirmative, then the person's inability is a mere inability. If the answer is negative, the inability is an unfreedom. When the *pre-emptive causation* of some inability of a person has occurred across the categories of causal factors, we can know without further enquiry that the inability is a mere inability if the pre-emptive set of conditions did not include any instances or products of anyone else's actions. If instead the set of conditions that did not include any such instances or products was the pre-empted set, the inability is an unfreedom during the interval (if any) between the time of its inception and the time at which it would have arisen if the pre-empted set of conditions had caused it. Thenceforward, however, it is a mere inability. In short, irrespective of the species of over-determination that might confront us when we endeavour to discover whether somebody is unfree-to-φ, the U Postulate yields unequivocal answers. Although the application of that postulate to specific situations can of course now and then be tricky because of uncertainties about the relevant facts, each prong of the postulate comes to grips with any ascertained facts in ways that are admirably clear-cut. At least at a theoretical level—as opposed to a concrete level at which theoretical standards are brought to bear on sometimes nebulous facts—the cruxes engendered by over-determination are not cruxes at all for my theory of freedom.

4. Acts, Omissions, and Causal Responsibility

Throughout the last section, my discussion has sought to indicate that among the causes of any state of affairs are not only its immediate antecedents but also the countless antecedents of those antecedents. The relationship of causality is transitive; that is, if X was a cause of Y and if Y was a cause of Z, then X was a cause of Z. When we endeavour to ascertain whether a person's lack of some freedom is causally attributable to other people's actions or is instead attributable exclusively to his own conduct and to natural processes, we have to ask not only whether other people's actions were directly implicated but also whether the products of their past actions were implicated in any way.

This final main section of the present chapter will later distinguish between actions and omissions rigorously, and will explain why omissions must receive special treatment. In the opening subsection, however, we may rely on an intuitive understanding of actions as we consider the extent of actions' causal contributions to restrictions on freedom.

4.1. Any Contribution is Enough

The paramount question to be addressed in this subsection is whether the contributions of a person's actions to any limits on some other person's liberty must pass a certain threshold of significance if those limits are to be correctly classifiable as unfreedoms. In pondering this question, we should recall the reasons for distinguishing between unfreedoms and mere inabilities in the first place. As has been indicated in Chapter 2 and again at the outset of this chapter, the basic reason for insisting on such a distinction is to avoid the conclusion that either the range of everyone's combinations of conjunctively exercisable freedoms or the range of everyone's combinations of consistent unfreedoms is infinite. That conclusion is indeed something to be avoided, since it would undermine this book's general claim that (at least in principle) the overall freedom of each person and of each society can be measured. Hence, a distinction between unfreedoms and mere inabilities is vital for the fundamental objective which I am pursuing.

To be sure, as has been noted near the beginning of this chapter, my specific way of posing that distinction—as a divide between the restrictions imposed by other people's actions and the restrictions imposed by oneself or by natural forces—has not yet been fully justified. Not until Chapter 5 will a set of arguments be advanced in support of that specific demarcation. Still, what should already be apparent is that my singling out of other people's actions as the sources of unfreedoms is based on the premise that the freedom-impairing effects of human intercourse (even remote and indirect human intercourse) are especially noteworthy for political philosophers. Although those philosophers are rightly attentive to all sorts of curbs on socio-political liberty, the distinctiveness of such liberty lies precisely in one's attribution of special significance to the curbs brought about by human interrelationships. Given as much, we have grounds for remaining alert to the freedom-constraining role of any such interrelationships even when that role is inconspicuous or attenuated. In the absence of reasons that countervail those grounds, then, we should accept that curtailments of a person's liberty arising partly from other people's actions will count as unfreedoms even if the causal contributions of those actions do not surpass any threshold of prominence that might be posited.

A further consideration militates against any insistence on such a threshold. Were we to contend that reductions in a person's liberty caused by other people's actions do not qualify as unfreedoms if the causal contributions of those actions are not salient, we would oblige ourselves to have recourse to evaluative judgements when staking off unfreedoms from mere inabilities. Although the evaluatively pregnant basis for such judgements would not necessarily be moral or political, it would indeed have to be evaluatively pregnant. Exactly what might constitute that basis is quite mysterious, for it could not reside in the special importance of human interrelationships as sources of constraints on people's freedom; after all, as has just been maintained, that special importance is a factor that weighs against the establishment of any threshold of causal significance. An alternative basis for the relevant evaluative judgements would therefore not only have to provide persuasive grounds for distinguishing between unfreedoms and mere inabilities by reference to its own particular conception of causal salience. In addition, it would have to override our reasons for drawing the unfreedoms/mere-inabilities distinction by reference to sheer causality rather than by reference to any conception of causal salience. Moreover, since those latter reasons are directly connected to the concept of sociopolitical liberty, any basis for judgements about salience that is capable of defeating those reasons must likewise be directly connected to that concept. Otherwise, far from yielding a more refined analysis of sociopolitical freedom, such a basis would amount to an extraneous change of topic. Whether any available principle could meet all these demands is exceedingly doubtful, to say the least. (Lest anything in this paragraph might somehow seem to bespeak a contrary view, I should note that at least in theory there is an obvious standard for measuring the sizeableness of any causal factor's contribution to some result R. If we can gauge the extent to which the existence of each such factor raised the *ex-ante* probability of an occurrence like R, we shall thereby have ascertained the relative salience of the factors in bringing about R. Throughout this subsection I implicitly rely on just such a measure of the prominence or inconspicuousness of various causes. Nevertheless, that way of quantifying causal significance is patently not the sort of evaluative principle to which this paragraph has referred. Rather, it is simply a precise means of expressing the fact that various causes partake of differing degrees of salience—a fact that is manifestly presupposed throughout my present discussion. A means of articulating that fact with exactitude does not go the slightest way toward establishing that anyone's actions which curtail anyone else's liberty must have surpassed a certain threshold of causal salience if the curtailment is to be classifiable as a state of unfreedom. Such a conclusion about a threshold of significance would be an outright non sequitur.)

What is more, there are no countervailing considerations that point in favour of grounding our distinction between unfreedoms and mere inabilities on judgements about the prominence of the contributions of other people's actions to various restrictions on liberty. Given that the focus of this subsection lies on actions as opposed to omissions, we need not be concerned here that taking account of inconspicuous causal contributions will be an unduly conjectural enterprise. Whereas omissions have to receive special treatment if we are to avoid inordinate speculativeness and other snags, actions and their effects—even their remoter effects—are generally much more clear-cut. Besides, in any context where the ascription of a minor causal role to some action would indeed be a matter of guesswork, we can either eschew the ascription or else attach a stringent probabilistic qualification to it. (Such a qualification would in turn get attached to our verdict that some constraint on a person's liberty is an unfreedom rather than a mere inability.) As we probe the sources of inabilities, we should of course be responsive to the facts of any situation but also to the limits on our ability to know the facts. Those limits are not very confining when we are concentrating on actions, but they do exist.

Nor should any worries about the issuance of unwarranted reproaches deter us from attributing decisive causal responsibility to somebody's action(s) that played only a tiny part in curbing someone else's freedom (a tiny part, that is, in comparison with the role of natural forces or of the latter person's own conduct). As has been observed in the opening portion of this chapter, the character of this book's enquiries is crucially different from the character of the enquiries undertaken by adjudicative officials. Those officials operate institutions that are charged with the practical task of holding people legally accountable—and often morally accountable as well—for their actions. For such officials, the meagreness or remoteness of a person's contribution to an untoward result is plainly a relevant consideration as they decide whether the person should be held legally responsible for that result. Admittedly, as was mentioned in my earlier remarks, these aspects of the matter of legal responsibility are frequently discussed by jurists as if they were causal issues, under headings such as 'proximate causation'. H. L. A. Hart and Tony Honoré, for example, have adopted just such an approach: '*A* hits *B* who falls to the ground stunned and bruised by the blow; at that moment a tree crashes to the ground and kills *B*. *A* has certainly caused *B*'s bruises but not his death.'[17] Nevertheless, in so far as the inconspicuousness or

---

[17] Hart and Honoré, *Causation*, 77. For an endorsement of Hart's and Honoré's position on this matter from a perspective largely at odds with theirs, see Peter Lipton, 'Causation outside the Law', in Hyman Gross and Ross Harrison (eds), *Jurisprudence: Cambridge Essays* (Oxford: Clarendon Press, 1992), 127, 138. For a sophisticated version of Hart's and Honoré's position that duly recognizes the distinction between causal responsibility and moral/legal responsibility, see Jonathan Bennett, 'Morality and Consequences', in Sterling McMurrin (ed.), *The Tanner Lectures on Human Values: 1981* (Cambridge: Cambridge University Press, 1981) [Bennett, 'Morality'], 45, 69–70, 71.

tenuousness of the causal role of someone's conduct is a factor that influences adjudicative decisions about his or her legal responsibility for some outcome, that factor is an object of normative assessments rather than of genuinely etiological investigations. No such assessments are requisite or pertinent in this book, since the aim herein is not to hold people accountable but to separate unfreedoms from mere inabilities. When a theorist pursuing the latter aim submits that somebody's modest or distant contribution to trammels on someone else's liberty is sufficient for the status of those trammels as instances of unfreedom, no blame whatsoever is thereby expressed. Far from deeming anyone to be culpable, we are simply concluding that the trammels in question derive from human interrelationships and that they are therefore of special interest to political philosophers. That theoretical conclusion has precious little to do with practical questions and decisions concerning the extent of the responsibilities that people owe to one another. Thus, because my theory of freedom is unburdened by the moral pressures that weigh on officials who have to reach judgements about punishments and compensatory remedies, we should have no qualms about imputing causal responsibility to any person whose actions were only minor elements in a set of conditions that minimally sufficed to curtail somebody else's liberty. We shall not thereby be condemning the person or doing anything else that affects his life adversely. There is accordingly no reason for us to feel squeamish or hesitant about treating his very modest role as a determinative factor in our analysis of the situation to which his actions contributed.

We should now contemplate a few examples that will help to clarify the implications of the arguments in this subsection. The central theme of those arguments is that the sheer remoteness or smallness of some person's causal contribution to a reduction in some other person's liberty is never per se a reason for ignoring that contribution when we are ascertaining whether the reduction consists in unfreedom. Although our enquiry might run afoul of serious empirical uncertainties about the nature and sequelae of the action(s) that apparently made the specified contribution, the outcome of our enquiry should be unequivocal if such uncertainties are absent. However modest the role of the action(s) may have been, we should regard it as enough to warrant our affixing the classification of 'unfreedoms' to any resultant curbs on someone's liberty. A meagre causal role is dispositive, for the purpose of gauging the applicability of that classification.

Consider, then, the following scenario. An obelisk or a statue or some other structure S was erected long ago near a mountain. Suppose that a landslide occurs and sends a stone hurtling against S; the stone ricochets off S and smashes into Andrew, incapacitating his left arm. Had S not been present, neither that stone nor any other stone in the landslide would have hit and disabled Andrew. Undeflected, the stones would have soared past him without harming him. (Let us assume that, if S had not been present, no natural stone formation nor any other natural structure would have been standing in its place.) In these circumstances, then, the presence of S was necessary for the sufficiency of a set of actual conditions that was minimally sufficient for the incapacitation of Andrew's arm. Therefore, because the presence of S was a product of someone else's actions, the incapacitation amounts to an array of unfreedoms rather than to an array of mere inabilities. In analysing this situation, we should not attach any importance to the fact that the actions which led to the presence of S were performed in the distant past. Nor should we be distracted by the fact that the role of those actions in curtailing Andrew's liberty was dwarfed by the role of natural forces. Though the avalanche was a much more prominent cause of the impairment of Andrew's freedom than was the erection of S many decades or centuries earlier, the avalanche was not sufficient for that impairment in the absence of S. It was therefore not sufficient for that impairment in the absence of the actions that gave rise to S in the remote past. The first prong of the U Postulate has thus been satisfied, since Andrew would now be able to make use of his left arm if the contribution of some other person(s) to the incapacitation of that arm had not occurred. Consequently, the curtailment of his liberty consists in unfreedom.

Many other examples could likewise be adduced to underscore the basic claim of this subsection: my claim that the meagreness or remoteness of the contribution of someone's actions to the constriction of somebody else's liberty is never a ground for ignoring that contribution when we are ascertaining whether the constriction has created unfreedoms. In every relevant scenario, somebody's actions are but-for causes of curbs on someone else's liberty, yet those actions are enormously overshadowed by other but-for causes in the form of natural occurrences or the latter person's own conduct. Suppose, for instance, that a short man Benjamin and a much taller man Nathan encounter each other near some trees and bushes. Benjamin is wielding a gun, and he orders Nathan to grasp some berries that are dangling overhead far beyond the short man's reach. Because Benjamin is so diminutive and so lacking in physical dexterity, he is wholly unable to gain hold of the berries without Nathan's assistance. Nathan, however, expostulates with Benjamin by pointing out that the berries are poisonous; anyone consuming them will quickly suffer paralysis from the waist down-ward. Benjamin, perhaps not believing Nathan or perhaps simply not caring about the ghastly potency of the berries, adamantly insists that he wishes to eat the berries and that he therefore wants the taller man to pick them for him. Benjamin warns that he will begin shooting within ten seconds if Nathan does not comply with his behests. Very reluctantly, the taller man submits to Benjamin's demands. He picks the berries and hands them over to Benjamin, who promptly gulps them down. Not long afterward, the short man undergoes the paralysing effects of his foolhardy repast. Has he thereby become unfree to perform the actions and combinations of actions that he thitherto could perform with his legs, or has he become merely unable to do so?

If we were engaged in an adjudicative enterprise whereby we had to apportion blame for the debilitation of Benjamin, we would be amply justified in ascribing full blame to Benjamin himself and in exonerating Nathan. However, as has been emphasized, the task of distinguishing between unfreedoms and mere inabilities has nothing to do with the attribution of guilt or innocence. It is etiological rather than censorious. A theorist undertaking that task in this context must focus not on Nathan's blameworthiness but on the causal status of his act of picking the berries. That act was plainly an element in the set of actual conditions that was minimally sufficient for the onset of Benjamin's paralysis. Moreover, even if it pre-empted the causal role of a similar act that would have been undertaken coercedly by a subsequent passer-by, that pre-empted occurrence would likewise have been an action performed by some person other than Benjamin. (Without the aid of such an action by a tall human being, Benjamin in the circumstances would not have been able to obtain the berries.) Hence, the pre-empted occurrence would likewise have endowed Benjamin's new incapacities with the status of unfreedoms. In sum, because Nathan's action or a similar action by some other tall person was essential for the chain of events that led to Benjamin's paralysis, the U Postulate classifies that paralysis as a state of unfreedom. In the absence of any action like Nathan's, Benjamin would have remained able to do all the things that his paralysis prevents him from doing. To be sure, Nathan's causal responsibility was greatly overshadowed by the causal role of the poisonous berries and especially by the causal role of Benjamin's own gun-toting threats and his own eager consumption of the poisonous fruit. Nonetheless, the relative inconspicuousness of Nathan's causal contribution is utterly immaterial here. The fact that his contribution was modest in comparison with that of some other factors is irrelevant; the fact that it was indeed an essential contribution is determinative.

As we ponder these and other examples, we should attend carefully to the causal issue that we are addressing. For the purpose of applying the U Postulate, strictly speaking, we are not asking whether any action(s) by some person P caused an event that eliminated some of the particular freedoms of another person Q; rather, we are asking whether P's action(s) caused the non-existence of some of Q's particular freedoms. To be sure, those two questions may seem indistinguishable, and the answer to each is usually the same as the answer to the other. Nevertheless, because we are taking account of small and remote causal contributions when we separate unfreedoms from mere inabilities, the two questions just delineated are occasionally divergent. The potential for a divergence between those questions becomes manifest in the following scenario. Suppose that Sarah has been flying her aeroplane and that she lands the vehicle in a natural meadow in order to go for a stroll through the surrounding countryside. While she is walking along, the aeroplane is destroyed by a small meteoroid that has survived its passage through the earth's atmosphere before plummeting into her craft. Sarah in the middle of an uninhabited region is now unable to reach the destination that she had been intending to visit, and she is also unable to do numerous other things that were possible for her with the use of her aircraft. She is not free to reach that destination, and she is not free to do those numerous other things. Has she been made unfree? On the one hand, the manufacture of her aeroplane by other people was plainly a but-for cause of the destruction of the plane by the meteoroid's impact. Had the manufacturing process not been carried out by those people—and had no comparable process been carried out by alternative people—Sarah would not have possessed an aeroplane, and thus there would not have been any such machine in the meadow for the meteoroid to demolish. The production of the plane by other people was thus an element in the set of actual conditions minimally sufficient for the devastation of the plane. Much the same can be said about the actions of other people that provided the fuel for Sarah's flying. Without those actions and without any similar actions by alternative people, the aeroplane would not have been operative and would thus not have been flown by Sarah to the place of its demolition. On the other hand, we should not rush to the conclusion that the destruction of that vehicle has rendered Sarah unfree in any respect. After all, although the actions of other people in manufacturing the vehicle were essential for its destruction (since it could not have been destroyed if it had never existed), they were not essential for the absence of Sarah's freedom to undertake a journey with an operative aeroplane. Had the actions of producing her plane and other planes never taken place, neither Sarah nor anyone else would have possessed such a vehicle, and thus she would not have been free to undertake a journey therewith. Likewise, if the actions of other people in producing fuel for aviation had not occurred, and if no similar actions by alternative people had occurred, Sarah would not have been free to fly her plane anywhere. In other words, whereas the processes of producing the vehicle and the fuel were but-for causes of the event by which Sarah *lost* her freedom to fly to her destination, they were not but-for causes of the fact that she *lacks* such a freedom. In the absence of those processes and any parallel processes of production, it would still be the case that Sarah lacks the specified freedom. Consequently, we have to conclude that Sarah is merely not-free-to-fly-to-her-destination and that she is not unfree-to-fly-there. Under the but-for test—which is the germane test for causation within the sway of the U Postulate's first prong—her inability has not resulted from any actions by other people, even though the loss of her ability did indeed partly result therefrom.

Note that the point made in the preceding paragraph can be suitably generalized as follows. If any action by some person is a but-for cause of the fact that some other person P is able to φ, that action will never in itself be a cause of the absence or limitedness of P's ability-to-φ. So generalized, the preceding paragraph's point is crucial for the tenableness of the distinction between unfreedoms and self-inflicted inabilities. After all, among the actual conditions minimally sufficient for the loss of any person's ability-to-φ is the fact that the person was brought into the world by the actions of other people. Had somebody not been born as a result of his parents' procreative acts or as a result of techniques of artificial conception, his subsequent loss of any ability would not have taken place. There would have been nothing for him to lose if he had never come into existence. Thus, unless we are alert to the potential divide between causing the elimination of an ability and causing the absence of an ability, we shall be tempted to conclude that every self-inflicted inability is partly due to the actions of other people and is consequently an unfreedom. If I jump off a cliff and thereby paralyse myself from the waist downward, my parents' acts of procreation were but-for causes of my loss of my ability-to-use-my-legs. Had my parents not begotten me, neither I nor my ability-to-use-my-legs would have existed; ergo, the loss of that ability could not have occurred. Yet, although my parents' acts of procreation played a but-for role in bringing about the *loss* of my ability, they have not played any such role in bringing about the *non-existence* of my ability. Had those acts never occurred, my ability would still have been non-existent. The proposition 'It is not the case that Matthew Henry Kramer can walk' would still have been true. Hence, the incapacity arising from my throwing myself off the cliff should not be classified as an instance of unfreedom. It should be classified as a mere inability which I have inflicted on myself. Much the same is true of other self-inflicted inabilities, which are categorizable as such despite the fact that the events leading up to them are causally attributable in part to acts of sexual intercourse by the parents of the people who have incurred the inabilities. Precisely because of the distinction highlighted in the pre-ceding paragraph—the distinction between other people's causing the extirpation of somebody's capacity and other people's causing the absence of somebody's capacity—the set of self-inflicted inabilities is not empty.

At any rate, the central thesis of this subsection is that even a tiny contribution by the actions of some person P to an inability of some other person Q is enough to warrant our designating that inability as an unfreedom. Of course, to say as much is to presuppose that the contribution was indeed a contribution. If P's actions made no differ-ence to the existence of Q's inability, then those actions played no causal role of the kind required by the U Postulate. Consider here a variant of the scenario involving Benjamin and Nathan and the berries. Suppose that Benjamin is able to reach the berries, but not as easily as the much taller man. When he orders Nathan to pick the berries for him, he is doing so out of laziness rather than because of a wholesale lack of any alternative means of obtaining the fruit. Were Nathan foolish enough to refuse to comply with the behest, Benjamin (after shooting Nathan) would straightaway gather the berries himself, with a bit of straining. Nathan is not foolish, however, and he reluctantly elects to follow Benjamin's orders. In these circumstances, then, his act of grasping the berries does not make a but-for contribution to the state of paralysis which Benjamin undergoes after eating the fruit that has been picked. Had Nathan not done what was demanded of him, Benjamin by his own efforts would still have obtained and con-sumed the berries and would therefore still have undergone their incapacitating effects. In sum, this variant of my earlier scenario depicts a situation of inter-categorial over-determination; Nathan's act of picking the berries is a pre-emptive cause, and Benjamin's act of picking them (which never occurs) is a pre-empted condition. In combination with the prevailing circumstances, including some of Benjamin's own subsequent actions, that pre-empted condition would have been sufficient to bring about his state of paralysis if the pre-emptive cause had not occurred. Accordingly, the first prong of the

U Postulate has not been satisfied. It is not the case that Benjamin would have retained the use of his legs if Nathan had declined to gather the berries. In other words, as has been remarked, Nathan's gathering of the berries did not contribute to Benjamin's paralysis in the fashion required under the U Postulate for the classifiability of the paralysis as a state of unfreedom.

Yet, whenever somebody's actions *have* made a contribution of the requisite sort (that is, a but-for contribution), the extent or salience of that contribution does not matter at all. Such is the view which we should take in regard to people's actions. As the rest of this section will argue, however, we should take an entirely different view in regard to omissions. Still, before we proceed to investigate the act/omission distinction, we should pause to note that some constraints on the freedom of countless individuals—constraints on the range of the combinations-of-conjunctively-exercisable-freedoms that are available to those individuals—are plainly owing to other people's actions and are therefore unproblematically recognizable as unfreedoms within my theory of negative liberty.

As was observed in Chapter 2, the actions that are sources of unfreedom need not be intentional in the sense of being aimed at producing their freedom-impairing effects. If someone's actions are such as to impose restrictions inadvertently on the liberty of somebody else, then those restrictions are straightforward unfreedoms despite the fact that they were not brought about deliberately. Similarly, if the 'impersonal' workings of social or political or economic institutions trammel people's liberty in various respects, the actions that diffusely constitute those workings are sources of unfreedom *pro tanto*. In particular, we should realize that many of the curbs on impecunious people's liberty are direct or indirect consequences of actions actually performed by other people or of actions that would be performed by those other people if certain circumstances arose. Ian Carter has made this point well: '[T]he money in one's possession partly determines whether or not others will physically prevent one from performing certain sets of actions. Thus, the tramp is physically prevented, not by his lack of money, but *because* of his lack of money, and *by other people*, from eating at the Ritz and then walking away unimpeded (assuming he is not thrown out first for bad dress).'[18] G. A. Cohen has offered an equally apt analysis from a Marxist perspective:

---

[18]   Carter, *Measure*, 235, emphases in original.

[I]f the structure of capitalism leaves the worker no [minimally acceptable] choice but to sell his labour power, then he is forced to do so by actions of persons. For the structure of capitalism is not in all senses self-sustaining. It is sustained by a great deal of intentional human action, notably on the part of the functionaries of the state. Since the state deliberately protects the property of the capitalist class, the structural constraint by virtue of which the worker must sell his labour power has enough human will behind it to satisfy the stipulation that where there is force, there are forcing human beings.[19]

Although my exposition of the act/omission distinction has not yet been unfolded, we should already recognize that the 'act' side of the demarcation comprises not only actual performances but also dispositions-to-perform-actions. As has been argued at length in Chapter 3, the readiness of a person P to act to prevent another person Q from exercising some combination of freedoms is as direct and important a trammel on Q's liberty as is any actual preventive action by P. If for example several policeman are prepared to prevent each person in their vicinity from vandalizing with impunity the premises that they are guarding, then each such person is unfree to engage in the following combination of activities: vandalism of the premises, and any activity ruled out by the punishment to be inflicted on everyone who commits such vandalism. Of course, if nobody attempts to commit any acts of vandalism, the dispositions of the policemen will remain unactivated.

---

[19] G. A. Cohen, *History, Labour, and Freedom* (Oxford: Clarendon Press, 1988), 258. For some important discussions of poverty and unfreedom, see Rodger Beehler, 'For One Concept of Liberty', 8 *Journal of Applied Philosophy* 27, 39–42 (1991); Stanley Benn and William Weinstein, 'Being Free to Act, and Being a Free Man', 80 *Mind* 194, 199–200 (1971); Carter, *Measure*, 234–6; G. A. Cohen, *Self-Ownership, Freedom, and Equality* (Cambridge: Cambridge University Press, 1995), 57–9; John Gray, 'On Negative and Positive Liberty', in *Liberalisms: Essays in Political Philosophy* (London: Routledge, 1989), 45, 61–2; David Miller, 'Constraints on Freedom', 94 *Ethics* 66, 80–6 (1983) [Miller, 'Constraints']. See also Stanley Benn, *A Theory of Freedom* (Cambridge: Cambridge University Press, 1988), 133–4; Marshall Cohen, 'Berlin and the Liberal Tradition', 10 *Philosophical Quarterly* 216, 224–6 (1960); William Connolly, *The Terms of Political Discourse*, 2nd edn (Princeton: Princeton University Press, 1983), 162–9; Keith Dixon, *Freedom and Equality* (London: Routledge & Kegan Paul, 1986), 27–9; Tim Gray, *Freedom* (London: Macmillan, 1991), 41–5; Will Kymlicka, *Contemporary Political Philosophy* (Oxford: Clarendon Press, 1990), 145–51; Andrew Levine, 'Foundations of Unfreedom', 88 *Ethics* 162 (1978); Ernest Loevinsohn, 'Liberty and the Redistribution of Property', 6 *Philosophy and Public Affairs* 226 (1976); Felix Oppenheim, *Political Concepts* (Chicago: University of Chicago Press, 1981), 158–9; Albert Weale, *Political Theory and Social Policy* (London: Macmillan, 1983), 52–4. Cf. D. A. Lloyd Thomas and Richard Norman, 'Liberty, Equality, Property: I & II', 55 (supp.) *Proceedings of the Aristotelian Society* 177 (1981).

Nevertheless, the dispositions themselves are actual, and their free-dom-curtailing effects are actual. The aforementioned combination of activities is not conjunctively performable by anyone within the sway of the policemen, and thus the overall liberty of everyone within their sway is diminished *pro tanto*.

Naturally, we shall sometimes not be in a position either to verify or to disprove the existence of an unactivated disposition. In such circumstances, we have to attach a probabilistic qualification to any ascription of unfreedom (or freedom) that is based on an affirmation of the disposition's existence (or inexistence). Still, the need for such a qualification also arises when we are not in a position either to verify or to disprove the occurrence of some action that is said to have caused an impairment of somebody's liberty. In such circumstances, we must attach a probabilistic caveat to any characterization of that impairment as a state of unfreedom, and we must likewise attach a caveat—an inverse caveat—to any characterization of the impairment as a mere inability. Epistemic limits do not uniquely bear on our knowledge of *dispositions*, by any means. Moreover, they certainly do not preclude us from confidently apprehending the existence of various unactivated dispositions in countless contexts.

Now, because dispositions-to-perform-actions are sources of unfreedom whenever they close off options or combinations of options for other people, the dispositions of officials and proprietors to keep impoverished people from gaining possession of sundry assets are sources of unfreedom for those indigent people. Of course, the unfreedom of poor people hardly derives exclusively from owners' and officials' *dispositions*. Multitudinous outright *actions* and products of actions, such as fences and walls, are likewise involved in blocking access to any number of resources and in thus giving rise to unfreedoms. Still, clearly among the pervasive sources of impoverished individuals' unfreedom are the dispositions of proprietors and officials to take action against those individuals if necessary in order to prevent them from stealing or defrauding with impunity. Those dispositions preclude each impoverished person from exercising certain freedoms conjunctively. (Of course, each wealthy person is likewise prevented from stealing or defrauding with impunity. However, unlike someone with scanty funds, a wealthy person can purchase access to manifold goods quite readily without having to resort to punishable misdeeds. Thus, although everyone undergoes the *pro-tanto* reductions in his or her overall freedom that have been described by this paragraph, those reductions will impinge more severely on the leeway of each needy person than on the leeway of each affluent person.)

Given that dispositions-to-perform-actions are located on the 'act' side of the act/omission divide, any causal contributions by them to the inabilities of indigent people are enough to invest those inabilities with the status of unfreedoms. No test or threshold of causal salience is pertinent. So long as some person's disposition-to-perform-an-action is a but-for cause of some inability of another person, the inability is an unfreedom irrespective of the disposition's prominence as a cause. Let us ponder an example that will highlight this point. Suppose that Joshua owns a farm that is devastated and rendered worthless by a medley of lightning bolts and cataclysmic floods in quick succession. Formerly wealthy, Joshua is now virtually penniless. He is barely able to satisfy his basic needs and is wholly unable to achieve a standard of living beyond the minimal satisfaction of those needs. Should we designate his inabilities as unfreedoms or as mere inabilities? Clearly, the most conspicuous causes of his plight were the destructive natural phenomena of lightning bolts and floods. Nonetheless, although those phenomena brought about Joshua's state of penury without the intervention of other people, the continuation of his destitution is by no means causally attributable solely to those natural forces (or solely to other natural forces). The people in the surrounding community, not least the officials entrusted with the duties of policing, are disposed to prevent Joshua from committing theft or fraud with impunity. Because those people are inclined to take preventive or punitive measures if Joshua attempts to gain possession of anybody's goods non-consensually, numerous options and combinations of options are closed off to him. His poverty thus consists in an array of unfreedoms, even though it originated exclusively from the workings of natural forces.

If we mildly embellish the narrative of Joshua's plight, the causal role of natural forces and of his own folly will even more markedly overshadow the causal role of other people's dispositions and actions. Suppose that Joshua is repeatedly admonished by the other residents in his community against locating his farm on a piece of land that is notoriously susceptible to lightning bolts and floods. They protractedly and vigorously remonstrate with him, and they warn him that they will not offer him any assistance in coping with disasters that might befall him if he recklessly disregards their advice. Despite all these exhortations, Joshua blithely proceeds to situate his farm on the ill-starred parcel of land. Thus, when he falls prey to the natural catastrophes that occur shortly after he has moved in, the slightly hard-hearted reaction of the people in his community is in keeping with their view that his troubles have been caused by his own obstinacy and of course also by the natural occurrences which he brazenly hazarded. Not only do they feel no moral responsibility for his plight, but they also feel that none of their actions has carried any causal responsibility for it whatsoever. Now, they are quite correct in believing that their actions have not been causally responsible for the *advent* of his woes, but they are wrong in so far as they believe that their actions or dispositions are not causally responsible for the *continuation* of his poverty. Although the most conspicuous causes of his current travails are his own heedlessness and the natural phenomena that initiated his state of indigence, the actions and the dispositions-to-perform-actions of the people in his community—most notably, their being disposed to prevent him from acquiring any of their assets non-consensually with impunity—are likewise some but-for causes of the persistence of his travails. As such, those dispositions and actions are enough under the U Postulate to get his state of penury classified as an array of unfreedoms. The fact that those but-for causes are over-shadowed by other but-for causes is immaterial.

Note that my characterization of Joshua's destitution as a situation of unfreedom is independent of any particular ethical or political theory that might assign moral responsibility for the plight of the poor. When we seek to apportion blame for the neediness of Joshua, we can quite plausibly affirm that the primary moral responsibility for his continuing hardships (and, of course, for the onset of his hardships) is assignable to him. Nevertheless, even when a victim of poverty is so unsympathetic by the lights of most moral theories, his impoverished state is correctly classifiable as a state of unfreedom—precisely because such a classification hinges on causal matters rather than on moral matters. Equally, the appositeness of that classification is independent of any particular economic theory about the principal determinants of poverty. A theory of that sort might single out certain factors as especially salient causes or as readily controllable and alterable causes. All such considerations are irrelevant to the U Postulate's demarcation between unfreedoms and mere inabilities. For the purpose of operationalizing that demarcation with reference to some inability of a person, we simply have to ask whether any actions or dispositions-to-perform-actions of any other person(s) are but-for causes of that inability. If the answer to that question is affirmative, then we can designate the inability as an unfreedom without enquiring further into the relative prominence or manipulability of the dispositions/actions that have contributed thereto. This point applies to inabilities associated with material want, plainly, as much as to inabilities of other types.

4.2. Separating Acts from Omissions

To set the stage for my next subsection, which will argue that omissions are never in themselves sources of unfreedom, this subsection expounds the basic division between acts and omissions. Let it be said at the outset that the terms 'act' and 'omission' are not entirely felicitous. Some philosophers turn instead to the phrases 'positive agency' and 'negative agency', and those phrases have much to commend them. The term 'omission' is particularly liable to mislead, since it tends to suggest an intentional refusal to act or a failure to act in the presence of a clear opportunity. Although the category of omissions as expounded below does encompass any deliberate refusals and any failures to take advantage of palpable opportunities, it extends further. It includes also any portion of the conduct of a person in which he or she does not perform any action of some specified type that is within his or her powers. Nevertheless, while the term 'omission' is certainly not ideal in all respects, every alternative term or phrase would likewise partake of shortcomings. Moreover, the contrasting labels 'acts' and 'omissions' are familiar not only in philosophy and law but also in ordinary discourse. Though the applications of those labels in this chapter will obviously be more precise and consistent than the applications thereof in the unreflective discourses of everyday life, the meanings which I attach to those terms are plainly similar in many ways to their ordinary meanings. Thus, so long as it is clear that 'act' and 'omission' as used by this chapter are elements of a technical parlance, their widespread familiarity is more of an advantage than a disadvantage; those terms are helpful preliminary signals, albeit imperfect signals, of the tenor of my distinction between their referents.

This subsection draws heavily on the work of Jonathan Bennett,[20]

[20] See Jonathan Bennett, 'Whatever the Consequences', 26 *Analysis* 83, 94–7 (1966); Bennett, 'Morality', *passim*; Bennett, *Events*, 218–21; Jonathan Bennett, 'Negation and Abstention: Two Theories of Allowing', in Bonnie Steinbock and Alastair Norcross (eds), *Killing and Letting Die*, 2nd edn (New York: Fordham University Press, 1994) [Bennett, 'Negation'], 230; Bennett, *Act*, Chs 4–8. One of the very few writers who have heretofore recognized even *en passant* the potential importance of Bennett's positive/negative distinction for theories of freedom is David Miller. See Miller, 'Constraints', at 73; David Miller, 'Reply to Oppenheim', 95 *Ethics* 310, 311–12 (1985) [Miller, 'Reply']; David Miller, *Market, State, and Community* (Oxford: Clarendon Press, 1990) [Miller, *Market*], 33–5. Miller, however, does not incorporate Bennett's distinction into his own theory of freedom.

The act/omission divide has figured quite prominently in contemporary whose exploration of the act/omission dichotomy is unsurpassed in contemporary philosophy for rigour and subtlety. My account of that dichotomy will not seek to reproduce all the layers and involutions of Bennett's arguments and his responses to critics, but his fundamental line of thought will serve admirably as a starting point for the special treatment of omissions in this chapter. (Bennett generally prefers the 'positive'/'negative' terminology because his discussion of this matter concentrates largely on propositions concerning human conduct rather than on human conduct itself. His focus and terminology are apposite for his purposes, but I have departed from them here.) Modifying some ideas put forward by Kant and A. J. Ayer, Bennett maintains that the key to the act/omission distinction is the relative numerousness of the ways in which a person P can behave in order to achieve some result E. If E is to be attained by some sort of action on the part of P, then the number of different ways in which P can behave while bringing about E is small—much smaller than if E is to be attained by an omission on the part of P. Now, if we wish to invoke such a criterion for staking off acts from omissions, we manifestly must rely on some metric for quantifying the ways in which P can behave. Unless we can fix on a standard that will in principle enable us to count the different modes of conduct in which P can engage, we shall not be able to make the comparisons required for distinguishing between acts and omissions. That is, we shall not be able to determine whether the number of ways in which P can behave while bringing about E is small or large as a proportion of the total number of ways in which P can behave. Bennett endeavours to supply the requisite metric—with elaborate arguments that will not be recounted here—by focusing on the sundry movements and the sundry stationary postures that can be adopted by a human body. For the application of such a metric, we must opt for a certain level of concreteness or abstraction in our specifications of the movements and positions that can be predicated of a person's body. Whatever the level for which we opt, its workability depends on our stopping well short of infinite concreteness and infinite divisibility; that is, the smallest spatio-temporal units in our specifications will not be infinitesimal. Now, if at a given level of

philosophical debates over the moral significance of two dichotomies: the distinction between doing and allowing, and the distinction between intended effects and foreseen effects. For a powerful recent contribution to the latter debate, with many pertinent citations to the literature, see Alison McIntyre, 'Doing Away with Double Effect', 111 *Ethics* 219 (2001). Most participants in the aforementioned debates, however, take the nature of the act/omission divide (as opposed to its moral significance) for granted.

concreteness we consider all the possible movements and stationary positions among which some person P can select at a particular juncture, and if we consider further whether each of those movements and positions would lead to a certain result E on which P's conduct has a bearing, we shall be able to distinguish pertinently between acts and omissions. If the movements and positions that would each lead to E are a very small proportion of the total array of movements and positions among which P can select at the specified juncture, then the bringing about of E by P is an act. If on the contrary the movements and positions that would each lead to E are a very large proportion of the total array of movements and positions among which P can select, then E occurs—if it does occur—by dint of P's omitting to do what is necessary to prevent it. In short, given that E occurs and that P's conduct has had some bearing on its occurrence, P's contribution to E was an action if nearly all of the movements and positions available to P would not have led to E; and P's contribution to E was an omission if nearly all of the movements and positions available to P would have led to E. (Of course, P's conduct will not have any bearing on the occurrence of myriad events and states of affairs. No act that could ever be performed by P would affect the continuation of the revolution of the planet Pluto around the sun, for example. If no act within P's power could ever help to promote or prevent the occurrence of E, then every element of his conduct is neither an act nor an omission in relation to E.)

One of the great advantages of Bennett's account of the act/omission divide is that it fully acknowledges a point which has sometimes been thought to cast doubt on that divide. That is, on the basis of Bennett's approach, we can easily recognize that virtually every mode of conduct classifiable as an omission is also an action. When P omits to do whatever is necessary to prevent E, he *pari passu* does something else that relates as an action to some other result. Indeed, save perhaps when P has been rendered unconscious, he will always be acting as well as omitting to act in various ways. What Bennett's exposition highlights is that the status of a mode of conduct as an omission or an action is not an intrinsic property. Rather, that status resides in a relation among the specified mode of conduct, other available modes of conduct, and some result(s) to which each course of conduct would or would not contribute. Because the aforementioned status is a complex relational property of this sort, and because every stretch of conduct stands in any number of the relevant relations, every stretch of conduct is an act in respect of some outcomes and an omission in respect of numerous others. As Bennett writes: '[T]here could not possibly be conduct which was, in itself, negative: it is an error to try to divide items of conduct into those that are and those that are not negative acts or refrainings or forbearances or omissions, as though we had "…is negative" or "…is a refraining" as a monadic predicate of acts.'[21] Far from being called into question by the fact that every omission-to-avert in relation to E_1 is likewise an act-to-promote in relation to E_2, my exposition of the act/omission distinction is reinforced by that very fact.

Another virtue of Bennett's explication of the act/omission dichotomy is its strict moral neutrality. When we classify some element of P's conduct as an action because it is one of the few modes of behaviour available to P that will lead to E rather than to not-E, or when we classify some element of P's conduct as an omission because it is one among a vast array of modes of behaviour available to P that will lead to E rather than to not-E, we are not thereby making any claim about the moral status of P's conduct or the moral status of E. In this respect, Bennett's division between acts and omissions is in keeping with the broader tenor and ambitions of this chapter. Although the ultimate justification for this book's specific way of distinguishing between unfreedoms and mere inabilities is partly moral-political—in an extremely abstract and expansive sense—the implementation of that distinction through the elaboration and application of appropriate causal criteria is an enterprise that does not depend on any further moral judgements. So this chapter has observed more than once. Thus, since the contrast between acts and omissions is of considerable importance in shaping the causal criteria developed herein, the moral neutrality of that contrast as analysed by Bennett is a major desideratum. After all, one of the principal objectives of this chapter is to avoid any conflation of causal responsibility and moral responsibility. Only by sedulously separating the one from the other can this book present a theory of freedom that will be valuable across the widest possible spectrum of political viewpoints. Bennett's analysis is to be welcomed for furthering that objective.

Let us now ponder the most frequently raised objection to Bennett's approach. Recall that, while bodily movements are key physical components of manifold types of conduct that are open to most people in various contexts, positions of stationariness are key physical components of other such types of conduct. In most circumstances and in relation to most consequences, a stretch of conduct that qualifies

---

[21] Bennett, *Act*, 86.

under Bennett's test as an action will involve some bodily move-
ment(s). Nevertheless, there will from time to time clearly be circumstances in which something that qualifies under his test as an action
does not involve any such movement(s) and instead consists in stark
stationariness.[22] Let us contemplate two scenarios, the first of which
has been propounded by Bennett himself and by several of his critics.
Suppose that, if Herman remains completely motionless in the sealed
room where he is standing, a fine metallic dust in the air will settle upon
the floor. Some of the dust will fall onto a tiny electronic device and
will close a circuit, triggering an explosion that will release some
hostages from a room where they have been detained. By contrast, if
Herman moves his body in any perceptible way, he will prevent the
fine dust from settling and will thereby avert an explosion. In these
circumstances, then, his remaining immobile is the only mode of
behaviour or just about the only mode of behaviour by which he can
set off an explosion near the other room. His remaining immobile will
thus qualify as an action by which he can achieve that result. Contrariwise, if he engages in any of the countless perceptible movements of his
body that are within his power, he will avert the explosion. Since those
movements are huge in number, any one of them will be classifiable as
his omission to do what is necessary for the occurrence of an explosion.
In sum, this scenario confronts us with a situation in which a posture of
utter stationariness is an action and in which any movement of Herman's body is an omission. According to some critics of Bennett, we
should be troubled by such an upshot.

In the scenario just broached—which I shall shortly endeavour to
defuse—we are not told whether Herman knows that an explosion will

---

[22] See Bennett, 'Morality', 66–9; Bennett, 'Negation', 239–41; Bennett, *Act*,
96–100, 112–14. For some of the critics of Bennett who have raised this point, see
Daniel Dinello, 'On Killing and Letting Die', in Bonnie Steinbock and Alastair
Norcross (eds), *Killing and Letting Die* (New York: Fordham University Press,
1994) [Dinello, 'Killing'], 192; Don Locke, 'The Choice Between Lives', 57
Philosophy 453, 463 (1982) [Locke, Choice']; Warren Quinn, 'Actions, Intentions,
and Consequences: The Doctrine of Doing and Allowing', in *Morality and Action*
(Cambridge: Cambridge University Press, 1993), 149, 157–8; Bernard Williams,
'Acts and Omissions, Doing and Not Doing', in Rosalind Hursthouse, Gavin
Lawrence, and Warren Quinn (eds), *Virtues and Reasons* (Oxford: Clarendon
Press, 1995) [Williams, 'Acts'], 331, 335. Though Judith Lichtenberg does not
criticize Bennett at all, she presupposes the equivalence of the act/omission and
movement/stationariness distinctions in her 'The Moral Equivalence of Action
and Omission', in Bonnie Steinbock and Alastair Norcross (eds), *Killing and
Letting Die* (New York: Fordham University Press, 1994) [Lichtenberg, 'Equivalence'], 210, 212–13.

ensue if he keeps his body still, and we are likewise not told whether he views such a result as desirable (or whether he would view such a result as desirable if he knew of it). To be sure, neither of those aspects of the situation is strictly relevant to the classifiability of his stationariness as an action and the classifiability of any movement of his as an omission. Nonetheless, the scepticism of Bennett's opponents might seem to be especially warranted if Herman does not know the implications of his conduct. The complaints by those opponents might appear even stronger in respect of a second scenario (of my own invention), where the agency of the person involved is highly attenuated. Suppose that Margaret is walking along when an earthquake erupts around her. While remaining fully conscious, she freezes out of fear. As she stands transfixed, all the ground around her crumbles violently; nothing but the spot on which she stands is spared from the destruction. Had she not frozen into immobility, then, she would have been killed or at least badly injured. Only because she abruptly desisted from walking is she on the lone piece of accessible land where she can be safe. Thus, in relation to the objective of staying alive in the unusual circumstances, her motionlessness must plainly be classified as an action—whereas any continuation of her ambling would have been properly classifiable as an omission. Anyone endorsing Bennett's approach to the act/ omission distinction must accept this conclusion, notwithstanding that Margaret has remained fully stationary out of sheer fear rather than as a result of any decision on her part.

How can Bennett's approach be defended against the objection which these narratives highlight? A small point to be noted initially is something mentioned at the outset of my consideration of that objection. That is, because actions as defined by Bennett will in relation to most outcomes in most circumstances involve bodily movements, we are bound to regard as somewhat odd the quite infrequent contexts in which actions as defined by him instead consist in motionlessness. Unaccustomedness should not be mistaken for incorrectness. Much more important, the whole objection which we are exploring is based on the very error which Bennett's analysis is designed to correct. In posing that objection, his critics wrongly presume that the property of being an action or being an omission is intrinsic—like the property of being immobile—rather than relational. As Bennett declares, the thesis underlying their complaints 'is quite worthless because it relies on the notion of negativeness *de re*, negativeness as a monadic property of concrete actions and events'.[23] In fact, as most of those

---

[23] Bennett, 'Morality', 67.

critics themselves elsewhere emphasize, hardly any omissions (as understood by Bennett or as understood in everyday discourse and legal discourse) are instances of motionlessness.[24] When a person omits to do something that is necessary to avert some result, he or she is typically engaging in bodily movements to do something else; very seldom is he or she remaining immobile like a mummy. However, once we discern that stationariness is not the essential characteristic of omissions that distinguishes them from actions, we need to specify some other characteristic that does so distinguish them. We can scarcely content ourselves with saying that an omission consists in not doing something that would have prevented a certain outcome. After all, any actions which are essential for that outcome will likewise consist in not doing anything that would have prevented it—that is, in not doing anything that would have been inconsistent with the performance of those essential actions. We therefore have to look for a more complex relation that can form a line of demarcation between omissions and actions. Bennett's specification of a multi-faceted relationship—the relationship between (1) any course of conduct for some person P that has some bearing on an upshot E, and (2) all the other courses of conduct which are possible for P and which will each promote or not promote E—is a singularly powerful and pertinent solution to this crux.

When the opponents of Bennett's approach purport to disprove his line of thought by pointing out that some instances of behaviour classified under his analysis as omissions will consist in bodily movements and that some instances of behaviour classified under his analysis as actions will consist in strict motionlessness, they are guilty of begging the question or of fallacious reasoning. Perhaps, as Bennett himself suggests, those opponents in their efforts to refute his approach are slipping back into thinking that the essential feature of every omission is the intrinsic property of stationariness. If so, they thereby beg the question against him by upbraiding him for departing from a non-relational conception of omissions (and actions) which his theory robustly rejects. In so doing, moreover, they fail woefully to shed any light on the problem that has motivated the development of his theory: namely, the problem residing in the fact that most omissions do not consist in stationariness, which therefore cannot correctly be singled out as the property that distinguishes omissions from actions. Alternatively, the writers who assail Bennett are perhaps simply assuming that a position of immobility cannot be sufficiently 'active' to count as an

[24] This is a central theme, for example, in Williams, 'Acts'.

action. Such an assumption is once again a begging of the question, since it is nothing more than a variant of the thesis that the status of an instance of conduct as an action or omission is a corollary of some intrinsic property. As a riposte to Bennett, a claim that all actions must involve bodily movements is no more effective than a claim that all omissions must involve the absence of bodily movements. In each case, the particular claim rests on the tenet that the defining property of every act as an act or of every omission as an omission is non-relational. Such a claim thus begs the question against Bennett, instead of engaging with his arguments. Under his analysis, the retention of a posture of stationariness by some person P can perfectly well count as an action, since it can be just about the only mode of conduct available to P that would lead to some specified result. Furthermore, as should be apparent from my remarks on actions and bodily movements in the first main section of Chapter 3, the notion that all actions must involve bodily movements is at odds even with a quotidian conception of actions. On this point, as on most other points, one's endorsement of Bennett's rigorous analysis is likewise an endorsement of common sense.

Let us now return to the scenarios with which I began this discussion of the objection concerning immobility. In particular, we should mull over the importance or unimportance of the outlook of the agent in each scenario. With regard to the first narrative, will the status of Herman's motionlessness as an action be affected at all by his knowledge or ignorance of the implications of his conduct? On the one hand, to be sure, that status is especially clear if Herman as he remains stationary is aware that he must do so in order to bring about an explosion. Given such knowledge, his retention of an immobile posture—which might very well require great doggedness—is directly oriented toward the end which it promotes, the occurrence of an explosion. When the narrative is embellished along these lines, the resistance of sceptics to classifying Herman's stationariness as an action should be minimal. Likewise, their resistance to classifying any perceptible movement by Herman as an omission should be minimal. If he does move, he will have omitted to do what he knows to be necessary for the attainment of an important objective. In that respect, his situation is similar to that of a studio model who is instructed by an artist to remain entirely still while he paints a full-length portrait of her. If the model scratches her nose or shifts her legs, the irascible artist could quite intelligibly chastise her: 'You have failed to do what I told you to do. I instructed you to keep still. How can I work properly if you decline to play your part in the production of this painting?!' Though such a rebuke can certainly be faulted for its petulance, it should not strike anyone as a misapplication of the concept of omissions.

On the other hand, despite what has just been said, we should not hesitate to affirm that the retention of a motionless posture by Herman is an action even if he is ignorant of the full implications of his conduct. Perhaps he remains stationary simply because he is musing on some deep intellectual problem or is recalling some fond memories. Even so, he is behaving in just about the only way available to him that is promotive of the occurrence of an explosion. In relation to that outcome, his stillness is an act, and any movement by him would be an omission to do what is requisite. His ignorance of the full significance of his remaining immobile does not disqualify the immobility as an action, any more than a comparable ignorance on the part of someone who performs various bodily movements. If Hannah presses against a wall and thereby engages in just about the only bodily movement that will lead to the disclosure of a secret passage within a house, her ignorance of the implications of her act of pressing is fully consistent with the status of that act as such. Many actions are characterized by inadvertence, in that their chief effects have not been envisaged and perhaps not desired by the people who perform the actions. In that respect, Herman's inadvertent triggering of an explosion (by remaining motionless) is no different from Hannah's inadvertent uncovering of the secret passage (by pressing against a certain part of the wall). If the latter bit of conduct should be classified as an action notwithstanding the unexpectedness of the consequences that flow from it—as it patently should—then the same is true of the former bit of conduct.

My scenario involving Margaret and the earthquake is slightly more perplexing, though not in any way that places in doubt the classifiability of some instances of stationariness as actions. To designate Margaret's terrified retention of an immobile posture as an action is problematic not because of the unmovingness of her stance but because of the attenuation of her agency. It is quite doubtful whether we can correctly describe her frozen position as an element of her conduct at all; it is more plausible to describe that position as something that happens to her than as something that she does. However, these difficulties are not at all distinctively connected with the fact that her action consists in motionlessness. Parallel difficulties can surround various actions that consist in bodily movements. For example, my second chapter has mentioned the scene in *Schindler's List* where a bulky German soldier bellows truculently at his Jewish victims when he orders them to march in a certain direction. Their first several steps after his screaming at them are impelled as much by instinctive reflexes as by any conscious choices. Whether those steps should be classified as actions at all is therefore quite problematic. The dubiousness of the classification stems of course not from the fact that the steps are bodily movements but from the fact that they are barely volitional. Much the same is true of Margaret's petrified immobility, which saves her life. If her failure to move is only problematically classifiable as an act, the difficulty stems not from the nature of that failure as an instance of stationariness but from its nature as a largely non-volitional reflex. In other words, the difficulty does not pertain to classifying her transfixed stillness as an act rather than as an omission; instead, the difficulty pertains to classifying that stillness as a portion of her conduct at all.

Let us close this subsection with a brief look at a few other misgivings that have been expressed by various writers about the act/omission distinction generally or about Bennett's construal of that distinction. Each of these queries is focused on a situation of over-determination or of multiple causes in protracted sequences. The first of these queries, contained in an attack on Bennett, has been raised by Don Locke among others: '[I]f Y swallows poison and X, instead of giving him an emetic or antidote, shoots him through the heart, we would surely say that X killed Y, though on Bennett's account he has merely let him die, inasmuch as almost any course of action would have resulted in Y's death.'[25] As should be clear from some of my earlier discussions, the scenario recounted by Locke depicts a situation of pre-emptive causation. The shot through the heart was a pre-emptive cause of Y's death, whereas the swallowing of the poison was a pre-empted condition that would in the circumstances have been sufficient to bring about his death if the shot through the heart had not occurred. Given that the shot did occur, the poison made no causal contribution to Y's death. If any set of actual conditions minimally sufficient for Y's death had included the swallowing of the poisonous liquid, it would also have had to include Y's survival up to the point when the lethal powers of the liquid could take effect. Since Y did not in fact survive that long, the swallowing of the poison was not a cause of his death. It was not a member of any set of actual conditions minimally sufficient for the fatality that in fact came about. Just as a fire cannot be causally responsible for the incineration of a house that has burned down before the fire reaches it, so too the ingestion of the poison could not be causally

---

[25] Locke, 'Choice', 463. For the slightly more elaborate original version of the example, which exhibits some regrettable inconsistency in the names attached to the parties, see Dinello, 'Killing', 193–4.

responsible for the demise of someone whose life had ended before the poison could wend its way through his body.

Hence, X conducted himself in just about the only available manner that would arrest the fatal workings of the poisonous substance by halting the life of Y before those workings could reach their culmination. In other words, Locke's retort to Bennett is doubly incorrect. Bennett's analysis does not generate the conclusion that X let Y die, and it does generate the conclusion that X acted in such a way as to kill Y. X did not let Y die, because in the circumstances the myriad possible routes for his allowing the death would each have involved his allowing the poison to continue its operations unchecked. Far from omitting to do what was necessary to terminate those operations, X pursued one of the few courses of action available to him that would indeed bring the effectiveness of those operations to an end. Similarly, he pursued one of the few available paths of conduct that would amount to his killing Y rather than to his merely letting Y die. By opting for that path of conduct, X brought it about that the only set of actual conditions minimally sufficient for Y's death was a set that included the shooting of the gun but not the swallowing of the poison. Because the shooting causally contributed to the death, and because that contribution did not consist in letting Y die—since it in fact excluded all the countless ways in which X could have let Y die from the workings of the poison—it had to amount to a killing.

Maybe someone will try to shore up Locke's criticism of Bennett by depicting a situation of duplicative causation rather than of preemptive causation. Suppose that, instead of shooting Y before the lethal effects of the poison have taken hold, X sends a bullet through his heart just as the poison's effects reach their culmination. We now confront a situation akin to that in which two fires arrive at exactly the same time rather than in succession. Here, according to the NESS test for causation, the poison in conjunction with the prevailing circumstances has indeed caused Y's death. Is a supporter of Bennett's analysis therefore logically committed to the view that X in this modified scenario has merely let Y die? Because of the adverb 'merely' in the foregoing question, the answer is negative. Although X has indeed let Y die, he has also killed Y. The status or character of his pattern of conduct is twofold. On the one hand, because X did not cut short the operations of the poisonous liquid before they reached the point of producing their fatal outcome, he acted in one of the numerous ways that would consist in his letting Y die. On the other hand, X likewise conducted himself in one of the few ways that would amount to his killing Y. His act of shooting Y through the heart was a key element in a set of actual conditions minimally sufficient for the occurrence of Y's death—a minimally sufficient set that did not encompass the ingestion of the poison. Thus, although X omitted to do what was necessary to prevent the deadly effect of the poisonous substance, he acted to do what was necessary to bring about Y's death independently of that substance. Whereas the former aspect of his conduct could materialize through manifold routes, the latter aspect could materialize only through a highly limited number of routes. Hence, once again Bennett's analysis yields the correct conclusions about the nature or status of X's conduct. If there is something odd about those conclusions in this context, it lies in the general oddness of duplicative causation; it does not lie in anything peculiar to the treatment of duplicative causation which my focus on the act/omission distinction inspires.

In any event, as should be clear from this chapter's earlier section on over-determination, problems such as those raised by Locke's original scenario or by my duplicative-causation version of his scenario do not really have to be addressed within the confines of this book. To see as much, let us presume that the poisonous substance and the gunshot would each be incapacitating rather than lethal. In Locke's original scenario suitably modified, then, X's gunshot disables precisely the same part of Y's body that would have been disabled by the poison if some more time had elapsed. In the duplicative-causation variant of that scenario, X's gunshot disables some part of Y's body at the very moment when that same part of his body is disabled by the ingested poison. Now, an investigation of the status of X's shooting as an act or an omission is almost certainly superfluous within this book—regardless of whether we are analysing a situation of pre-emptive causation or of duplicative causation. Although Y's swallowing of the poison was his own conduct, the poison itself or some component thereof was almost certainly the product of other people's actions. Without those actions and without similar actions by alternative people, no poison would have been available. Hence, given that the classification of a person's inability as an unfreedom hinges only on the existence and not on the salience of the causal contribution made by anyone else's actions, the role of other people's actions in producing the poisonous liquid would be sufficient for the status of Y's incapacitation as an array of unfreedoms.

When we look at some other expressed misgivings about the act/omission distinction, we shall find that—even in the absence of over-determination—enquiries into the 'act'/'omission' status of various elements of people's conduct are often dispensable in contexts where the causes involving such conduct are multiple. David Miller, while readily and commendably acknowledging the importance of Bennett's work, has advanced some doubts about the general sustainability of the act/omission distinction. He conjures up a scenario in which a large tree on Jones's plot of land is towering over a contiguous highway. Miller believes that each of the following two versions of the scenario is especially resistant to any straightforward categorization: 'In the first, the tree will blow down if (and only if) Jones tills the soil around it, weakening the roots. In the second, the tree will blow down if (and only if) Jones does not till the soil (doing which would allow moisture to penetrate). In each of these cases, would the tree's falling and the blocking of the highway result from an act or an omission?' Miller avows that Bennett's act/omission criterion could '[i]n theory' handle each of these two situations, but he provides no suggestions on how the criterion would or should be applied.[26] In fact, the resolution of each case is perfectly clear-cut. In the first situation, any conduct by Jones that leads to the toppling of the tree is an act as opposed to an omission, since quite a specific type of conduct is required—far more specific than what is required for the avoidance of the toppling. In the second situation, any conduct by Jones that leads to the toppling of the tree is an omission, since the type of conduct required is anything within a vast range that excludes only acts of extensive tilling.

In sum, Miller's scenarios pose no difficulties at all for the application of Bennett's act/omission schema. Furthermore, even if they were less tidily resolvable under that schema, they would not be troubling. After all, for the purposes of this book, we very likely do not have to ponder the 'act'/'omission' status of Jones's conduct in the period when the tree might topple. A tree growing on a parcel of land adjacent to a road has very likely been planted by some human being(s) in the past, whether by Jones or by some predecessor. If so, then the curtailment of the freedom of motorists by the toppling of the tree onto the highway is an increase in the unfreedom of each motorist affected. Each motorist is unfree, rather than merely not free, to drive past the point at which the tree is blocking the road. The planting of the tree, which was a human action, was a but-for cause of the tree's subsequent tumble onto the highway, even if those two events were separated by many decades. Since the causal contribution of anybody's action to some other person's inability does not have to surpass a threshold of salience or proximity in order to warrant our classifying the inability as an unfreedom, the curtailment of each motorist's liberty by the tum-

---

[26] Miller, 'Reply', 311, 312; Miller, *Market*, 33, 34.

bling down of the tree is a situation of unfreedom irrespective of whether any actions beyond the planting were involved. We therefore do not have to worry about categorizing Jones's behaviour in the period leading up to the fall of the tree. Regardless of the correct categorization of that behaviour, the tree's demise has imposed unfreedoms on motorists.

Miller challenges the view that a very distant or inconspicuous causal contribution by a human action is sufficient to warrant the designation of any resultant inability as an unfreedom.[27] He constructs a narrative in which a picnicker on a rocky hill casually tosses aside an apple. A seed from the apple takes root and develops into a tree over the course of several years. At some point, the tree precipitates a rockfall that traps an unfortunate person in a cave below. Miller stipulates that 'the fall wouldn't have occurred unless the apple had landed more or less where it did'. In these extraordinary circumstances, then, the trapping of the person in the cave is an event that not only greatly curtails her liberty but also greatly increases her unfreedom. Though the causal contribution by a human action was made long before the occurrence of the rockslide, it sufficed to endow the trapped person's new inabilities with the status of unfreedoms. Such, at least, is the conclusion for which this chapter has plumped in declining to lay down any threshold of causal conspicuousness or proximity for actions. Miller takes a contrary view. He submits that a characterization of the trapped person's plight as a situation of unfreedom 'seem[s] paradoxical because [it] clash[es] with our primary intuition that [unfreedoms] are obstacles attributable to human agency. In [the scenario of the rockslide] the result depends on a combination of natural factors and human behavior. But "human agency" means both more and less than [the causal contribution, however slight, of a human act]. It means that the humans in question knew what they were doing or, if not, that they should have done'. Miller adds that, although the tossing of the apple was a cause of the confinement of the person in the cave, such a result was 'neither willed nor intended nor foreseen (nor even perhaps capable of being foreseen)'.[28] Now, as has been argued in Chapter 2 and much more tersely in this chapter, the actions that give rise to unfreedoms are not perforce deliberately aimed at producing such effects. Nor must those constraining effects be foreseen or foreseeable in order to count as unfreedoms. When somebody's actions curtail someone else's liberty in a wholly and excusably

---

[27] Miller, 'Reply', 312–13; Miller, *Market*, 34–5.   [28] Miller, 'Reply', 312.

inadvertent manner—perhaps after an interval of many decades—the curtailment consists in unfreedom despite its utter unforeseeability. Just as there is no threshold for the significance or proximity of an action's causal contribution, so too there is no requirement of intentionality or foreseeability. Miller's insistence on such a requirement is based on his premise that the distinction between unfreedoms and mere inabilities is profoundly moral. Whereas I draw that distinction by reference to causal responsibility, Miller draws it by reference to moral responsibility. He maintains that unfreedoms arise only when any person P has limited the freedom of any other person in a way (maybe a fully justified or excusable way) for which P is morally responsible.

Although the current subsection is not the place for a full-scale rehearsal of the reasons for my austere methodological stance, we should glance here at Miller's rejection of such a stance. He writes: 'The view that the idea of freedom has no built-in evaluative force seems to me incredible. If showing that the enactment of a certain law increases or decreases freedom or that people in society A generally enjoy more freedom than people in society B were merely an exercise in technical classification, what purpose would it have? We are interested in deciding when obstacles are properly seen as [unfreedoms] because, other things being equal, we wish not to be [unfree]'.[29] In fairness to Miller, let us straightaway note that he is responding here to the extreme methodological position of Felix Oppenheim. His retort would undoubtedly have been more textured if he had been contesting a subtler position. Nonetheless, as his pronouncements stand, they purport to call into question any methodologically austere perspective that does not resort to a standard of moral responsibility as the touchstone for distinguishing between unfreedoms and mere inabilities. Regrettably, his comments in the context of his overarching argument run together two distinct questions. First, what is the nature or content of the criterion for staking off unfreedoms from mere inabilities, and, second, what is the justification for the content of that criterion? This book accepts that the ultimate justification for the pertinent criterion is partly moral-political, at a very high level of abstraction. However, the pertinent criterion itself is strictly non-normative, with a focus on causal responsibility rather than on moral responsibility. Only by conflating the two specified questions can Miller think that his moral-responsibility criterion is supported by his observations on the

[29] Miller, 'Reply', 313.

moral-political tenor of the justification for enquiring into the status of obstacles as unfreedoms.

The separability of those questions can best be highlighted if we shift our attention to a property that is uncontroversially non-normative and non-evaluative. One such property, apt for consideration here, is the speed with which human beings can run. Devices and techniques for measuring that property have been developed to a high level of technical refinement, to ensure that comparisons among people's performances are strictly accurate rather than misleading. Nevertheless, we would go badly astray if we were to surmise that the carrying out of those meticulous comparisons is 'merely an exercise in technical classification' (in Miller's words). Far from being an arid exercise in cataloguing, those elaborately precise comparisons are the means of ascertaining levels of excellence in an activity that pushes human endurance to its limits. Officials who monitor the efforts of runners in races go to great lengths to achieve accuracy in their measurements because those measurements serve as the bases for richly evaluative judgements about the relative proficiency of people in a gruelling sport. Prizes and plaudits and lucrative advertising contracts are conferred on certain runners by reference to those measurements. The attainment of rigorous accuracy is thus essential for the attainment of fairness in the distribution of sundry benefits. Consequently, the employment of devices and standards that enable such accuracy can be justified on normative and evaluative grounds, even though the devices and standards themselves are neither normative nor evaluative.

Of course, the analogy sketched in my last paragraph is only an analogy and is thus inevitably imperfect. Although evaluations of the relative performances of runners quite often encompass judgements about their fortitude and their competitive perseverance, no sensible person would think that assessments of runners' proficiency are as morally profound and significant as the judgements at which we arrive on the basis of our surveys of people's freedoms and unfreedoms. Somebody can be an admirable human agent without being a good runner, whereas no society can be admirable unless most of its inhabitants enjoy substantial degrees of overall liberty. All the same, notwithstanding the evident shortcomings of the analogy, the key point which it underscores is that a set of criteria can be strictly non-normative even if the justification for adopting and applying those criteria is of a moral-political character.

When we seek to ascertain whether an individual has been made unfree in some respect(s), we typically do so in order to reach exonerative or condemnatory judgements. We likewise often do so in order to gauge the efficacy of formal or informal mechanisms for averting some type(s) of unfreedom. Our findings also enable us to compare individuals in order to see whether instances of unfreedom of some kind are widely distributed or are confined largely to certain groups. Perhaps most notably, our enquiries into the existence of unfreedoms are steps toward the measurement of the overall freedom of each individual and of each society. Our measurements can form the bases for comparative judgements about societies' differing merits, and can also form the bases for determinations concerning the extent to which any given society's institutional arrangements are just. All of these uses (and other moral-political uses) to which our investigations of specific unfreedoms can be put are far more than a sterile 'exercise in technical classification'. If we deem those investigations to be worthwhile, one key reason is that they enable us to come up with solidly informed moral-political verdicts on certain questions. What may be even more important, they help us along the path toward coming up with such verdicts on a much wider array of questions—by helping to lay the groundwork for the measurement of each person's overall liberty. In other words, a prominent part of the justification for looking carefully into the existence or inexistence of various unfreedoms is moral-political. If our enquiries into the occurrence and frequency of those unfreedoms never led us to arrive at verdicts of the sort just mentioned, they would be largely pointless. Still, we should not rush to embrace Miller's conclusions. Nothing said here should incline us to think that the distinction between unfreedoms and mere inabilities must itself be defined in a manner that requires moral judgements for its application. Indeed, not least because of all the moral-political uses to which our discoveries of unfreedoms can be put, we should opt for a definition that does not leave those discoveries dependent on moral-political judgements. Clarity at every stage will be enhanced if we keep a firm separation between moral-political disputation and the matters of fact to which the disputation pertains. If the initial stage at which we categorize states of affairs as unfreedoms or as mere inabilities is already a stage that kindles moral-political controversies, then the focus of our subsequent debates will be less sharp. At any rate, from the sheer fact that the *justification* for staking off unfreedoms from mere inabilities in a certain fashion is partly political—at a high level of abstraction—we cannot validly infer that the *content* of the criterion for the unfreedoms/mere-inabilities distinction must itself be morally pregnant. Miller's suggestion to the contrary is erroneous. There is ample room for a criterion, such as a causal criterion, that can be applied without recourse to moral-political considerations. (More is said in other parts of this book about the general methodological issues raised fleetingly in this paragraph.)

Having eschewed Miller's conflation of the content of a criterion and the justification for that content, we can and should accept that any causal contribution by someone's actions to the impairment of somebody else's freedom is a source of unfreedom. Let us consider a further example that underlines how slight the causal contribution of an action can be. Suppose first that Fred and Mabel are near a cave into which Mabel wishes to descend. Fred assures her that he will prevent a large boulder from rolling down and blocking the narrow mouth of the cave. On the basis of that assurance, Mabel descends; she would not have gone into the cave without receiving such an undertaking. If Fred subsequently declines to avert the rock's motion—perhaps because of malice or remissness, or perhaps because he needs to attend to some other urgent task—his omission has clearly been preceded by his action of offering an assurance, an action that was a but-for cause of Mabel's entry into the cave. The contribution of his action to her confinement in the cave is sufficient to endow that confinement with the status of an array of unfreedoms. So much is obvious, but now let us look at a modified version of the scenario. Suppose that, although Fred and Mabel are both in the vicinity of the cave, they are not together. Indeed, Fred is not even aware of Mabel's presence at all, and he certainly does not offer any assistance or undertakings. Nonetheless, Mabel sees Fred at a distance and mistakenly assumes that he knows of her presence. Without bothering to extract any assurances or to communicate with him in any way, she presumes that he will stop any boulders from rolling into the mouth of the cave. She accordingly enters the cave with confidence that she is safe; had she not seen Fred or some other robust person in the general area, she would not have undertaken her speleological descent. When the boulder rolls down and occludes the mouth of the cave, has she been made unfree? On the one hand, it is manifest that the most salient causes of Mabel's captivity were her own foolishness and the operations of natural forces. On the other hand, Fred's action of strolling around the general area of the cave was a but-for cause of that captivity. Had Fred not been present in that area, Mabel would not have seen him and would therefore not have felt sufficiently secure to enter the cave. Consequently, although he was wholly unaware of her existence and although his lulling of her into a false sense of security was neither intentional nor negligent on his part, an action of his was a but-for cause of the severe impairment of her liberty. Thus, her plight is a situation of unfreedom; the causal contribution made by Fred's act of visiting the area of the cave was enough per se to trigger the applicability of the 'unfreedoms' side of the 'unfreedoms'/'mere-inabilities' dichotomy.

4.3. Why Omissions are Not Sources of Unfreedom

In this final subsection we must consider why omissions should be disregarded when we endeavour to apprehend whether people's inabilities are unfreedoms or not. The contrast here, of course, is with actions. When people's inabilities have been caused to even a slight extent by other people's actions or by the products of other people's actions, they *ipso facto* count as unfreedoms. More precisely, whenever at least one action (or any product of such an action) by at least one person is necessary for the existence of some inability of another person, that inability should be classified as an unfreedom. No such classification is warranted, however, if the only contribution to some inability of a person by anyone else is an omission or a set of omissions.

On the way to understanding why omissions must be put aside, we should initially glance at two false trails—two untenable lines of thought concerning the distinctiveness of omissions. First, as should be apparent from some of my previous remarks, the noteworthy difference between acts and omissions that necessitates a special approach to the latter is not a matter of morality or politics. We do not need to tackle here the question whether there are always some moral differences between contributing to the occurrence of E by doing something and contributing to the occurrence of E by omitting to do something. Although such a question is undoubtedly of importance in itself, and although it attracts attention from many philosophers who write on the act/omission distinction (including Bennett), it is beside the point within this chapter.

On the one hand, as has already been emphasized, the act/omission distinction as drawn by Bennett does not partake of any inherent moral significance. That aspect of it is one of its strengths, as far as this book is concerned. On the other hand, as Bennett himself illuminatingly observes,[30] his distinction is correlated—albeit quite imperfectly—with certain other distinctions that are indisputably of moral significance. One such distinction, for example, lies between courses of conduct that are relatively burdensome (for the person who chooses them) and courses of conduct that are relatively easy. Another such distinction lies between conduct that motivationally is highly focused and conduct that motivationally is much more diffuse. Now, while

---

[30] Bennett, *Act*, 74–7.

these distinctions and other morally pregnant distinctions do correlate imperfectly with the act/omission dichotomy, my concern in this book is with ensuring the measurability of overall freedom rather than with assessing the moral weight of considerations that support or discredit certain patterns of behaviour. Thus, even if there were always some moral difference between contributing to E by doing something and contributing to E by omitting to do something—because the contrasts that imperfectly correlate with the act/omission dichotomy might somehow always be disjunctively applicable, even though no single one of those contrasts would always be applicable—we could leave that whole matter aside. Of course, there is in fact no reason to think that a moral difference of the aforementioned kind does always obtain. There is every reason to agree with Bennett when he writes that the distinctions which correlate imperfectly with the act/omission dichotomy are 'merely frequent companions' of that dichotomy and are not invariable accompaniments, even disjunctively.[31] All the same, we can prescind from that topic here. Though my view is that Bennett is surely correct, this chapter will not attempt to substantiate that view. Even if he were wrong, my reasons for adopting a distinctive approach to omissions would be entirely unaffected, neither weakened nor strengthened.

One false trail to be avoided, then, is the notion that this subsection's discussions derive from a premise affirming some inherent or invariable moral difference between acts and omissions. Another false trail is the thesis that the very concept of causation applies differently between acts and omissions. Both the NESS test and the but-for test ascribe causal roles to omissions as well as to acts, and the questions asked by each test about omissions are exactly the same as the questions that are asked about acts. Nothing in this chapter is meant to suggest otherwise. My isolating of omissions for special treatment does not derive from any sense that the fundamental criteria for designating them as causes of inabilities are different from the criteria for so designating acts.

Some philosophers have challenged the claim that the fundamental criteria for causation are uniform between acts and omissions. Let us consider one example of such a challenge, from a sophisticated essay by Alison McIntyre on the moral responsibility of people for omissions. Although McIntyre is discussing the issue of moral responsibility, her division between acts and omissions is a division between causing and

---

[31] Bennett, *Act*, 142.

allowing, and her way of pinpointing the distinctiveness of omissions is focused on the matter of causal efficacy in contexts of over-determination.

If by omitting to perform some act A you have *allowed* some event E to occur, then it must be true that your doing A would have prevented E. However, if an action of yours has *caused* some event E, it need not be true that an alternative course of action by you would have prevented E. Thus, if you shoot Sam you can be morally responsible for causing him to be shot even if it is true that if you had refrained from shooting him, he still would have been shot by someone else who stood waiting nearby. In contrast, you can be morally responsible for allowing Sam to drown by refusing to toss him a life preserver only if tossing him a life preserver would have prevented him from drowning.[32]

McIntyre here envisages two situations of pre-emptive causality. Her comment about the first of those situations, in which someone shoots Sam, is entirely unexceptionable. As should be plain from my earlier exposition of pre-emptive causation—and in particular from my scenario of the criminal henchman who purchases drugs—McIntyre is unimpeachably correct in stating that the assailant caused Sam's death, even though the death would have been caused by someone else if the assailant had not committed his misdeed. The act of shooting was an element in a set of actual conditions minimally sufficient for the occurrence of the death. Under the NESS test, then, the act of shooting was unequivocally a cause of the death. To be sure, the but-for test would lead to a different verdict; yet, as was indicated in my initial presentation of those two tests, the fact that the but-for criterion would generate a different verdict in such a context is a principal reason for deeming that criterion to be inferior to the NESS standard. When we are probing the nature of causal relationships generally, and thus when our reflections on the matter are not bound by the peculiar constraints and requirements of the U Postulate, the NESS principle is always to

---

[32] Alison McIntyre, 'Compatibilists Could Have Done Otherwise: Responsibility and Negative Agency', 103 *Philosophical Review* 453, 463 (1994), emphases in original. Equally inadvisable is a later argument by McIntyre that treats a situation of pre-emptive causation as if it were a situation of duplicative causation; see MacIntyre, 'Compatibilists', 474–7. For some expressions of the erroneous view that omissions are not causes, see Bunzl, 'Overdetermination', 149; Lichtenberg, 'Equivalence', 221–2; Eric Mack, 'Bad Samaritanism and the Causation of Harm', 9 *Philosophy and Public Affairs* 230 (1980). On this point, I am in agreement with John Harris, 'The Marxist Critique of Violence', 3 *Philosophy and Public Affairs* 192 (1974). Harris, however, overlooks the difficulties that preoccupy me in this subsection.

be preferred to the but-for principle in the infrequent circumstances where the two standards lead to divergent conclusions. Hence, McIntyre's account of the shooting—an account that is obviously not inflected by the constraints and requirements of the U Postulate—is beyond reproach.

By contrast, her comment on her scenario of the bystander who refuses to rescue Sam from drowning is untenable. The unsustainability of her analysis will become palpable if the scenario is amplified slightly. (Let us designate this amplified scenario as 'S_1'.) Suppose that, if the bystander throws the life preserver to Sam, the drowning man will gratefully avail himself of it to keep afloat. He will make his way to a dock that is not far from the location where the waters nearly overwhelmed him. Unbeknownst to him and to the bystander, however, a thug who deeply dislikes Sam is hiding behind the dock. Just as Sam arrives, the thug will grab him and will hold his head under the water until he drowns. Sam's death from drowning will occur at approximately the same time at which Sam would have drowned if the bystander had not tossed the life preserver to him. In these circumstances, then, it is not the case that 'tossing him a life preserver would have prevented him from drowning' (in McIntyre's words). Now, while keeping in mind what would happen if the bystander were to be responsive to Sam's call for aid, let us assume that he will not in fact be responsive. If we apply the NESS criterion in order to ascertain whether his refusal to throw the life preserver is classifiable as a cause of Sam's death, the answer is clearly affirmative. His refusal is an element in a set of actual conditions minimally sufficient for the occurrence of the death. In the event of such a refusal, the thug's murderous actions will not take place and will be wholly pre-empted by the set of actual conditions that includes the bystander's unhelpfulness. In sum, McIntyre has gone astray in thinking that an omission cannot count as a cause of some untoward outcome in a situation of over-determination. Just as the NESS standard can lead us to designate an *action* as a cause in such a situation—as McIntyre herself explicitly accepts when mentioning the shooting of Sam—so too it can lead us to designate an *omission* as a pre-emptive cause. That is, an omission can qualify under the NESS criterion as a cause even though the outcome allowed by it would have come about through some other means if the omitted action had been performed.

Note that the S_1 scenario recounted in the preceding paragraph is crucially different from a scenario in which the throwing of the life preserver would have proved futile because Sam would not have been able to keep himself afloat with it. Let us designate that new scenario as

'S_2'. In the context of S_2, the refusal of the bystander to toss the life preserver—though reprehensible—would not count as a cause of Sam's death at all. No set of actual conditions minimally sufficient for the occurrence of the death would include the bystander's omission, since the omission was utterly redundant in the circumstances, and no minimally sufficient set includes any redundant members. Thus, whereas the refusal of the bystander was a pre-emptive cause of Sam's death in S_1, it would make no causal contribution whatsoever in S_2. We can know as much by applying the NESS standard straightforwardly to each case. McIntyre's remarks on omissions and over-determination are correct with reference to the kind of situation depicted in S_2, but they overlook the kind of situation depicted in S_1.

In short, my singling out of omissions for special treatment in this chapter is not due to any fundamental moral differences between acts and omissions, nor due to any differences of causal efficacy between them. No differences of the latter sort obtain, and any differences of the former sort would be irrelevant even if they did obtain. Why, then, is a separate subsection on omissions necessary? Why should we not adopt the same approach for omissions as for actions, and why therefore should we not attach the designation of 'unfreedom' to every inability of a person that is caused by any other person's omission(s)? Such a uniform approach, after all, would deal perfectly well with the basic problem that has prompted me to distinguish between unfreedoms and mere inabilities. That is, it would enable us to affirm that neither the range of the combinations of conjunctively exercisable freedoms nor the range of the combinations of consistent unfreedoms for each person is infinite in extent. After all, countless inabilities—such as the inability of each person to fly around and around every galaxy—are not traceable to anyone's omissions (or to anyone's actions, of course). Such inabilities would be classifiable as mere inabilities even if every inability caused in part by some omission(s) were to be classified as an unfreedom. In other words, even if omissions were placed fully on a par with actions as sources of unfreedoms, and thus even if the slightest or remotest causal contribution by any omission to an inability were enough to elicit the designation of 'unfreedom', the range of the combinations of consistent unfreedoms for each person would be finite. Hence, the measurability of everyone's overall liberty would not be threatened by the prospect of an infinitely large denominator in the fraction that expresses the freedom-measuring ratio for each person.

Nevertheless, for a number of reasons, any uniform approach to actions and omissions would undermine my theory of freedom. Such an approach would disregard the key divergence between actions and omissions. Whereas an action is an event that occurs, an omission is the fact that no action leading to some particular outcome has occurred. An ascription of an action to some person P is a more or less precise specification of something that she has done in furtherance of a certain upshot, whereas an ascription of an omission to P is in itself a relatively uninformative assertion that she has *not* done anything that would have furthered a certain upshot. As we have seen in my discussion of Bennett, the considerable informativeness of an ascription of an action to P derives from the fact that the ways in which she can position her body to perform the action are far fewer than the alternative ways in which she can position her body. Conversely, the relatively meagre informativeness of an ascription of an omission to P derives from the fact that the ways in which she can position her body without bringing about some specified result are far more numerous than the ways in which she can position her body to bring about that result. (Here and elsewhere, of course, the notion of positioning one's body is meant to encompass one's retention of any stationary posture as well as one's carrying out of any movements.) Now, because of this central difference between actions and omissions, we shall have to maintain that inabilities caused by other people's omissions but not directly or indirectly by other people's actions are mere inabilities rather than unfreedoms. In exploring this point, we should contemplate first the possibility of treating all omissions as potential sources of unfreedom, and then the possibility of treating only some omissions in that manner. As will be seen, each of those alternatives is unacceptable. Omissions have to be excluded as sources of unfreedom.

If we regard all omissions as potential sources of unfreedom when we endeavour to ascertain whether sundry inabilities are unfreedoms or not, at least two formidable difficulties will arise. In the first place, we shall have rendered our enquiries unmanageably speculative and tangled. After all, when we take into account the causal roles of omissions, we are pondering the diversion of resources from their actual uses to alternative uses. We are taking into account what would have happened if people had behaved differently in some respects from the ways in which they have actually behaved, and we are likewise taking into account what would have happened if various substances and materials had been employed differently. To be sure, so long as we are hypothesizing diversions of resources to alternative uses on a modest scale, we can have confidence in the veracity of our claims about the outcomes of the diversions. Those claims will not be unduly conjectural and will not enmesh us in severe complications pertaining to the incidental effects of the diversions. Contrariwise, if we are hypothesizing assignments of resources to alternative uses on a sweeping scale, our enquiries will consist of absurdly extensive guess-work. The resultant uncertainties are not just snarls that would thwart the practical implementation of any criteria for distinguishing between unfreedoms and mere inabilities; they are snarls that would thwart the coherent elaboration of those criteria at a theoretical level.

To a large degree, the problem of speculativeness in this context is a general problem that afflicts counter-factual conditionals. In so far as the antecedent (the 'if' clause) in a counter-factual departs markedly from actuality, we can only conjecture whether the consequent (the 'then' clause) follows therefrom or not. As David Lewis has remarked, 'the farther we depart from actuality, the more we lose control over our counterfactuals'.[33] In this respect, the uncertainties that attend our reflections on allocations of resources sweepingly different from any actual allocations are roughly similar to the uncertainties that attend our reflections on the outcome of the Second World War if Germany had declined to declare war on the United States in late 1941 and if Winston Churchill and Franklin Roosevelt had both been assassinated around that time. In important respects, however, the counter-factual musings required for the tracing of inabilities to complex omissions would be even more disconcertingly fanciful. Perhaps the most knotty problem is that a theorist engaged in such musings would have to be able to divine whether a host of unrealized technological developments could have been realized if they had been pursued with unremitting tenacity.

Suppose, for example, that societies throughout the world have devoted their extensive resources to countless uses that have resulted in a high standard of living for the large majority of human beings. Nevertheless, no one is able to embark on a journey to Mars or to any other planet, since the technology for interplanetary travel by people has not been developed. Suppose that, when gauging the overall liberty of each person, a theorist wants to separate unfreedoms from mere inabilities in accordance with my U Postulate while wanting also to treat all omissions as potential sources of unfreedom. Such a theorist will have to try to discern whether the technology for interplanetary travel could have been developed if massive quantities of resources (up to any levels compatible with the continued existence of civilization) had been devoted to that objective over a period of many years. If the answer to that question is affirmative, then the inability of each person to engage in interplanetary travel is a state of unfreedom. Contrariwise,

---

[33] Lewis, 'Postscripts', 173.

if the answer is negative, the aforementioned inability is a mere inability rather than an unfreedom. Exactly how a political philosopher or even a scientific expert could arrive at an answer to such a question with minimal confidence is not at all clear. Moreover, he would have to arrive at answers to myriad other questions on the frontiers of scientific exploration. For example, suppose that some people suffer from a disease that incapacitates their legs. The theorist depicted here would have to decide whether a cure for that disease could have been developed if vast amounts of resources had been dedicated to such an aim over a long period of time. If the answer to that question is affirmative, then the incapacitation of each person who suffers from the specified disease is a state of unfreedom. If the answer is negative, the incapacitation is an array of mere inabilities. Again, exactly how a political philosopher or anyone else could reach a minimally reliable answer to such a question is far from apparent—especially since he would also have to grapple with thousands and thousands of other scientific/technological questions, virtually none of which would be straightforwardly or uncontroversially answerable by leading experts in the relevant fields. Even the attachment of probabilistic qualifications to answers would very frequently be a matter of sheer guesswork.

In sum, unless we restrict the range of the omissions that are taken into account when we separate unfreedoms from mere inabilities, our enquiries will become ludicrously conjectural. If we are to be reasonably confident in our ascertainment of each person's unfreedoms, we have to avoid getting bogged down in quagmires of imponderables. Hopeless speculativeness, however, is not the only fatal drawback of which we would run afoul if we were to view all omissions as potential sources of unfreedom. In addition, such an approach would effectively mean that all the self-inflicted inabilities of every person are unfreedoms—since every such inability has been caused in part by other people's omissions.

To perceive why the self/other distinction would be effaced, we should briefly recall the nature of omissions. On the one hand, a stretch of conduct does not constitute an omission unless the omitted act was within the powers of the person to whom we ascribe the omission. As has already been mentioned, a person's conduct must have some bearing on the occurrence of a given outcome if that conduct is to be classifiable as an act or omission in relation to that outcome. If no action that a person could possibly perform would ever prevent some state of affairs—such as the continuation of the revolution of the planet Pluto around the sun—then the fact that the person does not do anything to preclude that state of affairs is not an omission on his part. If the conduct of someone is to be classifiable as an omission in relation to the emergence of some outcome E, there has to be a distinction for him or her between 'There was absolutely nothing that I could have done at any time to prevent E' and 'I did not do anything to prevent E'. On the other hand, when we accept that an action of a specified type must be within someone's abilities if his non-performance of that action is to be classifiable as an omission, we are not thereby accepting that the non-performance of the action must perforce have been aimed at allowing whatever the action in the circumstances would have averted. As was noted earlier, an omission that allows the occurrence of E is an omission regardless of whether it was intended to have any such effect. It may have been intentional, of course, but it may have been wholly inadvertent (perhaps because of remissness or perhaps because of innocent ignorance). Accordingly, as was also remarked earlier, we can correctly ascribe an omission to some person P even if he or she has not had any evident opportunity to perform the action(s) which he or she has omitted. So long as there was in fact some opportunity, it need not have been manifest to P at all.

Thus, if every omission were a potential source of unfreedom, all inabilities caused by one's own conduct would be unfreedoms even though some of those inabilities would not be due to other people's actions in any way. After all, unlike some naturally caused inabilities, every inability inflicted by a person upon himself is something that could have been averted by other people. Whenever a person curtails his own freedom without any contribution by anyone else's actions or by the products of anyone else's actions, certain omissions on the part of other people are nevertheless but-for causes of the curtailment. Had some other person(s) acted to prevent him from doing that which brought about the curtailment, it obviously would not have come about. Let us think back, for example, to the scenario of Fred and Mabel and the cave. Suppose that neither Fred nor anyone else apart from Mabel herself is within 20 miles of the cave when she descends. Neither he nor anyone else apart from Mabel herself knows of her whereabouts, and not even she is aware of the danger from the boulder. In these circumstances, no one other than Mabel has an opportunity to save her by the time she actually enters the cave. However, Fred and myriad other people had opportunities to save her at earlier junctures. Someone could have tracked her movements and could have been on the scene to keep the boulder from rolling down. Someone could have persuaded her not to journey into the cave, or could have forcibly prevented her if necessary. If no single person could have stopped her from undertaking that journey, then multiple people certainly could have. Their not having done so was a but-for cause of her confinement in the cave. This point applies, of course, regardless of her outlook when she trapped herself in the cave. Whether her imprisonment of herself was deliberate or wholly unwitting, it could have been forestalled by actions which other people did not in fact perform.

The preceding paragraph's argument applies *mutatis mutandis* to absolutely every impairment of a person's freedom by the person himself. Suppose, for instance, that Mabel has ascended a cliff instead of descending into a cave. If she jumps or stumbles over the brink of the cliff, and if she becomes physically paralysed as a result, and if all omissions are to be counted as sources of unfreedom, then her state of paralysis will be classifiable as a state of unfreedom. Any number of people could have watched over her as she strolled along the cliff; or, either through exhortation or through physical force, they could have prevented her from ascending the cliff at all. Their not having done so was a but-for cause of her paralysing plunge.

Manifestly, the underlying point made in the last couple of paragraphs applies not only to Mabel but to everyone else as well. Whenever anyone does something that reduces his own freedom, he has done something that could have been averted by the actions of other people. Their not having performed any of those actions was a but-for cause of the reduction in his freedom. Hence, if causal connections between their omissions and his inabilities were sufficient for the classification of his inabilities as unfreedoms, every one of his ostensibly self-inflicted inabilities would be an instance of unfreedom. There would be no such thing as a self-inflicted inability that would get classified under the U Postulate as a mere inability. What is so troubling about this is that the U Postulate as a central element in a political-philosophical theory of freedom is meant to distinguish between constraints on freedom imposed by other people and constraints on freedom imposed by oneself or by natural forces. If the first half of that dichotomy comprises all constraints which emanate from other people's omissions as well as constraints which emanate from other people's actions, then a significant portion of the latter half of the dichotomy—namely, the portion consisting of all constraints imposed by oneself and some constraints imposed by natural forces—will have disappeared. In sum, if we wish to sustain the basic role of the U Postulate, we cannot regard all omissions by other people as potential sources of unfreedom. The countless omissions that cause inabilities are not causes on which the division between unfreedoms and mere inabilities can hinge.

Should we, then, regard *some* omissions by other people as potential sources of unfreedom? Should we exclude some omissions but take account of others? An approach along these lines will presumably exclude omissions of coordinated arrays of actions if those arrays would have involved massive reallocations of resources on a humanity-wide scale or even a society-wide scale. Such a tack finesses the problem of inordinate conjecturalness that arises when all omissions are regarded as potential sources of unfreedom. At the same time, such a tack enables us to regard some omissions as such sources. Moreover, its line of demarcation between the included and excluded omissions is drawn by reference to epistemic considerations rather than by reference to moral considerations. It thereby realizes my aim of coming up with a morally neutral content for the criterion that separates unfreedoms from mere inabilities; any unfreedoms that owe their statuses as such to the included omissions will be identifiable as unfreedoms without recourse to moral judgements.

One major snag for such an approach is the likelihood of substantial second-order uncertainty. That is, not only are we frequently engaged in a speculative enquiry when we ask whether this or that outcome could have been averted by a massive humanity-wide reallocation of resources; in addition, we will often be engaged in a speculative enquiry when we seek to determine whether the foregoing question as applied to this or that outcome can be answered with an acceptable degree of definiteness (albeit probabilistic definiteness). Hence, we shall be faced with no easy task if we have to distinguish between omissions with solidly ascertainable consequences and omissions with consequences that are only conjecturally ascertainable. Let us put that problem aside, however. The chief drawback of the approach outlined in my last paragraph is that it hollows out the category of self-inflicted inabilities, just as we do when we regard *all* omissions as potential sources of unfreedom. Even if we can manage to specify the omissions that are to be excluded because of the unascertainableness of their consequences, we shall still be taking account of every omission that allows any person's curtailment of his own freedom. After all, in respect of any self-inflicted inability, we can say with certitude that sufficient monitoring and intervention by some other person(s) would have prevented its occurrence. In taking such a view, we are not grappling with unfathomable questions at the limits of technological progress, nor more generally are we pondering situations that diverge sweepingly from actuality. Epistemic concerns about undue guesswork provide no basis whatsoever for declining to advert to the omissions that enable anybody to harm herself. We can know perfectly straightforwardly that, if Fred and some other people had restrained Mabel from walking along the cliff, she would not have fallen off and paralysed herself. We can therefore know straightforwardly that their not having induced her to forgo that activity was a but-for cause of its freedom-impairing upshot. Such a claim is not at all akin to a conjectural claim about the feasibility of interplanetary travel in the event that massive amounts of resources had been devoted to such a development during a sustained period.

Note that, if a selective approach to omissions is to be based solely on epistemic concerns about the avoidance of excessive speculativeness, it will not only hollow out the category of self-inflicted inabilities but will also cut substantially into the category of natural inabilities. Many inabilities normally perceived as imposed by natural forces will have to be characterized as unfreedoms. Such a characterization will be required whenever the curtailment of anyone's freedom by the operations of natural forces could patently have been arrested or deflected or defused through the anticipatory actions of some other person(s). Attacks in the wild by sharks and bears, for example, will be among the incidents that give rise to unfreedoms (at least where the victims of those attacks have only been injured rather than killed); the victim of any such attack could have been prevented from going into the wild, or the attack itself could have been fended off by the efforts of several other people with guns if they had trailed the victim. To be sure, the distinction between unfreedoms and natural inabilities will not altogether lose its pertinence. As was noted earlier in this subsection, myriad inabilities—such as the incapacity of each person to fly around and around the galaxies—will continue to fall on the 'natural inabilities' side of that distinction. All the same, the range of the inabilities classifiable as mere-inabilities-imposed-by-natural-forces will be greatly diminished.

In short, if the basic role of the U Postulate is to be upheld, a selective approach to omissions cannot be based on purely epistemic considerations. A concern to eschew inordinate speculation will not per se keep the category of self-inflicted inabilities from being thoroughly eviscerated as a category of mere inabilities. A selective approach to omissions will therefore have to introduce some supplementary criteria for distinguishing between those omissions that are potential sources of unfreedom and those that are not. Such criteria might focus, for example, on the availability of ready opportunities for the carrying out of actions that could avert or remove inabilities. Thus, if Fred is actually on the scene to behold Mabel's descent into the cave, and if he could forestall the slide of the boulder without much difficulty, his decision against undertaking such an action will be sufficient to warrant the classification of her subsequent confinement as a state of unfreedom. Or—whether additionally or alternatively—perhaps the supplementary criteria would focus on the intentions of people who omit to perform actions that could have averted or removed the inabilities of other people. If Fred's failure to rescue Mabel was due to malice rather than to remissness (or to an urgent need to perform some other action), then her imprisonment in the cave is a state of unfreedom. Such is the conclusion to which we would be led by a supplementary criterion focused on intentions. Another possible criterion for the inclusion of some omissions might focus on what is normal or predictable. If an action of a certain type in circumstances of a certain kind would be usual as a matter of statistical frequency, then an omission to perform such an action in such circumstances is a potential source of unfreedom. That is, if anybody's omission is abnormal and if it plays a but-for causal role in the cabining of anyone else's liberty, the upshot of that cabining is *ipso facto* a state of unfreedom. So we would be asked to believe by a supplementary criterion focused on the typicalness of patterns of behaviour.

For two main reasons, we should reject any such attempts to resort to supplementary criteria for the purpose of salvaging an analysis that selectively includes omissions as sources of unfreedom. (We should therefore reject that whole line of analysis, of course.) In the first place, each supplementary criterion has a suspiciously ad-hoc air. Neither the criteria broached in the preceding paragraph nor any other colourable criterion can be justified on the basis of epistemic considerations, since each of them is meant to supplement such considerations. Likewise, no such criterion can be justified by reference to the concept of causation; the omissions excluded under any supplementary criterion are causes just as much as the omissions included. Each criterion therefore seems justified only as a contrivedly ad-hoc device for preserving the full significance of the U Postulate by ensuring that some self-inflicted inabilities are designated as mere inabilities. Nothing appears to warrant our drawing the line between excluded omissions and included omissions at the particular place prescribed by any such criterion.

More important is a second difficulty, which arises from the most evident way of addressing the problem of ad-hoc contrivedness. Each of the supplementary criteria can plausibly be justified on moral grounds. If for example we follow the first of those criteria in its focus on the easiness or burdensomeness of performing various acts, we are singling out a factor that is always relevant to the moral issue of the reasonableness or unreasonableness of omitting to perform those acts. Likewise, if we follow the second of the supplementary criteria in its focus on intentions, we shall be attending to a factor that is clearly of moral significance (indeed, according to many moral doctrines, a factor that is of paramount moral significance). Similarly, if we join the third criterion in looking for statistically anomalous behaviour that is freedom-impairing, we shall be concentrating on a factor that is quite closely connected with the dashing of legitimate expectations, which are always morally significant. Hence, each of the supplementary criteria can divest itself of its air of ad-hoc arbitrariness if it is presented as a morally pregnant standard. The overwhelming disadvantage of such a tack, however, is that it runs athwart the fundamental tenor of this book. It turns the distinction between unfreedoms and mere inabilities into a morally fraught divide, the application of which cannot be ascertained without recourse to moral judgements. We would not be able to draw that distinction comprehensively without first arriving at moral judgements about the reasonableness or unreasonableness of various patterns of behaviour. In a like vein, we would first have to arrive at moral judgements on issues such as the appropriateness of assimilating intentionality and recklessness or intentionality and gross negligence. We would similarly have to reach moral judgements on matters such as the level of abstractness or concreteness at which anybody's intentions are to be construed. Even the criterion concerning statistical frequency would require moral judgements, since it would oblige us to specify the frame of reference wherein normality is defined (one society, some portion of one society, all societies in the present, all societies either past or present, some subset of all societies?). Without that indispensable specification, which is profoundly normative, the statistical-frequency criterion cannot be applied determinately. By contrast, my book persistently argues that each person's freedoms and unfreedoms are to be detected through factual judgements rather than through moral judgements. That is, the relevant factors are abilities, inabilities, and causes of inabilities. Moral considerations such as those just mentioned are irrelevant. To be sure, as has been observed more than once, moral considerations at a highly abstract level are part of the ultimate justification for defining the factual issues along the lines developed in this book. Nonetheless, those issues are indeed factual. No moral judgements are required when we address them.

In short, if the general character of this book and the general function of the U Postulate are to be sustained, we shall have to rule out omissions as potential sources of unfreedom. Neither the inclusion of all omissions as such sources nor the inclusion of only some omissions is supportable; we have to conclude that, although many inabilities are caused in part by other people's omissions, those causal connections are never in themselves sufficient to warrant the classification of the inabilities as unfreedoms. Only the causal contributions of other people's *actions* (and of the products of their actions) are sufficient to warrant such a classification.

We should not worry that this restriction on the sources of unfreedom is inappositely confining within a theory that attaches special importance to the constraints on freedom imposed by human intercourse. Here we should recall that any causal contributions whatsoever by other people's actions or by the products of their actions are sufficient to endow inabilities with the status of unfreedoms. Think back to the example of a man who swallows some poisonous liquid that paralyses him. Suppose that someone sitting nearby is in possession of an antidote, which is fully effective if taken within 20 minutes of the ingestion of the poison. She blithely declines to administer the antidote to the man who has become incapacitated and fallen to the floor. That odious omission, which is manifestly a cause of the man's incapacities, is not in itself sufficient to endow those incapacities with the status of unfreedoms. However, the incapacities are almost certainly unfreedoms in any event, because the poisonous substance was almost certainly the product of other people's actions. In this scenario, then, as in many other circumstances, the fact that an omission does not count as a source of unfreedom is beside the point. Any causal contributions by some other person's actions, even if remote or inconspicuous, will place an inability on the 'unfreedoms' side of the division between unfreedoms and mere inabilities. Given that such causal contributions will so often be present when omissions are also involved, a theory that does not take account of omissions can hardly be accused of blinkeredness.

5. Conclusion

Although the NESS test is generally the best standard for ascertaining the existence of causal relations, the U Postulate makes the but-for test the operative standard when we wish to establish whether some inability of a person has been caused by at least one action of some other person(s). When two or more such actions are causally involved, not every one of them must meet the but-for requirement. Indeed, in unusual circumstances where two or more actions are duplicative causes or where one action is a pre-emptive cause and another is a pre-empted condition, none of those actions will on its own have satisfied the but-for requirement. However, given that in such circumstances the but-for test will have been satisfied by the fact that at least one action by some other person(s) occurred, the U Postulate's category of 'unfreedom' will be straightforwardly applicable. So long as the but-for criterion has been fulfilled in that manner, the possible slightness or remoteness of the causal contribution made by the relevant action(s) will not detract from the applicability of the category of 'unfreedom' at all. As a result, we should feel no misgivings about concluding that other people's omissions—as opposed to their actions—are not potential sources of unfreedom. Such a conclusion is essential for the accomplishment of the aims of this book, and it does not undesirably de-emphasize the unique importance of the constraints imposed by human beings on the freedom of one another. Hence, equipped with a suitable set of criteria for separating unfreedoms from mere inabilities, we are now ready to explore in depth the complexities of measuring the overall liberty of each person.

5

On Ascertaining the Extent of Everyone's Overall Freedom

This final chapter will draw on some of the ideas already adumbrated in this book, in an effort to specify the appropriate general formula for measuring the extent of each person's overall freedom. We shall begin by considering the central components of that formula, which have been touched upon intermittently since Chapter 2 but which must now be examined much more sustainedly. We shall then ponder the other principal elements of the formula, which profoundly influence its character. As we explore those additional elements, the importance of the distinction between the overall freedom and the particular freedoms of each person will be manifest. Most notably, the present chapter's focus on the measurement of overall liberty will involve an evaluative dimension that is altogether absent from investigations into the existence of particular liberties. Whereas the existence of any particular freedom is a strict matter of fact that can be verified or disconfirmed by reference to non-evaluative categories—albeit often with probabilistic qualifications—the extent of anyone's overall freedom is a matter that cannot be fully ascertained in the absence of evaluative assumptions. So, at any rate, the second half of this chapter will argue.

On the point just mentioned and on a number of other points, this chapter will be taking issue with positions adopted by Ian Carter. Indeed, in many respects my discussions amount to a critical dialogue with Carter—and with Hillel Steiner, whose trail-blazing stances on most of the topics discussed herein are similar to Carter's. Sometimes explicitly and sometimes more obliquely, quite a few of my analyses endeavour to rebut or defuse arguments that have been put forward by Carter and Steiner. Hence, it should be emphasized at the outset that this chapter is enormously indebted to their writings. Though my objections to aspects of their work are numerous and wide-ranging, the underlying purpose of the objections is to distil and amplify the invaluable insights which those two theorists have advanced.

1. Why a Ratio, and Why This Ratio?

As has been indicated in Chapter 2, the formula for the measurement of each person's overall freedom involves a complicated ratio, expressible as a fraction with the following numerator and denominator: the square of the range of each person's combinations of conjunctively exercisable freedoms, and the range of each person's combinations of conjunctively exercisable freedoms plus the range of each person's combinations of consistent unfreedoms. If we designate the range of each person's combinations of conjunctively exercisable liberties as 'F', and if we designate the range of each person's combinations of consistent unfreedoms as 'U', the freedom-measuring fraction—which will incorporate probabilistic qualifications and qualitative weightings, to be discussed later—is $F^2/(F+U)$.

Several prominent features of this ratio are in need of elucidation and defence. Why is the numerator of the fraction squared? How are the combinations of freedoms and the combinations of consistent unfreedoms tallied? How are the freedoms and unfreedoms themselves demarcated? These and other questions must receive adequate answers if the objective of measuring anyone's overall liberty is to be realizable even in principle. Before we address any of those inquiries, however, we should ponder a question that immediately calls for attention. Why does the formula for the measurement of overall freedom consist in a ratio at all? That is, why should we not be interested solely in the numerator of the specified fraction?

1.1. The Distinctiveness of Humanly Engendered Constraints

At first glance, the unsquared numerator of the fraction in the formula for measurements of overall freedom might seem to be the parameter on which we should be exclusively focused for such measurements. After all, once we ascertain the range of each person's combinations of conjunctively exercisable liberties, we apparently know everything that we need to know in order to gauge the extent of what each person is unprevented from doing and being and becoming and undergoing.

To proceed further by enquiring into the range of each person's combinations of consistent unfreedoms is to introduce an apparently extraneous consideration. At any rate, such is the view taken by theorists (including G. A. Cohen) who regard 'free' and 'unfree' as bivalent and who classify every inability as an unfreedom, regardless of whether it is naturally caused or humanly caused. For such theorists, the overall liberty of any person consists in the full array of opportunities—the full array of pathways for doing or being or becoming or undergoing various things—that are open to him or her. To identify and measure that array, we clearly do not have to ascertain what the person can*not* do or be or become or undergo. According to such theorists, then, the denominator of the fraction in my formula for measurements of overall freedom is irrelevant and misconceived. Indeed, if we were to accept their conception of unfreedom, we would likewise have to accept that the denominator of my fraction is infinitely large; hence, if one were to take account of the figure in that denominator for one's project of measuring each person's overall freedom, one would have to conclude that such a project is not possible even in principle.

As will be recalled from Chapter 2, the indispensability of avoiding an infinitely large element in the freedom-measuring fraction is precisely what motivates my adoption of a trivalent conception of freedom and unfreedom (that is, a conception which encompasses the predicate 'neither free nor unfree' alongside the predicates 'free' and 'unfree'). Thus, the topic of this subsection clearly has a bearing on that trivalent approach, which has been championed in this book precisely because my formula for measuring overall liberty involves the specified fraction rather than simply the numerator of that fraction. If the numerator alone were the relevant indicator of each person's overall liberty, one would obviously not have to worry about the spectre of an infinitely large denominator, and one would therefore not have to take any measures to fend off that spectre. Moreover, the connection between the aforementioned fraction and my trivalent conception of freedom/unfreedom is even closer than has just been implied. As was suggested near the outset of Chapter 4, my specific way of distinguishing between unfreedoms and mere inabilities is itself bound up with my reasons for insisting that the relevant measure of overall liberty is a ratio. In other words, the topic of this subsection is integrally linked not only to the general dichotomy between unfreedoms and mere inabilities, but also to the precise content of that dichotomy as defined by this book. (Seemingly at odds with what has just been said, the idea of measuring overall liberty as a ratio was first broached by Steiner, who robustly adheres to a bivalent conception of freedom and unfreedom.[1] However, as my second chapter has argued, Steiner errs in thinking that his positions on these matters are consistent. Although his rejection of Felix Oppenheim's idiosyncratic trivalent conception of freedom and unfreedom is warranted, the bivalent conception which he himself espouses is destructive of the coherence of his endeavours to measure overall liberty. No one who wishes to measure liberty as a ratio along the lines envisaged by Steiner or Carter or me can coherently endorse a bivalent conception of freedom and unfreedom. Indeed, because Steiner classifies mere inabilities as freedoms—unlike the theorists discussed in my last paragraph, who classify mere inabilities as unfreedoms—his position is especially problematic. For reasons discussed in Chapter 2, the numerator as well as the denominator of my fraction would be infinitely large if mere inabilities were classified as freedoms. Accordingly, even if Steiner were to take that numerator as the sole indicator of each person's overall liberty, he would find his project of measurement thwarted.)

Although theorists do not commit any outright errors when they decline to take account of unfreedoms at all for the purpose of measuring each person's overall liberty, their stance is unsatisfactory—at least within social and political philosophy—because it attaches no special importance whatsoever to constraints on freedom that have been engendered by human beings. Those constraints are treated as if they were on a par in every respect with constraints caused purely by natural forces. Since theorists who concentrate solely on the numerator of my fraction will pay no attention to what each person is unable to do or be or become or undergo, the *reasons* for the various inabilities of each person will likewise receive no attention. By default, then, humanly imposed limits on each person's freedom will remain wholly undistinguished from natural limits; all such limits will be lumped together as factors that constitute the unanalysed boundaries of these theorists' calculations. Consequently, these theorists in their approach to the measurement of overall liberty have failed to capture a central feature of socio-political freedom. That is, they have altogether failed to make clear that such freedom pertains distinctively—though not exclusively—to the multitudinous relationships between each person and other people. (N.B. Here as elsewhere throughout this book, my references to socio-political freedom are to non-normative liberty rather than to normative liberty. My infrequent references to

---

[1] See Hillel Steiner, 'Freedom and Bivalence', in Ian Carter and Mario Ricciardi (eds), *Freedom, Power, and Political Morality* (Basingstoke: Palgrave, 2001), 57.

normative freedom, chiefly to the normative freedom that consists in moral or legal permissibility, are specifically designated as such.)

Charles Taylor once complained that negative-liberty theorists understand the freedom of a human being as if it were the 'freedom of some physical object, say a lever'.[2] To be sure, Taylor's objection in its original context was misguided, not least because of his unattuned-ness to the distinction between the existence of anyone's particular liberties and the extent of anyone's overall liberty. Nevertheless, in the present context his complaint can be turned against the theorists who seek to measure each person's overall freedom without discriminating at all between the causes of the limits on that freedom. Their approach would be suitable for measuring the overall freedom of a lever. Like-wise, it might well be suitable for measurements of the overall freedom of a human being by physicists or engineers who are entirely uninter-ested in matters of social and political philosophy. When our focus is on socio-political freedom, however, we have to give some recognition to the distinctive importance of human interrelationships as sources of restrictions on that freedom.

Admittedly, the position propounded in my last couple of para-graphs is probably not justifiable in any way that ultimately escapes circularity.[3] That is, the arguments that support my claim about the distinctive importance of human interaction in the curbing of liberty— one or two of which will be presented shortly—are doubtless each based partly on a premise that imputes such importance to such inter-action. To come up with justificatory arguments that are not ultimately circular, someone would have to adduce a more profound dichotomy that pertinently comprehends the distinction between the human and the natural. No obvious candidates for that role come to mind. Instead, the chief dichotomies that might seem to be solid foundations for the human/natural distinction are in fact only contingently connected to it.

---

[2] Charles Taylor, 'What's Wrong with Negative Liberty', in Alan Ryan (ed.), *The Idea of Freedom* (Oxford: Oxford University Press, 1979), 175, 183. In more recent years, Taylor appears to have adopted a more favourable attitude toward the doctrine of negative liberty. See Charles Taylor, 'Plurality of Goods', in Mark Lilla, Ronald Dworkin, and Robert Silvers (eds), *The Legacy of Isaiah Berlin* (New York: New York Review Books, 2001), 113.

[3] On this point, I agree with Hillel Steiner, 'Freedom, Rights, and Equality: A Reply to Wolff', 6 *International Journal of Philosophical Studies* 128, 130 (1998). Steiner, however, makes the point in the context of his own bivalent conception of freedom and unfreedom. See also Hillel Steiner, 'How Free: Computing Personal Liberty', in A. Phillips Griffiths (ed.), *Of Liberty* (Cambridge: Cambridge University Press, 1983) [hereinafter cited as Steiner, 'Computing'], 73, 74–5.

Consider, for example, the thesis that humanly caused constraints on freedom are remediable whereas naturally caused constraints are not.[4] Anyone whose innate myopia has been corrected by eyeglasses or laser treatments will straightaway recognize the fallaciousness of the second half of this thesis. Indeed, the thesis as a whole is starkly unsustainable, as a simple scenario will reveal. Suppose that an industrial enterprise contaminates some land so badly that nobody will be free to grow anything thereon for decades (in the absence of major breakthroughs in the technology of detoxification, which—we may assume—will not occur). By reference to the remediability/irremediability dichotomy, the situation just mentioned is indistinguishable from a situation in which a similar level of contamination involving the same toxicants has occurred naturally. If no relevant technological advances take place, then each of these situations will remain irremediable for a long period; if such advances do take place, then each situation will have turned out to be remediable. Here and in a host of other situations, we find no correlation between the remediability/irremediability divide and the human/natural divide. To invoke the former dichotomy in justification of the latter is therefore to commit a non sequitur.

Equally unavailing as a non-circular foundation for the attribution of special importance to humanly caused constraints on freedom is any distinction between the myriad constraints that elicit resentment and the myriad constraints that do not have such an effect. Like the remediability/irremediability dichotomy, a dichotomy between resentment and its absence is only contingently correlated with the distinction between the human and the natural. Though many humanly imposed restrictions on a person's liberty do provoke disgruntlement, many instead elicit gratitude or indifference. If for example several railings effectively prevent me from plunging off a flight of stairs, I shall very likely be grateful for having been deprived of my freedom-to-plunge. Nor can this example be parried by someone who maintains that the presence of the railings will have increased my overall freedom by protecting me against some incapacitating injuries. Even if such a retort is true, it does not cast any doubt on the observation that some of my liberties have been removed; the chief point at issue here is focused on removals of particular liberties rather than on net decreases in overall liberty. Moreover, the claim about a net expansion of my overall liberty might well be false. If I am sufficiently nimble to be in no need of the railings' protection, then their

---

[4] In a different context I critically discuss this thesis in my *In the Realm of Legal and Moral Philosophy* (Basingstoke: Macmillan, 1999), 86–7.

obstructive presence will eliminate each instance of my freedom-to-plunge while conferring only some minor freedoms on me—such as the freedom to lean toward the side of the staircase in ways that would not be possible without the railings. Whether the railings in such circumstances have on balance enlarged or diminished my overall liberty is not a question with an answer too obvious to require any further investigation.

What is more, in situations of anomalous or adaptive preferences, any number of humanly imposed restrictions on freedom might not induce displeasure even though they are objectively detrimental and stifling. Indeed, a key reason for the negative-liberty theorists' insistence on the desire-independence of the existence of any particular unfreedoms is the very fact that some people become enamoured of countless constraints on what they can do and be and become. The spectre of contented slaves who feel no unhappiness over their shackles is what spurs negative-liberty theorists to highlight the potential division between trammels and resented trammels. Although slaves are usually far from contented, the possibility of contentment on their part is real and intelligible, and it must be acknowledged by any satisfactory theory of freedom. Less prodigious instances of adaptive preferences are not only possible but are also frequently actual. Because people do quite often adapt wholeheartedly to the limits placed on them by other people, an absence of resentment is not an adequate indicator of the absence of those limits—especially when the limits are beneficial, of course, but even when objectively they are harmfully confining.

Thus, if we are to associate the distinction between humanly caused obstacles and naturally caused obstacles with the distinction between resentment and a lack of resentment, the first half of the first of these distinctions must encompass only certain types of humanly caused obstacles: those which are perceived as harmful, especially but not exclusively those which are imposed maliciously or negligently or officiously.[5] (Although innocent unawareness on the part of someone who inflicts an injury will often avert resentment, it will not always do so. Suppose that John successfully courts Karen, with whom Peter has long been in love. Even if Peter recognizes that John had no grounds for knowing of his own feelings toward Karen, he might nonetheless

---

[5] An especially restrictive approach along these lines is adopted by Philip Pettit. See for example his 'On *Republicanism*: Reply to Carter, Christman and Dagger', 9/3 *The Good Society* 54, 55 (2000). For a more expansive variant of the same basic approach, see Bernard Williams, 'From Freedom to Liberty: The Construction of a Political Value', 30 *Philosophy and Public Affairs* 3 (2001). Cf. Stanley Benn, *A Theory of Freedom* (Cambridge: Cambridge University Press,

credibly feel resentment toward John.) Other humanly caused impediments—those which are not perceived as harmful, and those which are perceived as harmful but excusable—will have to be assimilated to the impediments imposed by natural forces. Now, although such an approach may be meritorious in certain respects, it clearly does not amount to a justification for ascribing special importance to humanly caused constraints generally. At most, it justifies the ascription of special importance to a subset of those constraints. That is, a focus on resentment cannot bear the justificatory burden that would be laid upon it by my formula for the measurement of overall freedom.

Indeed, such a conclusion is warranted not only because many humanly imposed restrictions on freedom arouse no resentment, but also because many natural restrictions do provoke the indignation of the people affected. To be sure, assertions to the contrary are not uncommon in the philosophical literature on freedom. Philip Pettit, for example, declares: 'We see only human beings as worthy of reactions like resentment and gratitude. To feel such reactions towards natural phenomena like the weather... or even towards non-human animals and their doings is, so most of us think, quite inappropriate.'[6] Pettit's confident employment of first-person plural pronouns is not sufficient to substantiate his claims. Perhaps hostile reactive attitudes toward animals are not very magnanimous, but they are frequently harboured. For example, when the ass of the soothsayer Balaam refused to proceed straight ahead on her journey with her master, he thrice beat her and screamed that 'you have made sport of me. I wish I had a sword in my hand, for then I would kill you'.[7] Resentment in response to inanimate natural phenomena is likewise quite common. As anyone familiar with the Book of Job will have gathered, people who believe in God or gods can become bitterly enraged at natural afflictions which they perceive as instances of divine persecution.

1988), 126, 133: '[B]ecause the concept of personal freedom is most at home in the context of complaints, grievances, claims, and justifications, this distinction [between unfreedom and mere inability] clarifies when someone's inability to φ will sustain at most a regret that he cannot do it, and when it can properly be the subject of a complaint that he is unfree to do it... [T]he primary functions of the concept of freedom in practical discourse [are] as a counter for expressing grievances, claiming rights, and defending interests.'

  [6] Philip Pettit, *A Theory of Freedom* (Cambridge: Polity Press, 2001), 13. For a classic expression of the view that reactive attitudes such as resentment are unique to interpersonal dealings, see P. F. Strawson, 'Freedom and Resentment', in *Freedom and Resentment and Other Essays* (London: Methuen, 1974), 1, especially at 9.
  [7] Numbers 22:29.

Similarly, even agnostics or atheists can fulminate against the indiscriminate harshness of the natural world when they have been divested of sundry freedoms by the ravages of floods or earthquakes or hurricanes or lightning bolts or tornados. Tirades against the indifference of the forces of nature toward human well-being and suffering are not confined to believers, by any means. In short, the distinction between resentment-eliciting trammels and resignation-eliciting trammels is only contingently correlated on each of its sides with the distinction between humanly induced trammels and naturally induced trammels. Consequently, however important the former distinction undoubtedly is, it hardly constitutes a suitable foundation for the latter.

Given that we almost certainly cannot succeed in our efforts to locate a non-circular justification for the attribution of special importance to the curbs on freedom that are products of human actions, we must rely on a justification that is ultimately circular. To say as much, however, is not to say that we must settle for a gross begging of the question. Arguments can still be marshalled to highlight the unacceptability of the stance adopted by theorists who contend that each person's overall liberty is to be measured with reference only to the numerator of my fraction (rather than with reference to the entire fraction).

Our measurements of overall liberty should be guided by the entirety of my fraction because we thereby acknowledge the relevant domain within which the enterprise of measurement is carried out: the domain of social and political philosophy. That domain covers the vast matrix of human interrelationships, which has been recognized as a distinctive object of investigation and reflection since ancient times. To come to grips with that matrix adequately, we must measure everyone's overall liberty not merely by gauging the range of the combinations-of-opportunities open to each person, but more complicatedly by also ascertaining the ratio between that range and the full range that would be available to each person in the absence of impediments caused by the actions of other people. By perceiving that what each person *can* do is a subset of what each person *could* do in the absence of the aforementioned impediments, and by taking that subset (expressed as a percentage) as a key element of the extent of each person's overall freedom, we emphasize that the humanly shaped aspects of the world are especially important components of the multifarious array of constraints within which the overall freedom of each person is possessed. Humanly imposed constraints do not only delimit the field of everyone's overall freedom as external boundaries—in the manner of natural constraints—but also cut into that field in a role that is accentuatedly diminutional rather than merely non-augmentative. We should single out the humanly imposed constraints as especially important because our questions about the extent of each person's overall freedom are broached within social and political philosophy. That is, although each such question of course concerns the range expressed in the numerator of my fraction, it also distinctively concerns the extent to which that range has been curtailed by the actions of other people. When we ask how free somebody is, we certainly are asking how many combinations of opportunities are open to him or her, but we are also asking how many combinations of opportunities have been closed off to him or her by the actions of other people. Precisely because our 'how free' question includes the latter inquiry, it arises within the realm of social and political philosophy rather than solely within the realm of physics and engineering.

No doubt, everything said in the last paragraph is ultimately question-begging. As has already been suggested, there is very likely not any way of taking a stand on the chief point at issue here—namely, on the question whether our calculations of each person's overall liberty should attach a special importance to the restrictions on freedom that have been caused by other people's actions—without presupposing the conclusion for which one is endeavouring to argue. Nonetheless, even if there is no wholesale escape from circularity in this dispute, the unappealing implications of the opposing side's stand can certainly be highlighted. Consider, for example, a scenario involving Melvin and Mildred. Melvin lives in some society *A* while Mildred lives in some society *B*, but each of them enjoys the same range of combinations of conjunctively exercisable freedoms as is enjoyed by the other. However, far more of the restrictions on the range enjoyed by Melvin are due to the actions of other people (not least the actions of governmental officials), whereas far more of the restrictions on the range enjoyed by Mildred are due to the operations of natural phenomena. For instance, whereas Mildred suffers from a natural incapacity that prevents her from walking for more than a few hundred meters, Melvin despite his natural physical robustness is persistently prevented by other people from walking for more than a few hundred meters. Now, in so far as theorists aim to gauge the overall liberty of each person by reference to the numerator alone in my fraction—rather than by reference to the full fraction—they are logically committed to the view that Melvin and Mildred enjoy exactly the same amount of overall liberty. Quite irrelevant in the eyes of the proponents of such a view is the fact that Melvin's opportunities are cabined much more severely by the actions of other people than are Mildred's opportunities. Having elided the distinction between naturally caused obstacles and humanly caused obstacles, these theorists have to maintain that the answer to a 'how free' question is precisely the same for Melvin as for Mildred.

To be sure, if these theorists were engineers interested only in the sheer physical latitude of human beings and levers, their way of calculating the overall freedom of Melvin and of Mildred would be appropriate. However, given that they are philosophers who purport to address matters of social and political philosophy, the conclusion about Melvin and Mildred that follows from their approach to the measurement of each person's overall freedom is a reason for rejecting that approach. Their conclusion about Melvin and Mildred completely obfuscates the special importance, for social and political philosophy, of the ways in which human conduct shapes the environments wherein people act and decide and develop. The conclusion reached by these theorists will have lumped together all obstacles, notwithstanding that a social/political philosopher who asks a 'how free' question about Melvin or Mildred has thereby posed an inquiry that discriminates among obstacles. Such an inquiry is in part distinctively about the extent to which the latitude of Melvin or Mildred is hemmed in by constraints that are attributable to the actions of other people. If we are to capture that dimension of the question, we shall have to concentrate on the entirety of my freedom-measuring fraction rather than only on its numerator.

1.2. Squaring the Numerator

In so far as social and political philosophers wish to focus exclusively on the numerator of my fraction, they are unacceptably neglecting the distinctive importance of the restrictions on each person's freedom that have been caused by other people's actions; but they are correct in sensing that the parameter expressed in the numerator is itself the dominant factor in each person's overall liberty. On the one hand, as has just been argued, a question about the overall liberty of anybody is always about the full ratio expressed in my fraction. When we ask how free some person is, we are asking not only about his combinations of conjunctively exercisable opportunities, but also distinctively about the limits placed on those combinations of opportunities by other people. The point of such a question—when posed by social and political philosophers—is to know how much has been closed off to a person by the actions of other people, as well as to know how much remains open to the person. On the other hand, the latter aspect of the question's point (that is, learning how much remains open to a person) is undoubtedly the primary aspect. Social and political philosophers should strive to ascertain the relative extent of the combinations of pathways that are withheld from each person by the actions and dispositions-to-perform-actions of other people, but they should even more keenly strive to ascertain the sheer range of the combinations of pathways that are available to each person.

Precisely because that range is the principal parameter to be gauged in our calculations of each person's overall freedom, the numerator of my fraction has to be squared. To say as much, of course, is equivalent to saying that the figure which specifies the aforementioned range must be multiplied by the following ratio: the ratio between that range itself and the full array of combinations of conjunctively exercisable opportunities that would be available to a person if all such combinations currently foreclosed by the actions of other people were open to her without removing any of the combinations that are now available. In other words, in the notation introduced near the outset of this chapter, $F^2/(F+U) = F \times F/(F+U)$. Through the multiplication of F by $F/(F+U)$, we lay paramount emphasis on each person's combinations of conjunctively exercisable freedoms. After all, the figure specifying the range of those combinations is the whole of the multiplicand and is a key component of the multiplier. At the same time, our multiplication effectively diminishes that figure to reflect the fact that the specified range coexists with a medley of combinations of consistent unfreedoms. The diminution as a percentage is equivalent to the ratio between the latter set of combinations and the two sets together. Thus, for example, if 40 per cent of the combinations of pathways comprised by those two sets are unavailable to a person because of the actions of other people—that is, if the range of a person's combinations of consistent unfreedoms is 40 per cent as large as the sum of that range itself plus the range of her combinations of conjunctively exercisable liberties—the figure representing the *available* combinations of pathways will be diminished by 40 per cent to yield the figure that represents the person's overall liberty. Were we not to effect such a reduction for the purpose of our calculations, we would neglect a factor that has an important bearing on any 'how free' question raised by social and political philosophers. That factor, of course, is the imposition of curbs on each person's liberty by the actions of other people. Contrariwise, we would exaggerate the importance of that factor if we were to go further by declining to square the numerator in my fraction. Squaring the numerator is the optimal way of acknowledging the centrality of the parameter expressed therein, while also acknowledging (through the retention of the denominator) that the existence of unfreedoms is something which must be reflected in our measurements of each person's overall liberty.

As will be seen presently, the squaring of the numerator in my fraction enables us to overcome some serious problems that would otherwise plague one's efforts to measure freedom by reference to that fraction. First, however, we should look at a crude example that will help to illuminate and underscore the general appropriateness of the squaring of the numerator. Let us consider a modified version of the scenario of Melvin and Mildred, with some accompanying numbers. Suppose that the range of the combinations of conjunctively exercisable freedoms available to Melvin can be represented as 12, and that the range of the combinations of consistent unfreedoms confronting him can be represented as 8.[8] Suppose further that the former range for Mildred can be represented as 6 and that the latter range for her can be represented as 4. We can straightaway conclude that Melvin is twice as free overall as is Mildred. By contrast, were the numerator in each of the relevant fractions not squared, our measurement of each person's overall freedom as a ratio would lead us to the conclusion that Mildred enjoys exactly the same degree of overall freedom as Melvin. Such a conclusion would slight the primary importance of the disparity between the numerators, which obviously represents a disparity between the arrays of alternatives open to Melvin and Mildred respectively. If that discrepancy between those arrays is to be captured adequately in our calculations, the numerator in each fraction will have to be squared. In other words, the figure representing the range of the combinations of conjunctively exercisable freedoms enjoyed by each person is not only the first term in a relevant ratio, but is also itself a multiplicand to be multiplied by that very ratio. The status of that figure as a separate multiplicand is indicative of the fact that the range which it represents is the foremost object of attention in our measurements of each person's overall freedom. (Note incidentally that, when the respective situations of Melvin and Mildred are accurately represented by the numbers specified above, my conclusion about their relative levels of overall freedom—my conclusion that Melvin is twice as free overall as is Mildred—will also be reached by someone

---

[8] What exactly is represented by '12' or '8'? As will be explained later, '12' represents the summed weights of all the combinations comprised by the range of Melvin's combinations of conjunctively exercisable liberties, while '8' represents the summed weights of all the combinations comprised by the range of his combinations of consistent unfreedoms. How the weights are to be determined is likewise a question that will be answered later.

who concentrates only on the numerators of the relevant fractions. After all, 12 is exactly twice as large as 6. However, if the numbers were changed slightly, my approach and the unfreedom-disregarding approach would no longer converge. For example, suppose that the range of the combinations of consistent unfreedoms confronting Mildred should be represented as 2 rather than as 4. The unfreedom-disregarding approach will still generate the verdict that Melvin is twice as free overall as Mildred, whereas my approach will now yield a contrary verdict. Though Melvin certainly still enjoys greater freedom overall than Mildred under my analysis, the ratio between their levels of freedom is now 7.2/4.5, that is, 8/5.)

In sum, the squaring of the numerator in the freedom-measuring fraction gives due recognition to the paramountcy of the squared parameter in our measurements of each person's overall liberty, without obliterating the importance of the distinction between naturally imposed constraints and humanly imposed constraints. In addition, the squaring of the numerator enables us to circumvent or defuse certain difficulties that would be formidable if the numerator were not squared. Let us explore two such cruxes.

Suppose that Gertrude is undertaking some speleological investigations. While walking around in a small cave, she is trapped by a natural landslide. Unable to get out, she has to remain within the cave's cramped confines. Now, according to the U Postulate, she is not unfree in any respect. She is not unfree to do or remain or become or undergo anything, because she cannot be unfree in any of those ways unless every set of conditions minimally sufficient to prevent her from doing or remaining or becoming or undergoing something is a set that includes some action(s) or disposition(s)-to-perform-some-action(s) on the part of some other person(s). Since it is not the case that every minimally sufficient set of preventive conditions does encompass some action(s) or disposition(s)-to-perform-some-action(s) on the part of some other person(s), however, Gertrude is merely not-free rather than unfree. Whatever she is thwarted from doing or remaining or becoming or undergoing, she is thwarted from doing or remaining or becoming or undergoing by sets of conditions that include only natural forces and natural limitations without any action(s) or disposition(s)-to-perform-some-action(s) on the part of any other person(s). Of course, she unquestionably is also prevented from doing many things by sets of conditions that encompass the actions and dispositions of other people, but she is not prevented *only* by sets that include such elements. Also precluding her from doing any of those things is the fact that she remains trapped by the soil and rocks that have blocked the exit from the cave. Because of her immurement in the cave by natural forces, the first prong of the U Postulate will not be satisfied whenever we inquire whether any of her inabilities should be classified as unfreedoms. Consequently, as has been stated, her situation is devoid of unfreedom. Hence, if we were to calculate her overall liberty by reference to my fraction without squaring its numerator, we would have to conclude that she enjoys perfect liberty: a ratio of 1/1 (the figure in the numerator divided by itself, since the sum in the denominator would consist of that figure plus zero). No one else's overall freedom could ever attain to a higher ratio, and virtually everyone else's overall freedom would consist in a lower ratio. Accordingly, in any ranking of people based on the varying degrees of liberty that they enjoy, Gertrude trapped in a small cave would be at the pinnacle. She would be a paradigmatic instance of a truly free person. To avoid such a ludicrous assessment of her situation, we have to square the numerator in my fraction whenever we measure someone's overall freedom. So long as we take such a step, we shall almost certainly find that most people enjoy higher levels of freedom—indeed, much higher levels— than does Gertrude. What this example vividly reveals is that, if we were to rely on my fraction with an unsquared numerator, we would be woefully failing to grasp that the dominant factor in the overall liberty of each person is the range of the combinations-of-conjunctively-exercisable-freedoms available to him or her. Because that range is very small for Gertrude, her overall liberty is severely constricted. Although the combinations of consistent unfreedoms that confront each person do have an important bearing on his or her overall freedom, they are of secondary importance. Unless we recognize that that latter factor is only of subordinate importance—and therefore unless we recognize that the principal element of anyone's overall liberty is the range of her combinations of conjunctively exercisable freedoms— we shall arrive at ridiculous judgements when we look at situations such as that of Gertrude. Squaring the numerator in the freedom-measuring fraction is the key to a principled repudiation of those risible judgements.

Another conundrum that must be handled by any satisfactory project of measuring each person's overall freedom as a ratio has been perceptively highlighted by Martin van Hees.[9] Van Hees recounts a couple of scenarios to illustrate the basic problem that he has discerned; we shall here probe a modified version of the more trouble-

---

[9] Martin van Hees, *Legal Reductionism and Freedom* (Dordrecht: Kluwer, 2000), 123, 132–3.

some of those scenarios. Suppose that some illness incapacitates its victims and prevents them from ever walking again. Let us presume that there are 100,000 people who suffer from this illness, each of whom would be capable of walking again if the malady could be cured. Now suppose that some scientists have at last come up with a cure for the incapacitating disease. However, because several of the ingredients in the curative medication are extremely rare, and because for several years (and perhaps for ever) there will not be any means of producing those ingredients artificially, only 100 effective doses of the medication can be prepared. Let us assume that every one of the sufferers of the disease has been informed of this medical break-through, and let us assume highly credibly that each of them will desire and strive to get one of the doses. We can also assume that each of them has an equal opportunity to get a dose, since the government that sponsored the research has elected to distribute the doses free of charge to the 100 sufferers whose names are drawn in a lottery. Once the lottery has taken place and the doses have been distributed and admin-istered, of course, 100 erstwhile victims of the disease will each have regained the freedom-to-walk, while 99,900 less fortunate people will remain unable to use their legs. Before the lottery has been held, then, the probability that any particular victim will regain his freedom-to-walk is one in one thousand or 0.001, and the probability that any particular victim will remain unable to walk is 0.999. Let us initially concentrate on the pre-lottery stage as we ponder this example.

On the one hand, there is no doubt that this scenario is troubling for anyone who maintains that the overall socio-political freedom of each person should be measured as a ratio that takes account of unfreedoms. Van Hees has deftly unearthed a genuine problem. On the other hand, the very aspect of the scenario that makes it so vexing is much less problematic when the numerator in the freedom-measuring fraction is squared. To see as much, we must first look carefully at the crux posed by the scenario.

Throughout the pre-lottery period, each victim of the disease has a 0.001 chance of acquiring a host of new freedoms and a 0.999 chance of incurring a host of new unfreedoms. (The new unfreedoms, if they are incurred, will not be new inabilities. Instead, they are pre-existent inabilities that will no longer be due purely to natural causes but will now be due partly to the actions and dispositions-to-perform-actions of other people. They will have changed from mere inabilities into unfreedoms. Of course, omissions are obviously involved as well in the withholding of the medication from any invalid who does not prevail in the lottery. Omissions are never in themselves sources of unfreedom.

However, the omissions are here combined with actions and dispositions-to-perform-actions, as the governmental officials in control of the medication are fully prepared to block all efforts by any invalid or his relatives to obtain an unauthorized dose.) Hence, although the potential new combinations of conjunctively exercisable freedoms and the potential new combinations of consistent unfreedoms will be extensionally equivalent, the figure representing each set of combinations will carry far greater weight in the denominator of my freedom-measuring fraction than in the numerator. Whereas that figure in the numerator will be precipitously reduced by a stringent probabilistic qualification, it will not be reduced at all in the denominator—because it will be apportioned between the two elements of the denominator, with a stringent probabilistic qualification and a light probabilistic qualification that will add up to 1. Thus, the development of medical science will effectively have reduced the overall liberty of each victim of the disease, even while creating new opportunities for the acquisition of countless freedoms and combinations of freedoms. Such is the counter-intuitive conclusion that presses itself on theorists who seek to measure the overall freedom of anyone as a ratio. That is, because of the role of probabilities in our calculations (a role that will be examined further in this chapter), such theorists – including me – have to accept that the availability of new opportunities can sometimes decrease the overall liberty of a person who is faced with those opportunities.

If the numerator in the freedom-measuring fraction were left unsquared, the difficulty just outlined would be especially disconcerting when the figure which accurately represents the range of an invalid's potential new combinations of conjunctively exercisable opportunities is very large. (That figure, of course, also represents the range of his potential new combinations of consistent unfreedoms.) Suppose, for example, that that figure is 2 million. In that event, we would be adding 2 million to the denominator of the fraction and only 2,000 to the numerator. Given that in those circumstances each person suffering from the disease has a small chance of vastly expanding his range of abilities and no chance of losing any of his current abilities, the huge disparity between the addition to the numerator and the addition to the denominator is outlandish. Should we really subscribe to the preposterous notion that any sufferer in such a situation has undergone a sharp impairment of his overall freedom? Fortunately, that notion can and must be rejected when the numerator in the freedom-measuring fraction is squared, as it should be. Instead of adding 2,000 to the numerator, we shall be adding more than 4 million. (Because the numerator is squared all at once, each of the components thereof is multiplied not only by itself but simultaneously by every other component. Accordingly, an addition of 2,000 to the pre-squared numerator will increase the squared numerator by more than 4 million, since the pre-squared figure for each victim of the disease has previously been greater than zero. Given that the previous figure has almost certainly been far greater than zero, the increase in the squared numerator will almost certainly be far greater than 4 million.)

To be sure, the salutary impact of the squaring of the numerator will be less substantial when the figure representing the potential new combinations of conjunctively exercisable freedoms is lower. (The figure will vary in relation to the curative potency of the medication and in relation to the innate capacities of each victim; but, largely for ease of exposition, those sources of variability can be put aside here as we focus on the role of probabilistic qualifications.) Nevertheless, even when the figure is very low—reduced by a stringent probabilistic qualification to a level below 1—the squaring of the numerator will usually ensure that the potential availability of the new combinations of freedoms is measured by us as an augmentation of the level of each invalid's overall liberty. Because the figure that represents the potential new combinations and the figure for the rest of the pre-squared numerator will add up to more than 1 even after any probabilistic discounting, the smallness of the figure for the new combinations after such discounting is consistent with quite a substantial increase in the squared numerator as a whole.

Of course, to say that the squaring of the numerator will usually produce the outcome described in the last paragraph is not to say that it will always guarantee the occurrence of such an outcome. Suppose that the probability of attaining the new combinations of conjunctively exercisable freedoms is staggeringly small for each invalid. Perhaps there is only one effective dose of medication for a disease that afflicts 80 million people, and the recipient of the one dose is to be selected by a lottery. In respect of such a situation, the disparity between the impact of the probabilistic qualification in the numerator of the freedom-measuring fraction and the impact of the probabilistic qualifications in the denominator will very likely outweigh the salutary effects of the squaring of the numerator. In such circumstances, then, the prospect of acquiring the new combinations of freedoms will have lowered each invalid's overall liberty. Now, let us note that each invalid in such circumstances will face a vanishingly small chance of gaining new combinations of freedoms and an overwhelmingly high chance of incurring new combinations of consistent unfreedoms. Hence, the only thing odd about registering this emergent state of affairs as a reduction in each sick person's overall liberty is that any new unfreedoms arising from the development of a cure will not consist in new inabilities; what has changed is not the existence of those inabilities but the causal responsibility for them. Still, as has been argued in the preceding subsection, our measurements of anybody's overall liberty should be inflected by the fact that some of his inabilities are caused by other people's actions and dispositions-to-perform-actions. The correct answer to a 'how free' question about any person will partly depend on the extent to which other people's actions have been causally responsible for the framework of constraints within which the person leads his life. One central concern (albeit only one central concern) of such a question is specifically the degree to which a person has been impeded or left unimpeded by other people. If we are to capture the distinctive importance of humanly imposed constraints, we shall have to put up with some mildly odd results in a small proportion of van Heesian situations—results whose strangeness is kept firmly in check, at any rate, by the squaring of the numerator in the freedom-measuring fraction.

Of course, once the situation of the invalids in the original scenario has moved to the post-lottery stage, the squaring of the numerator will no longer make any difference to the change that we measure in the overall liberty of each invalid whose name has not been drawn. Between the time before the medication has been developed and the time after the 100 doses of the medication have been administered to the lottery winners, each ill person not fortunate enough to receive a dose will have undergone a substantial reduction in his overall freedom. The range of his combinations of conjunctively exercisable freedoms will be the same at the later time as at the earlier time—which is why the squaring of the numerator does not make a difference to the change that we measure—but the range of his combinations of consistent unfreedoms will have enlarged considerably between those two junctures. Moreover, as has been suggested, that latter range will have expanded significantly even though none of the sufferers of the disease has acquired any new inabilities. Now, although this verdict delivered by one's measurement of each person's overall liberty as a ratio is admittedly rather counter-intuitive, it conveys in this peculiar context the distinctive importance of the fact that certain inabilities of a person are due to other people's actions. Furthermore, the strangeness of the verdict is due largely to the way in which the example has been constructed. Some prominent features of the example (such as the key role of natural shortages in limiting the number of doses of the medication that can be prepared, and the use of a randomized lottery as the means of selecting the recipients of the doses) have been designed to accentuate the discomfort that might be felt in response to my analysis of the post-lottery situation. If those features are suitably modified, my verdict on the unlucky invalids' lot will seem much more straightforward.

Suppose, for example, that the dearth of effective doses of the medication is due not to any limitations on the availability of the requisite natural resources, but to a deliberate effort by governmental officials to ensure that most of the invalids remain crippled by their illness. Because of medical breakthroughs and the abundant presence of the materials needed for the manufacture of the medication, doses sufficiently numerous to cure all the sufferers of the disease could be produced without great expense. Nevertheless, the officials in charge of the research withhold this information and instead convey the impression that, because of a paucity of essential natural resources, only 100 doses of the medication can be prepared. Perhaps the officials (or their administrative superiors) feel that many of the people debilitated by the disease are potentially subversive and dangerous, and that they should therefore be kept in an enfeebled condition that reduces their harmfulness. Or perhaps the officials want a large pool of incapacitated victims of the disease as subjects for future medical experimentation. Whatever may be the nefarious purpose that lies behind the dissimulation and the calculated refusal to help people who could in fact quite readily be cured, that refusal preserves their inabilities which are thereby transformed from mere inabilities into unfreedoms. The invalids now are invalids not merely because of natural forces, but largely because of the actions and dispositions-to-perform-actions of other people. (Though omissions are obviously implicated here as well, the machinations of the officials are actions, and their readiness to do what is necessary to ensure the success of those machinations is crucial for their malign enterprise—just as the readiness of the police and other people to prevent criminals from stealing goods with impunity is crucial for the secure ownership of those goods.) In these circumstances, where the continued incapacitation of each uncured victim of the illness is due to the actions of other people, it is more specifically due to the ruthless and deceitful actions of other people. As a consequence, we should feel no unease about measuring each victim's overall liberty in a way that takes account of his plight as an array of unfreedoms. Indeed, if a reply to a 'how free' question about each victim does not characterize his plight in that fashion, it will *pro tanto* be an inadequate reply. The fact that no victim has incurred any new inabilities is beside the point.

Now, the modified version of the van Heesian example should certainly not lead us to infer that actions which produce unfreedom must be malicious or even that they must be deliberate. As has been argued in previous chapters, a person's inabilities are unfreedoms if they are causally attributable to *any* actions performed by other people. The domain of political and social philosophy comprehends all the interrelationships among people constituted by their sundry doings, whether those doings be malevolent or benign, and whether they be intentional or inadvertent. That domain patently encompasses all supportive and cooperative endeavours, and it likewise plainly includes the wholly unforeseen consequences of people's actions; to a large extent, in fact, the institutions of socio-political life are composed of such endeavours and such consequences. Hence, since the divide between unfreedoms and mere inabilities is defined by reference to the domain of political and social philosophy, it is not the case that an action must be calculated or evil to qualify as a potential source of unfreedom. What we should instead infer from the modified van Heesian example, then, is that any unease felt in connection with my analysis of the original version of that example is due to inessential factors that do not impinge on the basic character of the depicted situation. Those factors—such as the salient causal role of natural shortages in limiting the quantity of the available medication, and the randomness of the procedure for selecting people to be cured—do not affect the status of each uncured person's continued incapacitation as a condition caused in part by the actions and dispositions-to-perform-actions of other people. Because the continued incapacitation is so caused, it is correctly classified as a state of unfreedom. Accordingly, the sets of particular inabilities arising from that state are combinations of consistent unfreedoms that must be entered into the denominator of the freedom-measuring fraction when we gauge each invalid's overall liberty.

At any rate, although the squaring of the numerator in that fraction does not have a bearing on my analysis of the contrast between the overall freedom of each uncured person in the period prior to the development of the medication and the overall freedom of each such person in the period after the administration of all the attainable doses, it does have a highly salutary bearing on one's efforts to gauge the overall freedom of people in countless contexts. It enables us to avert or transcend a number of snags that would gravely weaken the cogency of any measurements carried out on the basis of my fraction with an unsquared numerator. Even more important, it enables us to gauge each person's situation in a way that is accurately responsive to the point of a 'how free' question. An appropriate answer to such a question about anyone must reflect the range of the combinations-of-conjunctively-exercisable-freedoms which he enjoys, but it must do so only to a certain extent—namely, to the precise extent of the ratio between that range and the range of the combinations of conjunctively exercisable freedoms that would be enjoyed by him if all of his current combinations of such freedoms were retained while his combinations of consistent unfreedoms were surmounted. Let us henceforth symbolize the former range as 'R_1' and the latter as 'R_2'. By measuring R_1 as a proportion of R_2, we ascertain the degree to which the former is to count as the property which we designate as somebody's overall socio-political freedom. On the one hand, somewhat like the theorists such as Cohen whose position I contested in the preceding subsection, we should deem R_1 to be a crucial factor in itself as the central constituent of a person's overall liberty. On the other hand, to give due weight to unfreedoms as aspects of the socio-political environment in which any combinations of conjunctively exercisable freedoms are available, R_1 should be classified as a person's overall liberty only to the extent specified above. If when confronted with a 'how free' question we wish to join Cohen in highlighting the importance of R_1, and if when confronted with such a question we wish to join Steiner and Carter in highlighting the status of R_1 as a subset of R_2, then we should answer the question by bringing together those two factors—the figure for R_1, and the ratio of R_1/R_2—as a multiplicand and a multiplier. In other words, we arrive at a figure for the overall freedom of a person by reducing the figure for the person's R_1 to reflect the extent to which his R_1 falls short of exhausting his R_2. We shall thereby have captured both the insight motivating the approach favoured by Cohen and the equally sound insight motivating the approach favoured by Steiner and Carter.

1.3. Size Matters

Having looked at some of the broad characteristics of my freedom-measuring fraction, we should now probe in greater depth the means by which that fraction is to be applied (in principle, though undoubtedly not yet in practice). Let us begin with a problem that has often been perceived as an especially formidable obstacle to the measurement of anyone's overall liberty.[10] How are particular freedoms and

[10] See for example Will Kymlicka, *Contemporary Political Philosophy* (Oxford: Clarendon Press, 1990) [Kymlicka, *Contemporary*], 140–1; Onora O'Neill, 'The Most Extensive Liberty', 80 *Proceedings of the Aristotelian Society* 45, 50 (1979).

unfreedoms individuated, so that we can apprehend the number and sizes of the combinations-of-conjunctively-exercisable-freedoms and of the combinations-of-consistent-unfreedoms over which my fraction quantifies?

As Carter has astutely recognized,[11] the key to dealing adequately with this problem lies in taking a step similar to one of the steps taken in my fourth chapter's discussion of the act/omission distinction. That is, we have to come up with spatio-temporal units by dividing space analytically into finite regions and time analytically into finite stretches. We likewise have to divide objects, most notably the bodies of human beings, analytically into units of matter. A project of measuring any person's overall liberty, then, will consist in ascertaining the sets of spatial regions that can be occupied by his body and by concomitant objects during some specified span of time. Some of the available patterns of the positioning of his body and concomitant objects in the spatial regions over time are movements of various sorts, and some are instances of stationariness. If we know the combinations-of-such-patterns among which a person can select, then we know the range of his combinations of conjunctively exercisable freedoms. And if we know the sundry combinations-of-such-patterns that are closed off to a person by dint of other people's actions, then we know the range of his combinations of consistent unfreedoms. Carter admirably summarizes the basic technique that underlies the measurement of freedom:

[W]e need to divide space and time into equally sized units, and matter into equally sized units that are at least as small as the units of space. Depending on their size, physical objects will then consist in varying numbers of units of matter, and what we shall be interested in measuring is, for any particular unit of matter, the number of space-time units in which it might be located ... [W]e shall be counting possible 'occupyings'. Space and time must be thought of as an immobile *grid*, made up of a finite series of spatio-temporal *regions*. A physical object of a standard volume can then be seen as a potential occupant of one or another spatio-temporally fixed region.[12]

If an irresistible impetus completely overpowers a person during a given stretch of time, then the spatial regions through which his body passes are the only set of spatial units which he is able to occupy during that time. Much the same can be said about a person who has been rendered thoroughly immobile. During the period of incapacitation, the spatial regions in which his stationary body is located are the only

---

[11] Ian Carter, *A Measure of Freedom* (Oxford: Oxford University Press, 1999) [Carter, *Measure*], 183–8.

[12] Carter, *Measure*, 184, emphases in original.

array of spatial units that he is capable of occupying. By contrast, whenever a person does enjoy a certain degree of choice concerning the positioning of his body and concomitant objects during some span of time, he will be able to select among sets of spatial regions in which he can locate the various units of matter. The range of the combinations-of-regions open to him for occupation is the range of his combinations of conjunctively exercisable freedoms during that span. Conversely, the range of the combinations-of-regions shut off to him by the actions of other people is the range of his combinations of consistent unfreedoms during the specified period.

Something that will probably spring to the mind of the reader straightaway is the question of how large the elementary spatial regions and temporal spans should be. What are the units of our measurements? Three preliminary observations will lead into a reply to this question. First, the optimal size for each uniform region or span will vary in accordance with the purposes of our analyses. Astronomers do not preposterously measure the distance between the Milky Way and other galaxies in inches, and someone endeavouring to gauge levels of socio-political freedom must likewise opt for units of measurement that are suited to his or her specific aims. In a lot of ordinary contexts, where we are not even attempting to engage in comprehensive surveys of people's freedoms and unfreedoms, and where we instead are carrying out some quite narrowly focused comparisons or enquiries that allow us to leave most freedoms/unfreedoms out of any direct consideration, we can happily avail ourselves of units of measurement that would be unacceptably coarse and imprecise in certain other contexts. Indeed, most discussions of the various scenarios propounded by philosophers who write about socio-political freedom are guided by just such rough-hewn units of measurement. As we can infer from the nature of those discussions, the fine-grained exactitude required for systematic measurements and comparisons is not similarly necessary for many other purposes—even for many other purposes of philosophers in the course of writing on these topics. As Carter correctly remarks, our spatio-temporal units should be 'smaller than any of the distances of the movements (or differences in sizes of objects) that we are interested in measuring'. He continues: 'But the only absolute requirement . . . is that the space-time units be of an equal size. This equal size might be increased for practical purposes, as long as one is aware that the measurements one is producing increase in roughness along with increases in the size of the units.'[13] In short,

---

[13] Carter, *Measure*, 186.

although minute precision is essential for the success of some projects, it is often dispensable. Indeed, it would sometimes be a distracting encumbrance—if our units of measurement were ludicrously smaller than what our purposes would require. Hence, to insist on minute precision in an appropriate context, as I shortly shall, is not to make the mistake of insisting on it in all contexts.

Second, my concern throughout this chapter is to indicate how the measurement of each person's overall freedom can and should proceed in principle. Practical obstacles to the implementation of systematic measurements are not addressed herein. My aim is not to suggest that a project involving comprehensive measurements and comparisons will be feasible in practice; instead, my aim is to show that there are no conceptual or theoretical barriers to a project of that sort. The conceptual coherence of such a project, rather than its practical realizability, is what this chapter seeks to uphold. Accordingly, when we endeavour to fix upon a pertinent size for the spatio-temporal units with which we can gauge each person's overall liberty, we should not be swayed at all by the fact that measurements which use very small units might turn out to be unmanageable if we were actually to try to perform them with our current technology. Such considerations are irrelevant to my discussions, which offer general conceptual claims rather than concrete instructions with an eye toward the execution of those instructions. To be sure, given that a scheme of measurement fully suitable in principle for the ascertainment of people's levels of socio-political liberty will very likely not be suitable at present for large-scale practical applications, we should recognize the importance of questions about surrogate metrics that will lend themselves to such applications. If a metric does lend itself to such applications, and if the findings generated by it are reasonable approximations of the findings that would be generated by an ideal scheme of measurement, then it clearly should receive serious attention from political philosophers. Carter does in fact devote considerable attention to metrics that might serve as proxies for an ideal scheme.[14] As he remarks, however, we cannot know whether a metric is a fitting surrogate until we have gained a good sense of the system of calibrations for which we are proposing to substitute it—and until we have satisfied ourselves of that system's coherence. '[T]he choice between [surrogate] metrics will be arbitrary unless we have a standard on the basis of which such a choice is to be made. Any "second-best" metric will be flawed from the start if we do not succeed in refuting the widely raised objection that the quantifica-

---

[14] Carter, *Measure*, 269–87.

tion of [freedoms] is a theoretical non-starter. Approximate measurements are, after all, approximations to *something*.'[15] Thus, while the task of practical implementation is unquestionably a matter that warrants close investigation, the abstract conceptual focus of this chapter is a means of coming to grips with issues that are at least as important. After all, unless we are confident that the objective of measuring each person's overall freedom is coherent at a conceptual level, we cannot be confident that there are any genuine practical issues to be addressed.

Third, when we seek to specify the appropriate size of the spatial regions and temporal spans that make up the grid by reference to which we can conduct systematic measurements and comparisons of people's levels of overall liberty, we should keep in mind the reasons for resorting to such a grid in the first place. The problem to be overcome by one's reliance on a spatio-temporal grid is that of infinite divisibility. Because space and time can analytically be divided into infinitesimally small units, we might seem to have no basis for individuating actions and other occurrences, and we therefore might seem to have no basis for individuating the freedoms that pertain to those actions and occurrences. If we can continue to subdivide spatial regions and temporal stretches indefinitely, we may appear drawn to the conclusion that occurrences and freedoms will prove infinitely numerous and that they will consequently prove insusceptible to being measured through counting. If we had to accept such a conclusion, we would of course likewise have to accept that the enterprise of gauging anyone's overall liberty is chimerical. Because such an enterprise ultimately depends on one's counting of freedoms and combinations of freedoms, it would be irretrievably doomed (in principle as well as in practice) if every process of such counting were inherently subject to hopeless incompletion. Nobody's overall liberty could ever be calculated—not even in principle, much less in practice—and, *a fortiori*, nobody's overall liberty could ever meaningfully be compared with that of anybody else. Clearly, then, we have to repel the threat posed by infinite divisibility. We should do so not by denying that space and time are infinitely divisible (a point that can here remain an open question or even a question with an affirmative answer), but by stipulating that the regions of space and stretches of time which form the grid for our measurements are never infinitesimal in size. Whatever our purposes in any of our enquiries may be, they will always necessitate the use of units of measurement that are not infinitely small. Yet, so long as we do distinguish perspicuously between the infinite divisibility of space or

---

[15] Carter, *Measure*, 171, emphasis in original.

time and the non-infinitesimal size of the aforementioned units, we can in principle embark unproblematically on the task of ascertaining people's levels of overall liberty. As Carter writes: 'While it is true that space and time can in theory be divided up indefinitely, then, the division of space and time into equal finite units allows us to represent what we do as a matter of fact see as the possibility of greater or lesser possibilities of movement. The fact that a finite quantity of space can be divided up indefinitely is not something that stops us from saying that it is greater or smaller than another finite quantity of space.'[16] What should be underscored here is that any size larger than infinitesimalness will suffice to avert the problem of endless divisibility and incompletion. If the aims of some of our analyses require the use of tiny units of measurement, we need not be worried at all. Such an eventuality may of course detract from the practical operationalizability of those analyses, but it will not impair their conceptual coherence. Whereas infinitesimalness is insuperably problematic even at a level of theoretical principle, tininess is not.

Keeping these three preliminary observations prominently in mind, we should now return to the question that triggered them. What is the appropriate size for the calibrations employed in the project of measurement whose coherence this chapter aspires to vindicate? We know that the answer to this question will not preordain or inflect our answers to questions about other projects of measurement, and we similarly know that our reply should not be oriented toward the practical workability—as opposed to the theoretical intelligibility—of the project directly under examination. Equally, we know that the requisite size of each unit of measurement will be untroubling even if it is very small, so long as it is not infinitesimal. Partly on the basis of all these considerations, then, we should perceive that the requisite size will indeed be very small. More specifically, it will have to be small enough to accommodate some extremely important motions such as the laryngeal motions that constitute a person's speaking and the cerebral motions that constitute a person's becoming angry or becoming sad or having certain thoughts. In line with Carter's words (quoted slightly earlier) that our units of measurement should be 'smaller than any of the distances of the movements... that we are interested in measuring', we should divide space and time sufficiently finely to enable us to gauge the extent to which anyone can speak on a variety of topics and develop a variety of emotions and thoughts. If we rely on a coarser grid with spatio-temporal elements too large to be attuned to

[16] Carter, *Measure*, 185.

laryngeal and cerebral motions, we shall overlook many crucial free-doms and unfreedoms; and we shall therefore arrive at distortive estimations of people's levels of overall liberty. Hence, although the exact size of each element in the grid does not have to be specified here, we can know that it will be small indeed.

A handful of potential objections, from differing perspectives, must be parried before we move on. Perhaps the most obvious query is that, if we have recourse to units of measurement small enough to allow us to discriminate among cerebral movements and among laryngeal movements, our efforts to take account of much larger movements will be like the efforts of astronomers who are so addle-headed as to measure distances between galaxies in inches. Faced with an objection along these lines, we should fall back upon all three of my preliminary observations. First, the fact that such minute units are necessary for the comprehensive measurement of everyone's overall liberty does not mean that they are necessary for many less ambitious enquiries and comparisons. Even when our investigations require cardinal measure-ments, the units of the relevant metric can often be much rougher than the units of the ideal metric that would structure a truly thoroughgoing investigation. Of course, sometimes our purposes will require meticu-lous precision approximating that of an ideal set of measurements; but often a considerably less exacting degree of meticulousness will suffice. Thus, everything said here about an ideal set of measurements is fully consistent with the view that any method of enquiry broadly analo-gous to measuring the distances between galaxies in inches would be asinine.

Second, although the need for a grid sufficiently fine-grained to track cerebral and laryngeal motions will doubtless render infeasible the practical implementation of my project of measuring each person's overall freedom, it goes no way toward impairing that project's coher-ence. To acknowledge that the enterprise of measurement would be forbiddingly difficult and unwieldy—too forbiddingly difficult and unwieldy to be undertaken in any full-scale way for quite some time—is decidedly not to concede that it would be impossible in principle. Though the putting of that enterprise into practice with its tiny units of measurement would at present be plainly unmanageable, the enterprise is perfectly sustainable at a theoretical level. And, third, the reason for its theoretical sustainability lies in the difference between tininess and infinitesimalness. Very small though our units of measurement would have to be in any full-scale computation of everyone's overall liberty, they would not be infinitely small. Their minuteness would give rise to daunting practical complexities and gnarls if we actually attempted to engage in such a computation, but it does not give rise to the downright unintelligibility of measurements carried out with infinitely small gradations. Measurements with infinitesimal gradations would be no measurements at all. They would be conceptually impossible. By contrast, although wide-ranging measurements based on my ideal spatio-temporal grid might be practically unmanageable, they would be conceptually impeccable.

Let us turn to quite a different objection, then. Instead of highlighting the infeasibility of a project of systematic measurements with such tiny units, someone might aver that the reason for adopting those units is itself dubious. We must resort to such units because we cannot otherwise take account of laryngeal and cerebral motions when we measure each person's freedom; but, a critic might retort, an effort to take account of such motions in a project of measuring each person's overall freedom is misconceived. Because the potential movements of a person's larynx or of the cells in his brain are so formidably minute in comparison with the potential movements of his body over large distances in sundry directions, the unpreventedness of various laryngeal and cerebral movements does not in itself contribute anything worthy of notice to a person's overall liberty. Any such contribution to a person's physical latitude is trifling, and thus it can very safely be disregarded altogether when we gauge the extent of that latitude. Such is the position affirmed by Carter, for example, in regard to the mental processes of each person: 'Mental acts cannot themselves be members of the set of acts that are taken into account by measurements of overall empirical freedom: even where such acts are conceived in physical terms, their "extensiveness" will be trivial.'[17] He likewise acknowledges that '[f]reedom of speech...would appear to be represented by [Carter's approach to measurement] as contributing very little to our overall freedom, given that the exercising of one's freedom of speech involves only small movements of one's tongue and vocal chords'.[18]

The foregoing objection is coupled by Carter with a related line of argument. He contends that our measurements of people's levels of liberty will in any event give due weight to freedoms of thought and speech, since the removal of any such freedoms would almost inevitably involve the removal of many other freedoms as well. If someone lacks particular freedoms of thought and utterance, he has almost certainly been deprived of much of his overall liberty—because he

[17] Carter, *Measure*, 206.
[18] Carter, *Measure*, 205.

will almost certainly have been deprived of numerous freedoms to use his body in ways that are physically much more far-reaching than laryngeal and cerebral movements. Rarely is it the case that a person's ability to utter particular statements or to experience particular emotions can be eliminated in isolation; in just about any ordinary context, the expunction of such an ability can be accomplished only through the imposition of tight limits on what a person can do. Thus, according to Carter, the vital role of freedoms of speech and freedoms of thought will be registered in our measurements without our having to chart laryngeal and cerebral movements.[19] Hence, he would argue, there is generally no need for units of measurement as fine-grained as I have proposed.

Full replies to these paired Carterian objections will not emerge until the second half of this chapter. In the meantime, let us note the following points. The first of these two most recent objections is correct as far as it goes, but it thereby reveals that the measuring of each person's overall liberty cannot be wholly non-evaluative. As was mentioned at the outset of this chapter, and as will be argued sustainedly later, we have to invoke certain evaluative assumptions when we gauge the extent of the overall freedom of anyone. To be sure, the purely physical dimensions of a person's latitude (and of the humanly imposed curtailments of his latitude) are the primary parameters that must be ascertained in the course of our measuring his overall liberty. Nonetheless, evaluative assumptions play an important role—albeit a subordinate role—in the process of measurement. The existence or non-existence of any particular freedom is strictly a matter of fact, but the level of someone's overall freedom is a partly evaluative phenomenon. So, at least, the latter half of this chapter will argue. On the basis of the arguments therein, we can respond to the first of the Carterian queries by attaching heavy evaluative multipliers to the numerical expressions of any freedoms that are of especially great significance for a typical person who possesses them.

My riposte to the second Carterian line of argument will likewise unfold later. Suffice it for now to say that that line of argument is an *ignoratio elenchi*, and that even on its own terms it does not succeed. In so far as Carter establishes anything with that line of argument, he establishes that someone deprived of freedoms of speech or thought will also have been deprived of many other freedoms. What he needs to establish, however, is quite different. He has to show that the very fact that someone is endowed with a full array of freedoms of speech and

[19] Carter, *Measure*, 205–8.

thought will have added greatly to her overall liberty; yet, given the general tenor and limits of his theory, Carter cannot establish (indeed, cannot with consistency *seek* to establish) that very point. Moreover, as will be remarked subsequently, even the claim for which he does argue—his claim about situations in which people have been deprived of the aforementioned freedoms—is false with reference to some quite credible and important circumstances. In sum, like the first Carterian objection to my position concerning the size of the ideal units of measurement for gauging people's levels of liberty, the second Carterian objection does not deliver any telling blows. It does not supply any reason for a retraction of my thesis that those units should be small enough to register laryngeal and cerebral motions.

1.4. On Interaction

As has just been seen, certain aspects of my approach to the measurement of freedom can fruitfully be developed as responses to some weaknesses in Carter's approach that have been exposed in earlier chapters. His failure to take adequate account of freedoms of thought is something that received attention in my third chapter's discussion of freedoms and unfreedoms that pertain to 'becomings'. Becoming angry or becoming sad is something that a person can be free or unfree to do—irrespective of whether those 'becomings' affect her capacity to perform actions—and our calculations of the person's overall liberty ought to reflect as much.

In the present subsection, we can again take some of the criticisms of Carter within my third chapter as a point of departure. Especially in that chapter's discussion of the freedom-impairing effects of a threatening person's conduct, but also in its discussion of Carter-versus-Cohen on the notion of collective unfreedom, we found that Carter's theory does not satisfactorily handle the potential interaction of people with one another and the potential interaction of people with objects. The problems that we encountered in those portions of Chapter 3 are distinct, and we shall have to ponder them here separately. When we looked at Carter's analysis of threats, we discovered that his analysis has to be supplemented with his account of joint actions; and we likewise discovered that that latter account has to be amplified in some crucial respects. In the present subsection, without a specific focus on threats, we shall consider afresh the amplifications that are needed in his account. Different, though not entirely unrelated, is the lacuna that became apparent when we looked at Carter's remarks on Cohen's concept of collective unfreedom. Because of the general tenor of Carter's theory, his comments on collective unfreedom neglect some major causal consequences of people's choices and actions. To rescue those consequences from obscurity, and to incorporate them properly into our measurements of people's levels of overall freedom, we have to move away from Carter's strictly non-evaluative conception of the freedom-measuring enterprise.

1.4.1. Non-Causal Interaction   Carter certainly takes account of the causal consequences of people's conduct, and indeed he classifies them—for the purposes of his measurements—as actions which people can be free or not free to undertake.[20] However, as we have glimpsed in my third chapter's discussion of joint actions, his calculations of levels of overall liberty do not similarly advert to some of the non-causal aspects of people's interaction with other people and objects. To be sure, he does recognize the occurrence of joint actions, whereby people can do things together which none of them could do individually. If two people can push a car for a certain distance along a road during a certain period of time, and if neither of them could move the car at all on his own, then their pushing is a joint action. Carter explicitly maintains that any person's freedom to participate in such an action is to be incorporated into our calculations of the person's overall liberty. Each such particular freedom will add to the person's level of overall liberty an amount that 'will be represented by the number we assign to the combination of equal spatio-temporally specified event-units that constitute the moving of the car... divided by the number of agents whose basic actions are necessary in order for that movement to be brought about—in this case, two'.[21] However, when Carter recognizes the occurrence of joint actions and when he includes them among the contents of people's freedoms and unfreedoms, he is not really moving beyond his causal model. On the contrary, he characterizes a joint action as 'a single action that is causally generated by the separate coordinated basic actions of two individuals'.[22] That is, he perceives such an action as a simultaneous causal consequence of the coordinated actions that give rise to it.

Though many collaborative actions (including all of those discussed in my third chapter) can be subsumed under Carter's model if it is construed expansively, some instances of collaboration or interaction

[20] Carter, *Measure*, 178–83.
[21] Carter, *Measure*, 250.
[22] Ibid.

cannot be so subsumed. As a result, his theory cannot do justice to each person's freedom of assembly. Let us take up this matter by examining his treatment of political demonstrations mounted by disgruntled citizens. We shall assume that the protestors who assemble on the town square are not causally responsible for the presence of one another. That is, no one played any role in convincing anyone else to show up, and everyone would have made an appearance even if nobody else had bothered to go. Had any one of them turned out to be alone on the town square with his placards, he would still have gone through the same chants and marches. In these circumstances, then, even a highly expansive understanding of Carter's model of joint actions will not lead to the verdict that the demonstration by the dissidents is a joint action. After all, nobody is causally responsible for the presence of any of his fellow protestors, and nobody performs any bodily movements that he would not have performed in the absence of his companions. By the lights of the Carterian model, therefore, the demonstration is not a joint action but is instead simply an array of individual actions. Carter himself unequivocally declares that street protests are to be so classi-fied, whether or not they partake of the special features that I have outlined. He submits that a political demonstration 'is identical, for the purposes of freedom measurement, to the set of coordinated actions (of the separate individuals) which generate it'.[23] In other words, if we leave aside any causal consequences that might flow from a protest—such as the liberalization of a stern regime—each participant's freedom is wholly unaffected by any other participant's freedom to turn up and march. If Jane herself is unprevented from attending and marching and chanting, her overall freedom is not increased by the fact that other people also are unprevented. After all, her possession of freedoms to engage in the sundry bodily movements of marching and chanting does not hinge on anyone else's enjoyment of parallel freedoms; and since her possession of those freedoms is the only aspect of the demonstra-tion itself (as opposed to its possible causal consequences) that is relevant to her overall liberty, the level of her overall liberty is unaffected by anyone else's enjoyment of parallel freedoms.

The chief problem with this Carterian view is that it altogether obscures the importance, and indeed the existence, of each person's freedom of assembly. The non-causal interaction that constitutes a person's assembling with other people is not among the contents of her freedoms and unfreedoms that can be acknowledged as such by Carter. Only the bodily movements and the positions of stationariness

---

[23] Carter, *Measure*, 257.

that can be undertaken by the person herself in the course of the assembling—along with the causal consequences of those movements and those positions of stationariness—are among the contents of her freedoms and unfreedoms, according to Carter. If we are to remedy this blind spot in his theory, we shall have to grasp the key role of any person's surroundings as elements of what the person is free to do or be or become. That is, we have to grasp that a person's actions and states consist not only in the positioning of her own body within spatio-temporal regions, but also in the presence of any other objects (not least other people's bodies) which accompany that positioning. This point emerged in Chapter 3's discussion of joint actions, which insisted on the distinction between what a person does when he talks to himself and what a person does when he talks to someone else. Even if his laryngeal movements and gestures are exactly the same in the two situations, his actions are not the same. If he can talk either to himself or to someone else, then he enjoys a freedom which he does not enjoy if he cannot talk to anyone but himself. A corresponding point applies to any dissident who will march and chant against some governmental policy. If she can engage in those activities (with the same bodily movements) either by herself or in the presence of other demonstrators, she enjoys a set of freedoms which she does not enjoy if she cannot engage in those activities with anyone but herself.

How, then, do we incorporate these relational properties of actions into our calculations of each person's overall liberty? What we are trying to ascertain when we take notice of those properties is the variegatedness of the actions or states that are available to a person P at particular times. That variegatedness can be cashed out along strictly quantitative lines if we deal with the surrounding objects in much the same way as we deal with P's own body. That is, we have to divide those objects analytically into bits of matter, and we have to divide space and time analytically into regions within which those bits of matter can be positioned and among which they can move. The differing numbers and identities of the bits of matter that can accompany P's body in its potential actions and states, and the differing ways in which those bits can occupy the surrounding spatial regions through stretches of time, are the determinants of the variegatedness of those potential actions and states. In adopting this approach, of course, we should be striving not for the practical realizability of our measurements but for their realizability in principle. As a practical matter, this latest twist on the task of gauging each person's overall liberty is a further ground for thinking that the comprehensive fulfilment of that task lies well beyond our current powers. As a theoretical matter, however, this latest twist introduces a lot of formidable complexities without rendering the fulfilment of the aforementioned task incoherent or impossible in principle.

Of course, at any given juncture a person's options for that juncture will be largely fixed, in the respect on which we are now concentrating. If other demonstrators are gathered on the town square at noon for a rally to protest some governmental policy, then Jane's options concerning her body's occupation of spatial regions on the town square at that time do not include potential actions performed in the absence of the other protestors. Jane can probably affect the positioning and movements of her fellow dissidents to some degree, and she might even be able to induce some or all of them to leave. At least initially, however, her actions on the town square (if any) will have to be performed in the presence of those dissidents. Conversely, if at noon the town square is empty of people, then Jane does not at that time enjoy the option of carrying out chants and marches in the presence of other demonstrators. She might shortly thereafter enjoy that option, if other people turn up because of her efforts or independently of her efforts; but at noon she does not have such an option. The only actions available to her at that time on the town square are actions undertaken in the presence of no one other than herself. Hence, if we focus only on what Jane at some time t_1 is free to do at that time, my present discussion might not seem to be of great importance. However, as has been explained in my second chapter, just about any person is not only free at some time t_1 to do certain things at t_1, but is also free at t_1 to do various things at later times such as t_2 and t_3. When the temporal prospectivity of many of Jane's freedoms comes into focus, we can see that the role of the things in her surroundings as elements of her actions is potentially of major importance. (Often included among the things in her surroundings, of course, are other people.)

Jane at t_1 will very likely not be able to do much to rearrange her surroundings-at-t_1, but at t_1 she may well be able to influence the presence and positioning of the things that will be in her surroundings at t_2 or t_3. If Jane arrives at the town square at noon and finds nobody else there, then at least for a little while her chanting and strutting on the town square will have to be conducted in the presence of no one other than herself. Throughout the morning she has clearly been free to chant and parade by herself at noon on the town square. After all, anything which she actually does at noon is something which she has been free to do then. Had she not been free throughout the morning to chant and parade by herself on the town square at noon, she could not have engaged in those exploits there by herself at noon. In addition, however, she may well have been free during some portion of the morning to chant and parade on the town square at noon in the presence of other dissidents. That is, during some portion of the morning she may well have been able to take steps to arrange for the presence of other demonstrators on the town square at noon. Let us suppose that Jane for part of the morning is in fact able to take such steps, and that throughout the specified period of the morning (which we may designate as '$t_1 \rightarrow t_2$') she therefore enjoys the following two freedoms: (1) the freedom during $t_1 \rightarrow t_2$ to march and chant by herself on the town square at noon, and (2) the freedom during $t_1 \rightarrow t_2$ to march and chant in the presence of other dissidents on the town square at noon. We can further suppose that the bodily movements available to Jane on the town square at noon will be the same irrespective of the presence or absence of other protestors. For example, given the inclinations and agility of the other protestors who might be present, they will not lift her up onto their shoulders or allow her to shove them. In respect of these circumstances, then, Carter cannot accept that the two freedoms mentioned above are indeed distinct freedoms. According to his theory, each of those freedoms is the liberty of Jane during $t_1 \rightarrow t_2$ to move or position her body in various ways on the town square at noon. In the circumstances—so Carter must maintain—the presence or absence of other dissidents while Jane marches and chants on the town square at noon is something that has no bearing on the content of her freedom-during-$t_1 \rightarrow t_2$-to-engage-in-marching-and-chanting-on-the-town-square-at-noon. Thus the freedoms (1) and (2), between which I have distinguished on the basis of the presence or absence of the other dissidents, are for Carter indistinguishable. In his eyes, the content of either of those freedoms is exactly the same as the content of the other. In sum, when we take account of the temporal prospectivity of many liberties, the blind spot in Carter's theory becomes salient. If we are to do justice to each person's freedom of assembly, we shall have to eschew Carter's approach in favour of the approach outlined here.

What is more, when we shift our scrutiny from ascriptions of freedom and look instead at ascriptions of unfreedom, a further implication of my present discussion becomes visible. That implication can become clear not least when the two temporal indices in an ascription of unfreedom—that is, the time at which the unfreedom exists, and the time of the event or state to which it pertains—are simultaneous or virtually simultaneous. To discern this point, we should probe afresh the scenario of the demonstrators. If 20 other dissidents are on the town square when Jane arrives at noon, then she is unfree to carry out her protests on the square at noon in the presence of nobody other than herself, and more broadly she is unfree to carry out her protests on the square at noon in the presence of fewer than 20 other people. The actions of the other dissidents in gathering on the town square at noon have made her unfree in those respects even though they have made her free to carry out her protests on the square at noon in the presence of 20 other people. Although she is undoubtedly delighted by that freedom and indifferent to those unfreedoms, they are unfreedoms all the same. As has been noted at several junctures in this book, a person's attitude toward her freedoms and unfreedoms does not affect their status as such. (Of course, to say as much is obviously not to deny that the status of Jane's unfreedoms as unfreedoms would be even more vivid if they arose in a setting where they were unwelcome. Suppose for example that Jane is a keen admirer of natural beauty, and that at noon she is sitting in a meadow to enjoy its bucolic charmingness. If 20 other people are present throughout the meadow at noon, then Jane is not free to sit there at that time in the presence of nobody other than herself. Even if the presence of those other people does not interfere at all with her ability to move her body and to remain stationary, and even if the other people refrain from making any irksome noise, she might resent the fact that she is unfree to exult in the splendour of the natural scenery on her own.)

When Jane arrives on the town square at noon and finds exactly 20 other demonstrators present, she is unfree to chant and march on the town square at noon in the presence of fewer than 20 other people. Is she also unfree to chant and march on the town square at noon in the presence of *more* than 20 other dissidents? The answer to this question will depend on the reason for the fact that no more than 20 protestors other than Jane have come. If the reason is simply that no one else was inclined to turn up, then the omission of everyone else to attend has not rendered Jane unfree in the respect just mentioned. After all, as has been argued in Chapter 4, omissions are not sources of unfreedom. By contrast, if the reason for the non-appearance of further protestors is that they have been prevented from attending the demonstration by the actions of other people—perhaps by repressive governmental officials, for example, or perhaps by bad traffic jams—then Jane has indeed been rendered unfree to chant and march in their presence on the town square at noon. What makes them unfree to attend the demonstration at noon has also made her unfree to attend at noon in their presence.

In more than one respect, then, the implications of the present discussion are quite far-reaching. A key point remains to be considered, however, before we can move on. If we are to take account of the things in a person's surroundings (most notably the other people in her surroundings) as elements of her potential actions and states, we have to know how the surroundings themselves are to be delimited. We have to know which things can contribute to the variegatedness of the actions and states that are available to a person, and which things are irrelevant to that variegatedness. Only thus can we know whether some apparently distinguishable options count as genuinely distinguishable options or not.

On the one hand, the domain of things that can contribute to the variegatedness of a person's potential actions and states must be bounded. In the absence of extremely unusual circumstances, for example, it cannot be the case that the character of Jane's marching and chanting on the square of a Massachusetts town at noon is affected in any relevant way by someone's decision about lifting a teacup to a shelf at that very hour in the parlour of a house in Tibet. Jane's bodily position vis-à-vis the teacup at noon will be affected by the Tibetan person's decision whether to lift the cup or not, but the range of things which Jane is free to do at that hour will not be defined by reference to the teacup's positioning or movements. Her overall liberty is not affected at all by the decision about the lifting of the cup. If the only alternative to a Carterian disregard of Jane's freedom of assembly were a position that commits us to holding that the movement of the cup is a component of her marching and chanting, we would do well to side with Carter. (Note that the present topic is importantly different from the topic under consideration in Chapter 3's discussion of the opportunities that are in effect posed by people throughout the world for future joint actions with anyone else in the world. There the question was not how actions are to be defined; the question, rather, was when and how certain opportunities for actions exist. When I argued there that just about anyone in Massachusetts would have opportunities to perform future joint actions with just about anybody elsewhere in the world, I certainly did not suggest that the current movements of everybody throughout the world are elements of the current actions of everybody else throughout the world.)

On the other hand, when we delimit the domain of things that can contribute to the variegatedness of a person's potential actions and states, we should be careful not to draw the boundaries too tightly. In particular, we should not presume that geographical proximity is a necessary condition for the membership of things in that domain. Not least because of the reach of modern technology, the surroundings that contain elements of one's actions are not perforce confined to the spatial regions that are close to one's own body. Suppose that an entertainer engages in musical and histrionic performances that are broadcast on radio through much of the world. Suppose further that, whenever the broadcasts of the performances are sent through the airwaves, the religious fanatics who operate a tyrannical Taliban-like regime in some distant land shut down the machinery there that would receive and air the broadcasts. One result of this censorship, of course, is that all or most of the hapless people who live under the sway of the monstrous regime are unfree to listen to the broadcasts on their radios. In addition, however, the entertainer herself is rendered unfree to communicate with those people via radio. She has been deprived of opportunities to convey her spoken and sung words to people who would have listened to those words with pleasure if they had not been blocked from doing so. Preventive actions by the governmental officials, rather than disinclinations-to-listen on the part of the downtrodden citizens, are what thwart the entertainer from expressing herself to those citizens. (Were there no censorship, and were disinclinations-to-listen instead the reason for the failure of the entertainer to reach the citizens with her broadcasts, their omissions would not render her unfree in any respect.) In these circumstances, then, the officials' preventative interference reduces the variegatedness of the actions available to the entertainer and thus reduces her overall liberty by removing some of her combinations of conjunctively exercisable freedoms and by confronting her with some new combinations of consistent unfreedoms.

Of course, Carter might seek to accommodate this example within his own theory of freedom. That is, he might maintain that the broadcasts of the entertainer's speeches and songs to the potential members of her audience are causal consequences of her actions of speaking and singing and are therefore themselves to be classified (by measurers of freedom) as some of her potential actions. Such a move would not be objectionable at all from my perspective, and it would largely enable Carter to acknowledge the importance of each person's freedom of communication and freedom of interaction with other people. However, such a move should also lead us to question why Carter has taken such a restrictive view of each person's freedom of assembly, in his discussions of political demonstrations. If the communication of the entertainer's words to her audience is to be classified (by measurers of freedom) as an array of her actions, why does not a similar point apply to each participant in a demonstration? When each protestor appears at a political rally, she makes herself visible and audible to her fellow protestors – indeed, more directly so than the entertainer to the audience in a far-off land. Why should we not accordingly classify as some of her actions the impressions that she makes on the eyes and ears and brains of her fellow dissidents? Their seeing and hearing her are causal consequences of the bodily movements involved in her appearing at the demonstration and in her chanting and strutting once she is there. In sum, if Carter opts for the line of analysis delineated in this paragraph, he will have gone a long way toward embracing my view of the components of human intercourse that are to be counted as elements of each person's potential actions.

At any rate, whether or not Carter pursues the course just suggested, we still face the task of delimiting the domain of the things that are to count as elements of any person's potential actions. How do we set the boundaries to a person's surroundings, by reference to which her actions are partially defined? As has been indicated, geographical proximity is not in itself the sole touchstone through which we can answer this question. In fact, the key to an answer lies in my preceding paragraph's remarks about Carter's analysis. As has been suggested in that paragraph, even non-causal interaction among people—and between people and things—is causal in some respects. Even when the presence of Jane at a political demonstration is not a NESS condition for the participation or the ambulatory movements of the other dissidents who are present, it is a NESS condition for their seeing and hearing her and for her seeing and hearing them. At least one aspect of her attendance at the demonstration, such as her location in some area or her speaking aloud, is a NESS condition for at least one aspect of the states or actions of other dissidents (such as their mental/visual/aural states in seeing and hearing her). Conversely, at least one aspect of the presence of the other dissidents at the demonstration is a NESS condition for at least one aspect of Jane's states or actions, such as her mental/visual/aural states in seeing and hearing those other participants. By contrast, nothing pertaining to her attendance at the demonstration is a NESS condition for anything pertaining to the lifting of the teacup in Tibet, or vice versa—save in wildly fanciful circumstances that need not be contemplated here. (Note that the causal relata mentioned here are intrinsic properties rather than relational properties. Although the relevant mental/visual/aural states are of course made possible by the relationship of proximity between Jane and the other protestors, those states are not themselves relational properties. Were relational properties to be included among the causes and effects that bear on my present point, a contrived property such as Jane's physical position vis-à-vis the Tibetan teacup would be included. In that event, of course, my delimitation of the domain of the things that count as elements of a person's actions would be no delimitation at all; nothing would be excluded from any such domain, since everything stands in some relation or another to everything else, however contrived. Thus, if my delimitation of such a domain for anyone's actions is to be pertinent and effective, the causal relationships that form the domain must lie between intrinsic properties rather than between relational properties.)

In short, when we wish to determine the boundaries of a person's surroundings that contain the external elements of her actions and states, we have to ask about the causal relationships between the person and anything beyond the spatial regions which her own body occupies. If any intrinsic property of some potential action or state of hers is a NESS condition for some intrinsic property of anything beyond her, then that thing beyond her is an element of her potential action or state. That external thing is to be taken into account when we gauge the variegatedness of the actions and states that are available to her. Likewise, if any intrinsic property of something beyond her during some period of time is a NESS condition for an intrinsic property of some potential state of hers or for an intrinsic property of her performance of some potential action(s), then that thing beyond her is an element of her potential states and actions during the specified period of time. Its positioning is to be taken into account when we gauge the variegatedness of the states and actions that are available to her.

Under the disjunctive criterion just specified, geographical proximity between a person and any external things will typically be of major importance in determining whether those things count as components of her potential states and actions; but it will not always be of unique importance. Let us return for a moment to the example of the entertainer whose singing and recitations are broadcast on radio to countries throughout the world. At least one aspect of her action of singing or reciting is a NESS condition for at least one aspect of the state (the mental and aural state) of each person in her audience. The status of each potential member of her audience as such is therefore to be taken into account when we gauge the variegatedness of the actions of singing and reciting which she can carry out. When the ruthless Taliban-like autocrats block her broadcasts from being aired in their country, they prevent her from encompassing within her actions the citizens in that unhappy land who would have listened to her. The autocrats render her unfree in certain respects by reducing the reach of her actions and thus by reducing the variegatedness of her potential actions. But for the obstructiveness of those despots, at least one intrinsic property of the actions of the entertainer would be causally linked to at least one intrinsic property of the state of each person who is thwarted by the tyrants from hearing her. Precisely because what is being suppressed is a causal connection of that sort, each person affected is a component of the entertainer's potential performances.

1.4.2. The Burden of Responsibility My third chapter took exception not only to some facets of Carter's analysis of joint actions, but also—in a later portion of the chapter—to some facets of his analysis of collective unfreedom. In particular, we looked at a situation in which the following conditions obtain: (1) each person in a group of people is free to escape from a cell or room in which they are all interned; (2) each person's freedom-to-escape will cease to exist if any other member of the group exercises his or her parallel freedom-to-escape; (3) despite the fact that the continuation of each person's freedom-to-escape is conditional on the non-exercise of anyone else's homologous freedom, there is only an extremely low likelihood that any member of the group will lose his freedom-to-escape; and (4) the exercise of the freedom-to-escape by anyone would require very little effort. While the first three of these conditions constitute a predicament of collective unfreedom, the upshot of the fourth condition is that Carter's attempts to unpack the phenomenon of collective unfreedom are inapplicable to the depicted situation. On the one hand, if the exercise of the freedom-to-escape by anyone would involve laborious and protracted toil on her part, that particular freedom would not add enormously to anyone's overall liberty—since it would be included in relatively few of each person's combinations of conjunctively exercisable freedoms. Given such a state of affairs, Carter can correctly maintain that his approach to the measurement of each person's overall liberty will quite suitably reflect the straitened circumstances of each person caught in a plight of collective unfreedom. On the other hand, his approach produces far less impressive results when the fourth condition above obtains. If each person in a predicament of collective unfreedom can easily exercise her freedom-to-escape (provided that nobody else has extinguished that freedom by escaping ahead of her, of course), then Carter's analysis will yield the conclusion that the overall liberty of each such person is impaired very little indeed by that predicament. Not even a *pro-tanto* reduction in anyone's overall liberty, save to a trifling extent, can be acknowledged within Carter's theory. As my third chapter has contended, his analysis certainly seems to be overlooking something important. Though his approach does not blind us to anything of much significance in connection with some situations such as that of the users on a huge telephone network, it does neglect a highly significant aspect of the situation of the people in the dungeon.

We are now in a position to apprehend further grounds for my third chapter's rejection of Carter's stance on this matter. In any situation of collective unfreedom like the one on which we principally focused in that chapter, the people affected are components of the actions of one another. Confined to a room or cell, they are in proximity with one another and are indeed very likely motivated chiefly by their feelings toward one another. (Recall that the most plausible basis for each person's disinclination to leave the place of imprisonment is his sense of solidarity with the other captives or his desire to avoid being seen as a selfish coward by the others.) In these circumstances, then, the positioning of each person is something by reference to which the potential actions of every other person in the room are partially defined. Hence, although the captor has in one respect increased the variegatedness of the actions available to each hostage—by enabling each one to seal the others impregnably in the room through his or her departure—he has in another respect decreased the variegatedness of those available actions, by disabling each hostage from departing without sealing the others impregnably in the room. Because the kidnapper stands ready to prevent any captive from effecting a departure that does not imprison her fellow captives, each person in the room is unfree (rather than merely not free) to carry out such a departure.

That is, the *pro-tanto* reduction in everyone's overall liberty consists not only in each captive's loss of some combinations of conjunctively exercisable freedoms, but also in each captive's incurring of some additional combinations of consistent unfreedoms. Whereas each hostage's loss of some combinations of conjunctively exercisable liberties is offset (at least partially, and perhaps more than partially) by her gain of certain other such combinations, each hostage's incurring of additional combinations of consistent unfreedoms is not offset by her shedding of any other such combinations. To be sure, if the kidnapper would irreversibly relent and allow each of his victims to leave the room without entrapping the others, he would deprive each of them of her ability to imprison the others, and he would consequently remove from each victim some of her current combinations of conjunctively exercisable liberties. However, he would not be imposing on each victim any additional unfreedoms. Like other omissions, his omission to act upon his original threat would not give rise to any unfreedoms; when combinations of liberties are eliminated by a stark omission, no commensurate unfreedoms are thereby engendered. Accordingly, when the captor in fact refuses to relent, he does not thereby disemburden his hostages of any unfreedoms—because no unfreedoms would have been imposed on them by his relenting, and thus because there was no prospect of unfreedoms of which the hostages can be disemburdened by the captor's unyieldingness. His adamancy creates or sustains some unfreedoms without relieving anyone of other unfreedoms.

My last two paragraphs have analysed the situation of the hostages in terms that should be largely congenial to Carter. Though the treatment of the status of each hostage as a component of the actions of every other hostage has gone beyond anything stated explicitly by Carter, the analysis has remained purely quantitative. As was mentioned earlier, the notion of variegatedness is cashed out here along quantitative lines. To say that the captor has reduced *pro tanto* the variegatedness of the actions available to his victims is to say that he has reduced *pro tanto* the sheer number of actions that are available to them. To be sure, my way of individuating each person's actions partly by reference to the states and positioning of other people's bodies is more attentive to the role of external objects as components of actions than are some of Carter's remarks on political demonstrations and the like. Nevertheless, when Carter submits that the causal consequences of each person's actions are themselves to be classified as actions (for the purpose of measuring each person's overall liberty), he is adopting an approach that can yield verdicts largely similar to my own—if the proponent of that approach is alert to the full range of causal consequences that flow from anyone's actions.

What has become clear both here and in Chapter 3 is that pinning down the upshot of a situation of collective unfreedom is a gnarledly complicated task. *Pro-tanto* decreases in each affected person's overall liberty are countervailed to varying degrees by *pro-tanto* expansions. Indeed, the complexities of the situation are more formidable than has been suggested in my last few paragraphs, since the newly precluded actions and states and the newly available actions and states are more numerous than those paragraphs have intimated. Let us presume that, in the scenario which we have been pondering, there are ten hostages in the room. While the kidnapper prevents each hostage from effecting a departure that would not immure any of the other hostages, he also prevents each of them from effecting a departure that would cause the immurement of exactly eight of the other hostages—and he also prevents each of them from effecting a departure that would cause the immurement of exactly seven of the other hostages, and so forth. For each captive, the kidnapper has ruled out a number of distinct though related actions. Whether we convey these complexities by characterizing them as matters of the variegatedness of the actions available to each captive, or whether we instead proceed in more of a Carterian vein by characterizing the complexities as matters of the causal consequences of each captive's potential actions, we shall find that the impact of a situation of collective unfreedom on the overall liberty of each person involved is highly complicated indeed.

Still, despite the intricacy of the effects, the balance between *pro-tanto* diminutions and *pro-tanto* increases in each captive's overall liberty will generally be tilted in favour of the diminutions—because of a facet of my project of measurement that has not yet been discussed more than fleetingly, a facet that differentiates my own project quite sharply from Carter's. Let us for a moment prescind from the complications broached in my last paragraph. In that event, the captor has reduced *pro tanto* the overall liberty of each of the victims by preventing any of them from departing without trapping everyone else, and he has enlarged *pro tanto* the overall liberty of each of the victims by enabling any one of them to effect a departure that will trap everyone else. What has not yet been mentioned is that, when each of these developments is gauged as an increment or a decrement in each person's overall freedom, it will be attached to a qualitatively-oriented multiplier. As will be outlined in the second half of this chapter, every item in each combination of conjunctively exercisable liberties will be associated with a multiplier which reflects the significance of that item for the human being whose particular freedom it is. Similarly, each combination of consistent unfreedoms will be associated with a multiplier that reflects the significance of the deprivation. An item in a combination of conjunctively exercisable freedoms will be weighted heavily by a qualitatively-oriented multiplier if it is especially important for a typical human being. A less important item will be weighted less heavily. Conversely, a combination of consistent unfreedoms will be weighted heavily by a qualitatively-oriented multiplier if its lack of conjunctive exercisability is especially damaging for a typical human being. A combination of consistent unfreedoms whose status as such is less detrimental for a typical person will be weighted less heavily. To be sure, as we shall observe later, these qualitatively-oriented weightings do not alter the fact that a project of measuring everyone's freedom is an enterprise focused primarily on physical parameters. All the same, those weightings can play a decisive role in a knotty situation involving many competing considerations that bear on the overall liberty of everybody affected.

In the scenario of the kidnapper and the hostages, of course, there are many such competing considerations. Of particular importance to a typical human being is the option of avoiding responsibility for the permanent imprisonment of other innocent human beings. Because of the nefarious designs of the kidnapper, no hostage enjoys that option except at the cost of remaining permanently imprisoned herself. In other words, no hostage can exercise *in toto* any combination of opportunities comprehending both the responsibility-avoiding option and the option of escaping from the cell in which she has been confined; those options are not conjunctively exercisable. Every such combination is something which each captive is unfree to carry out. Given the loathsomeness of her choice (if any) between an extremely disagreeable future of confinement for herself and an extremely distasteful involvement in the entombment of other innocent people, we should attach heavy weight to the fact that she is unfree to eschew both prongs—rather than only one prong—of that choice. When we gauge how much her unfreedom in that respect adds to her total unfreedom, we shall be attaching some substantial qualitatively-oriented multipliers to the closed-off combinations of options (which will be numerous, since my present point applies to every combination which encompasses the two options specified above and which satisfies the first clause of the U Postulate).

By contrast, each captive's ability to imprison other innocent people, which is now included in many of her combinations of conjunctively exercisable freedoms, will be associated with a much lower qualitatively-oriented multiplier. On the one hand, such an ability might not be wholly without value to a typical human being, at least when he or she who possesses it can at no great cost refrain from exercising it. Though the *exercise* of a freedom-to-trap-other-innocent-people would be repellent to a typical human being, the possession of that freedom itself is somewhat different. On the other hand, notwithstanding that such a freedom (as opposed to the exercise thereof) might commend itself to a typical human being, it is far less estimable than the freedom to refrain at reasonable cost from becoming responsible for the entombment of other innocent people. Accordingly, the qualitatively-oriented weighting that should be given to a liberty of the former sort is considerably less than the qualitatively-oriented weighting that should be given to any combination of consistent unfreedoms that involves the negation of a liberty of the latter sort. Because of this disparity between the qualitatively-oriented multipliers, the balance between the *pro-tanto* decreases and the *pro-tanto* increases in the overall liberty of each person affected by a serious predicament of collective unfreedom—like the predicament of the ten people confined in the room—will amount to an all-things-considered decrease. In sum, even though my theory ascribes particular freedoms and unfreedoms only to individuals and not to groups, the constraining effects of a plight of collective unfreedom are fully registered in my approach to the measurement of liberty.

1.5. Combinations of Consistent Unfreedoms

In the closing remarks of the preceding subsection, we have glanced at one feature of the role of unfreedoms that should receive further explication. More generally, the nature of combinations of consistent unfreedoms and their place in my formula for the measurement of liberty should receive some elucidation. The phrase 'combination of consistent unfreedoms' is used throughout this book to designate any set of opportunities which are not conjunctively exercisable by a person P and which would be conjunctively exercisable by P in the absence of the preventive effects of some action(s) performed by some other person(s)—or in the absence of the preventive effects of any action(s) that would be performed by some other person(s) if P were to attempt to exercise those opportunities conjunctively. A combination of opportunities can lack conjunctive exercisability for either or both of two main reasons. First, it might be the case that at least one of the opportunities in the combination is itself classifiable as an unfreedom under the U Postulate. If so, then the opportunity or opportunities in question will have rendered unperformable the combination as a whole. All of the other opportunities in the combination may well be performable both individually and conjunctively, but the combination cannot be performed in its entirety—precisely because it includes at least one opportunity that has been ruled out by somebody else's actions. A second main reason for the absence of conjunctive exercisability can apply in addition to the first reason or in lieu of it. Whether or not a combination of opportunities for somebody includes any single opportunity that has been closed off by some action(s) of some other person(s), it can include two or more opportunities which are unperformable in tandem because of some action(s) of some other person(s). We have encountered many examples of this state of affairs throughout this book. As has been noted, for instance, most well-enforced legal prohibitions operate in practice not through anticipatory preventive steps but through *ex-post* punishments and remedies. Each person under the sway of a well-enforced prohibition on doing X is free to perform the proscribed act and is also free to do anything that would be ruled out by the penalty for performing that act; but he or she cannot exercise those freedoms in tandem. Because the prohibition is well-enforced, a person's exercise of the former freedom excludes her exercise of the latter. Hence, any combination of opportunities containing both of those particular freedoms is not a conjunctively exercisable set. Its conjunctive exercisability has been ruled out for each citizen by the actions which other people (that is, legal officials) do undertake or are prepared to undertake.

Of course, when a combination of consistent unfreedoms is made up of just one item, only the first of the two foregoing reasons for its lack of conjunctive exercisability will ever be applicable. In regard to any larger combination, however, either or both of the reasons can be applicable. To be sure, the term 'unfreedoms' in the phrase 'combination of consistent unfreedoms' might be slightly misleading, since many such combinations will comprise elements that are not individually unfreedoms. That somewhat cumbersome phrase is meant to convey the fact that, even when opportunities have not been individually closed off by anyone else's actions, they may well have been closed off as a package. When they have been closed off as a package by somebody else's actions, just as much as when they have been closed off individually, they render unperformable any combination of opportunities of which they together are members. Our focus in respect of unfreedoms, for the purpose of measuring each person's overall liberty, is therefore squarely on combinations rather than on individual opportunities.

Thus, when indicating the greater or lesser importance of a combination of opportunities that lacks conjunctive exercisability for someone as a result of the actions of some other person(s), we attach a qualitatively-oriented multiplier to the combination as a whole rather than to any of the individual elements thereof. What the multiplier reflects is the significance of the fact that the combination cannot be exercised in its entirety. We should not attempt to reflect the significance of the ostensible fact that each opportunity which composes such a combination is not exercisable; after all, each of the elements in many a combination *can* be exercised individually, even though some or all of them cannot be exercised together. Assigning qualitatively-oriented weights to the individual elements in a combination of consistent unfreedoms—rather than to each such combination as a whole—would consequently be misconceived. By contrast, we do indeed assign such weights to the individual items in combinations of conjunctively exercisable liberties. Every item in any combination of that latter sort is itself a liberty. No combination of conjunctively exercisable freedoms ever contains any elements that are individually unfreedoms; all such elements are freedoms individually as well as conjunctively. Hence, the weight to be attached to any such combination is nothing separate from the weights to be attached to the freedoms that are its constituents. (As will be observed later in this chapter, however, those weights are themselves affected by the relationships of diversity and complementarity among individual freedoms.) In sum, with regard to any combination of consistent unfreedoms, the basic point of application for a qualitatively-oriented multiplier is the combination as a whole. With regard to any combination of conjunctively exercisable liberties, contrariwise, the basic point of application for a qualitatively-oriented multiplier is each liberty in the combination.

Now, we characterize combinations of conjunctively exercisable freedoms and combinations of consistent unfreedoms partly by reference to the presence or absence of the property of conjunctive exercisability. What exactly is that property? To apprehend the answer to this question, we should recall that there are two key temporal components of any freedom or unfreedom: the time at which the freedom or unfreedom exists, and the time of the occurrence or state to which the freedom or unfreedom pertains. When we ascribe a freedom or an unfreedom to anyone, we explicitly or implicitly incorporate those two temporal indices into our ascription. Many freedoms/unfreedoms existing at some moment t pertain to some actions or states that would arise at t or at junctures very shortly after t (if at all), whereas other freedoms/unfreedoms existing at that moment pertain to actions or states that would arise at later junctures (if at all). In any full-scale measurement of every person's overall liberty, the temporal components of each freedom and unfreedom must be specified with considerable precision. With those components suitably specified, and with the spatial components of the content of each freedom also suitably specified, we can then determine whether or not any particular freedoms of some person can be exercised conjunctively.

To say that two or more freedoms can be exercised conjunctively is to say that they can be exercised together either simultaneously or sequentially. Some freedoms of any person P will clearly be exercisable simultaneously: for example, the freedom of P at some moment t_1 to walk along a certain path at t_1, and the freedom of P at t_1 to whistle at t_1, and the freedom of P at t_1 to wave his right hand at t_1. By contrast, if P cannot sing and whistle at the same time, then the freedom of P at t_1 to sing at t_1 is not exercisable simultaneously with his freedom at t_1 to whistle at t_1 and is therefore not exercisable simultaneously with the combination of the three freedoms delineated just above. Nevertheless, the freedom of P at t_1 to sing at some later moment t_2 can be exercised simultaneously with those three freedoms, since P's whistling at *t1* does not preclude his singing at t_2. Likewise, although the freedom of P at t_2 to sing at t_2 is not exercisable simultaneously with any of the other freedoms mentioned here—because it is possessed by P at a time later than the time at which the other freedoms are possessed by him—it is exercisable conjunctively with those freedoms, since it can be exercised together with them sequentially. In sum, all of the following freedoms (and therefore any subset of them) will be exercisable conjunctively: the freedom of P at t_1 to walk along a certain path at t_1; the freedom of P at t_1 to whistle at t_1; the freedom of P at t_1 to wave his right hand at t_1; the freedom of P at t_1 to sing at t_2; and the freedom of P at t_2 to sing at t_2. Similarly, if we were to omit from the foregoing list the freedom of P at t_1 to whistle at t_1, and if we were to replace it with the freedom of P at t_1 to sing at t_1, the list would again contain a conjunctively exercisable set of liberties.

Having noted that conjunctively exercisable liberties can be exercised together either simultaneously or sequentially, we now need to determine how (in principle) we can tell whether some combination of liberties is conjunctively exercisable or not. For purposes of illustration, let us focus on the liberties recounted in the preceding paragraph. An enquiry into the conjunctive exercisability of those liberties should begin with the liberties held at the earliest moment, t_1. To ascertain whether those liberties are conjunctively exercisable, we need to judge whether the actuality of the event or the state-of-affairs to which each liberty pertains is consistent with the actuality of the event or the state-of-affairs to which each of the other liberties pertains. That question in turn is to be answered by reference to the positioning of objects in spatio-temporal regions. Any occurrence or state-of-affairs ensuing from the exercise of a liberty will consist in the positioning of one or more objects in just such regions. Thus, for example, if the freedom of P at t_1 to walk along a certain path at t_1 is exercised by P, then P's body will be moving through regions of space along the path at t_1. If he exercises his freedom at t_1 to whistle at t_1, his mouth and lungs will be positioned and moving in various spatial regions at t_1. (Remember that, in any full-scale measurement of each person's overall liberty, the spatio-temporal regions that serve as the units of measurement will be very small in order to register minute movements of the body.) If the relevant movement of P's body through the spatial regions along the path at t_1 is consistent with the relevant positioning of his mouth and lungs in certain spatial regions at t_1, then his freedom at t_1 to walk along the path at t_1 is exercisable conjunctively with his freedom at t_1 to whistle at t_1. Parallel enquiries into the consistency between the content of each of P's freedoms and the content of each of his other freedoms will reveal which of those freedoms can be exercised conjunctively. Each of those contents, of course, is cashed out as the occupation of various spatio-temporal regions by objects, most notably including P's body. Of course, when enquiries of this sort are undertaken in application to the freedoms of P that were listed in the preceding paragraph, they will probably seem somewhat heavy-handed and pedantic. After all, in the absence of unusual circumstances—such as a shuddersome lack of physical dexterity on the part of P—the relations of consistency and inconsistency between the contents of those freedoms are quite evident without any detailed investigation. Nonetheless, in application to many other freedoms, enquiries along the lines sketched here will be essential for revealing the presence or absence of conjunctive exercisability. At any rate, even when no detailed investigations are necessary, the basic focus of the enquiries outlined here is correct. That is, whenever we wish to discover whether any particular freedoms are conjunctively exercisable by some person, we have to ask about the positioning of objects in spatio-temporal regions. If the positioning of objects entailed by the exercise of each liberty is consistent with the positioning of objects entailed by the exercise of each of the other liberties, then the whole set of liberties is conjunctively exercisable; and, if there is instead any inconsistency, then conjunctive exercisability is missing.

When some set of opportunities for a person P does not partake of conjunctive exercisability, and when a but-for reason for the absence of conjunctive exercisability lies in the actions of other people, the set is one of P's combinations of consistent unfreedoms (whether any of its elements are individually unfreedoms or not). We should note that, to be classifiable as a combination of consistent unfreedoms, a set of opportunities for P must satisfy the first prong of the U Postulate. That is, such a classification presupposes that the set would be conjunctively exercisable by P in the absence of some preventive action(s) by some other person(s). If instead at least one array of minimally sufficient conditions for the lack of conjunctive exercisability does not include any action(s) by anyone else, then the set of opportunities does not count as a combination of consistent unfreedoms—even if some of its elements are individually unfreedoms, and even if many of its subsets are classifiable as combinations of consistent unfreedoms. Suppose for example that a set of opportunities contains the following members: P's opportunity at t_1 to walk along a certain path at t_1, P's opportunity at t_1 to sing at t_1, P's opportunity at t_1 to whistle at t_1. Let us suppose that the first of these opportunities has been negated by the presence of other people who will block P's way and prevent him from walking along the path at all. In that case, the first member of the set is an unfreedom rather than a freedom. Nevertheless, the set as a whole does not qualify as a combination of consistent unfreedoms. Its second and third members are not conjunctively exercisable, and the reason for the lack of conjunctive exercisability is not the actions of anyone else but the limitedness of P's capacities. Thus, although three subsets of this set of opportunities will qualify as combinations of consistent unfreedoms—namely, the first opportunity on its own, and the first opportunity in combination with either of the other two opportunities—the set as a whole does not so qualify. It is not the case that the set as a whole would be conjunctively exercisable in the absence of the people who are obstructing the path, and therefore it is not the case that the set as a whole satisfies the first prong of the U Postulate. Hence, although P is not free to exercise the three opportunities in the set conjunctively, he is likewise not *unfree* to exercise them conjunctively (even though he is of course unfree to exercise the opportunity-to-walk-along-the-path, which has been negated as an opportunity for him).

One major reason for taking note of the point made in the preceding paragraph is its highlighting of the fact that, when my theory deals with any combination of consistent unfreedoms, our primary focus lies on the whole combination rather than on the individual elements thereof. We have seen as much already, and we shall return to this observation more than once. Another reason for the importance of the preceding paragraph's point is that it underlines why the denominator of my freedom-measuring fraction will be finite. Were it not the case that the first prong of the U Postulate must be satisfied by every genuine combination of consistent unfreedoms as an overarching set, then the range of such combinations would be infinite. Consequently, of course, the denominator in my fraction for measuring anyone's overall liberty would be infinite. After all, if any set of opportunities that includes some item(s) closed off by other people's actions can be classified as a combination of consistent unfreedoms even though the set as a whole does not satisfy the first prong of the U Postulate, then such combinations and their elements will abound endlessly. Let us think back, for example, to the situation of P whose efforts to walk along a certain path at t_1 will be thwarted by people who are blocking the path. Any set of options for P that includes his squelched opportunity at t_1 to walk along the path at t_1 will not be conjunctively exercisable, and the absence of conjunctive exercisability is due at least partly to the actions of other people. Accordingly, if the first prong of the U Postulate were not a constraint on what can count as a combination of consistent unfreedoms, absolutely any set of options that encompasses P's squelched opportunity would so count. One such combination would be a set containing his squelched opportunity plus the opportunity to soar around every galaxy five times. Another such combination would be a set containing the squelched opportunity plus the opportunity to soar in a different direction around every galaxy ten times. And so forth. P's combinations of consistent unfreedoms would be utterly unlimited in their range, and the denominator of my fraction for measuring his overall liberty would thus be infinitely large. Hence, when one insists that the first prong of the U Postulate must be satisfied by every combination of consistent unfreedoms as an overarching set, one's insistence is doubly warranted. In the first place, when judging whether a set of opportunities is a combination of consistent unfreedoms, our paramount concern—in connection with the measurement of each person's overall liberty—is with the performability of the whole combination. Consequently, just as any qualitatively-oriented multiplier and any probabilistic qualification should attach to the whole combination, so too the U Postulate's tests for separating unfreedoms from mere inabilities must be satisfied by the whole combination. (However, those tests must also be applied to the elements and subsets of each combination. Although the second prong of the U Postulate need not be satisfied by any element or subset short of a whole combination, the fact of its being so satisfied is the most common reason for deeming a whole combination to be a combination of consistent unfreedoms.) In the second place, moreover, my insistence on the satisfaction of the U Postulate's tests by any veritable combination of consistent unfreedoms in its entirety is essential for the very coherence of the idea of measuring each person's overall liberty as a ratio. If we failed to require the satisfaction of the first prong of the U Postulate by every combination of consistent unfreedoms as a whole, we would have to conclude that the range of such combinations is completely without bounds. We would therefore have to conclude that the measurement of each person's overall liberty is impossible even in principle. An avoidance of such an upshot is a highly salutary result of a requirement that is also independently justifiable.

Before we move to the next subsection, we should mull over one further point—a point that is relevant not only to combinations of consistent unfreedoms but also to combinations of conjunctively exercisable freedoms. If we leave aside for now the bearings of qualitatively-oriented multipliers and probabilistic qualifications, how is each combination of either type to be weighed? That is, how are the multifarious combinations expressed in numerical terms? To answer such a question, we must consider how the elements in any combination of either type are to be individuated. Plainly, the elements are to be individuated through the individuation of their contents, and the contents are individuated through our division of space into regions, our division of time into spans, and our division of objects into portions of matter. For any full-scale measurement of each person's overall liberty, as we have seen, the spatio-temporal regions and the portions of matter will be very small—small enough to register every relevant movement and every instance of stationariness, including cerebral processes and laryngeal vibrations. Of key importance here is that, whatever be the exact size of each region of space, it must be the same size as that of every other such region. A parallel point must be true of the portions of matter and the stretches of time, which must every one be of a uniform mass or a uniform duration respectively. Only thus can our analytical divisions of space and time and matter serve as units of measurement, as Carter has rightly emphasized.[24]

Making use of suitable units of measurement, we must ask how many ways a person can position objects in space during a specified span of time. That question is to be answered by reference to the number of portions of matter involved, the number of differing arrays of spatial regions that can be occupied by those portions of matter within the specified temporal span, and the roles of other objects in the surroundings of the person whose freedom is being gauged. (As was argued earlier, the roles of those other objects in variegating the options available to the person are themselves to be cashed out along purely spatio-temporal lines.) In other words, within any enterprise of systematically measuring each person's overall liberty, every particular freedom pertains precisely to the occupation of an array of spatio-temporal regions by portions of matter. A freedom that pertains to some different array of regions or to some different portions of matter is a distinct freedom, even if there is a substantial overlap between its content and the contents of some of the freedoms from which it is distinct. For example, a person's freedom to extend his arm almost fully is distinct from his freedom to extend it fully, because the spatial regions that would be occupied by the arm as a result of his exercise of the former freedom are not identical to the spatial regions that would be occupied by the arm as a result of his exercise of the latter freedom— even though the two sets of regions overlap to a far greater degree than they diverge. Thus, the contents of the liberties in any combination of conjunctively exercisable liberties are the sundry distinct ways in which a person can position bits of matter in arrays of spatial regions

[24] Carter, *Measure*, 186.

through some period of time. Inasmuch as those ways can occur together either simultaneously or sequentially, the freedoms that pertain to them are conjunctively exercisable. Of course, because the spatial regions and the portions of matter that serve as our ideal units of measurement are tiny, the numbers associated with most combinations of conjunctively exercisable freedoms will be vast. However, though huge, the numbers will be finite; consequently, the coherence of the enterprise of measurement is secure, irrespective of how humblingly far beyond our current technological powers the execution of that enterprise might lie in practice.

The ways in which a person P can position bits of matter in spatial regions are of course not limited to the ways in which she can occupy space and move through space with her body. In addition, the causal consequences of her potential bodily movements and postures are among the things which she is free to bring about. Those potential consequences themselves would consist in the positioning of bits of matter in spatial regions, and accordingly the measurement of their extent proceeds in exactly the same fashion as the measurement of the extent to which her body can occupy differing arrays of spatial regions. Furthermore, the objects potentially in her surroundings—not least the other people who may be present—will have partially defined what she can do and be and become and undergo. In so far as those objects can vary with regard to their presence or absence and with regard to the specific patterns in which they occupy spatial regions, they variegate her doings and becomings and undergoings. Hence, a comprehensive project of measuring her overall liberty must not only take account of all the ways in which she can bring about the occupation of matrices and concatenations of spatial regions by portions of matter. Additionally, it must take account of the potential positionings of objects in her surroundings that partially define and thereby variegate the aforementioned ways that are open to her.

In short, if we temporarily pretermit the roles of qualitatively-oriented multipliers and probabilistic qualifications in our calculations, the question with which this line of discussion began three paragraphs ago is now answerable (at an abstract level). Each of P's combinations of conjunctively exercisable liberties is expressed numerically as a sum of the numbers assigned to its individual freedoms. Each such freedom in turn is expressed numerically as the product of two factors: the number of units of matter whose positioning would be involved in the course of any potential action or state or process to which the freedom pertains; and the number of spatial regions among which those units of matter would be arrayed or moved during the specified action or state or process. As has been indicated, freedoms are individuated by two main sets of considerations that relate to their contents. (For the sake of minimizing the unwieldiness of my prose, I shall here refer only to potential actions and shall leave aside potential states and processes. P's actions should here be understood to include the causal consequences of her bodily postures and movements.) First, if the spatio-temporal regions or the portions of matter that would be involved in some potential action by P are different from those that would be involved in some other potential action of hers—even if there is a very considerable overlap—then the freedom that pertains to the former action is distinct from the freedom that pertains to the latter. Second, if the objects that would be in her surroundings during one of her potential actions are different or differently positioned from those that would be in her surroundings during another of her potential actions, then the freedom that pertains to the former action is distinct from the freedom that pertains to the latter. When freedoms so individuated are expressed numerically and summed, the upshot is the weight to be ascribed to the combination which comprises those freedoms. (Once again, the analysis in this paragraph—and indeed throughout this closing line of discussion in the current subsection—prescinds from the effects of qualitatively-oriented multipliers and probabilistic qualifications. Those effects have been explored already, and will be investigated at greater length presently.)

The parameters to be ascertained for P's combinations of consistent unfreedoms are similar to those for her combinations of conjunctively exercisable liberties. That is, each opportunity comprised within such a combination—whether the opportunity has been individually closed off by other people's actions or not—is to be expressed numerically by reference to the factors outlined above. The numbers so assigned to the opportunities are then to be added up, and the resultant sum is the purely quantitative weight for each combination of consistent unfreedoms as a whole. When the figure representing each such combination for P is duly modified by a qualitatively-oriented multiplier and a probabilistic qualification, and when that modified figure is added to the figures representing her other combinations of consistent unfreedoms, the upshot is the numerical expression of the full range of such combinations for P.

1.6. Causation and Probability

Like Carter, this chapter has maintained that the causal consequences of each person's potential doings and becomings and undergoings are to be included among the things which the person is free or unfree to bring about. Those consequences, in other words, are among the things to which her freedoms and unfreedoms pertain. Now, on the one hand, we could classify those causal consequences as elements of the doings or becomings or undergoings from which they ensue. Were we to go down that route, the purely quantitative weight associated with each action or becoming or undergoing would reflect the physical dimensions of its causal consequences in accordance with the pattern of calculation outlined in the preceding subsection. On the other hand, nevertheless, for reasons that will become clear in this subsection, we should opt to treat the causal consequences as some separate contents of freedoms/unfreedoms rather than as some components of such contents. Before we consider that point more closely, however, we should ponder how far those consequences are to be taken into account at all.

1.6.1. Potential Chains of Causation: How Far?   This question about the extent to which causal consequences should get entered into our calculations is something that must be addressed here because of the boundlessness of those consequences, as Carter recognizes.[25] After all, not only the immediate effects of what a person does or becomes or undergoes are causally related thereto; also causally related thereto, as can be gathered from Chapter 4, are all the effects of those effects *ad infinitum*. Given as much, however, we clearly need a way of delimiting the range of the potential consequences that will be included among the contents of a person's liberties. For one thing, if we could not set boundaries to that range, we would have to accept that both the numerator and the denominator in the fraction that expresses anyone's overall liberty are infinitely large. Since the causal consequences taken into account would be endless, the items in anyone's combinations of conjunctively exercisable freedoms and the items in her combinations of consistent unfreedoms would likewise be endless. To every one of the causal consequences that would flow from anything which P is free (or unfree) to do, there would correspond a freedom (or an unfreedom); the interminable proliferation of potential consequences would therefore ensure the interminable proliferation of freedoms and unfreedoms.

Another principal reason for laying restrictions on the length of the causal concatenations that are covered by our measurements of each

---

[25] Carter, *Measure*, 188–9.

person's overall liberty—a reason closely related to the point just made—is that the absence of such restrictions would endue those measurements with an outlandish degree of speculativeness. Since the causal chains would extend indefinitely into the future, we would have to conjecture about occurrences that might unfold aeons and aeons from now. Even the attachment of probabilities to those envisaged occurrences would be a matter of ungrounded guesswork; the probability of the correctness of any of those probabilities would itself be unknowable. We would thus find ourselves adrift on a sea of surmises, even more disconcertingly than we would if we allowed that unfreedoms can arise from other people's omissions as well as from their actions. Thus, given that Chapter 4 declined to countenance the speculativeness involved in tracing unfreedoms to omissions, we should plainly eschew the speculativeness involved in charting causal series without limits.

Note that this point about the avoidance of inordinate conjecturalness is perfectly consistent with my frequent distinction in this chapter between what is possible in principle and what is possible in practice. Although the sheer number of variables to be ascertained in the course of comprehensively measuring anyone's overall liberty will have rendered such an enterprise forbiddingly complicated in practice, the carrying out of that enterprise is possible in principle, and it would become possible in practice if enough people and resources were devoted to developing and employing some appropriate technology for it. Moreover, we can meaningfully seek to carry out partial measurements that will stand as rough approximations of some of the findings in an ideally comprehensive set of measurements. By contrast, the objective of charting causal chains that stretch millions of years into the future is an aim of which the fulfilment would require little short of omniscience. In principle as well as in practice, such an aim could not be accomplished satisfactorily without the assistance of an all-knowing Deity. In principle as well as in practice, we would lack any grounds for minimal confidence in the accuracy of our ludicrously distant predictions. As has been indicated, furthermore, the attachment of probabilistic qualifications would not avail us; such qualifications would be as dubiously conjectural as the propositions which they would qualify. We would have no basis for knowing whether our predictions are rough approximations of the truth or not.

This problem clearly stands in need of a solution, and the last couple of paragraphs in summarizing a major aspect of the problem have pointed the way toward the best tack for disposing of it. Although my discussion proceeding at a high level of abstraction cannot specify a precise cut-off point for the inclusion of causal consequences among the things which a person is free or unfree to bring about, the key consideration is the need to avoid crippling uncertainty and fancifulness. When we can judge with confidence that some particular consequences are highly likely to ensue if a person exercises this or that freedom, we should incorporate those consequences (with probabilistic qualifications) into our calculations of the person's combinations of conjunctively exercisable liberties. Similarly, we should incorporate such consequences into our calculations of a person's combinations of consistent unfreedoms when we can judge with confidence that those consequences would be highly likely to ensue from the exercise of any opportunity contained in such a combination. (This wording is meant to apply irrespective of whether the opportunity is individually open to the person or is closed off to her by other people's actions.) Moreover, we should also take account of causal consequences even if they are not highly likely to ensue from the exercise of an opportunity, so long as we can confidently assign probabilities to their ensuing. For example, although the probability of a twelve on any particular throw of a pair of fair dice is low, it can be assigned precisely. A specification of such an outcome, accompanied by a stringent probabilistic qualification, will therefore be among our specifications of the potential causal consequences of a person's exercise of her freedom to throw some pair of dice. A substantial degree of second-order confidence of this sort is the crucial factor that must be present for the incorporation of potential causal consequences into our calculations. In the absence of such confidence, a project of measuring each person's overall liberty would be completely unmoored and unworkable; it would fail to keep the components of the liberty-measuring fraction from expanding limitlessly on the basis of airy speculations.

To be sure, at an abstract level we cannot pinpoint with exactitude the degree of second-order confidence that is sufficient for the inclusion of various potential causal consequences among the contents of a person's freedoms or unfreedoms. The threshold degree of confidence will vary to some extent among different types of contexts, and will likewise vary in response to developments in the prevailing methodological canons of the natural and social sciences. As a result, the measurement of each person's overall freedom will be subject to a modest amount of vagueness or uncertainty at its edges, even in principle. Given that we have to encompass many potential causal consequences of any person's doings in our reckoning of the things which the person is free or unfree to bring about, and given that there is no firmly context-transcendent line to be drawn between those potential consequences that are to be encompassed and those that are not, the precise location of the periphery of each person's overall freedom will be a matter about which reasonable people can disagree. Still, for at least three reasons, the troublesomeness of this observation is very small indeed. First, of course, the decision between inclusion and exclusion will be clear-cut in regard to most potential causal consequences. The area of vagueness is at the penumbra of the freedom-measuring enterprise, and does not mar the perspicuousness of that enterprise's core. Second, any controversy arising in that penumbral area will not be moral/political, but will instead centre on epistemic queries and on scientific or social-scientific issues concerning the unfolding of events. Hence, this paragraph's remarks on the equivocal status of some potential causal consequences do not clash at all with my repeated insistence that the existence of each particular freedom or unfreedom is something that can be ascertained without any reliance on moral or evaluative assumptions. Third, the fact that reasonable people might well disagree about the status of some potential causal consequences is fully compatible with the attainment of rigorous consistency in one's own treatment of such consequences. What is vital is not the formation of a consensus among all theorists who might endeavour to gauge the overall freedom of each person. What is vital, rather, is the consistent handling of potential causal consequences by any given theorist. One should strive to treat assimilable cases uniformly and divergent cases differently in order to achieve the consonance between cases that is essential for the illuminatingness of any scheme of measurements and rankings. Just as the units of measurement within any tenable approach to ascertaining the extent of everyone's overall liberty must be uniform in size, so too one's classification of causal consequences must display regularity in differentiating among some cases and in drawing parallels between others. Such regularity is crucial not only for the avoidance of confusion and distortions within one's own scheme of measurement, but also for the fruitfulness of comparisons with other credible schemes; unless a system of measurement is consistent within itself, no genuinely illuminating contrasts can be drawn between its own conclusions and the conclusions of cognate systems that are also consistent. These advantages of one's attainment of rigorous consistency within one's own set of classifications go a very long way towards offsetting the drawbacks of the peripheral area of disaccord between that set and other reasonable ways of classifying potential causal consequences.

1.6.2. Probabilistic Qualifications   In much of the foregoing discussion of potential causal consequences, and also in many other parts of this book, the role of probabilistic qualifications has figured saliently. In principle as well as in practice, any endeavour to measure people's levels of liberty must make extensive use of such qualifications, since most ascriptions of particular freedoms and unfreedoms are probabilistic. Although the relevant probabilities are often very high, they usually fall short of 1; accordingly, our claims about the existence of particular freedoms or unfreedoms are usually accompanied by probabilistic qualifications, which nonetheless frequently remain implicit (especially when the probabilities are extremely high).

The attachment of probabilistic qualifications to attributions of particular freedoms and unfreedoms is straightforward, but the matter becomes somewhat more complicated when we ponder how such qualifications are to be reflected in our calculations of anyone's overall liberty. On the one hand, to be sure, no really serious complexities arise in connection with any person's combinations of conjunctively exercisable freedoms. The numerical expression of each freedom in every such combination is multiplied by the probability of that freedom's existence. When the resultant product has also been multiplied by the applicable qualitatively-oriented weighting, it is then an element in the combination to be added up with all of the other elements therein. Once we have arrived at a sum of those elements, we have come up with a preliminary figure that represents the combination as a whole. Such a figure is then multiplied by the probability that the exercise of each of the freedoms in the combination would be consistent with the exercise of each of the other freedoms therein. We thus get a final numerical expression of the combination, which can be added up with the numerical expressions of the person's other combinations of conjunctively exercisable liberties.

Things become more involuted when we turn our attention to the combinations of consistent unfreedoms that confront any person *P*. A chief source of the intricateness is the fact that there are two main ways in which any apparent set of opportunities can prove not to be a combination of consistent unfreedoms. It can prove to be a combination of conjunctively exercisable liberties, or it can prove to be a set that lacks conjunctive exercisability without satisfying the first prong of the U Postulate. With an eye towards the first of these eventualities, we need to know the probability that the opportunities in the set under consideration will not be exercisable together by *P*. With an eye towards the second of the stated eventualities, we need to know the probability that natural forces and *P*'s own conduct will not be sufficient (in the absence of other people's actions) to eliminate *P*'s ability to avail himself of the specified set of opportunities conjunctively. In short, we need to ascertain the probability that the following two conditions obtain: a set of opportunities is not conjunctively exercisable by *P*, and at least one action by some person(s) other than *P* is a causally necessary condition for the lack of conjunctive exercisability.

If a combination of consistent unfreedoms for *P* consists of only one item which is itself an unfreedom, then the role of the probabilistic qualification is clear-cut. The qualification to be attached to the whole combination is the probability that the single item is indeed an unfreedom—in other words, the probability that it is closed off as an opportunity and that a causally necessary condition for its being closed off is at least one action by some person(s) other than *P*. When a combination consists of two or more items that are individually unfreedoms, the role of the probabilistic qualification becomes more complicated. Indeed, not very much can be said at an abstract level, since the exact upshot in each case will depend on the relationship (particularly on the degree of independence) between the constraints that close off opportunities to *P*. What can be said, however, is that the probabilistic qualification attaching to the whole combination will never be lower than the product of the following two factors: the probability pr_1 that the element of the combination most likely to be an unfreedom is indeed an unfreedom, and the probability pr_2 that no other opportunity or set of opportunities in the combination will have been deprived of exercisability or conjunctive exercisability in a fashion that leaves the first prong of the U Postulate unsatisfied. If pr_1 is lower than the probability pr_3 that two or more opportunities in the combination do not partake of conjunctive exercisability and that a causally necessary condition for their lack of conjunctive exercisability is at least one action by some person(s) other than *P*, then we can know that the probabilistic qualification attaching to the combination as a whole will never be lower than the product of pr_2 and pr_3. (Note that the only probabilistic qualification entered into our final calculations is the one that attaches to the entire combination of consistent unfreedoms. Though we have to assign probabilities to the individual elements along the way, those probabilities are subsumed into the overarching qualification.)

Essentially the same points apply to any combination of consistent unfreedoms in which not every item is individually an unfreedom. For any such combination in which at least one element is individually an unfreedom, the lowest probabilistic qualification attaching to the entire combination will be either the product of pr_1 and pr_2 or the product of pr_2 and pr_3, whichever is the higher. In respect of any combination of consistent unfreedoms in which no element is individually an unfreedom, the lowest probabilistic qualification for the whole combination will be the product of pr_2 and pr_3. Of course, whether or not a combination of consistent unfreedoms for P is made up of items that are individually unfreedoms, we might discover that more than one subset of the items has been divested of conjunctive exercisability because of the actions of other people. Whenever more than one such subset is present, each of them is associated with a probability that it lacks conjunctive exercisability and that at least one action by somebody other than P was causally necessary for the absence of conjunctive exercisability. In these circumstances, the highest such probability is the value of pr_3.

Arcane and abstract though these remarks on probabilistic qualifications might seem to some readers, the importance of those qualifications should be evident from several of the earlier portions of this book. For example—by no means the only example—an alertness to the role of those qualifications enables us to perceive that the ostensible divergence between the negative conception and the civic-republican conception of liberty is *au fond* a difference of emphasis concerning the means by which the overall liberty of virtually everyone can be promoted. Civic republicans highlight the need for bolstering the security of various freedoms, and they plump for institutional arrangements that can help to cultivate and sustain such security. In so doing, they propose to enhance the overall freedom of virtually everyone by increasing the probability of the existence of certain freedoms (and thus in effect by increasing the probabilistic qualifications that can correctly be attached to one's ascriptions of any number of particular liberties). Although the civic republicans resort to quite a different vocabulary in order to express their aspirations, those aspirations can be understood and accommodated perfectly well within the analytical/terminological framework devised here for the purpose of measuring freedom. So long as we grasp the function and significance of probabilistic qualifications, we can recognize how the civic-republican proposals bear directly on each person's overall liberty. Despite the penchant of journalists and some philosophers for a division between liberty and security, the latter side of that division is in fact an aspect of the former. Because most ascriptions of freedom or unfreedom carry probabilistic qualifications (albeit often only implicitly), and because those implicit or explicit qualifications are squarely incorporated into our measurements of each person's overall freedom, an increase in the security of somebody's pursuit of various projects is *pro tanto* an increase in the property which we measure as her overall freedom.

Now, before we move on, we should note the deliberately narrow focus of my comments in this subsection. Throughout the present discussion and my earlier discussions of the probabilistic qualifications that attach to claims about freedom, I have sought to avoid taking any stands on metaphysical questions concerning the ultimate nature and groundings of probabilities. Just as Chapter 4 has dodged many of the metaphysical questions that surround the concept of causation, my remarks in the current subsection and elsewhere have endeavoured to sidestep the corresponding medley of metaphysical questions that surround the concept of probability. In particular, this subsection's analysis has not tried in any way to determine whether probabilities are ultimately purely epistemic limitations or whether instead they are ontologically grounded (perhaps in some possible-worlds meta-physic). Immensely interesting though such issues are, they are beside the point here—since my aim in this discussion, as in Chapter 4, has been to delineate some general criteria and methods on the basis of which a project of measuring each person's overall liberty can be operationalized. For someone striving to accomplish such an aim, an investigation of the metaphysical status of probabilities would be as gratuitous and distracting as it would be in a textbook on statistics where the aim is to expound laws of probability for the purpose of guiding statistical inferences. Regardless of the ultimate groundings of our probabilistic qualifications, they express the confidence with which we can attribute particular freedoms and unfreedoms to people, and they thereby impinge on what we measure as each person's overall liberty.

Anyone's rational confidence in propounding a proposition will of course depend largely on the information at his or her disposal. From whose perspective, then, should the probabilistic qualifications in any ascriptions of freedoms and unfreedoms be set? Plainly, the qualifica-tions that are invoked in a truly comprehensive project of measure-ment should be set from the perspective of the people who have sufficient information—and therefore sufficiently advanced technol-ogy—to carry out such a project. Although the germane information would be staggeringly enormous and complex, it would be finite both in quantity and in intricacy; the idea of a perspective rooted in such information is thus eminently coherent, even if the gathering of the information will remain far beyond our powers well into the future. In present-day settings, where any enquiries into people's levels of overall liberty will fall markedly short of ideal comprehensiveness, the appropriate perspective for the fixing of probabilities is that of the people whose relevant knowledge most closely approximates the knowledge required for thoroughgoing measurements. In this respect, then, Carter is correct when he submits that the applicable probabilities are to be set by reference to the vantage point of 'the best-informed person'.[26]

Considerably less persuasive, however, is Carter's suggestion that the pertinent vantage point is occupied more specifically by the best-informed person *at the time of the existence of the freedom that is being measured*. Of course, when the time just stated is the same as the juncture at which the freedom is being measured, Carter's suggestion is manifestly correct. However, in respect of any situation in which those two junctures do not coincide, his contention lacks cogency. Carter maintains that his approach to this matter is warranted because it enables us to engage undistortively in inter-temporal comparisons of people's levels of overall liberty: '[W]e may be interested in comparing the freedom of agents who themselves have different temporal locations . . . [W]here [the time of the existence of the freedom that is being measured] is some time in the past, then in order to put such assessments of past degrees of freedom on all fours with assessments of present degrees of freedom (so as to allow for valid intertemporal comparisons of freedom), we should disregard any consequences of basic actions about which we have come to know only with hindsight.'[27]

For three principal reasons, Carter's stance on this specific point should be rejected. First, although his position might be sensible if we had solid grounds for thinking that the superior knowledgeableness of the retrospective viewpoint (over the prospective viewpoint) will generally skew our inter-temporal comparisons of levels of freedom, we do not in fact have any such grounds. Skewing would indeed occur if the retrospective viewpoint enabled us to detect many additional freedoms but few additional unfreedoms and mere inabilities. Skewing would likewise occur, of course, if the retrospective viewpoint instead enabled us to descry many additional unfreedoms and mere inabilities but few additional freedoms. In either of these two situations, our inter-temporal comparisons among people's levels of overall liberty would indeed be distortive if we were not to heed Carter's admonition. In the first situation we would be overestimating the relative extent of

---

[26] Carter, *Measure*, 189.
[27] Ibid.

the freedom of people in the past—that is, their levels of freedom in comparison with the levels of freedom enjoyed by people in the present. In the second situation, obviously, our mistake would lie in the opposite direction. Though in each case our estimates of the bygone levels of freedom might in themselves be especially accurate, they would mislead us when they are laid alongside our estimates of the current levels of freedom. However, there is no reason, certainly no manifest reason, for thinking that the superiority of the retrospective vantage point will in fact bias our inter-temporal comparisons in either of the two directions sketched here. In the absence of any arguments to the contrary from Carter, we can assume that the epistemic advantages of the retrospective viewpoint will enable us to discern more readily both the presence of various freedoms and the absence of various other freedoms in some earlier era. Though we will very likely be in a position to know that certain things which might have appeared impossible at the time were actually possible, we shall also very likely be in a position to know that certain things which seemed possible at the time were actually impossible. To be sure, the balance between these corrective effects might not be exactly even; there might turn out to be a slight tilt in one direction or the other. Nevertheless, in the absence of any arguments for presuming otherwise, we have no basis for fearing that such a tilt will be pronounced (and thus significantly distortive). Hence, even if there were no other reasons for querying Carter's position on this issue, our reasons for accepting his position would be meagre.

Second, we should not leave utterly unchallenged the assumption that the retrospective viewpoint will in fact be superior to the pro-spective viewpoint in all or most respects. On the one hand, it will undoubtedly be superior in *some* respects, along the lines mentioned in my last paragraph. Furthermore, it might conceivably be superior in all or most respects. On the other hand, the likelihood that all or nearly all the advantages lie in favour of the retrospective orientation is pretty low. When people are on the scene at the time of the existence of the freedom which they are measuring, they will ordinarily be in a position to detect certain facets of the situation that remain concealed from the gaze of later investigators. To be sure, this point should not be pressed particularly hard. People looking into the past will typically enjoy a number of epistemic advantages over people on the scene, and their advantages might well outweigh their disadvantages (maybe quite substantially). Nevertheless, we cannot safely predict that our weighing up of a backward-looking perspective's benefits and draw-backs will always yield the conclusion that the former exceed the latter.

Third, and perhaps most important, any claims about the outlooks of people in some quondam age are themselves probabilistic; our knowledge of their outlooks is no more immune to uncertainties than our knowledge of other aspects of their situation. Hence, if we take those outlooks (or, more precisely, the best-informed outlooks among them) as our benchmark for specifying the probabilistic qualifications that are operative when we ascribe freedoms and unfreedoms to the people in that past age, we shall have to add further probabilistic qualifications in order to reflect the possibility of errors in our understanding of those outlooks. Thus, while trying to place the two sides of a comparison between the present and the past 'on all fours'—in Carter's words—we would be introducing a new element of uncertainty into one of those sides. On the former half of the comparison would be freedom-ascribing statements endowed with probabilistic qualifications, while on the latter half would be freedom-ascribing statements endowed with probabilistic qualifications attached to additional probabilistic qualifications.

To be sure, if some commendably thorough measurements of people's levels of overall liberty at t_1 have been undertaken at t_1, and if equally thorough measurements of people's levels of overall liberty at t_2 have been undertaken at t_2, then the germane perspective for specifying the probabilistic qualifications within each set of measurements is the perspective of the measurers at the time of the existence of the freedom that has been gauged. Typically, however, an inter-temporal comparison will involve sets of measurements that are undertaken at a single time t (though with divergent temporal orientations, of course). For any such comparison, the appropriate perspective for the fixing of probabilities in each set of measurements is that of the best-informed measurers at t.

Now, lest the last several paragraphs convey a misleading impression, this section should close by briefly clarifying the point of contention that has been addressed in those paragraphs. Not in dispute is the notion that the relevant probability of any particular freedom's existence is the probability thereof at the time of the freedom's actual or ostensible existence. Let us designate that time as 'm'. The probability at m that the specified freedom exists at m, rather than the probability at any later time that that freedom existed at m, is what should be reflected in the probabilistic qualification attached to any ascription of that particular freedom for the purpose of an inter-temporal comparison. What is in dispute is not that point, then, but the matter of the perspective from which the relevant probability should be ascertained. Whereas Carter maintains that the pertinent viewpoint is always occupied by the best-informed person at the time of the actual or ostensible existence of the freedom in question, my discussion has argued that the pertinent viewpoint is instead that of the best-informed person at the time when the particular freedom gets taken into account by liberty-measuring calculations. We are disagreeing not about the temporal location of the relevant probability, but about the temporal location of the perspective from which that probability is to be gauged.

2. Measurement and Evaluation

In the second half of this chapter, we turn to the aspect of the freedom-measuring enterprise that most sharply distinguishes my own approach from that of Carter and Steiner (who, on this topic, are in virtually complete agreement with each other). As has been declared at the outset of this chapter and at other junctures in this book, we should distinguish carefully between enquiries into the existence of anyone's particular freedoms/unfreedoms and enquiries into the extent of anyone's overall liberty. Whereas enquiries of the former type do not depend on evaluative assumptions, enquiries of the latter type do indeed integrally involve such assumptions. To be sure, when we ask a 'how free' question about anyone, we are asking primarily about the purely physical scope of the person's latitude and about the purely physical scope of the confinedness that has been imposed on the person by other people; but we are also asking about the qualitative significance of the combinations of conjunctively exercisable freedoms and the combinations of consistent unfreedoms which respectively make up that latitude and that confinedness. To omit the evaluative component altogether is to misconstrue the import of the 'how free' question, or so the rest of this chapter will argue.

Some other negative-liberty theorists have maintained that ascertaining the extent of anyone's overall freedom is a partly evaluative endeavour, though their arguments typically differ substantially from the arguments that will be marshalled here. Quite closely aligned with me is G. A. Cohen, who has highlighted the dichotomy between the existence of anybody's particular freedoms and the extent of anybody's overall liberty: 'Reference to a man's desires is irrelevant to the question "What is he free to do?", but it is, I believe, relevant to the question "How much freedom (comprehensively) does he have?", and consequently to the politically crucial question of comparing the amounts of freedom enjoyed in different societies.'[28] To be sure, the quoted passage goes slightly astray by concentrating on desires rather than on objective values—which include the value of being free to pursue what one strongly desires, but which are by no means limited to that value. Moreover, Cohen has not subsequently expanded on the basic insight which he tersely articulates in this passage. Nonetheless, that insight is of key importance for my own approach to the measurement of freedom. Likewise noteworthy in adumbrating broadly the same conception of overall freedom are a few remarks by Isaiah Berlin. Though his comments on the overall freedom of people are brief and somewhat vaporous, he grasped that evaluative considerations must inform our answers to any 'how free' questions. He submitted that two of the factors which determine 'the extent of my freedom' are 'how important in my plan of life, given my character and circumstances, [the possibilities open to me] are when compared with each other' and 'what value not merely the agent, but the general sentiment of the society in which he lives, puts on the various possibilities'.[29] In a similar vein is the comment that 'freedom ultimately depends...on how many doors are open, how open they are, upon their relative importance in my life'.[30] Along essentially the same lines is a pronouncement by Berlin near the end of his famous essay on negative and positive liberty, where he asserted that '[t]he freedom of a society' depends in part on 'the number and importance of the paths' that are kept open to people therein.[31] Fuzzy though his analyses may have been, then, he prefigured the general position that will be defended below.

That position has been attacked by some other negative-liberty theorists, however, who have contended that the enterprise of measur-

---

[28] G. A. Cohen, 'Illusions about Private Property and Freedom', in John Mepham and David Hillel-Ruben (eds), *Issues in Marxist Philosophy*, iv (Hassocks: Harvester Press, 1981), 223, 231. For a similar position, see Lawrence Crocker, *Positive Liberty* (The Hague: Martinus Nijhoff, 1980), 45, 47: 'While I think the negative account could do perfectly well without mentioning desire in the case of freedom to perform particular actions, desire may not be quite so easily dispensed with from an account of the total freedom of a person...The better course is to take desirability and related matters as affecting the contribution an alternative makes to [a person's overall] liberty.'

[29] Isaiah Berlin, *Four Essays on Liberty* (Oxford: Oxford University Press, 1969) [Berlin, *Four Essays*], 130 n. 1.

[30] Berlin, *Four Essays*, xxxix.

[31] Berlin, *Four Essays*, 166.

ing each person's overall liberty is strictly non-evaluative. Van Hees is one of the theorists who have delivered such attacks, but Carter and Steiner have presented the most sustained set of arguments against the view that 'how free' questions are partly evaluative. They have affirmed that a starkly non-evaluative approach can surmount the numerous difficulties that beset it, and they have sought to show that the invocation of evaluative considerations will give rise to errors and absurdities. My responses to Carter and Steiner will therefore have to be both defensive and offensive. On the one hand, this chapter will argue that—so long as a firm distinction is maintained between questions about the extent of a person's overall freedom and questions about the existence of a person's particular liberties or unfreedoms— my reliance on evaluative assumptions can withstand all the challenges launched by Carter and Steiner. Equally, I shall argue that any wholesale eschewal of evaluative assumptions in the measurement of freedom leads to unacceptable results which Carter and Steiner themselves are keen to avoid.

Let it be emphasized straightaway that the defensive and offensive strategies just mentioned are not accompanied here by any attempt to establish that my conception of overall freedom as a partly evaluative phenomenon can be derived from some deeper premise or set of premises. What was said of the human/natural distinction earlier in this chapter is applicable here (*mutatis mutandis*) to my conception of overall freedom. Any effort to derive that conception from some profounder point of departure would almost certainly be patently question-begging and would thus be futile. Hence, instead of seeking to provide a derivation, this chapter takes as given that the level of each person's overall liberty is indeed determined in part by evaluative considerations. It then endeavours to show that, when properly formulated, such a thesis is not problematic in the ways suggested by Carter and Steiner; and it further endeavours to show that that thesis enables us to deal handily with certain difficulties that are stumbling stones for Carter and Steiner. Both that defensive point and that offensive point will have lent some vital confirmatory support to my conception of overall freedom, but neither of them is a ground from which that conception is strictly deducible. This book does not pretend to reveal any ground of that sort. No such ground is needed for the sustainment of a thesis that proves to be indispensable for any satisfactory theory of socio-political freedom.

2.1. Basic Ideas and Defences

In the first half of this chapter, we have looked at how qualitatively-oriented multipliers are to be incorporated into our calculations of levels of overall liberty. Those points do not have to be recapitulated here. Instead, we need to probe the multipliers themselves. That is, this subsection will outline the basic considerations that underlie each multiplier, and it will venture to demonstrate that those considerations when suitably understood are not vulnerable to the objections that have been broached by Carter and Steiner.

2.1.1. Qualitative Considerations   The fundamental idea motivating the introduction of qualitatively-oriented multipliers has already been stated. When a 'how free' question is posed about anyone, an accurate answer will be focused primarily on the purely physical dimensions of the person's combinations of conjunctively exercisable freedoms and combinations of consistent unfreedoms, but will also be focused on the objective importance of those combinations (and their elements) for the person. Several aspects of this general idea must be fleshed out. What is meant by my saying that the purely physical dimensions of a person's latitude and confinedness will be the primary determinants of her level of overall liberty? Concomitantly, what is meant by the obvious corollary that the qualitative weightings attached to freedoms and to combinations of consistent unfreedoms are to play only a subordinate role in our calculations of people's levels of liberty? How can the importance of freedoms and unfreedoms be both object-ive and 'for the person'? What in any event are the relevant touchstones for gauging that importance? Do the desires of a person bear on the significance which we should attribute to her freedoms and unfreedoms?

The primacy of the purely physical dimensions of a person's overall freedom lies in the fact that the lowest value for any qualitatively-oriented multiplier is 1. Though such a multiplier might occasionally not increase the numerical expression of some particular freedom or some combination of consistent unfreedoms, it never decreases that numerical expression. Even when the possession of a particular freedom of some anomalous type is typically of disvalue for a human being, the qualitatively-oriented multiplier associated with any freedom of that type is not negative or zero. As has been indicated, such a multiplier never takes a numerical value lower than 1. If it does not make an augmentative difference to the weight of some particular freedom, then it makes no difference at all; it never makes a diminutional difference. Every freedom or unfreedom will be registered in our calculations at least to the extent of its physical dimensions. A failure to insist on this point would be a failure to recognize that 'how free' questions are primarily about those dimensions. Even when some person P comes to possess some unusual freedoms that are typically without value for anyone who is endowed with them, they will have warranted larger numbers in our answers to 'how free' questions about P than would be warranted if those freedoms were eliminated while everything else remained the same. After all, by contributing to the range of things which P is able to do or be or become, every such freedom of hers contributes *pro tanto* to her overall liberty. Consequently, the physical ambit of every such freedom must be fully taken into account when we endeavour to calculate how free P is.

Qualitatively-oriented weightings, then, occupy a subordinate place in our measurements. They never lower the numbers at which we arrive through our enquiries into the purely physical scopes of each person's freedoms and unfreedoms. Knowing as much, we must now consider how they perform their augmentative role. If we are employing such weightings to reflect the objective importance of freedoms and unfreedoms, what exactly are we trying to capture? Importance here is to be understood by reference to certain ideals that are promoted by freedom in a content-independent fashion. Each particular freedom is to be assessed as relatively significant or relatively insignificant in accordance with its greater or lesser tendency to foster those ideals.

Carter has argued lengthily and persuasively in favour of the view that freedom partakes of content-independent valuableness.[32] That is, not only are many of P's particular freedoms valuable for P because of their specific contents, but in addition her overall liberty is valuable for her independently of any of those specific contents. While leaving open the possibility that the content-independent valuableness of

---

[32] His main arguments are presented in the second chapter of Carter, *Measure*. For a somewhat earlier version of those arguments, see Ian Carter, 'The Independent Value of Freedom', 105 *Ethics* 819 (1995). For some broadly similar arguments, see Peter Jones and Robert Sugden, 'Evaluating Choice', 2 *International Review of Law and Economics* 47, 52–5 (1982) [Jones and Sugden, 'Choice']. Cf. Richard Flathman, *The Philosophy and Politics of Freedom* (Chicago: University of Chicago Press, 1987) [Flathman, *Freedom*], Ch. 8; Amartya Sen, 'Markets and Freedoms: Achievements and Limitations of the Market Mechanism in Promoting Individual Freedoms', 45 *Oxford Economic Papers* 519, 523–4 (1993).

freedom is exhausted (or is outweighed by the content-independent disvalue of freedom) above some high level, Carter convincingly maintains that—at least up to a certain level—freedom is invested with content-independent instrumental valuableness and content-independent constitutive valuableness. His powerful arguments in support of these conclusions will not be recounted fully here, but we should look very briefly at the conclusions themselves. (Carter also argues that freedom partakes of intrinsic valuableness. We shall put that claim aside simply because it does not posit any connection between freedom and other valuable states.)

Freedom is instrumentally valuable in that it tends to promote certain other desiderata, and the instrumental valuableness is content-independent in that it is characteristic of anyone's overall liberty and not merely of some of her particular liberties. The desiderata promoted are those of individual development and well-being. What bestows content-independent valuableness on freedom in the further-ance of those desiderata is the inability of human beings to anticipate exactly which paths they will aim to take in the future and which present things will turn out to be serviceable for the attainment of future objectives. Because human beings are far from omniscient, and because they and their circumstances tend to undergo numerous vicis-situdes, the content-dependent valuableness of any particular freedom may turn out to be lower or greater than it seems at the time of the particular freedom's existence. What currently appear to be attractive opportunities may prove to be trifling or even detrimental, and what currently seem to be inconsequential options may prove to be some highly rewarding paths. In sum, the insurmountable finitude of our knowledge can lead us astray in our judgements about the content-dependent valuableness of this or that freedom. Accordingly, at least up to a certain level of overall liberty, we shall be more likely to develop ourselves fruitfully if we enjoy more freedoms rather than fewer. Since nobody at present can infallibly identify the particular freedoms that are most advantageous for us, our lives will generally go better if our combinations of conjunctively exercisable freedoms are plentiful rather than cabined—even if the cabining would be carried out with the best of intentions by knowledgeable people. Abundant freedoms generally enable us to flourish through experimentation and through the consequent adaptation of our activities, notwithstanding that many of the particular freedoms will go unexercised, and notwithstanding that some of them when exercised will turn out to be profitless. Thus, as has been widely recognized at least since the time of John Stuart Mill, freedom as a phenomenon that overarches its myriad instances and combinations of instances is possessed of a distinctive instrumental value as a facilitator of progress.

Before we proceed to glance at the content-independent constitutive valuableness of freedom, one or two caveats should be entered. As has already been noted, Carter readily acknowledges that additional combinations of liberties beyond some high level might not enhance the content-independent valuableness of a person's overall liberty and might even detract from it. He also readily acknowledges that, even below the high level just mentioned, the emergence of certain additional combinations of liberties for a person might carry some quantum of content-specific disvalue for her that outweighs their enhancement of the content-independent valuableness of her overall liberty. That content-specific disvalue, moreover, might be easily foreseeable and might therefore unequivocally warrant our averting the emergence of the new combinations of liberties. Hence, Carter's arguments are not meant to suggest that we should always try to increase each person's overall freedom (at least up to some high level). Rather, they are simply meant to reveal that any accurate cost/benefit assessment of new combinations of conjunctively exercisable freedoms must take into account the contributions by those new combinations to the content-independent valuableness of a person's overall liberty.

Freedom partakes of content-independent constitutive valuableness, in that it is an integral constituent of something else that is intrinsically good. Specifically, it is a key ingredient of individual autonomy. An autonomous person gains and retains her status as such not only by arriving at most of her decisions in a reasonably reflective manner that bespeaks her self-determination, but also by having been free to behave in any number of ways that are contrary to the ways in which she actually behaves. In so far as the options open to a person have been tightly constricted, she has lacked the room necessary for achieving and exhibiting full-fledged autonomy. Even in the extremely unlikely event that the hemmed-in person has been unaware of the confines of her situation and has reached appropriate decisions for apt reasons that are independent of her dearth of alternatives, her unawareness of the constraints on her latitude is itself a defect in her rational autonomy. Furthermore, even if there is no element of serious unawareness on her part, she has at most attained the affirmative aspect of autonomy without attaining its declinatory aspect. That is, although *ex hypothesi* she has persistently arrived at proper decisions for proper reasons, she has not been in a position to decide against following many contrary paths. She has not enjoyed a substantial set of opportunities to exert herself as a choosing agent with some degree of control over what she does and what happens to her. The exercise of any genuinely autonomous agency consists in abundant refusals— whether implicit or explicit—as well as in affirmative choices made for apposite reasons. As Carter states: '[T]he more freedom we have, the greater the sense in which we can be called agents, and thus responsible for what we do, because the greater the number of times that we can [tacitly or expressly] say "no".'[33]

What is crucial about each of the two types of valuableness just delineated is that each of them can be imputed to freedom on content-independent grounds. Though each type of valuableness is applicable to numerous particular freedoms in a content-dependent manner, each type is also characteristic of overall freedom as a property that comprehends its countless instances. So Carter argues, and his arguments are powerful. Thus, if we in our evaluations of the significance of various particular freedoms make our judgements by reference to precisely the desiderata that are associated with freedom in a content-independent fashion, we shall not be shifting from one analysandum to another. We shall not be changing the topic of discussion from the extent of each person's overall freedom to something else.

The purpose of our evaluations is to ascertain how much is qualitatively contributed by each particular liberty of some person P to her overall freedom. In other words, we are seeking to determine the bearing of each liberty on the appropriate answer to a 'how free' question about P. To be sure, as has been insisted, such a question is primarily about the physical dimensions of her opportunities and constrainedness; but, as has also been insisted, such a question is likewise about the qualitative importance of those physical states. We now can see that the matter of importance is gauged by recourse to desiderata—such as individual development and well-being and autonomy—which are not chosen at random but which instead are distinctively engendered by freedom itself, instrumentally or constitutively. A 'how free' question in its qualitative aspect is an inquiry about the extent to which P's state of overall freedom promotes the desiderata that are integrally associated with overall freedom as a general attribute. Of course, a suitable answer to that question in its qualitative aspect will focus especially on the sheer physical scope of P's combinations-of-conjunctively-exercisable-freedoms and combinations-of-consistent-unfreedoms. After all, the desiderata that serve as our touchstones of qualitative significance are linked to freedom in a content-independent fashion—which means that they are linked to

---

[33] Carter, *Measure*, 58.

overall freedom as a sheer physical property. However, a suitable answer to the 'how free' question must also take account of the content-specific ways in which P's sundry liberties contribute to the realization of those desiderata (and the content-specific ways in which her combinations of consistent unfreedoms would have contributed to that realization if the conjunctive exercisability of each such combination had not been eliminated by the actions of other people). For that purpose, plainly, we have to make reference not merely to the physical magnitude of her liberties but also to their qualitative types. If we neglect such qualitative considerations when we answer a 'how free' question about P, we shall be missing the full import of the question—which concerns all the ways in which her freedoms promote the ideals that are distinctively connected with freedom. Those ideals are promoted by her freedoms qua constituents of her overall liberty, but they are also promoted by her freedoms qua particular opportunities that pertain to specific actions or states or processes.

In short, when we wish to gauge the significance of P's particular freedoms in order to assign each of them a qualitatively-oriented multiplier for our measurements of P's overall liberty, we should base our judgements of significance on each freedom's content-dependent tendency to foster the desiderata with which any person's liberty has content-independent ties. (Incidentally, as should be evident from Chapter 3's account of the distinction between the value of one's φ-ing and the value of one's particular freedom-to-φ, a freedom-to-φ can have a content-dependent tendency to advance the aforementioned desiderata even though φ-ing itself might have no such tendency. For example, one's autonomy will generally be bolstered through one's possession of the freedom to commit suicide in this or that manner, even though the exercise of such a freedom would scarcely sustain one's autonomy.) The matter addressed here, of course, is not *whether* evaluative considerations affect the level of each person's overall liberty. As has already been observed, the character of everyone's overall freedom as a partly evaluative phenomenon is taken as given throughout my discussion. Instead, the matter addressed here is *which* evaluative considerations affect the extent of each person's overall liberty. I have focused on the content-independent connections between freedom and certain ideals in order to answer this latter question, which asks us to single out the pertinent evaluative considerations non-arbitrarily. By looking for those content-independent connections, we can avoid arbitrariness and can base the evaluative dimension of the freedom-measuring enterprise on the distinctive value-engendering roles of freedom itself.

A query immediately arises, however. Given that Carter's arguments for the content-independent instrumental valuableness of freedom highlight the inability of human beings to tell exactly which particular freedoms will be valuable for them and which will not, we may seem to lack an adequate basis for judging the significance of particular freedoms in the way just described. Since measurers of freedom will be subject to the same general limits on their knowledge as everyone else, how can we discern what apparently lies beyond the ken of other people? Fortunately, the problem posed by this question is much less troubling than it might at first seem. Nobody has ever denied that some particular freedoms are qualitatively more important than others,[34] nor has anyone denied that we can frequently know with a high degree of confidence which freedoms are especially valuable. What Carter aptly emphasizes is the fallibility of our judgements about qualitative significance; to underscore that fallibility, however, is not to suggest that people suffer from outright ignorance in these matters. Although we should surely accept that freedom is endowed with content-independent valuableness partly because of the proneness of human beings to err when they esteem or depreciate certain particular freedoms, we should hardly conclude therefrom that no judgements about the significance of particular freedoms can reasonably be made and confirmed. People sometimes go astray when reaching such judgements—a point whose importance should be neither underestimated nor overestimated—but very often their judgements prove to be correct.

Moreover, two features of the qualitative side of a freedom-measuring enterprise provide further grounds for thinking that the fallibility of human judgements about the significance of particular freedoms is not a bar to a proper reliance on such judgements when we gauge each person's overall liberty. First, as will be discussed presently, our judgements are about the importance of various freedoms *for a typical human being*. Though those judgements are brought to bear on the situation of this or that particular individual, they are not tailored to any individual's peculiar needs and views (except in a limited way that will be recounted shortly). Thus, one's assessments of the qualitative significance of freedoms will not be plagued by the uncertainties attendant on the personal predilections and idiosyncrasies of anyone whose overall freedom is being measured.

---

[34] When Will Kymlicka attacks the view that 'each ... freedom is as important as any other', he is assailing a position that has never been adopted by anyone. Kymlicka, *Contemporary*, 140.

Second, many of the relevant assessments are initially reached for fairly broad types of freedoms rather than for the countless instances of those types. Only subsequently do the assessments get applied to particular instances. Hence, since qualitative judgements at the level of broad freedom-types will normally be more reliable than such judgements at the level of freedom-tokens or narrower freedom-types, the assessments required in a liberty-measuring enterprise will warrant quite a robust level of confidence. When we appraise the significance of the freedom-to-read, for example, we are less likely to commit any notable errors than when we appraise the significance of some more specific varieties of that freedom (such as the freedom to read a pornographic magazine versus the freedom to read a novel by Proust). Accordingly, if our appraisals of the more specific varieties are governed to a considerable extent by our appraisal of the broader category, we shall have gone a long way toward defusing any difficulties posed by the finitude of human knowledge and foresight. To be sure, given the multifariousness of the particular freedoms whose significance will have to be assessed, subcategorizations and some case-by-case evaluations will be unavoidable. Nevertheless, the subcategorizations and case-by-case judgements will emerge within a framework of broad classifications that can provide steadying guidance to most of our fine-grained determinations.

Remaining to be elucidated are two aspects of the fundamental idea that underlies the incorporation of qualitatively-oriented weightings into our measurements of each person's overall liberty. As was declared at the outset of this discussion, such weightings reflect the objective importance of particular freedoms for the person who possesses them. Although the pertinent touchstones for gauging the importance of the freedoms have been singled out, we have not yet seen in exactly what sense the importance is objective or in exactly what sense that importance is for the person who possesses the freedoms. Let us take the latter of these two unexplored topics first. The key point here is that the importance of the freedoms of any person P is evaluated by reference to her interests rather than by reference to the interests of her society or the interests of humankind. We are asking how beneficial the freedoms are for her, rather than how beneficial her possession or exercise of those freedoms is for other people. To be sure, as has been noted and as will be discussed at greater length in a moment, P's interests are defined objectively as those of a typical human being. Nonetheless, the focus is on her rather than on other people who might be affected by her possession or exercise of her freedoms. Furthermore, since one of the interests of a typical person resides in being free to satisfy his or her strongly felt desires, P's intense desires (even if idiosyncratic) will be taken into account as we evaluate the significance of her freedoms for the promotion of her general well-being. If for example P harbours a fanatical desire to wiggle her thumbs daily in certain patterns as devotional exercises for some obscure religion to which she subscribes,[35] her freedom to wiggle her thumbs in those patterns will be assigned a greater significance than would be assigned thereto if she did not adhere to her peculiar creed. In these crucial respects, then, the importance of each particular freedom is assessed as its importance for the person who is endowed with the freedom.

Fully consistent with what has just been said is the objective character of the requisite assessments. Those assessments are objective in at least three respects, two of which have already been indicated. First, as has just been remarked, the interests of the possessor of any freedoms are identified objectively as those of a typical human being. Although the ability to act upon keen desires will be included among the things that are in the interest of a typical person—which means that we do have to pay some attention to P's desires when we gauge the significance of her freedoms—many of her objectively defined interests are desire-independent. For example, regardless of whether P has any inclination to exercise her ability-to-read, that ability will be appraised at a high level of significance. Irrespective of P's preferences, such an ability is manifestly promotive of the desiderata that are distinctively associated with freedom; and, since a tendency to promote those desiderata is precisely what we are looking for when we evaluate the importance of particular freedoms, P's ability-to-read will receive a heavy qualitative weighting even if that ability is seldom or never exerted. Conversely, if the actions or dispositions-to-perform-actions of other people deprive P of that ability, or if (perhaps by way of a well-enforced legal prohibition on reading) they prevent her from exercising her ability-to-read in conjunction with different freedoms of hers, her new combinations of consistent unfreedoms will receive heavy qualitative weightings even if she is indifferent to what she has lost. In sum, the objectivity of my evaluations of particular freedoms will

---

[35] This well-known example is broached in Richard Arneson, 'Freedom and Desire', 15 *Canadian Journal of Philosophy* 425, 427 (1985); Arneson's approach to the example is markedly different from my own. Note, incidentally, that my claim about a typical person's interest in being free to satisfy her keenly felt desires is not equivalent to a claim about a typical person's interest in satisfying such desires. Though the latter thesis entails the former, there is no entailment in the opposite direction. On the importance of the distinction between the two theses, see Joseph Raz, *The Morality of Freedom* (Oxford: Clarendon Press, 1986), 143–4.

have left plenty of room for gaps between what is in P's interests and what P believes to be in her interests.

A second central aspect of the objectivity of those evaluations is also apparent from what has been argued already in this subsection. As has been maintained, the ideals that serve as the linchpins for our scale of importance are distinctively associated with freedom in the sense of having content-independent connections therewith. Those ideals have not been chosen at large or at the discretion of the measurer of freedom. Even more plainly, they have not been chosen on the basis of the predilections of the person whose freedom is being measured. They inform any apposite answer to a 'how free' question precisely because they are linked to freedom in a content-independent fashion, and precisely because the evaluative dimension of such a question is therefore to be construed as oriented toward those ideals rather than toward any other ideals. Hence, when we accept that overall freedom is a partly evaluative property, we are certainly not accepting that the choice of values for our judgements about the significance of particular freedoms is a matter of arbitrary discretion. That choice is settled by the bearings of freedom itself.

Third, especially since many of the aforementioned judgements will involve the subsumption of particular freedoms under fairly broad freedom-types, the questions which those judgements address are objective in the sense that many of them lend themselves to uniquely correct answers. Furthermore, even if some question does not lend itself to a uniquely correct answer, it will lend itself to a set of answers which are each correct and which are thus distinguishable from countless incorrect responses. Thus, each evaluation required for the measurement of any person's overall liberty is objective, either inasmuch as it is uniquely correct or inasmuch as it falls within a circumscribed range of correct assessments. In other words, this third aspect of evaluative objectivity consists in determinate correctness.

My claims about the determinate correctness of one's appropriate evaluations are more controversial than the rest of this discussion of objectivity, for a general sense of doubt about the context-transcendent solidity of evaluative judgements and normative judgements is what lies behind some of the resistance to the idea that such judgements are necessary for ascertaining the levels of people's overall liberty. Let us note that an insistence on *determinate* correctness is by no means equivalent to an insistence on *demonstrable* correctness. While rejecting the notion that the truth-values of most evaluative propositions are indeterminate, one should not hesitate to acknowledge that the truth-values of some such propositions are indemonstrable; that is, the truth-values of some evaluative propositions cannot be demonstrated in ways that would elicit a consensus among all or nearly all reasonable people who competently ponder those propositions. Disagreements among reasonable people, pertaining to some of those propositions, are ineliminable. Nevertheless, we should not presume that the insurmountability of such disagreements is always or usually a sign of indeterminacy. For one thing, when two or more assessments of a certain situation (two or more ordinal rankings of the importance of certain freedoms, for example) are equally correct while other contrary assessments are wrong, the disagreements among reasonable people can occur entirely within the range of correct evaluations. Moreover, the ineliminability of such disagreements relating to this or that evaluation is perfectly consistent with the unique correctness of one side in the disagreements. Only a conflation of indemonstrability and indeterminacy could lead anyone to infer otherwise. Of course, to say as much is not to suggest the existence of some mysterious entities to which our true evaluative judgements correspond. Rather, when we insist that one position in some intractable evaluative debate between reasonable people is uniquely correct, we should simply maintain that evaluative argumentation can in principle yield a verdict that is superior to every other verdict on the topic of that debate. Such a thesis is itself an evaluative claim rather than an instance of metaphysical speculation.[36]

Now, nothing in the preceding paragraph should be taken to imply that the truth-values of evaluative propositions are never indeterminate. There is no reason to deny the possibility of indeterminacy altogether. All the same, we have solid grounds for thinking that the truth-values of the evaluative judgements required for the measurement of anyone's overall liberty will generally be determinate. In the first place, as has been indicated, those judgements concern what is valuable for a typical human being rather than for all human beings. Although most evaluative propositions purporting to apply instead to what is valuable for all people would be straightforwardly false, and although some such propositions would be straightforwardly true, many of them would have murky truth-values. Considerably less problematic are evaluative propositions with a sharper focus. In addition, as has also been indicated already, our judgements will be

---

[36] The views expressed in this paragraph have been heavily influenced by Ronald Dworkin, 'Objectivity and Truth: You'd Better Believe It', 25 *Philosophy & Public Affairs* 87 (1996)—though Dworkin's article focuses on normative judgements more than on evaluative judgements. I have written at greater length on these matters, with a focus on normative judgements, in my *In Defense of Legal Positivism* (Oxford: Oxford University Press, 1999), 152–61.

oriented toward a clear-cut set of basic desiderata—individual matur-ation, well-being, and self-determination—by reference to which the degrees of importance of sundry liberties are gauged for the purpose of coming up with qualitatively-oriented multipliers in a freedom-measuring enterprise. Similarly, because of the emphasis on fairly broad freedom-types for the fixing of those multipliers, most of the requisite evaluations can be thin in the Rawlsian sense. That is, most of the evaluations derive from evaluations of freedom-types, and the freedom-types bear straightforward connections—whether supportive or unsupportive—to the desiderata which serve as our lodestars. Free-doms that fall within those types can be assessed as instances thereof.

For essentially the same reasons that have just been rehearsed, the controversies surrounding the freedom-measuring evaluations will very likely never be radical. Notwithstanding the distinction between determinacy and demonstrability, the factors that help to ensure the determinacy of the evaluations' truth-values will likewise help to avert or allay serious disagreements. Nonetheless, some degree of controversy is virtually inevitable, and it might prove to be exten-sive. Even though the points of contention are evaluations rather than full-blooded normative prescriptions, and even though the sweep of the evaluations has been cabined in the ways outlined by my last paragraph, the chances of a thorough consensus on those points of contention are exceedingly low. There surely remains room for dis-agreements among reasonable measurers of freedom. Should we find this situation troubling?

Let us first note that the evaluative judgements for specifying the qualitatively-oriented multipliers are not the only point at which a freedom-measuring project leaves room for divergences of views among reasonable people. As has already been discussed in this chapter, such divergences will arise as well when we take into account the potential causal consequences of the actions that can be performed by someone (and of the actions that could have been performed by someone if they had not been closed off to her by other people). Determining which of the potential causal consequences are to be included in one's analysis and which of them are to be excluded is a task that will almost inevitably fail to generate consentaneity among reasonable measurers of freedom. Though many of the decisions about including or excluding the potential causal consequences will be clear-cut—as will many of the requisite evaluations of the significance of particular freedoms—a number of those decisions will be controver-sial. Hence, the sheer fact that the qualitative component of a freedom-measuring project will give rise to disagreements among reasonable people is not a distinctive vice of that component. Any measurer of freedom who wants to take account of the potential causal consequences of people's actions will have to resign himself to the prospect of such disagreements. The strong likelihood of the occurrence of those disagreements is not an adequate ground for declining (quite foolishly) to enter the potential causal consequences into one's calculations; it is similarly not an adequate ground for declining to incorporate qualitative considerations into a freedom-measuring enterprise. In each case, what is crucial is not the eliciting of unanimity among all competent participants in a debate over the minutiae of the correct approach to measuring freedom. What is crucial, rather, is to strive for consistency in one's own approach. When approaches are consistent within themselves and when they diverge from one another on sundry matters of detail, their implications can fruitfully be compared.

Yet, although the evaluative side of a freedom-measuring project is not the only facet of such a project that will engender controversies among reasonable people, it is distinctive in generating controversies that are indeed evaluative. That point is in need of some explanation and defence. After all, at more than one juncture, this book has emphasized its avoidance of evaluative or normative assumptions when engaging in various analyses. Such an emphasis emerged in Chapter 2, for example, with my rejection of moralized accounts of freedom and with my general insistence that the existence of any particular freedom or unfreedom is ascertainable without recourse to evaluative or normative assumptions. A similar emphasis emerged in Chapter 4, with my repudiation of the view that the contents of the criteria for tracing causal connections are evaluative or normative. Given the methodological austerity of this book heretofore, why has this chapter unfurled an approach to the measurement of freedom that squarely invokes evaluative assumptions (in a subordinate but quite prominent role)? Why should we be prepared to acquiesce in the occurrence of evaluative controversies at this stage, whereas they have hitherto not been countenanced?

The answer to these questions should be evident. At every stage in this book where evaluative and normative assumptions have been eschewed, the topic under examination has been the existence of particular freedoms or unfreedoms. Moralized accounts of freedom are unacceptable precisely because they maintain that moral considerations—such as the illegitimacy of some prevented activity or the legitimacy of some preventive interference—determine whether particular instances of freedom or unfreedom exist as such.[37] Likewise, moralized criteria for the ascription of causal responsibility are unacceptable precisely because those criteria settle whether particular instances of unfreedom exist as such (or whether instead some inabilities of a person are mere inabilities). Because the existence of any particular freedom is a matter of some ability of a person, and because the existence of any particular unfreedom is a matter of some inability of a person and the sources thereof, any evaluative and normative considerations are beside the point. Things are very different when we shift our attention to ascertaining the extent of a person's overall liberty. In gauging that extent, we are seeking to answer a 'how free' question; and, as has been submitted throughout this chapter, any such question is partly evaluative. Though evaluative factors are secondary to physical magnitudes in determining the level of anyone's overall freedom, those factors do shape the condition of a person about which we are inquiring when we ask how free the person is. Hence, whereas evaluative or normative disputation pertaining to the existence of particular freedoms/unfreedoms would be a sign and a fount of confusion, a certain amount of evaluative disputation pertaining to the levels of people's overall liberty is quite predictable and pertinent. Perhaps some of the participants in that disputation will adopt positions that are misguided in various respects, but their sheer invocation of evaluative considerations is not in itself a category mistake of any sort. On the contrary, their resort to evaluative concerns and concepts is in accordance with the nature of the phenomenon under investigation. When a partly evaluative property is one's analysandum, one must make evaluative judgements in order to treat of the matter thoroughly. If the differing sets of such judgements put forward by various analysts are consistent within themselves, the divergences among those sets—and thus the divergences among the analysts' answers to any number of 'how free' questions—can structure a rewarding debate.

2.1.2. Objections Parried   So far, this chapter has outlined (at an abstract level) how qualitatively-oriented multipliers are to be specified, and how they are to be incorporated into our measurements. It

---

[37] Often this mistake derives from a failure to distinguish between the question whether some person *P* has been made unfree to do some action *x* and the question whether *P* has been coerced into abstaining from doing *x*. See for example Flathman, *Freedom*, 203–4.

has also suggested why such multipliers are needed at all. That last point, which consists in explaining the importance of the fact that the overall freedom of each person is in part an evaluative property, will receive sustained attention throughout the rest of this chapter. To a degree, of course, that point can be grounded on appeals to common sense. As Carter himself takes pains to underscore,[38] the attempts by political philosophers to incorporate evaluative considerations into their accounts of overall liberty have been legion. In diverse ways, those philosophers have presumed that 'how free' questions cannot be answered satisfactorily without some reliance on evaluative judgements. In so presuming, they have followed the beckoning of common sense; they have felt that the inclusion of evaluative assessments is necessary for 'measurements that are isomorphic with our common-sense comparisons of freedom'.[39]

Still, common sense can lead us astray in regard to complex problems of political philosophy. Something more is needed. Thus, the remainder of this chapter will adopt a defensive line of analysis and then an offensive line of analysis in vindication of the common-sense impression that 'how free' questions are partly evaluative. In the present subsection, we shall look at most of the criticisms posed by Carter and Steiner against the incorporation of evaluative assessments into one's measurements of the level of each person's overall liberty. My concern in scrutinizing those criticisms is solely to ponder whether they land any telling blows against the evaluative approach developed in this chapter. My discussion of those criticisms will not consider their appositeness as objections to other evaluative approaches. Quite a few of the previous attempts by philosophers to draw on evaluative considerations for measuring and comparing levels of freedom have been misguided. Many of Carter's and Steiner's strictures are undoubtedly warranted as ripostes to those previous theories. All the same, the aim here is neither to defend other theories against the aforesaid strictures nor to applaud Carter and Steiner for exposing the weaknesses of some of those theories. Rather, as has been indicated, the lone aim is to determine whether their animadversions on other evaluative accounts of freedom are effective as objections to my own position.

After the defensive rejoinders that occupy our attention in this subsection, the next subsection will go on the offensive by arguing that a partly evaluative approach to the measurement of freedom is essential for the adequate handling of certain matters that lead to

---

[38] Carter, *Measure*, 121–4.
[39] Carter, *Measure*, 121.

unacceptable conclusions when handled by a wholly non-evaluative approach. Although Carter and Steiner have been alert to some of the difficulties that will be discussed, they have overestimated their ability to fend off or defuse those difficulties. In short, not only shall we find that a partly evaluative conception of the freedom-measuring enterprise can withstand the challenges that have been mounted against it, but we shall also find that it avoids the shortcomings of any alternative conception.

2.1.2.1. Every Freedom Counts as a Freedom

We shall examine Steiner's and Carter's criticisms in an order that largely corresponds to the order in which I have presented the general features of my partly evaluative approach to the measurement of freedom. Let us begin, then, with the objection that has figured most saliently in Steiner's remarks—and less conspicuously in Carter's remarks—on the incorporation of evaluative considerations into one's freedom-measuring calculations.[40] While acknowledging that 'our first reactions strongly incline us to the view that the significance of the actions which we are or are not free to do must enter into our estimations of how free we are and not just how valuable the freedom we have is',[41] Steiner warns against succumbing to any such inclination. His central concern is that some qualitatively-oriented multipliers will be negative. He contends that the variations in the significance of freedoms 'can be either negative or positive. If saving another person's life is a highly significant act, it seems reasonable to think that the act of taking another's life is not perspicuously graded as "insignificant" but rather (infelicitously) as "anti-significant"'. Steiner accordingly infers that, if we were to base our measurements partly on evaluative considerations, 'all acts...would be assigned positive or negative numbers representing the valuation of their significance or anti-significance'.[42] Steiner observes that the use of negative multipliers would mean that the overall liberty of a person can sometimes be reduced by her gaining of certain new freedoms even while she does not lose any of her existing freedoms or acquire any new unfreedoms. He rightly declares that such an implication is absurd, and that the use of negative multipliers must therefore be ruled out.

---

[40] The objection is raised in Steiner, 'Computing', 80–83; and in Hillel Steiner, *An Essay on Rights* (Oxford: Blackwell, 1994) [Steiner, *Essay*], 46–8. It is endorsed in Carter, *Measure*, 130–1.

[41] Steiner, *Essay*, 45.

[42] Steiner, 'Computing', 81.

However, he believes that such a move is unavailable to theorists who advocate the use of qualitatively-oriented multipliers at all:

[I]t is thus necessary to exclude the use of negative numbers from our valuational assignments to listed actions. But how can this be done? For as was just noted, whatever positive value we assign to an act of life-saving, it would not make sense that an act of life-taking be assigned merely a lower positive value. If it were, this would have the utterly absurd consequence that a sufficiently large number of life-taking acts would be equal or greater in value than one life-saving act.[43]

Three major missteps undermine the soundness of Steiner's argument. First, in each of the quoted passages Steiner commits an error similar to a mistake which my third chapter has revealed in the work of Carter and others. That is, he fails to distinguish adequately between the value of the freedom-to-do-X and the value of doing X. In each passage, Steiner suggests that a qualitatively-oriented multiplier expresses the value of doing X. In fact, however, any such multiplier expresses the value of being free-to-do-X. As has been indicated in Chapter 3, the difference between those two values is noteworthy precisely in connection with detrimental actions. Someone might attach considerable value to the freedom-to-engage-in-suicide, for example, even though she shudders at the thought of exercising that freedom. Thus, from the premise that the performance of X would be harmful, we cannot validly infer that the freedom-to-perform-X is of negative value. Steiner commits a non sequitur in drawing such an inference, or in conflating that premise and that inference.

Second, Steiner wrongly presumes that the relevant values are to be gauged by reference to the interests of people other than the person whose freedoms are under consideration. His examples of life-saving acts as highly valuable and life-taking acts as highly detrimental are clearly founded on such a presumption. In fact, however, the importance of any particular freedom is to be gauged by reference to the objectively defined interests of the person who possesses that freedom. Very few freedoms indeed are of no value or of negative value to a typical human being who is endowed with them; the freedom-to-take-someone-else's-life would hardly ever be of no value or of negative value to the possessor of such a freedom, even though she might very likely blanch at the thought of exercising it.

To be sure, we need not and should not think that absolutely every particular freedom is of some positive value to any typical human being

---

[43] Ibid.

who possesses it. One can imagine circumstances in which some particular freedom would probably be of negative value for a typical human being. For example, suppose that a narrow path with a steep bank on each side is not fenced at all to prevent people from plunging down either of the stony banks. The presence of a suitably high barrier on one side or the other of the path would remove the freedom of a typical person to topple down the inclination on that side, but would probably not thereby deprive her of anything valuable. (If someone derives gratification from the risk of tumbling over onto rocks and mud, she still has the opportunity to hazard such a risk on the other side of the path.) At any rate, although there doubtless can be some particular freedoms that are of negative value or of no value to any typical person who is possessed of them, they are rare—far rarer than the particular freedoms of a person that are of negative value or no value for other people. We can easily recognize as much when we keep in mind the distinction between the value of doing X and the value of being free-to-do-X.

Third, and most important, Steiner inadvisably takes for granted that every partly evaluative approach to the measurement of freedom must attach negative weightings or zero weightings to some liberties. In other words, he inadvisably assumes that every partly evaluative approach will decline to assign primacy to the purely physical dimensions of each person's overall freedom. His whole attack therefore fails to land any blow at all against my own partly evaluative approach, which does indeed assign primacy to the physical dimensions of everyone's overall liberty by insisting that the level of any qualitatively-oriented multiplier can never be lower than 1. If a multiplier were to be given a lower numerical value, the freedom associated therewith would not be counted to the full extent of its physical proportions and would perhaps be counted negatively. Such an upshot would be utterly unacceptable, as Steiner correctly proclaims with regard to unfreedoms: '[I]t makes no sense to say that my being prevented from doing [something] is an instance of unfreedom but, because it lacks significance, that prevention cannot be counted in estimating the extent to which I'm unfree. Instances, as was suggested, necessarily count in the computation of whatever they instantiate.'[44] Admirable though this pronouncement is, Steiner draws from it an erroneous conclusion. He asserts that, because 'an action's significance or eligibility [that is, attractiveness] has no bearing on *whether* a person is free to do it . . . it cannot have any bearing on *how much* freedom he has if he

---

[44] Steiner, *Essay*, 46.

is free to do it'.[45] Steiner's premise in this compressed argument is solid, but his conclusion is a non sequitur. Instead of inferring that the significance of any particular freedom has no bearing at all on the extent of that freedom's contribution to a person's overall liberty, we should infer that it never has any *diminutional* bearing on that contribution. As has been stated, every freedom or unfreedom must count at least to the full extent of its physical proportions. A qualitatively-oriented multiplier can increase the weight of a freedom or an unfreedom beyond its purely physical dimensions, but can never reduce that weight. To assume that such a multiplier can play a diminutional role is to assume that the unimportance or disvalue of a particular freedom affects the very existence of that freedom as such. Steiner is right to denounce any assumption along those lines—but he errs in thinking that his denunciation is inconsistent with a partly evaluative conception of the freedom-measuring enterprise. One should wholeheartedly endorse his insistence that '[w]e must and do distinguish between whether we have a freedom and what that freedom is worth',[46] while realizing that that insistence requires no more than the disallowance of any diminutional role for each qualitatively-oriented multiplier.

2.1.2.2. No Change of Subject

Carter repeatedly maintains that any partly evaluative approach to the measurement of freedom will have sought to gauge the extent of each person's overall liberty by reference to factors that are independent of the concept of liberty. Though he is unquestionably correct in his characterization of some previous evaluative treatments of this topic, he seeks to go further by presenting his retort to those previous theories as a general claim about all evaluative conceptions of freedom. His most striking line of argument against a partly evaluative approach to measurement (which he labels as a 'hybrid approach') is as follows:

[T]he hybrid approach has the following rather startling implication: that the degree of one's freedom is a function both of the degree of one's freedom and of the importance of that freedom in terms of other goods. No doubt it is important to provide overall evaluations of freedom in such a way as to combine these two variables. What certainly cannot be the case is that the measurement of these two variables in combination is identical to the measurement of one of them.[47]

---

[45] Ibid., emphases in original.
[46] Steiner, *Essay*, 48.
[47] Carter, *Measure*, 145.

Carter's argument is fallacious, for it damagingly trades on an equivocation that has to some degree been harmlessly present in one or two of my own strands of argument in this chapter. Let us distinguish here between a person's overall freedom as calculated without the use of any qualitatively-oriented multipliers and a person's overall freedom as calculated with such multipliers. The first of these quantities or phenomena can be designated as 'Fr_1', and the second can be designated as 'Fr_2'.

When this chapter slightly earlier maintained that the desiderata invoked as touchstones for our evaluative judgements are themselves distinctively associated with freedom, the referent of that claim was Fr_1 rather than Fr_2. Obviously, those touchstones are specially linked to Fr_2, since the level of Fr_2 is determined in part by them. However, my claim about the distinctive association of the desiderata with freedom was not focused on that uninterestingly obvious relationship, but instead on the less obvious point that the desiderata bear content-independent connections to Fr_1 (instrumental and constitutive connections which Carter himself has so perceptively highlighted). Precisely because of those connections, Fr_2 is not determined in any way by ideals that are extrinsic to the value-engendering roles of Fr_1.

Though my earlier argument is wholly unharmed and is indeed illuminated by the distinction between Fr_1 and Fr_2, Carter's argument in the quotation above does not similarly withstand scrutiny. Let us substitute 'Fr_1' or 'Fr_2' for each instance of 'freedom' in the opening sentence of that quotation, to produce a claim that would actually be endorsed by a proponent of the so-called hybrid approach: '[T]he degree of one's Fr_2 is a function both of the degree of one's Fr_1 and of the importance of that Fr_1 in terms of other goods.' Although the phrase 'other goods' somewhat misleadingly makes no mention of the distinctive ties between the specified goods and Fr_1, it can be condoned for the moment. More important is that the reformulated sentence makes clear that the rest of the argument in the original quotation does not follow. It is not the case that the proponent of the hybrid approach is ridiculously trying to combine the numerical expression of Fr_1 with qualitatively-oriented multipliers in order to arrive at the numerical expression of Fr_1. Rather, such a proponent is combining those factors in order to arrive at the numerical expression of Fr_2. Carter has begged the question against the hybrid approach by assuming that its adherents must be seeking to ascertain the level of Fr_1 rather than of Fr_2. In his eyes, of course, only the former phenomenon should be labelled as 'freedom'. However, since his stance on that matter is a key point of contention between his opponents and himself, he cannot legitimately ascribe that same stance to his opponents when he states what they are endeavouring to ascertain. Only by engaging in that question-begging ascription does he make his opponents' aspiration seem preposterous and incoherent. When their aspiration is correctly understood—when we grasp that a partly evaluative approach will respond to a 'how free' question about anyone by aiming to find the level of the person's Fr_2—the preposterousness and incoherence dissolve.

Equally objectionable are Carter's broader and persistent suggestions that a partly evaluative approach will have introduced some extraneous considerations into the freedom-measuring enterprise. Carter articulates his general view in the following passage:

> [T]he values being referred to [within a partly evaluative approach to the measurement of liberty] must be values other than freedom. Otherwise, all that we would be saying is that the extent of a person's freedom is a function of the value of her available actions in terms of freedom, in which case the value-based approach would amount to no more than a tautology.[48]

Before we fix upon the main shortcoming in this passage, let us note that an inattentiveness to the distinction between Fr_1 and Fr_2 has led Carter to misstate his point slightly. While the first and third instances of 'freedom' in the quoted passage each refer to Fr_1, the second instance of that word refers to Fr_2. Thus, the challenge for the partly evaluative approach is not really the avoidance of a tautology, but instead the avoidance of a collapse of Fr_2 into Fr_1—and a consequent collapse of the partly evaluative approach into a non-evaluative approach.

However, the chief weakness in this latest passage is somewhat different. Carter implies that we face a stark dichotomy between looking only at Fr_1 and looking also at desiderata that have nothing to do with Fr_1. In fact, as has been emphasized repeatedly herein, our alternatives are not so polarized. Although the desiderata on the basis of which we evaluate the significance of particular freedoms are not themselves elements of Fr_1, they are not chosen at large without reference to Fr_1—for they are connected to it in content-independent ways. Thus, when we invoke those desiderata as evaluative bases for gauging Fr_2, we are not changing the subject of discussion from the measurement of freedom to something else. We are instead recognizing that the overall freedom of any person, which we seek to ascertain when we answer a 'how free' question about that person, is a partly evaluative property; and we are likewise recognizing that, in order to

---

[48] Carter, *Measure*, 120.

avoid a shift to a new subject of discussion, the touchstones for the subordinate evaluative component of the freedom-measuring enterprise must be distinctively linked to the dominant physical component. By apprehending the content-dependent tendencies of a person's Fr_1 to promote the desiderata with which anyone's Fr_1 has content-independent connections, we come up with qualitatively-oriented multipliers that can be combined with the elements of the person's Fr_1 to yield the quantity that comprises all the content-dependent contributions and content-independent contributions of her Fr_1 to her overall liberty (Fr_2). That state of overall liberty is primarily determined by the physical scope of the person's latitude and by the curtailments of that scope through the actions of other people, but is also partly determined by the various concrete ways in which the components of her latitude are promotive of certain ideals with which the latitude as a whole is persistently connected. A 'how free' question is an inquiry about the latter aspect of a person's overall liberty as well as about the former aspect.

2.1.2.3. Arbitrary Charges

In the course of striving to rebut the so-called hybrid approach to the measurement of freedom, Carter contends that such an approach will be dogged by arbitrariness.[49] 'A problem with the hybrid approach ...is posed by the indeterminacy of the relative weights of the quantitative and qualitative assessments of a person's available actions when it comes to producing overall measurements of freedom.' He poses what he takes to be a rhetorical question: 'Who is freer, on the hybrid approach, when one person has ten options each of which is of moderate, little, or no value, and another has two options each of which is of great value?' Carter presents the gist of his attack in the following passage:

There is surely no well-grounded, nonarbitrary basis for specifying whether *any given number of actions* is less than, equals, or outweighs *any given action value* in terms of freedom...Neither will it do to suggest that one of these two dimensions should have lexical priority over the other...Lexical priority is simply one among the many possible ways of combining the two variables—like the claim that one variable should count for, say, 40 per cent of a person's overall freedom. What seems to be lacking in our ordinary notion of freedom, including in the ordinary notion of freedom of those who support the value-based approach, is a *reason* for assigning lexical priority to one

[49] Carter, *Measure*, 136–9.

particular dimension, or for saying that it counts for 40 per cent, or 60 per cent, or 10 per cent.[50]

One regrettable feature of Carter's remarks is his apparent assumption that the relative contributions of the physical facet and the qualitative facet of each particular freedom to a person's overall liberty will be uniform across all of her freedoms. There is absolutely no warrant for such an assumption, at least in connection with my own conception of the freedom-measuring enterprise. Under my approach, qualitatively-oriented weightings are attached to particular freedoms and to combinations of consistent unfreedoms. The relative contributions of the physical and the qualitative are bound to vary from one freedom-type to the next. In respect of instances of the freedom-to-speak or the freedom-to-read, for example, the relative contribution of the qualitatively-oriented multiplier will be considerably heavier than in respect of instances of certain other freedom-types. Thus, although the specification of an *across-the-board* percentage for the relative contribution of the physical facet or the qualitative facet would indeed be arbitrary, there is no such element of arbitrariness in my approach to measurement. Under my approach, the relative weight of the qualitative dimension will be uniform across all or most instances of each freedom-type but not across all freedom-types.

More generally, Carter's remarks are regrettable in insisting that a freedom-measuring project which takes into account both physical factors and qualitative factors is doomed to indeterminacy when it combines those sets of factors. My earlier exposition of my approach to measurement has offered a number of reasons for thinking that the evaluative judgements required under that approach will generally have determinate truth-values; I have likewise suggested why the evaluative disputation surrounding those judgements will probably be quite cabined and manageable. Instead of rehearsing those points afresh, my present discussion will supplement them with a few methodological and substantive observations focused on the matter that worries Carter.

His main concern is that we lack any reason for setting the size of a qualitatively-oriented multiplier at this or that specific level rather than at some other specific level. Such a complaint overlooks the basic method that informs Carter's own theorizing—the method of reflective equilibrium.[51] In adopting such a method, we begin with the knowledge that no qualitatively-oriented multiplier can ever fall

[50] Carter, *Measure*, 137, emphases in original.
[51] Carter, *Measure*, Ch. 4.

below 1. That lower limit, of course, follows from the primacy of the physical aspect of freedom and the secondariness of the qualitative aspect. Given such a minimum for the magnitude of any qualitatively-oriented multiplier, we must proceed to specify a numerical value for every such multiplier in order to bring our final calculations of people's levels of overall liberty into line with common-sense comparisons among those levels—common-sense comparisons to which Carter rightly attaches great importance. (Those paradigmatic comparisons can be among individuals' levels of overall liberty or among societal levels.) We must be prepared to amend the qualitatively-oriented multipliers which we assign to particular freedoms, in light of the implications of those assignments for the common-sense comparisons whose soundness we tentatively take for granted; and we must like-wise be prepared to abandon or modify our acceptance of various common-sense comparisons, in light of the implications of those com-parisons for our assignments of qualitatively-oriented multipliers. In other words, the appropriate balance between the physical and the qualitative for each particular freedom is struck through an overarch-ing process of mutual adjustments. One's reason for striking the bal-ance at the specified level for any particular freedom, rather than at some lower or higher level, is precisely that it fits smoothly into the structure—the equilibrium—yielded by that overarching process. On the basis of that smooth fit for every particular freedom, we can be confident that we have singled out the partly evaluative property for which we are looking. In sum, by starting with a medley of common-sense comparisons which we provisionally endorse as sound, and by starting as well with the knowledge that the minimum numerical value for any qualitatively-oriented multiplier is 1, we can proceed through a vast array of mutual adjustments in order to generate reasons for fixing the numerical values of our multipliers at specific levels. A determin-ation of the relative weights of the physical dimension and the qualita-tive dimension for each particular freedom is not doomed to arbitrariness.

Furthermore, Carter's distribution of the burden of proof on this matter is itself a begging of the question. Carter presumes that, unless a reason can be adduced for setting each qualitatively-oriented multi-plier at a specific level, we should take account only of the physical dimensions of each freedom or unfreedom when we measure any person's overall liberty. However, unless Carter is begging the question by presupposing here that the overall liberty of any person is not a partly evaluative property, he is in effect maintaining that every one of our qualitatively-oriented multipliers should be set at 1 except when we have reasons for adopting some alternative numerical value. What could be more patently arbitrary than the attachment of a qualitatively-oriented multiplier of 1 to every particular freedom and every combination of consistent unfreedoms? From the perspective of someone who regards the overall liberty of each person as a partly evaluative property—a perspective which Carter manifestly does not share, but which he should not here be assuming away—a proposal for the uniform evaluative weighting of every freedom and every combination of consistent unfreedoms is an arbitrary elision of all qualitative differences.

Of course, nothing just said is meant to suggest that a partly evaluative approach to the measurement of freedom would be unweakened if we could not supply any reasons for fixing the numerical values of qualitatively-oriented multipliers at specific levels. On the contrary, exactly because the provision of adequate reasons is crucial for rescuing such an approach from arbitrariness, the penultimate paragraph above (in combination with some of my earlier discussions) has argued that solid reasons will indeed be available. My present aim, then, has not been to imply that Carter is wrong to press for reasons that underlie the specific numerical values of qualitatively-oriented multipliers. Rather, my aim has been to show that he begs the question by presuming that the inability of analysts to come up with such reasons—if they were indeed unable to come up with such reasons—would lead us to the conclusion that the overall freedom of each person is Fr_1.[52] As has been stated, someone who subscribes to a partly evaluative conception of the freedom-measuring enterprise will view Carter's conclusion as tantamount to a proposal that every qualitatively-oriented multiplier in our calculations should be assigned a numerical value of 1. A proposal along those lines would partake of no less arbitrariness than would any proposal for alternative numerical values, if we could not offer any reasons for setting the multipliers at specific levels. Hence, instead of being led to Carter's conclusion, the champion of the partly evaluative conception would be led to conclude that our endeavours to measure the overall liberty of each

---

[52] In fairness to Carter, I should note that he earlier recognizes that his attack on evaluative approaches to the measurement of freedom can lead to conclusions other than his own. Carter, *Measure*, 129. Yet he clearly appears to think that, if the proponents of those approaches were to accept the soundness of his attack, they would have to abandon their conception of overall liberty. As I am here arguing, those proponents could retain their conception while abandoning the idea that anyone's overall liberty is measurable in ways that do not partake of arbitrariness.

person are doomed to arbitrariness. Though such a conclusion would be dismaying, it would not warrant our accepting that we should really be trying to ascertain no more than a person's Fr_1 when we measure her overall liberty. What we should be trying to ascertain is her Fr_2. At any rate, fortunately, we can reject both Carter's conclusion and the dismaying conclusion about arbitrariness that has just been sketched. We can reject each of those inferences because each of them derives from the premise that we cannot adduce reasons for setting our qualitatively-oriented multipliers at specific levels; such a premise, as has been argued, is false. We can accordingly be abundantly optimistic about the prospects for success, at least in principle, of a partly evaluative freedom-measuring project.

Let us notice a further respect in which Carter begs the question while impugning some partly evaluative approaches to measurement. He submits that such approaches land us in controversies that ought to be skirted by a measurer of freedom:

We should be surprised if we were to discover that after a person has committed herself to a particular *definition* of overall freedom, she nevertheless has to express a *further* commitment (i.e. to a certain way of combining the [physical and qualitative] variables) before she can make judgements about who is freer than whom. If this were so, then judgements about overall freedom would be hotly contested by different individuals *who nevertheless agreed over the definition of overall freedom*. It is not clear that we can tolerate such differences in judgement in the way in which we tolerate similar subjective differences in judgements about restaurants.[53]

We should initially glance at two minor aspects of this passage. First, the phrase 'hotly contested' is hyperbolic. On the one hand, to be sure, there will almost inevitably arise disagreements over the settings of various qualitatively-oriented multipliers—just as there will almost inevitably arise disagreements over the inclusion of various potential causal consequences among the contents of the myriad freedoms that are to be covered by one's calculations, whether one's approach to measurement is evaluative or non-evaluative. On the other hand, as has been maintained in some of my earlier discussions, the disagreements over the qualitatively-oriented multipliers should prove to be quite contained and fruitful. So long as each participant in the debate strives for consistency within his own array of multipliers, the differences among the participants should give rise to more light than heat.

Second, the word 'subjective' near the end of the passage is at best vacuous and at worst dogmatically unsupported. It is vacuous if it

[53] Carter, *Measure*, 138, emphases in original.

simply indicates that the differences of judgement among the participants in an evaluative debate are indeed differences of judgement. Much more likely, however, is that the word is meant to suggest the absence of objective reference points for such a debate. After all, in an unquoted passage Carter declares (justifiably) that judgements about the quality of restaurants are sheer expressions of preferences and are not claims about objective properties of overall goodness. Hence, when he posits an analogy between those judgements and our evaluative judgements about the significance of particular freedoms, he is quite plainly telling us that judgements of the latter sort are likewise expressions of preferences unmoored to objective standards. As has already been contended, someone who adheres to such a view of the evaluative disputes about the significance of particular freedoms has thereby moved too quickly from a correct observation concerning indemonstrability to an unsupported inference concerning indeterminacy. Though disagreements among the reasonable people who participate in such disputes are generally ineliminable, that fact alone does not warrant the conclusion that there are no determinately correct answers to the questions around which the disputes swirl.

More striking than either of the foregoing two objectionable features of the passage quoted above is the question-begging assumption that pervades it. Carter supposes that, if theorists agree on a conception of overall freedom, we ought to be surprised by the occurrence of any evaluative controversies among them as they seek to answer 'how free' questions. Now, such controversies will indeed be surprising if the conception on which the theorists agree is Carter's. Under his conception, there is no need for them to come up with any qualitatively-oriented multipliers, and thus there is no occasion for them to disagree about the numerical values of such multipliers. However, the occurrence of evaluative controversies among theorists who try to answer 'how free' questions will not be even slightly surprising if the conception of overall liberty on which they agree is mine rather than Carter's. Under my conception, qualitatively-oriented multipliers are essential for the measurement of each person's overall freedom; accordingly, the efforts of measurers to ascertain the level of anybody's overall freedom will almost inevitably be marked by some evaluative disputation. Far from being surprising, such disputation is an utterly predictable consequence of the fact that the measurers are endeavouring to gauge the extent of a partly evaluative property. Hence, when Carter admonishes us that that disputation would be surprising and intolerable if it were to occur among people who agree on a conception of overall freedom, his admonitions make sense only if the shared conception is non-evaluative—in which case he is begging the question here against any conception with an evaluative component. Someone who espouses a partly evaluative approach can retort that, if theorists concur on a conception of overall freedom and do not engage in evaluative disputation over qualitatively-oriented multipliers, they have almost certainly embraced the wrong conception.

2.2. Unto the Breach

What has been said so far in reply to Steiner and Carter might seem somewhat inconclusive. Although we have found that their animadversions on evaluative approaches to the measurement of freedom do not tell against my own approach, my ripostes heretofore have concentrated on parrying those animadversions. This chapter has not yet mounted any sustained counter-attacks. It has therefore perhaps not yet made clear why a partly evaluative conception of overall freedom is to be preferred to a non-evaluative conception. Any such unresolvedness will be dispelled in the present subsection, where we shall ponder a number of respects in which Steiner's and Carter's non-evaluative approaches to the measurement of freedom are gravely unsatisfactory. As will be seen, their approaches do not deal well at all with some of the basic issues and phenomena that prompt people to be interested in measuring overall freedom in the first place. We can accordingly conclude that my partly evaluative approach not only withstands Steiner's and Carter's onslaughts; it also enables us to overcome several problems that confound their own theories. It is not merely a coherent alternative to their position, but also a preferable alternative.

We shall look in depth at two areas that pose special difficulties for Steiner and Carter: freedoms of speech and thought, and the importance of the diversity of one's freedoms. We have glimpsed at the first of these areas in the initial half of this chapter, where I indicated that it would be treated at some length in the current half. What has also surfaced in the initial half of this chapter is another problem that would be discussed in detail here if I had not analysed it sufficiently there— the problem of giving due weight to the potential causal consequences of a person's actions in some circumstances of collective unfreedom. As we have seen, Carter cannot adequately take account of those causal consequences, and therefore he cannot suitably capture what is objectionable about some situations of collective unfreedom. He rightly wants to avoid having to ascribe combinations of consistent unfreedoms to groups of people rather than to individuals, but he cannot explain why the individuals in certain special situations of collective unfreedom are correct in believing that their overall liberty has been significantly abridged. To explain how the overall liberty of each of them has indeed been constricted, we must avail ourselves of qualitatively-oriented multipliers to take into consideration the importance of avoiding responsibility for the imprisonment of other innocent people. We can then give due weight to the fact that, in some circumstances of collective unfreedom, nobody involved can exercise the liberty-to-avoid-the-aforesaid-responsibility in conjunction with exercising the liberty-to-escape-imprisonment-himself. Without the use of qualitatively-oriented weightings, we would be led to the conclusion that the *pro-tanto* curtailment of everyone's overall liberty in such a situation of collective unfreedom is surpassed by the *pro-tanto* enhancement thereof (an enhancement residing in the new ability of each person to effect the permanent captivity of his comrades). With the use of those weightings, we can abjure such an outlandish conclusion and can perceive that there has been a net reduction in everyone's overall freedom.

In short, in respect of some situations of collective unfreedom— which have been discussed much more lengthily in the first half of this chapter and in Chapter 3—the application of qualitatively-oriented multipliers is essential if our measurements of individuals' levels of overall liberty are to yield credible results. We shall find in this subsection that such multipliers are similarly essential in other contexts. Neither Steiner nor Carter, despite sedulous efforts, can properly come to grips with the importance of freedoms of speech and thought or with the importance of the diversity of one's freedoms. Consequently, each of them will have failed to supply credible answers to many of the 'how free' questions that must be addressed by any theory of socio-political liberty.

2.2.1. The Significance of Small Movements   Steiner and Carter in their calculations of each person's overall liberty cannot register the importance of freedoms of speech and thought, because the laryngeal and cerebral motions to which those freedoms pertain are so small. Faced with my claim (made in the first half of this chapter) that the spatio-temporal units in any comprehensive system of measurement must be small enough to enable us to chart the potential occurrence of tiny motions involving tiny parts of the body, Steiner and Carter with their eschewal of qualitatively-oriented multipliers would insist that freedoms-to-engage-in-such-motions expand anyone's overall liberty only to a paltry degree. As Carter acknowledges: 'Freedom of speech . . . would appear to be represented by the [non-evaluative] approach as contributing very little to our overall freedom, given that the exercising of one's freedom of speech involves only small movements of one's tongue and vocal chords. And yet, we intuitively feel, freedom of speech contributes a great deal to our overall freedom.'[54] As he states in one of his early articles, we are not inclined to think that 'the extent of freedom represented by ordinary freedoms of speech is . . . the extent of movement of the tongue and vocal chords necessary for their exercise'.[55]

Now, before we scrutinize Carter's principal way of trying to get around this problem, we should ponder one partial route of escape to which his discussion refers only obliquely and fleetingly (if at all). Given that the causal consequences of the potential actions of a person are among the things which she is free to bring about, the causal consequences of her utterances will be among the things which she is free to bring about. A great many causal consequences can flow from an utterance. For example, Marc Antony's stirring funeral oration in *Julius Caesar* let slip the dogs of war in its immediate aftermath. When the causal consequences of a person's potential utterances are taken into account, the sizeableness of the contributions made by her freedoms-of-speech to her overall liberty is much more evident—regardless of whether one's approach to measuring her overall liberty is non-evaluative or partly evaluative. Hence, the highlighting of those consequences would go some way toward defusing my criticism of Carter and Steiner for their slighting of the aforementioned contributions.

Nonetheless, such a rejoinder on their part would plainly fall well short of a full defence against my criticism. It would do nothing to underline the weightiness of freedoms-of-speech in circumstances where the probable causal consequences of speaking are negligible. For example, if a religious zealot delivers orations on a corner of the open-air market in Cambridge, England, he will typically bring about only a few trifling causal consequences through his declamations. He will of course cause certain vibrations in the air and in people's ears, and he will probably cause some people to grimace or to walk a bit more hurriedly than they otherwise would. On the whole, however,

---

[54] Carter, *Measure*, 205.
[55] Ian Carter, 'The Measurement of Pure Negative Freedom', 40 *Political Studies* 38, 48 (1992). For a similar point, see Tim Gray, *Freedom* (London: Macmillan, 1991) [Gray, *Freedom*], 126–7.

the effects produced by his harangues will be close to nil. Hence, in respect of such circumstances, and in respect of countless other circumstances in which the exercise of a person's freedoms-to-speak would not yield any major effects, Steiner and Carter are committed to the view that the specified freedoms add virtually nothing to the person's overall liberty.

Perhaps because the line of defence suggested on behalf of Steiner and Carter in the penultimate paragraph above would be largely or wholly inapplicable to many contexts—and perhaps because in any event such a defence would not capture at all the consequence-independent importance of being able to speak—the principal tack adopted by Carter himself is quite different. As has been briefly outlined in the first half of this chapter, he concentrates on the fact that someone who has been deprived of her freedom-to-speak will usually have been deprived of quite a few other freedoms as well. 'Where agent A is rendered unfree to speak, then, there is very likely to be a great reduction in A's freedom *in an overall sense*. For A will as a result be unfree to perform certain bodily movements, or will at least be deprived of access to the physical space (through which the sound waves would have travelled) which would otherwise have been directly causally linked to A's body.'[56] If a person has been divested altogether of her ability to speak, perhaps as a result of the clamping of a hand on her mouth or the stuffing of a gag down her throat, she will typically have undergone other severe impairments of her bodily mobility as well. Similarly, if she has retained her ability-to-speak but has been segregated from all other people and has thus been deprived altogether of her ability to communicate with anyone else, the segregation itself is a massive constriction of her freedom. Hence, Carter contends, the importance of freedoms-of-speech will be duly registered in the calculations undertaken by theorists who favour a non-evaluative approach to the measurement of each person's overall liberty. If those freedoms are missing, then usually a lot of other freedoms and combinations of freedoms will be missing as well. Their absence will amount to a sharp reduction in the overall liberty of the person who lacks them.

Carter's attempt to accommodate the importance of freedoms-of-speech within his analysis suffers from two main weaknesses. First, as has been stated *en passant* in my earlier discussion of this matter, Carter's argument is aimed at establishing the wrong point (even if we assume that his establishing of that point is otherwise unassailable).

---

[56] Carter, *Measure*, 206, emphasis in original.

What Carter needs to uphold is the thesis that a person's possession of sundry freedoms-of-speech will have contributed substantially to her overall liberty. What he tries to uphold instead, however, is the thesis that the removal of sundry freedoms-of-speech from a person will usually derogate substantially from her overall liberty because the removal will usually also take away many of her other freedoms. Not only is there no relationship of entailment between the latter thesis (Thesis B) and the former (Thesis A); what is more, Carter advances Thesis B precisely because he believes that it will help to compensate for his rejection of Thesis A. As he indicates, he hopes that 'the force of this objection [that is, an objection focused on what has been characterized here as Carter's repudiation of Thesis A] is greatly diminished once we take into account [Thesis B]'.[57] Hence, even if his argument were unimpeachable in all other respects, it would serve to highlight the inconsistency between Thesis A and his own approach to the measurement of freedom. He cannot uphold a thesis that would strike most people as a basic corollary of any satisfactory conception of socio-political liberty.

Second, as should be evident from my phrasing in the last couple of paragraphs, Carter's Thesis B presents a claim about what is usually or typically the case rather than about what is always the case. In most circumstances, the only ways of stopping some person P altogether from speaking will involve the elimination of many of her other liberties as well; but in quite a number of circumstances, including certain contexts that are perfectly credible, such an effect will not occur. As Carter himself avouches, 'one can think of restrictions on freedom of speech that are not accompanied by the removal of other freedoms'. He colourfully acknowledges that some curbs on P's freedom of speech can operate 'in a way analogous to so-called smart bombs, eliminating only certain specific targets while leaving all other freedoms intact'.[58] To be sure, some of those conceivable curbs are quite far-fetched. For example, we can easily imagine a situation in which P's ability to speak has been largely or wholly expunged through the installation of devices into her throat which prevent P from speaking but which do not otherwise impinge on her potential actions (apart from averting the causal consequences that would have flowed from her potential utterances). Much the same could be true of electronic signals transmitted with great precision, or of a special potion that paralyses her vocal chords without otherwise impeding her from

[57] Carter, *Measure*, 205.
[58] Carter, *Measure*, 207.

performing various actions. In respect of each of these situations, the narrow targetedness of the means of preventing *P* from speaking has rendered inapplicable the argument by Carter that was summarized in my penultimate paragraph above. Another slightly fanciful situation to which his argument does not apply is that of an invalid who can speak but who has otherwise been paralysed since birth. Any number of utterances are the only actions which such an incapacitated person can perform. Hence, if her ability to engage in such utterances is removed—perhaps through the clamping of a hand on her mouth or the stuffing of a gag down her throat—her ability to undertake other actions will not have been affected at all. She could not do anything else before, and she cannot do anything else now. She has lost only her freedoms-of-speech, and thus she has lost very little by Carter's reckoning.

Some other scenarios to which Carter's riposte does not apply are more credible. For example, think again of the religious zealot who delivers bombastic sermons on a corner of the Cambridge open-air market. Suppose that, because of the ambient noise, he cannot make himself heard by more than a very small number of people unless he uses a megaphone or some other amplifying device. If his device is taken away from him—perhaps by the police or by irate pedestrians— he will no longer be able to express himself to many people in the vicinity of the market. Nevertheless, his abilities to engage in other types of actions will be almost completely unaffected. Indeed, even his ability to move his vocal chords in myriad ways will have remained entirely intact. Thus, in respect of this plausible situation involving a substantial reduction in the extent to which somebody can communicate his ideas to other people, Carter has to maintain that the effect on the person's overall liberty is trifling. (Nor can Carter point to a notable decrease in the causal consequences that would flow from the zealot's rants. We can very safely assume that, apart from creating vibrations in more pairs of ears, the megaphone or other amplifying device had not augmented the effectiveness of the preacher's sermonizing. The higher level of decibels had undoubtedly engendered more widespread annoyance among passers-by, but it had not enhanced the appeal of the proselytizing.)

To discern another relevant and credible situation, involving the elimination of a person's very ability-to-speak rather than just her ability to communicate her words widely, we should dispense with the assumption that the extirpation of her ability is due to the actions of other people. Suppose that a person *P* has suffered a stroke or some other malady that has robbed her of the ability-to-speak without depriving her of any of her other abilities. We shall continue here to put aside the causal consequences of her potential utterances, which she is no longer free to bring about (unless she can use alternative means of communication to bring some or all of those consequences about). We shall therefore have to conclude that, under Carter's non-evaluative approach to measuring the liberty of *P*, she has undergone hardly any reduction in her overall freedom. Of course—if we suppose, perhaps inaccurately, that no causal responsibility for *P*'s malady is traceable to the actions of other people—this conclusion about her overall liberty might not seem unpalatable to theorists who hold that natural constraints and obstacles are not restrictions on anybody's freedom. Steiner is one of those theorists. However, in Chapter 2 and elsewhere I have argued on independent grounds against such a conception of freedom, and in any event Carter professes to be agnostic on issues of that sort. Thus, with regard to this eminently believable situation in which *P*'s ability to speak has been extinguished by natural forces, as much as with regard to any situation in which that ability of hers has been extinguished by the actions of other people, we should conclude that the loss of her capacity to speak is a curtailment of her overall freedom. If we want to shun the Carterian view that that curtailment is negligible, we shall have to forswear the non-evaluative approach to measuring each person's overall liberty.

These remarks on the difficulties faced by Steiner and Carter in dealing adequately with freedoms of speech are applicable *a fortiori*—and *mutatis mutandis*—to the difficulties faced by them in dealing with freedoms of thought. (I am here using the term 'thought' broadly to refer to all mental activity, rather than just to reasoning and reflection.) As has been discussed in my third chapter, Carter has to maintain that freedoms of thought contribute to a person's overall liberty only in so far as thoughts are indispensable for the performance of various actions. He accordingly has to ignore any impairment of a person's overall liberty that results when the person has been deprived of freedoms-of-thought that were not indispensable for her performance of various actions. Indeed, as has been noted, Carter explicitly denies that mental processes themselves are to be taken into account at all by a freedom-measuring enterprise. '[E]ven where such acts are conceived in physical terms, their "extensiveness" will be trivial.'[59] He is therefore committed to the view that the ability to become sad and the ability to become angry and the ability to feel exalted will not be among the particular freedoms that are entered into our calculations,

[59] Carter, *Measure*, 206.

save in so far as those abilities are necessary for the performance of certain actions. Much the same can be said about the ability to read and the ability to contemplate philosophical issues. Although some of those abilities are doubtless necessary for the performance of some actions, and although they will be reflected to that extent in Carterian measurements of anyone's overall freedom, those abilities in themselves will not be recorded by Carterian measurements at all.

Suppose, for example, that Mary hits Martha on the head and causes a brain injury which prevents Martha from reading but which does not otherwise interfere with her mental faculties. According to Carter's theory, the fact that Martha has been deprived of her ability-to-read does not in itself have any bearing on her overall liberty whatsoever. To be sure, that ability was probably an integral component of some of her erstwhile abilities to perform various physical actions. Her losses of her abilities to carry out those actions will be registered in our measurements of her overall liberty, and to that extent the loss of her ability-to-read will be indirectly registered. However, that latter loss will not be included as a separate item in our calculations at all. Under Carter's approach, reading per se—as opposed to any number of bodily movements that normally accompany reading—is not something which anyone can ever be free or unfree to do. Hence, the ability-to-read is never in itself a freedom, and an inability-to-read that has resulted from other people's actions is never in itself an unfreedom. Neither an ability of that sort nor an inability of that sort ever in itself enlarges or diminishes a person's overall liberty. Only in the indirect fashion explained above does a person's gaining or losing of the ability-to-read have such an effect. Consequently, if Martha in becoming newly unable-to-read has not become newly unable to perform any other activities, Carter will have to conclude that Mary has not made her unfree in any respect. He will have to reach the same conclusion if the blow by Mary has made Martha unable-to-become-sad or unable-to-become-angry or unable-to-become-cheerful without having made her newly unable to perform any activities. He will likewise have to reach that conclusion if Mary has cabined Martha's thoughts not through a blow but through a sophisticatedly precise form of mind-control that shuts down some mental function(s) without shutting down any others.

As the most recent quotation above reveals, Carter adopts his strange position on this matter because he feels that the motions of the cerebral processes involved in mental functioning are in themselves too trivially small to be perceptible blips on the radar screen of a freedom-measuring project. Far too slight to be noticed by a Carterian measurer of freedom is the difference between moving one's outer body in certain ways while one reads a book and moving one's outer body in those same ways while one only seems to read a book. From the perspective of such a measurer, that is, the difference just mentioned is far too slight to warrant our taking into account a person's ability-to-read as a separate item in our tallying of the person's overall liberty. Anyone who regards Carter's stance on this topic as unacceptable will have to repudiate his strictly non-evaluative approach to the measurement of freedom. We must avail ourselves of some sizeable qualitatively-oriented multipliers to offset the minuteness of the physical proportions of the processes to which any freedoms-of-thought pertain. Those freedoms will then weigh heavily in our calculations of anyone's overall liberty. We can thereby capture the momentous importance of such freedoms for any typical human being who is endowed with them (and for any typical human being who has been deprived of them). The fact that a partly evaluative approach to the measurement of freedom can indeed capture that importance is a very strong point in its favour.

2.2.2. The Spice of Life   Another aspect of the freedom of each person that eludes the framework of Carter's theory is the importance of the diversity of anybody's particular liberties. Carter himself explicitly recognizes how important that diversity is, and he rightly sees it as one key facet of the broader interplay among freedoms: '[I]f one adopts [an evaluative] approach, one should not look in isolation at the single actions available to a person in order to fix their weights, since the way in which specific options are combined may well be relevant to their values. For example, certain freedoms may constitute complementary goods, such as the freedom to drive a car and the freedom to buy petrol; and other freedoms, when all of the same kind, may have diminishing marginal value.'[60] Although the first sentence in this quotation runs together the desirability of doing *X* and the desirability of being free to do *X*, the passage is otherwise an admirable statement of some of the basic ways in which the values of particular freedoms interact. Carter proceeds to expand on the factor of diversity by noting that the monotonous homogeneity of one's particular freedoms will lessen the evaluatively weighted contribution which each such freedom makes to one's overall liberty:

[60] Carter, *Measure*, 124.

We feel that some increases in choice add very little to our freedom, even where those increases involve the addition of a large number of options each of which, when viewed in isolation, may be of considerable value. For example, we feel intuitively that the freedom to use one of ten Ford Escorts does not give us ten times more freedom than the freedom to use a single Ford Escort, and that the choice between twenty-one brands of soap powder in a supermarket does not give us three times more freedom than the choice between seven such brands.[61]

On the one hand, the second sentence in this quotation vividly and unobjectionably offers some examples to illustrate the thesis that a dearth of diversity among a person's particular freedoms will frequently lower the evaluatively weighted contribution which each freedom makes to the person's overall liberty. On the other hand, the first sentence in the quotation is much more dubious. Interpreted very generously, it simply formulates the general thesis which the next sentence aptly illustrates. Interpreted more warily, however, it maintains that proponents of evaluative approaches to the measurement of freedom believe that the dreary homogeneity of particular liberties will not only have lowered the evaluative weighting of each liberty but will also have removed some of the liberties from our calculations altogether. This suspicious construal of the sentence is, alas, borne out by the statement that immediately follows the quoted passage. That statement attributes an untenable view to proponents of evaluative approaches: 'Given these last examples, it would seem that in order to make a difference to an agent's overall freedom, a new option must be *significantly different* from the options the agent already has.'[62]

In fairness to Carter, it should straightaway be conceded that the statement just quoted is accurate as a thumbnail summary of the views held by some other theorists who have adopted evaluative approaches to the measurement of freedom. Such theorists have gone astray by mistakenly presuming that the significance of the differences among particular freedoms can bear on the very existence of some of those freedoms as such, rather than only on the magnitude of the qualitatively-oriented multipliers that are to be attached to those freedoms' numerical expressions. For example, Richard Norman, from whom Carter has borrowed the scenario involving brands of detergent, writes as follows: 'My freedom is not increased by the availability of a large number of options if there is, as we say, "nothing to choose between

---

[61] Ibid., footnotes omitted.
[62] Ibid., emphasis in original.

them". A notorious example is the availability of innumerable brands of some commodity [such as pork pies].'[63] Norman and any like-minded theorists have failed to assign primacy to the physical aspect of each person's overall liberty. That is, they have failed to insist that every particular freedom or unfreedom must be counted in our calculations at least to the full extent of its physical dimensions. They have in effect allowed that the numerical values of qualitatively-oriented multipliers can fall below 1. Indeed, in respect of any new particular freedoms of a person P that are not significantly different from those already possessed by P, Norman ascribes a numerical value of 0 to the qualitatively-oriented multipliers that are associated with those new freedoms. He in effect maintains that the absence of significant differences undoes the status of each of the new freedoms as a freedom—as something, in other words, that must be registered when we tally P's overall liberty. Steiner and Carter are fully justified in objecting to such a claim. *Pace* Norman, we should not place ourselves in the position of saying that somebody who gains new liberties while losing none and while acquiring no new unfreedoms might nevertheless be no freer than before. My own partly evaluative conception of the freedom-measuring enterprise rejects Norman's position just as firmly as do Steiner and Carter, of course. Thus, although Carter is warranted in replying as he does to the champions of some alternative evaluational conceptions of freedom, he has stumbled in implying that all such conceptions are tainted by the vice to which he rightly takes exception. My own partly evaluative approach emphasizes, rather than denies, that every one of P's liberties will figure as an element in one or more of her combinations of conjunctively exercisable freedoms.

Heretofore, however, this discussion of the diversity of freedoms has been entirely defensive. My concern so far has been once again to distinguish my own conception of the freedom-measuring enterprise from other evaluative conceptions—conceptions which do not assign primacy to the physical aspect of each person's overall liberty, and

[63] Richard Norman, *Free and Equal* (Oxford: Oxford University Press, 1987), 38. The example of the multiple detergents is presented in Richard Norman, 'Liberty, Equality, Property: II', 55 (supp.) *Proceedings of the Aristotelian Society* 193, 201 (1981). For positions similar to that of Norman, see Ian Hunt, 'Freedom and Its Conditions', 69 *Australasian Journal of Philosophy* 288, 298 (1991); Jones and Sugden, 'Choice', 56–64; Marlies Klemisch-Ahlert, 'Freedom of Choice: A Comparison of Different Rankings of Opportunity Sets', 10 *Social Choice and Welfare* 189 (1993). For a corrective to those positions, see Gray, *Freedom*, 33–4. More ambiguous are William Connolly, *The Terms of Political Discourse*, 2nd edn (Princeton: Princeton University Press, 1983), 171–72; Christine Swanton, *Freedom: A Coherence Theory* (Indianapolis: Hackett, 1992), 100–3.

which therefore do not properly distinguish between those matters that affect the existence of a person's particular liberties and those matters that affect the extent of her overall freedom. What we have not yet seen is why Carter's own treatment of this topic is inadequate. To affirm that my partly evaluative approach does not run afoul of the errors which Carter reprehends in other evaluative approaches is not yet to reveal any shortcomings in his own non-evaluative stance. Let us turn, then, to those shortcomings.

As we consider Carter's position, we should recognize that it ensues from his agreement with the thesis that the diversity of a person's particular freedoms has a substantial bearing on the extent to which each of those freedoms contributes to the person's overall liberty. Carter does not reject that thesis, but instead strives to show that it can be accommodated by his non-evaluative approach to the measurement of freedom. As we shall behold, however, his argument in support of his stance is fallacious. He is sensible in acknowledging the importance of the diversity of particular freedoms, but he errs in thinking that that importance can be captured suitably (or indeed at all) by his non-evaluative conception of the freedom-measuring enterprise.

To explain why the homogeneity of a person's freedoms will tend to reduce the extent of the contribution made by each of those freedoms to the person's overall liberty, Carter seeks to come to grips with the notion that someone can be free to do the same thing in different ways.[64] Here he has in mind a medley of examples such as a choice between different brands of detergent for the washing of clothes, a choice between a red car and a blue car for travelling to a certain destination, and a choice between different routes of the same length for bicycling to a swimming pool. In each case, a person can choose among similar means of achieving the same result—a result that in turn will open up further choices. In each scenario, the specified result is something which the person is free to bring about. Let us concentrate on the example of a person P who can bicycle by different routes to a swimming pool. Suppose that P is initially not free to get to the pool at all, because every relevant route is blocked. She is therefore not initially free to perform the various activities, such as swimming and diving, that would be possible for her at the pool. Suppose that a route R_1 subsequently becomes open to her. She is now free to bicycle down R_1 and is therefore free to get access to the pool and to engage in sundry activities there. Later still, a few other routes of equal length

---

[64] Carter, *Measure*, 191–204.

(R_2, R_3, and R_4) likewise become open to her. She can now choose among the routes whenever she wishes to pay a visit to the swimming pool. Now, what Carter has to explain within his purely non-evaluative framework is why the opening up of R_1 increased P's overall liberty more than did the subsequent opening up of R_2 or R_3 or R_4. He has to explain the decreasing marginal weight of each new alternative. In addressing that point, as has been mentioned, he propounds an unsustainable line of argument.

Carter argues that we must avoid the double counting of certain freedoms. More specifically with reference to the example outlined above, he aims to avoid duplications relating to the result that can be achieved by P in different ways. He first broaches his line of reasoning in the following passage:

Once we come to consider the fact of there being different ways of doing the same thing, we can see that one [set of events which somebody can bring about] might *overlap* with another. In such a case, each of the two sets of events that the agent is free to bring about will have in common a particular subset of events [for example, P's arrival at the swimming pool and her activities at the pool], and we should like to avoid double counting the agent's freedom to bring about that subset. Therefore ... the weight deriving from the extensiveness of the above-mentioned subset of events ought not to be assigned to more than one [of the sets of events which the agent is free to bring about].[65]

This passage quite plainly suggests that, if a freedom to perform some action can itself be brought about via any one of two or more separate paths by a person, its inclusion in the person's combinations of conjunctively exercisable freedoms is to be confined to the combinations that contain one of those paths as opposed to the other(s). Thus, in the example on which we are concentrating, P's freedom to arrive at the swimming pool and her freedoms to undertake aquatic activities there are apparently to be included only in her combinations of conjunctively exercisable liberties that contain her liberty to bicycle along R_1. Those freedoms are apparently not to be comprehended as well by any similar combinations that contain her liberty to bicycle along R_2, R_3, or R_4.

Carter therefore believes that he has fathomed in purely non-evaluative terms the importance of the diversity of anybody's particular freedoms. Although such diversity has a bearing on the overall liberty of the person who is endowed with those freedoms, that bearing is not due to qualitative considerations. Rather, Carter contends, the

---

[65] Carter, *Measure*, 198, emphasis in original.

impact on the person's overall liberty stems from the sheer fact that homogeneous freedoms will make available a narrower range of actions than will heterogeneous freedoms. As he writes:

[W]hen two physical components appear similar, it is likely to be the case that many of the events they are a means to bringing about are identical. Indeed, the *less* significant the difference between them appears to be, the *greater* the set of actions they are both a means to performing is in practice likely to be. Thus, there would appear to be a law of 'diminishing marginal freedom' with respect to the acquisition of options which are not significantly different from those one already has—not because we should discount those additional options themselves (why should we do that, if they differ to *some* degree?), but simply because they provide us with diminishing marginal extents of available action.[66]

Any suggestions by Carter along these lines are mistaken. On the one hand, he has been far more attentive than any previous theorist to the fact that the overall freedom of each person is summed over the person's combinations of conjunctively exercisable freedoms and her combinations of consistent unfreedoms rather than over her separate freedoms and unfreedoms. On the other hand, he appears here to be forgetting that very insight. Although P's freedom to dive into the swimming pool at a certain time is obviously identical with itself as a particular freedom, its status as a member of a set changes from one combination of P's conjunctively exercisable liberties to the next. Given that that particular freedom is included in a combination of her conjunctively exercisable liberties which encompasses her freedom to bicycle to the pool along R_1, it is a member of that precise combination (which we may designate as 'C_1'). Given that that freedom of P to dive into the swimming pool at a certain time is also included in a combination of her conjunctively exercisable liberties which encompasses her freedom to bicycle to the pool along R_2—after all, those two freedoms are indeed conjunctively exercisable—it is likewise a member of *that* combination (which we may designate as 'C_2'). Hence, when we take account of that particular freedom of hers once in C_1 and again in C_2, no illegitimate double counting whatsoever is involved. We first enter that freedom into our calculations in its status as an element of C_1, and we then enter it into our calculations in its status as an element of C_2. In neither case are we summing over the freedom as an item unto itself; in each case, rather, we are embracing it in our calculations as a member of a set. Although that particular freedom is always identical with itself as a freedom, its status as an element of C_1 is not identical with its status as an element of C_2. Far from indulging in some improper double counting, then, we in our calculations have to register the presence of that freedom both in its former status and in its latter status if we are to avoid the omission of any elements from C_1 or C_2. Of course, reservations about double counting would be justified if our freedom-measuring enterprise were summing over individual freedoms directly. However, those reservations are in fact baseless because our final calculations never sum over individual freedoms directly but only over combinations. In short, as has been stressed, freedoms enter our measurements only as members of sets.

Consequently, Carter is wrong when he suggests that any particular freedom of a person that can be brought about by her via two or more alternative paths is to be included only in her combinations of conjunctively exercisable liberties that comprehend one of those paths, which is to be singled out in opposition to the other pathway(s). The freedom of P to dive into the swimming pool at a certain time will be an element in each combination-of-her-conjunctively-exercisable-liberties that encompasses any freedom of hers to pursue *any* path by which she can render possible her act of diving at that time. Her freedom-to-dive will of course be an element in C_1, but it will also be an element in C_2—and in C_3 and C_4, which respectively contain her freedom to bicycle to the pool along R_3 and her freedom to bicycle to the pool along R_4. In each case, the freedom-to-dive gains a place in our calculations as a member of a combination that is distinct from each of the other combinations in which the freedom-to-dive is also included. Because none of those combinations of conjunctively exercisable liberties is identical with any of the others, the status of the freedom-to-dive as an element in each combination is not identical with its status as an element in any of the other combinations. Accordingly, when we take account of that freedom in each of its multiple statuses, we are not engaging in any dubious duplication.

Let us see this point in a slightly more formal presentation. To facilitate the exposition, in this paragraph only, I shall assume away all of P's particular freedoms other than her freedoms to bicycle by four different routes to the swimming pool and her freedom to dive into the pool at a certain time. The latter freedom will be designated here as 'b', and the former freedoms—the freedom to bicycle along R_1, the freedom to bicycle along R_2, the freedom to bicycle along R_3, and the freedom to bicycle along R_4—will be designated respectively as 'a_1', 'a_2', 'a_3', and 'a_4'. P therefore enjoys the following four combinations of conjunctively exercisable liberties:

$$C_1\{a_1,\ b\} \quad C_2\{a_2,\ b\} \quad C_3\{a_3,\ b\} \quad C_4\{a_4,\ b\}$$

When we take account of b in C_1, we are taking account of it not as an independent item but as b-qua-element-in-combination-with-a_1. Likewise, when we take account of b in C_2, we are taking account of it not as an independent item but as b-qua-element-in-combination-with-a_2. And so forth. Though b is of course identical to itself, b-qua-element-in-combination-with-a_1 is hardly identical to b-qua-element-in-combination-with-a_2. Were we to omit b from its role as a member of C_2 or C_3 or C_4 when we gauge P's overall freedom, we would not be remedying a situation of double counting; instead, we would be distorting our perception of the combinations of conjunctively exercisable liberties which P in fact enjoys.

In short, by espousing a purely non-evaluative approach to the measurement of freedom, Carter is without the theoretical resources needed for explaining the importance of the diversity of particular liberties. Once his pronouncements on double counting are exposed as erroneous, he cannot distinguish in any pertinent way between the opening up of R_1 as a route to the swimming pool for P and the subsequent opening up of R_2. As should be evident by now, he cannot aptly draw a distinction between those two occurrences by maintaining that P's freedom-to-dive-into-the-swimming-pool-at-a-certain-time should be included only in C_1 and not in C_2. That freedom of hers is exercisable in conjunction with her freedom to travel to the pool along R_2, and it therefore belongs in C_2 (and in C_3 and C_4) just as much as in C_1. Nor can Carter maintain that the physical proportions of the contents of the freedoms in C_1 are larger than those of the contents of the freedoms in C_2. After all, most of the elements in either of those full combinations of conjunctively exercisable liberties are also contained in the other, and the contents of the freedoms that are not shared between those combinations—the content of the freedom-to-bicycle-along-R_1 and the content of the freedom-to-bicycle-along-R_2—are of equivalent physical dimensions. C_1 and C_2 are indistinguishable on the basis of physical sizeableness, the only basis on which Carter can seek to discriminate between them. Therefore, despite his inclination to the contrary, he is logically committed to the view that P's acquisition of the freedom-to-travel-along-R_1 did not increase her overall liberty to a greater degree than her subsequent acquisition of the freedom-to-travel-along-R_2.

How, then, can we duly recognize and explain the disparity between the upshot of the first of those new freedoms for P and the upshot of the second? If we share Carter's belief that such a disparity obtains, how can we avoid his fate of being obliged to deny its existence? Plainly, the way out of this quandary lies in the adoption of a partly evaluative approach to the measurement of freedom. When we attach qualitatively-oriented multipliers to the numerical expressions of a person's particular freedoms, we can adjust their weights in light of the other freedoms which the person enjoys. Carter himself indicates as much, in the passages quoted at the outset of this subsection. Thus, when P acquires the freedom-to-travel-to-the-swimming-pool-via-R_2, theorists who measure her overall liberty should assign a considerably lower qualitatively-oriented weighting to that freedom than they have assigned to her freedom-to-travel-to-the-pool-via-R_1. They should do so precisely because P is already endowed with the freedom-to-travel-via-R_1 by the time she gains the freedom-to-travel-via-R_2. Likewise, all the other freedoms contained in C_2 should receive considerably lower qualitatively-oriented weightings than those assigned to the corresponding freedoms in C_1. For example, P's freedom-to-dive-at-a-certain-time-t qua element of C_2 will be assigned a much lower qualitatively-oriented multiplier than her freedom-to-dive-at-t qua element of C_1. Again, the reason for the discrepancy is the very fact that she is already endowed with that particular freedom qua element of C_1 by the time she becomes endowed with it qua element of C_2. That freedom in its new status as a member of C_2 is not nearly as ground-breaking for her—not nearly as promotive of her autonomy—as it has been in its status as a member of C_1. (Note that this point about the promotion of her autonomy is independent of her inclination or disinclination to avail herself of the particular freedom.) With a partly evaluative approach to the measurement of P's overall liberty, we can use qualitatively-oriented multipliers to reflect this very difference between the particular freedom in its already-existing status and that freedom in its new status. By contrast, Carter with his non-evaluative approach cannot register such a difference or indeed any difference between C_1 and C_2 that has a bearing on P's overall liberty. He should follow his intuition that there are differences of exactly that sort, and he should abandon his non-evaluative conception of the freedom-measuring enterprise.

3. Conclusion

Having begun with two postulates that delineate the necessary and sufficient conditions for the existence of particular freedoms and unfreedoms, and having explored numerous facets and implications of those postulates, this book has closed with a chapter-long account of the property of overall freedom. Throughout the volume, a central theme has been the dichotomy between the strictly non-evaluative task of ascertaining the existence of particular freedoms or unfreedoms and the partly evaluative task of measuring someone's overall liberty. Nearly all previous evaluative approaches to the measurement of freedom have failed to heed that dichotomy sufficiently. In a markedly different fashion, Carter too has blurred that very distinction which he himself has done so much to highlight. In his case, of course, the misstep does not lie in suggesting that the existence of particular freedoms or unfreedoms will hinge on evaluative considerations; rather, he goes astray by obscuring the respects in which the extent of anyone's overall liberty does hinge on such considerations. As the second half of this chapter has argued, my conception of each person's overall liberty as a partly evaluative property is not only able to withstand all of Carter's challenges, but is also able to overcome the difficulties that plague his own theory—difficulties that become especially acute in any context where the partly evaluative character of each person's overall freedom becomes especially palpable.

Of course, when we recognize that the level of each person's overall liberty is partly determined by evaluative considerations, we are not thereby maintaining that that level is itself a product of moral/political principles. Normative concerns, such as principles of justice, operate not as fundamental determinants of the property of overall freedom but only at a subsequent stage where that property has emerged as a basic distribuendum. The evaluative aspect of each person's overall freedom is not to be conflated with the normative tenor of the principles that prescribe how freedom (or other desiderata) should be distributed. Hence, as has been discussed in my opening chapter, this book sets the stage for normative disputation instead of participating therein directly. Specifically, it sets the stage by elucidating the nature of one of the key distribuenda that will be governed by the principles on which the disputation is focused. I have sought to sharpen that disputation by helping to clarify what it is about.

Of course, no clarificatory effort can be entirely unaffected by moral/political considerations. In particular, any theory of socio-political freedom must take a stand on the question whether restrictions created by human beings are in some way to be treated differently from restrictions created purely by natural forces. My own stand on that question—my view that special treatment is indeed essential—has been evident since my opening chapter's presentation of the U Postulate and has generated the need for my fourth chapter. What ultimately justifies that stand, as the present chapter has made clear, is a moral/political premise concerning the distinctive importance of the ways in which human actions shape the settings wherein people live and behave. Nonetheless, although such a premise is undoubtedly moral/political, it is so only at a rarefied height of abstraction. It leaves unaddressed and wholly unresolved the countless issues that are at stake in the normative disputation to which the preceding paragraph has referred. It is a premise that delimits the domain of social and political philosophy without pre-deciding or professing to pre-decide the outcomes of any of the myriad debates conducted within that domain. Thus, although this book has endeavoured at length to analyse one of the foremost concepts in political thought, it is in some respects a prolegomenon to works of political philosophy that go beyond it by entering the aforementioned debates.

In relation to normative matters, then, this book has not really sought to supply answers to various questions; it has instead sought to bestow greater precision on some of the questions themselves. In dealing with analytical matters, however, my discussions have been much more assertive. Throughout the volume, the aim has been not only to clarify certain positions on the nature of freedom but also to uphold them and to marshal arguments in favour of them. Those arguments have been oriented in part toward the common-sense comparisons (among people's levels of overall liberty) on which Carter has rightly laid emphasis. They have also been guided in part by considerations of internal consistency and exactitude and capaciousness, with an eye toward the sustainment of subtle and illuminating distinctions wherever possible. Although those standard virtues of philosophical analysis do not in themselves fully determine the direction of one's theorizing, they are indispensable lodestars. Any acceptable theory must partake of them to a very high degree. Finally, the arguments in this book have been oriented towards my paramount objective of presenting freedom as a property that is both rigorously measurable and partly evaluative. That objective, which gains its importance as the means of rendering fully intelligible many of the accounts of justice to which this book serves as a prolegomenon, has shaped a number of aspects of my theory. It has come to the fore, of course, in the current chapter. The first half of this chapter has dwelt more on freedom's rigorous measurability whereas the second half has dwelt more on freedom's partly evaluative character, but the chapter as a whole has attempted to provide a unified analysis of the central concept that structures this book. It has sought to convey the quality of freedom.

Index